W9-CZV-996

Fodor's 97

Scotland

" *"When it comes to information on regional history, what to see and do, and shopping, these guides are exhaustive."*

—*USAir Magazine*

"Usable, sophisticated restaurant coverage, with an emphasis on good value."
—Andy Birsh, *Gourmet Magazine* columnist

"Valuable because of their comprehensiveness."
—*Minneapolis Star-Tribune*

"Fodor's always delivers high quality...thoughtfully presented...thorough."
—*Houston Post*

"An excellent choice for those who want everything under one cover."
—*Washington Post* "

Fodor's Travel Publications, Inc.
New York • Toronto • London • Sydney • Auckland
http://www.fodors.com/

Fodor's Scotland '97

Editor: Matthew Lore

Area Editor: Beth Ingpen, with the assistance of Gilbert Summers

Editorial Contributors: Steven Amsterdam, Robert Andrews, Carmen Anthony, David Brown, Audra Epstein, Laura M. Kidder, Heidi Sarna, Helayne Schiff, Mary Ellen Schultz, M.T. Schwartzman (Gold Guide editor), Dinah Spritzer, Gilbert Summers.

Creative Director: Fabrizio La Rocca

Associate Art Director: Guido Caroti

Photo Researcher: Jolie Novak

Cartographers: David Lindroth, Inc.; Mapping Specialists

Cover Photograph: Catherine Karnow/Woodfin Camp

Text Design: Between the Covers

Copyright

ISBN 0-679-03282-7

Special Sales

Fodor's Travel Publications are available at special discounts for bulk purchases for sales promotions or premiums. Special editions, including personalized covers, excerpts of existing guides, and corporate imprints, can be created in large quantities for special needs. For more information, contact your local bookseller or write to Special Marketing, Fodor's Travel Publications, 201 East 50th Street, New York, NY 10022. Inquiries from Canada should be directed to your local Canadian bookseller or sent to Random House of Canada, Ltd., Marketing Department, 1265 Aerowood Drive, Mississauga, Ontario L4W 1B9. Inquiries from the United Kingdom should be sent to Fodor's Travel Publications, 20 Vauxhall Bridge Road, London, England SW1V 2SA.

PRINTED IN THE UNITED STATES OF AMERICA

10 9 8 7 6 5 4 3 2 1

CONTENTS

ON THE ROAD WITH FODOR'S

WE'RE ALWAYS THRILLED to get letters from readers, especially one like this:

It took us an hour to decide what book to buy and we now know we picked the best one. Your book was wonderful, easy to follow, very accurate, and good on pointing out eating places, informal as well as formal. When we saw other people using your book, we would look at each other and smile.

Our editors and writers are deeply committed to making every Fodor's guide "the best one"—not only accurate but always charming, brimming with sound recommendations and solid ideas, right on the mark in describing restaurants and hotels, and full of fascinating facts that make you view what you've traveled to see in a rich new light.

About Our Writers

Our success in achieving our goals—and in helping to make your trip the best of all possible vacations—is a credit to the hard work of our extraordinary writers and editors.

The information in these pages is largely the work of **Beth Ingpen.** A longtime editorial contributor to *Fodor's Scotland,* Beth works as a freelance editor and writer. She was previously publishing manager with the Royal Society of Edinburgh, Scotland's premier learned society, and spent lunchtimes soaking up that city's culture, particularly in its art galleries and concert halls. She has recently become an expert at holidays with small children, with their very different needs and interests. She is assisted by her husband, **Gilbert Summers,** a native Scot who has spent the last 14 years writing numerous guidebooks and articles about his home country. His aim is to make visitors realize that there is a much more diverse nation behind the "haggis and tartan" image (Gilbert has never worn a kilt in his life). They live out

in the barley fields in the rural northeast, within sight of the sea.

New this Year

This year we've reformatted our guides to make them easier to use. Each chapter of *Scotland '97* begins with brand-new recommended itineraries to help you decide what to see in the time you have; a section called When to Tour points out the optimal time of day, day of the week, and season for your journey. You may also notice our fresh graphics, new in 1996. More readable and more helpful than ever? We think so—and we hope you do, too.

New Takes on the Northern Highlands

Beth Ingpen and Gilbert Summers now cover the whole of the far north coast. They take us to Caithness, at the very north of Scotland, a place they describe as "space, big skies, and distant blue hills beyond endless rolling moors," and to Cape Wrath at its northwestern tip, named by the Vikings.

On the Web

Also check out Fodor's Web site (http://www.fodors.com/), where you'll find travel information on major destinations around the world and an ever-changing array of travel-savvy interactive features.

How to Use this Book

Organization

Up front is the **Gold Guide.** Its first section, **Important Contacts A to Z,** gives addresses and telephone numbers of organizations and companies that offer destination-related services and detailed information and publications. **Smart Travel Tips A to Z,** the Gold Guide's second section, gives specific information on how to accomplish what you need to in Scotland as well as tips on savvy traveling. Both sections are in alphabetical order by topic.

Chapters in *Scotland '97* are arranged by region. Each city chapter begins with an Exploring section, which is subdivided by neighborhood; each subsection recommends a walking or driving tour and lists sights in alphabetical order. Each regional chapter is divided by geographical area; within each area, towns are covered in logical geographical order, and attractive stretches of road and minor points of interest between them are indicated by the designation En Route. Throughout, Off the Beaten Path sights appear after the places from which they are most easily accessible. And within town sections, all restaurants and lodgings are grouped together.

To help you decide what to visit in the time you have, all chapters begin with recommended itineraries; you can mix and match those from several chapters to create a complete vacation. The A to Z section that ends all chapters covers getting there, getting around, and helpful contacts and resources.

At the end of the book you'll find Portraits, including a chronology and a brand-new addition on the surge in the number of films set in Scotland.

Icons and Symbols

★   Our special recommendations
✕   Restaurant
⌾   Lodging establishment
✕⌾   Lodging establishment whose restaurant warrants a detour
⚠   Campgrounds
♨   Rubber duckie (good for kids)
☞   Sends you to another section of the guide for more info
⊠   Address
☎   Telephone number
℻   Fax number
☉   Opening and closing times
▣   Admission prices (those we give apply only to adults; substantially reduced fees are almost always available for children, students, and senior citizens)

Numbers in white and black circles—②
and ❷, for example—that appear on the maps, in the margins, and within the tours correspond to one another.

Dining and Lodging

The restaurants and lodgings we list are the cream of the crop in each price range. Price charts appear in the Pleasures and Pastimes section that follows each chapter introduction.

Hotel Facilities

We always list the facilities that are available—but we don't specify whether they cost extra. When pricing accommodations, always ask what's included.

Assume that hotels operate on the **European Plan** (EP, with no meals) unless we note that they use the **Full American Plan** (FAP, with all meals), the **Modified American Plan** (MAP, with breakfast and dinner daily), or the **Continental Plan** (CP, with a Continental breakfast daily).

Restaurant Reservations and Dress Codes

Reservations are always a good idea; we note only when they're essential or when they are not accepted. Book as far ahead as you can, and reconfirm when you get to town. Unless otherwise noted, the restaurants listed are open daily for lunch and dinner. We mention dress only when men are required to wear a jacket or a jacket and tie. Look for an overview of local habits under Dining in Smart Travel Tips A to Z and in the Pleasures and Pastimes section that follows each chapter introduction.

Credit Cards

The following abbreviations are used: **AE**, American Express; **D**, Discover; **DC**, Diners Club; **MC**, MasterCard; and **V**, Visa.

Please Write to Us

You can use this book in the confidence that all prices and opening times are based on information supplied to us at press time; Fodor's cannot accept responsibility for any errors. Time inevitably brings changes, so always confirm information when it matters—especially if you're making a detour to visit a specific place. In addition, when making reservations be sure to mention if you have a disability or are traveling with children, if you prefer a private bath or a certain type of bed, or if you have specific dietary needs or any other concerns.

Were the restaurants we recommended as described? Did our hotel picks exceed your expectations? Did you find a museum we recommended a waste of time? If you have complaints, we'll look into them and revise our entries when the facts warrant it. If you've discovered a special place that we haven't included, we'll pass the information along to our correspondents and have them check it out. So send your feedback, positive *and* negative, to the Scotland Editor at 201 East 50th Street, New York, New York 10022—and have a wonderful trip!

Karen Cure
Editorial Director

Scotland

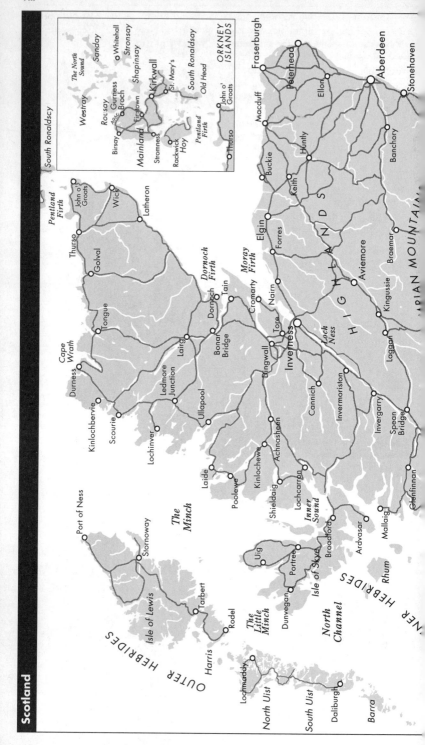

Europe

Reykjavik
ICELAND

NORW
Bergen

SCOTLAND

NORTHERN
IRELAND
Edinburgh

North
Sea

Sk

Belfast
IRELAND   *Irish
            Sea*
Dublin   UNITED
          KINGDOM

DENMA

WALES

ENGLAND   NETHERLANDS

Cardiff

Hamb

Amsterdam

London   The Hague
                   Rotterdam

ATLANTIC
OCEAN

English Channel

Brussels
BELGIUM

G E

Bonn

Paris
         LUXEMBOURG

Frankfurt

F R A N C E   Zürich

Bern
SWITZERLAND

LIECHTE

Lyon

Milan

PORTUGAL

Madrid

Marseille   Nice   Monte
                   Carlo
                   MONACO

ANDORRA

Floren

Lisbon

Barcelona

Corsica

S P A I N

Seville   Granada

*Balearic
Islands*

Sardinia

Tyrr.

Gibraltar

Mediterranean Sea

MOROCCO   ALGERIA

0   400 miles
0   600 km

TUNISIA

IMPORTANT CONTACTS A TO Z

An Alphabetical Listing of Publications, Organizations, and Companies that Will Help You Before, During, and After Your Trip

A

AIR TRAVEL

The major gateway to Scotland is **Glasgow Airport** (☎ 0141/887–1111). Flying time is 6½ hours from New York, 7½ hours from Chicago, and 10 hours from Los Angeles.

CARRIERS

Carriers serving Scotland include **American Airlines** (☎ 800/433–7300), **British Airways** (☎ 800/247–9297), **Continental** (☎ 800/525–0280), **Delta** (☎ 800/221–2121), **Northwest Airlines** (☎ 800/447–4747), **TWA** (☎ 800/892–4141), **United** (☎ 800/241–6522), and **Virgin Atlantic** (☎ 800/862–8621).

FROM THE U.K.➤ **British Airways** (☎ 0181/897–4000; outside London, 0345/222111) flies from Heathrow, **Air UK** (☎ 0345/666777) flies from Stansted, and **British Midland** (☎ 0181/754–7321 or 0345/554554) also flies from Heathrow.

COMPLAINTS

To register complaints about charter and scheduled airlines, contact the U.S. Department of Transportation's **Aviation Consumer Protection Division** (✉ C-75, Washington, DC 20590, ☎ 202/366–2220). Complaints about lost baggage or ticketing problems and safety concerns may also be logged with the **Federal Aviation Administration (FAA) Consumer Hotline** (☎ 800/322–7873).

CONSOLIDATORS

For the names of reputable air-ticket consolidators, contact the **United States Air Consolidators Association** (925 L St., Suite 220, Sacramento, CA 95814, ☎ 916/441–4166, FAX 916/441–3520). For discount air-ticketing agencies, *see* Discounts & Deals, *below.*

PUBLICATIONS

For general information about charter carriers, ask for the Department of Transportation's free brochure **"Plane Talk: Public Charter Flights"** (✉ Aviation Consumer Protection Division, C-75, Washington, DC 20590, ☎ 202/366–2220). The Department of Transportation also publishes a 58-page booklet, **"Fly Rights,"** available from the Consumer Information Center (✉ Supt. of Documents, Dept. 136C, Pueblo, CO 81009; $1.75).

For other tips and hints, consult the Consumers Union's monthly **"Consumer Reports Travel Letter"** (✉ Box 53629, Boulder, CO 80322, ☎ 800/234–1970; $39 1st year).

WITHIN SCOTLAND

Although a small country, Scotland has a significant internal air network. Contact **British Airways Express** (☎ 0345/222111) for details of flights from Glasgow, Edinburgh, Aberdeen, and Inverness to the furthest corners of the Scottish mainland and to the islands. Check out details of discounts and passes: For example, British Airways has in the past offered a Highland Rover Pass in the winter season, which gave substantial savings on a total of 5 flights around Scotland.

AIRPORT TRANSFERS

Two companies, **Lothian Regional Transport** (☎ 0131/555–6363) and **Guide Friday** (☎ 0131/556–2244), run buses between **Edinburgh Airport**'s main terminal building and Waverley Bridge, in center city and within easy reach of several hotels. The buses run every 30 minutes on weekdays (9–5) and less frequently (roughly every hour) during off-peak hours and on weekends. The trip takes about 30 minutes (about 45 minutes during rush hour). Single fare for Lothian Regional Transport is £3.20; for Guide Friday, £3.40.

Express buses run from **Glasgow Airport** to near the Glasgow Central railway station (☎ 0141/204–2844) and to the Glasgow Buchanan Street bus station (☎ 0141/332–7133). There is service every 15 minutes throughout the day. The fare is about £2.

B

BETTER BUSINESS BUREAU

For local contacts in the hometown of a tour operator you may be considering, consult the **Council of Better Business Bureaus** (✉ 4200 Wilson Blvd., Suite 800, Arlington, VA 22203, ☎ 703/276–0100, FAX 703/525–8277).

BICYCLING

TOURS

Ian Pragnell of **Bespoke Highland Tours** (✉ The Bothy, Camusdarach, Inverness-shire, PH39 4NT, ☎ 01687/450272) arranges treks throughout the Highlands and the islands for cyclists of all abilities. Scottish **Border Trails** (✉ Drummore, Venlaw High Rd., Peebles, EH45 87RL, ☎ 01721/720336, FAX 01721/723004) runs off-road mountain bike treks in the Borders and vehicle-supported road tours on which your luggage is ferried between stops. **Wildcat Mountain Bike Tours** (✉ 15A Henderson St., Bridge of Allan, Stirling, FK9 4HN, ☎ FAX 01786/832321) sells guided, vehicle-supported tours throughout Scotland for novices and experts.

ORGANIZATIONS

Cyclists' Touring Club (✉ National Headquarters, Cotterell House, 69 Meadrow, Godalming, Surrey, GU7 3HS, England, ☎ 01483/417217) actively campaigns for better cyclist facilities throughout the United Kingdom. It publishes a members magazine, route maps, and guides.

Sustrans Ltd. (✉ 53 Cochrane St., Glasgow, G1 1HL, ☎ 0141/552–8241) is a nonprofit organization dedicated to providing environmentally friendly routes for cyclists, notably in and around cities.

PUBLICATIONS

The Scottish Tourist Board's free brochure "Adventure and Special Interest Holidays," published annually, lists prepackaged vacations that may include cycling; its free "**Cycling in Scotland**" brochure has some suggested routes and practical advice. More detailed information on routes is given in the guidebook **Cycling in Scotland & North-East England,** published by Sigma Press and available from the Scottish Tourist Board. The Ordnance Survey Landranger series of maps, which shows gradient, is invaluable for cyclists.

BUS TRAVEL

FROM ENGLAND

For timetables, contact **National Express** (✉ Buchanan Street Bus Station, Killermont St., Glasgow, G2 3NP, ☎ 0990/808080, FAX 0141/332–8055). Travel centers and travel agents also have

details, and some travel agents sell tickets.

WITHIN SCOTLAND

For information on the country's bus network contact any bus station or the **Travel Center** (✉ Buchanan Street Bus Station, Glasgow G2 3NP, ☎ 0141/332–7133); **S.M.T.** (St. Andrew Bus Station, Edinburgh, EH1 3DU, ☎ 0131/558–1616); and **Edinburgh and Scotland Information Centre** (✉ 3 Princes St., Edinburgh, EH2 2QP, ☎ 0131/557–1700).

C

CAR RENTAL

The major car-rental companies represented in Scotland are **Alamo** (☎ 800/327–9633; in the U.K., 0800/272–2000), **Avis** (☎ 800/331–1084; in Canada, 800/879–2847), **Budget** (☎ 800/527–0700; in the U.K., 0800/181181), **Dollar** (☎ 800/800–4000; in the U.K., 0990/565656, where it is known as Eurodollar), **Hertz** (☎ 800/654–3001; in Canada, 800/263–0600; in the U.K., 0345/555888), and **National InterRent** (sometimes known as Europcar InterRent outside North America; ☎ 800/227–3876; in the U.K., 01345/222–525). Rates in Scotland begin at $24 a day and $99 a week for an economy car with unlimited mileage. This does not include tax on car rentals, which is 17.5%.

RENTAL WHOLESALERS

Contact **Auto Europe** (☎ 207/828–2525 or

800/223–5555), **Europe by Car** (☎ 800/223–1516; in CA, 800/252–9401), or the **Kemwel Group** (☎ 914/835–5555 or 800/678–0678).

THE CHANNEL TUNNEL

For information, contact **Le Shuttle** (in the U.S., ☎ 800/388–3876; in the U.K., 0990/353535), which transports cars, or **Eurostar** (in the U.S., ☎ 800/942–4866; in the U.K., 0345/881881), the high-speed train service between London (Waterloo) and Paris (Gare du Nord). Eurostar tickets are available in the U.K. through **InterCity Europe,** the international wing of BritRail (⌧ Victoria Station, London, ☎ 0171/834–2345 or 0171/828–0892 for credit-card bookings), and in the United States through **Rail Europe** (☎ 800/942–4866) and **BritRail Travel** (☎ 800/677–8585).

CHILDREN & TRAVEL

FLYING

Look into **"Flying with Baby"** (⌧ Third Street Press, Box 261250, Littleton, CO 80163, ☎ 303/595–5959; $4.95 includes shipping), cowritten by a flight attendant. **"Kids and Teens in Flight,"** free from the U.S. Department of Transportation's Aviation Consumer Protection Division (⌧ C-75, Washington, DC 20590, ☎ 202/366–2220), offers tips on children flying alone. Every two years the February issue of **Family Travel Times**

(☞ Know-How, *below*) details children's services on three dozen airlines. **"Flying Alone, Handy Advice for Kids Traveling Solo"** is available free from the American Automobile Association (AAA) (⌧ send stamped, self-addressed, legal-size envelope: Flying Alone, Mail Stop 800, 1000 AAA Dr., Heathrow, FL 32746).

KNOW-HOW

Family Travel Times, published quarterly by Travel with Your Children (⌧ TWYCH, 40 5th Ave., New York, NY 10011, ☎ 212/477–5524; $40 per year), covers destinations, types of vacations, and modes of travel.

LOCAL INFORMATION

The Scottish Tourist Board's two accommodation guides, *Hotels & Guest Houses* and *Bed & Breakfast,* indicate establishments which welcome children and have facilities for them, such as cots and high chairs. It is wise to mention the age of your children when booking accommodation—some of the more upscale country house hotels, in particular, do not allow children under a certain age, e.g. 12, to stay. On the other hand, you may well find that as soon as you arrive at your hotel or guest house, the children are warmly welcomed and a box of toys appears. Many tourist information centers have leaflets on activities for children in the surrounding area.

TOUR OPERATORS

Contact **Grandtravel** (⌧ 6900 Wisconsin Ave., Suite 706, Chevy Chase, MD 20815, ☎ 301/986–0790 or 800/247–7651), which has tours for people traveling with grandchildren ages 7–17; **Families Welcome!** (⌧ 4711 Hope Valley Rd., Durham, NC 27707, ☎ 919/489–2555 or 800/326–0724); or **Rascals in Paradise** (⌧ 650 5th St., Suite 505, San Francisco, CA 94107, ☎ 415/978–9800 or 800/872–7225).

CRUISING

Cunard Line (555 5th Ave., New York, NY 10017, ☎ 212/880–7500 or 800/528–6273) operates the *Queen Elizabeth* (QE2) on the only regular transatlantic crossings sailing between New York City and Southampton, England, from April through December. Very occasionally, this liner visits Glasgow.

SPECIAL-INTEREST CRUISES

Hebridean Island Cruises Ltd. (⌧ Acorn Park, Skipton, North Yorkshire, BD23 2UE, ☎ 01756/701338) offers 6- or 8-night luxury cruises aboard the MV *Hebridean Princess* around the Scottish islands, including visits to Orkney and Shetland on two of the cruises. The **National Trust for Scotland** (⌧ Cruise Manager, National Trust for Scotland, 5 Charlotte Square, Edinburgh, EH2 4DU, ☎ 0131/226–5922) runs a regular cruise program with lectures on natural history, etc. The destination changes each year, but may well include the West Coast or Northern Isles the year you wish to visit. The **Scottish Tourist Board's** free brochure, "Watersports," includes details of many charter firms operating among the islands.

U.S. CITIZENS

The **U.S. Customs Service** (✉ Box 7407, Washington, DC 20044, ☎ 202/927–6724) can answer questions on duty-free limits and publishes a helpful brochure, "Know Before You Go." For information on registering foreign-made articles, call 202/927–0540 or write U.S. Customs Service, Resource Management, 1301 Constitution Ave. NW, Washington, DC 20229.

COMPLAINTS➤ Note the inspector's badge number and write to the commissioner's office (✉ 1301 Constitution Ave. NW, Washington, DC 20229).

CANADIANS

Contact **Revenue Canada** (✉ 2265 St. Laurent Blvd. S, Ottawa, Ontario K1G 4K3, ☎ 613/993–0534) for a copy of the free brochure **"I Declare/Je Déclare"** and for details on duty-free limits. For recorded information (within Canada only), call 800/461–9999.

COMPLAINTS

To register complaints under the provisions of the Americans with Disabilities Act, contact the U.S. Department of Justice's **Disability Rights Section** (✉ Box 66738, Washington, DC 20035, ☎ 202/514–0301 or 800/514–0301, FAX 202/307–1198, TTY 202/514–0383 or 800/514–0383). For airline-related problems, contact the U.S. Department of Transportation's **Aviation Consumer Protection Division** (☞ Air Travel, *above*). For complaints about surface transportation, contact the Department of Transportation's **Civil Rights Office** (✉ 400 7th St., SW, Room 10215, Washington DC, 20590 ☎ 202/366–4648).

GETTING AROUND

Hertz (☎ 800/654–3131) can provide hand controls for their cars at its rental offices in Glasgow and Edinburgh. With advance notice, British Rail staff will assist passengers with disabilities; inquire at any British Rail area office.

LOCAL INFORMATION

In Britain, the nonprofit **Holiday Care Service** (✉ 2nd Floor, Imperial Buildings, Victoria Rd., Horley, Surrey RH6 7PZ, England, ☎ 01293/774–535) provides a hotel reservation service and free information and advice on holidays for people with special needs. **The Scottish Tourist Board** (✉ 23 Ravelston Terr., Edinburgh, EH4 3EU, Scotland, ☎ 0131/332–2433) has information on accommodations and transportation. Another useful source is

Disability Scotland (✉ Princes House, 5 Shandwick Place, Edinburgh, EH2 4RG, ☎ 0131/229–8632). A guidebook from the **National Trust for Scotland** (✉ 5 Charlotte Sq., Edinburgh, EH2 4DU, ☎ 0131/226–5922) details facilities for people with disabilities who visit its various historic houses and monuments.

ORGANIZATIONS

TRAVELERS WITH HEARING IMPAIRMENTS➤ The **American Academy of Otolaryngology** (✉ 1 Prince St., Alexandria, VA 22314, ☎ 703/836–4444, FAX 703/683–5100, TTY 703/519–1585) publishes a brochure, "Travel Tips for Hearing Impaired People."

TRAVELERS WITH MOBILITY PROBLEMS➤ Contact the **Information Center for Individuals with Disabilities** (✉ Box 256, Boston, MA 02117, ☎ 617/450–9888; in MA, 800/462–5015; TTY 617/424–6855); **Mobility International USA** (✉ Box 10767, Eugene, OR 97440, ☎ and TTY 541/343–1284, FAX 541/343–6812), the U.S. branch of a Belgium-based organization (☞ *below*) with affiliates in 30 countries; **MossRehab Hospital Travel Information Service** (☎ 215/456–9600, TTY 215/456–9602), a telephone information resource for travelers with physical disabilities; the **Society for the Advancement of Travel for the Handicapped** (✉ 347 5th Ave., Suite 610, New York, NY 10016, ☎ 212/447–7284, FAX 212/725–8253; membership $45); and

THE GOLD GUIDE / IMPORTANT CONTACTS

Travelin' Talk (✉ Box 3534, Clarksville, TN 37043, ☎ 615/552–6670, FAX 615/552–1182) which provides local contacts worldwide for travelers with disabilities.

TRAVELERS WITH VISION IMPAIRMENTS➤ Contact the **American Council of the Blind** (✉ 1155 15th St. NW, Suite 720, Washington, DC 20005, ☎ 202/467–5081, FAX 202/467–5085) for a list of travelers' resources or the **American Foundation for the Blind** (✉ 11 Penn Plaza, Suite 300, New York, NY 10001, ☎ 212/502–7600 or 800/232–5463, TTY 212/502–7662), which provides general advice and publishes "Access to Art" ($19.95), a directory of museums that accommodate travelers with vision impairments.

IN THE U.K.

Contact the **Royal Association for Disability and Rehabilitation** (✉ RADAR, 12 City Forum, 250 City Rd., London EC1V 8AF, ☎ 0171/250–3222) or **Mobility International** (✉ rue de Manchester 25, B-1080 Brussels, Belgium, ☎ 00–322–410–6297, FAX 00–322–410–6874), an international travel-information clearinghouse for people with disabilities.

PUBLICATIONS

Several publications for travelers with disabilities are available from the **Consumer Information Center** (✉ Box 100, Pueblo, CO 81009, ☎ 719/948–3334). Call or write for its free catalog

of current titles. The Society for the Advancement of Travel for the Handicapped (☞ Organizations, *above*) publishes the quarterly magazine **"Access to Travel"** ($13 for 1-year subscription).

The 500-page **Travelin' Talk Directory** (✉ Box 3534, Clarksville, TN 37043, ☎ 615/552–6670, FAX 615/552–1182; $35) lists people and organizations who help travelers with disabilities. For travel agents worldwide, consult the **Directory of Travel Agencies for the Disabled** (✉ Twin Peaks Press, Box 129, Vancouver, WA 98666, ☎ 360/694–2462 or 800/637–2256, FAX 360/696–3210; $19.95 plus $3 shipping).

TRAVEL AGENCIES & TOUR OPERATORS

The Americans with Disabilities Act requires that all travel firms serve the needs of all travelers. That said, you should note that some agencies and operators specialize in making travel arrangements for individuals and groups with disabilities, among them **Access Adventures** (✉ 206 Chestnut Ridge Rd., Rochester, NY 14624, ☎ 716/889–9096), run by a former physical-rehab counselor.

TRAVELERS WITH MOBILITY PROBLEMS➤ Contact **Accessible Journeys** (✉ 35 W. Sellers Ave., Ridley Park, PA 19078, ☎ 610/521–0339 or 800/846–4537, FAX 610/521–6959), an escorted-tour operator exclusively for travelers with mobility impair-

ments; **Flying Wheels Travel** (✉ 143 W. Bridge St., Box 382, Owatonna, MN 55060, ☎ 507/451–5005 or 800/535–6790), a travel agency specializing in European cruises and tours; **Hinsdale Travel Service** (✉ 201 E. Ogden Ave., Suite 100, Hinsdale, IL 60521, ☎ 708/325–1335), a travel agency that benefits from the advice of wheelchair traveler Janice Perkins; and **Wheelchair Journeys** (✉ 16979 Redmond Way, Redmond, WA 98052, ☎ 206/885–2210 or 800/313–4751), which can handle arrangements worldwide.

TRAVELERS WITH DEVELOPMENTAL DISABILITIES➤ Contact the nonprofit **New Directions** (✉ 5276 Hollister Ave., Suite 207, Santa Barbara, CA 93111, ☎ 805/967–2841).

TRAVEL GEAR

The **Magellan's** catalog (☎ 800/962–4943, FAX 805/568–5406), includes a section devoted to products designed for travelers with disabilities.

DISCOUNTS & DEALS

AIRFARES

For the lowest airfares to Scotland, call 800/FLY–4–LES.

CLUBS

Contact **Entertainment Travel Editions** (✉ Box 1068, Trumbull, CT 06611, ☎ 800/445–4137; $28–$53, depending on destination), **Great American Traveler** (✉ Box 27965, Salt Lake City, UT 84127, ☎ 800/548–2812;

$49.95 per year), **Moment's Notice Discount Travel Club** (✉ 7301 New Utrecht Ave., Brooklyn, NY 11204, ☎ 718/234-6295; $25 per year, single or family), **Privilege Card** (✉ 3391 Peachtree Rd. NE, Suite 110, Atlanta, GA 30326, ☎ 404/262-0222 or 800/236-9732; $74.95 per year), **Travelers Advantage** (✉ CUC Travel Service, 49 Music Sq. W, Nashville, TN 37203, ☎ 800/548-1116 or 800/648-4037; $49 per year, single or family), or **Worldwide Discount Travel Club** (✉ 1674 Meridian Ave., Miami Beach, FL 33139, ☎ 305/534-2082; $50 per year for family, $40 single).

DISCOUNT PASSES

See Train Travel, *below.*

HOTEL ROOMS

For hotel room rates guaranteed in U.S. dollars, call **Steigenberger Reservation Service** (☎ 800/223-5652).

STUDENTS

Members of Hostelling International–American Youth Hostels (☞ Students, *below*) are eligible for discounts on car rentals, admissions to attractions, and other selected travel expenses.

PUBLICATIONS

Consult **The Frugal Globetrotter,** by Bruce Northam (✉ Fulcrum Publishing, 350 Indiana St., Suite 350, Golden, CO 80401, ☎ 800/992-2908; $16.95 plus $4 shipping). For publications that tell how to find the lowest prices on plane tickets, *see* Air Travel, *above.*

Also see Fodor's **Affordable Great Britain** (available in bookstores, or ☎ 800/533-6478; $17).

AUTO CLUBS

If you belong to a motoring organization, look into reciprocal membership benefits, including breakdown assistance, available with the Automobile Association (AA) in Britain. If your auto club doesn't have such an arrangement, consider taking out an associate membership in the **AA** (✉ Fanum House, Basingstoke, Hants, RG2I 2EA, ☎ 01256/20123, FAX 01256/492440) or the **Royal Automobile Club** (✉ RAC House, Bartlett St., Box 10, Croydon, Surrey, CR2 6XW, ☎ 0181/686-2525), available to overseas visitors. Their large touring departments offer a wealth of detailed information about motoring in Britain.

MAPS

The best general purpose touring map is the Scottish Tourist Board's Touring Map of Scotland (5 miles to the inch), widely available in bookshops, tourist information centers, or direct from the Scottish Tourist Board (☞ Visitor Info, *below*). Any bookshop in the main cities will usually sell a good range of maps. For walking or getting to know a smaller area, the Ordnance Survey Landranger series (1:50,000) cannot be beaten and, again, is widely available.

E

To contact the police, fire brigade, ambulance service or coast guard, dial 999 from any telephone. No coins are needed for emergency calls from public telephone boxes.

F

Car-ferry services to and from Scotland's main islands are operated by **Caledonian MacBrayne** (CalMac, main office: ✉ The Ferry Terminal, Gourock, ☎ 01475/650100, FAX 01475/637607; for reservations, ☎ 01475/650000, FAX 01475/637607); **Western Ferries** (☎ 0141/332-9766); and **P & O Ferries** (Orkney and Shetland Services, Box 5, Jamieson's Quay, Aberdeen, ☎ 01224/572615, FAX 01224/574411).

G

ORGANIZATIONS

The **International Gay Travel Association** (✉ Box 4974, Key West, FL 33041, ☎ 800/448-8550, FAX 305/296-6633), a consortium of more than 1,000 travel companies, can supply names of gay-friendly travel agents, tour operators, and accommodations.

PUBLICATIONS

The premier international travel magazine for gays and lesbians is **Our World** (✉ 1104 N. Nova Rd., Suite 251,

THE GOLD GUIDE / IMPORTANT CONTACTS

Daytona Beach, FL 32117, ☎ 904/441–5367, FAX 904/441–5604; $35 for 10 issues). The 16-page monthly **"Out & About"** (☎ 212/645–6922 or 800/929–2268, FAX 800/929–2215; $49 for 10 issues and quarterly calendar) covers gay-friendly resorts, hotels, cruise lines, and airlines.

TOUR OPERATORS

Hanns Ebensten Travel (✉ 513 Fleming St., Key West, FL 33040, ☎ 305/294–8174), one of the nation's oldest operators in the gay market, and **Toto Tours** (✉ 1326 W. Albion Ave., Suite 3W, Chicago, IL 60626, ☎ 312/274–8686 or 800/565–1241, FAX 312/274–8695) offer group tours to worldwide destinations.

TRAVEL AGENCIES

The largest agencies serving gay travelers are **Advance Travel** (✉ 10700 Northwest Fwy., Suite 160, Houston, TX 77092, ☎ 713/682–2002 or 800/292–0500), **Islanders/Kennedy Travel** (✉ 183 W. 10th St., New York, NY 10014, ☎ 212/242–3222 or 800/988–1181), **Now Voyager** (✉ 4406 18th St., San Francisco, CA 94114, ☎ 415/626–1169 or 800/255–6951), and **Yellowbrick Road** (✉ 1500 W. Balmoral Ave., Chicago, IL 60640, ☎ 312/561–1800 or 800/642–2488). **Skylink Women's Travel** (✉ 2460 W. 3rd St., Suite 215, Santa Rosa, CA 95401, ☎ 707/570–0105 or 800/225–5759) serves lesbian travelers.

H
HEALTH

MEDICAL ASSISTANCE COMPANIES

The following companies are concerned primarily with emergency medical assistance, although they may provide some insurance as part of their coverage. For a list of full-service travel insurance companies, *see* Insurance, *below.*

Contact **International SOS Assistance** (✉ Box 11568, Philadelphia, PA 19116, ☎ 215/244–1500 or 800/523–8930; Box 466, Pl. Bonaventure, Montréal, Québec H5A 1C1, ☎ 514/874–7674 or 800/363–0263; 7 Old Lodge Pl., St. Margarets, Twickenham, TW1 1RQ, England, ☎ 0181/744–0033), **Medex Assistance Corporation** (✉ Box 5375, Timonium, MD 21094-5375, ☎ 410/453–6300 or 800/537–2029), **Traveler's Emergency Network** (✉ 3100 Tower Blvd., Suite 3100A, Durham, NC 27702, ☎ 919/490–6065 or 800/275–4836, FAX 919/493–8262), **TravMed** (✉ Box 5375, Timonium, MD 21094, ☎ 410/453–6380 or 800/732–5309), or **Worldwide Assistance Services** (✉ 1133 15th St. NW, Suite 400, Washington, DC 20005, ☎ 202/331–1609 or 800/821–2828, FAX 202/828–5896).

I
INSURANCE

IN THE U.S.

Travel insurance covering baggage, health, and trip cancellation or interruptions is available from **Access America** (✉ 6600 W. Broad St., Richmond, VA 23230, ☎ 804/285–3300 or 800/334–7525), **Carefree Travel Insurance** (✉ Box 9366, 100 Garden City Plaza, Garden City, NY 11530, ☎ 516/294–0220 or 800/323–3149), **Near Travel Services** (✉ Box 1339, Calumet City, IL 60409, ☎ 708/868–6700 or 800/654–6700), **Tele-Trip** (✉ Mutual of Omaha Plaza, Box 31716, Omaha, NE 68131, ☎ 800/228–9792), **Travel Guard International** (✉ 1145 Clark St., Stevens Point, WI 54481, ☎ 715/345–0505 or 800/826–1300), **Travel Insured International** (✉ Box 280568, East Hartford, CT 06128, ☎ 203/528–7663 or 800/243–3174), and **Wallach & Company** (✉ 107 W. Federal St., Box 480, Middleburg, VA 22117, ☎ 540/687–3166 or 800/237–6615).

IN CANADA

Contact **Mutual of Omaha** (✉ Travel Division, 500 University Ave., Toronto, Ontario M5G 1V8, ☎ 800/465–0267 (in Canada) or 416/598–4083).

L
LODGING

The Scottish Tourist Board publishes two *Where to Stay* guides updated annually, **Hotels & Guest Houses** (£6.99) and **Bed & Breakfast** (£4.99), which give detailed information of facilities provided, and classify and grade the accommodation (☞ Lodging Ratings *in* Smart Travel Tips, *below*). The various area tourist boards also publish separate accommodation listings for their areas, annually, which can be obtained either from the Scottish Tourist Board or from the individual area tourist authority.

For information on hotel consolidators, *see* Hotel Rooms *in* Discounts and Deals, *above*.

APARTMENT & VILLA RENTAL

Among the companies to contact are **Europa-Let** (⊠ 92 N. Main St., Ashland, OR 97520, ☎ 541/482–5806 or 800/462–4486, FAX 541/482–0660), **Property Rentals International** (⊠ 1008 Mansfield Crossing Rd., Richmond, VA 23236, ☎ 804/378–6054 or 800/220–3332, FAX 804/379–2073), **Rent-a-Home International** (⊠ 7200 34th Ave. NW, Seattle, WA 98117, ☎ 206/789–9377 or 800/488–7368, FAX 206/789–9379, rentahome-international@msn.com), and **Vacation Home Rentals Worldwide** (⊠ 235 Kensington Ave., Norwood, NJ 07648, ☎ 201/767–9393 or 800/633–3284, FAX 201/767–5510).

CAMPING

Camping is an economical option for budget travelers. Consult the free British Tourist Authority booklet *Camping and Caravan Parks in Britain,* or *Forestry Commission*

Camping and Caravan Sites (free from the **Forestry Commission,** ⊠ 231 Corstorphine Rd., Edinburgh, EH12 7AT, Scotland, ☎ 0131/334–0303). For help planning a bicycle camping trip, contact the **Camping and Caravanning Club** (⊠ 11 Lower Grosvenor Pl., London, SW1W 0EY, England).

FARMHOUSE AND CROFTING HOLIDAYS

A popular option for families with children is a farmhouse holiday, combining the freedom of bed-and-breakfast accommodations with the hospitality of Scottish family life. Information is available from the **British Tourist Authority** or the **Scottish Tourist Board** (*see* Visitor Info, *below*), from **Scottish Farmhouse Holidays** (⊠ 5 Drumtenant, Ladybank, Fife, KY7 7UG, Scotland, ☎ 01337/830451, FAX 01337/831301), and from the **Farm Holiday Bureau** (⊠ National Agricultural Centre, Stoneleigh, Warwickshire, England CV8 2LZ, ☎ 01203/696909).

HOME EXCHANGE

Some of the principal clearinghouses are **HomeLink International/Vacation Exchange Club** (⊠ Box 650, Key West, FL 33041, ☎ 305/294–1448 or 800/638–3841, FAX 305/294–1148; $78 per year), which sends members five annual directories, with a listing in one, plus updates; and **Intervac International** (⊠ Box 590504, San Francisco, CA 94159, ☎ 415/

435–3497, FAX 415/435–7440; $65 per year), which publishes four annual directories.

HOTELS

Some recommended groupings of hotels include **Scotland's Commended Hotels** (⊠ 54 High St., Dunblane, Perthshire, FK15 9AY, ☎ 01786/825550), **The Tartan Collection** for hotels and restaurants in the Northeast (⊠ Migvie House, North Silver St., Aberdeen, AB1 1RJ, ☎ 01224/848813, FAX 01224/848805), and **Scotland Deluxe,** which also covers guest houses and bed-and-breakfast (⊠ Sandy Rd., Seamill, West Kilbride, Ayrshire, KA23 9NN, ☎ 01294/823131, FAX 01294/823179).

M
MONEY

ATMS

For specific foreign **Cirrus** locations, call 800/424–7787; for foreign **Plus** locations, consult the Plus directory at your local bank.

CURRENCY EXCHANGE

If your bank doesn't exchange currency, contact **Thomas Cook Currency Services** (☎ 800/287–7362 for locations). **Ruesch International** (☎ 800/424–2923 for locations) can also provide you with foreign banknotes before you leave home and publishes a number of useful brochures, including a "Foreign Currency Guide" and "Foreign Exchange Tips."

WIRING FUNDS

Funds can be wired via **MoneyGram℠** (for locations and information in the U.S. and Canada, ☎ 800/926–9400) or **Western Union** (for agent locations or to send money using MasterCard or Visa, ☎ 800/325–6000; in Canada, 800/321–2923; in the U.K., 0800/833833; or visit the Western Union office at the nearest major post office).

P

PACKING

For strategies on packing light, get a copy of *The Packing Book,* by Judith Gilford (✉ Ten Speed Press, Box 7123, Berkeley, CA 94707, ☎ 510/559–1600 or 800/841–2665, FAX 510/524–4588; $7.95 plus $3.50 shipping).

PASSPORTS & VISAS

U.S. CITIZENS

For fees, documentation requirements, and other information, call the State Department's **Office of Passport Services** information line (☎ 202/647–0518).

CANADIANS

For fees, documentation requirements, and other information, call the Ministry of Foreign Affairs and International Trade's **Passport Office** (☎ 819/994–3500 or 800/567–6868).

PHOTO HELP

The **Kodak Information Center** (☎ 800/242–2424) answers consumer questions about film and photography. The *Kodak Guide to Shooting Great Travel Pictures* (available in bookstores; or contact Fodor's Travel Publications, ☎ 800/533–6478; $16.50 plus $4 shipping) explains how to take expert travel photographs.

S

SAFETY

"Trouble-Free Travel," from the AAA, is a booklet of tips for protecting yourself and your belongings when away from home. Send a stamped, self-addressed, legal-size envelope to Trouble-Free Travel (✉ Mail Stop 75, 1000 AAA Dr., Heathrow, FL 32746).

SENIOR CITIZENS

EDUCATIONAL TRAVEL

The nonprofit **Elderhostel** (✉ 75 Federal St., 3rd Floor, Boston, MA 02110, ☎ 617/426–7788), for people 55 and older, has offered inexpensive study programs since 1975. Courses cover everything from marine science to Greek mythology and cowboy poetry. Costs for two- to three-week international trips—including room, board, and transportation from the United States—range from $1,800 to $4,500.

Interhostel (✉ University of New Hampshire, 6 Garrison Ave., Durham, NH 03824, ☎ 603/862–1147 or 800/733–9753), for travelers 50 and older, has two- to three-week trips; most last two weeks and cost $2,000–$3,500, including airfare.

LODGING

Scottish Highland Hotels (☎ 0131/557–2368 in Scotland) have a special year-round "Golden Times" package offering one-third off regular rates.

ORGANIZATIONS

Contact the **American Association of Retired Persons** (✉ AARP, 601 E St. NW, Washington, DC 20049, ☎ 202/434–2277; annual dues $8 per person or couple). Its Purchase Privilege Program secures discounts for members on lodging, car rentals, and sightseeing.

Additional sources for discounts on lodgings, car rentals, and other travel expenses, as well as helpful magazines and newsletters, are the **National Council of Senior Citizens** (✉ 1331 F St. NW, Washington, DC 20004, ☎ 202/347–8800; annual membership $12) and Sears's **Mature Outlook** (✉ Box 10448, Des Moines, IA 50306, ☎ 800/336–6330; annual membership $14.95).

SIGHTSEEING

The **Scottish Tourist Guides Association** (✉ Mrs. Catherine Martindale, Secretary General, 6 Springfield Avenue, Uddingston, Glasgow, G71 7LY) has members throughout Scotland, who are fully qualified professional tourist guides able to offer walking tours in the major cities, half- or full-day tours or extended tours throughout Scotland, driver-guiding, and special study tours. Many of the guides have at least one second language other than English. Fees are negotiable with individual guides, a list of whom can be obtained from the above address.

SPORTS

The Scottish Tourist Board can provide details of companies offering sports-related holidays in Scotland.

STUDENTS

GROUPS

The major tour operators specializing in student travel are **Contiki Holidays** (✉ 300 Plaza Alicante, Suite 900, Garden Grove, CA 92640, ☎ 714/740–0808 or 800/266–8454) and **AESU Travel** (✉ 2 Hamill Rd., Suite 248, Baltimore, MD 21210-1807, ☎ 410/323–4416 or 800/638–7640).

LODGING

HOSTELS➤ In the United States, contact **Hostelling International–American Youth Hostels** (✉ 733 15th St. NW, Suite 840, Washington, DC 20005, ☎ 202/783–6161, FAX 202/783–6171); in Canada, **Hostelling International–Canada** (✉ 205 Catherine St., Suite 400, Ottawa, Ontario K2P 1C3, ☎ 613/237–7884); and in the United Kingdom, the **Youth Hostel Association of England and Wales** (✉ Trevelyan House, 8 St. Stephen's Hill, St. Albans, Hertfordshire, AL1 2DY, ☎ 01727/855215 or 01727/845047). Membership (in the U.S., $25; in Canada, C$26.75; in the U.K., £9.30) gives you access to 5,000 hostels in 77 countries that charge $5–$40 per person per night.

In Scotland, information is available from **The Scottish Youth Hostels Association** (✉ 7 Glebe Crescent, Stirling, FK8 2JA, ☎ 01786/451181, FAX 01786/450198). A list of independent hostels and bunkhouses is available from **Independent Backpackers' Hostels Scotland** (✉ Croft Bunkhouse and Bothy, Portnalong, Isle of Skye, IV47 8SL, ☎ 01478/640254).

UNIVERSITY HOUSING➤ For information on staying in college and university dormitories, contact the **Scottish Universities Accommodation Consortium** (SUAC, Box 808, Edinburgh, EH14 4AS, ☎ 0131/449–4034), **British Universities Accommodation Consortium** (BUAC, Box 1188, University Park, Nottingham, NG7 2RD, England, ☎ 0114/950–4571), or the **Higher Education Accommodation Consortium** (HEAC, 36 Collegiate Crescent, Sheffield, S10 2BP, England, ☎ 0114/268–3759).

ORGANIZATIONS

A major contact is the **Council on International Educational Exchange** (✉ mail orders only: CIEE, 205 E. 42nd St., 16th Floor, New York, NY 10017, ☎ 212/661–1450, info@ciee.org). The **Educational Travel Centre** (✉ 438 N. Frances St., Madison, WI 53703, ☎ 608/256–5551 or 800/747–5551, FAX 608/256–2042) offers rail passes and low-cost airline tickets, mostly for flights that depart from Chicago.

In Canada, also contact **Travel Cuts** (✉ 187 College St., Toronto, Ontario M5T 1P7, ☎ 416/979–2406 or 800/667–2887).

PUBLICATIONS

Check out the **Berkeley Guide to Great Britain & Ireland** (available in bookstores; or contact Fodor's Travel Publications, ☎ 800/533–6478; $18.95 plus $4 shipping).

T

TELEPHONES

The country code for Great Britain is 44. For local access numbers abroad, contact **AT&T USADirect** (☎ 800/874–4000), **MCI** Call USA (☎ 800/444–4444), or **Sprint** Express (☎ 800/793–1153).

OPERATORS AND INFORMATION

To call the operator, dial 100; directory inquiries (information), 192; international directory inquiries, 153.

TOUR OPERATORS

Among the companies that sell tours and packages to Scotland, the following are nationally known, have a proven reputation, and offer plenty of options.

GROUP TOURS

SUPER-DELUXE➤ **Abercrombie & Kent** (✉ 1520 Kensington Rd., Oak Brook, IL 60521-2141, ☎ 708/954–2944 or 800/323–7308, FAX 708/954–3324) and **Travcoa** (✉ Box 2630, 2350 S.E. Bristol St., Newport Beach, CA 92660, ☎ 714/476–2800 or 800/992–2003, FAX 714/476–2538).

DELUXE➤ **Globus** (✉ 5301 S. Federal Circle, Littleton, CO 80123-2980, ☎ 303/797–

2800 or 800/221–0090, FAX 303/795–0962), **Maupintour** (⊠ Box 807, 1515 St. Andrews Dr., Lawrence, KS 66047, ☎ 913/843–1211 or 800/255–4266, FAX 913/843–8351), and **Tauck Tours** (⊠ Box 5027, 276 Post Rd. W, Westport, CT 06881, ☎ 203/226–6911 or 800/468–2825, FAX 203/221–6828).

FIRST-CLASS➤ **Brendan Tours** (⊠ 15137 Califa St., Van Nuys, CA 91411, ☎ 818/785–9696 or 800/421–8446, FAX 818/902–9876), **British Airways Holidays** (☎ 800/247–9297), **Caravan Tours** (⊠ 401 N. Michigan Ave., Chicago, IL 60611, ☎ 312/321–9800 or 800/227–2826), **CIE Tours** (⊠ Box 501, 100 Hanover Ave., Cedar Knolls, NJ 07927-0501, ☎ 201/292–3899 or 800/243–8687), **Collette Tours** (⊠ 162 Middle St., Pawtucket, RI 02860, ☎ 401/728–3805 or 800/832–4656, FAX 401/728–1380), **Insight International Tours** (⊠ 745 Atlantic Ave., #720, Boston, MA 02111, ☎ 617/482–2000 or 800/582–8380, FAX 617/482–2884 or 800/622–5015), and **Trafalgar Tours** (⊠ 11 E. 26th St., New York, NY 10010, ☎ 212/689–8977 or 800/854–0103, FAX 800/457–6644).

PACKAGES

Independent packages are available from major tour operators and airlines. Contact **American Airlines Fly AAway Vacations** (☎ 800/321–2121), **British Airways Holidays** (☞ Group Tours, *above*), **Continental Vacations** (☎ 800/634–5555), **Delta Dream Vacations** (☎ 800/872–7786), and **United Vacations** (☎ 800/328–6877). Other packagers include **Celtic International Tours** (⊠ 1860 Western Ave., Albany, NY 12203, ☎ 518/463–5511 or 800/833–4373), **CIE Tours** (☞ Group Tours, *above*), **DER Tours** (⊠ 11933 Wilshire Blvd., Los Angeles, CA 90025, ☎ 310/479–4140 or 800/782–2424), **Five Star Touring** (⊠ 60 E. 42nd St., #612, New York, NY 10165, ☎ 212/818–9140 or 800/792–7827, FAX 212/818–9142), and **Jet Vacations** (⊠ 1775 Broadway, New York, NY 10019, ☎ 212/474–8740 or 800/538–2762). **Funjet Vacations,** based in Milwaukee, Wisconsin, and **Gogo Tours,** based in Ramsey, New Jersey, sell packages only through travel agents.

FROM THE U.K.

Get Active in Scotland (☎ 01738/444–144) offers a range of activities, from white-water rafting to painting, and **Mackay's** (⊠ 30 Frederick St., Edinburgh, EH2 2JR, ☎ 0131/226–4364) has self-catering accommodations from luxury homes to croft cottages.

THEME TRIPS

Travel Contacts (⊠ Box 173, Camberley, GU15 1YE, England, ☎ 0127/667–7217, FAX 0127/663477), which represents 150 tour operators, can satisfy virtually any special interest in Scotland. **Journeys Thru Scotland** (⊠ Box 116, Sheridan, OR 97378, ☎ 800/828–7583, FAX 503/843–4557) arranges tours that focus on golf, castles and gardens, and weaving, spinning, and knitting.

ADVENTURE➤ For strictly hiking, try **Above the Clouds Trekking** (⊠ Box 398, Worcester, MA 01602-0398, ☎ 800/233–4499 or 508/799–4499) and **Himalayan Travel** (⊠ 112 Prospect St., Stamford, CT 06901, ☎ 203/359–3711 or 800/225–2380, FAX 203/359–3669). **Francine Atkins' Scotland Ireland** (⊠ 2 Ross Ct., Trophy Club, TX 76262, ☎ 817/491–1105 or 800/742–0355, FAX 817/491–2025) arranges fishing, golfing, shooting, and hunting trips.

BARGE/RIVER CRUISES➤ **European Waterways** (⊠ 140 E. 56th St., #4C, New York, NY 10022, ☎ 212/688–9489 or 800/217–4447, FAX 212/688–3778 or 800/296–4554, cellular@interport.net) represents barges that carry 6–12 passengers; hot air ballooning and bicycling are available from most barges. For barge tours of Scotland, contact **Alden Yacht Charters** (⊠ 1909 Alden Landing, Portsmouth, RI 02871, ☎ 401/683–1782 or 800/662–2628, FAX 401/683–3668) and **Le Boat** (Box E, Mawood, NJ 07507, ☎ 201/342–1838 or 800/922–0291).

BEER➤ **MIR Corporation** (⊠ 85 S. Washington St., #210, Seattle, WA 98104, ☎ 206/624–7289 or 800/424–7289, FAX 206/624–7360, mir@igc.apc.org) has packages for beer lovers.

BICYCLING➤ Contact **Uniquely Europe** (✉ 2819 1st Ave., #280, Seattle, WA 98121-1113, ☎ 206/441-8682 or 800/426-3615, FAX 206/441-8862).

FISHING➤ For fishing packages throughout Scotland, try **Rod & Reel Adventures** (✉ 3507 Tully Rd., #B6, Modesto, CA 95356-1052, ☎ 209/524-7775 or 800/356-6982, FAX 209/524-1220).

GOLF➤ A wide array of packages are sold by **Francine Atkins' Scotland Ireland** (☞ Adventure, *above*), **Golf International** (✉ 275 Madison Ave., New York, NY 10016, ☎ 212/986-9176 or 800/833-1389, FAX 212/986-3720), **Golfpac** (✉ Box 162366, Altamonte Springs, FL 32716-2366, ☎ 407/260-2288 or 800/327-0878, FAX 407/260-8899), **ITC Golf Tours** (✉ 4134 Atlantic Ave., #205, Long Beach, CA 90807, ☎ 310/595-6905 or 800/257-4981), and **Stine's Golftrips** (✉ Box 2314, Winter Haven, FL 33883-2314, ☎ 941/324-1300 or 800/428-1940, FAX 941/325-0384, golftrip@cris.com). The **Scottish Golf and Travel Service** (✉ 12 Rutland Sq., Edinburgh, EH1 2BB, ☎ 800/847-8064, FAX 800/546-3510) arranges golf holidays throughout Scotland. Upscale golf holidays with gourmet dining are available from **Fenwick & Lang** (✉ 900 4th Ave., #1201, Seattle, WA 98164, ☎ 206/382-1384 or 800/243-6244).

HOMES AND GARDENS➤ **Coopersmith's England** (✉ Box 900, Inverness, CA 94937, ☎ 415/669-1914, FAX 415/669-1942) wines and dines you with gourmet meals and books your accommodations in castles, historic country inns, and manor houses.

HORSEBACK RIDING➤ **FITS Equestrian** (✉ 685 Lateen Rd., Solvang, CA 93463, ☎ 805/688-9494 or 800/666-3487, FAX 805/688-2943) has tours for every level of rider.

HORTICULTURE➤ Amateur and professional gardeners alike should contact **Expo Garden Tours** (✉ 101 Sunrise Hill Rd., Norwalk, CT 06851, ☎ 203/840-1441 or 800/448-2685, FAX 203/840-1224).

LEARNING➤ **Earthwatch** (✉ Box 403, 680 Mount Auburn St., Watertown, MA 02272, ☎ 617/926-8200 or 800/776-0188, FAX 617/926-8532, info@earthwatch.org) recruits volunteers to serve in its EarthCorps as short-term assistants to scientists on research expeditions. **Natural Habitat Adventures** (✉ 2945 Center Green Ct., Boulder, CO 80301, ☎ 303/449-3711 or 800/543-8917, FAX 303/449-3712) and **Smithsonian Study Tours and Seminars** (✉ 1100 Jefferson Dr. SW, Room 3045, MRC 702, Washington, DC 20560, ☎ 202/357-4700, FAX 202/633-9250) offer tours focused on natural history and culture. **National Audubon Society** (✉ 700 Broadway, New York, NY 10003, ☎ 212/979-

3066, FAX 212/353-0190, travel@audubon.org) has a train tour on board the Royal Scotsman.

NATURAL HISTORY➤ **Questers** (✉ 381 Park Ave. S, New York, NY 10016, ☎ 212/251-0444 or 800/468-8668, FAX 212/251-0890) explores the wild side of Scotland's Outer Islands and Highlands in the company of expert guides.

TRAIN TOURS➤ **Abercrombie & Kent** (☞ Group Tours, *above*) books guests on the luxurious Royal Scotsman train tours.

VILLA RENTALS➤ Contact **Villas International** (✉ 605 Market St., San Francisco, CA 94105, ☎ 415/281-0910 or 800/221-2260, FAX 415/281-0919).

WALKING➤ Tours operated by **Backroads** (✉ 1516 5th St., Berkeley, CA 94710-1740, ☎ 510/527-1555 or 800/462-2848, FAX 510/527-1444, goactive@Backroads.com) and **Wilderness Travel** (✉ 801 Allston Way, Berkeley, CA 94710, ☎ 510/548-0420 or 800/368-2794, FAX 510/548-0347, info@wildernesstravel.com) meander through the highlands and islands of Scotland. **Butterfield & Robinson** (✉ 70 Bond St., Toronto, Ontario, Canada M5B 1X3, ☎ 416/864-1354 or 800/678-1147, FAX 416/864-0541, info@butterfield.com) and **Country Walkers** (Box 180, Waterbury, VT 05676-0180, ☎ 802/244-1387 or 800/464-9255, FAX 802/

244–5661) have tours focusing on Scotland's cities and countryside. **English Lakeland Ramblers** (⌧ 18 Stuyvesant Oval #1A, New York NY 10009, ☎ 212/505–1020 or 800/724–8801, ℻ 212/979–5342) arranges walking and hiking tours that focus on literature, culture and natural history. **Walking the World** (⌧ Box 1186, Fort Collins, CO 80522, ☎ 303/225–0500) roams the Highlands, the Cairngornm Mountains, and Loch Ness with travelers 50 years old and older.

PUBLICATIONS

Contact the USTOA (☞ Organizations, *above*) for its **"Smart Traveler's Planning Kit."** Pamphlets in the kit include the "Worldwide Tour and Vacation Package Finder," "How to Select a Tour or Vacation Package," and information on the organization's consumer protection plan. Also get copy of the Better Business Bureau's **"Tips on Travel Packages"** (⌧ Publication 24-195, 4200 Wilson Blvd., Arlington, VA 22203; $2).

ORGANIZATIONS

The **National Tour Association** (⌧ NTA, 546 E. Main St., Lexington, KY 40508, ☎ 606/226–4444 or 800/755–8687) and the **United States Tour Operators Association** (⌧ USTOA, 211 E. 51st St., Suite 12B, New York, NY 10022, ☎ 212/750–7371) can provide lists of members and information on booking tours.

DISCOUNT PASSES

BritRail Passes are available from most travel agents or from **BritRail Travel International** offices (⌧ 1500 Broadway, New York, NY 10036, ☎ 212/575–2667; 94 Cumberland St., Toronto, Ontario M5R 1A3, ☎ 416/482–1777). Note that EurailPasses are not valid in Britain.

In London, contact the British Rail Travel Centre (⌧ Euston Station, London, NW1 1DF, ☎ 0171/387–7070).

SCENIC ROUTES

A luxury private train, the **Royal Scotsman,** does scenic tours, partly under steam power, with banquets en route. Book through Abercrombie & Kent (⌧ Sloane Square House, Holbein Pl., London SW1W 8NS, ☎ 0171/730–9600; or 1420 Kensington Rd., Oak Brook, IL 60521, ☎ 312/954–2944 or 800/323–7308); cost ranges from $1,950 for three days to $4,980 for seven days. **Waterman Railways** offers occasional Pullman rail cruises, partly steam-hauled, on the **Cock o' the North** and **Monarch of the Glen** (£399 from London); every passenger gets a window seat, and overnights are in hotels. Details are available from the London (Euston) Travel Center; book through **Waterman Railways** (⌧ Box 4472, Lichfield, Staffordshire, WS13 6RU, ☎ 01543/254076).

For travel apparel, appliances, personal-care items, and other travel necessities, get a free catalog from **Magellan's** (☎ 800/962–4943, ℻ 805/568–5406), **Orvis Travel** (☎ 800/541–3541, ℻ 703/343–7053), or **TravelSmith** (☎ 800/950–1600, ℻ 415/455–0554).

ELECTRICAL CONVERTERS

Send a self-addressed, stamped envelope to the **Franzus Company** (⌧ Customer Service, Dept. B50, Murtha Industrial Park, Box 142, Beacon Falls, CT 06403, ☎ 203/723–6664) for a copy of the free brochure "Foreign Electricity Is No Deep, Dark Secret."

For names of reputable agencies in your area, contact the **American Society of Travel Agents** (⌧ ASTA, 1101 King St., Suite 200, Alexandria, VA 22314, ☎ 703/739–2782), the **Association of Canadian Travel Agents** (⌧ Suite 201, 1729 Bank St., Ottawa, Ontario K1V 7Z5, ☎ 613/521–0474, ℻ 613/521–0805) or the **Association of British Travel Agents** (⌧ 55-57 Newman St., London, W1P 4AH, ☎ 0171/637–2444, ℻ 0171/637–0713).

The U.S. Department of State's American Citizens Services office (⌧

Room 4811, Washington, DC 20520; enclose SASE) issues **Consular Information Sheets** on all foreign countries. These cover issues such as crime, security, political climate, and health risks as well as listing embassy locations, entry requirements, currency regulations, and providing other useful information. (Travel warnings that counsel travelers to avoid a country entirely are issued in extreme cases.) For the latest information, stop in at any U.S. passport office, consulate, or embassy; call the interactive hot line (☎ 202/647–5225, FAX 202/647–3000); or, with your PC's modem, tap into the department's computer bulletin board (☎ 202/647–9225).

IN THE U.S.

British Tourist Authority (⊠ 551 5th Ave., Suite 701, New York, NY 10176, ☎ 212/986–2200 or 800/462–2748 FAX 212/986–1188).

IN CANADA

British Tourist Authority (⊠ 111 Avenue Rd., Suite 450, Toronto, Ontario M5R 35B, ☎ 416/925–6326).

IN THE U.K.

Scottish Tourist Board (⊠ 23 Ravelston Terr., Edinburgh, EH4 3EU, ☎ 0131/332–2433; ⊠ 19 Cockspur St., London, SWIY 5BL, ☎ 0171/930–8661).

For current conditions and forecasts, plus the local time and helpful travel tips, call the **Weather Channel Connection** (☎ 900/932–8437; 95¢ per minute) from a Touch-Tone phone.

The *International Traveler's Weather Guide* (⊠ Weather Press, Box 660606, Sacramento, CA 95866, ☎ 916/974–0201 or 800/972–0201; $10.95 includes shipping), written by two meteorologists, provides month-by-month information on temperature, humidity, and precipitation in more than 175 cities worldwide.

THE GOLD GUIDE / IMPORTANT CONTACTS

SMART TRAVEL TIPS A TO Z

Basic Information on Traveling in Scotland and Savvy Tips to Make Your Trip a Breeze

A

AIR TRAVEL

If time is an issue, **always look for nonstop flights,** which require no change of plane. If possible, **avoid connecting flights,** which stop at least once and can involve a change of plane, even though the flight number remains the same; if the first leg is late, the second waits.

For better service, **fly smaller or regional carriers,** which often have higher passenger satisfaction ratings. Sometimes they have such in-flight amenities as leather seats or greater legroom and they often have better food.

Don't automatically think you must go to London to reach Scotland by air. Frankfurt Airport is quoting under 45 minutes' transfer time compared with 75 minutes at London Heathrow; Amsterdam and Paris airports also offer direct links to Glasgow and Edinburgh. Of course, don't forget you can also **fly direct to Glasgow, and at least in the charter market, to Prestwick and Edinburgh.**

CUTTING COSTS

The Sunday travel section of most newspapers is a good place to look for deals.

CONSOLIDATORS➤ Consolidators buy tickets for scheduled flights at reduced rates from the airlines, then sell them at prices below the lowest available from the airlines directly—usually without advance restrictions. Sometimes you can even get your money back if you need to return the ticket. Carefully read the fine print detailing penalties for changes and cancellations. If you doubt the reliability of a consolidator, **confirm your reservation with the airline.**

DISCOUNT PASSES➤ At certain (less popular) times of year, airlines may offer travel passes covering a certain number of flights within Scotland, which offer considerable savings over the cost of the flights booked individually. Inquire immediately before your arrival in Scotland as to what is available.

FARE WARS➤ If you intend to fly to Scotland from London, **take advantage of the current fare wars** on internal routes—notably between London's three airports and Glasgow/Edinburgh. At press time, Ryanair leads the field between London Stansted (with its excellent rail links from London's Liverpool Street Station) and Glasgow Prestwick. They currently offer fares from as low as £29 one way. When you reach Prestwick, another worthwhile bargain awaits rail travelers: For only £5 you can get a ticket for any rail destination in Scotland. The railway station is adjacent to the main Prestwick terminal building.

MAJOR AIRLINES➤ The least-expensive airfares from the major airlines are priced for round-trip travel and are subject to restrictions. Usually, you must **book in advance and buy the ticket within 24 hours** to get cheaper fares, and you may have to **stay over a Saturday night.** The lowest fare is subject to availability, and only a small percentage of the plane's total seats is sold at that price. It's smart to **call a number of airlines,** and **when you are quoted a good price, book it on the spot**—the same fare may not be available on the same flight the next day. Airlines generally allow you to change your return date for a $25 to $50 fee. If you don't use your ticket, you can apply the cost toward the purchase of a new ticket, again for a small charge. However, most low-fare tickets are nonrefundable. To get the lowest airfare, **check different routings.** If your destination has more than one gateway, **compare prices to different airports.**

FROM THE U.K.➤ To save money on flights, **look into an APEX or Super-Pex ticket.** APEX tickets must be booked in advance and have certain restrictions. Super-PEX tickets can be purchased right at the airport.

ALOFT

AIRLINE FOOD➢ If you hate airline food, **ask for special meals when booking.** These can be vegetarian, low-cholesterol, or kosher, for example; commonly prepared to order in smaller quantities than standard fare, they can be tastier.

JET LAG➢ To avoid this syndrome, which occurs when travel disrupts your body's natural cycles, try to maintain a normal routine. At night, **get some sleep.** By day, move about the cabin to **stretch your legs, eat light meals, and drink water—not alcohol.**

SMOKING➢ Smoking is not allowed on flights of six hours or less within the continental United States. Smoking is also prohibited on flights within Canada. For U.S. flights longer than six hours or international flights, **contact your carrier regarding their smoking policy.** Some carriers have prohibited smoking throughout their system; others allow smoking only on certain routes or even certain departures of that route.

B
BICYCLING

Because Scotland's main roads are continually being upgraded, it is easier than ever for bicyclists to access the network of quieter rural roads in such areas as Dumfries and Galloway, the Borders, and much

of eastern Scotland, especially Grampian. Still, care must be taken in getting from some town centers to rural riding areas, so if in doubt, ask a local. In a few areas of the Highlands, notably in northwestern Scotland, the rugged nature of the terrain and limited population have resulted in the lack of side roads, making it more difficult—sometimes impossible—to plan a minor-road route in these areas.

The best months for cycling in Scotland are May, June, and September, when the roads are often quieter and the weather is usually better. Winds are predominantly from the southwest, so plan your route accordingly.

A variety of agencies are now promoting "safe routes" for recreational cyclists in Scotland. These routes are signposted, and the agencies have produced maps or leaflets showing where they run. Perhaps best known is the Glasgow–Loch Lomond–Killin Cycleway, which makes use of former railway track beds, forest trails, quiet rural side roads, and some main roads. The Glasgow to Irvine Cycle Route runs south and west of Glasgow and links with the Johnstone and Greenock Railway Path. In Edinburgh there is the Innocent Railway Path from Holyrood Path to St. Leonards. Contact the relevant tourist board for more information.

BIKES ON BUSES

Although some rural bus services will trans-

port cycles if space is available, you usually can't count on getting your bike on a bus. Be sure to check well in advance with the appropriate bus company.

BIKES ON FERRIES

Bicycles can be taken without any restrictions on car and passenger ferries in Scotland, and it is not generally necessary to book in advance. The three main ferry service operators (☞ Ferry Travel *in* Important Contacts A to Z, *above*) are Caledonian MacBrayne, which charges £1 per journey for accompanied bicycles; Western Ferries, which carries accompanied bicycles free; and P & O Ferries, which charges from £6.20 to £10.40 in addition to the cost of a passenger ticket. On car ferries, check cycles early so that they can be loaded through the boat's car entrance.

BIKES ON TRAINS

Scotrail strongly advises making a reservation for you and your bike at least a month in advance. On several trains, reservations are compulsory. A leaflet containing the latest information is available through Scotrail and can be picked up at most manned train stations within Scotland.

CYCLING OFF-ROAD

People in Scotland were cycling off-road long before the mountain bike was invented. Sometimes they cycled over rights of way in the Highlands; sometimes they biked cross-country to shorten the time taken to climb less

THE GOLD GUIDE / SMART TRAVEL TIPS

accessible high hills. The growing popularity of mountain biking, however, has forced the Scots to focus on the suitability and availability of routes.

Scotland's legal position on off-road cycling is complex. Cycling is covered by road traffic laws because a bike is classified as a vehicle. In a strict legal sense, cycling off-road is only possible on specifically designated cycle tracks, routes that have a common-law right of way for cycles, or routes that have the consent of the landowner. Legally, cyclists are not allowed on pedestrian rights of way, but many landowners don't mind if cyclists use them. Nevertheless, it is best for off-road cyclists to seek local advice when planning routes.

BUS TRAVEL

FROM ENGLAND

Coaches (as long-distance and touring buses are usually called) provide the cheapest way to travel between England and Scotland; fares are approximately one-third of the rail fares for comparable trips. About 20 companies operate service between major cities, including National Express. Journey time between London and Glasgow or Edinburgh is 8 to 8¼ hours. The main London terminal is Victoria Coach Station, but some Scottish companies use Gloucester Road Coach Station in west London, near the Penta Hotel. Many people travel to Scotland by coach; in summer a reservation three

or four days ahead is advisable. At press time, fares were £100 for a one-way, first-class ticket and £80 for an economy fare.

PASSES

On bus routes, Tourist Trail Pass offers complete freedom of travel on any National Express or Scottish Citylink services throughout the mainland UK. Four different permutations give up to 15 days travel in 30 consecutive days. It is available from Scottish Citylink offices, most bus stations, and any National Express appointed agent.

WITHIN SCOTLAND

The country's bus network is extensive. Bus service is comprehensive in cities, less so in country districts. **Express service links main cities and towns,** connecting, for example, Glasgow and Edinburgh to Inverness, Aberdeen, Perth, Skye, Ayr, Dumfries, and Carlisle; or Inverness with Aberdeen, Wick, Thurso, and Fort William. These express services are very fast, and fares are quite reasonable.

For town, suburban, or short-distance journeys, you normally buy your ticket on the bus, from a paybox or the driver. Sometimes you need exact change. For longer journeys—for example, Glasgow–Inverness—it is usual to reserve and pay at the bus station booking office.

BUSINESS HOURS

BANKS

Banks are open weekdays 9:30–3:30, some days to 4:45. Some

banks have extended hours on Thursday evenings, and a few are open on Saturday mornings. Some also close for an hour at lunchtime. The major airports operate 24-hour banking services seven days a week.

SHOPS

Usual business hours are Monday–Saturday 9–5:30. Outside the main centers, most shops observe an early closing day once a week, often Wednesday or Thursday—they close at 1 PM and do not reopen until the following morning. In small villages, many also close for lunch. Department stores in large cities stay open for late-night shopping (usually until 7:30 or 8) one day a week. Apart from some newsstands and small food stores, many shops are closed on Sunday except in larger towns and cities, where main shopping malls may be open.

C

CAMERAS, CAMCORDERS, & COMPUTERS

IN TRANSIT

Always **keep your film, tape, or disks out of the sun;** never put these on the dashboard of a car. Carry an extra supply of batteries, and **be prepared to turn on your camera, camcorder, or laptop computer for security personnel** to prove that it's real.

X-RAYS

Always **ask for hand inspection at security.** Such requests are virtually always honored at U.S. airports, and are usually accommodated abroad. Photographic film becomes clouded after successive exposure to airport X-ray machines. Videotape and computer disks are not harmed by X-rays, but **keep your tapes and disks away from metal detectors.**

CUSTOMS

Before departing, **register your foreign-made camera or laptop with U.S. Customs.** If your equipment is U.S.-made, call the consulate of the country you'll be visiting to find out whether it should be registered with local customs upon arrival.

CAR RENTAL

If you're traveling to more than one country, make sure your rental contract permits you to take the car across borders and that the insurance policy covers you in every country you visit. Remember that unlike cars in the United States or the rest of Europe, British cars have the steering wheel on the right. Therefore, you may want to leave your rented car in Britain and pick up a left-side drive when you cross the Channel.

CUTTING COSTS

If you're flying to Scotland and plan to spend some time first in Edinburgh, don't pick up your car until you're ready to leave the city; otherwise, arrange to pick up and return your car at the airport. And carefully weigh the convenience of renting a car from a major company with an airport

branch against the savings to be had from a local company with offices in town.

To get the best deal, **book through a travel agent who is willing to shop around.** Ask your agent to **look for fly-drive packages,** which also save you money, and **ask if local taxes are included** in the rental or fly-drive price. These can be as high as 20% in some destinations. Don't forget to find out about required deposits, cancellation penalties, drop-off charges, and the cost of any required insurance coverage.

Also **ask your travel agent about a company's customer-service record.** How has it responded to late plane arrivals and vehicle mishaps? Are there often lines at the rental counter, and—if you're traveling during a holiday period—does a confirmed reservation guarantee you a car?

Always **find out what equipment is standard** at your destination before specifying what you want; automatic transmission and air-conditioning are usually optional—and very expensive. You may, however, consider paying extra for an automatic if you are unfamiliar with manual transmissions. Driving on the left side of the road will probably be enough to worry about.

Be sure to **look into wholesalers**—companies that do not own their own fleets but rent in bulk from those that do and often offer better rates than tradi-

tional car-rental operations. Prices are best during off-peak periods; rentals booked through wholesalers must be paid for before you leave the United States.

INSURANCE

When driving a rented car, you are generally responsible for any damage to or loss of the rental vehicle. Before you rent, **see what coverage you already have** under the terms of your personal auto insurance policy and credit cards.

If you do not have auto insurance or an umbrella insurance policy that covers damage to third parties, purchasing CDW or LDW is highly recommended.

Collision policies that car-rental companies sell for European rentals typically do not cover stolen vehicles. Before you buy additional coverage for theft, find out if your credit card or personal auto insurance will cover the loss.

LICENSE REQUIREMENTS

In Scotland your own driver's license is acceptable. An International Driver's Permit is a good idea; it's available from the American or Canadian automobile associations, or, in the United Kingdom, from the AA or RAC.

SURCHARGES

Before you pick up a car in one city and leave it in another, **ask about drop-off charges or one-way service fees,** which can be substantial. Note, too, that some rental agencies charge extra if you return the car before the time specified on your contract. To avoid a hefty refueling fee, **fill the tank just before you turn in the car**—but be aware that gas stations near the rental outlet may overcharge.

THE CHANNEL TUNNEL

The "Chunnel" is the fastest way to cross the English Channel short of flying—35 minutes from Folkestone to Calais, 60 minutes from motorway to motorway, or 3 hours from Waterloo, London, to Paris's Gare du Nord. It consists of two large 50-kilometer- (31-mile-) long train tunnels, and a smaller service tunnel running between them. The Tunnel is reached from exit 11a of the M20/A20. Tickets for either Tunnel service can be purchased in advance (☞ Important Contacts A to Z, *above*).

CHILDREN & TRAVEL

When traveling with children, **plan ahead** and **involve your youngsters** as you outline your trip. **Pack things to keep them busy** en route (☞ Children & Travel *in* Important Contacts A to Z). On sightseeing days, try to **schedule activities of special interest to your children**, like a trip to a zoo or a playground. If you **plan your itinerary around festivals,** you'll never lack for things to do. In addition, **check local newspapers for special events** mounted by public libraries, museums, and parks.

BABY-SITTING

For recommended local sitters, **check with your hotel desk.** Many bed-and-breakfast landladies will be happy to baby-sit while you go out for a meal, but this should not be relied upon.

DRIVING

If you are renting a car, don't forget to **arrange for a car seat when you reserve.** Sometimes they're free.

FLYING

As a rule, infants under two not occupying a seat fly at greatly reduced fares and occasionally for free. If your children are two or older **ask about special children's fares.** Age limits for these fares vary among carriers. Rules also vary regarding unaccompanied minors, so again, check with your airline.

BAGGAGE➤ In general, the adult baggage allowance applies to children paying half or more of the adult fare. If you are traveling with an infant, **ask about carry-on allowances** before departure. In general, for infants charged 10% of the adult fare you are allowed one carry-on bag and a collapsible stroller, which may have to be checked; you may be limited to less if the flight is full.

SAFETY SEATS➤ According to the FAA, it's a good idea to **use safety seats aloft** for children weighing less than 40 pounds. Airline policies vary. U.S. carriers allow FAA-approved models but usually require that you buy a ticket, even if

your child would otherwise ride free, since the seats must be strapped into regular seats. However, some U.S. and foreign-flag airlines may require you to hold your baby during takeoff and landing—defeating the seat's purpose. Other foreign carriers may not allow infant seats at all, or may charge a child rather than an infant fare for their use.

FACILITIES➤ When making your reservation, **request children's meals or freestanding bassinets** if you need them; the latter are available only to those seated at the bulkhead, where there's enough legroom. If you don't need a bassinet, **think twice before requesting bulkhead seats**—the only storage space for in-flight necessities is in inconveniently distant overhead bins.

GAMES

Milton Bradley and Parker Brothers have travel versions of some of their most popular games, including Yahtzee, Trouble, Sorry, and Monopoly. Prices run $5 to $8. Look for them in the travel section of your local toy store.

LODGING

Most hotels allow children under a certain age to stay in their parents' room at no extra charge; others charge them as extra adults. Be sure to **ask about the cutoff age.**

Although there is no general policy regarding hotel rates for children in Scotland, Milton Hotels allow children under 14 to stay for free in their parents' room. Many also have adjoining family rooms. Embassy Hotels allow up to two children under 16 to stay free when sharing their parents' room and offer a 25% discount for children occupying their own rooms.

CRUISES

Many of the crossings from North America to Europe are repositioning sailings for ships that cruise the Caribbean in winter and European waters in summer. Sometimes rates are reduced, and fly/cruise packages are usually available.

Check the travel pages of your Sunday newspaper or contact a travel agent for lines and sailing dates.

To get the best deal on a cruise, **consult a cruise-only travel agency.**

CUSTOMS & DUTIES

To speed your clearance through customs, **keep receipts for all your purchases abroad** and **be ready to show the inspector what you've bought.** If you feel that you've been incorrectly or unfairly charged a duty, you can **appeal assessments in dispute.** First ask to see a supervisor. If you are still unsatisfied, **write to the port director** your point of entry, sending your customs receipt and any other appropriate documentation. The address will be listed on your receipt. If you still don't get satisfaction, you can take your case

to customs headquarters in Washington.

IN SCOTLAND

Entering the United Kingdom, a traveler 17 or over can take in (1) 200 cigarettes or 100 cigarillos or 50 cigars or 250 grams of tobacco; (2) one liter of alcohol over 22% volume or two liters of alcohol under 22% volume or two liters of fortified or sparkling wine; (3) two liters of still table wine; (4) 60 ml of perfume and 250 ml of toilet water; (5) other goods to a value of £145 (no pooling of exemptions is allowed).

IN THE U.S.

You may bring home $400 worth of foreign goods duty-free if you've been out of the country for at least 48 hours and haven't already used the $400 allowance, or any part of it, in the past 30 days.

Travelers 21 or older may bring back 1 liter of alcohol duty-free, provided the beverage laws of the state through which they reenter the United States allow it. In addition, regardless of their age, they are allowed 100 non-Cuban cigars and 200 cigarettes. Antiques, which the U.S. Customs Service defines as objects more than 100 years old, are duty-free. Original works of art done entirely by hand are also duty-free. These include, but are not limited to, paintings, drawings, and sculptures.

Duty-free, travelers may mail packages valued at up to $200 to themselves and up to $100

to others, with a limit of one parcel per addressee per day (and no alcohol or tobacco products or perfume valued at more than $5); on the outside, the package must be labeled as being either for personal use or an unsolicited gift, and a list of its contents and their retail value must be attached. Mailed items do not affect your duty-free allowance on your return.

IN CANADA

If you've been out of Canada for at least seven days, you may bring in C$500 worth of goods duty-free. If you've been away for fewer than seven days but for more than 48 hours, the duty-free allowance drops to C$200; if your trip lasts between 24 and 48 hours, the allowance is C$50. You cannot pool allowances with family members. Goods claimed under the C$500 exemption may follow you by mail; those claimed under the lesser exemptions must accompany you.

Alcohol and tobacco products may be included in the seven-day and 48-hour exemptions but not in the 24-hour exemption. If you meet the age requirements of the province or territory through which you reenter Canada, you may bring in, duty-free, 1.14 liters (40 imperial ounces) of wine or liquor *or* 24 12-ounce cans or bottles of beer or ale. If you are 16 or older, you may bring in, duty-free, 200 cigarettes, 50 cigars or cigarillos, and 400 tobacco sticks or 400 grams of manufactured tobacco. Alcohol and tobacco must accompany you on your return.

An unlimited number of gifts with a value of up to C$60 each may be mailed to Canada duty-free. These do not affect your duty-free allowance on your return. Label the package "Unsolicited Gift—Value Under $60." Alcohol and tobacco are excluded.

D

DINING

In a country so involved in the tourism industry, "all day" meal places are becoming quite widespread. The normal lunch period, however, is 12:30–2:30. A few places offer "high tea"—one hot dish and masses of cakes, bread and butter, and jam, served with tea only, around 5:30–6:30.

DISABILITIES & ACCESSIBILITY

In Scotland, many hotels offer facilities for wheelchair users, and special carriages are beginning to appear on intercity and long-distance trains. However, since much of Scotland's beauty is found in hidden hills and corners "off the beaten track," renting a car is probably a better option.

When discussing accessibility with an operator or reservationist, ask hard questions. Are there any stairs, inside *or* out? Are there grab bars next to the toilet *and* in the shower/tub?

How wide is the doorway to the room? To the bathroom? For the most extensive facilities, meeting the latest legal specifications, **opt for newer accommodations,** which more often have been designed with access in mind. Older properties or ships must usually be retrofitted and may offer more limited facilities as a result. Be sure to **discuss your needs before booking.**

DISCOUNTS & DEALS

You shouldn't have to pay for a discount. In fact, you may already be eligible for all kinds of savings. Here are some time-honored strategies for getting the best deal.

LOOK IN YOUR WALLET

When you **use your credit card to make travel purchases,** you may get free travel-accident insurance, collision damage insurance, medical or legal assistance, depending on the card and bank that issued it. Visa and MasterCard provide one or more of these services, so **get a copy of your card's travel benefits.** If you are a member of the AAA or an oil-company-sponsored road-assistance plan, always **ask hotel or car-rental reservationists for auto-club discounts.** Some clubs offer additional discounts on tours, cruises, or admission to attractions. And don't forget that auto-club membership entitles you to free maps and trip-planning services.

DIAL FOR DOLLARS

To save money, **look into "1-800" discount reservations services,** which often have lower rates. These services use their buying power to get a better price on hotels, airline tickets, and sometimes even car rentals. When booking a room, always **call the hotel's local toll-free number** (if one is available) rather than the central reservations number—you'll often get a better price. Ask the reservationist about special packages or corporate rates, which are usually available even if you're not traveling on business.

JOIN A CLUB?

Discount clubs can be a legitimate source of savings, but you must use the participating hotels and visit the participating attractions in order to realize any benefits. Remember, too, that you have to pay a fee to join, so **determine if you'll save enough to warrant your membership fee.** Before booking with a club, **make sure the hotel or other supplier isn't offering a better deal.**

GET A GUARANTEE

When shopping for the best deal on hotels and car rentals, **look for guaranteed exchange rates,** which protect you against a falling dollar. With your rate locked in, you won't pay more even if the price goes up in the local currency.

SENIORS CITIZENS & STUDENTS

As a senior-citizen traveler, you may be eligible for special rates, but you should mention your senior-citizen status up front. If you're a student, or under 26, you can also get discounts, especially if you have an official ID card (☞ Senior-Citizen Discounts *and* Students on the Road, *below*).

FUEL AVAILABILITY AND COSTS

Though costs have been remarkably stable in recent years, **expect to pay a good deal more for gasoline than in the United States,** about £2.50 a gallon (55p a liter) for unleaded—up to 10p a gallon higher in remote rural locations. Remember, too, that the British Imperial gallon is about 20% more in volume than the U.S. gallon. What you may find confusing is that although service stations advertise prices by the gallon (mainly for the benefit of the conservative British who continue to resist metrication), pumps actually measure in liters. A British gallon is approximately 4.5 liters.

Most gas stations stock 4-star (97 octane), unleaded and super unleaded, plus diesel. Service stations are located at regular intervals on motorways and are usually open 24 hours a day, though stations elsewhere usually close from 9 PM to 7 AM, and in country areas many close at 6 PM and all day on Sunday.

RULES OF THE ROAD

The most noticeable difference for the visitor is that when **in Britain,**

you drive on the left. This takes a bit of getting used to, but it doesn't take very long, particularly if you're driving a British car where the steering and mirrors will be adjusted for U.K. conditions. **Give yourself time to adjust to driving on the left**—especially if you pick up your car at the airport and are still suffering from jet lag.

One of the most complicated questions facing visitors to Britain is that of speed limits. In urban areas, except for certain freeways, it is generally 30 miles per hour (mph), but it is 40 mph on some main roads, as indicated by circular red signs. In rural areas the official limit is 60 mph on ordinary roads and 70 mph on motor-ways—and traffic police can be hard on speeders, especially in urban areas. In other respects procedures are similar to those in the United States.

TYPES OF ROADS

A very good network of superhighways, known as motorways, and divided highways, known as dual carriage-ways, extends through-out Britain, though in the remoter areas of Scotland where the motorway has not penetrated, travel is noticeably slower. Motorways shown with the prefix "M" are mainly two or three lanes in each direction, without any right-hand turns. If you'll be cover-ing longer distances, these are the roads to use, though inevitably you'll see less of the countryside. Service

areas are at most about an hour apart. Dual carriageways, usually shown on a map as a thick red line (often with a black line in the center) and the prefix "A" followed by a number perhaps with a bracket "T" (for exam-ple, A304[T]), are similar to motorways, except that right turns are sometimes permit-ted and you'll find both traffic lights and traffic circles on them.

The vast network of other main roads, which typical maps show as either single red "A" roads, or narrower brown "B" roads, also numbered, are for the most part the old coach and turnpike roads built for horses and carriages in the last century or earlier. Travel along these roads is a bit slower because passing is more difficult, and your trip will take longer than it would take along a motorway. On the other hand, you'll see much more of Scotland.

Minor roads (shown as yellow or white on most maps, unlettered and unnumbered) are the ancient lanes and by-ways of Britain, roads that are not only living history but a superb way of discovering the real Scotland. You have to drive along them slowly and carefully. On single-track roads, found in the north and west of Scotland, there isn't room for two vehicles to pass, and you must use a passing place if you meet an oncoming car or tractor, or if a car behind wishes to overtake.

THE GOLD GUIDE / SMART TRAVEL TIPS

Never hold up traffic on single-track roads; it is considered extremely bad manners.

F
FERRY TRAVEL

With so many islands, plus the great Firth of Clyde waterway, ferry services in Scotland are of paramount importance. Most of these now transport vehicles as well as foot passengers, although a number of the smaller ones are passengers only.

The main operator is Caledonian MacBrayne Ltd., known generally as Calmac. Services extend from the Firth of Clyde, where there is an extremely extensive network, right up to the northwest of Scotland and all of the Hebrides. Calmac offers an Island Rover runabout ticket, which is ideal for touring holidays in the islands, as well as an island-hopping scheme called Island Hop-scotch, and inclusive holidays under the name Hebridean Drive-away which include ferries, accommodation and some meals.

The Dunoon–Gourock route on the Clyde, as well as a run from Islay (Port Askaig) to Jura is served by Western Ferries.

P & O Ferries operates a car ferry for Orkney between Scrabster (near Thurso) or Aberdeen and Stromness (on the main island of Orkney, called Mainland) and for Shetland between Aberdeen and Lerwick. The main ferries, the *St. Clair* and the *St. Sunniva*, have cabin accommodations and sail five times a week in each direction.

G
GAY & LESBIAN TRAVEL

Outside the main cities, at least a sector of Scottish society is a little Calvinistic and not given to much in the way of open expression of heterosexuality, let alone anything else. In short, Scotland isn't California. However, most Scots also have an attitude of "live and let live," so it is unlikely you will encounter problems or any real hostility.

H
HEALTH

No particular shots are necessary for visiting Scotland from the USA. If you are traveling in the Highlands and islands in summer, **pack some midge repellent and antihistamine cream** to reduce swelling: the Highland midge is a force to be reckoned with.

I
INSURANCE

Travel insurance can protect your monetary investment, replace your luggage and its contents, or provide for medical coverage should you fall ill during your trip. Most tour operators, travel agents, and insurance agents sell specialized health-and-accident, flight, trip-cancellation, and luggage insurance as well as comprehensive policies with some or all of these coverages. Comprehensive policies may also reimburse you for delays due to weather—an important consideration if you're traveling during the winter months. Some health-insurance policies do not cover preexisting conditions, but waivers may be available in specific cases. Coverage is sold by the companies listed in Important Contacts A to Z; these companies act as the policy's administrators. The actual insurance is usually underwritten by a well-known name, such as The Travelers or Continental Insurance.

Before you make any purchase, **review your existing health and homeowner's policies** to find out whether they cover expenses incurred while traveling.

BAGGAGE

Airline liability for baggage is limited to $1,250 per person on domestic flights. On international flights, it amounts to $9.07 per pound or $20 per kilogram for checked baggage (roughly $640 per 70-pound bag) and $400 per passenger for unchecked baggage. Insurance for losses exceeding the terms of your airline ticket can be bought directly from the airline at check-in for about $10 per $1,000 of coverage; note that it excludes a rather extensive list of items, shown on your airline ticket.

COMPREHENSIVE

Comprehensive insurance policies include all the coverages described above plus some that may not be available in more specific policies. If you have purchased an expensive vacation, especially one that involves travel abroad, comprehensive insurance is a must; **look for policies that include trip delay insurance,** which will protect you in the event that weather problems cause you to miss your flight, tour, or cruise. A few insurers will also sell you a waiver for preexisting medical conditions. Some of the companies that offer both these features are Access America, Carefree Travel, Travel Insured International, and TravelGuard (☞ Insurance *in* Important Contacts A to Z).

FLIGHT

You should **think twice before buying flight insurance.** Often purchased as a last-minute impulse at the airport, it pays a lump sum when a plane crashes, either to a beneficiary if the insured dies or sometimes to a surviving passenger who loses his or her eyesight or a limb. Supplementing the airlines' coverage described in the limits-of-liability paragraphs on your ticket, it's expensive and basically unnecessary. Charging an airline ticket to a major credit card often automatically provides you with coverage that may also extend to travel by bus, train, and ship.

HEALTH

Medicare generally does not cover health care costs outside the United States; nor do many privately issued policies. If your own health insurance policy does not cover you outside the United States, **consider buying supplemental medical coverage.** It can reimburse you for $1,000–$150,000 worth of medical and/or dental expenses incurred as a result of an accident or illness during a trip. These policies also may include a personal-accident, or death-and-dismemberment, provision, which pays a lump sum ranging from $15,000 to $500,000 to your beneficiaries if you die or to you if you lose one or more limbs or your eyesight, and a medical-assistance provision, which may either reimburse you for the cost of referrals, evacuation, or repatriation and other services, or automatically enroll you as a member of a particular medical-assistance company. (☞ Health *in* Important Contacts A to Z.)

TRIP

Without insurance, you will lose all or most of your money if you cancel your trip regardless of the reason. Especially if your airline ticket, cruise, or package tour is nonrefundable and cannot be changed, it's essential that you **buy trip-cancellation-and-interruption insurance.** When considering how much coverage you need, look for a policy that will cover the cost of your trip plus the nondiscounted price of a one-way airline ticket should you need to return home early. Read the fine print carefully, especially sections that define "family member" and "preexisting medical conditions." Also

consider default or bankruptcy insurance, which protects you against a supplier's failure to deliver. Be aware, however, that if you buy such a policy from a travel agency, tour operator, airline, or cruise line, it may not cover default by the firm in question.

L

LANGUAGE

"Much," said Doctor Johnson, "may be made of a Scotchman if he be caught young." This quote sums up—even today—the attitude of some English people to the Scots language. They simply assume that their English is superior. Since they speak the language of Parliament and much of the media, their arrogance is understandable. The Scots have long been made to feel uncomfortable about their mother tongue and have only themselves to blame, being until recently actively encouraged—at school, for example—to ape the dialect of the Thames Valley ("Standard English") in order to "get on" in life.

The Scots language (that is, Lowland Scots, not Gaelic) was a northern form of Middle English and in its day was the language used in the court and in literature. It borrowed from Scandinavian, Dutch, French, and Gaelic. After a series of historical body blows—such as the decamping of the Scottish Court to England after 1603 and the printing of the King James Bible in English

THE GOLD GUIDE / SMART TRAVEL TIPS

but not in Scots—it declined as a literary or official language. It survives, in various forms, virtually as an underground language spoken at home, in shops, on the playground, the farm, or the quayside among ordinary folk, especially in its heartland, in northeast Scotland. (There they describe Scots who use the brayed diphthongs of the English Thames Valley as speaking with a *bool in the mou*—marble in the mouth!)

Plenty of Scots speak English with only an accent and virtually all will "modulate" either unconsciously or out of politeness into understandable English when conversing with a nondialect speaker. As for Gaelic, that belongs to a different Celtic culture and, though threatened, hangs on in spite of the Highlands depopulation.

LODGING

In many small towns and villages there are inns and hotels that offer central heating, rooms with bath or shower and telephone and television, and other comforts at competitive prices. But **rural Scotland is bed-and-breakfast land,** and, because Scottish breakfasts are nothing if not hearty, these lodging places represent a very good value. Indeed, they can be hard to beat, especially since most offer genuinely warm hospitality, as well as home cooking and comforts. The Scottish Tourist Board's

Scotland: Hotels and Guest Houses (£8.99 by mail) and *Scotland Bed and Breakfast* (£6.99) together give details of more than 4,000 bed-and-breakfasts.

APARTMENT & VILLA RENTAL

If you want a home base that's roomy enough for a family and comes with cooking facilities, **consider taking a furnished rental.** This can also save you money, but not always—some rentals are luxury properties (economical only when your party is large). Home-exchange directories list rentals—often second homes owned by prospective house swappers—and some services search for a house or apartment for you (even a castle if that's your fancy) and handle the paperwork. Some send an illustrated catalog; others send photographs only of specific properties, sometimes at a charge; up-front registration fees may apply.

HOME EXCHANGE

If you would like to find a house, an apartment, or some other type of vacation property to exchange for your own while on holiday, **become a member of a home-exchange organization,** which will send you its updated listings of available exchanges for a year, and will include your own listing in at least one of them. Arrangements for the actual exchange are made by the two parties involved, not by the organization.

HOTELS

Hotels in the larger cities are generally also good. Glasgow and Edinburgh boast a number of superior establishments, as well as an extensive range of good hotels in all other price categories.

If you are touring around, you are not likely to be stranded: In recent years, even in the height of the season—July and August—hotel occupancy has run at about 80%. On the other hand, if you arrive in Edinburgh at festival time or some place where a big Highland Gathering or golf tournament is in progress, your choice of accommodations will be extremely limited, and your best bet will be to try for a room in a nearby village. To secure your first choice, **it's always good to reserve in advance,** either through a travel agent at home, directly with the facility, or through local Information Centers (see the individual city or regional chapters), making use of their "Book-a-Bed-Ahead" services. Telephone bookings made from home should be confirmed by letter, and country hotels expect you to turn up by about 6 PM.

RATINGS

Scotland was the first part of the United Kingdom to run a national "Classification and Grading Scheme" to take some of the guesswork out of booking accommodations. Though Fodor's does not use this rating system, you will see it in Scottish publications, and when you are considering a hotel, guest house, or bed-and-breakfast, make sure that you pay close attention to its classification and its grading. The classification part is easy. The number of crowns from zero to five tells you the range of the establishment's facilities. Zero crowns (confusingly described as "Listed") is basic, five crowns luxury. The grading part is actually more important. It purports to assess the quality of the place objectively. Very roughly, the ordinary is "Approved," the good "Commended," the very good "Highly Commended," and the "De Luxe" the best of all. Thus a two-crown "Highly Commended" is probably better value all around than a four-crown "Approved." The awards are part of the accommodations listing in the Where to Stay guides distributed at most tourist information centers. Not all establishments participate, but the scheme is becoming popular.

M

MAIL

Airmail letters to the United States and Canada cost 41p, postcards 35p, aerograms 36p. Letters and postcards to Europe under 20 grams cost 30p (25p to other European Union member countries). Within the U.K. first-class letters cost 25p, second-class letters and postcards 19p.

RECEIVING MAIL

If you're uncertain where you'll be staying, you can **arrange to have your mail sent to American Express.** The service is free to cardholders; all others pay a small fee. You can also collect letters at any post office, by addressing them to Poste Restante at the post office you nominate. In Edinburgh, a convenient central office is St. James Centre Post Office, St. James Centre, Edinburgh, EH1 3SR, Scotland.

MONEY

Britain's currency is the pound sterling, which is divided into 100 pence (100p). Notes are issued in the values of £50, £20, £10, and £5 (also £1 in Scotland). Coins are issued to the values of £1, 50p, 20p, 10p, 5p, 2p, and 1p. Scottish coins are the same as English ones, but Scottish notes are issued by three banks: the Bank of Scotland, the Royal Bank of Scotland, and the Clydesdale Bank. They have the same face values as English notes, and English notes are interchangeable with them in Scotland. Scottish £1 notes are no longer legal tender outside Scotland. English banks and post offices will exchange them for you, but fewer and fewer English shops are accepting them.

At press time (spring 1996), the exchange rate for the pound sterling was 63p to the dollar.

ATMS

CASH ADVANCES>
Before leaving home, **make sure that your**

credit cards have been **programmed for ATM use** in Scotland. Note that Discover is accepted mostly in the United States. Local bank cards often do not work overseas either; **ask your bank about a Visa debit card,** which works like a bank card but can be used at any ATM displaying a Visa logo.

TRANSACTION FEES>
Although fees charged for ATM transactions may be higher abroad than at home, Cirrus and Plus exchange rates are excellent, because they are based on wholesale rates offered only by major banks.

COSTS

A man's haircut will cost £4 and up; a woman's anywhere from £10 to £20. It costs about £1.50 to have a shirt laundered, from £5 to dry-clean a dress, and from £8 to dry-clean a man's suit. A local newspaper will cost you about 35p and a national daily, 45p. A pint of beer is around £1.60, and a serving of whisky about the same. A cup of coffee will run from 50p to £1, depending on where you drink it; a ham sandwich, £2; lunch in a pub, £4 and up (plus your drink).

A theater seat will cost from £5 to £30 in Edinburgh and Glasgow, less elsewhere. Nightclubs will take all they can get from you. For dining and lodging costs, *see* each chapter under that heading.

EXCHANGING CURRENCY

For the most favorable rates, **change money at**

banks. You won't do as well at exchange booths in airports or rail and bus stations, in hotels, in restaurants, or in stores, although you may find their hours more convenient. To avoid lines at airport exchange booths, **get a small amount of the local currency before you leave home.**

TAXES

VAT➤ The British sales tax, VAT (Value Added Tax), is 17.5%. The tax is almost always included in quoted prices in shops, hotels, and restaurants. Overseas visitors to Scotland can reclaim the VAT on goods by using the Foreign Exchange Tax-Free Shopping arrangements, available only in participating shops. To **get a VAT refund,** you must complete a Tax-Free Shopping form at the shop where the goods are purchased (take your passport with you) and then present the form and the goods to HM Customs and Excise as you leave Great Britain.

Details on how to get a VAT refund and a list of stores offering tax-free shopping are available from the British Tourist Authority (☞ Visitor Info *in* Important Contacts A to Z, *above*).

TRAVELER'S CHECKS

Whether or not to buy traveler's checks depends on where you are headed; **take cash to rural areas and small towns, traveler's checks to cities.** The most widely recognized checks are issued by

American Express, Citicorp, Thomas Cook, and Visa. These are sold by major commercial banks for 1%–3% of the checks' face value—it pays to **shop around.** Both American Express and Thomas Cook issue checks that can be countersigned and used by either you or your traveling companion, and they both provide checks, at no extra charge, valued in pounds. So you won't be left with excess foreign currency, **buy a few checks in small denominations** to cash toward the end of your trip. Before leaving home, **contact your issuer for information on where to cash your checks** without a incurring a transaction fee. Record the numbers of all your checks, and keep this listing in a separate place, crossing off the numbers of checks you have cashed.

WIRING MONEY

For a fee of 3%–10%, depending on the amount of the transaction, you can have money sent to you from home through Money-Gram^{SM} or Western Union (☞ Money Matters *in* Important Contacts A to Z). The transferred funds and the service fee can be charged to a Master-Card or Visa account.

P

PACKING FOR SCOTLAND

Travel light. Porters are more or less wholly extinct these days (and very expensive where you can find them).

In Scotland **casual clothes are de rigueur,** and very few hotels or restaurants insist on jackets and ties for men in the evenings. If you expect to attend some gala occasion, you may need evening wear. For summer, lightweight clothing is usually adequate, except in the evenings, when you'll need a jacket, sweater, or cardigan. A water-proof coat or parka is essential. Drip-dry and crease-resistant fabrics are a good bet, since only the most presti-gious hotels have speedy laundering or dry-cleaning service.

Many visitors to Scotland appear to think it necessary to adopt a Scottish costume. It is not. Scots themselves do not wear tartan ties or Balmoral "bunnets" (caps), and only an enthusiastic minority prefer the kilt for every-day wear.

Bring an extra pair of eyeglasses or contact lenses in your carry-on luggage, and if you have a health problem, **pack enough medication** to last the trip or have your doctor write you a prescription using the drug's generic name, because brand names vary from country to country (you'll then need a duplicate pre-scription from a local doctor). It's important that you **don't put prescription drugs or valuables in luggage to be checked,** for it could go astray. To avoid problems with customs officials, carry medica-tions in the original packaging. Also, don't forget the addresses of offices that handle refunds of lost traveler's checks.

ELECTRICITY

To use your U.S.-purchased electric-powered equipment, **bring a converter and an adapter.** The electrical current in Scotland is 220 volts, 50 cycles alternating current (AC); wall outlets take plugs with two round oversize prongs and plugs with three prongs.

If your appliances are dual-voltage, you'll need only an adapter. Hotels sometimes have 110-volt outlets for low-wattage appliances near the sink, marked FOR SHAVERS ONLY; don't use them for high-wattage appliances like blow-dryers. If your laptop computer is older, carry a converter; new laptops operate equally well on 110 and 220 volts, so you need only an adapter.

LUGGAGE

Airline baggage allowances depend on the airline, the route, and the class of your ticket; ask in advance. In general, on domestic flights and on international flights between the United States and foreign destinations, you are entitled to check two bags. A third piece may be brought on board, but it must fit easily under the seat in front of you or in the overhead compartment. In the United States, the FAA gives airlines broad latitude regarding carry-on allowances, and they tend to tailor them to different aircraft and operational conditions. Charges for excess, oversize, or overweight pieces vary.

If you are flying between two foreign destinations, note that baggage allowances may be determined not by piece but by weight— generally 88 pounds (40 kilograms) in first class, 66 pounds (30 kilograms) in business class, and 44 pounds (20 kilograms) in economy. If your flight between two cities abroad *connects* with your transatlantic or transpacific flight, the piece method still applies.

SAFEGUARDING YOUR LUGGAGE➣ Before leaving home, **itemize your bags' contents** and their worth, and label them with your name, address, and phone number. (If you use your home address, cover it so that potential thieves can't see it readily.) Inside each bag, **pack a copy of your itinerary.** At check-in, **make sure that each bag is correctly tagged** with the destination airport's three-letter code. If your bags arrive damaged—or fail to arrive at all—file a written report with the airline before leaving the airport.

PASSPORTS & VISAS

If you don't already have one, **get a passport.** It is advisable that you **leave one photocopy of your passport's data page with someone** at home and keep another with you, separated from your passport, while traveling. If you lose your passport, promptly call the nearest embassy or consulate and the local police; having the data page information can speed replacement.

U.S. CITIZENS

All U.S. citizens, even infants, need only a valid passport to enter Great Britain for stays of up to 90 days. Application forms for both first-time and renewal passports are available at any of the 13 U.S. Passport Agency offices and at some post offices and courthouses. Passports are usually mailed within four weeks; allow five weeks or more in spring and summer.

CANADIANS

You need only a valid passport to enter Great Britain for stays of up to 90 days. Passport application forms are available at 28 regional passport offices, as well as post offices and travel agencies. Whether for a first or a renewal passport, you must apply in person. Children under 16 may be included on a parent's passport but must have their own to travel alone. Passports are valid for five years and are usually mailed within two to three weeks of application.

S
SENIOR-CITIZEN DISCOUNTS

Scotland offers a wide variety of discounts and travel bargains for men over 65 and women 60 and over. **Look into the Senior Citizen Railcard;** it's available in all major railway stations and offers one-third off all rail fares. Travelers

SMART TRAVEL TIPS

THE GOLD GUIDE / SMART TRAVEL TIPS

over 60 are eligible for the Discount Coach Card, which provides one-third off all long-distance National Express or Scottish Citylink coach fares in Britain.

Many hotels advertise off-season discounts for senior citizens, and some offer year-round savings. Budget-minded seniors may also **consider overnight accommodations at a university or college residence hall** (☞ Students *in* Important Contacts A to Z, *above*).

For discounted admission to hundreds of museums, historic buildings, and attractions throughout Britain, senior citizens need show only their passport as proof of age. Reduced-rate tickets to theater and ballet are also available.

To qualify for age-related discounts, **mention your senior-citizen status up front** when booking hotel reservations, not when checking out, and before you're seated in restaurants, not when paying the bill. Note that discounts may be limited to certain menus, days, or hours. When renting a car, **ask about promotional car-rental discounts**—they can net even lower costs than your senior-citizen discount.

STUDENTS ON THE ROAD

To save money, **look into deals available through student-oriented travel agencies.** To qualify, you'll need to have a bona fide student ID card. Mem-

bers of international student groups are also eligible (☞ Students *in* Important Contacts A to Z).

GETTING AROUND

A Student Coach Card from National Express, available to full-time students aged 17 and older, provides one-third off all long-distance coach fares in Britain; contact any National Express agent in Britain with evidence of student status. Those 16–25 are eligible for the same reduction via the National Express Discount Coach Card.

LODGING

UNIVERSITY HOUSING➢ Many universities and colleges throughout Britain open their halls of residence to visitors during vacation periods—that is, from mid-March to mid-April, from July to September, and during the Christmas holidays. Campus accommodations—usually single rooms with access to lounges, libraries, and sports facilities—include breakfast and generally cost about $30 per night. Locations vary from city centers to bucolic lakeside parks.

T
TAXIS

In Edinburgh, Glasgow, and the larger cities, taxis with their "Taxi" sign illuminated can be hailed in the street, or booked by telephone. Elsewhere, most communities of any size at all have a taxi service; your hotel or landlady will be able to supply telephone numbers. Very often you will find

an advertisement for the local taxi service in public phone booths.

TELEPHONES

LONG-DISTANCE

To call Scotland from the United States you do not dial the initial 0 of the area code, but when calling city to city within Scotland, you must dial the 0. Cellular phone numbers, the 0800 toll-free code and local-rate 0345 numbers do not have a 1 after the initial 0.

To make international calls *from* Scotland, you must use the international access code 00. To call North America, dial 00–1–area code–number.

The long-distance services of AT&T, MCI, and Sprint make calling home relatively convenient, but in many hotels you may find it impossible to dial the access number. The hotel operator may also refuse to make the connection. Instead, the hotel will charge you a premium rate—as much as 400% more than a calling card—for calls placed from your hotel room. To avoid such price gouging, travel with more than one company's long-distance calling card—a hotel may block Sprint but not MCI. If the hotel operator claims that you cannot use any phone card, ask to be connected to an international operator, who will help you to access your phone card. You can also dial the international operator yourself. If none of this works, try calling your phone company collect in the

United States. If collect calls are also blocked, call from a pay phone in the hotel lobby. Before you go, **find out the local access codes** for your destinations.

Some restaurants and most hotels add a service charge of 10%–15% to the bill. In this case you are not expected to tip. If no service charge is indicated, add 10% to your total bill, but always check first. Taxi drivers should also get 10%, hairdressers and barbers 10%–15%. You are not expected to tip theater or movie theater ushers, elevator operators, or bartenders in pubs.

A package or tour to Scotland can make your vacation less expensive and more hassle-free. Firms that sell tours and packages reserve airline seats, hotel rooms, and rental cars in bulk and pass some of the savings on to you. In addition, the best operators have local representatives available to help you at your destination.

A GOOD DEAL?

The more your package or tour includes, the better you can predict the ultimate cost of your vacation. Make sure you know exactly what is covered, and **beware of hidden costs.** Are taxes, tips, and service charges included? Transfers and baggage handling? Entertainment and excursions? These can add up.

Most packages and tours are rated deluxe,

first-class superior, first class, tourist, or budget. The key difference is usually accommodations. If the package or tour you are considering is priced lower than in your wildest dreams, **be skeptical.** Also, **make sure your travel agent knows the accommodations** and other services. Ask about the hotel's location, room size, beds, and whether it has a pool, room service, or programs for children, if you care about these. Has your agent been there in person or sent others you can contact?

BUYER BEWARE

Each year a number of consumers are stranded or lose their money when operators—even very large ones with excellent reputations—go out of business. To avoid becoming one of them, take the time to **check out the operator**—find out how long the company has been in business and ask several agents about its reputation. Next, **don't book unless the firm has a consumer-protection program.** Members of the USTOA and the NTA are required to set aside funds for the sole purpose of covering your payments and travel arrangements in case of default. Non-member operators may instead carry insurance; look for the details in the operator's brochure—and for the name of an underwriter with a solid reputation. Note: When it comes to tour operators, **don't trust escrow accounts.** Although there are laws governing those of charter-flight operators,

no governmental body prevents tour operators from raiding the till.

Next, **contact your local Better Business Bureau and the attorney general's offices** in both your own state and the operator's; have any complaints been filed? Finally, **pay with a major credit card.** Then you can cancel payment, provided that you can document your complaint. Always **consider trip-cancellation insurance** (☞ Insurance, *above*).

BIG VS. SMALL➤ Operators that handle several hundred thousand travelers per year can use their purchasing power to give you a good price. Their high volume may also indicate financial stability. But some small companies provide more personalized service; because they tend to specialize, they may also be more knowledgeable about a given area.

USING AN AGENT

Travel agents are excellent resources. In fact, large operators accept bookings made only through travel agents. But it's good to **collect brochures from several agencies** because some agents' suggestions may be skewed by promotional relationships with tour and package firms that reward them for volume sales. If you have a special interest, **find an agent with expertise in that area;** ASTA can provide leads in the United States. (Don't rely solely on your agent, though; agents may be unaware of small-niche operators, and some special-interest travel companies only sell direct.)

SINGLE TRAVELERS

Prices are usually quoted per person, based on two sharing a room. If traveling solo, you may be required to pay the full double-occupancy rate. Some operators eliminate this surcharge if you agree to be matched up with a roommate of the same sex, even if one is not found by departure time.

TRAIN TRAVEL

If you plan to travel by train in Scotland, **consider purchasing a BritRail Pass.** Prices begin at $235 for eight days of second-class travel and $325 for eight days of first-class travel. Passes good for longer periods of time are also available, as are a Flexipass, a BritRail Senior Pass, and a BritRail Kids Pass. Remember that Eurail-Passes are not honored in Scotland.

Many travelers assume that rail passes guarantee them seats on the trains they wish to ride. Not so. You need to **book seats ahead even if you are using a rail pass;** seat reservations are required on some European trains, particularly high-speed trains, and are a good idea on trains that may be crowded—particularly in summer on popular routes. You will also need a reservation if you purchase overnight sleeping accommodations.

DISCOUNT PASSES

To save money, **look into rail passes.** But be aware that if you don't plan to cover many miles, you may come out ahead by buying individual tickets. Standard passes are available for eight days ($299 in first class and $219 in second class), for 15 days ($489 and $339), and one month ($715 and $495). Britrail Flexipasses allow you to travel for 4 days in an 8-day period, 8 days in a 15-day period, or 15 days of a 30 day period. You pay $249, $389, and $575 for the Flexipass in first class, $189, $269, and $395 for second class.

The BritFrance Rail Pass covers both France and Britain (and hovercraft Channel crossings); cost for unlimited travel on any 5 days of a 15-day period is $359 in first class, $259 in second class; $539 and $399 for any 10 days in a 30-day period.

The Britrail Youth Pass and Britrail Youth Flexipass are available for second-class travel for those under 26 on their first travel day; fares for the Youth Pass are $179, $269, $339 and $395 for 8, 15, 22, and 30 days. The Youth Flexipass is $155 for 4 days of travel in an 8 day period, $219 for 8 days in a 15 day period, and $309 for 15 days in a two-month period. Or try the Freedom of Scotland Travel Pass, for 8, 15, and 22 days of consecutive travel for $145, $205, and $259, respectively; with the pass you also travel free on Caledonian MacBrayne's west coast ferries (except to Raasay and Scalpay), and for 33% less on many bus routes. The Freedom of Scotland Flexipass, good for 8 days out of 15, costs $185.

Although some passes may be purchased in Scotland, **you must purchase many passes stateside;** they're sold by travel agents as well as Britrail or Rail Europe (☞ Important Contacts A to Z and Senior-Citizen Discounts, *above*). Eurail-Passes are not valid in Great Britain.

FROM ENGLAND

There are two main rail routes to Scotland from the south of England. The first, the west coast main line, runs from London Euston to Glasgow Central; it takes four or five hours to make the 400-mile trip to central Scotland, and service is frequent and reliable, with one train every two hours on average. Useful for daytime travel to the Scottish Highlands, and equipped with an excellent restaurant car, is the direct train to Stirling and Aviemore, terminating at Inverness. For a restful route to the Scottish Highlands, take the overnight sleeper service, with air-conditioned, soundproof sleeping carriages, which runs from London Euston, departing in late evening, to Perth, Stirling, Aviemore, and Inverness, where it arrives the following morning; family compartments are available.

The second route is the east coast main line from London King's Cross to Edinburgh; it provides the quickest trip to the Scottish capital, and between 8 AM and 6 PM there are 16 trains to Edinburgh, three of them through to Aberdeen. Limited-stop expresses like the *Flying Scotsman* make the 393-mile London to Edinburgh journey in around four hours. Connecting services to most parts of Scotland—particularly the Western Highlands—are often better from Edinburgh than from Glasgow.

Trains from elsewhere in England are good: There is regular service from Birmingham, Manchester, Liverpool, and Bristol to Glasgow and Edinburgh. From Harwich (the port of call for ships from Holland, Germany, and Denmark), you can travel to Glasgow via Manchester. But it is faster to change at Peterborough for the east coast main line to Edinburgh. **Reservations for all sleeper services are essential.**

WITHIN SCOTLAND

Scotland has a rail network extending all the way to Thurso and Wick, the most northerly stations in the British Isles. Lowland services, most of which originate in Glasgow or Edinburgh, are generally fast and reliable. A shuttle makes the 50-minute trip between the cities every half hour. (For information about Edinburgh's and Glasgow's train stations, *see* Chapters 3 and 4, respectively.)

Some lines in Scotland—all suburban services and lines north and west of Inverness—operate on one class only (standard). Long-distance services carry buffet and refreshment cars. One word of caution: **There are very few trains in the Highlands on Sundays.**

FARES

Train fares vary according to class of ticket purchased and distance traveled. The fare system is complex. Before you buy your ticket, be sure to stop at the Information Office/Travel Centre first and request the lowest fare to your destination and information about any special offers. Find out about InterCity Saver, Supersaver, Super-APEX and APEX tickets, and about the Family Railcard if children are with you. Note that your ticket does *not* guarantee you a seat. For that you need a seat reservation, which must be made and paid for separately at a cost of £1 *per train* on your itinerary (that is, £2 if you need to book seats on two trains). You can opt to sit facing toward or away from the engine, and in a smoking or no-smoking compartment.

SCENIC ROUTES

Although many routes in Scotland run through extremely attractive countryside, several stand out: from Glasgow to Oban via Loch Lomond; to Fort William and Mallaig via Rannoch (ferry connection to Skye); from Edinburgh to Inverness via the Forth Bridge and Perth; from Inverness to Kyle of Lochalsh and to Wick; and from Inverness to Aberdeen.

TRAVEL AGENTS

If you want a travel agent to make all the arrangements, make sure he or she is a SCOTS—an acronym which stands for Special Counsellor on Tourism in Scotland. The North American market is important enough to the Scottish Tourist Board to run a special training program for travel agents working in the United States and Canada.

TRAVEL GEAR

Travel catalogs specialize in useful items that can **save space when packing** and make life on the road more convenient. Compact alarm clocks, travel irons, travel wallets, and personal-care kits are among the most common items you'll find. They also carry dual-voltage appliances, currency converters and foreign-language phrase books. Some catalogs even carry miniature coffeemakers and water purifiers.

U

U.S.
GOVERNMENT

The U.S. government can be an excellent source of travel information. Some of this is free and some is available for a nominal charge. When planning your trip, **find out what government materials are available.** For just a couple of dollars, you can get a variety of publications from the Consumer Information

Center in Pueblo, Colorado. Free consumer information also is available from individual government agencies, such as the Department of Transportation or the U.S. Customs Service.

W
WHEN TO GO

The Scottish climate has been much maligned (sometimes with justification). You can be unlucky: You may spend a summer week in Scotland and experience nothing but low clouds and drizzle. But on the other hand, you may enjoy calm Mediterranean-like weather even in early spring and late fall.

Generally speaking, Scotland is three or four degrees cooler than southern England. The east is drier and colder than the west; Edinburgh's rainfall is comparable to Rome's, while Glasgow's is more like that in Vancouver—yet the cities are only 44 miles apart.

All visitors comment on the long summer evenings, which grow longer still as you travel north. Dawn in Orkney and Shetland in June is at around 1 AM, no more than an hour or so after sunset. Winter days are very short.

Scotland has few thunderstorms and little fog, except for local mists near coasts. But there are often variable winds that reach gale force even in summer. They blow away the hordes of gnats and midges, the curse of the western Highlands.

CLIMATE

What follows are average daily maximum and minimum temperatures for major cities in Scotland.

Climate in Scotland

ABERDEEN

Jan.	43F	6C	May	54F	12C	Sept.	59F	15C
	36	2		43	6		49	9
Feb.	43F	6C	June	61F	16C	Oct.	54F	12C
	36	2		49	9		43	6
Mar.	47F	8C	July	63F	17C	Nov.	47F	8C
	36	2		52	11		40	4
Apr.	49F	9C	Aug.	63F	17C	Dec.	45F	7C
	40	4		52	11		36	2

EDINBURGH

Jan.	43F	6C	May	58F	14C	Sept.	61F	16C
	34	1		43	6		49	9
Feb.	43F	6C	June	63F	17C	Oct.	54F	12C
	34	1		49	9		45	7
Mar.	47F	8C	July	65F	18C	Nov.	49F	9C
	36	2		52	11		40	4
Apr.	52F	11C	Aug.	65F	18C	Dec.	45F	7C
	40	4		52	11		36	2

GLASGOW

Jan.	41F	5C	May	59F	15C	Sept.	61F	16C
	34	1		43	6		49	9
Feb.	45F	7C	June	65F	18C	Oct.	56F	13C
	34	1		49	9		43	6
Mar.	49F	9C	July	67F	19C	Nov.	49F	9C
	36	2		52	11		38	3
Apr.	54F	12C	Aug.	67F	19C	Dec.	45F	7C
	40	4		52	11		36	2

HIGHLANDS

Jan.	43F	6C	May	58F	14C	Sept.	61F	16C
	32	0		43	6		49	9
Feb.	45F	7C	June	63F	17C	Oct.	56F	13C
	34	1		49	9		43	6
Mar.	49F	9C	July	65F	18C	Nov.	49F	9C
	36	2		52	11		38	3
Apr.	52F	11C	Aug.	65F	18C	Dec.	45F	7C
	40	4		52	11		34	1

ORKNEY ISLANDS

Jan.	43F	6C	May	54F	12C	Sept.	58F	14C
	36	2		43	6		49	9
Feb.	43F	6C	June	58F	14C	Oct.	52F	11C
	36	2		47	8		45	7
Mar.	45F	7C	July	61F	16C	Nov.	47F	8C
	38	3		50	10		41	5
Apr.	49F	9C	Aug.	61F	16C	Dec.	45F	7C
	40	4		50	10		38	3

THE GOLD GUIDE / SMART TRAVEL TIPS

1 Destination: Scotland

THE PRIDE OF SCOTLAND

ON SOME OLD RECORDINGS of Scottish songs still in circulation, you may run across *Roamin' in the Gloamin'* or *I Love a Lassie* or one of the other comic ditties of Harry Lauder, a star of the music halls of the 1920s. With his garish kilt, short crooked walking stick, rich rolling *R*s, and *pawky* (cheerfully impudent) humor, chiefly based on the alleged meanness of the Scots, he impressed a Scottish character on the world. But his was, needless to say, a false impression and one the Scots have been trying to stamp out ever since.

How, then, do you characterize the Scots? Temperamentally, they are a mass of contradictions. They have been likened, not to a Scotch egg, but to a soft-boiled egg: a dour hard shell, a mushy middle. The Scots laugh and weep with almost Latin facility, but to strangers they are reserved, noncommittal, in no hurry to make an impression. Historically, fortitude and resilience have been their hallmarks, and there are streaks of both resignation and pitiless ferocity in their makeup, warring with sentimentality and love of family. Very Scottish was the instant reaction of an elderly woman of Edinburgh 200 years ago, when news arrived of the defeat in Mysore in India and of the Scottish soldiers being fettered in irons, two by two: "God help the puir chiel that's chained tae oor Davie."

The Scots are in general suspicious of the go-getter. "Whiz kid" is a term of contempt. But they are by no means plodders, though it is true to say that they are determined and thorough, respecting success only when it has been a few hundred years in the making. Praise of some bright ambitious youngster is quenched with the sneer: "Him? Ah kent (knew) his faither."

Yet this is the nation that built commerce throughout the British Empire, opened wild territories, and was responsible for much of humankind's scientific and technological advancement, a nation boastful about things it is not too good at and shamefacedly modest about genuine achievements. Consider the following extract from a handout about the Edinburgh School of Medicine: "If one excepts a few discoveries such as that of 'fixed air' by Black, of the diverse functions of the nerve-roots by Bell, of the anaesthetic properties of chloroform by Simpson, of the invention of certain powerful drugs by Christison and of the importance of antiseptic procedures by Lister, the influence of Edinburgh medicine has been of a steady constructive rather than a revolutionary type."

Among things that strike most newcomers to Scotland are the generosity of the Scots; their obsession with respectability; their satisfaction with themselves and their desire to stay as they are; and, above all, their passionate love of Scotland. An obstinate refusal to go along with English ideas has led to accusations that the nation has a head-in-the-sand attitude toward progress. But the Scots have their own ideas of progress, and they jealously guard the institutions that remain unique to them.

When it comes to education, Scotland has a proud record. The nation boasted four universities—St. Andrews, Aberdeen, Glasgow, and Edinburgh—when England had only two: Oxford and Cambridge. The *lad o' pairts* (man of talents)—the poor child of a feckless father and a fiercely self-sacrificing mother, sternly tutored by the village *dominie* (schoolmaster) and turned loose at the age of 13 with so firm a base of learning that he rose to the very top of his profession—this type of lad is a phenomenon of Scottish social history. The sacrifices that boys made as a matter of course to further their education are an old Scottish tradition. "Meal Monday," the midsemester holiday at a Scottish university, is a survivor of the long weekend that once enabled students to return to their distant homes—on foot—and replenish the sack of "meal" (oatmeal) that was their only subsistence.

It is a British cliché that an English education teaches you to think and a Scottish education stuffs your head with information. The average Scot does appear to be better informed than his English neighbor and to discuss facts rather than ideas. Scots pride themselves on their international outlook and on being better linguists than the English. The Scots get on well with foreigners, and they offer strangers a kindly welcome and a civility not often found in the modern world.

Just as the Scots have their own traditions in education, so is their legal system distinct from England's. In England the police both investigate crime and prosecute suspects. In Scotland there is a public prosecutor directly responsible to the Lord Advocate (equivalent to England's Attorney General), who is himself accountable to Parliament.

For the most part, however, you will notice few practical differences except in terminology. The barrister in England becomes an advocate in Scotland. Law-office nameplates designate their occupants "S. S. C." (Solicitor to the Supreme Court) or "W. S." (Writer to the Signet); cases for prosecution go before the "procurator fiscal" and are tried by the "sheriff" or "sheriff-substitute." The terms are different in England, and procedures are slightly different, too, for Scotland is one of the few countries that still bases its legal system on the old Roman law.

Crimes with picturesque names from ancient times remain on the statute book: *hamesucken,* for example, means assaulting a person in his home. In criminal cases Scotland adds to "Guilty" and "Not Guilty" a third verdict: "Not Proven." This, say the cynics, signifies "Don't do it again."

The Presbyterian Church of Scotland—the "Kirk"—is entirely independent of the Church of England. Until the 20th century it was a power in the land and did much to shape Scottish character. There are still those who can remember when the minister visited houses like an inquisitor and put members of the families through their catechism, punishing or reprimanding those who were not word-perfect. On Sunday morning the elders patrolled the streets, ordering people into church and rebuking those who sat at home in their gardens.

Religion in Scotland, as elsewhere, has lost much of its grip. But the Kirk remains influential in rural districts, where Kirk officials are pillars of local society. Ministers and their wives are seen in all their somber glory in Edinburgh in springtime, when the General Assembly of the Kirk takes place, and, for a week or more, Scottish newspapers devote several column-inches daily to the deliberations.

THE EPISCOPALIAN CHURCH of Scotland has bishops, as its name implies (unlike the Kirk, where the ministers are all equal), and a more colorful ritual. Considered genteel, Episcopalianism in Scotland has been described rather sourly by the Scottish novelist Lewis Grassie Gibbon as "more a matter of social status than theological conviction . . . a grateful bourgeois acknowledgment of anglicisation."

Of the various nonconformist offshoots of the established Kirk, the Free Kirk of Scotland is the largest. It remains faithful to the monolithic unity of its forefathers, promoting the grim discipline that John Knox promoted long ago. The Free Kirk is strong in parts of the Outer Hebrides—Lewis, Harris, and North Uist. On Sunday in these areas no buses run, all the shops are shut, and there is a general atmosphere of a people cowering under the wrath of God. Among the fishing communities, especially those of the Northeast from Buckie to Peterhead, evangelical movements, such as the Close Brethren and Jehovah's Witnesses, have made impressive inroads.

Other than religion, Scotland on the whole is mercifully free of the class consciousness and social elitism that so often amuse or disgust foreign residents in England. But its turbulent history has left Scotland a legacy of sectarian bigotry comparable to that of Northern Ireland. Scotland's large minority population of Roman Catholics is still to some extent underprivileged. Catholics tend to stick together, Protestants to mix only with Protestants. Even the two most famous soccer teams in Scotland—Rangers and Celtic—are notorious for their sectarian bias.

A word, finally, is needed on the vexed subject of nomenclature. A "scotchman" is a nautical device for "scotching," or clamping, a running rope. It is not a native of Scotland. Though you may find some rather more conservative people refer to themselves as Scotchmen and consider themselves Scotch, most prefer Scot or Scotsman and call themselves Scottish or Scots.

There are exceptions to this rule. Certain internationally known Scottish products are Scotch. There is Scotch whisky, Scotch wool, Scotch tweed, Scotch mist (persistent drizzling rain). A Scotch snap is a short accented note followed by a longer one—a phrase that is characteristic of Scottish music, though certainly not unique to it. A snack food of a hard-boiled egg wrapped in sausage-meat and rolled in crumb coating, then fried, is a Scotch egg.

You may include the Scots in the broader term British, but they dislike the word *Brits,* and nothing infuriates them more than being called English. Nonetheless, there are a lot of Anglo-Scots, that is, people of Scottish birth who live in England or are the offspring of marriages between Scottish and English people. The term Anglo-Scots is not to be confused with Sassenachs, the Gaelic word for Saxon, which is applied facetiously or disdainfully to all the English. But at the same time, English people who live in Scotland remain English to their dying day, and their children after them. Similarly, the designation of North Britain for Scotland, which crept in during Victorian times, has now crept out again. It survives only in the names of a few North British hotels. Scots feel that it denies their national identity, and there are some who, on receiving a letter with "N. B." or "North Britain" in the address, will cross it out and return the envelope to the sender.

WHAT'S WHERE

Edinburgh

Scotland's capital makes a strong first impression—Edinburgh Castle looming from the crags of an ancient volcano; the Royal Mile stretching from the castle to the Palace of Holyroodhouse; the neoclassical monuments perched on Calton Hill; Arthur's Seat, a small mountain with steep slopes, little crags, and spectacular vistas over the city and the Firth of Forth. Like Rome, Edinburgh is built on seven hills, and it has an Old Town district that retains striking evidence of a colorful history. Medieval Old Town, with its winding closes (narrow, stone-arched walkways) contrasts sharply with the Georgian New Town and its planned squares and streets. But Edinburgh offers more than just a unique architectural landscape—it's a cosmopolitan capital, rich in museums, pubs, and culture. It's the site of the famous International Festival, when tourists and performers descend upon the city in late summer to celebrate the arts. Even more obvious to the casual stroller during this time is the refreshingly irreverent Edinburgh Festival Fringe, unruly child of the official festival, which spills out of halls and theaters all over town.

Glasgow

Glasgow, Scotland's largest city, suffered gravely from the industrial decline of the 1960s and '70s, but recent efforts at commercial and cultural renewal have restored much of the style and grandeur it had in the 19th century, at the height of its economic power. Now it is again a vibrant metropolitan center with a thriving artistic life—so much so that it is to be UK City of Architecture and Design in 1999. Glasgow is a very convenient touring center, too, in easy reach of the Clyde coast to the south and with excellent transportation links to the rest of Scotland.

The Borders and the Southwest

The Borders area comprises the great rolling hills, moors, wooded river valleys, and farmland that stretch south from Lothian, the region crowned by Edinburgh, to England. All the distinctive features of Scotland—paper currency, architecture, opening hours of pubs and stores, food and drink, and accent—start right at the border; you won't find the Borders a diluted version of England. The Dumfries and Galloway region south of Glasgow is a hilly and sparsely populated area, divided from England by the Solway Firth; it's a region of somber forests and radiant gardens, where the palm, in places, is as much at home as the pine. The county seat is Dumfries, associated with Robert Burns (he spent the last years of his life here) in much the same way as the Borders are with Sir Walter Scott.

Fife and Angus

Fife, northwest of Edinburgh, has the distinction of being the sunniest and driest part of Scotland. This area is one of sandy beaches, fishing villages, and windswept cliffs, hills, and glens. The industrial west may hold little interest, but the east coast is home to the ancient university and golf town of St. Andrews, with its romantic stone houses and seaside ruins. Angus, whose main city, Dundee, is an industrial port, stretches to the northeast into the North Sea. The Angus glens provide scenic hikes through secluded plateaus surrounded by hills and mountains.

Aberdeen and the Northeast

Aberdeen, Scotland's third-largest city, is a sophisticated city built largely of glittering granite, and is a main port of North Sea oil operations. The Grampian region spreads out to the west, the terrain changing from coastline—some of the United Kingdom's wildest shorelines of high cliffs and sandy beaches—to farmland to forests to hills. Here, the Grampian mountains and the Cairngorms, beautiful regions of heather and forest, granite peaks and deep glens, are popular for hill walking in warm weather and skiing in cold weather. The northeast is also known for its wealth of castles and whisky distilleries.

The Central Highlands

The main towns of Perth and Stirling are easily accessible gateways to the Central Highlands, the rugged and spectacular terrain stretching north from Glasgow. This may not be the famed Highlands of the north, but there's plenty of wild country to be experienced in the Central Highlands; here you'll find lush green woodlands and lochs. Especially in the Trossachs, deep lochs shimmer at the foot of gently sloping hills covered in birch, oak, and pine. Loch Lomond (*loch* is Scots for lake), Scotland's largest, is here; Sir Walter Scott's poems about the area have ensured its popularity as a tourist destination.

Argyll and the Isles

Argyll, a remote, sparsely populated group of islands in western Scotland that form part of the Inner Hebridean archipelago, is a transitional area between the Highlands and Lowlands, an environment ranging from lush landscapes to treeless islands, sea lochs to wooded hills. Oban, the hub of transportation for Argyll, is the main sea gateway for Mull and the Southern Islands. The Island of Mull has a rolling green landscape and its capital,

Tobermory, has brightly painted houses that give it a Mediterranean look. Iona, near Mull, is Scotland's most important Christian site, with an abbey and a royal graveyard. The Isle of Islay is synonymous with whisky—it produces seven malts. Jura is covered with wild mountains. Sweeping southward, the long Kintyre peninsula is a wonderland of sea views, spectacular sunsets, and prehistoric monuments. Arran is more developed than most southern isles, with mist-shrouded mountains in the north and farmland in the south.

Around the Great Glen

The Great Glen cuts through the Southern Highlands from Inverness to Fort William and is surrounded by Scotland's tallest mountains and greatest lochs; it is considered by many to be the most dramatic, captivating landscape in Scotland. Of its lochs, the most famous is Loch Ness. Inverness, on the Moray Firth, is a major shipping port and the last substantial outpost as you head north. East of Fort William, Glen Nevis is home to Ben Nevis, Britain's highest peak. Serious climbers come from far and wide to scale it.

The Northern Highlands

The Highlands, a remote and wild area of Scotland, are the source of the country's most breathtaking scenery. The great surprises to unprepared visitors are the changing terrain and the stunning effects of light and shade, cloud, sunshine, and rainbows. In a couple of hours you may pass from heather, bracken, and springy turf to granite rock and bog, to serrated peak and snow-water lake, to the red Torridon sandstone of Wester Ross, and the flowery banks of Loch Ewe and Loch Maree. Sea inlets are deep and fjordlike. The black shapes of the isles cluster like basking whales on the skyline. Cliffs where quartzite gleams above crescents of hard sand lead around a northern shore that looks from the air as though it had been trimmed by an axe. Gaelic-speaking natives on the Isle of Skye live in villages along the coast; the varied interior has forested glens, hills of heather, rocky waterfalls, and the Cuillin Mountains. The Outer Hebrides, also known as the Western Isles, arc outward to the Atlantic; this is possibly the most rugged part of Scotland, with frequent wind and rain, and an often inhospitable landscape where anything that grows seems a gift. In between are hidden coves with awe-striking white sand beaches and turquoise waters. Westward, the next stop is North America.

The Northern Isles

The nearly unceasing wind in the Northern Isles create a challenging climate that contributes to the feeling that you've reached the end of the world. Orkney, a grouping of almost 70 islands, 20 of them inhabited, has the greatest concentration of prehistoric sites in Scotland. The treeless Mainland, Orkney's major island, strikes a peculiar mix between farmland and prominent stone-age relics, including phenomenally well-preserved standing circles, brochs (circular towers), and tombs. Shetland's islands, with their dramatic vertical cliffs on the coastline and barren moors in the interior, aren't as rugged as you might think; the harshest winter weather is kept in check by the Gulf Stream. Winter days are sometimes no more than five hours long, while beautiful summer days last almost 20 hours, with a persistent twilight known as the "summer dim." There are few trees to be found, and no spot is farther than 3 miles from the blue-black sea. North Sea oil has brought great wealth to the Shetlands: some of Scotland's best roads are here, the buses are modern, and most homes are recently built.

PLEASURES AND PASTIMES

Cultural Festivals

The Edinburgh International Festival is the spectacular flagship of mainstream cultural events, from theater to comedy skits. In fact, the capital suffers from Festival overkill in late August, partly due to the size of the Fringe, the less formal and more unruly part of the official festival. This huge grab bag of performances spreads out of halls and theaters onto the streets of the capital. Also adding to the throng are the Edinburgh Military Tattoo and a range of smaller events such as the Book Festival and the Jazz Festival. Earlier in the year, rival Glasgow holds the increasingly influential MayFest. This broad-based festival is international and eclectic in content, and delivered with all the panache and local support now associated with the city. Folk festivals are also held in many places at various times of the year, as are themed festivals. One example is the Fife Festival of Food and Wine, bringing cheer to bleak March.

Cycling and Hiking

Cycling is an ideal way to see the country. A mountain bike with street tires is as good a touring bike as the traditional, slouch-forward road bikes. But a good bike does not a successful tour make: You will need to build up your endurance for longer rides, and outfit and equip yourself appropriately. Don't forget that although some terrain may be flat, as in the Northern Isles, the conditions may be hazardous—strong winds or thick mist.

If you prefer to use your own two feet, hiking is a superb pursuit for getting to know Scotland's varied landscape of low-lying glens and major mountains. From Edinburgh's Arthur's Seat to Ben Nevis, Britain's tallest peak, Scotland offers an unlimited number of walking and hiking possibilities.

Dining

Scottish restaurants are noted for helpful attention and modest prices, rather than for their exotic or imaginative cuisine. City Scots usually take their midday meals in a pub, wine bar, bistro, or department store restaurant (which might not serve alcohol and which might ban smoking). When traveling, the Scot generally eats inexpensively and quickly at a country pub or village tearoom. Places like Glasgow, Edinburgh, and Aberdeen, of course, offer restaurants of cosmopolitan character and various price levels; of these, the more notable tend to open only in the evening. You will come across restaurants that offer a "Taste of Scotland" menu, full of oddly named traditional dishes often cooked and served in traditional pots and pans. The Taste of Scotland scheme, initiated by the Scottish Tourist Board, has helped—almost by accident—to preserve some of the Scots language, especially the names for a variety of traditional dishes. Most smaller towns and many villages have at least one restaurant where—certainly if a local is in charge—the service is a reminder of a Highland tradition that ensured that no stranger could travel through the country without receiving a welcome.

To start the day with a full stomach, try a "traditional Scottish breakfast," which consists of bacon and fried eggs, served with sausage, fried mushrooms and tomatoes, and, often, fried bread or potato scones. Most places also serve kippers (smoked herring). All this is in addition to juice, porridge, cereal, toast, and other bread products. It is possible to eat a healthier breakfast—fruit, for example, is on most hotel menus—but the high-cholesterol temptations are conventional in Scotland.

Distillery Tours

The process of producing whisky is closely monitored by the British government. It is strictly commercially licensed and takes place only in Scotland's distilleries (and, in Scotland, the product is most definitely spelled "whisky," without an "e"). Many distilleries place strong emphasis on visitor facilities and attempt to inject some drama and excitement into a process that is visually undramatic but nevertheless requires skill, method, and large-scale investment. A typical visit includes some kind of audiovisual presentation and a tour and then a dram is usually offered. No tour of Speyside is complete without taking in at least one distillery.

Golf

Scotland is often called the "home of golf" and, brushing aside any suggestion that the game probably originated in the Low Countries, claims it for her own. Certainly, Scotland has a number of very old established courses, often lying close to town centers, where, had it not been for the early rights of golfers, the land would have been swallowed up by developments long ago. Now, with more than 400 golf courses—some world-famous—Scotland is a destination for golfers the world over. St. Andrews is such a popular spot for golfers that reservations need to be made up to a year in advance for summer play. Courses are also located in the major urban centers: 20 courses are within or close to Edinburgh, while seven courses are within Glasgow.

Pubs

The Scots enjoy their pub culture. Whether you join in a lively political discussion in a bar in Glasgow, or enjoy folk music and dancing in a rural pub in the Highlands, you'll find that a public house is the perfect site to experience the Scottish spirit and, of course, enjoy a pint or a wee dram. Most bars sell two kinds of beer—lager and ale. Lager (try Tennent's or McEwan's), most familiar to American drinkers, is light-colored, heavily carbonated, and served cold. Ale (try McEwan "80 Shilling" and Caledonian "80") is dark, semi-carbonated, and served just below room temperature. All pubs also carry any number of single-malt and blended whiskies.

Scenic Drives

One of the best ways to see Scotland is to rent a car and drive. The following are some of our favorite scenic routes: the road west of Aberdeen into Royal Deeside, on either bank of the River Dee (Aberdeen); the east bank of Loch Ness, from Fort Augustus to Inverness via Dores (Around the Great Glen); the route between Brig o' Turk and Aberfoyle in the Trossachs (Central Highlands); and the Drumbeg road, north of Lochinver (Northern Highlands). For planned routes, ☞ Great Itineraries, *below*.

Shopping

The best buys in Britain in general are antiques, craft items, woolen goods, china, men's shoes, books, confectionery, and toys. In Scotland, many visitors go for tweeds, designer knitwear, Shetland and Fair Isle woolens, tartan rugs and fabrics, Edinburgh crystal, Caithness glass, malt whisky, Celtic silver, and pebble jewelry. The Scottish Highlands bristle with old *bothies* (farm buildings) that have been turned into small crafts workshops where visitors are welcome—but not pressured—to buy attractive handmade items of bone, silver, wood, pottery, leather, and glass. Handmade chocolates, often with whisky or Drambuie fillings, and the traditional "petticoat tail" shortbread in tin boxes are popular; so, too, at a more mundane level, are boiled sweets in jars from particular localities—Berwick cockles, Jethart snails, Edinburgh rock, and similar crunchy items. Dundee cake, a rich fruit mixture with almonds on top, and Dundee marmalades and heather honeys are among the other eatables that visitors take home from Scotland.

NEW AND NOTEWORTHY

Accommodation: Scotland Deluxe

The Scottish Tourish Board operates a classification and grading scheme for accommodation in Scotland. Whether you are considering a tiny bed and breakfast or a grand hotel, you should be able to check its grading. Some of the top-graded smaller establishments have formed an association called Scotland Deluxe to promote their high quality. A number of these places are featured in this guide—Crolinnhe in Fort William and Sunbank House Hotel in Perth, for instance. Akin to the "Leading Hotels of the World," Scotland Deluxe operates as a network of referrals and has its own brochure as well.

Fare Wars and Air Travel

If you intend to fly to Scotland from London, take advantage of the fare wars on these internal routes—notably between London's three airports and Glasgow/Edinburgh. At press time (spring, 1996), Ryanair (☎ 0171/435–7101) leads the field between London Stansted (with its excellent rail links from London's Liverpool Street Station) and Glasgow Prestwick. They currently offer fares from as low as £29 one way. When you reach Prestwick, another worthwhile bargain awaits rail travelers: For only £5 you can get a ticket for any rail destination in Scotland. The railway station is adjacent to the main Prestwick terminal building.

Gallery of Modern Art

In urban news, Glasgow's new Gallery of Modern Art has recently opened in one of the most impressive Georgian buildings in the city center, the former Stirling Library, with its classical columns and facade. It houses works by famous Scots and international artistic innovators.

Hogmanay

With roots going back to the pagan era, Hogmanay (☞ Festivals and Seasonal Events, *below*) not long ago was *the* winter celebration in Scotland. Up to the 1950s children in some parts of Scotland would hang up their stockings on the night of December 31, rather than at Christmas. Since then, the influence of the mostly English-controlled media and the commercial pressures to conform have led the Scots to as enthusiastic a celebration of Christmas as the English. But Hogmanay has not died out as a night of celebration and overindulgence north of the Border, and today it's undergoing something of a revival. If you are in Scotland at the end of December, unless you have an invitation to a private party with Scottish friends, then Edinburgh is the place to be celebrate this most Scottish of all celebrations. A program of events starts on December 30, runs through Hogmanay itself (the 31st) and continues into New Years' Day—often a very quiet day north of the Border, as the natives nurse their sore heads.

Mad Cow Disease

The so-called "mad cow disease" (or BSE, bovine spongiform encephalopathy) and its possible link with the human equivalent, CJD (Creutzfeldt-Jakob disease), was one of the major stories out of the United Kingdom in 1996. Scottish farmers have pointed out that Scottish beef is usually grass-fed and (comparatively) BSE-free. However, the reputation of prime Scottish beef—much of it exported to Europe's top restaurants—has suffered along with that of the rest of the United Kingdom's beef supply. In short, nobody can say for certain that all beef is absolutely safe, so you'll need to decide for yourself. One thing is certain: It is certainly not worth postponing your Scottish trip. You will find plenty of locals still eating high-quality beef. Besides, the range of other food—from wild game to seafood—means that it is easy to avoid beef on the menu, if you choose.

Skye Road Bridge

Last year, a 1,800-foot-long road bridge, one of the longest balanced cantilever bridges in the world, opened over the Kyleakin Narrows at Kyle of Lochalsh, replacing the five-minute ferry crossing to the Isle of Skye. (Since then, news of the bridge has become a staple in Scottish newspapers, which report on continuing protests over tolls: Residents of Skye object to paying £4.30 every time they use the bridge.) If you are an incurable romantic and want to go "over the sea to Skye" (in the words of a Scottish song), you still can. Fifteen miles south of the bridge, pick up the car ferry between Maillaig on the mainland, at the end of the famous "Road to Isle," and Armadale on Skye, which has the Clan Donald Centre nearby. Using the bridge one way and the ferry the other makes for a good round trip.

Scotland's Lighthouse Museum

In Grampian, in the northeast of Scotland, an important new museum has just opened that tells the story of Scotland's lighthouses. Scotland's Lighthouse Museum, perhaps a bit esoteric at first glance, is a major exposition of Scotland's maritime heritage, situated in Fraserburgh on a breezy headland amid all the paraphernalia of a workaday fishing town, and overlooked by a 16th-century castle.

Tall Ships Race

Aberdeen is still talking about 1991's Cutty Sark Tall Ships Race, which returns in 1997 from July 12 to 15. The gathering of the world's finest and largest sailing vessels is visually spectacular, especially as they parade offshore before beginning their race to Trondheim in Norway across the North Sea. Since the road between Edinburgh and Aberdeen is all divided highway, Scotland's most northerly city is only a couple of hours above the central belt of Scotland by car.

FODOR'S CHOICE

Buildings and Monuments

★ **The facade of Marischal College, Aberdeen.** This ornate facade was built in 1891, and is part of the second-largest granite building in the world.

★ **The Black House at Arnol, the Isle of Lewis in the Outer Hebrides (Northern Highlands).** Built without mortar and thatched on a timber framework without eaves, this house is a good example of a rare type of traditional Hebridean home.

★ **The Georgian House, Edinburgh.** In New Town's Charlotte Square, this house is decorated in period style to demonstrate the lifestyle of an affluent family living in the late 18th century.

★ **Traquair House, near Walkerburn (Borders).** This is said to be the oldest continually occupied house in Scotland. Be sure to sample the ale that is brewed on site in an 18th-century brewhouse.

★ **The Standing Stones of Callanish, Lewis (Northern Highlands).** This series of monoliths is considered second only to Stonehenge in England, and is thought to have been used for astronomical observations.

★ **Torosay Castle, Isle of Mull (Argyll and the Isles).** One of Mull's best-known castles, Torosay has a friendly air and gives visitors the run of much of the house.

★ **Blair Castle, Perthshire (Central Highlands).** A few minutes north of the Pass of Killiecrankie, Blair Castle, one of Scotland's most highly acclaimed, is the Duke of Atholl's ancestral home. Inside are military artifacts and a fine collection of furniture and paintings.

Lodging

★ **Auchterarder House, Auchterarder (Central Highlands).** This secluded Victorian country mansion offers bedrooms with original furnishings and views of the Perthshire countryside. $$$$

★ **Kildrummy Castle, Kildrummy (Aberdeen and the Northeast).** An old Victorian country house is the peaceful setting for attentive service and award-winning cuisine. $$$$

★ **Roman Camp, Callander (Central Highlands).** A former hunting lodge set on 20 acres of gardens with river frontage (fishing available) is the setting for antique-filled rooms and an excellent restaurant. $$$$

★ **Channings, Edinburgh.** This elegant hotel is made up of five Edwardian terraced houses; those facing north provide wonderful views of Fife. $$$

★ **Clifton House, Nairn (Great Glen).** This unique hotel has original works of art, antique furnishings, and famed cuisine. $$$

★ **Cringletie House, Peebles (Borders).** Turrets and crow-step gables lend a traditional Scottish baronial style to this hotel, whose accommodations are simple and comfortable; the food is its major achievement. $$$

Museums and Visitor Centers

★ **Auchindrain Museum (Argyll).** This 18th-century communal tenancy farm has been restored to illustrate early farming life in the Highlands.

★ **Burrell Collection (Glasgow).** Pollock County Park is the setting for one of Scotland's finest art collections, with exhibits ranging from Egyptian, Greek, and Roman artifacts to stained glass and French Impressionist paintings.

⭐**Paisley Museum and Art Gallery (Glasgow).** Paisley, part of the Greater Glasgow suburban area, is home to this museum that tells the story of the woolen Paisley Shawl, and describes the famous Paisley pattern and weaving techniques.

⭐**Scottish Fisheries Museum (Fife).** In Anstruther, this museum illustrates the life of Scottish fishermen through documents, artifacts, paintings, and quayside floating exhibits.

⭐**Scotland's Lighthouse Museum (Aberdeenshire).** Scotland's first lighthouse was built at Fraserburgh in the 1780s on top of a 16th-century castle. A climb to its topmost gallery can now form part of an information-packed visit to this museum on the history, science, and role of lighthouses over the centuries.

⭐**Carnegie Birthplace Museum (Edinburgh and the Lothians).** In Dunfermline, the birthplace of Andrew Carnegie tells his life story.

Dining

⭐**The Old Monastery, Buckie (Aberdeen).** The setting is a Victorian former religious establishment, and the theme is ever present, from the Cloisters Bar to the Chapel Restaurant. Local specialties include fresh river fish and Aberdeen Angus beef. *$$–$$$$*

⭐**Auchterarder House, Auchterarder (Central Highlands).** This dining room filled with sparkling glassware is attached to a fine hotel (☞ above) and serves excellent cuisine. *$$$$*

⭐**The Atrium, Edinburgh.** This restaurant is a good place to go for pre- or post-theater dinner (the Traverse Theatre is next door) to sample Scottish ingredients combined in unusual ways; the menu changes daily. *$$$*

⭐**The Cellar, Anstruther (Fife).** The fact that this place is popular with locals is a good sign. Come here for top-quality fish, beef, and lamb, cooked in a simple, straightforward fashion. *$$$*

⭐**The Ubiquitous Chip, Glasgow.** With one of the best wine cellars in the city, this unique restaurant is set in a courtyard with a fountain, a pleasant spot for fresh Scottish game and produce. *$$*

GREAT ITINERARIES

Scottish tourist authorities have developed numerous tourist trails that encompass everything from Scotland's brooding castles to its pungent whisky distilleries. However, you should probably avoid these thematic trails during the height of summer, when crowds and buses tend to swarm the best-known sights. The following itineraries, conceived independently of the Tourist Board, are offered as a guide in planning individual travel. For more travel suggestions, be sure to consult the three itineraries recommended in each chapter.

The Seaways of the West

From Glasgow, you and your rental car can escape into the Western Highlands in under two hours, using a short ferry crossing to save time. Then, if it isn't raining, you'll discover why the romantic landscapes of the west, with their vanished clans and tales of Bonnie Prince Charlie, continue to hold an intense fascination for visitors.

DURATION➤ 4 to 6 Days

THE MAIN ROUTE➤ **1 to 2 Nights:** Go west from Glasgow on the A8 along the south bank of the meandering River Clyde to reach Wemyss Bay on the A78. Catch the ferry for the old-fashioned holiday resort of Rothesay on the island of Bute. Tour the hinterland and leave the island via the five-minute Rhubodach–Colintraive ferry and enjoy the typical western scenery around Cowal.

1 Night: Go south to Lochgilphead, take a quick peek at the Caledonian Canal, then head for Tarbert and the peninsular Mull of Kintyre. If you crave island scenery, you can hop across to the tiny island of Gigha. Otherwise, continue south toward Campbeltown.

1 to 3 Nights: Return north through Lochgilphead and head for Oban, a busy ferryport where tartan kitsch and tour buses form the backdrop. Cross from Oban to the dramatic Isle of Mull, eventually arriving at the tiny Isle of Iona, the ancient burial place of Scottish kings. Leave Iona and Mull via the Fishnish–Lochaline ferry, then loop north toward Acharacle for magnificent views of the small isles of Rhum, Eigg, and Muck.

1 to 3 Nights: If time permits continue west to Mallaig, a ferryport with connections to the rugged and wild Isle of Skye. Otherwise, head east to Fort William, taking the A82 southward toward the famous Loch Lomond before returning to Glasgow.

Anything But the Main Route

If you're on a whirlwind tour of Scotland, this driving tour offers discriminating adventurers the chance to skirt the tourist horde while still experiencing some of the country's better-known sights. This nearly circular tour starts in Dunfermline and ends in either Perth or Edinburgh, but it could be done in either direction. (A good road map is indispensable.)

DURATION➤ 4 to 7 Days

THE MAIN ROUTE➤ **1 to 2 Nights:** From Dunfermline, the ancient capital of Scotland and the birthplace of Andrew Carnegie, take the A823 northwest. This soon cuts through the green and rounded Ochil Hills, giving good views of the nearby Highlands. You can browse for antiques in Auchterarder before continuing to the pleasant Highland-edge town of Crieff (another good spot for bargain hunters).

1 to 2 Nights: From Crieff follow the A822 north into the Highlands through the Sma'Glen, but keep your eyes open for a sign marked GLEN QUAICH and KENMORE. This route rises through moors before zigzagging steeply down to the east end of Loch Tay. Head to Fortigall to join, a little way east, the B846. Take this high road over the hills to Tummel Bridge, then go east to join the main and busy A9 (there is no other option here). At Dalwhinnie take the A86 (via Loch Laggan) to cosmopolitan Fort William.

1 Night: From Fort William take the A82 north past Loch Lochy to Fort Augustus. Leave the busy A82 and keep to the scenic east bank of Loch Ness—home to the fabled and feared Loch Ness Monster (locals call her Nessie). Continue to Inverness.

1 to 3 Nights: From Inverness take the A96 and then the A939 to Cawdor Castle, the haunting ground of Shakespeare's Macbeth. Continue south on the A939 and cross the wilds of Dava Moor to reach handsome Grantown-on-Spey. Continue toward Tomintoul and the Royal Deeside region (also known as Castle Country), stopping off at one of the region's many dramatic keeps—perhaps the castles at Corgarff, Balmoral, or Braemar. You can detour along the A93 to Aberdeen, a pleasant but commercial port city. Otherwise, rejoin the A9 and head south to Pitlochry, home to the Edradour Distillery, which claims to be the smallest single-malt distillery in Scotland. Head south along the banks of the River Tummel, joining the B867 at Dunkeld. Continue south for Perth and Edinburgh.

The Highlands and Islands by Bike

Happiness is zooming down a steep coastal hill with horizon-wide views of the rugged Highlands. Biking the eastern side of Scotland, around Aberdeen, is saner since the landscape is mostly soft and gentle. But in the coastal Highlands, from Oban to the Isle of Skye to Inverness, the country turns raw and wild. Cycling in this environment requires more than a little stamina, though dining and lodging facilities are generally closely spaced. The following itinerary starts in Glasgow and ends in Inverness. Some sections take advantage of specially designated cycle routes; others follow main and secondary roads where you must be wary of vehicular traffic. No matter what time of year you visit, bring rain gear.

DURATION➤ 8 to 14 Days

THE MAIN ROUTE➤ **1 Night:** From Glasgow take the train to Paisley to link with the Glasgow–Irvine Pedestrian and Cycle Route (maps available from Tourist Information Centers). From Paisley via Lochwinnoch and Kilwinning, the next 30 miles lead through tame countryside to Androssan, where you can catch a summer ferry to Brodick, on Arran island.

1 to 2 Nights: From Brodick follow the A841 clockwise around the island; or, if you're short on time, turn north toward Lochranza, where there's a frequent summer-only ferry to Claonaig. Continue to the quiet town of Kennacraig or larger Tarbert.

1 to 2 Nights: If time permits, follow the B8024 clockwise around Knapdale for

outstanding views of the Hebridean islands. Otherwise, continue north from
Tarbert along the western bank of Loch
Gilp. Your final destination in either case
is the small, very pleasant town of Lochgilphead.

1 to 2 Nights: Take the minor road (B840)
northeast to Ford at the southern end of
Loch Awe, Scotland's longest loch. You
can make a quick detour to Carnasserie
Castle, just off the A816, or continue
along the loch's northwestern side to the
B845 junction. Follow the B845 to Taynuilt,
where there's an unlabeled back road to
Oban via Glen Lonan.

1 Night: North of Oban there are summer
ferries to Craignure, on the Isle of Mull.
On Mull, follow the A849 south past
Torosay and Duart castles, then circle
northward on the B8035 to reach Fishnish Pier, connected by ferry during summer with Lochaline. On the mainland,
follow the A884 north to Strontian or
Salen.

1 Night: Continue north along the coast,
past Loch Ailort, to the A830 junction.
Head west, either to Arisaig or Mallaig.

1 to 3 Nights: Summer ferries connect
Mallaig with the rugged Isle of Skye. If
you're pressed for time, head north on the
A851, then east on the A850 for Kyle of
Lochalsh—a five-minute ferry ride from
the mainland. Otherwise, the A850 leads
northwest to the lovely town of Portree
and to the wild, spectacular seascapes of
northern Skye. When you're ready, back-
track to the Kyle of Lochalsh ferry.

1 to 2 Nights: Continue northeast via the
villages of Plockton and Stromeferry. It's
a demanding uphill ride around the banks
of Loch Carron, but there's plenty of accommodation in Lochcarron, and the subsequent ride between Ardarroch and
Shieldaig is spectacular. So, too, is the
short ride between Shieldaig and Torridon.
From Torridon, bike 20 miles to
Achnasheen and continue by bike or train
to Inverness.

FESTIVALS AND SEASONAL EVENTS

DEC. 30–JAN. 1➤ **Hogmanay** (Edinburgh Tourish Information, ☎ 0131/557–1700), Edinburgh's ancient, still thriving alternative to Christmas.

JAN. 25➤ Burns Night dinners and other entertainments are held in memory of Robert Burns in Glasgow, Ayr, Dumfries, Edinburgh, and many other towns and villages.

MAY➤ **Glasgow Mayfest** (Festival Dir., 18 Albion St., Glasgow, G1 1LH, ☎ 0141/552–8000), Glasgow's answer to the Edinburgh Festival, is a citywide international festival of theater, dance, music, and street events.

MID-MAY➤ The **Perth Festival of the Arts** (☎ 01738/21031) offers orchestral and choral concerts, drama, opera, recitals, and ballet throughout Perth, Tayside.

MID-AUG.–EARLY SEPT.➤ The **Edinburgh International Festival** (21 Market St., Edinburgh, EH1 1BW, ☎ 0131/226–4001), which runs for three weeks, is the world's largest festival of the arts. After dark is the **Edinburgh Military Tattoo** (22 Market St., Edinburgh, EH1 1DF, ☎ 0131/225–1188), a display of military expertise.

SEPTEMBER➤ The **Braemar Royal Highland Gathering** (Princess Royal and Duke of Fife Memorial Park, Braemar, Grampian, ☎ 01339/755377) hosts kilted clansmen from all over Scotland.

2 Scotland: The Home of Golf

Golfing Throughout the Country

By John
Hutchinson

John
Hutchinson
worked for
many years
with the
Scottish Tourist
Board and is
an expert on
the history and
lore of sport in
Scotland.

THERE ARE MORE THAN 400 GOLF COURSES in Scotland and only 5 million local residents, so the country has probably the highest concentration of courses to people anywhere in the world. Some of these courses are world famous as venues for major championships, and any golfer coming to Scotland will probably want to play the "famous names" sometime in his or her career. Telling your friends in the clubhouse back home that you got a birdie at the Road Hole on the Old Course in St. Andrews, where Lyle, Faldo, and Jacklin have played, somehow carries more weight in terms of prestige than an excellent round at an obscure but delightful little course that no one has ever heard of.

So, by all means, play the championship courses and get your prestige, but remember they are championship courses and, therefore, they are difficult; you may enjoy the actual game itself much more at an easier, if less well-known, location. Remember, too, that everyone else wants to play them, so booking can be more of a problem, particularly on peak days during the summer. Do book early, or, if you are staying in a hotel attached to a course, get them to book for you.

There has always been considerable debate as to who invented golf, but there is no doubt that its development into one of the most popular games in the world stems from Scotland. Like many other games that involve hitting a ball with a stick, golf evolved during the Middle Ages and gradually took on its present form.

The first written reference to golf, variously spelled as "gowf" or "goff," was as long ago as 1457, when James II of Scotland declared that both golf and football should be "utterly cryit doune and nocht usit" because they were distracting his subjects from their archery practice. Mary Queen of Scots, it seems, was fond of golf. When in Edinburgh, she played on Leith Links and on Bruntsfield Links, perhaps the oldest course in the world where the game is still played. When in Fife, she played at Falkland near the palace and at St. Andrews itself.

Golf must surely rank as one of Scotland's earliest cultural exports. In 1603, when James VI of Scotland also became James I of England, he moved his court to London. With him went his golf-loving friends, and they set up a course on Blackheath Common, then on the outskirts of London.

Golf clubs as we know them today first began in the middle of the 18th century. The earliest written evidence of the existence of a club is of the Honourable Company of Edinburgh Golfers, now residing at Muirfield, in 1744, and of the Royal and Ancient at St. Andrews in 1754. From then on, clubs sprang up all over Scotland: Royal Aberdeen (1780), Crail Golfing Society (1786), Dunbar (1794), and the Royal Perth Golfing Society (1824).

By the early years of the 19th century, golf clubs had been set up in England, and the game had begun to be carried all over the world by enthusiastic Scots. With them, these Scottish golf missionaries took their knowledge not only of golf, but of golf courses. Scotland is fortunate in that large parts of its coastline are natural golf courses, and the origins of bunkers and the word *links* are to be found in the sand dunes of the Scottish shore. But other countries were not so fortunate. The natural terrain did not exist, and courses had to be designed and created. Willie Park of Musselburgh (who laid out Sunningdale), James Braid, and C. K. Hutchison (whose crowning glory is at Gleneagles Hotel) are some of the best known of Scotland's golf architects.

Golf has always had a peculiar classlessness in Scotland. It is a game for everyone, and for centuries towns and cities in Scotland have had their own golf courses for the enjoyment of the citizens. The snobbishness and exclusivity of golf clubs in some parts of the world have few echoes here.

Many of the important changes in the design and construction of balls and clubs were pioneered by the professional players who lived and worked around these town courses and who made the balls and clubs themselves. The original balls, called "featheries," were leather bags stuffed with boiled feathers. When, in 1848, the gutta percha ball, called a *guttie,* was introduced, there was considerable friction, particularly in St. Andrews, between the makers of the two rival types of ball. The gutta percha proved superior and was in general use until the invention of the rubber-core ball in 1901.

Clubs were traditionally made of wood: shafts of ash, later hickory, and heads of thorn or some other hardwood like apple or pear. Heads were spliced then bound to the shaft with twine. Players generally managed with far fewer clubs than today. About 1628 the marquis of Montrose, a great golf enthusiast, had a set of clubs made for him in St. Andrews that illustrate the range of clubs used in Stuart times: "Bonker clubis, a irone club, and twa play clubs."

Caddies—the word comes from the French *cadet,* a young boy, and was used, particularly in Edinburgh, for anyone who ran messages—carried the players' clubs around, usually under the arm. Golf carts did not come into fashion in Britain until the 1950s.

The technology of golf may change, but its addictive qualities are timeless. Toward the end of the 18th century, an Edinburgh golfer called Alexander McKellar regularly played golf all day and refused to stop even when it grew dark. One night his wife carried his dinner and nightcap on Bruntsfield Links where he was playing in an attempt to shame him into changing his ways. She failed.

And the addiction continues.

Where to Play

Scotland's courses are well spread throughout the country in all areas but the far northern Highlands and some of the islands, so finding a holiday golf course is never a problem. The country's main golfing areas are outlined below. Some suggestions are also given for the things nongolfers could do in an area. For more information region by region, *see* Outdoor Activities and Sports *in* Chapters 3 through 12.

The Stewartry
Starting at the very southern border, the first of these areas is a delightful part of Scotland set in the rich farmlands around Dumfries, a golfing holiday area since Victorian times.

Powfoot and Southerness are excellent links courses with magnificent views over the Solway Firth, while inland, Dumfries and Moffat have long-established courses that provide excellent golf in a clean invigorating environment. There are also several fine nine-hole courses in the area.

Ayrshire and the Clyde Coast
Lying just an hour to the south of Glasgow either by car or by train, Ayrshire and the Clyde Coast has been a holiday area for Glaswegians for generations. Few people need an introduction to the famous names of Turnberry, Royal Troon, Prestwick, or Western Gailes, all excellent links courses along this coast. In addition, there are at least 20 courses

in the area within an hour's drive. Remember, too, that at major locations, such as Turnberry, Troon, and Ayr, there are several different courses to play from the same base.

East Lothian

The sand dunes that stretch eastward from Edinburgh along the southern shore of the Firth of Forth made an ideal location for some of the earliest golf courses in the world. Muirfield is perhaps the most famous course in the area, but around it are more than a dozen more, at Gullane, North Berwick, Dunbar, and Aberlady and, nearer Edinburgh, at Longniddry, Prestonpans, and Musselburgh. All are links courses, many with views to the island of the Firth of Forth and northward to Fife, and if you weary of the East Lothian courses, just 20 or so miles away there are nearly 30 more within the city of Edinburgh.

Fife

Few would dispute the claim of St. Andrews to be the Home of Golf, holding as it does the Royal and Ancient, the organization that governs the sport worldwide. Golf has been played in the area since the very beginning, and to play in Fife is for most golfers a cherished ambition. St. Andrews itself has a wide range of full 18-hole courses in addition to the famous Old Course, and along the shores of the Firth of Forth is a string of ancient villages, each with its harbor, ancient red-roofed buildings, and golf course. In all, there are about 30 in the area.

Perthshire

The first inland golfing area to be considered, Perthshire has a variety of really excellent courses developed specifically for holiday golf and for visitors, rather than for large numbers of local club members. Gleneagles Hotel is, of course, the most famous of these golf resort hotels. Its facilities are considered outstanding when compared with those anywhere in the world. But other courses in the area, set on the edges of beautiful Highland scenery, will delight any golfer. Crieff, Taymouth, and other courses are in the mountains; Blairgowrie and Perth are set amid the rich farmlands nearer the sea.

Angus

East of Perthshire, north of the city of Dundee, is a string of excellent courses along the shores of the North Sea and inland into the foothills of the Grampian Mountains. The most famous course in Angus is probably Carnoustie, one of several British Open Championship venues in Scotland, but there are many more along the same stretch of coast from Dundee northward as far as Stonehaven. Golfers who excel in windy conditions will particularly enjoy the breezes blowing eastward from the sea. Inland Edzell, Forfar, Brechin, and Kirriemuir all have courses nestling in the farmlands of Strathmore.

Aberdeenshire

The city of Aberdeen, Scotland's third largest, is particularly known for its sparkling granite buildings and the amazing displays of roses each summer. It also offers a good range of courses for the golfer. Aberdeen itself has four major courses, and to the north, as far as Fraserburgh and Peterhead, there are five others, including the popular Cruden Bay. Royal Deeside has three, and in the rich farmlands to the north are three more with at least six nine-hole courses as well.

Speyside

Set on the main A9 road an hour south of Inverness amid the Cairngorm Mountains, the valley of the River Spey is one of Scotland's most attractive all-year sports centers, with winter skiing and in summer, sailing and canoeing, pony-trekking, fishing, and some excellent golf. The main courses in the area are Newtonmore, Grantown on Spey, and Boat of Garten, all fine inland courses with wonderful views of the surrounding mountains and challenging golf provided by the springy turf and the heather. For a change of pace, the Moray Firth courses, with their seaside attractions, are only an hour's drive away.

Moray Coast

No one can say that the Lowlands of Scotland have a monopoly of Scotland's fine seaside golf courses. The Moray Coast, stretching eastward from Inverness, has some spectacular sand dunes, and these have been adapted to create stimulating and exciting links courses.

The two courses at Nairn have long been known to golfers famous and unknown. Charlie Chaplin regularly played here. But in addition there are a dozen courses looking out over the sea from Inverness as far along as Banff and Macduff and several inland amid the fertile Moray farmland.

Dornoch Firth

North of Inverness, the east coast is deeply indented with firths along whose shores are to be found some excellent and relatively unknown golf courses. Royal Dornoch has recently been "discovered" by international golf writers, but knowledgeable golfers have been making the northern pilgrimage for well over a hundred years. There are half a dozen excellent links courses around Dornoch and inland, another Victorian golfing holiday center, Strathpeffer, preserves much of the atmosphere these gentlemen of a past age set out to achieve.

Courses Around the Country

Most courses welcome visitors with the minimum of formalities, and some at surprisingly low cost. (Out of season, a few clubs still use the "honest box," in which you drop your fees!) Admittedly, there are at least a few clubs that have always been noted for their exclusive air, and there are newer golf courses emerging as part of exclusive leisure complexes. These are exceptions to the long tradition of recreation for all. Golf in Scotland is usually a very democratic game, played by ordinary folk as well as the rich and leisured. Here is a selection of clubs that welcome visitors. Just three short pieces of advice (particularly for North Americans): 1) In Scotland the game is usually played fairly quickly, so please don't hang about if others are waiting; 2) caddy carts are hand-pulled carts for your clubs, not the electric golf carts that are more familiar to U.S. golfers and rarely available in Scotland; and 3) when they say "rough" they really mean "rough."

Balgownie, Royal Aberdeen Golf Club. This old, established club (1780) is the archetypal Scottish links course: long and testing over uneven ground, with the frequently added hazard of a sea breeze. Prickly gorse is inclined to close in and form an additional hurdle. The course is tucked behind the rough, grassy sand dunes, and there are surprisingly few views of the sea. One historical note: In 1783, this club originated the five-minute-search rule for a lost ball. ☎ 01224/702221. *18 holes. Yardage: 6,372. Par 70. Fees: £37/round, £48 daily. Weekend restrictions, letter of introduction required. Advance reservations. Facilities: practice area, catering.*

Ballater. This club has a holiday atmosphere and a course laid out along the river flats of the River Dee. Originally opened in 1906, the club makes maximum use of the fine setting between river and woods and is ideal for a relaxing round of vacation golf. The variety of shops and pleasant walks in nearby Ballater make this a good place for nongolfing partners. ☎ 013397/55567 or 012297/55658. *18 holes. Yardage: 5,638. Par 67. Fees: weekdays, £17/round, £26 daily; weekends,*

£20/round, £30 daily. Visitors welcome daily. Advance reservations. Facilities: practice area, caddy carts, catering.

Banff, Duff House Royal Gold Golf Club. Although it is within moments of the sea, this club is a curious blend of a coastal course with a parkland setting. The course, which is only minutes from Banff center, lies within the parkland grounds of Duff House, an Adam mansion that was donated to the town. The club has inherited the ancient traditions of seaside play (golf records here go back to the 17th century). Mature trees and gentle slopes create a pleasant playing atmosphere. ☎ *01261/812075. 18 holes. Yardage: 6,161. Par 69. Fees: weekdays, £14/round, £18 daily; weekends, £20/round, £26 daily. Advance reservations. Facilities: practice area, caddy carts, catering.*

Boat of Garten. Possibly one of the greatest "undiscovered" courses in Scotland, Boat of Garten was designed by famous golf architect James Braid. Each of the 18 holes is individual: Some cut through birchwood and heathery rough, most have long views to the Cairngorms and a strong Highland ambience. An unusual feature is the preserved steam railway that runs along part of the course. The occasional puffing locomotive can hardly be considered a hazard. ☎ *01479/831282. 18 holes. Yardage: 5,837. Par 69. Fees: weekdays, £20 daily; weekends, £25 daily. Starting sheet used on weekends. Advance reservations. Facilities: caddies, caddy carts, catering.*

Callander. Another course well worth seeking out, Callander was designed by Tom Morris and has a scenic upland feel. Pine and birch woods and hilly fairways offer fine views, and the tricky moorland layout demands accurate hitting off the tee. ☎ *01877/330090. 18 holes. Yardage: 5,125. Par 66. Fees: weekdays, £17/round, £22.50 daily; weekends, £22.50/round, £28 daily. Facilities: practice area, caddies, caddy carts, catering.*

Carnoustie. Home in former days of the British Open Championship, the extensive coastal links around Carnoustie have been played for generations. Carnoustie was also once a training ground for golf coaches, many of whom went to the United States. The choice municipal course here is therefore full of historical snippets and local color, as well as being tough and full of interest. ☎ *01241/853789. 18 holes. Yardage 6,936. Par 74. Fees: £45/round, £135 3 days, £200 5 days. Visitors welcome except Sat. morning, Sun. before 11:30 AM. Advance reservations. Facilities: caddies, caddy carts (May–Oct.), catering.*

Cruden Bay. Another east coast Lowland course sheltered behind the extensive sand hills, this one offers a typical Scottish golf experience. Runnels and valleys, among other hazards, on the challenging fairways ensure plenty of excitement, and some of the holes are rated among the finest anywhere in Scotland. Like Gleneagles and Turnberry, this course owes its origins to an association with the grand railway hotels that were built in the heyday of steam. Unlike the other two, however, Cruden Bay's railway hotel and the railway itself have gone, though the course has only gotten better. ☎ *01779/812285. 18 holes. Yardage: 6,370. Par 71. Fees: weekdays, £30 daily; weekends, £40 daily; £120 weekly; £200 for 2 weeks. Visitors welcome weekdays, restricted weekends. Advance reservations. Facilities: practice area, caddy carts, catering.*

Dornoch. This course, which was laid out by Tom Morris in 1886 on a sort of coastal shelf behind the shore, has matured to become one of the world's finest. Its location in the north of Scotland, though less than an hour's drive from Inverness Airport, means that it is far from overrun even in peak season. It may not have the fame of a Gleneagles or a St. Andrews, but if time permits, Dornoch is a memorable golfing experience. The little town of Dornoch, behind the course, is both sleepy and charming. ☎ *01862/810219. 18 holes. Yardage 6,581. Par 70. Fees: weekdays, £40/round, £100 3 days; weekends, £45/round. Advance reservations. Max handicap: men 24, women 35. Facilities: practice area, caddies, caddy carts, catering.*

Dunbar. This ancient golfing site by the sea even has a lighthouse at the 9th hole. It's a good choice for a typical east coast Lowland course within easy reach of Edinburgh. ☎ *01368/862317. 18 holes. Yardage: 6,426. Par 71. Fees: weekdays, £30 daily; weekends, £40 daily. Visitors welcome after 9:30 AM except Thurs. Advance reservations. Facilities: practice area, caddies (by reservation), catering.*

Fraserburgh. A northeast town with extensive links and dunes that seem to have grown up around the course rather than the other way around. Be prepared for a hill climb and a tough finish. ☎ *01346/518287. 18 holes (4 additional for warm-up). Yardage: 6,279. Par 70. Fees: weekdays, £11/round, £14 daily; weekends, £15/round, £20 daily. Facilities: practice area, catering.*

Girvan. An old established course with play along a narrow coastal strip and a more lush inland section beside the Water of Girvan—the neighborhood river that constitutes a particular hazard at the 15th, unless you are a big hitter. This is quite a scenic course, with good views of the Clyde estuary. ☎ *01465/714346. 18 holes. Yardage: 5,078. Par 65. Fees: £11/round, £18 daily. Visitors welcome daily. Facilities: caddy carts, catering.*

Killin. A splendidly scenic course, typically Highland, with a roaring river, woodland birdsong, and backdrop of high green hills. There are a few surprises, including two blind shots to reach the green at the 4th. The village of Killin is very attractive, almost alpine in feel, especially in spring when the hilltops may still be white. ☎ *01567/820312. 9 holes. Yardage: 2,410. Par 65. Fees: £11/round, £14 daily. Facilities: caddy carts, club hire, catering.*

Ladybank. Fife is famous for its choice of coastal courses, but this one offers an interesting contrast: Though Ladybank is laid out on fairly level ground, the fir woods, birches, and heathery rough give it a Highland flavor among the gentle Lowland fields. Qualifying rounds of the British Open are played here when the main championship is played at St. Andrews. ☎ *01337/830814. 18 holes. Yardage: 6,641. Par 71. Fees: Oct.–Apr. weekdays, £17/round, £24 daily; weekends, £20/round, £28 daily. May–Sept. weekdays, £26/round, £35 daily; weekends, £28/round, £38 daily. Visitors welcome daily. Advance reservations essential. Facilities: practice area, caddy carts, catering.*

Leven. Another fine Fife course used as a British Open qualifier, this one also feels like the more famous St. Andrews, with hummocky terrain and a tang of salt in the air. The 1st and 18th share the same fairway. ☎ *01333/428859. 18 holes. Yardage: 6,436. Par 71. Fees: weekdays, £20/round, £30 daily; weekends, £24/round, £36 daily. Visitors welcome except Sat. Advance reservations. Facilities: catering.*

Lossiemouth, Moray Golf Club. Discover the mild airs of the "Moray Riviera," as Tom Morris did in 1889 when he was inspired by the lie of the natural links. There are two courses plus a six-hole minicourse. There is lots of atmosphere here, with golfing memorabilia in the clubhouse, as well as the tale of the British prime minister, Lord Asquith, who took a holiday in this out-of-the-way spot, yet still managed to be attacked by a crowd of militant suffragettes at the 17th. All other hazards on these testing courses are entirely natural. ☎ *01343/813330. 18 holes each (6 separate). Yardage: 6,643, 6,005. Par 71, 69. Fees: Old Course, weekdays, £22/round, £32 daily; weekends, £33/round, £43 daily. New Course, weekdays, £17/round, £22 daily; weekends, £22/round, £27 daily. Joint ticket (one round on each course), £27 weekdays, £38 weekends. Facilities: practice area, caddy carts, catering.*

Machrihanish, by Campbeltown. This is a western course that many enthusiasts discuss in hushed tones—a kind of out-of-the-way golfers' Shangri-La. It was laid out in 1876 by Tom Morris on the links around the sandy Machrihanish Bay. The drive of the first tee is across the beach to reach the green—an intimidating start to a memorable series of very individual holes. If you are short on time, consider flying from Glasgow to nearby Campbeltown, the last town on the long peninsula of Kintyre. ☎ *01586/810277. 18 holes. Yardage: 6,228. Par 70. Fees: Sun.–Fri., £20/round, £30 daily; Sat. £35 daily; £120 weekly. Advance reservations. Facilities: practice area, caddy carts, catering.*

Nairn. Widely regarded in golfing circles as a truly great course, Nairn dates from 1887 and is the regular home of Scotland's Northern Open. Huge greens, aggressive gorse, a beach hazard for five of the holes, a steady prevailing wind, and distracting views across the Moray Firth to the northern hills make play here a memorable experience. ☎ *01667/453208. 18 holes. Yardage: 6,722. Par 72. Fees: weekdays, £35/round; weekends, £42/round. Advance reservations. Facilities: practice area, caddies, caddy carts, catering.*

Rosemount, Blairgowrie Golf Club. Well known to native golfers looking for an exciting challenge, Rosemount's 18 are laid out in the fir woods, which certainly bring a wild air to the scene. You may encounter a browsing roe deer if you stray too far. There are also, however, wide fairways and at least some large greens. ☎ *01250/872622. 18 holes. Yardage: 6,556. Par 72. Fees: weekdays, £35/round, £48 daily; weekends, £40/round. Visitors welcome Mon., Tues., Thurs. Facilities: practice area, caddies, caddy carts, catering.*

3 Edinburgh and the Lothians

Scotland's capital makes a strong first impression—Edinburgh Castle looming from the crags of an ancient volcano; neoclassical monuments perched on Calton Hill; Arthur's Seat, a small mountain with steep slopes, little crags, and spectacular vistas over the city and the Firth of Forth. Like Rome, Edinburgh is built on seven hills, and it has an Old Town district that retains striking evidence of a colorful history. But Edinburgh offers more than just a unique historical and architectural landscape—it's a cosmopolitan capital, rich in museums and culture.

By Gilbert
Summers

THE FIRST-TIME VISITOR TO SCOTLAND may be surprised that the country still has a capital city at all, thinking perhaps that the seat of government was drained of all its resources and power after the union with England in 1707. Far from it. The Union of Parliaments brought with it a set of political partnerships—such as separate legal, ecclesiastical, and educational systems—that Edinburgh (-*burgh* is always pronounced *burra* in Scots), as former seat of the Scottish parliament, assimilated and integrated with its own surviving institutions. In the trying decades after the union, many influential Scots, both in Edinburgh and beyond, went through an identity crisis, but out of the 18th-century difficulties grew the Scottish Enlightenment, during which great strides were made by educated Scots in medicine, economics, and science.

By the mid-18th century, it had become the custom for wealthy Scottish landowners to spend the winter in town houses in the Old Town of Edinburgh, huddled between the high castle rock and the Royal Palace below. In the tall crowded buildings of old Edinburgh, the well-to-do tended to have their rooms on the middle floors, while the "lower orders" occupied dwellings on the top and ground floors. Such an overcrowded arrangement bred plenty of unsavory and odorous hazards (more on this later), but it also bred ideas. Uniquely cross-fertilized in the coffeehouses and taverns, intellectual notions flourished among a people determined to remain Scottish yet deprived of their identity in a political sense. One result was a campaign to expand and beautify the city, to give it a look worthy of its subsequent nickname, Athens of the North. Thus was the New Town of Edinburgh built, with broad streets and gracious buildings creating a harmony that even today's throbbing traffic cannot obscure.

Edinburgh today is the second-most-important financial center in the United Kingdom. Its residents come from all over Britain—not least of all because the city regularly ranks near the top of surveys that measure "quality of life"—and New Town apartments in fashionable streets sell for considerable amounts of money. In some senses the city is showy and materialistic, but Edinburgh still supports several learned societies, many of which have their roots in the Scottish Enlightenment: The Royal Society of Edinburgh, for example, established in 1783 "for the advancement of learning and useful knowledge," is still an important forum for interdisciplinary activities, both in Edinburgh and in Scotland as a whole, publishing scientific papers, holding academic symposia and meetings, and administering research fellowships in many Scottish universities. Hand in hand with the city's academic and scientific life is a rich cultural life, with the Edinburgh International Festival attracting lovers of all the arts. Running for three weeks from late August into September, this is simply one of the top cultural and artistic festivals in the world. It attracts talent from all parts of the globe: top orchestras and conductors, international dance troupes and ballet companies, and leading opera and theater performers.

Thousands of years ago, an eastward-grinding glacier encountered the tough basalt plug or core of an ancient volcano. It swept around the core, scouring steep cliffs and leaving a trail of material like the tail of a comet. This material formed a ramp, gently leading down from the rocky summit. On this *crag* and *tail* would grow the city of Edinburgh. The lands that rolled down to the sea were for centuries open country, between Castle Rock and the tiny community clustered by the shore that grew into Leith, Edinburgh's seaport. By the 12th century Edinburgh had become a walled town, still perched on the hill. Its shape was becoming clearer: like a fish with its head at the castle, backbone running down the ridge, with "ribs" leading briefly off on either side. The backbone gradually became the continuous thoroughfare now known as the Royal Mile, and the ribs became the closes (alleyways), some still surviving, that were the scene of many historic incidents. By the early 15th century Edinburgh had become the undisputed capital of Scotland. The bitter defeat of Scotland at Flodden in 1513 (when Scotland aligned itself with France against England) caused a new defensive city wall to be built. Though the castle escaped, the city was burned by the English earl of Hertford under the orders of King Henry VIII of England. By the time that Mary, Queen of Scots, returned already widowed from France, in 1561, the guest house of the Abbey of Holyrood had grown to become the Palace of Holyroodhouse. Mary's legacy to the city included the destruction of most of the earliest buildings of Edinburgh Castle, held by her supporters after she was forced to flee her homeland.

By the end of the 18th century the grand New Town was taking shape, though it never was taken as far as the sea at Leith, which had been the original intention. Victorian suburbs added to the gradual sprawl. Despite the expansion, the guardian castle remained the focal point. Princes Street—a master stroke in city planning—was built up only on one side, allowing magnificent views of the great rock on which the fortress stands. The result for today's visitor is a skyline of sheer drama and an aura of grandeur. Edinburgh Castle watches over the city, frowning down on Princes Street, now the main downtown shopping area, as if disapproving of its modern razzmatazz. Its ramparts still echo with gunfire each day when the traditional one o'clock gun booms out over the city, startling unwary shoppers. To the east, the top of New Town's Calton Hill is cluttered with sturdy neoclassical structures, somewhat like an abandoned set for a Greek tragedy.

These theatrical elements give a unique identity to downtown, but turn a corner, say, off George Street, and you will see, not an endless cityscape, but blue sea and a patchwork of fields. This is the county of Fife, beyond the inlet of the North Sea called the Firth of Forth—a reminder, like the Highlands to the northwest glimpsed from Edinburgh's highest points, that the rest of Scotland lies within easy reach.

Pleasures and Pastimes

Bicycling
Edinburgh is a fairly compact, if hilly, city, and bicycling is a good way to get around, though careful route planning may be needed to avoid traffic. The East Lothian countryside, with its miles of twisting roads and light traffic, is within cycling distance of the city.

Dining
Edinburgh's restaurants offer a sophisticated, diverse mix of traditional and exotic cuisines, from Scottish to Mexican, Thai, Chinese, Greek, and Russian. It's worth investigating the set-price business lunches many restaurants offer, which are often a good value.

Golf
Golf courses abound—there are about 20 courses within or close to the city (not including the easily accessible East Lothian courses), many of which welcome visitors.

Lodging
Edinburgh offers a variety of accommodations, many in traditional Georgian properties, some even in the New Town, only a few minutes from

downtown. There are also a number of upscale hotels in the downtown area, each with an international flavor.

Nightlife and the Arts

Edinburgh is world renowned for its flagship arts event, the **Edinburgh International Festival,** now in its 51st year, and there is no escaping a sense of theater if you visit the city from August to early September. The annual festival has attracted all sorts of international performers since its inception in 1947. (Technically, 1997 is the festival's 50th anniversary, but the 50th festival was, in fact, in 1996.) Even more obvious to the casual stroller during this time is the refreshingly irreverent **Edinburgh Festival Fringe,** unruly child of the official festival, which spills out of halls and theaters and onto the streets all over town. At other times throughout the year professional and amateur groups alike offer a range of cultural options appropriate to a capital city, even if Edinburgh's neighbor and rival city, Glasgow, has the reputation of being more lively.

Edinburgh's nightlife is quite varied and includes dinner dances, discos, Scottish musical evenings, and *ceilidhs* (roaming bands of homicidal clog dancers, pronounced *kay*-lees). Jazz and folk music in general are wide-ranging. In quiet-living Edinburgh, there are no nightclubs of the cabaret-and-striptease variety.

Shopping

To make the most of shopping in Edinburgh you will need at least two days, in part because the town's most interesting shops are distributed among several districts. Edinburgh's downtown has the usual chain stores, lined up shoulder to shoulder and offering identical goods. But within a few yards, down some of the side streets, you'll find shops offering more exclusive wares, such as designer clothing, unique craft items, 18th-century silverware, and wild-caught, smoked Scottish salmon.

As the capital city and an important tourist center, Edinburgh features a cross section of Scottish specialties, such as tartans and tweeds, rather than products peculiar to the Edinburgh area. Once you venture into Edinburgh's "villages"—perhaps Stockbridge, Bruntsfield, Morningside, or even the Old Town itself—you will find many unusual stores specializing in single items, such as antique clocks, and designer knitwear using the finest Scottish wool or cashmere. In many cases the goods sold in these stores are unavailable elsewhere in Scotland.

If you are interested in antiques, Edinburgh should be a productive hunting ground. Scotland has a strong tradition of distinctive furniture makers, silversmiths, and artists; top-quality examples of their work can still be found, at a price. Most reputable dealers are able to arrange transport abroad for your purchases if you buy something too bulky to fit into your luggage.

EXPLORING EDINBURGH AND THE LOTHIANS

The Old Town, which bears a great measure of symbolic weight as the "heart of Scotland's capital," is for lovers of atmosphere and history. The New Town, by contrast, is for those visitors who appreciate the unique architectural heritage of Edinburgh's Enlightenment. If you belong in both categories, don't worry—the Old and the New Towns are only yards apart. The Old and the New are the essence of Edinburgh, even if, away from this central core, Victorian expansion and urban sprawl have greatly increased the city's dimensions. But Edinburgh, as cities go, is still compact, and much of the interesting city-center environment can be covered on foot.

The countryside outside Edinburgh—Midlothian, West Lothian and East Lothian, collectively called "the Lothians"—can be reached very quickly by bus or car, and its hills, green fields, beaches, and historic houses and castles offer a chance to escape from the Festival crush at the height of summer.

Great Itineraries

Edinburgh's spectacular setting usually means a good first impression—you can be there for a day and think you know the place, as even a cursory bus tour will enable you to grasp the layout of castle, Royal Mile, Old Town, New Town, and so on. However, if your taste is more for leisurely strolling through the nooks and crannies of the Old Town closes, then three or four days might be a better time allocation.

IF YOU HAVE 2 DAYS

To start you off, make your way to **Edinburgh Castle**—not just the battlements—and spend some time there, just for its sense of history. Certainly, take a city bus tour as well. Your list of must-sees should also have the **National Gallery of Scotland** and, unless it is winter, the **Georgian House** for an idea of life in the New Town.

IF YOU HAVE 5 DAYS

Five days allows plenty of time for Old Town exploration, including the important museums of **Huntly House** and the People's Story (located in the **Canongate Tolbooth**), and for a walk around the New Town with its **Scottish National Portrait Gallery** and the **Scottish National Gallery of Modern Art,** both well worth an hour or two. You should also have plenty of time for shopping, not only in areas close to the city center like Rose Street and Victoria Street, but also in some of the less "touristy" areas like Bruntsfield. Make a foray down to **Leith,** to check out its array of eating places. You could also hop on a bus out to Midlothian to see the stunning stone carving in **Rosslyn Chapel** at Roslin, and visit the **Edinburgh Crystal Visitor Centre** at Penicuik for crystal bargains. Consider spending another half day traveling out to South Queensferry, to admire the Forth road and rail bridges, then visit palatial **Hopetoun House** with its wealth of portraits and fine furniture.

IF YOU HAVE 8 DAYS

In addition to a thorough exploration of Edinburgh's Old and New Towns, museums and galleries, and a shopping trip or two, in eight days you will not only have time to explore **Leith,** Roslin, and South Queensferry, but also to make the two side trips suggested in this chapter. Allow at least a day for each trip, so you have time to enjoy stately homes such as **Dalmeny House** for its Rothschild Collection of sumptuous French furniture; a historic ruin such as **Linlithgow Palace,** with its Mary Queen of Scots connection; or the magnificently sited **Castle Campbell. Gullane,** with its splendid East Lothian beach, is a good place to walk in the footsteps of Robert Louis Stevenson. **Andrew Carnegie's Birthplace Museum** at Dunfermline; Dunbar, with its **John Muir Country Park**; or the delightful market town of **Haddington,** with the nearby **Lennoxlove House** (which also boasts Mary Queen of Scots associations) are other highlights of the side trips. If it is festival time, however, you can probably take in shows, concerts, and exhibitions for eight days solidly and hardly stray from the city center.

The Old Town

Time and progress (of a sort) have swept away some of the narrow closes and tall tenements of the Old Town, but enough remain for the visitor to imagine the original shape of Scotland's capital. Probably every visitor to the city tours the castle, which is more than can be said for many of the city's residents. Its popularity as an attraction is due not only to the castle's historic and symbolic value, but also to the outstanding views offered from its battlements. Immediately below the Castle Esplanade the Royal Mile starts, running roughly west to east, from the castle to the Palace of Holyroodhouse, the queen's official residence in Scotland. Its name changes as it progresses, from Castlehill to Lawnmarket, High Street, and Canongate.

A Good Walk

Numbers in the text correspond to numbers in the margin and on the Edinburgh, West Lothian and the Forth Valley, and Midlothian and East Lothian exploring maps.

Start your exploration of the Old Town at **Edinburgh Castle** ①. After exploring its extensive complex of buildings, and admiring the view from the battlements, set off down the first part of the Royal Mile, calling in en route at your choice of the museums and other interesting ports of call: **Castlehill** ② and Cannonball House, the Outlook Tower and Camera Obscura, the Scotch Whisky Heritage Centre, the Tolbooth Kirk (*kirk* means church), the Upper Bow, Gladstone's Land, and The Writers' Museum.

At the junction of Lawnmarket with George IV Bridge, turn right then right again into Victoria Street, which winds down to the historic **Grassmarket** ③, where parts of the old city walls still stand. Retrace your steps to George IV Bridge, then detour again southward to see the National Library of Scotland, the **Kirk of the Greyfriars** ④ and the little statue of the faithful Greyfriars Bobby. In Chambers Street, at the foot of George IV Bridge, the impressive galleries of the **Royal Museum of Scotland** ⑤ have enough variety to interest all ages.

Returning to the junction of George IV Bridge with the Royal Mile, turn right (eastward) down High Street for **Parliament House** ⑥, the **High Kirk of St. Giles** ⑦, the Mercat Cross, and the elegant City Chambers, bringing a flavor of the New Town's neoclassicism to the Old Town's severity. Further down on the right is the Tron Kirk, with the **Museum of Childhood** beyond. John Knox House and the Netherbow Arts Centre are two further attractions on this section of the Royal Mile, which immediately afterward becomes the Canongate.

A short distance up the Canongate on the left is **Canongate Tolbooth** ⑧; **Huntly House** ⑨ is opposite, and the **Canongate Kirk** ⑩ and Acheson House are nearby. This walk ends, as it started, on a high point: the **Palace of Holyroodhouse** ⑪, full of historic and architectural interest, with some fine paintings, tapestries and furnishings to admire.

TIMING

The walk could be accomplished in a day, but in order to give the major sights—the castle, Palace of Holyroodhouse, and Royal Museum of Scotland—the time they deserve, and also see at least some of the other attractions properly, you should allow two days. We suggest that you end the first day with an afternoon in the Royal Museum of Scotland, and spend the second afternoon at Holyroodhouse.

Sights to See

Canongate. Named for the canons who once ran the abbey at Holyrood, now the site of Holyrood Palace, Canongate extends from High Street to the palace. In Scots, "gate" means "street." Canongate itself was originally an independent "burgh," another Scottish term used to refer to a community with trading rights granted by the monarch. Canon-

Exploring Edinburgh

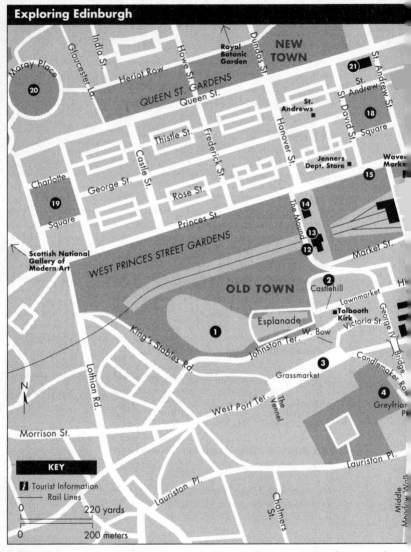

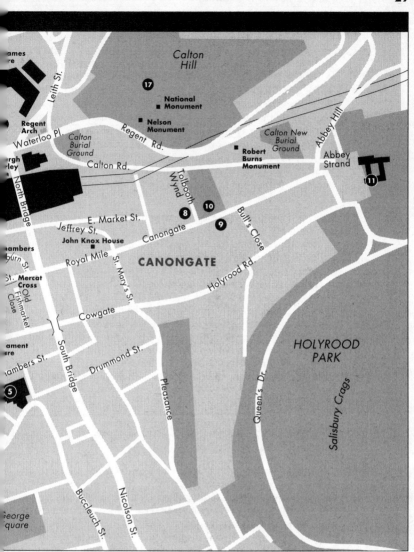

Calton
Hill

⑰

National
■ Monument

■ Nelson
Monument

Leith St.

Regent
Arch

Waterloo Pl.

Regent Rd.

Calton
Burial
Ground

Calton New
Burial
Ground

Abbey Hill

Calton Rd.

North Bridge

Tolbooth
Wynd

■ Robert
Burns
Monument

Abbey
Strand

⑪

E. Market St.

⑧ ⑩

⑨

Bull's Close

Jeffrey St.

Canongate

■ John Knox House

CANONGATE

Royal Mile

St. Mary's St.

Holyrood Rd.

Chambers

burn St.

St.

Mercat
Cross

Old
Fishmarket
Close

Cowgate

HOLYROOD
PARK

ament
are

South Bridge

Drummond St.

⑤

hambers St.

Pleasance

Queen's Dr.

Salisbury Crags

George
quare

Buccleuch St.

Nicolson St.

gate is home to ☞ **Canongate Kirk,** ☞ **Canongate Tolbooth,** ☞ **Huntly House,** and ☞ **Acheson House.**

⑩ Canongate Kirk. The graveyard of the church (built in 1688) is the burial place of some notable Scots, including Adam Smith, author of *The Wealth of Nations* (1776), who once lived in 17th-century Panmure House nearby. You can also visit the grave of the undervalued Scots poet Robert Fergusson. The fact that Fergusson's grave is even marked is due to the efforts of the much more famous Robert Burns. On a visit to the city Burns was dismayed to find the grave had no headstone, so he commissioned an architect—by the name of Robert Burn—to design one. (Burn reportedly took two years to complete the commission, so Burns, in turn, took two years to pay.) Burn also designed the Nelson Monument, the tall column on Calton Hill to the north, which you can see from the graveyard.

Before you leave, look for the monument to Robert Burns himself, also on Calton Hill and visible from the graveyard; it is the circular temple below Regent Road (☞ The New Town, *below*). Devotees of Burns will want to visit one other grave. Against the eastern wall of the graveyard is a bronze sculpture of the head of Mrs. Agnes McLehose, "Clarinda" of the copious correspondence Burns engaged in while confined to his lodgings with an injured leg in 1788. Burns and Mrs. McLehose—an attractive and talented woman who had been abandoned by her husband—exchanged passionate letters for some six weeks that year, Burns signing his name "Sylvander"; Mrs. McLehose, "Clarinda." The missives were dispatched across town by a postal service that delivered them for a penny an hour. The curiously literary affair ended when Burns left Edinburgh to take up a farm tenancy and marry Jean Armour.

Opposite Canongate graveyard is **Acheson House** (c. 1633), once a fine town mansion, which, like so much of the property in the Canongate, fell on hard times. It has been restored, as has Moray House, which dates from 1628, a little farther up the street.

⑧ Canongate Tolbooth, where Canongate's town council once met, now houses a museum, the People's Story, which focuses on the lives of "ordinary" people from the 18th century to today and describes how this now in some ways rather sterile street once bustled with the activities of the various tradesmen needed to supply life's essentials in the days before superstores. Special displays include a reconstruction of a cooper's workshop and a 1940s kitchen. ✉ *Canongate Tolbooth,* ☎ *0131/225–2424, ext. 4057.* 🎫 *Free.* ☼ *June–Sept., Mon.–Sat. 10–6, Sun. during festival 2–5; Oct.–May, Mon.–Sat. 10–5.*

NEED A BREAK?   You can get a good cup of tea and a sticky cake (a quintessentially Scottish indulgence) from **Clarinda's** (✉ 69 Canongate) or the **Abbey Strand Tearoom** (✉ The Sanctuary, Abbey Strand), near the palace gates.

❷ Castlehill. Witches were brought here in the late 16th century to be burnt at the stake, as a bronze plaque recalls. The cannonball embedded in the west gable of **Cannonball House** was, so legend says, fired from the castle during the Jacobite rebellion in 1745 led by Bonnie Prince Charlie, the most romantic of the Stuart pretenders to the British throne. Most authorities agree on a more prosaic explanation, however, saying it was a height marker for Edinburgh's first piped water-supply system, installed in 1681.

In **Outlook Tower** the **Camera Obscura** offers armchair views of the city. The 17th-century tower was significantly altered in the 1840s and

1850s with the installation of the present system of lenses, which, on a clear day, project an image of the city onto a white concave table. ✉ *Castlehill,* ☎ *0131/226–3709.* 🎫 *£3.30.* ☉ *Apr.–Oct., weekdays 9:30–6, weekends 10–6; Nov.–Mar., daily 10–5.*

The mysterious process that turns malted barley and spring water into one of Scotland's most important exports is revealed at the **Scotch Whisky Heritage Centre.** Although whisky-making is not in itself packed with drama, the center manages an imaginative presentation using models and tableaux viewed while riding in low-speed barrel-cars. At one point visitors find themselves inside a huge vat surrounded by bubbling sounds and malty smells. ✉ *358 Castlehill,* ☎ *0131/220–0441.* 🎫 *£4.20.* ☉ *Daily 10–5:30 (extended hours in summer).*

The Gothic **Tolbooth Kirk,** built in 1842–44 for the General Assembly of the Church of Scotland church, boasts the tallest spire in the city—240 feet.

At the intersection at the end of Castlehill, look for the **Upper Bow** on the right, immediately east of where Johnston Terrace joins the Lawnmarket. This was once the main route westward from town and castle. Before Victoria Street was built, in the late 19th century, Upper Bow led down into a narrow dark thoroughfare coursing between a canyon of tenements. All traffic struggled up and down this steep slope from the Grassmarket, which joins the now-truncated West Bow at its lower end.

NEED A BREAK? There are a number of atmospheric pubs and restaurants in this section of the Royal Mile. Try the **Jolly Judge** (✉ James Ct.), a friendly pub where bright firelight brightens the dark-wood beams.

❶ **Edinburgh Castle.** Recent archaeological investigations have established that the rock on which the castle stands was inhabited as far back as AD 1000, in the latter part of the Bronze Age. There have been fortifications here since the mysterious people called the Picts first used it as a stronghold in the 3rd and 4th centuries BC. The Picts were dislodged by Saxon invaders from northern England in 452 BC, and for the next 1,300 years the site saw countless battles and skirmishes.

The castle has been held by Scots and Englishmen, Catholics and Protestants, soldiers and royalty; during the Napoleonic Wars it even contained French prisoners of war, whose carvings can still be seen on the vaults under the great hall. In the 16th century, Mary, Queen of Scots, gave birth in the castle to the future James VI of Scotland, who was also to rule England as James I. In 1573 the castle defended Mary as rightful Catholic queen of Scotland; it was her last stronghold and was virtually destroyed by English artillery.

The oldest surviving building in the complex—in fact, in all the city—is the tiny 11th-century **St. Margaret's Chapel,** named in honor of Saxon Queen Margaret, who had persuaded her husband, King Malcolm, to move his court from Dunfermline to Edinburgh because the latter's environs—the Lothians—were occupied by Saxon settlers with whom she felt more at home, or so the story goes. (Dunfermline was surrounded by Celts.) The chapel was the only building spared when the castle was razed in 1313 by the Scots, having won it back from their English foes. Also worth seeing are the **crown room,** which contains the **regalia of Scotland**—the crown, scepter, and sword that once graced the Scottish monarch; the **old parliament hall;** and **Queen Mary's apartments,** where she gave birth to James. The **great hall** features a collection of arms and armor and has an impressive vaulted, beamed ceiling.

There are several military features of interest, including the **Scottish National War Memorial,** the **Scottish United Services Museum,** and the famous 15th-century Belgian-made cannon **Mons Meg.** This enormous piece of artillery has been silent since 1682, when it exploded while firing a salute for the duke of York; it now stands in an ancient hall behind the Half-Moon Battery, the curving ramparts that give Edinburgh Castle its distinctive appearance from miles away. Contrary to what you may hear from locals, it is not *Mons Meg* but the battery's time gun that goes off with a bang every weekday at 1, frightening visitors and reminding Edinburghers to check their watches.

The **Esplanade,** the huge forecourt of the castle, was built in the 18th century as a parade ground, using earth from the foundation of the Royal Exchange (now the City Chambers) to widen and level the area. Although it now serves as the castle parking lot, it comes alive with color each year during the festival, when it is used for the Tattoo, a magnificent military display and pageant. ☎ *0131/668–8600.* 💷 *£5.50.* ⏰ *Apr.–Sept., daily 9:30–5:15; Oct.–Mar., daily 9:30–4:15.*

NEED A BREAK?   At the castle, **Mills Mount Restaurant** serves coffee, light lunches, and afternoon teas in bright premises with panoramic views over the city.

George IV Bridge. It is not immediately obvious that this is in fact a bridge, as buildings are closely packed most of the way along both sides. But these buildings extend several stories below street level, as can be seen by looking over the short lengths of parapet. The **National Library of Scotland,** founded in 1689, has a superb collection of books and manuscripts on the history and culture of Scotland, and also mounts regular exhibitions. ✉ *George IV Bridge,* ☎ *0131/226–4531.* 💷 *Admission to exhibitions free.* ⏰ *Mon., Tues., Thurs., Fri. 9:30–8:30, Wed. 10–8:30, Sat. 9:30–1; exhibitions Mon.–Sat. 10-5.*

❸ Grassmarket. Down in the Grassmarket, which for centuries was, as its name suggests, an agricultural market, there are now numerous bars and restaurants which make this a hub of activity at night.

Sections of the Old Town wall can be approximately traced on the north (castle) side by a series of steps that runs steeply up from Grassmarket to Johnston Terrace above. By far the best-preserved section of the wall, however, is to be found by crossing to the south side and climbing the steps of the lane called **The Vennel.** Here you can see a section of the 16th-century **Flodden Wall,** which comes in from the east and turns southward at Telfer's Wall, a 17th-century extension. From here there are outstanding views northward to the castle.

The **cobbled cross** marks the site of the town gallows. Among those hanged here were many 17th-century Covenanters. Judges were known to issue the death sentence for these religious reformers with the words, "Let them glorify God in the Grassmarket."

Victoria Street leads up to George IV Bridge from the northeast corner of the Grassmarket and is a 19th-century addition to the Old Town. Its shops offer antiques, new designer clothing, and high-quality giftware.

❼ High Kirk of St. Giles. Originally the city's parish church, St. Giles's became a cathedral in 1633 and is now often called St. Giles's Cathedral. There has been a church on the site since AD 854, although most of the present structure dates from 1829. The spire, however, was completed in 1495. The **Chapel of the Order of the Thistle,** bearing the belligerent national motto NEMO ME IMPUNE LACESSIT ("No one provokes me with impunity"), was added in 1911. ✉ *High St.,* ☎ *0131/*

225–4363. ✉ Kirk admission free. Thistle Chapel donation: £1. ☉ Mon.–Sat. 9–5 (until 7 in summer), Sun. 1–5 (services 8 AM, 10 AM, 11:30 AM, 6 PM, 8 PM).

High Street. One of the four streets making up the Royal Mile, High Street contains some of the Old Town's most impressive buildings and sights, which merit individual entries. However, there are also other, less obvious historic relics to be seen. Near Parliament Square, look on the west side for a heart set in cobbles. This marks the site of the vanished **Tolbooth,** the center of city life from the 15th century until the building's demolition in 1817. This ancient civic edifice, formerly housing the Scottish parliament and used as a prison from 1640 onward, inspired Sir Walter Scott's novel *The Heart of Midlothian.* Nearly every city and town in Scotland once had a tolbooth. Originally a customs house where tolls were gathered, the name came to mean "town hall" and later "prison" because detention cells were located in the basement.

Another landmark in Old Town life can be seen just outside Parliament House. The **Mercat Cross** (*mercat* means market), a focus of public attention for centuries, is still the site of royal proclamations. The cross itself is modern, but part of its shaft is as old as the city.

Across High Street from St. Giles's Cathedral are the **City Chambers,** now the seat of local authority. Designed by John Adam in 1753, the chambers were originally known as the Royal Exchange and intended to be a place where merchants and lawyers could conduct business. Note that the building drops 12 stories to Cockburn Street on its north side.

A *tron* is a weigh beam used in public weigh houses, and the **Tron Kirk** was named after a salt tron that used to stand nearby. The kirk itself was built after 1635, when St. Giles's became an Episcopal cathedral for a brief time. In this church in 1693 a minister offered an often-quoted prayer for the local government: "Lord, hae mercy on aa [every] fool and idiot, and particularly on the Magistrates of Edinburgh."

Two blocks past the North Bridge–South Bridge junction on High Street is the ☺ **Museum of Childhood,** a celebration of toys that even adults will enjoy. The museum offers a collection of childhood memorabilia, vintage toys, and dolls, as well as a reconstructed schoolroom, street scene, fancy-dress party, and nursery. This often (cheerfully) noisy museum was the first in the world to be devoted solely to the history of childhood. ✉ 42 High St., ☎ 0131/225–2424, extension 4142. ✉ Free. ☉ June–Sept., Mon.–Sat. 10–6, Sun. during 2–5; Oct.–May, Mon.–Sat. 10–5.

The ☺ **Brass Rubbing Centre,** down a close opposite the Museum of Childhood, provides all the materials children (and adults) need to create do-it-yourself replicas from original Pictish stones and markers, rare Scottish brasses, and medieval church brasses. No experience is needed for this pastime, which children find quite absorbing. ✉ Trinity Apse, Chalmers Close, ☎ 0131/556–4364. ✉ Free but a charge (50p–£17) is made for every rubbing. ☉ June–Sept., Mon.–Sat. 10–6 (Sun. during festival 12–5); Oct.–May, Mon.–Sat. 10–5.

It is not certain that Scotland's severe religious reformer (1514–72) lived at **John Knox House,** but mementos of his life are on view inside. This distinctive dwelling offers a glimpse of what Old Town life was like in the 16th century. The projecting upper stories were once commonplace along the Royal Mile, darkening and further closing in the already narrow passage. Look for the initials of former owner James Mossman and his wife, carved into the stonework on the "marriage lintel." Mossman was goldsmith to Mary, Queen of Scots, and was hanged in 1573 for his allegiance to her. ⊠ *45 High St.,* ☎ *0131/556–2647.* ☞ *£1.75.* ⊘ *Mon.–Sat. 10–5 (last admission 4:30).*

You would once have passed out of the safety of the town walls through a gate called the **Netherbow Port.** Look for the brass studs in the street cobbles that mark its location. A plaque outside the **Nether-bow Arts Centre** depicts the gate. The Arts Centre has a gallery and theater with a regular program of exhibitions and productions. ⊠ *43 High St.,* ☎ *0131/556–9579* ☞ *Free.* ⊘ *Mon.–Sat. 10–5 (last admission 4:30), and for evening performances.*

NEED A BREAK?

The **café** (⊘ 10–5) at the Netherbow Arts Centre is an excellent stop at any time of day, serving breakfast, morning coffee with home bakes, lunches ranging from a full cooked meal to a bowl of soup, and delicious afternoon teas.

❾ Huntly House. Dating from 1570, now a museum of local history, its exhibits include collections of Scottish pottery and Edinburgh silver and glassware. ⊠ *142 Canongate,* ☎ *0131/529–4143.* ☞ *Free.* ⊘ *June–Sept., Mon.–Sat. 10–6, Sun. during festival 2–5; Oct.–May, Mon.–Sat. 10–5.*

❹ Kirk of the Greyfriars. Built on the site of a medieval monastery, Greyfriars church was where the National Covenant was signed in 1638, declaring the independence of the Presbyterian Church in Scotland from government control. The covenant plunged Scotland into decades of civil war. A visitor center and audiovisual presentation tell the story. ⊠ *Greyfriars Pl.,* ☎ *0131/225–1900.* ☞ *Free.* ⊘ *Easter–Oct., weekdays 10:30–4:30, Sat. 10:30–2:30; Nov.–Easter, Thurs. 1:30–3:30.*

At the corner of George IV Bridge and Candlemaker Row, near the Greyfriars church, stands one of the most photographed sculptures in Scotland, *Greyfriars Bobby.* This famous Skye terrier kept vigil beside his master's grave in the churchyard for 14 years, leaving only for a short time each day to be fed at a nearby pub after the one-o'clock salute from the castle.

Lawnmarket. The second of the streets that make up the Royal Mile was formerly the site of the produce market for the city, with, once a week, a special cloth sale of wool and linen. The narrow six-story tenement known as **Gladstone's Land,** just beside the Assembly Hall, is a survivor from the 17th century, demonstrating typical architectural features, including an arcaded ground floor and an entrance at second-floor level (livestock sometimes inhabited the ground floor). It is furnished in the style of a 17th-century merchant's house. ⊠ *Lawnmarket,* ☎ *0131/226–5856.* ☞ *£2.60.* ⊘ *Apr.–Oct., Mon.–Sat. 10–5, Sun. 2–5. Last admission 4:30* PM.

Close by Gladstone's Land, down another close, is **The Writers' Museum,** housed in a building known as Lady Stair's House, a good example of 17th-century urban architecture. Built in 1622, it evokes Scotland's literary past with exhibits on Sir Walter Scott, Robert Louis Stevenson, and Robert Burns. ⊠ *Off Lawnmarket,* ☎ *0131/225–2424, ext. 4901.* ☞ *Free.* ⊘ *June–Sept., Mon.–Sat. 10–6, Sun. during festival 2–5; Oct.–May, Mon.–Sat. 10–5.*

⓫ Palace of Holyroodhouse. The official residence of the queen when she is in Scotland can be seen through the elaborate wrought-iron gates at the end of Canongate. When the royal family is not in residence, you can go inside for a conducted tour.

The highlights include the **King James Tower,** the oldest surviving section, which contains the rooms of Mary, Queen of Scots, on the second floor, and Lord Darnley's rooms below. Though much has been altered, there are fine fireplaces, paneling, plasterwork, tapestries, and 18th-century furniture throughout the structure. Along the front of the palace, between the two main towers, are the duchess of Hamilton's room and the Adam-style dining room.

Along the southern side of the palace are the **Throne Room** and other drawing rooms now used for social and ceremonial occasions. At the back of the palace is the **King's Bedchamber.** Another notable attraction is the **Picture Gallery,** which has a huge collection of portraits of Scottish monarchs (some of the royal figures honored here are actually fictional, and the likenesses of others are purely imaginary). All the portraits were painted by a Dutch artist, Jacob De Witt, who signed a contract in 1684 with the Queen's Cashkeeper Hugh Wallace that bound him to deliver 110 pictures within two years, for which he received an annual stipend of £120. Surely one of the most desperate scenes in the palace's history is that of the Dutch artist feverishly turning out potboiler portraits at the rate of one a week for two years.

The palace came into existence originally as a guest house for the Abbey of Holyrood, which was founded in 1128 by Scottish king David I. Look for the brass letters "SSS" set into the road at the beginning of Abbey Strand (the continuation of the Royal Mile beyond the traffic circle). The letters stand for "sanctuary" and recall the days when the former abbey served as a retreat for debtors (until 1880, when the government stopped imprisoning people for debt). Curiously, the area of sanctuary extended across what is now Holyrood Park, so debtors could get some fresh air without fear of being caught by their creditors. Oddest of all, however, was the agreement that after debtors checked in at Holyrood they were able to go anywhere in the city on Sunday. This made for great entertainment on Sunday evening as midnight approached: the debtors raced back to Holyrood before the stroke of 12, often hotly pursued by their creditors. The poet Thomas de Quincey and the comte d'Artois, brother of the deposed King Louis XVIII of France, were only two of the more exotic of Holyrood's denizens.

After the Union of the Crowns in 1603, when the Scottish Royal Court packed its bags and decamped for England, the building fell into decline. Oliver Cromwell, the Protestant Lord Protector of England, who had conquered Scotland, ordered the palace rebuilt after a fire in 1650, but the work was poorly carried out and lasted only until the restoration of the monarchy, after Cromwell's death. When Charles II ascended the British throne in 1660, he ordered Holyrood rebuilt in the architectural style of Louis XIV (the French Sun King), and that is the palace that visitors see today.

In 1688 an anti-Catholic faction ran riot within the palace, and in 1745 the palace was occupied by Prince Charles Edward Stuart, during the last Jacobite campaign. After the 1822 visit of King George IV, in more peaceable times, the palace sank into decline once again. But Queen Victoria and her grandson King George V renewed interest in the palace: The buildings were once more refurbished and made suitable for royal residence. ☎ *0131/556–7371. Recorded information* ☎ *0131/556–1096.* 🎫 *£5.* ☉ *Apr.–Oct., Mon.–Sat. 9:30–5:15, Sun. 9:30–4:30; Nov.–Mar., daily 9:30–3:45; closed during royal and state visits.*

Behind the palace lie the open grounds and looming crags of Holyrood Park, which enclose Edinburgh's mini-mountain, **Arthur's Seat** (822 feet). The park was the hunting ground of early Scottish kings. The views of the city and the surrounding area from the top of Arthur's Seat are breathtaking.

<table>
<tr><td>OFF THE
BEATEN PATH</td><td>**DUDDINGSTON** – Tucked behind Arthur's Seat—about an hour's walk from Princes Street via Holyrood Park—this little community (formerly of brewers and weavers) has an interesting church with a Norman doorway and a watchtower that was built to keep body snatchers out of the graveyard. The church overlooks Duddingston Loch, popular with birdwatchers, and moments away is an old-style pub called the Sheep's Heid Inn, which offers a variety of beers and the oldest skittle alley in Scotland. *LRT Bus 42 or 46.*</td></tr>
</table>

❻ Parliament House. The seat of Scottish government until 1707, when the crowns of Scotland and England were united, Parliament House is partially hidden by the bulk of St. Giles's. It's now the home of the Supreme Law Courts of Scotland. Parliament Hall inside is remarkable for its hammer beam roof and its display of portraits by major Scottish artists. ✉ *Parliament Sq.,* ☎ *0131/225–2595.* 🖾 *Free.* ☉ *Weekdays 10–4:30.*

❺ Royal Museum of Scotland. Occupying an imposing Victorian building in Chambers Street, which leads off from George IV Bridge, the Royal Museum of Scotland displays a broad collection drawn from natural history, archaeology, and scientific and industrial history. The great Main Hall, with its soaring roof, is architecturally interesting in its own right but will be enhanced by a major extension, to be completed in 1998. ✉ *Chambers St.,* ☎ *0131/225–7534.* 🖾 *Free.* ☉ *Mon.–Sat. 10–5 (Tues. until 8), Sun. 12–5.*

The New Town

At the dawn of the Scottish Enlightenment, in the 18th century, the city fathers busied themselves with various schemes to improve the capital. By that time Edinburgh's insanitary ambience—created primarily by the crowded conditions in which most people lived—was becoming notorious. The well-known Scots fiddle tune "The Flooers (flowers) of Edinburgh" was only one of many ironic references to the capital's unpleasant atmosphere, which greatly embarrassed the Scot James Boswell, biographer and companion of the English lexicographer Dr. Samuel Johnson. In his *Journal of a Tour of the Hebrides,* Boswell recalled that on retrieving the newly arrived Johnson from his grubby inn in the Canongate, "I could not prevent his being assailed by the evening effluvia of Edinburgh. . . . Walking the streets at night was pretty perilous and a good deal odoriferous. . . ."

To help remedy this sorry state of affairs, in 1767 James Drummond, the city's Lord Provost (Scots for mayor), urged the town council to hold a competition to design a new district for Edinburgh. The winner was an unknown young architect named James Craig. His plan was for a grid of three main east–west streets, balanced at either end by two grand squares. These streets survive today, though some of the buildings lining them were altered by later development. Princes Street is the southernmost, with Queen Street to the north and George Street as the axis, punctuated by St. Andrew and Charlotte squares. A map reveals the district's symmetry, unusual in Britain.

A Good Walk

Start your walk on **The Mound** ⑫, the sloping street that joins the Old and New towns. Two galleries immediately east of this great linking ramp, the **National Gallery of Scotland** ⑬ and the **Royal Scottish Academy** ⑭, are the work of W. H. Playfair (1789–1857), an architect whose neoclassical buildings contributed greatly to Edinburgh's title, "the Athens of the North."

At the foot of the Mound is Edinburgh's most famous street, **Princes Street.** The north side is now one long sequence of chain stores whose unappealing modern fronts can be seen in almost any large British town. Luckily the other side of the street is occupied by well-kept gardens, which act as a wide green moat to the castle on its rock. Walk east until you reach the Gothic spire of the **Scott Monument** ⑮, built in 1844 in honor of Scotland's most famous author, Sir Walter Scott (1771–1832). Opposite is that most Edinburgh of institutions, Jenners department store. Further east, **Register House** ⑯, opposite the main post office, marks the end of Princes Street.

The monuments on **Calton Hill** ⑰, growing ever more noticeable ahead as you walk east along Princes Street, can be reached by first continuing along Waterloo Place, the eastern extension of Princes Street. There is some fine neoclassically inspired architecture on this street, all designed as a piece by Archibald Elliott. The Regent Bridge or, more precisely, the Regent Arch—a simple, triumphal, Corinthian-column conceit on top of the bridge—was intended as a war memorial. The road then continues in a single sweep through the Calton Burial Ground to the screen walling at the base of Calton Hill. On the left you'll see steps that lead to the hilltop. Drivers—or walkers who don't feel up to the steep climb—can take the road farther on to the left, which loops up the hill at a more leisurely pace.

Leaving Calton Hill, you may wish to continue east along Regent Road, perhaps as far as the Robert Burns Monument, to admire the views westward of the castle and of the facade of the former Royal High School (directly above you). Then retrace your steps to the Waterloo Place traffic lights and make your way to **St. Andrew Square** ⑱ by cutting through the St. James Centre shopping mall, across Leith Street, and then through the bus station. After admiring the interior of the Royal Bank of Scotland on the eastern side of the square, walk west along George Street.

The essence of the New Town spirit survives in **Charlotte Square** ⑲, at the western end of George Street, and especially in the **Georgian House,** a faithfully restored, furnished recreation of the home of an 18th-century Edinburgh family, and West Register House. To explore further, choose your own route northward, down to the wide and elegant streets centering on **Moray Place** ⑳. Then make your way back eastward along Queen Street to visit the **Scottish National Portrait Gallery** ㉑.

TIMING

Although this walk could be done in a morning (with a prompt start), if you want to get the most out of the National Gallery of Scotland and the National Portrait Gallery, allow at least an hour for each. The Portrait Gallery has a good restaurant, so one option is to arrive in time for lunch, then spend the afternoon there.

Sights To See

⑰ **Calton Hill.** Robert Louis Stevenson's favorite view of his beloved city was from the top of this hill, a worthwhile reward for the climb. The architectural styles represented by the extraordinary collection of monuments include the Gothic—the Old Observatory, for example—and the neoclassical. Under the latter fall William Playfair's monument to his talented uncle, the philosopher and mathematician John Playfair, as well as his cruciform **New Observatory.** The piece that commands the most attention, however, is the so-called **National Monument,** often referred to as "Edinburgh's [or Scotland's] Disgrace." Intended to copy Athens's Parthenon, this monument for the dead of the Napoleonic Wars was started in 1822 to the specifications of a design by the ubiquitous Playfair. But in 1830, only 12 columns later, money ran out, and the columned facade became a monument to high aspirations and poor fund-raising. The tallest monument on Calton Hill is the 100-foot-high **Nelson Monument,** completed in 1814 in honor of Britain's naval hero. ☎ *0131/556–2716.* ✉ *Admission Nelson Monument: £1.20* ☉ *Apr.–Sept., Mon. 1–6, Tues.–Sat. 10–6; Oct.–Mar., Mon.–Sat. 10–3.*

⓳ Charlotte Square. The centerpiece of the New Town opens out at the western end of George Street. Note the palatial facade of the square's north side, designed by Robert Adam. It is considered one of Europe's finest pieces of civic architecture; here you will find the **Georgian House,** which the National Trust for Scotland has furnished in period style to show the elegant domestic arrangements of an affluent family of the late 18th century. The hallway was designed to accommodate sedan chairs, in which 18th-century grandees were carried through the streets. A refreshing feature of the house is the absence of restraining guide ropes (but please do not touch the furnishings). ✉ *7 Charlotte Sq.,* ☎ *0131/225–2160.* ✉ *£3.60.* ☉ *Apr.–Oct., Mon.–Sat. 10–5, Sun. 2–5 (last admission 4:30).*

In the middle of the west side of the square, the former St. George's Church now fulfills a different role, as **West Register House,** an extension of the original Register House on Princes Street. ✉ *Charlotte Sq.,* ☎ *0131/556–1400.* ✉ *Free.* ☉ *Weekdays 10–4 (exhibitions) and 9–4:45 (research room).*

NEED A BREAK?   Try **Bianco's** (✉ 9–11 Hope St., ☎ 0131/226–2047), close to the Georgian House, for coffee and croissants. You rarely have to wait in line; the atmosphere is relaxed; the seats are comfortable; and the coffee, by Edinburgh standards, is very good.

George Street. With its variety of upmarket shops and handsome Georgian frontages, this is a more pleasant, less crowded street than Princes Street for the pedestrian. The **statue of King George IV,** at the intersection of George and Hanover streets, recalls the visit of George IV to Scotland in 1822; he was the first British monarch to do so since King Charles II, in the 17th century. By the 19th century Scotland was perceived at Westminster, distant English seat of Parliament, as being almost civilized enough for a monarch to visit in safety.

The ubiquitous Sir Walter Scott turns up farther down the street. It was at a grand dinner in the **Assembly Rooms** (between Hanover and Frederick streets) that Scott acknowledged having written the *Waverley* novels (the name of the author had hitherto been a secret.) You can meet Scott once again, in the form of a plaque just downhill, at 39 Castle Street, where he lived from 1797 until his death.

NEED A BREAK?   The little restaurant on the upper floor at **James Thin** bookshop (✉ 57 George St., ☎ 0131/225–4495) is ideally placed for enjoying a cup of coffee or light lunch, while reading your latest holiday purchase.

Jenners. Edinburgh's equivalent of London's Harrod's department store, Jenners is noteworthy not only for its high-quality wares and good restaurants, but also because of the building's interesting architectural detail—baroque on the outside, with a mock-Jacobean central well inside. The female caryatids decorating the exterior were said to have been placed in honor of the predominantly female customers of the store, one of the earliest department stores ever to be established. ⊠ *4 Princes St.,* ☎ *0131/225–2442.* ⊙ *Mon.–Sat. 9–5:30, Thurs. until 7:30.*

OFF THE
BEATEN PATH **LEITH** – Edinburgh's ancient seaport has been revitalized in recent years, with the restoration of those fine commercial buildings that survived an earlier, and insensitive, redevelopment phase. It is worth exploring the lowest reaches of the Water of Leith, an area where pubs and restaurants now proliferate. ⊠ *Reach Leith by walking down Leith St. and Leith Walk, from the east end of Princes St. (20–30 mins brisk walking), or take a bus: LRT Buses 7, 10, 14, 16, 17, 22, 25, 32, 34, 35, 52, or 87, or circle route 2/12.*

㉖ Moray Place. Twelve-sided Moray Place, with its "pendants," Ainslie Place and Randolph Crescent, lying between Charlotte Square and the Water of Leith to the north, was laid out in 1822 by the Earl of Moray. It is a fine example of an 1820s development, with imposing porticos and a central secluded garden (for residents only). From the start the houses were planned to be of particularly high quality, and the curving facades are still very pleasing today.

⑫ The Mound. The Mound originated in the need for a dry-shod crossing of the muddy quagmire that was left behind when Nor' Loch, the body of water below the castle, was drained (the railway now cuts through this area). The work is said to have been started by a local tailor, George Boyd, who tired of struggling through the mud en route from his New Town house to his Old Town shop. The building of a ramp was under way by 1781, and by the time of its completion, in 1830, "Geordie Boyd's mud brig" (bridge), as the street was first known, had been built up with an estimated 2 million cartloads of earth dug from the foundations of the New Town.

⑬ National Gallery of Scotland. This impressive gallery, recently renovated at vast expense to show the William Playfair–designed building in its full glory, has a wide selection of paintings, from the Renaissance to the Post-Impressionist period, with works by Velázquez, El Greco, Rembrandt, Turner, Degas, Monet, and Van Gogh, among others, as well as a fine collection of Scottish art. ⊠ *The Mound,* ☎ *0131/556–8921.* ⊡ *Free.* ⊙ *Mon.–Sat. 10–5 (extended during festival), Sun. 2–5. Print Room, weekdays 10–noon and 2–4, by arrangement.*

⑯ Register House. Scotland's first custom-built archives depository, Register House was partly funded by the sale of estates forfeited by Jacobite landowners, following their last rebellion in Britain (1745–46). Work on the building, designed by Robert Adam, Scotland's most famous neoclassical architect, started in 1774. The statue in front is of the Duke of Wellington. ⊠ *Princes St.,* ☎ *0131/556–6585.* ⊡ *Free.* ⊙ *Weekdays, legal collection 9:30–4:30, historical collection 9–4:30.*

NEED A
BREAK?
Immediately west of Register House is the **Café Royal** (17 W. Register St.), which has good beer and lots of character, with ornate tiles and stained glass contributing to the atmosphere.

OFF THE
BEATEN PATH **ROYAL BOTANIC GARDEN** – These 70-acre gardens have the largest rhododendron and azalea collection in Britain. There is also a convenient cafeteria and a shop on the premises. To reach the gardens, only 10–15 minutes walk from the New Town, walk down Dundas Street, the continuation of Hanover Street, and turn left across the bridge over the Water of Leith, Edinburgh's small-scale river. ⊠ *Inverleith Row,* ☎ *0131/552–7171,* 𝔽𝔸𝕏 *0131/552–0382.* ⊡ *Free (voluntary donation for greenhouses).* ⊙ *Mar., Apr., Sept., and Oct., daily 10–6;*

May–Aug., daily 10–8; Nov.–Feb., daily 10–4. Shop, café, and exhibi-tion areas, Mar.–Oct., daily 10–5, Nov.–Feb., daily 10–3:30, closed Dec. 25, Jan. 1.

⑭ Royal Scottish Academy. This most imposing building, with columned facade overlooking Princes Street, is used for the RSA Annual Exhibition of paintings, sculpture, and prints. Immediately before the Annual Exhibition, art students have their own exhibition, while the various Scottish societies of artists—watercolorists, etc.—have exhibitions earlier or later in the year. ⊠ *Princes St.,* ☎ *0131/225–6671.* ☜ *Admission charges vary depending on exhibition.* ☉ *Annual Exhibition: Late-Apr.–July, Mon.–Sat. 10–5, Sun. 2–5; open for other exhibitions at various times throughout the year.*

⑱ St. Andrew Square. The most notable building on this square, which terminates George Street at its eastward end, is the headquarters of the **Royal Bank of Scotland;** take a look inside at the lavish decor of the central banking hall. In the distance, at the other end of George Street, on Charlotte Square, you can see the copper dome of the former St. George's Church. In Craig's symmetrical plan for the New Town, a matching church was intended for the bank's site, but Sir Lawrence Dundas, a wealthy and influential baronet, somehow managed to acquire the space for his town house. The grand mansion was later converted into the bank. The church originally intended for the site, St. Andrew's, is a little farther down George Street on the right. ⊠ *St. Andrew Square,* ☎ *0131/556–8555.* ☜ *Free.* ☉ *Weekdays 9:15–4:45, Tues. opens at 10.*

⑮ Scott Monument. An unmistakable 200-foot-high Gothic spire looming over Princes Street, it was built in 1844 in honor of Scotland's most famous author, Sir Walter Scott (1771–1832), author of *Ivanhoe, Waverley,* and many other novels and poems. (Note the marble statue of Scott and his favorite dog.) When Scott died, public sentiment demanded a grand acknowledgment of the work of the then wildly popular writer. After much delay the committee supervising the construction of a suitable memorial announced a competition for its design. (If in doubt about how to proceed with any civic development, the burghers of Edinburgh usually hold a competition.) After the Gothic structure that you now see was chosen, the committee was somewhat dismayed to learn that the design, submitted under a pseudonym, turned out to be not the work of a prestigious architect, but rather that of a carpenter and self-taught draftsman, George Meikle Kemp. A well-traveled man, Kemp incorporated elements of France's Rheims Cathedral into his design for the monument. ⊠ *Princes St.,* ☎ *0131/225–2424.* ☜ *£1.20.* ☉ *Apr.–Sept., Mon.–Sat. 9–6 (last admission 5:45); Oct.–Mar., Mon.–Sat. 9–3.*

OFF THE BEATEN PATH   **SCOTTISH NATIONAL GALLERY OF MODERN ART** – Close to the New Town in a handsome former school building on Belford Road, this magnificent gallery features paintings and sculpture, including works by Picasso, Braque, Matisse, and Derain. ⊠ *Belford Rd.,* ☎ *0131/556–8921.* ☜ *Free.* ☉ *Mon.–Sat. 10–5, Sun. 2–5 (extended during the festival).*

NEED A BREAK?   The **Gallery of Modern Art** (⊠ Belford Rd., ☎ 0131/556–8921) has a deservedly popular basement restaurant that serves a whole-food menu. In summer, you can sit at tables on the terrace outside.

㉑ Scottish National Portrait Gallery. A magnificent red sandstone Gothic building on Queen Street houses this must-visit institution. The gallery contains a superb Gainsborough and portraits by the Scottish artists

Ramsay and Raeburn. ⊠ *Queen St.,* ☎ *0131/225–7534.* 🖪 *Free.* ☉ *Mon.–Sat. 10–5, Sun. 2–5.*

OFF THE
BEATEN PATH
EDINBURGH ZOO – On an 80-acre site on the slopes of Corstorphine Hill, Edinburgh's Zoo offers traditional zoo delights plus animal contact and handling sessions in the main season, as well as its ever-popular Penguin Parade (held daily in summer). ⊠ *Corstorphine Rd., beside Post House Hotel (4 mi west of city),* ☎ *0131/334-9171.* 🖪 *£5.50.* ☉ *Apr.–Sept., Mon.–Sat. 9–6, Sun. 9:30–6; Mar. and Oct., Mon.–Sat. 9–5, Sun. 9:30–5; Nov.–Feb., Mon.–Sat. 9–4:30, Sun. 9:30–4:30.*

DINING

Be sure, particularly at festival time, to make reservations well in advance. Also, be warned that there is an element of "it'd be fun to open a restaurant" about Edinburgh's eating scene; restaurants can open and close with the passing of a season.

It is possible to eat well in Edinburgh without spending a fortune. Even those restaurants that are ranked in the $$$$ category could be squeezed into the top of the $$$ range, depending on what you order. A service charge of 10% may be added to your bill, though this practice is not adhered to uniformly. If no charge has been added and you are satisfied with the service, a 10% tip is appropriate.

Dining hours in Edinburgh are much the same as in the rest of Great Britain, with the main rush at lunchtime from 1 to 2, and at dinner, from 8 to 9.

WHAT TO WEAR

Restaurants in Edinburgh tend to be casual. Generally, the more expensive places prefer a jacket and/or tie; we tell you where this is advisable.

CATEGORY	COST*
$$$$	over £30
$$$	£20–£30
$$	£15–£20
$	under £15

per person for a three-course meal, including VAT and excluding drinks and service

$$$$ ✕ **The Grill Room.** Set in the Edwardian splendor of the Balmoral Hotel, the Grill Room has established itself at the top end of Edinburgh's dining scene. The Oriental-themed room has a luxurious ambience created by a green marble floor, Chinese lacquer wall panels, and an abundance of silver and crystal. The seating is particularly comfortable, and the tables are widely spaced, which makes it a great place for a private conversation or romantic dinner. The service is formal but relaxed, with no pressure to finish. As its name suggests, the restaurant specializes in grills, which you can see being cooked on the open grill, but there is also an extensive à la carte menu. ⊠ *Princes St.,* ☎ *0131/556–6727. Reservations essential. Jacket and tie. AE, DC, MC, V.*

$$$$ ✕ **L'Auberge.** A number of Edinburgh restaurants take the best Scottish food and prepare it French style, but L'Auberge is French through and through. A romantic feel prevails: a large number of tables are set for two. The menu is all in French with only a cursory translation; owner-manager Monsieur Daniel will be glad to explain the recipes to you in detail. The menu changes frequently, but you may be able to choose, for example, the terrine of seafood, the guinea fowl with mushrooms and claret sauce, or venison with Armagnac. The impressive wine list

is, not surprisingly, French and includes excellent dessert wines. ⊠ *56–58 St. Mary St.,* ☎ *0131/556–5888. AE, DC, MC, V. Closed Dec. 25–26, Jan. 1.*

$$$$ ✕ **Pompadour.** Insulated by arched windows and lilac drapes from the
★   bustle of west-end Princes Street, the Pompadour aims to impress. The decor, with its subtle plasterwork and rich murals, is inspired by the court of Louis XV, as may be expected in a restaurant named after the king's mistress, Madame de Pompadour. The cuisine is also classic French, with top-quality Scottish produce completing the happiest of alliances. The extensive, well-chosen wine list complements such dishes as sea bass with crispy leeks and caviar butter sauce, whole lobster with mustard and cheese, or loin of venison with potato pancakes. This is the place to go if you want a festive night out. It's more relaxed and informal at lunchtime. ⊠ *Caledonian Hotel, Princes St.,* ☎ *0131/459–9988. Jacket and tie. AE, DC, MC, V. No lunch weekends.*

$$$ ✕ **The Atrium.** With its cream-color tented fabric ceiling, smart cream cotton chair covers, and wrought-iron candlesticks and unusual candelabra, the Atrium is a distinctive setting for pre- or post-theater dinner (the Traverse Theatre is right next door). The chef-proprietor Andrew Radford uses typical Scottish ingredients in very atypical combinations: Curly kale, once the staple of every Scottish rural home, may be married with beef, bacon, and shallots, and salmon might be presented with zucchini, red pepper, and Parmesan. The menu changes daily, but there is always a vegetarian option. The wine list has recently been extended to include dessert wines. ⊠ *10 Cambridge St. (beneath Saltire Ct.),* ☎ *0131/228–8882. AE, MC, V.*

$$$ ✕ **Beehive Inn.** One of the oldest pubs in the city, the Beehive snuggles in the Grassmarket, under the majestic shadow of the castle. Some 400 years ago the Beehive was a coaching inn, and outside the pub's doors once stood the main set of city gallows, where over the centuries numerous executions were held. Now it's a good spot for a quick lunch. The upstairs **Rafters** restaurant lies hidden in an attractive and spacious attic room, crammed with weird and wonderful junk. Open only for dinner, it features mostly steaks and fish: Try the charcoal-grilled trout with Drambuie and oregano sauce, or veal pan fried with thyme and mushrooms. ⊠ *18/20 Grassmarket,* ☎ *0131/225–7171. AE, DC, MC, V.*

$$$ ✕ **Kelly's.** This Scottish restaurant with a French influence is slightly off the beaten path on the south side of the city but still only a short taxi ride or 20-minute walk from the center. The entrance to this former bakery, difficult to spot in a line of residential properties, leads into a pine-furnished, peach-tinted room with only 9 or 10 tables. The ambience is intimate, ideal for a quiet discussion over an unhurried meal. Among the fine choices are smoked Scottish salmon with mushrooms in Pernod sauce and Border lamb cutlets with a Grand-Marnier-and-rosemary glaze. ⊠ *46 W. Richmond St.,* ☎ *0131/668–3847. AE, MC, V. Closed Sun.–Tues. Lunch during festival only.*

$$$ ✕ **Martins.** Don't be put off by the look of this restaurant from the
★   outside. It's tucked away in a little back alley between Frederick and Castle streets and has a typically forbidding northern facade. All's well inside, though, and the menu emphasizes organically grown local products. The best Scottish salmon, venison, fish, and west-coast shellfish appear in various forms—poached, baked, roasted, and in casseroles—usually with inventive sauces. Starters may include rabbit liver and mushrooms with wild-mushroom sauce or terrine of rabbit and chicory with orange. There's also a far-famed cheese board. This is the place for serious eating in an unstuffy atmosphere, and lunches are an excellent value. The wine list is serious but affordable and includes an excellent choice of half-bottles. Smoking is not permitted.

✉ *70 Rose St. North La.,* ☎ *0131/225–3106. Reservations essential. AE, DC, MC, V. Closed Sun. and Mon. No lunch Sat.*

$$$ ✕ **Merchants.** On a street running below George IV Bridge and only moments from the Grassmarket and looming Edinburgh Castle, Merchants is competent and reliable. The decor is gently understated, with pinewood flooring, crisp white tablecloths, cane chairs, and exposed beams. Light jazz plays in the background. A sophisticated fixed-price menu (lunch £9.50, dinner £15.50–£18.50) in French and English has such adventurous moments as veal in dill and coriander; lamb chops with raspberry-and-mint sauce; and herbed roulade of beef filled with prawns and avocado mousse, with orange-and-tarragon vinaigrette. ✉ *17 Merchant St.,* ☎ *0131/225–4009. Reservations essential. AE, DC, MC, V.*

$$$ ✕ **Spices.** As its name implies, this restaurant specializes in spicy foods drawn from places like India, Persia, Zanzibar, and Goa. Try the *murgh reshmee* (barbecued chicken breast) kebab, the lamb *pukhraj* (with pistachios), or the *jhinga imlidhar* (king prawns with tamarind and spices). Don't be afraid to experiment with Spice's phenomenal menu—all dishes have individually chosen and freshly ground spices, a world away from standard restaurant curry. The stylish russet decor with black chairs is complemented with carved wooden screens and attentive service. Health-conscious people will appreciate Spice's no-smoking dining area. ✉ *110 West Bow,* ☎ *0131/225–5028. MC, V. Closed Sun.*

$$$ ✕ **Vito.** Like La Lanterna (☞ *below*), this is a basement restaurant, but here you'll find a whitewashed wine cellar with vaulted ceiling, arches, and nooks and crannies for intimate meals. The vaguely rustic Italian decor complements the genuinely Italian cuisine (there's a southern Italian owner and northern Italian chef, so all regions are featured on the menu). Dishes include king prawns in a sauce of tomato, cream, and brandy, and veal stuffed with cheese and ham. The separate bar area is a good place for a quiet drink before dinner. ✉ *55A Frederick St.,* ☎ *0131/225–5052. AE, DC, MC, V.*

$$$ ✕ **The Witchery by the Castle.** As the name indicates, a somewhat eerie ambience—complete with flickering candlelight—reigns here. The lugubrious, cavernous interior is festooned with cauldrons and broomsticks and decorated with cabalistic insignia. The inspiration for this spooky haunt derives from the fact that some 300 years ago hundreds of witches were executed on the Castlehill, barely a few dozen yards from where you will be seated. There's nothing spooky about the food, however, with fine venison, duck, lamb, salmon, and fillet steak among the specialties. There's a £21.95 fixed-price dinner menu. ✉ *352 Castlehill, Royal Mile,* ☎ *0131/225–5613. Reservations essential. AE, DC, MC, V.*

$$ ✕ **Buntoms Thai Restaurant.** A room in the Linden Hotel was converted into this authentic-looking Thai restaurant by the addition of genuine Thai wall coverings and antiques. You can leave Georgian New Town at the door and be transported halfway around the world with such savory delights as hot-and-sour squid and mushroom salad, seafood cooked with broccoli in oyster sauce, or spiced chicken fried with cashew nuts and onions (one of this restaurant's best offerings). Don't come here if you're on a tight schedule—each dish is prepared fresh, but it's definitely worth the wait, and you'll want to savor each bite. ✉ *Linden Hotel, 9–13 Nelson St.,* ☎ *0131/557–4344. Reservations essential. AE, DC, MC, V. No lunch Sun.*

$$ ✕ **Jackson's.** Intimate and candlelit in a historic Old Town close, Jackson's offers good Scots fare, including excellent Aberdeen Angus steaks and Border lamb. Seafood and vegetarian specialties are always on the menu. The decor is rustic, with lots of greenery, stone walls, pine farmhouse-style tables and chairs, and fresh flowers. The wine list includes 60 malt whiskies and some Scottish country wines to complete the Scottish experience. ⊠ *2 Jackson Close, 209–213 High St., Royal Mile,* ☎ *0131/225–1793. AE, MC, V. No lunch weekends.*

$$ ✗ **Kweilin.** This pleasant family-run restaurant in Edinburgh's sedate New Town is popular with the city's Chinese community, as well as with tourists. The decor is traditional Chinese, with several large paintings depicting scenes from the Kwangsi province, of which Kweilin is the capital. There are always several suggested menus for two, three, or four diners, which are recommended; but you can, of course, select your own combinations of dishes. The fixed-menu offerings are a good value, starting at £16.50 per person and going up to £26.50 a head for the Executive Choice menu. ⊠ *19–21 Dundas St.,* ☎ *0131/ 557–1875. AE, MC, V.*

$$ ✗ **La Lanterna.** This inconspicuous basement-level trattoria serves
★ wholesome and straightforward pastas—among them tagliatelle carbonara and spaghetti *mare* (with seafood)—and other Italian dishes. The family who runs the business is cheerful; their unaffected approach is popular and packs in the customers. The decor is pine-walled and postcard-pinned. Seats are comfortable, though tables are set close. The restaurant is well located in the city center, two minutes from Princes Street. ⊠ *83 Hanover St.,* ☎ *0131/226–3090. AE, MC, V. Closed Sun.*

$$ ✗ **Lancers.** This intimate Indian restaurant, decorated with rosewood tables and chairs, is located in the Stockbridge area of Edinburgh, just a short taxi ride from the city center. It's on a fairly busy road, but external distractions are blocked out by window blinds, which add to the sense of intimacy. The feel of this place is a little like that of an officers' mess in Bengal, which is entirely appropriate, since it was named after the famed Bengal Lancers, who fought with such distinction alongside the British army in every quarter of the globe. As a simple introduction to Bengali cuisine, you could try the vegetarian (or nonvegetarian) *thali* (a sampler tray including rice, lentils, curries, and more); those already initiated to the delights of this cuisine can pick and choose among varieties of *pasandas* (lamb fillet kabobs), *kormas* (braised meat or vegetables), *tikkas* (cutlets), and *bhundas*. ⊠ *5 Hamilton Pl.,* ☎ *0131/332–3444 or 0131/332– 9559. AE, MC, V.*

$$ ✗ **Old Orleans.** A first in Edinburgh: Cajun cooking, served with real Southern panache, plus Mexican and American dishes that include red snapper and alligator. Choose the spareribs (they come with a large bib and finger bowl of hot water). Decor is typical New Orleans: trellis and metalwork, brass instruments, and travel-related items; the music is blues and jazz. There is also a large, mirrored, American-style bar. ⊠ *30 Grindlay St.,* ☎ *0131/229–1511. AE, DC, MC, V.*

$–$$ ✗ **Alan's Chinese Restaurant.** This restaurant specializes in Cantonese fare and provides a wealth of choices: The menu runs five pages, and offers a selection of duck, chicken, beef, pork, and vegetarian creations, in addition to the seafood dishes that head the list. The walls are adorned with backlit Chinese scenes, and a large fish tank stands proudly in the middle of the restaurant, dividing it into two pleasant, comfortably sized dining rooms. Fixed-menu dinners are priced from £13.50 to £18.50 per person for five courses. ⊠ *217 High St., Royal Mile,* ☎ *0131/225–2999. AE, MC, V.*

$–$$ ✗ **Doric Tavern.** Do not be put off by the rather tatty entrance staircase plastered with posters and playbills: Inside this café–bistro bar, the stripped wood floor, dark wood tables, and navy velvet curtains create a superbly subdued, languid atmosphere. The menu always features a daily special—like roast pigeon salad with raspberry vinegar dressing—and a selection of fresh fish poached with basil and cream. Lunch can be anything from a large salad, perhaps with strips of venison, to chicken with tarragon or a wild mushroom stir-fry. If you still can't decide, try the fixed-price lunch (£8.50–£11.75) or dinner (£16.75), both excellent values. ⊠ *15/16 Market St.,* ☎ *0131/225–1084. AE, MC, V. Restaurant closes 11 PM (last orders 10:30), wine bar open until 1 AM.*

$–$$ ✕ **Hendersons.** This was Edinburgh's original vegetarian restaurant, long before it was fashionable to offer wholesome, meatless creations. If you haven't summoned the courage to try an authentic haggis while in Scotland, come here to sample a vegetarian version. The **Bistro Bar** owned by the same proprietors around the corner in Thistle Street is open Sunday 12–6. ⊠ *94 Hanover St.,* ☎ *0131/225–2131. AE, DC, MC, V. Closed Sun. except during festival.*

$–$$ ✕ **Howie's.** This simple neighborhood bistro doesn't have a liquor license, but you can bring your own bottle. The steaks are tender Aberdeen beef, the Loch Fyne herring are sweet-cured to Howie's own recipe, and the clientele is lively. ⊠ *75 St. Leonard's St.,* ☎ *0131/668–2917 or 0131/313–3334. MC, V. No lunch Mon. Branches also at* ⊠ *208 Bruntsfield Place,* ☎ *0131/221–1777(lunch and dinner daily) and* ⊠ *63 Dalry Rd.,* ☎ *0131/313–3334; both branches are licensed.*

$–$$ ✕ **Kalpna.** This vegetarian Indian restaurant is on the city's south side,
★ close to the university. Don't be put off by the unremarkable facade among an ordinary row of shops, or by the low-key decor enlivened by Indian prints and fabric pictures: The food is unlike anything you are likely to encounter elsewhere in the city. If you can't decide what you want to eat, order an anapurna thali, a sampler tray that here generally comes with curried vegetables or meats complimented with coconut, peas, melt-in-the-mouth halva, fresh coriander, and a touch of garlic. Kalpna tends to fill up as the evening progresses, so book ahead if you want to eat after 8. At lunchtime and in the early evening (except perhaps at festival time) you can usually just drop in. ⊠ *2/3 St. Patricks Sq.,* ☎ *0131/ 667–9890. MC, V. Closed Sun., Dec. 25–26, Jan. 1.*

$–$$ ✕ **Loon Fung.** Seafood is the specialty of this Cantonese restaurant. Delicious dishes include jumbo king prawns with garlic sauce and black pepper, fresh mussels with ginger and black bean sauce, and fried oysters with ginger and spring onions. The Loon Fung is small, friendly, and candlelit, with rapid service. The green and pink decor is relaxing, although tables are quite closely spaced. For two or more people, the set menus are a good value. A take-out menu is available. ⊠ *32 Grindlay St.,* ☎ *0131/229–5757. AE, MC, V.*

$–$$ ✕ **Peter's Cellars.** With a traditional "country cottage" look, complete with wooden booths, flowered curtains, and well-spaced tables, this cellar wine bar-cum-restaurant is a casual, relaxing venue. The food, though not elaborate, is carefully cooked with some imaginative touches. Try the seafood ragout, pork kebabs with plum sauce, or supreme of chicken stuffed with pineapple and cream cheese. The fixed-price lunch (£7.95) and dinner (£15.95) are good deals. ⊠ *11– 13 William St.,* ☎ *0131/226–3161. AE, MC, V.*

$–$$ ✕ **Pierre Victoire.** Edinburgh has five branches of this very popular bistro chain. All are fairly chaotic, enjoyable eateries serving healthy portions of French country cooking at low prices. The fish is fresh and especially good. Try the baked oysters with bacon and hollandaise. ⊠ *38 Grassmarket,* ☎ *0131/226–2442 (open daily);* ⊠ *10 Victoria St.,* ☎ *0131/225–1721 (closed Sun.);* ⊠ *8 Union St.,* ☎ *0131/557–8451;* ⊠ *5 Dock Pl., Leith,* ☎ *0131/555–6178 (closed Sun. evening);* ⊠ *17 Queensfery St.,* ☎ *0131/226–1890 (closed Sun.). MC, V.*

$–$$ ✕ **Waterfront Wine Bar and Bistro.** In the heart of Leith, the Waterfront, one of the city's longest-established wine bars, is always busy with a local crowd in their twenties and thirties, so don't come here if you want a quiet meal *à deux.* Blackboards listing wines and daily specials hang on the stone walls, surrounded by shipping memorabilia.

Edinburgh Dining and Lodging

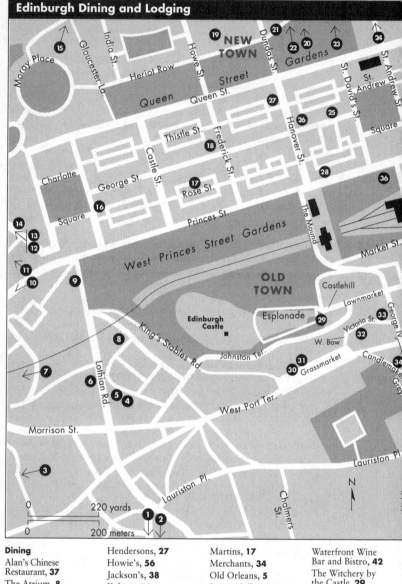

Dining

Alan's Chinese Restaurant, **37**
The Atrium, **8**
L'Auberge, **46**
Beehive Inn, **30**
Buntoms Thai Restaurant, **23**
The Doric Tavern, **35**
The Grill Room, **36**

Hendersons, **27**
Howie's, **56**
Jackson's, **38**
Kalpna, **54**
Kelly's, **48**
Kweilin, **21**
Lancers, **15**
La Lanterna, **26**
Loon Fung, **4**

Martins, **17**
Merchants, **34**
Old Orleans, **5**
Peter's Cellars, **11**
Pierre Victoire, **14, 31, 33, 40, 41**
Pompadour, **9**
Spices, **32**
Vito, **18**

Waterfront Wine Bar and Bistro, **42**
The Witchery by the Castle, **29**

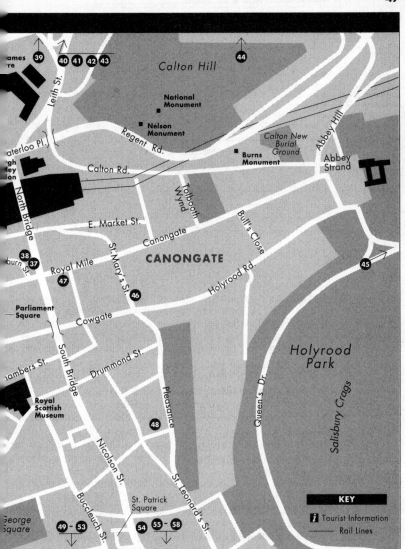

Lodging

Albany, **43**

Ashdene House, **49**

Balmoral Hotel, **36**

Caledonian, **9**

Channings, **12**

Classic Guest House, **50**

Crannoch But & Ben, **13**

Drummond House, **24**

Edinburgh Grand Sheraton, **6**

Ellesmere Guest House, **2**

George Intercontinental, **25**

Holiday Inn Crown Plaza, **47**

Howard Hotel, **22**

Jarvis Mount Royal Hotel, **28**

Lodge Hotel, **10**

Mrs. Coleman, **51**

Mrs. Graham, **52**

Mrs. Valerie Livingstone, **45**

Norton House, **3**

Roselea House, **53**

Roxburghe, **16**

Royal Terrace, **44**

17 Abercrombie Place, **20**

Sibbet House, **19**

Silverburn Steading, **1**

Stakis Edinburgh Grosvenor Hotel, **7**

Stuart House, **39**

Teviotdale House, **55**

Thrums Private Hotel, **58**

Turret Guest House, **57**

Grilled sardines with rosemary butter, wild mushrooms (in season), pan-fried pigeon breasts with strawberry and orange sauce, and fillets of sea bass in white wine and cream sauce are examples of the food on offer. ⊠ *1a Dock Pl., Leith,* ☎ *0131/554–7427. Reservations essential on weekends. AE, MC, V.*

LODGING

If you are planning to stay in the area during the festival, be sure to reserve several months in advance. Also note that weekend rates in the larger hotels are always much cheaper than midweek rates, so if you want to stay in a plush hotel, come on the weekend.

CATEGORY	COST*
$$$$	over £110
$$$	£80–£110
$$	£50–£80
$	under £50

All prices are for a standard double room, including service, breakfast, and VAT.

$$$$ ★ 🏨 **Balmoral Hotel.** The attention to detail in the elegant rooms and the sheer élan that has re-created the Edwardian heyday of this former grand railroad hotel all contribute to the Balmoral's growing popularity. Staying here, below the impressive clock tower marking the east end of Princes Street, gives a strong sense of being at the center of Edinburgh life. The hotel's main restaurant is the plush and stylish Grill Room (☞ Dining, *above*). ⊠ *Princes St., EH2 2EQ,* ☎ *0131/556–2414,* 🆔 *0131/557–8740. 189 rooms with bath, 21 suites. 2 restaurants, bar, wine bar, indoor pool, health club. AE, DC, MC, V.*

$$$$ ★ 🏨 **Caledonian.** A conspicuous block of red sandstone beyond the west end of Princes Street Gardens, "the Caley" was built as the flagship hotel of the Caledonian Railway, and its imposing Victorian decor has been faithfully preserved. The public area has marbled green columns and an ornate stairwell with a burnished-metalwork balustrade. Rooms are exceptionally large and well appointed, and the generous width of the corridors reminds guests that this establishment was designed in a more sumptuous age. ⊠ *Princes St., EH1 2AB,* ☎ *0131/459–9988,* 🆔 *0131/225–6632. 236 rooms with bath. 2 restaurants, in-room VCRs. AE, DC, MC, V.*

$$$$ 🏨 **Edinburgh Grand Sheraton.** Built in 1985, this property underwent a major refurbishment in 1993, when two new restaurants were added: the brasserie-style **Terrace,** overlooking Edinburgh Castle and Festival Square, and the intimate **Grill Room,** serving fine fish, game, and Scottish beef. Guest rooms are well above average size, and many of them are decorated in traditional style with tartan furnishings and prints of old Edinburgh. The grandest rooms face the castle. You can enjoy piano music in the bar and lounge area, and there's a shopping gallery to browse in. A ground-floor reception area features a sweeping grand staircase. The hotel's popularity with locals, especially after work and in the evening before and after concerts at Usher Hall, across the street, testifies to its continuing part in Edinburgh's social life. ⊠ *1 Festival Sq., EH3 9SR,* ☎ *0131/229–9131,* 🆔 *0131/228–4510. 264 rooms with bath. 2 restaurants, bar, indoor pool, health club. AE, DC, MC, V.*

$$$$ ★ 🏨 **George Intercontinental.** Part of this hotel served as an insurance-company office during the 19th century, and the splendidly ornate business hall remains intact as the Carvery Restaurant, the less expensive of the two dining rooms. The hotel's modern extension, added in 1972, is carefully blended with the original structure (1881), and the George retains a more intimate feeling than you'd expect from a large hotel.

Major renovations throughout 1994–5 helped make the guest rooms, with reproduction-antique furnishings, light, airy, and immaculate; sizes range from adequate to spacious, and the desks are unusually large. The best rooms are at the back of the hotel, high up and looking north over the New Town roofs to the Firth of Forth and to Fife beyond. But even rooms overlooking George Street southward, with bird's-eye views of the 18th-century surroundings, are quiet. The central location, only yards from the financial center of St. Andrew Square, has only one disadvantage: difficult parking. The pricey French-style **Le Chambertin** restaurant has excellent food; its sommelier is one of only two members of the Guild of Master Sommeliers in Scotland. ✉ *19–21 George St., EH2 2PB,* ☎ *0131/225–1251,* FAX *0131/226–5644. 195 rooms with bath. 2 restaurants, bar, minibars. AE, DC, MC, V.*

$$$$ 🏨 **Holiday Inn Crown Plaza.** Although it was built late in the 1980s, this modern hotel blends into its surroundings among the ancient buildings on the Royal Mile. Its location is a good reason to stay here. Guest rooms are spacious, neat, and plain—practical rather than luxurious. ✉ *80 High St., Royal Mile, EH1 1TH,* ☎ *0131/557–9797,* FAX *0131/557–9789. 238 rooms with bath. Restaurant, indoor pool, health club, meeting rooms. AE, DC, MC, V.*

$$$$ 🏨 **Howard Hotel.** The Howard, close to Drummond Place, is a good
★ example of a New Town building, elegant and superbly proportioned. It is also small enough to offer personal attention; the hotel will be appreciated by those who enjoy a private club atmosphere. All guest rooms are spacious and furnished with antiques and original works of art, and some overlook the garden. ✉ *32 Great King St., EH3 6QH,* ☎ *0131/557–3500,* FAX *0131/557–6515. 16 rooms with bath. Restaurant. AE, DC, MC, V.*

$$$$ 🏨 **Jarvis Mount Royal Hotel.** Perched above the ground-floor shops on Princes Street, overlooking Edinburgh Castle and the Princes Street Gardens, the entrance to the Mount Royal is almost hidden between two of the city's major stores (Jenners and Marks & Spencer) and could easily be overlooked. Guest rooms have wood furnishings and pastel color schemes; the best views are from the rooms at the front of the hotel. ✉ *52 Princes St., EH2 2DQ,* ☎ *0131/225–7161,* FAX *0131/220–4671. 156 rooms with bath. Restaurant. AE, DC, MC, V.*

$$$$ 🏨 **Norton House.** This magnificent 1861 manor house was once the home of the Usher brewing family and still has the feeling of a private country home. Situated on idyllic grounds on the outskirts of Edinburgh, the Norton House provides a lovely alternative to downtown lodgings, yet is easily accessible from the city center. The elegant and refurbished reception area is graced by marble pillars; a striking wooden staircase leads to the upper floors. The airy guest rooms are decorated with modern furniture and delicate pastel shades. Guests can choose between two restaurants—the Conservatory, with its fine views of the gardens, offers decent Continental food, while the Norton Tavern offers a bistro-type menu. ✉ *Ingliston, EH28 8LX,* ☎ *0131/333–1275,* FAX *0131/333–5305. 47 rooms with bath. 2 restaurants, bar, train station and airport shuttle, free parking. AE, DC, MC, V.*

$$$$ 🏨 **Roxburghe.** As you sit in a deep leather armchair, the ticking of an antique clock in the background, and look out over the trees of Charlotte Square, it is easy to forget you are in the heart of Edinburgh's financial center, half a minute from Princes Street. The furniture, which includes many antique pieces, has the sheen of generations of polish. In the rooms, Adam fireplaces and ornate plasterwork complement the hotel's harmonious Georgian architecture. This country-house-come-to-town moves nearer modern times with its busy bar and informal ground-floor restaurant, **The Melrose Room,** but becomes positively overdone in its excessively draped main dining room downstairs. (The food, unlike the decor, is forgettable.) Not as expensive as the Sheraton or the Caledonian, the Roxburghe is hard to beat for a convenient location, though it can be a little noisy. ✉ *38 Charlotte Sq., EH2 4HG,* ☎ *0131/225–3921,* ℻ *0131/220–2518. 75 rooms with bath. Restaurant, bar, coffee shop. AE, DC, MC, V.*

$$$$ ⊞ **Royal Terrace.** More than 150 years ago, the renowned Edinburgh
★ architect Playfair designed the street called Royal Terrace as a tribute to King George IV. Most of the impressive Georgian homes on this block, their upper floors commanding views across the Firth of Forth to Fife, were owned by merchants. The present hotel consists of a half dozen of these original merchant houses, combined to create one of the most luxurious lodgings in the city. The unassuming exterior gives no hint of the sybaritic interior. But inside sumptuousness immediately prevails: The reception area is deeply carpeted and adorned with a massive pair of chandeliers and an eclectic collection of objets d'art. All rooms are furnished to an equally high standard and include telephones in the marble bathrooms. The best rooms—commanding the view across the city to the Forth—are on the top floors at the front. ✉ *18 Royal Terr., EH7 5AQ,* ☎ *0131/557–3222,* ℻ *0131/557–5334. 93 rooms with bath. Restaurant, bar, pool, health club. AE, DC, MC, V.*

$$$ ⊞ **Channings.** Five Edwardian terraced houses make up this elegant
★ hotel in an upscale neighborhood just minutes from the west end of Princes Street. Quiet rooms with restrained colors, antiques, and great views of Fife (from those facing north) set an elegant, refined tone. The **Brasserie** offers excellent value, especially at lunchtime; try the crab cakes with crayfish bisque. ✉ *12–16 South Learmonth Gardens, EH4 IEZ,* ☎ *0131/315–2226,* ℻ *0131/332–9631. 48 rooms with bath or shower. Restaurant. AE, DC, MC, V.*

$$$ ⊞ **Stakis Edinburgh Grosvenor Hotel.** This attractive, comfortable hotel in the West End comprises several converted terrace houses and is distinguished by an elegant Victorian facade. Guests are pampered as soon as they enter the large reception area, which is furnished with ample Chesterfield armchairs. The single rooms are fairly small, and the doubles are just adequate. All are brightly decorated with peach curtains and floral bedspreads; the furniture is made of dark wood. First- and second-floor bedrooms have high ceilings with attractive plaster cornices. Just a short walk from the West End's shopping district, the hotel is convenient to the Haymarket railway station. ✉ *Grosvenor St., EH12 5EA,* ☎ *0131/226–6001,* ℻ *0131/220–2387. 188 rooms with bath. Restaurant, 2 bars. AE, DC, MC, V.*

$$ ⊞ **Albany.** Three fine Georgian houses with many original features have been carefully converted into this comfortable city-center hotel. Rooms have high ceilings, neutral color schemes, and plain brown furnishings. Multicolored bedspreads match the curtains, a pleasant complement to the furniture. At press time (spring 1996), the hotel was about to undergo a major refurbishment. There's a good restaurant in the basement and a bar with piano. ✉ *39 Albany St., EH1 3Q4,* ☎ *0131/556–0397,* ℻ *0131/557–6633. 20 rooms with bath. Restaurant, bar. AE, DC, MC, V.*

$$ ⊞ **Drummond House.** Many hotels would be put to shame by the ac-
★ commodations at this top-of-the-range guest house in the heart of the New Town, within walking distance of the city center. The Georgian terraced house has spacious rooms, sumptuously decorated and furnished with swagged curtains, canopied beds, and antique furniture—all in elegant taste to suit the age of the house. Smoking is not permitted inside Drummond House, but guests can smoke while strolling through the several acres of private gardens across the road, open only to Drummond Place residents, which guests are welcome to use. ✉ *17*

Drummond Pl, EH3 6PL, ☎ FAX 0131/557–9189. 4 rooms with bath or shower. Dining room. MC, V.

$$ ★ **Lodge Hotel.** This stone detached Georgian house is easy to find on the main A8 Edinburgh–Glasgow road, a 15-minute walk from Princes Street. It is furnished in period style, with swagged curtains and canopied beds. The spacious bedrooms are stocked with fresh flowers and fruit as well as a decanter of sherry. Downstairs, there is a cocktail bar and peaceful pink-and-gray sitting room. The dining room has well-spaced tables covered with crisp white cloths and a menu that features fresh Scottish produce. ✉ *6 Hampton Terr., West Coates, EH12 5JD, ☎ 0131/337–3682, FAX 0131/313–1700. 12 rooms with shower. Dining room, no-smoking rooms. MC, V.*

$$ **Roselea House.** Another south-side bed-and-breakfast guest house, on the main route from the south, the Roselea is easy to find. The Victorian house is decorated in "a touch of tartan," and there is a sitting room for guests. ✉ *11 Mayfield Rd., EH9 2NG, ☎ 0131/667–6115, FAX 0131/667–3556. 7 rooms with bath or shower. AE, MC, V.*

$$ ★ **17 Abercrombie Place.** An exceptional standard is set at this bed-and-breakfast in the center of the New Town. The Georgian terraced house has shuttered windows and antique furniture and rugs (some used as wall hangings). The host, a keen golfer, and the hostess, a lawyer, both enjoy meeting guests and are very helpful. ✉ *17 Abercrombie Place, EH3 6LB, ☎ 0131/557–8036, FAX 0131/558–3453. 5 rooms with bath or shower. Dining room. MC, V.*

$$ ★ **Sibbet House.** The late-18th-century Georgian elegance of this small terraced town house in Edinburgh's New Town has been enhanced by careful attention to drapery, decor, and period antique furniture. Prices are reasonable, it is non-smoking throughout, and breakfasts are traditionally Scottish and sustaining, to say the least. You must eat out in the evenings, but all kinds of restaurants are only a few minutes' stroll away. This establishment also offers a facility that few others can match—the host plays the bagpipes (but only on request). ✉ *26 Northumberland St., EH3 6LS, ☎ 0131/556–1078, FAX 0131/557–9445. 4 rooms with bath or shower. MC, V.*

$$ **Thrums Private Hotel.** There is a pleasing mix of the modern and traditional in this detached Victorian house. It is small, cozy, and quiet, yet surprisingly close to downtown. ✉ *14–15 Minto St., EH9 1RQ, ☎ 0131/667–5545, FAX 0131/667–8707. 15 rooms, 8 with bath. Restaurant, bar. MC, V. Closed Christmas wk and 1 wk in Jan.*

$–$$ **Teviotdale House.** This is a small, family-run and -owned hotel in the genteel south side. The hosts, the Covilles, are friendly, and the house is a warm retreat on a tree-lined street away from but within reach of city-center bustle (a 30-minute walk from Charlotte Sq.). Individually decorated rooms and innovative, appetizing home cooking make this a pleasant, reasonable budget alternative to center-city hotels. The establishment is entirely non-smoking. ✉ *53 Grange Loan, EH9 2ER, ☎ FAX 0131/667–4376. 7 rooms, 5 with en suite bath, 2 with private bath. Dining room. AE, MC, V.*

$ **Ashdene House.** On a quiet residential street on the south side, only 10 minutes from the city center by bus, this Edwardian house is a first-class bed-and-breakfast where smoking is not permitted. Bedrooms are decorated without frills or flounces—just modern furnishings and floral fabrics—but in the downstairs public areas, deep, rich color schemes complement the age of the house. The owners are particularly helpful in arranging tours and evening theater entertainment, and they will recommend local restaurants. There is ample parking on the street and in a lot. ✉ *23 Fountainhall Rd., EH9 2LN, ☎ 0131/667–6026. 5 rooms with shower. Free parking. No credit cards.*

$ ⌂ **Classic Guest House.** It is easy to find this Victorian terraced house, on a main route from the south into Edinburgh. The decor is modern classic: stripped pine floors throughout, elegant chinoiserie in the dining room, and pastel florals in the warm bedrooms. Smoking is not permitted. ⌧ *50 Mayfield Rd., EH9 2NH,* ☎ *0131/667–5847. 4 rooms, 3 with en suite shower, 1 with private bath. Dining room. MC, V.*

$ ⌂ **Crannoch But & Ben.** This top-of-the-range bed-and-breakfast offers private facilities, a comfortable residents' lounge, and good hearty breakfasts. Only 3 miles from the city and on a good bus route, it's also particularly convenient for the airport. ⌧ *467 Queensferry Rd., EH4 7ND,* ☎ *0131/336–5688. 2 rooms with bath. No credit cards.*

$ ⌂ **Ellesmere Guest House.** Yet another Victorian terraced house, this bed-and-breakfast is close to the King's Theatre and several good restaurants. Its first-class rooms have modern furniture with pleasant pastel floral bedspreads and curtains; one room has a four-poster bed. Guests can relax in the comfortable sitting room, but the owners prefer that they not smoke. Ellesmere is stocked with brochures covering things to do in Edinburgh. ⌧ *11 Glengyle Terr., EH3 9LN,* ☎ *0131/229–4823,* ℻ *0131/229–5285. 6 rooms with bath. No credit cards, but dollar checks are accepted.*

$ ⌂ **Mrs. Coleman.** This bed-and-breakfast is in an elegant Victorian detached house, which still has many period trimmings, such as the original plaster cornices in many of the spacious rooms. The decor is marked by cheerful colors and floral fabrics, and the furnishings are modern. The owners are particularly friendly and helpful. ⌧ *54 Craigmillar Park, EH16 5PS,* ☎ *0131/668–3408. 3 rooms with shower. No credit cards.*

$ ⌂ **Mrs. Graham.** It may be difficult to find a parking space on the quiet
★ back street where this Victorian terraced house is situated, but it's easy enough to take Bus 3, 31, 69, 80, or 81 here, south from the city center. The spotlessly clean bed-and-breakfast has antique furniture complemented by beautiful kilim rugs and wall hangings. ⌧ *18 Moston Terr., EH9 2DE,* ☎ *0131/667–3466. 2 rooms share 1 bathroom. No credit cards.* ☉ *May–Oct.*

$ ⌂ **Mrs. Valerie Livingstone.** This is a modern terraced villa close to Arthur's Seat, with fine views over the Firth of Forth. Mrs. Livingstone maintains a high standard of accommodation and meals. Smoking is not permitted. ⌧ *Ceol-na-mara, 50 Paisley Crescent, EH8 7JQ,* ☎ *0131/ 661–6337. 3 rooms. Dining room. No credit cards.* ☉ *Apr.–Oct. and Dec. 25–Jan 1.*

$ ⌂ **Silverburn Steading.** Just outside Edinburgh in a rural setting at the foot of the Pentland Hills, this bed-and-breakfast makes a relaxing base to return to after a day sightseeing in the city center, only 20 minutes away by car. Ask for a room at the back if traffic noise bothers you. ⌧ *Silverburn, Penicuik, Midlothian, EH26 9LJ,* ☎ *01968/678420. 2 rooms with bath. MC, V.*

$ ⌂ **Stuart House.** Within 15 minutes' walk of the city center, this bed-
★ and-breakfast is in a Victorian terraced house with some fine plasterwork. The decor suits the structure: Bold colors, floral fabrics, and generously curtained windows combine with antique and traditional-style furniture and chandeliers to create an opulent ambience. Smoking is not permitted. ⌧ *12 E. Claremont St., EH7 4JP,* ☎ *0131/557–9030,* ℻ *0131/557–0563. 7 rooms with bath or shower. AE, MC, V.*

$ ⌂ **Turret Guest House.** On a quiet residential street on the south side, this bed-and-breakfast is close to bus routes as well as the Commonwealth Pool and Holyrood Park. Cheerful and cozy, it has modern furnishings, but many of the building's Victorian cornices, paneled doors, and high ceilings remain. ⌧ *8 Kilmaurs Terr., EH16 5DR,* ☎ *0131/667– 6704,* ℻ *0131/668–1368. 6 rooms, 4 with shower. No credit cards.*

NIGHTLIFE AND THE ARTS

The Arts

The List, available from newsagents throughout the city, and *What's On in Edinburgh,* available from the Information Centre (☞ Important Addresses and Numbers in Edinburgh Essentials, *below*) carry the most up-to-date details about cultural events. *The Scotsman,* an Edinburgh daily, also carries reviews in its arts pages on Monday and Wednesday. Tickets are generally available from the relevant box office in advance; in some cases, from certain designated travel agents; or at the door, although concerts by national orchestras often sell out long before the day of the performance.

The **Edinburgh International Festival** (1997: Aug. 10–30), the premier arts event of the year, has for 50 years attracted performing artists of international caliber to a celebration of music, dance, and drama. *Edinburgh Festival Office: ⊠ 21 Market St., EH1 1BW, ☎ 0131/226–4001, FAX 0131/225–1173.*

The **Edinburgh Festival Fringe** offers many theatrical and musical events, some by amateur groups (you have been warned) and is more of a grab bag than the official festival. During festival time it's possible to arrange your own entertainment program from morning to midnight and beyond, if you do not feel overwhelmed by the variety available. *Edinburgh Festival Fringe Office: ⊠ 180 High St., EH1 1QS, ☎ 0131/226–5257 or 0131/226–5259, FAX 0131/220–4205.*

The **Edinburgh Film Festival** (1997: Aug. 10–24) is yet another aspect of this busy summer festival logjam. *Edinburgh Film Festival Office, at the Filmhouse, ⊠ 88 Lothian Rd., EH3 9BZ, ☎ 0131/228–4051, FAX 0131/229–5501. Box office, ☎ 0131/228–4051.*

The **Edinburgh Military Tattoo** (1997: Aug. 1–23) may not be art, but it is certainly entertainment. It is sometimes confused with the festival itself, partly because the dates overlap. This celebration of martial music and skills is set on the castle esplanade, and the dramatic backdrop augments the spectacle. Dress warmly for late-evening performances. Even if it rains the show most definitely goes on. *Edinburgh Military Tattoo Office: ⊠ 22 Market St., EH1 1QB, ☎ 0131/225–1188, FAX 0131/225–8627.*

Away from the August-to-September festival overkill, the **Edinburgh Folk Festival** (⊠ Box 528, EH10 4DU, ☎ 0585/559870) usually takes place around Easter each year. This 10-day event blends performances by Scottish and international folk artists of the highest caliber.

Dance

Edinburgh has no ballet or modern-dance companies of its own, but visiting companies perform from time to time at the King's Theatre or Royal Lyceum (☞ *below*).

Film

Apart from cinema chains, Edinburgh has the excellent two-screen **Filmhouse** (⊠ 88 Lothian Rd., ☎ 0131/228–6382; box office, 0131/228–2688), the best venue for modern, foreign-language, offbeat, or simply less-commercial films. Its diverse monthly program is available from the box office and at a variety of other locations throughout the city (at the Tourist Centre, for example, or in theater foyers).

The **Cameo** (⊠ 38 Home St., ☎ 0131/228–4141) has three extremely comfortable theaters, a bar, and late-night specials (Thurs.–Sat., 11:30 PM). The family-owned and -run **Dominion** (⊠ Newbattle Terrace, ☎

0131/447–2660) offers one of the most pleasant alternatives to the larger commercial cinemas.

Modern Theater

The **Traverse Theatre** (✉ Cambridge St., ☎ 0131/228–1404) has developed a solid reputation as a venue for stimulating new work—though it has toned down its previously avant-garde approach.

The **Netherbow Arts Centre** (✉ 43 High St., ☎ 0131/556–9579) includes modern plays in its program of music, drama, and cabaret. The **Theatre Workshop** (✉ 34 Hamilton Pl., ☎ 0131/225–7942), hosts fringe events during the Edinburgh Festival and modern, community-based theater all year.

Music

The **Usher Hall** (✉ Lothian Rd., ☎ 0131/228–1155) is Edinburgh's grandest concert hall, venue for the Scottish National Orchestra during its winter season (October–March). Intimate in scale and used generally for smaller recitals and chamber music is the **Queen's Hall** (✉ Nicolson St., ☎ 0131/668–2019). You can find popular musicians and groups at the **Playhouse** (☞ *below*).

For jazz enthusiasts the main focus of entertainment is the **International Jazz Festival** (✉ 116 The Canongate, Edinburgh, EH8 8DD, ☎ 0131/557–1642), held each August, but live jazz can also be found in the city throughout the year. Consult *The List* for information.

Traditional Theater

Edinburgh has three main theaters. The **Royal Lyceum** (✉ Grindlay St., ☎ 0131/229–9697) shows traditional plays and contemporary works, often transferred from or prior to their London 'West End' showings. The **King's** (✉ Leven St., ☎ 0131/229–1201) has a program of contemporary and traditional dramatic works. **Edinburgh Festival Theatre** (✉ Nicolson St., ☎ 0131/529–6000) is the city's newest theater and hosts a variety of theatrical and musical entertainment.

The **Playhouse** (✉ Greenside Pl., ☎ 0131/557–2692) hosts mostly popular artists and has a Christmas pantomime. At Musselburgh, on the eastern outskirts of Edinburgh, the **Brunton Theatre** (✉ Brunton Hall, High St., Musselburgh, ☎ 0131/665–2240) offers a regular program of performances. At the **Church Hill Theatre** (✉ Morningside Rd., ☎ 0131/447–7597), local dramatic societies mount productions of a high standard.

Nightlife

The Edinburgh and Scotland Information Centre above Waverley Market (☞ Edinburgh A to Z, *below*) can supply information on various types of nightlife, especially on spots offering dinner-dances. *The List* gives a lot of information on the music scene.

Casinos

The following are all private clubs that offer free membership on 48 hours' notice: **Stanley Berkeley** (✉ 2 Rutland Pl., ☎ 0131/228–4446); **Stanley Martell** (✉ 7 Newington Rd., ☎ 0131/667–7763); and **The Stanley** (✉ 5b York Pl., ☎ 0131/556–1055). The **Stakis Regency Casino** (✉ 14 Picardy Pl., ☎ 0131/557–3585), whose restaurant is highly rated, charges a £10 membership fee (identification is required).

Pubs/Bars

Abbotsford (✉ 3 Rose St., ☎ 0131/225–1894) offers five real ales (changing all the time), bar lunches, and lots of Victorian atmosphere. **Drum and Monkey** (✉ 80 Queen St., ☎ 0131/538–8111), with cozy dark wood booths and a maroon color scheme, is just the place for soup and sandwich lunches with a pint of Old Wallop beer. There is a bistro restaurant downstairs.

Milne's Bar (⊠ 21–25 Rose St., ☎ 0131/225–6738) is known as the poets' pub because of its popularity with the Edinburgh literati. Pies and baked potatoes go well with seven real ales and varying guest beers. Victorian advertisements and photos of old Edinburgh give it an old-time feel.

Tiles (⊠ 1 St. Andrew Sq., ☎ 0131/558–1507, closed Sun.), a converted banking hall, gets its name from the wealth of tiles covering the walls. The ceiling is elaborate plasterwork. The large selection of real ales is complemented by a choice of bar meals or a *table d'hôte* menu specializing in fresh Scottish poultry, game, and fish.

Discos/Nightclubs

Many Edinburgh discos offer reduced admission and/or less expensive drinks for early revelers. Consult *The List* for special events.

The Citrus Club (⊠ Grindlay St., ☎ 0131/229–6697) offers a variety of music, usually spun by good quality DJs, on Wednesday, Friday, and Saturday nights from 10 PM–3 AM.

Minus One (⊠ Carlton Highland Hotel, North Bridge, ☎ 0131/556–7277) has a DJ on Friday and live music on Saturday. The sounds here are mainstream, for groovers of all generations. It's open Friday and Saturday 10 PM–3 AM. Free entry before 11 PM.

Red Hot Pepper Club (⊠ 3 Semple St., ☎ 0131/229–7733) moves to mainstream music Friday and Saturday 10 PM–4 AM.

Folk Clubs

There are always folk performers in various pubs throughout the city. **Edinburgh Folk Club** (☎ 0131/652–1471 for venue) regularly arranges live folk music in a variety of venues.

Scottish Evenings and Ceilidhs

Several hotels feature traditional Scottish-music evenings in the summer season, including the **Carlton Highland Hotel** (⊠ North Bridge, ☎ 0131/556–7277) and the **King James Hotel** (⊠ Leith St., ☎ 0131/556–0111), which produces **Jamie's Scottish Evening.** Contact the hotels for information.

The Scottish Experience (⊠ 12 High St., ☎ 0131/557–9350) offers a banquet with a haggis ceremony, and Scottish singing and dancing.

Cocktail Bars

Harry's Bar (⊠ 7b Randolph Pl., ☎ 0131/539–8100) is in a basement and decorated with Americana. Despite the disco music, it is hugely popular with locals. Harry's is open Monday–Saturday noon–1 AM, Sunday 7 PM–1 AM.

L'Attache (⊠ Beneath the Rutland Hotel, 1 Rutland Pl., ☎ 0131/229–3402), another basement bar, has live folk and rock music Sunday–Thursday 8 PM–1:30 AM, Friday and Saturday 8 PM–2 AM.

Madogs (⊠ 38A George St., ☎ 0131/225–3408) was one of Edinburgh's first all-American cocktail bar-restaurants. It's popular with professionals after work and has live music most weeknights. It's open Sunday 6:30 PM–2 AM, Monday–Thursday noon–2 AM, and Friday and Saturday noon–3 AM. No sneakers.

OUTDOOR ACTIVITIES AND SPORTS

Edinburgh has shared in the fitness boom of the past decade, as can be noted in **Holyrood Park,** where at almost any time of day or night joggers run the circuit around Arthur's Seat. The **Royal Commonwealth Pool** (⊠ Dalkeith Rd., ☎ 0131/667–7211), the largest swimming pool in the city, is part of a complex that includes a fitness center and a cafeteria. **Meadowbank Stadium** (northeast of the city center, ☎ 0131/661–5351) has facilities for more than 30 different track and indoor sports.

Some of the larger Edinburgh hotels have their own fitness centers, including the **Calton Highland** (⊠ North Bridge, ☎ 0131/556–7277; pool, gymnasium, snooker, squash, massage), **Edinburgh Grand Sheraton** (⊠ Lothian Rd., ☎ 0131/229–9131; pool, gymnasium, £12.50 day charge for nonresidents), **Royal Scot** (⊠ Glasgow Rd., ☎ 0131/334–9191; pool, gymnasium, £10 day charge for nonresidents), and **Forth Bridges Moat House** (⊠ South Queensferry, ☎ 0131/469–9955; pool, gymnasium, snooker, squash). Most facilities are free to guests, though there may be a charge for snooker and squash. The facilities are generally open to nonguests only through private membership.

Bicycling

Cycles may be hired from **Sandy Gilchrist Cycles** (⊠ 1 Cadzow Pl., ☎ 0131/652–1760), **Recycling** (⊠ 31–33 Iona St., Leith, ☎ 0131/553– 1130 or 467–7775), and **Central Cycle Hire** (⊠ 13 Lochrin Pl., ☎ 0131/ 228–6333). Rates in summer are about £25 per week for a 3-speed, £35– 50 for a 10-speed, and £50–£60 for a mountain bike. Recycling, under the name "Great Bikes, No Bull," runs a sell-and-buy-back scheme for longer periods (say, more than two weeks), which can save you money.

Golf

The Tourist Centre will provide local details, and the Scottish Tourist Board offers a free leaflet on golf in Scotland, available from the Edinburgh and Scotland Information Centre (☞ Edinburgh A to Z *below*). "SSS" indicates the "standard scratch score," or average score.

The following courses are open to visitors:

Braids (⊠ 3 mi south of Edinburgh, ☎ 0131/447–6666). Course 1: 18 holes, 5,731 yards, SSS 68. Course 2: 18 holes, 4,832 yards, SSS 63.
Carrick Knowe (⊠ 5 mi west of Edinburgh, ☎ 0131/337–1096). 18 holes, 6,229 yards, SSS 70.
Craigentinny (⊠ 3 mi east of Edinburgh, ☎ 0131/554–7501). 18 holes, 5,418 yards, SSS 68.
Liberton (⊠ Kingston Grange, 297 Gilmerton Rd., ☎ 0131/664– 8580). 18 holes, 5,229 yards, SSS 166.
Lothianburn (⊠ Biggar Rd., ☎ 0131/445–2206). 18 holes, 5,750 yards, SSS 69.
Portobello (⊠ Stanley St., ☎ 0131/669–4361). 9 holes, 2,410 yards, SSS 32.
Silverknowes (⊠ Silverknowes Pkwy., ☎ 0131/336–3843). 18 holes, 6,210 yards, SSS 70.
Swanston (⊠ Swanston Rd., ☎ 0131/445–2239). 18 holes, 4,825 yards, SSS 64.
Torphin Hill (⊠ Torphin Rd., ☎ 0131/441–1100). 18 holes, 5,025 yards, SSS 66.

For information on golfing throughout Scotland, *see* Chapter 2.

Skiing

At Hillend on the southern edge of the city is the longest artificial ski slope in the United Kingdom—go either to ski (equipment can be hired on the spot) or to ride the chairlift for fine city views. ⊠ *Biggar Rd.,* ☎ *0131/445–4433.* ▨ *Chairlift: £1.* ☉ *Apr.–Aug. weekdays 9:30– 9, weekends 10–6; Sept.–Mar., Mon.–Sat. 9:30–9, Sun. 9:30–7.*

Soccer and Rugby

The **Heart of Midlothian Football Club** (soccer) is based at Tynecastle (☎ 0131/337–6132) and its rival club **Hibernian** at Easter Road (☎ 0131/337–2346). Murrayfield Stadium, home of the **Scottish Rugby Union** (☎ 0131/346–5000), is the venue for Scotland's international rugby matches, played in early spring. During that time of year, crowds of good-humored rugby fans from Ireland and Wales add greatly to the atmosphere in the streets of Edinburgh.

SHOPPING

Shopping Districts

Princes Street

Despite its renown as a shopping street, Princes Street in the New Town may disappoint many visitors with its dull, anonymous modern architecture, average chain stores, and fast-food outlets. It is, however, one of the best spots to shop for tartans, tweeds, and knitwear—especially if your time is limited—and the view upward toward the castle is still magnificent.

Holding their ground amid more ordinary stores in Princes Street are a few gems, the most noteworthy being **Jenners** (⊠ 4 Princes St., ☎ 0131/225–2442), Edinburgh's last surviving independent department store, opposite the Scott Monument. Claiming to be the world's oldest department store (established in 1838), Jenners is housed in a handsome Victorian (and later) building, graced outside with caryatids that emphasize the importance of women to the business. Although you can buy almost anything here, the store does specialize in china and glassware and in upmarket tweeds and tartans. Its **Food Hall** features Scottish products—shortbreads and Dundee cakes, honeys and marmalades, many available in attractive gift packs—as well as a range of high-quality groceries. **The Scotch House** (⊠ 39–41 Princes St., ☎ 0131/556–1252) is popular with overseas visitors for its top-quality (if top-price) clothing and accessories.

Across the road from Jenners is an upscale shopping mall, the **Waverley Market.** This mall includes designer-label boutiques, and shops that sell Scottish woolens and tweeds, whisky, and confections.

Rose Street

One block north of Princes Street, Rose Street has many smaller specialty shops; part of the street is a traffic-free pedestrian zone, so it's a pleasant place to browse. **Alistir Tait** (⊠ 116a Rose St., ☎ 0131/225–4105) offers a collection of high-quality antique and fine jewelry, silver, clocks, and crystal. If you plan to do a lot of hiking or camping in the Highlands or the Islands, you may want to look over the selection of outdoor clothing, boots, jackets, and heavy- and lightweight gear at **Tiso** (⊠ 121 Rose St., ☎ 0131/225–9486).

George Street

The shops here tend to be fairly upscale. London names, such as Laura Ashley, Liberty, and Waterstones bookshop, are prominent, though some of the older independent stores continue to do good business. Try **Waterstons** (⊠ 35 George St., ☎ 0131/225–5690), not to be confused with Waterstones bookshop, not only for stationery but also for an excellent selection of small gift items. **Grays** (⊠ 89 George St., ☎ 0131/225–7381) is a long-established ironmonger and hardware store that believes in old-fashioned service. The jeweler **Hamilton and Inches** (⊠ 87 George St., ☎ 0131/225–4898), established in 1866, is a silver- and goldsmith, worth visiting not only for its modern and antique gift possibilities, but also for its late-Georgian interior, designed by David Bryce in 1834—all gilded columns and elaborate plasterwork.

The streets crossing George Street—Hanover, Frederick, and Castle— are also worth exploring. **Dundas Street,** the northern extension of Hanover Street, beyond Queen Street Gardens, features several antiques shops. **Howe Street** (beyond Frederick St.) has **Touch Wood** (⊠ 19 Howe St., ☎ 0131/557–6382) for hand-crafted pine; **Linens Fine** (⊠ 22 Howe St., ☎ 0131/225–6998) for a wonderful selection of embroidered and embellished bed linen, tablecloths, cushion covers, and such; and **In House** (⊠ 28 Howe St., ☎ 0131/225–2888) for designer furnishings and collectibles at the forefront of modern design. **Thistle Street,** originally George Street's "back lane," or service area, has several boutiques and more antiques shops.

The Royal Mile

As may be expected, many of the shops along the Royal Mile in the Old Town sell what may be politely or euphemistically described as tourist-ware. Careful exploration, however, will reveal some worthwhile establishments. **Geoffrey (Tailor) Highland Crafts** (⊠ 57–59 High St., ☎ 0131/557–0256) can clothe you in full Highland dress, with kilts made in its own workshops.

In addition to offering a good selection of whiskies, tartans, and tweeds, shops on the Royal Mile cater to highly specialized interests and hobbies. For example, one store offers a large selection of playing cards, and another is devoted to doll houses and doll furniture.

Victoria Street/West Bow/Grassmarket

Close to the castle end of the Royal Mile, just off George IV Bridge, the specialty shops of Victoria Street are contained within a small area. Follow the tiny West Bow to Grassmarket for more specialty stores. The interior design shop **Ampersand** (⊠ 18 Victoria St., ☎ 0131/226– 2734) stocks a large selection of sundry collectibles, mostly jugs, plates, lamps, and vases, as well as unusual fabric by the meter. **Kinnels** (⊠ 36 Victoria St., ☎ 0131/220–1150) combines a specialty coffee and tea shop with a relaxed, old-world coffee house, complete with a display of newspapers dating back to the early 1800s. **Bill Baber** (⊠ 66 Grassmarket, ☎ 0131/225–3249) is one of the most imaginative of the many Scottish knitwear designers, and a long way from the conservative pastel "woollies" stocked by some of the large mill shops. Back up Victoria Street, try **Byzantium** (⊠ 9A Victoria St., ☎ 0131/225– 1768) for an eclectic mix of antiques, crafts, clothes—and an excellent coffee shop on the top level.

Stockbridge

North of Princes Street, on the way to the Botanic Gardens, this is an oddball shopping area of some charm, particularly on St. Stephen Street. To get to Stockbridge, walk down Frederick Street and Howe Street north away from Princes Street, then turn left onto North West Circus Place.

Stafford Street/William Street

This is a small, upscale shopping area in a Georgian setting. **Studio One** (⊠ 10–16 Stafford St., ☎ 0131/226–5812) has a well-established and comprehensive inventory of kitchen goods and gift articles. **Something Simple** (⊠ 10 William St., ☎ 0131/225–4650) stocks clothes for all occasions, including some designer names. **The Extra Inch** (⊠ 16 William St., ☎ 0131/226–3303) stocks a full selection of clothes European size 38 and over. To get to this neighborhood, walk to the west end of Princes Street and along its continuation, Shandwick Place, then turn into Stafford Street. William Street crosses Stafford halfway down.

Department Stores

In contrast to other major cities, Edinburgh has few true department stores. However, in the city center you will find **Jenners** (⊠ 4 Princes St., ☎ 0131/225–2442), Edinburgh's oldest department store, which specializes in traditional Scottish clothing and has a justly famous food hall. **Frasers** (⊠ west end of Princes St., ☎ 0131/225–2472) is a part of Britain's largest chain of department stores. The ubiquitous **John Lewis** (⊠ 69 St. James Centre, ☎ 0131/556–9121), specializing in furniture and household goods, pledges that they are "Never Knowingly Undersold." Unlike Jenners, Frasers and John Lewis are not local, independently owned firms, and the goods are similar to those stocked in other, United Kingdom–wide branches. The High Street multiples, **Marks and Spencer** (⊠ 54 Princes St., ☎ 0131/225–2301), **Littlewoods** (⊠ 91 Princes St., ☎ 0131/225–1683), **British Home Stores** (⊠ 64 Princes St., ☎ 0131/226–2621), and so on, are also represented on Princes Street. However, even given the competition, if you plan a morning or a whole day wandering from department to department, trying on beautiful clothes, buying crystal or china, or stocking up on Scottish food specialties, with a break for lunch at an in-store restaurant, then Jenners is the store to choose.

Arcades and Shopping Centers

Like most large towns Edinburgh has succumbed to the fashion for "under one roof" shopping. If you dislike a breath of fresh air (or a wonderful view) between shops—or if it's raining—try **Waverley Market** (east end of Princes St.), which offers three floors of shops and a fast-food area. The **St. James Centre** (east end of Princes Street) has recently undergone extensive refurbishment, but its gathering of chain stores is still unremarkable. **Cameron Toll** (bottom of Dalkeith Rd.) shopping center, on the south side of the city, caters to local residents, with food stores and High Street brand names. The newest shopping center at **South Gyle** (on the outskirts of the city near the airport) is based on a typical U.S.-style shopping mall. Here you will find the High Street brand names again, including a huge Marks and Spencer.

Clothing Boutiques

Edinburgh is home to several top-quality designers (although, it must be said, probably not as many as are found in Glasgow, the country's fashion center), some of whom make a point of using Scottish materials in their creations, such as **Bill Baber** (☞ *above*). Well-heeled Edinburgh also has a branch of **Droopy and Brown** (⊠ 37–39 Frederick St., ☎ 0131/225–1019), whose distinctive clothing—from silk ball gowns and wedding dresses to flowing cord skirts and matching jackets, and pretty cotton print summer dresses—is guaranteed to make the wearer stand out from the crowd. **Judith Glue** (⊠ 60–64 High St., ☎ 0131/556–5443) stocks brilliantly patterned Orkney knitwear, as well as distinctive crafts, cards, candles.

If you are shopping for children, especially those who fit the tousled-tomboy mold, try **Baggins** (⊠ 12 Deanhaugh St., Stockbridge, ☎ 0131/315–2011) for practical, reasonably priced clothes made from natural fibers. All the clothes here are made to the owner's design in the store-cum-workshop.

Scottish Specialties

If you want to identify a particular tartan, several of the shops in Princes Street will be pleased to assist. The **Clan Tartan Centre** (⊠ 70–74 Bangor Rd., Leith, ☎ 0131/553–5100) has extensive displays of various aspects of tartanry. For craftware, use as your quality guide the **Royal Mile Living Craft Centre** (✉ 12 High St., ☎ 0131/557–9350). Here, crafts are made on the premises, and you can talk to the craftspeople as they work. The range of items available includes hand-woven tartan, kilts, bagpipes, silver, pottery, and Aran knitwear; there is also the Taste of Scotland coffee shop. **Edinburgh Crystal** (✉ Eastfield, Penicuik, ☎ 01968/675128) makes fine glassware that is stocked by many large stores and gift shops in the city center, but you can also visit its premises (visitor center, restaurant, and shop) at Penicuik, just south of the city.

Antiques

Antiques dealers tend to cluster together, so it may be easier to concentrate on one area—St. Stephen Street, Bruntsfield Place, Causewayside, or Dundas Street, for example—if you are short of time. **Joseph Bonnar** (✉ 72 Thistle St., ☎ 0131/226–2811) is a specialist in antique jewelry in the heart of the New Town. **Hamilton and Inches** (☞ George Street, *above*) also sells fine antique jewelry and silverware. Look into **Hand in Hand** (✉ 3 North West Circus Pl., ☎ 0131/226–3598) for beautiful antique textiles.

Bookstores

As a university city and cultural center, Edinburgh is well endowed with excellent bookshops, some of the most central being **James Thin, The Edinburgh Bookshop** (✉ 57 George St., ☎ 0131/225–4495; and 53 South Bridge, ☎ 0131/556–6743), and **Waterstones** (✉ 83 George St., ☎ 0131/225–3436; ✉ 13/14 Princes St., ☎ 0131/556–3034; and ✉ 128 Princes St., ☎ 0131/226–2666). All stock a wide range of guides and books giving information about every aspect of Edinburgh life, and all have extended opening hours (until 10 PM on certain nights), including Sunday.

SIDE TRIPS

West Lothian and the Forth Valley

The Lothians is the collective name given to the swath of countryside surrounding Edinburgh. This excursion explores West Lothian and the Forth Valley west of Edinburgh, as well as some of the territory north of the River Forth. In a round-trip of about 70 miles (**Castle Campbell**, at 30 miles from Edinburgh, is the farthest afield), it is possible to see plenty of the central belt of Scotland and to skirt the edge of the Central Highlands. The river Forth snakes across a widening floodplain on its descent from the Highlands, and by the time it reaches the western extremities of Edinburgh, it has already passed below the mighty Forth bridges and become a broad estuary. This is the excursion to take if you incline toward castles and stately homes, because they sprout thickly on both sides of the Forth.

Cramond

This compact settlement on the coast west of the city is the place to watch summer sunsets over the Firth of Forth, with the Cramond Inn nearby offering refreshment. The River Almond joins the main estuary here. Its banks, once the site of mills and works, now offer pleasant leafy walks and plenty to interest the industrial archaeologist.

Dalmeny House

The first of the stately homes clustered on the western edge of Edinburgh, **Dalmeny House** is the home of the Earl and Countess of Rosebery. This 1815 Tudor Gothic pile displays among its sumptuous contents the best of the family's famous collection of 18th-century French furniture. (Much of this collection was formerly displayed at Mentmore, the country seat 40 miles north of London, which belonged to the present earl's grandfather, Baron Mayer de Rothschild.) Highlights include the library; the drawing room, with its tapestries and highly wrought French furniture; the Napoleon Room; and the Vincennes and Sevres porcelain collections. ⊠ *B924, by South Queensferry (7 mi west of Edinburgh),* ☎ *0131/331–1888.* 🎫 *£3.50.* ⊙ *July–early Sept., Sun. 1–5:30, Mon. and Tues. noon–5:30. Last admission 4:45.*

South Queensferry

★ ㉓ This pleasant little waterside community, a former ferry port, is totally dominated by the **Forth bridges,** which cross the Firth of Forth at this point. The **Forth Rail Bridge** was opened in 1890 and is 2,765 yards long, except on a hot summer's day when it expands by about another yard! Its neighbor is the 1,993-yard-long Forth Road Bridge, opened in 1964.

Hopetoun House

㉔ The palatial premises of **Hopetoun House,** home of the marquesses of Linlithgow, are considered to be among the Adam family's finest designs. The pile was started in 1699 to the original plans of Sir William Bruce, then enlarged between 1721 and 1754 by William Adam and his son Robert. There is a notable painting collection, and the house has decorative work of the highest order, plus all the paraphernalia to amuse visitors: nature trail, restaurant, stables, museum, garden center. Much of the wealth that created this sumptuous building came from the family's mining interests. ⊠ *West of South Queensferry,* ☎ *0131/331– 2451.* 🎫 *£4.20.* ⊙ *Apr.–Sept., daily 10–5:30 (last admission 4:30).*

House of the Binns

㉕ The 17th-century General Tam Dalyell transformed a fortified stronghold into a gracious mansion, the **House of the Binns** (the name derives from *ben,* the Scottish word for hill). The present exterior dates from around 1810 and shows a remodeling into a kind of mock fort with crenelled battlements and turrets. Inside there are magnificent plaster ceilings in Elizabethan style. ⊠ *Off A904, 4 mi east of Linlithgow,* ☎ *0131/226– 5922.* 🎫 *£3.10.* ⊙ *May–Sept., Sat.–Thurs. 1:30–5:30 (last tour 5 PM).*

Blackness

㉖ The castle of **Blackness** stands like a grounded gray hulk on the very edge of the Forth. A curious 15th-century structure, it has had a varied career as a strategic fortress, state prison, powder magazine, and youth hostel. The countryside is gently green and cultivated, and open views extend across the blue Forth to the distant ramparts of the Ochil Hills. ⊠ *B903, 4 mi northeast of Linlithgow,* ☎ *0131/668–8600.* 🎫 *£1.50.* ⊙ *Apr.–Sept., Mon.–Sat. 9:30–6, Sun. 2–6; Oct.–Mar., Mon.–Wed. and Sat. 9:30–4, Thurs. 9:30–noon, Sun. 2–4.*

Linlithgow

㉗ On the edge of Linlithgow Loch stands the splendid ruin of **Linlithgow Palace,** birthplace of Mary, Queen of Scots (1542). Burned, perhaps by accident, by Hanoverian troops during the last Jacobite rebellion in 1746, this impressive shell stands on a site of great antiquity, though nothing for certain survived an earlier fire in 1424. The palace gatehouse is from the early 16th century, and the central courtyard's elaborate fountain dates from around 1535, but the halls and great rooms are cold echoing stone husks. ⊠ *South shore of Linlithgow Loch,* ☎ *0131/668–8600.* 🎫 *£2.* ⊙ *Apr.–Sept., Mon.–Sat. 9:30–6, Sun. 2–6; Oct.–Mar., Mon.–Sat. 9:30–4, Sun. 2–4.*

West Lothian and the Forth Valley

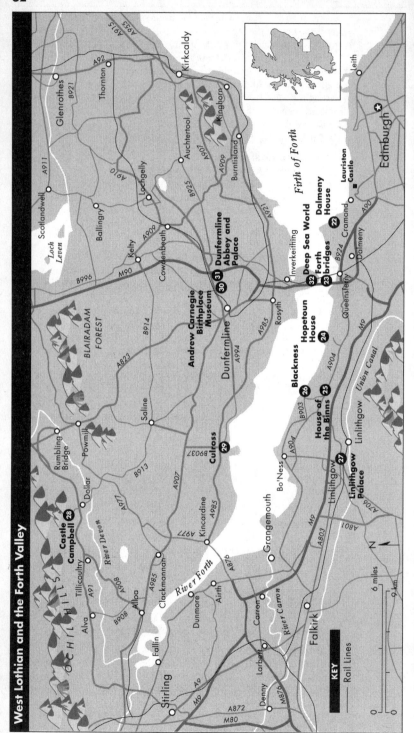

KEY

—— Rail Lines

The **Four Marys** (✉ 67 High St., Linlithgow) specializes in uncompli-
cated but wholesome pub lunches.

From the M9 you will begin to gain tempting glimpses of the Highland hills to the northwest and the long humped wall of the Ochil Hills,
across the river-plain to the north. The **River Carron,** which flows
under the M9, gave its name to the *carronade,* a kind of cannon manufactured in Falkirk, a few minutes to the southwest. You will also notice the apocalyptic complex of Grangemouth Refinery (impressive by
night), which you may also smell if the wind is right (or wrong!). The
refinery processes North Sea crude, but was originally sited here because of the now extinct oil-shale extraction industry of West Lothian, pioneered by a Scot, James "Paraffin" Young. This landscape may
not be the most scenic in Scotland, but it has certainly played its role
in the nation's industrial history.

The Ochil Hills

The scarp face of the Ochil Hills looms unmistakably, an old fault line,
bearing up the harder volcanic rocks in contrast to the softer coal measures immediately around the River Forth. The steep Ochils provided
grazing land and water power for Scotland's second-largest textile
area. Some mills still survive in the so-called Hillfoots towns on the
scarp edge east of Stirling. Several walkers' routes run into the narrow
chinks of glens here. Behind Alva is **Alva Glen** (park near the converted
Strude Mill, at the top and eastern end of the little town). A little farther east is the **Ochil Hills Woodland Park,** which provides access to
Silver Glen. The **Mill Glen,** behind Tillicoultry (pronounced tilly-*coot*-
ree), and its giant quarry, fine waterfalls, and interesting plants is another option for energetic explorers.

Dollar

This *douce* (Scots for well-mannered or gentle) and tidy town below
the slopes lies at the mouth of Dollar Glen. At first sight, the tilting
slopes seem an unlikely terrain for wheeled vehicles. By following
㉘ signs for **Castle Campbell,** however, you will find a road that angles
sharply up the east side of the wooded defile. The narrow road ends
in a parking lot from which it's only a short walk to Castle Campbell,
high on a great sloping mound in the center of the glen. With the green
woods below, bracken hills above, and a view that on a clear day stretches
right across the Forth Valley to the tip of Tinto Hill near Lanark, this
is certainly the most atmospheric fortress within easy reach of Edinburgh. Formerly known as Castle Gloom, Castle Campbell stands out
among Scottish castles for the sheer drama of its setting. The sturdy
square of the tower house survives from the 15th century, when this
site was first fortified by the Earl of Argyll. Other buildings and en-
closures were subsequently added, but the sheer lack of space on this
rocky eminence ensured that there were never any drastic changes. The
castle is associated with the earls of Argyll, as well as with John Knox,
the fiery religious reformer, who preached here. It also played a role
in the religious wars of the 17th century, having been captured by Oliver
Cromwell in 1654 and garrisoned with English troops. ✉ *Dollar Glen,
1 mi north of Dollar,* ☎ *0131/668–8600.* ⚑ *£2.* ☉ *Apr.–Sept.,
Mon.–Sat. 9:30–6, Sun. 2–6; Oct.–Mar., Mon.–Wed. and Sat. 9:30–
4, Thurs. 9:30–noon, Sun. 2–4.*

Culross

㉙ On the muddy shores of the Forth, **Culross** is one of the most remarkable little towns in all of Scotland. It once had a thriving industry and export trade in coal and salt (the coal was used in the salt-panning
process). It also had, curiously, a trade monopoly in the manufacture
of baking *girdles* (griddles). But as local coal became exhausted, the

impetus of the Industrial Revolution passed it by and other parts of the Forth Valley prospered. Culross became a backwater town, and the merchants' houses of the 17th and 18th centuries were never replaced by Victorian developments or modern architecture. In the 1930s, the very new and then very poor National Trust for Scotland started to buy up the decaying properties. With the help of a variety of other agencies, these buildings were conserved and brought to life. Many of the National Trust properties are today lived in by ordinary citizens. A few—the Palace, Study, and Town House—are open to the public. With its mercat cross, cobbled streets, tolbooth, and narrow wynds, Culross is now a living museum of a 17th-century town. ☎ *0131/226–5922. Admission to Palace, Study, and Town House £3.60. Study and Town House ☉ Apr.–Sept. daily, 1:30–5 (Oct., weekends 11–5); Palace ☉ Apr.–Sept. daily, 11–5 (last admission 4).*

Dunfermline

This town was once the world center for the production of damask linen; the **Dunfermline District Museum** (✉ Viewfield Terrace, ☎ 01383/721–814) tells the full story. Today the town is better known as the birthplace of millionaire philanthropist Andrew Carnegie. Undoubtedly Dunfermline's most famous son, Carnegie endowed the town with a library, health and fitness center, spacious park, and, naturally, a Carnegie Hall, still the focus of culture and entertainment. The 1835 weaver's cottage in which Carnegie was born is now the **Andrew Carnegie Birthplace Museum.** Don't be misled by the cottage's exterior. Inside it opens into a larger hall, where documents, photographs, and artifacts tell Carnegie's fascinating life story. You will learn such obscure details as the claim that Carnegie was only the third man in the United States to be able to translate Morse code by ear as it came down the wire! ✉ *Moodie St.,* ☎ *01383/724302.* ☜ *£1.50.* ☉ *Apr.–Oct., Mon.–Sat. 11–5, Sun. 2–5; Nov.–Mar., daily 2–4.*

Also of note in the town are the **Dunfermline Abbey and Palace** complex. The abbey was founded by Queen Margaret, the English wife of the Scots King Malcolm Canmore (1057–93). Some Norman work can be seen in the present church, where Robert the Bruce lies buried. The palace grew from the abbey guest house and was the birthplace of Charles I. Dunfermline was the seat of the Royal Court of Scotland until the end of the 11th century, and its central role in Scottish affairs is explored by means of display panels dotted around the drafty but hallowed buildings. ✉ *Monastery St.,* ☎ *0131/668–8600.* ☜ *£1.50.* ☉ *Apr.–Sept., Mon.–Sat. 9:30–6, Sun. 2–6; Oct.–Mar., Mon.–Wed., and Sat. 9:30–4, Thurs. 9:30–noon, Sun. 2–4.*

North Queensferry

The former ferry port on the north side of the Forth dropped almost into oblivion after the Forth Road Bridge opened, but was dragged abruptly back into the limelight when the hugely popular **Deep Sea World** arrived in the early 1990s. This sophisticated "aquarium"—for want of a better word—on the Firth of Forth offers a fascinating view of underwater life. Go down a clear acrylic tunnel for a diver's eye look at more than 5,000 fish, including a posse of 8-foot sharks, and visit the exhibition hall with displays and an audiovisual presentation on local marine life. Pirates also feature prominently in displays and tableaux. Ichthyophobes will feel more at ease in the adjacent café and gift shop. ✉ *North Queensferry,* ☎ *01383/411411.* ☜ *£5.50.* ☉ *Apr.–Oct., daily 10–6; Nov.–Mar., weekdays 10–4, weekends and holidays 10–6. Closed Dec. 25.*

West Lothian and the Forth Valley A to Z

ARRIVING AND DEPARTING

By Bus. Bus services link most of this area, but working out a detailed itinerary by bus would be best left to your travel agent or guide.

By Car. Leave Edinburgh by Queensferry Road—the A90—and follow signs for the Forth Bridge. Beyond the city boundary at Cramond take the slip road, B924, for South Queensferry, watching for signs to Dalmeny House. From Dalmeny, follow the B924 for the descent to South Queensferry. The B924 continues westward under the approaches to the suspension bridge and then meets the A904. On turning right, onto A904, follow signs for Hopetoun House. The House of the Binns and Blackness Castle are also signed from the A904. From Blackness, take the B903 to its junction with the A904. Turn left for Linlithgow on the A803. At this point it's best to join the M9, which will speed you westward. Follow Kincardine Bridge signs off the motorway, cross the Forth and take the A977 north from Kincardine, formerly a trading port and distillery center. Take the A985 to Alloa, get on the A908 (signed Tillicoultry) for a short stretch, and then pick up the B908 (signed Alva).

At this point you'll be leaving the industrial northern shore of the Forth behind and entering the Ochil Hills, which you can explore by following the A91 eastward at Alva; squeezed between the gentle River Devon and the steep slopes above, the road continues to Dollar, where you should follow signs to Castle Campbell. From the castle, retrace your route to A91 and turn left. Just a few minutes outside Dollar, turn right onto a minor road (signed Rumbling Bridge). Then turn right onto the A823. Follow A823 through Powmill (signs for Dunfermline); turn right off A823, following the signs for Saline (a pleasant if undistinguished village), and take an unclassified road due south to join the A907. Turn right, and then within a mile go left on the B9037, which leads down to Culross. Take the B9037 east to join the A994, which leads to Dunfermline. From here, follow Edinburgh signs to the A823 and return via North Queensferry and the Forth Road Bridge (toll: 40p).

By Train. Dalmeny, Linlithgow, and Dunfermline all have rail stations, and can be reached from Edinburgh Waverley Station.

VISITOR INFORMATION

The tourist information center at **Tillicoultry** can provide information on the region's textile establishments as well as a *Mill Trail* brochure, which can lead you to mill shops offering bargain woolen and tweed goods.

Midlothian and East Lothian

In spite of the finest stone carving in Scotland (at **Rosslyn Chapel**), associations with Sir Walter Scott, outstanding castles, and miles of varied rolling countryside, Midlothian, the area immediately south of Edinburgh, for years remained off the beaten tourist path. Perhaps a little in awe of sophisticated Edinburgh to the north and the well-manicured charm of the stockbroker belt of nearby upmarket East Lothian, Midlothian remained quietly preoccupied with its own workaday little towns and dormitory suburbs.

As for East Lothian, it started with the advantage of golf courses of world-rank, most notably Muirfield, plus a scattering of stately homes and interesting hotels. Red-pantiled and decidedly middle class, it is an area of glowing grainfields in summer and quite a few discreetly polite STRICTLY PRIVATE signs at the end of driveways. Still, it has plenty of interest for the visitor, including photogenic villages, active fishing harbors, and vistas of pastoral Lowland Scotland, a world away (but much less than an hour by car) from bustling Edinburgh.

Roslin

★ ㉝ A pretty little U-shaped miners' village, with its rows of stone-built terraced cottages, Roslin is famous for the extraordinary **Rosslyn Chapel.** Conceived by Sir William Sinclair and dedicated to St. Matthew in 1450, the chapel is outstanding for the quality and variety of the stone carving inside. Human figures, animals, and plants are all included, covering almost every square inch of stonework. The chapel was actually never finished. The original design called for a cruciform structure, but only the choir and parts of the east transept walls were completed. ⊠ *Roslin, off A703, 7½ mi south of Edinburgh,* ☎ *0131/440–2159.* ✑ *£2.25.* ☉ *Mon.–Sat. 10–5, Sun. noon–4:45 (restricted hours in winter).*

Penicuik

㉞ There are fine views of the Pentland Hills beyond this town, but its chief attraction for the tourist is the **Edinburgh Crystal Visitor Centre.** You may have seen this distinctive style of glassware in Edinburgh's upscale shops. Guided tours reveal the stages involved in the manufacture of cut crystal. In addition, groups of 6–12 people can pre-book a VIP tour (adults over 18 only). This includes the chance to blow a glass bubble and also to cut your own piece of glass, which will then be polished and given to you as a keepsake. Advance booking is essential for this tour. The Visitor Centre itself has crystal pieces on display, as well as an audiovisual exhibition on the production of crystal. ⊠ *Eastfield, Penicuik, 10 mi south of Edinburgh,* ☎ *01968/675128.* ✑ *Admission to center free. Tours: £2; VIP tour: £20.* ☉ *Mon.–Sat. 9–5, Sun. 11–5. Tours weekdays 9:15–3:30.*

The Pentlands

This unmistakable range of hills immediately south of Edinburgh has the longest artificial ski slope in Britain, at Hillend, and an all-year chairlift that provides magnificent views (even to nonskiers). There are several other access points along the A702 running parallel to the hills—the best is Flotterstone (where there is a parking lot, pub, and easy, quiet road-walking).

NEED A
BREAK?   The **Old Bakehouse** (☎ 01968/660830) at West Linton, southwest of Penicuik on the A702, serves home-cooked fare in quaint, wood-beamed rooms. Danish open sandwiches are the specialty, but home-made soups and a hot main course are also included on the menu. Tuesday through Sunday, lunch is served noon–2:30, and on Fridays and Saturdays you can also have dinner 6–9.

Newtongrange

㉟ This former mining community is the location for the **Scottish Mining Museum,** where, in the buildings of a now-closed colliery, you can learn something about the history of Scotland's coal miners. You can visit various buildings in the complex and view the giant winding engine, and also see a reconstruction of a modern mechanized coalface. Realistic tableaux in the mine's former offices relate the power that the mining company had over the lives of the individual workers in a frighteningly autocratic system that survived well into the 1930s. The mining company owned the houses, shops, and even the pub. Newtongrange was in fact the largest planned mining village in Scotland. The scenery is no more attractive than you would expect, though the green Pentland Hills are still in view in the distance. ☎ *0131/663–7519.* ✑ *£2.50.* ☉ *Mar.–Oct. daily 10–4.*

Borthwick

㊱ Set in green countryside with scattered woods and lush hedgerows, the little village of Borthwick is dominated by **Borthwick Castle,** which dates

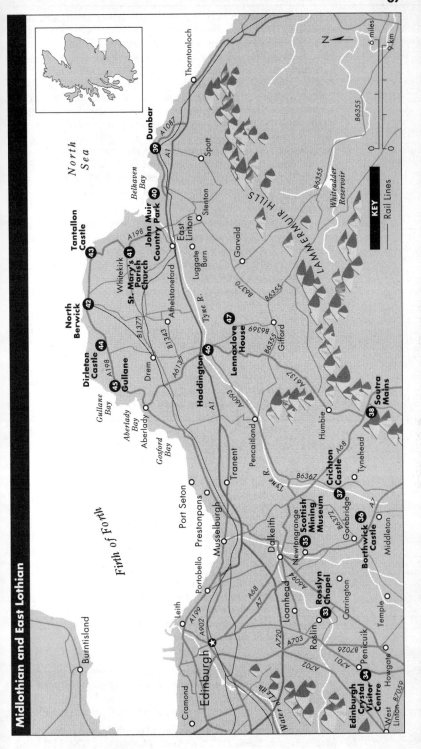

Midlothian and East Lothian

North Sea

Firth of Forth

LAMMERMUIR HILLS

KEY
Rail Lines

Burntisland
Cramond
Edinburgh
Leith
Portobello
Musselburgh
Prestonpans
Port Seton
Cockenzie
Tranent
Pencaitland
Dalkeith
Loanhead
Roslin
Carrington
Temple
Middleton
Gorebridge
Tynehead
Humbie
Gifford
Garvald
Spott
Stenton
East Linton
Athelstaneford
Drem
Aberlady
Gullane
North Berwick
Whitekirk
Dunbar
Thorntonloch
Spott
Belhaven Bay
Gullane Bay
Aberlady Bay
Gosford Bay
Luggate Burn
Haddington
Tyne R.
Penicuik
Howgate
West Linton

34 Edinburgh Crystal Visitor Centre
33 Rosslyn Chapel
35 Scottish Mining Museum
36 Borthwick Castle
37 Crichton Castle
38 Soutra Mains
39 Dunbar
40 John Muir Country Park
41 St. Mary's Parish Church
42 North Berwick
43 Tantallon Castle
44 Dirleton Castle
45 Gullane
46 Haddington
47 Lennoxlove House

Newtongrange
Newbattle
Whiteadder Reservoir

A1, A198, A199, A902, A720, A703, A701, A702, A68, A7, A6137, A6093, A6094, B1377, B1343, B1347, B6370, B6369, B6355, B6367, B6372, B7026, B7059, A1087, A6124 from the 15th century and is still occupied (it is now a hotel, ☞ *below*). This stark, tall, twin-towered fortress is associated with Mary, Queen of Scots. She came here on a kind of honeymoon with her ill-starred third husband, the Earl of Bothwell. Their already dubious bliss was interrupted by Mary's political opponents, often referred to as the Lords of the Congregation, a confederacy of powerful nobles who were against the queen's latest liaison and who instead favored the crowning of her young son James. Rather insensitively, they laid siege to the castle while the newlyweds were there. The history books relate that Mary subsequently escaped disguised as a man. She was not free for long, however. It was only a short time before she was defeated in battle and imprisoned. She languished in prison for 21 years before Queen Elizabeth of England signed her death warrant (1587). Bothwell's fate was equally gloomy: He died insane in a Danish prison.

LODGING

$$$–$$$$ 🏰 **Borthwick Castle.** There are hotels with castle names; and there are
★   hotels inside what once were castles; and then there is Borthwick, which is firstly a castle and only secondly a place where you can stay. This 15th-century fortress was already taking guests half a century before Columbus discovered the Americas. Nowhere else in Scotland offers the extraordinary experience of staying as a part of history. Your "bedchamber," be reassured, is warm and comfortable, fully equipped with bath or shower (the plumbing is not 15th-century). You eat fine food, not in a restaurant, but in a magnificent vaulted room, the Great Hall, lit by candles and the gleam of a log fire. ✉ *North Middleton, Midlothian, EH23 4QY,* ☎ *01875/820514,* ℻ *01875/821702. 10 bedchambers with bath or shower. AE, DC, MC, V. Closed Jan.–mid-March.*

Crichton Castle

③⑦ Like Borthwick Castle, **Crichton Castle** is set in attractive, rolling Lowland scenery, interrupted here and there with patches of woodland: It is possible to reach this castle from Borthwick Castle by taking a peaceful walk through the woods (there are signposts along the way). Crichton was a Bothwell family castle; Queen Mary attended the wedding here of Bothwell's sister, Lady Janet Hepburn, to Mary's natural brother, Lord John Stewart. Of particular interest in the extensive ruin is the curious arcaded range with its diamond-faceted stonework. This particular geometric pattern cut into the stone is unique in Scotland and is thought to have been inspired by Renaissance styles on the Continent, particularly Italy. The oldest part of the work is the 14th-century keep (square tower). ✉ *B6367, 7 mi southeast of Dalkeith,* ☎ *0131/668-8600.* ▨ *£1.20.* ☉ *Apr.–Sept., Mon.–Sat. 9:30–6, Sun. 2–6.*

En Route   Follow the A68 south, away from Edinburgh, to the very edge of the Lammermuir Hills. Just beyond the junction with the A6137 you'll come
③⑧ to a spot called **Soutra Mains.** There's a small parking lot here, from which you can enjoy glorious unobstructed views extending northward over the whole of the Lothian plain.

Gifford

With its 18th-century kirk and mercat cross, Gifford is a good example of a tweedily respectable, well-scrubbed, red-pantile-roofed East Lothian village.

Dunbar

In the days before tour companies started offering package deals to the
③⑨ Mediterranean, **Dunbar** was a popular holiday resort. Now a bit faded, the primary draws are some spacious Georgian-style properties, characterized by the astragals, or fan-shaped windows, above the doors; the symmetry of the house fronts; and the parapeted roof lines. Though

not the popular seaside playground it once was, Dunbar does still have an attractive beach and a picturesque harbor.

John Muir Country Park

40 Taking in the estuary of the River Tyne winding down from the Moorfoot Hills, the **John Muir Country Park** offers varied coastal scenery: rocky shoreline, golden sands, and the mixed woodlands of Tyninghame, teeming with wildlife. Dunbar-born John Muir (whose family emigrated to the United States when he was a child) founded the U.S. National Park system. Only recently has the work of this early conservationist been acknowledged in his native Scotland.

Whitekirk

41 The unmistakable red sandstone **St. Mary's Parish Church,** with Norman tower, stands on a site occupied since the 6th century. It was a place of pilgrimage in medieval times because of its healing well. Behind the kirk, in a field, stands a tithe barn. Tithe barns originated in the practice of giving to the church a proportion of local produce, which then required storage space. At one end of the structure is a 16th-century tower house, which at one point in its history accommodated visiting pilgrims. The large three-story barn was added to the tower house in the 17th century. ⊠ *A198.* ☞ *Free.* ☉ *Early morning to late evening.*

North Berwick

42 The pleasant little seaside resort of **North Berwick** manages to retain a small-town personality even when it's thronged with city visitors on warm summer Sunday afternoons. Munching on ice cream, the city folk stroll on the beach and in the narrow streets or gape at the sailing craft in the small harbor.

43 Rising on a cliff beyond the flat fields east of North Berwick, **Tantallon Castle** is a substantial ruin defending a headland with the sea on three sides. The red sandstone is pitted and eaten by time and sea-spray, with the earliest surviving stonework dating from the late-14th century. The fortress was besieged in 1529 by the cannons of King James V. (Rather inconveniently, the besieging forces ran out of gunpowder.) Cannons were used again, to deadlier effect, in a later siege during the Civil War in 1651. Twelve days of battering with the heavy guns of Cromwell's General Monk greatly damaged the flanking towers. However, much of the curtain wall of this former Douglas stronghold survives. ⊠ *A198, 3 mi east of North Berwick,* ☎ *0131/668–8600.* ☞ *£2.* ☉ *Apr.–Sept., Mon.–Sat. 9:30–6, Sun. 2–6; Oct.–Mar., Mon.–Wed. and Sat. 9:30–4, Thurs. noon–4, Sun. 2–4.*

Dirleton

44 Set right in the center of this small village is 12th-century **Dirleton Castle,** surrounded by a high outer wall. Within the wall you'll find a 17th-century bowling green, set in the shade of yew trees and surrounded by a herbaceous flower border that comes ablaze with color in high summer. Dirleton Castle was occupied in 1298 by King Edward I of England, as part of his campaign for the continued subjugation of the unruly Scots. ⊠ *A198,* ☎ *0131/668–8600.* ☞ *£2.* ☉ *Apr.–Sept., Mon.–Sat. 9:30–6, Sun. 2–6; Oct.–Mar., Mon.–Sat. 9:30–4, Sun. 2–4.*

Gullane

45 Very noticeable along this coastline are the golf courses of East Lothian, laid out wherever there is available links space. **Gullane,** surrounded by them, is ultrarespectable, its inhabitants clad mostly in expensive golfing sweaters. **Muirfield,** venue for the Open Championship, is nearby, as is **Greywalls,** now a hotel (☞ *below*), but originally a private house designed by Sir Edwin Lutyens. Away from the golf, Gullane's beach, well within driving distance of the city, offers opportunities for restful summer evening strolls.

LODGING

$$$$ 🏨 **Greywalls.** This is the ideal hotel for a golfing vacation: comfortable, with attentive service and award-winning modern British cuisine that makes the most of local produce. The house itself is an architectural treasure. Edward VII used to stay here, as have Nicklaus, Trevino, Palmer, and a host of other golfing greats. Decorated using stylish fabrics from the likes of Nina Campbell, Colefax and Fowler, and Osborne and Little, shades of restful green predominate. ⊠ *Muirfield, Gullane, EH31 2EG,* ☎ *01620/842144,* ℻ *01620/842241. 22 rooms with bath. Restaurant, putting green, tennis court. AE, DC, MC, V.* ☺ *Apr.–Oct.*

Haddington

One of the best-preserved medieval street plans in the country can be explored in **Haddington.** Among the many buildings of architectural or historical interest is the Town House, which was designed by William Adam in 1748 and enlarged in 1830. A wall plaque at the Sidegate recalls the great heights of floods from the River Tyne. Beyond is the medieval Nungate footbridge, with the Church of St. Mary a little way upstream.

Just to the south of Haddington is **Lennoxlove House,** which displays items associated with Mary, Queen of Scots. A turreted country house, part of it dating from the 15th century, Lennoxlove is a cheerful mix of family life and Scottish history. Housed in the beautifully decorated rooms are collections of portraits, furniture, and porcelain. ⊠ *B6369, 1 mi south of Haddington,* ☎ *01620/823720,* ℻ *01620/825112.* 🏨 *£3.* ☺ *May–Sept., Wed., Sat., and Sun. 2–5.*

Midlothian and East Lothian A to Z

ARRIVING AND DEPARTING

By Bus. City bus services run out as far as Swanston and the Pentland Hills. S.M.T. buses run to towns and villages throughout Midlothian and East Lothian. For details of all services, inquire at the St. Andrew Square Bus Station (☎ 0131/556–8464) in Edinburgh.

By Car. Leave Edinburgh via the A701 (Liberton Rd.). At the not-very-picturesque community of Bilston, turn left to Roslin on the B7006. From Roslin return to the A703 for Penicuik. From Penicuik, take the A766 and A702, which runs beneath the Pentland Hills to West Linton. Then follow the B7059 and the A701 to Leadburn and then Howgate. Get onto the A6094 for a few minutes, then turn right onto the B6372 and continue past Temple, an attractive village on the edge of the Moorfoot Hills, toward Gorebridge.

At the junction of B6372 with A7, just before Gorebridge, you have a choice. If your interests tend toward social history, turn left and drive 2 miles to reach Newtongrange. If you instead turn right, after a few moments' travel south you will see a sign for Borthwick. Take a left onto an unclassified road off A7, and a few minutes later, Borthwick Castle appears. From Borthwick, take the B6372 and turn right onto the A68. Just beyond the village of Pathhead you'll see signs to Crichton Castle. Having detoured to the castle, follow the A68 south, away from Edinburgh, to the very edge of the Lammermuir Hills. Just beyond the junction with the A6137 at Soutra Mains there's a small parking lot from which to enjoy the view. Make your way back to the A6137 and turn right onto it; turn right again onto the B6355, go through Gifford and head east for the junction with the B6370, which leads to Dunbar.

West of Dunbar, on the way back to Edinburgh, the A1087 leads to the sandy reaches of Belhaven Bay, signposted from the main road, and to the John Muir Country Park. From the park, drive north on the A198 (a right turn off the A1), to reach Whitekirk, Tantallon Castle, and North Berwick. Dirleton, with its own massive castle, and Gullane, surrounded by golf courses, follow. A198 eventually leads to Aberlady, from which you can take the A6137 south to the former county town of Haddington and, by way of the B6369, Lennoxlove House. Return to the A1 at Haddington and head west back to Edinburgh. From Haddington it's about 15 miles back to center city.

By Train. There is no train service in Midlothian. In East Lothian, North Berwick has a train station with regular services from Edinburgh.

EDINBURGH A TO Z

Arriving and Departing

By Bus
Scottish Citylink Coaches (☎ 0990/505050, FAX 0141/332–8055) and **National Express** (☎ 0990/808080, FAX 0141/332–8055) provide bus service to and from London. The main terminal, St. Andrew Square Bus Station, is only a couple of minutes (on foot) north of Waverley rail station, immediately east of St. Andrew Square. Long-distance coaches must be booked in advance from the booking office in the terminal. Edinburgh is approximately eight hours by bus from London.

By Car
Downtown Edinburgh centers on Princes Street, which runs east–west. Drivers from the east coast will come in on A1, Meadowbank Stadium serving as a landmark. The highway bypasses the suburbs of Musselburgh and Tranent; therefore, any bottlenecks will occur close to downtown. From the Borders the approach to Princes Street is by A7/A68 through Newington, an area offering a wide choice of accommodations. From Newington the east end of Princes Street is reached by North Bridge and South Bridge. Approaching from the southwest, drivers will join the west end of Princes Street (Lothian Rd.), via A701 and A702, and those coming west from Glasgow or Stirling will meet Princes Street from M8 or M9, respectively. A slightly more complicated approach is via M90—from Forth Road Bridge/Perth/east coast; the key road for getting downtown is Queensferry Road, which joins Charlotte Square close to the west end of Princes Street.

By Plane
At present, Edinburgh Airport offers no transatlantic flights. **Glasgow Airport** (☎ 0141/887–1111, ext. 4552), 50 miles west of Edinburgh, is now the major point of entry into Edinburgh for transatlantic flights (☞ Glasgow A to Z *in* Chapter 4).

Edinburgh Airport (☎ 0131/333–1000), 7 miles west of the city, has airlinks throughout the United Kingdom—London Heathrow/Gatwick/Stansted/Luton, Aberdeen, Birmingham, Bristol, Dundee, East Midlands, Humberside, Kirkwall (Orkney), Leeds/Bradford, Manchester, Norwich, Shetland, Southampton, and Belfast in Northern Ireland—as well as with a number of European cities, including Amsterdam, Brussels, Copenhagen, and Dublin. There are flights to Edinburgh Airport virtually every hour from London's Gatwick and Heathrow airports; it's usually faster and less complicated to fly through Gatwick (which has excellent rail service from London's Victoria Station). Airlines serving Edinburgh include British Airways, British Midland, Air UK, BusinessAir, Easyjet, Servisair, Sabena, Aer Lingus, and Air France.

Prestwick Airport (☎ 01292/479822), southwest of Glasgow, after some years of eclipse by Glasgow Airport, is beginning to come back into the reckoning, not least because of the activities of **Ryanair** (☎ 0171/435–7101), a company which has sparked off a major price war on the Anglo-Scottish routes (i.e. between London and Glasgow/Edinburgh). It offers (at time of writing) unbeatable, no-frills, rock-bottom air fares between London Stansted and Prestwick.

BETWEEN EDINBURGH AIRPORT AND THE CITY CENTER

There are no rail links to the city center, despite the fact that the airport sits between two main lines. By bus or car you can usually make it to Edinburgh in a comfortable half hour, unless you hit the morning or evening rush hours (7:30–9 AM and 4–6 PM).

By Bus: Two companies, **Lothian Regional Transport** (☎ 0131/555–6363) and **Guide Friday** (☎ 0131/556–2244), run buses between Edinburgh Airport's main terminal building and Waverley Bridge, in center city and within easy reach of several hotels. The buses run every 30 minutes on weekdays (9–5) and less frequently (roughly every hour) during off-peak hours and on weekends. The trip takes about 30 minutes (about 45 minutes during rush hour). Single fare for Lothian Regional Transport is £3.20, for Guide Friday, £3.40.

By Limousine: The following Edinburgh firms provide chauffeur-driven limousines to meet flights at Edinburgh Airport: **David Grieve Chauffeur Drive** (✉ 101 Gorgie Rd., ☎ 0131/337–7770; about £30), **Scothire Chauffeur Drive** (✉ 46 Ladywell Ave., ☎ 0131/334–9017; £25), and **Sleigh Ltd.** (✉ 6 Devon Pl., ☎ 0131/337–3171; about £30–£40).

By Rental Car: There is a good choice of car rental companies operating from the terminal building. The cost is from £40 a day, depending on the firm. If you choose to plunge yourself into Edinburgh's traffic system, take care on the first couple of traffic circles (called roundabouts) you encounter on the way into town from the airport—even the most experienced drivers find them challenging. By car the airport is about 7 miles west of Princes Street downtown and is clearly marked from A8. The usual route to downtown is via the suburb of Corstorphine.

By Taxi: These are readily available outside the terminal. The trip takes 20–30 minutes to center city, 15 minutes longer during morning and evening rush hours. The fare is roughly £15. Note that because of a local regulation, airport taxis picking up fares from the terminal are any color, not the typical black cabs, although these do take fares going to the airport.

BETWEEN GLASGOW AIRPORT AND EDINBURGH

By Bus and Train: Scottish Citylink Coaches (☎ 0990/505050, FAX 0141/332–8055) buses leave Glasgow Airport every hour at quarter to the hour and five minutes past the hour to travel direct to Edinburgh's St. Andrew Square Bus Station. The trip takes one hour and 10 minutes, and costs about £6. There is also a bus at 25 minutes past the hour going to Edinburgh, which requires a change of bus at Glasgow's Buchanan Street Bus Station. On Sundays, there is one bus per hour direct to Edinburgh, leaving on the hour. A somewhat more pleasant option is to take a cab from Glasgow Airport to Glasgow's Queen Street Train Station (15 minutes, £12) and then take the train to Waverley Station in Edinburgh. Trains leave about every 30 minutes; the trip takes 50 minutes and costs £6.70. Check times on weekends. Another, less expensive alternative—best for those with little luggage—is to take the bus from Glasgow Airport to Glasgow's Buchanan Bus Station, walk five minutes to the Queen Street train station, and catch the train to Edinburgh.

By Taxi: Taxis to downtown Edinburgh take about 70 minutes and cost around £70.

By Train

Edinburgh's main train station, **Waverley,** is downtown, below Waverley Bridge and around the corner from the unmistakable spire of the Scott Monument. Recorded information on services to King's Cross Station in London is available over the telephone for weekday service (☎ 0131/557–3000). For information on all other destinations or for other inquiries, call 0131/556–2451. King's Cross Station can be reached by dialing 0171/278–2477. Travel time from Edinburgh to London by train is as little as 4½ hours for the fastest services.

Edinburgh's other main station is **Haymarket,** about four minutes (by rail) west of Waverley. Most Glasgow and other western and northern services stop here. Haymarket can be slightly more convenient for visitors staying in hotels beyond the west end of Princes Street.

Getting Around

By Bus

Lothian Regional Transport, operating dark-red-and-white buses, is the main operator within Edinburgh. The **Edinburgh Freedom Ticket** (£2), allowing unlimited one-day travel on the city's buses, can be purchased in advance. More expensive is the **Tourist Card** (£5 for 2 days, £1.50 each additional day), available in units of 2 to 13 days, which gives unlimited access to buses (except Airlink) and includes vouchers for savings on tours and entrance fees. ⊠ *27 Hanover St.,* ☎ *0131/555— 6363.* ☉ *Mar.–Oct., Mon.–Sat. 8 AM–7 PM, Sun. 9–4:15; Nov.–Feb., Mon.–Sat. 8–6, closed Sun.*

S.M.T. (⊠ St. Andrew Square Bus Station, ☎ 0131/558–1616), operating green and cream buses, provides much of the service between Edinburgh and the Lothians and offers day tours around and beyond the city. You will also see other bus companies, including **Eastern Scottish, Lowland Scottish,** and **Midland Scottish** (all part of First Bus Co., along with S.M.T.) and **Fife Scottish,** which operate routes into and out of Edinburgh to other parts of Scotland.

By Car

Driving in Edinburgh has its quirks and pitfalls, but competent drivers should not be intimidated. Metered parking in the center city is scarce and expensive, and the local traffic wardens are alert. Note that illegally parked cars are routinely wheel-clamped and towed away, and getting your car back will be expensive. After 6 PM the parking situation improves considerably, and you may manage to find a space quite near your hotel, even downtown. If you park on a yellow line or in a resident's parking bay, be prepared to move your car by 8 AM the following morning, when the rush hour gets under way.

Princes Street is usually considered the city center. The street runs east–west; motorists using the A1 east-coast road enter the city from the east end of Princes Street. Using the city bypass, it is possible to reach key points to the west, such as the airport or the Forth Road Bridge (gateway to the north), from many parts of the outskirts and from East Lothian without getting tangled up in downtown traffic.

By Taxi

Taxi stands can be found throughout the downtown area; the following locations are the most convenient: the west end of Princes Street, South St. David Street, and North St. Andrew Street (both just off St.

Andrew Sq.), Waverley Market, Waterloo Place, and Lauriston Place. Alternatively, hail any taxi displaying an illuminated FOR HIRE sign.

By Train
Edinburgh has no urban or suburban rail systems.

Contacts and Resources

Car-Rental Agencies
Avis (☎ 0131/333–1866), **Alamo** (☎ 0131/344–3250), **Europcar** (☎ 0131/344–3114), and **Hertz** (☎ 0131/344–3260) have booths at the airport.

Consulates
American Consulate General (✉ 3 Regent Terr., ☎ 0131/556–8315).

The London office of the **Canadian High Commission** (☎ 0171/258–6316) can provide local information for visitors.

Emergencies
For **police, ambulance,** or **fire,** dial 999. No coins are needed for emergency calls made from pay phones.

Guided Tours
EXCURSIONS

Both **Lothian Regional Transport** and **Scotline Tours** (☞ Orientation Tours, *below*) offer day trips to destinations such as St. Andrews and Fife or the Trossachs and Loch Lomond.

ORIENTATION TOURS

Scottish Tourist Guides (contact Bob Motion, ✉ 14 East Court, Thistle Foundation, Niddrie Mains Rd., Edinburgh, EH16 4ED, ☎ FAX 0131/661–7977), endorsed by the Scottish Tourist Board, offers knowledgeable guides appropriate for an individual or a group. The tours are wide ranging and flexible.

Lothian Regional Transport's Edinburgh Classic Tour provides a worthwhile introduction to the Old and New Towns. The ticket is a bargain because it is valid on any other Lothian bus (except Airlink and night buses) for the remainder of the day. There are frequent departures from Waverley Bridge (outside the rail station) and other points around the city. Open-top buses operate in suitable weather. This is a flexible, show-up-and-hop-on service, meaning that you can get off the bus at any attractions you may want to see more closely. Allow an hour for the complete tour. You can buy tickets from the Lothian Regional Transport office on Hanover Street (☞ Getting Around, *above*), or you can buy them from the driver. 🎫 £5.

Scotline Tours' City Tour offers a comprehensive introduction to the city, as well as visits to Edinburgh Castle, the High Kirk of St. Giles, and the Palace of Holyroodhouse. Allow at least four hours for the entire tour. Scotline also offers a range of day tours to points beyond the city. ✉ 87 High St., ☎ 0131/557–0162. 🎫 £9. Call 8 AM–11 PM for reservations.

Guide Friday, Ltd., also offers an orientation tour. It runs less frequently than Lothian Regional Transport's equivalent, but you may enjoy riding through the streets of Edinburgh on one of Guide Friday's cheerful open-top, double-decker buses. The commentaries provided tend to be more colorful than accurate. The minimum tour time is one hour and buses leave from Waverley Bridge. ✉ Reception Centre, Waverley Station, ☎ 0131/556–2244. 🎫 £6.50.

Scottish Tourist Guides (☎ 0131/661–7977; ☞ Orientation Tours, *above*) can supply guides (in 19 languages) who are fully qualified and will meet clients at any point of entry into the United Kingdom or Scotland.

Scottish Tourist Guides (☞ Orientation Tours, *above*) will design tours tailored to your interests; it also offers a special Nightlife Tour. The **Cadies and Witchery Tours** (☞ *below*) operates a Ghosts and Ghouls tour through the narrow Old Town alleyways and closes with costumed guides and other theatrical characters showing up en route.

Robin's Edinburgh Tours, run by an Edinburgh native, offers a number of tours built around specific themes, such as Georgian Edinburgh, Robert Burns in Edinburgh, and Holyrood Royal Park, as well as a range of talks and slide shows. ⊠ *66 Willowbrae Rd.,* ☎ *0131/661– 0125.* 🖃 *From £4.*

The **Cadies and Witchery Tours,** fully qualified members of the Scottish Tourist Guides Association, have since 1983 steadily built a reputation for combining entertainment and historical accuracy in their lively, enthusiastic, and varied walking tours through the Old Town. ☎ *0131/225–6745.* 🖃 *£5.*

Hospital
Edinburgh Royal Infirmary (⊠ 51 Lauriston Pl., ☎ 0131/536–1000) is south of the city center—down George IV Bridge and then to the right.

Late-Night Pharmacies
You can find out which pharmacy is open late on a given night by looking at the notice posted on every pharmacy-shop door. A pharmacy— or "dispensing chemist"—is easily identified by its sign, showing a green cross on a white background.

Boots (⊠ 48 Shandwick Pl., west end of Princes St., ☎ 0131/225–6757) is open Monday–Saturday 8–9, Sunday 10–5.

Lost and Found
To retrieve lost property, try the **Lothian and Borders Police Headquarters** (⊠ Fettes Ave., ☎ 0131/311–3131).

Maps
Several excellent city maps are available at bookshops. Particularly recommended: the *Bartholomew Edinburgh Plan,* with a scale of approximately 4 inches to 1 mile, by the once-independent and long-established Edinburgh cartographic company John Bartholomew and Sons Ltd.

Post Offices
The post office in the St. James Centre is the most central (⊠ St Andrew Sq., ☎ 0131/556–0478. ☉ Mon. 9–5:30, Tues.–Fri. 8:30–5:30, Sat. 8:30–6). Other main post offices in the city center are at 40 Frederick Street and 7 Hope Street. Many newsagents also sell stamps.

Travel Agencies
American Express ⊠ 139 Princes St., ☎ 0131/225–7881. **Thomas Cook** ⊠ 79a Princes St., ☎ 0131/220–4039.

Visitor Information
Edinburgh and Scotland Information Centre, adjacent to Waverley Station (follow the TIC signs in the station and throughout the city) offers an accommodations service (Book-A-Bed-Ahead) in addition to the more typical services offered. ⊠ *3 Princes St.,* ☎ *0131/557–1700,*

FAX *0131/557–5118.* ☉ *May, June, Sept., Mon.–Sat. 9–8, Sun. 10–8; July, Aug., Mon.–Sat. 9–9, Sun. 10–9; Oct.–Apr., Mon.–Sat. 9–6, Sun. 10–6.*

Complete information is also available at the tourist-information desk at **Edinburgh Airport.** ☎ *0131/333–1000.* ☉ *Apr.–Oct., Mon.–Sat. 8:30 AM–9:30 PM, Sun. 9:30–9:30; Nov.–Mar., weekdays 8:30–6, weekends 9–5.*

The List, a publication available from city-center bookshops and news-agents, and *What's On in Edinburgh,* from the Edinburgh and Scotland Information Centre, both list information about all types of events, from movies and theater to sports. *The Scotsman,* a national newspaper published in Edinburgh, is good for both national and international news coverage, as well as for reviews and notices of upcoming events in Edinburgh and elsewhere in Scotland.

Where to Change Money

Most city-center banks have a **bureau de change** (usual banking hours are weekdays 9:30–4:45). The bureau de change at the Tourist Centre, Waverley Market is open on Sunday from May to September. There are also bureaux de change at **Waverley Rail Station, Edinburgh Airport,** and **Frasers** department store (west end of Princes Street).

4 Glasgow

Recent efforts at commercial and cultural renewal have restored much of the style and grandeur Glasgow had in the 19th century, at the height of its economic power. Again a vibrant metropolitan center with a thriving artistic life and notable civic buildings, Scotland's largest city is to be the "UK City of Architecture and Design" in 1999. It is a convenient touring center, as well, in easy reach of the Clyde coast to the south and with excellent transportation links to the rest of Scotland.

By John
Hutchinson

Updated by
Gilbert
Summers

IN THE DAYS WHEN BRITAIN still had an empire, Glasgow pronounced itself the Second City of the Empire. The people of Glasgow were justifiably proud of their city, since it was there that Britain's great steamships (including the 80,000-ton *Queen Elizabeth*) were built. The term *Clydebuilt* (from Glasgow's River Clyde) became synonymous with good workmanship and lasting quality. It was also the Glaswegians who built the railway engines that opened up the Canadian prairies, the South African veldt, the Australian plains, and the Indian subcontinent. Scots engineers were to be found wherever there were engines (and so it was perhaps no coincidence that even Captain Kirk on the Starship *Enterprise* had to say, "Beam me up, Scottie" to his engineer).

Scholars have argued for years about what the name Glasgow means (pronounce it to rhyme with *toe* and stress the first syllable), but, generally, "dear green place" is the interpretation that finds most favor today. Most suitable it is, too, for a town that, despite industrialization, has more city parks than anywhere else in Britain, and even the famous River Clyde is now clean enough for trout and salmon.

Glasgow first came into prominence in Scottish history somewhere around 1,400 years ago, and typically for this rambunctious city it was all to do with an argument between a husband and his wife. One of the local chieftains suspected, with some justification, that his wife had been having an affair, so he crept up on the suspect, one of his knights, and took from him a ring that she had rather foolishly given her lover—foolishly, because it had originally been given to her by her husband. The furious husband flung the ring into the River Clyde, then told his wife the next day that he wanted her to wear it that evening. The lady was distraught and called on the local holy man, Mungo, to help. Clearly a useful man to have in a tricky situation, Mungo sent a monk out fishing, and the first bite the monk had was a salmon with the ring in its mouth. Whether the lady learned her lesson or called on Mungo's services regularly after that, history does not relate.

Mungo features in two other legends: one of a pet bird that he nursed back to life and another, of a bush or tree, the branches of which he used to relight a fire. Tree, bird, and the salmon with a ring in its mouth are all to be found on the city of Glasgow's coat of arms, together with a bell that Mungo brought from Rome. Mungo is now the city's patron saint. His tomb is to be found in the mighty medieval cathedral that bears his name.

Glasgow led a fairly quiet existence in the Middle Ages. Its cathedral was the center of religious life, and although the city was made a Royal Burgh in 1175 by King William the Lion, its population was never more than a few thousand. What changed Glasgow irrevocably and laid the foundations for its immense prosperity was the Treaty of Union between Scotland and England in 1707. This allowed Scotland to trade with the essentially English colonies in America, and with their expansion Glasgow prospered. In came cotton, tobacco, and rum; out went various Scottish manufactured goods and clothing. The key to it all in the early days was tobacco, and the prosperous merchants were known as the "tobacco lords." It was they who ran the city, and their wealth laid the foundation stone for the manufacturing industries of the 19th century.

As Glasgow prospered, so her population grew. The "dear green place" became built over. The original medieval city around the cathedral and the High Street expanded westward. The 18th-century Merchant City, today the subject of a great deal of refurbishment, lies just to the south and west of George Square, and the houses of the merchants are even farther westward, along the gridiron pattern of Glasgow's streets up the hill toward Blytheswood Square.

But the city is not known as an 18th-century city; that honor is left to Edinburgh, in the east. Rather, Glasgow is known as one of the greatest Victorian cities in Europe. The population grew from 80,000 in 1801 to more than 700,000 in 1901, and with this enormous growth there developed also a sense of exuberance and confidence that is reflected in its public buildings. The City Chambers, built in 1888, are an extravaganza of marble and red sandstone, a clear symbol of the Victorian merchants' hopes for the future.

Yet, always at the forefront of change, Glasgow boasts, side by side with the overtly Victorian, an architectural vision of the future in the work of Charles Rennie Mackintosh. The Glasgow School of Art, the Willow Tearoom, and the churches and school buildings he designed point clearly to the clarity and simplicity of 20th-century lines.

Today, Glasgow has taken the best of the past and adapted it for the needs of the present day. The "dear green places" still remain in the city-center parks; the medieval cathedral stands proud, as it has done for 800 years; the Merchant City is revived and thriving; the Victorian splendor has been cleaned of its grime and will look good for many years to come; and the cultural legacy of museums and performing arts lives on stronger than ever. To cap it all, its superb location also makes it an ideal base from which to enjoy day tours of the Scottish countryside. Burns Country, the gardens of Galloway, the islands of the Clyde, Loch Lomond, the Trossachs, and Argyll are only about an hour or so from the city center, as is Edinburgh.

Pleasures and Pastimes

Dining
The restaurants of Glasgow have diversified over the past several years; as a result, this is one of the cities in Scotland where you'll find Chinese, Italian, and Indian food in addition to the usual French and Scottish offerings. Glasgow also has a strong café culture: Visit one or two to get a feel for this important part of the city. Pubs are also good bets for cheap lunches.

Lodging
Glasgow is now better equipped with hotels of all categories than it has ever been. The city has become a major business destination in the past several years, with the Scottish Conference and Exhibition Centre serving as the focal point. There are now some big city-center hotels (including the Hilton and Marriott) of both expensive and moderate character, and some good and reasonable small hotels and guest houses in the suburbs (in most cases, transportation into town is quick and dependable). All the larger hotels have restaurants open to nonguests.

Shopping
The old image of industrial Glasgow has changed considerably in recent years as the city has strenuously shrugged off its poor-cousin-to-Edinburgh label. Glaswegians are clotheshorses, and you'll find some of the world's best clothes at the many stores and malls which have helped to improve Glasgow's stature as a shopping city. Princes Square is a particularly good place to go if you're looking to enhance your wardrobe (and are willing to break the bank to do it).

EXPLORING GLASGOW

The city center is relatively flat, making for easy walking between such sights as the ancient cathedral; Provand's Lordship, the oldest house in Glasgow; the High Street; and the center of medieval activity, the Merchant City, which developed as Glasgow prospered. The River Clyde, on which Glasgow's trade across the Atlantic developed, is always at the center of the city, cutting it in half and offering often surprising views across to the buildings on the other side.

In the quieter, slightly hillier western part of the city is the University of Glasgow and that other "forgotten" side of Glasgow, unjustly perceived as a grimy center of heavy industry.

Great Itineraries

Glasgow is not like Edinburgh and its layout cannot be read in a single glance. However, its city center is a straightforward grid of streets that reward exploration on foot, and a visitor would do well to note the often ornate detailing above eye-level. Glasgow's strengths are, first, its wealth of cultural sites and, second, the best shopping in Scotland. To allow time to make the most of both, you could easily plan for four or five days.

IF YOU HAVE 2 DAYS

Glaswegians are particularly proud of the **Burrell Collection** in **Pollok Country Park,** so it should top your list of must-sees. The **cathedral** offers a historic focus, while Buchanan Street's shops, including the Princes Square development, offer the best of the city's commercial offerings. If time permits, add in the Charles Rennie Mackintosh material at the **Hunterian Art Gallery.** At the end of your days, remember Glasgow's pubs and clubs offer great entertainment till late in the evening.

IF YOU HAVE 5 DAYS

Five days allows enough time to add to the brief tour Glasgow's other key museums and cultural attractions: the new **Glasgow Gallery of Modern Art** in the city center or the **St. Mungo Museum** to the east. Toward the western edge of the city, the cluster of museums by the Kelvingrove Park (**Kelvingrove, Hunterian Art Gallery,** and **Museum of Transport**) need at least a day in themselves. For a good day trip out of the city, take the train to **Weymss Bay** (it's about an hour ride from Glasgow city center), and from there take the ferry to the **Isle of Bute,** home to the spectacular Victorian Gothic **Mount Stuart** house.

IF YOU HAVE 10 DAYS

Ten days based in Glasgow will allow you to thoroughly explore all of its museums (you may well want to visit the **Burrell Collection** more than once). Shopping in Princes Square can easily occupy at least a morning, while Buchanan Street and Sauchiehall Street will also reward the inveterate shopper. In the event you feel you have exhausted the city's possibilities, make time for at least one of the recommended side trips. The Clyde Coast and Ayrshire can take up at least two days—possibly three if you make the most of all the opportunities it offers: **Mount Stuart** house on the **Isle of Bute**; **Ayr** and **Alloway,** which will delight Robert Burns enthusiasts; while **Culzean Castle**—its Georgian elegance a sharp contrast to Mount Stuart—is another essential stop. Travel up the Clyde Valley to **Lanark** to spend a morning at New Lanark, the now-restored site of an 18th-century social experiment in improving the lives of mill workers; you will also be able to enjoy beautiful walks along the waterfall-dotted River Clyde here. **Biggar** will fill an afternoon or more with its fascinating museums, including Moat Park, which has an unusually fine embroidery collection.

Medieval Glasgow and the Merchant City

In this central part of the city there are not only surviving medieval build-ings, but also some of the best examples of the architectural confidence and exuberance that so characterized the Glasgow of 100 years ago. Today this area is experiencing a renaissance and a newfound appreciation.

A Good Walk

Numbers in the text correspond to numbers in the margin and on the Glasgow and Glasgow Excursions: Ayrshire and the Clyde Valley exploring maps.

George Square ①, the focal point of Glasgow's business district, is the natural starting point for any walking tour. It's in the very heart of Glasgow and convenient to the Buchanan Street bus and underground sta-tions and parking lot, as well as to the Queen Street railway station. After viewing the **City Chambers** ② on the east side of the square, leave George Square by the northeast corner and head eastward through a not particularly pretty part of the city along George Street, past the University of Strathclyde. Turn left at High Street, then go up the hill to **Glasgow Cathedral** ③, the **St. Mungo Museum and Cathedral Visi-tor Center,** and the fascinating if macabre **Necropolis** ④ burying ground just off Cathedral Square.

Opposite the cathedral, across Castle Street, is **Provand's Lordship** ⑤, Glasgow's oldest house. Retrace your steps down Castle Street and High Street. Look for the Greek goddess Pallas on top of the imposing gray sandstone building on the right, the former Bank of Scotland building, before reaching the Tolbooth Steeple at **Glasgow Cross** ⑥. Continue east along London Road (under the bridge) about a quarter of a mile and you'll come to **The Barras** ⑦ ("barrows", or pushcarts), Scotland's largest indoor market. Turn down Greendyke Street from London Road to reach **Glasgow Green** ⑧ by the River Clyde, with the **People's Palace** ⑨ museum of social history as its centerpiece.

Go back to Greendykes Street, past the new St. Andrew's Square de-velopment—with the magnificent St. Andrew's Church (1750) as its centerpiece—then via Saltmarket northwards to Tolbooth Steeple. Continue westward along Trongate. This is where the powerful "to-bacco lords" who traded with the Americas presided. On the right, down Albion Street, are the offices of Glasgow's daily papers, the *Herald* and the *Evening Times*. On the left, jutting out into Trongate, is the Tron Steeple, all that remains of a church burned down in 1793 when a joke by the local chapter of the Hell-Fire Club (young aristocratic trouble-makers) got a little out of hand. The rebuilt church has now been con-verted into the Tron Theatre.

Continue down the Trongate, then turn right into Hutcheson Street. This is Glasgow's **Merchant City,** with many handsome restored Geor-gian and Victorian buildings. At the end of the street, just south of George Square, look for **Hutcheson's Hall** ⑩, a visitor center, shop, and regional office for the National Trust for Scotland. Turn west onto Ingram Street and left down Glassford Street to see the **Trades House** on the right, which has a facade built in 1791 to designs by Robert Adam. Turn right along Wilson Street to reach Virginia Street, another favorite haunt of Glasgow's tobacco merchants. At No. 33, a former tobacco exchange survives, now an indoor shopping center. Nearby, **Virginia Court** ⑪, now somewhat faded, also echoes those far-off days. Walk northward up Virginia Street back to Ingram Street. To the left you'll have a good view down to the elegant Royal Exchange Square and the **Royal Ex-change** itself. Once a meeting place for merchants and traders, in April 1996 it became the **Glasgow Gallery of Modern Art** ⑫. Royal Ex-

Exploring Glasgow

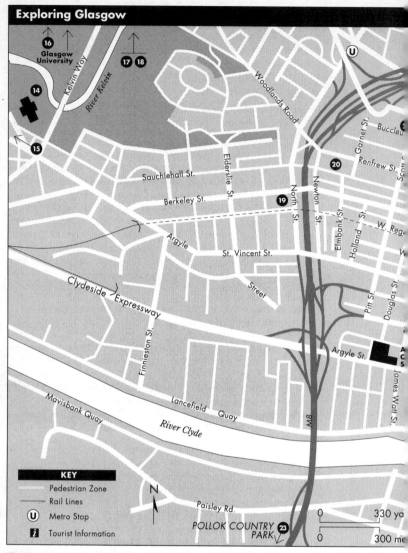

KEY

~~~ Pedestrian Zone

——— Rail Lines

Ⓤ Metro Stop

🛈 Tourist Information

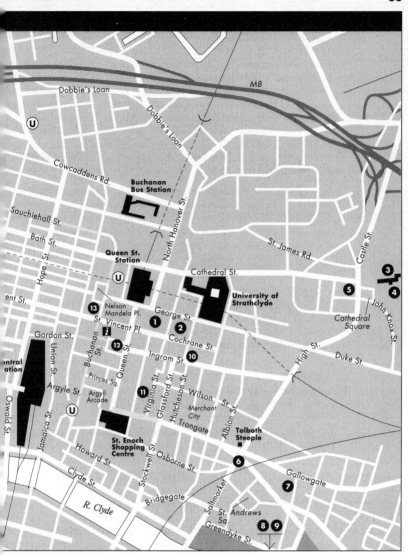

change Square leads, for pedestrians, westward to the pedestrian-zone shopping area of Buchanan Street. The Princes Square shopping mall on the east side has a particularly good selection of specialty shops.

Make your way down to Argyle Street. Looking to the west, you'll see the large railway bridge supporting the tracks going into **Central Station.** The depot is known as the Heilanman's Umbrella, because it was the point of meeting and shelter for so many Highlanders who had moved to Glasgow in search of better economic opportunities in the last century. Pause to look at the lovely iron arcading of **Gardner's Warehouse** at 36 Jamaica Street. Head north up Union Street and note the extraordinary architecture of Nos. 84–100, the so-called **Egyptian Halls,** designed and built in 1871 by Alexander "Greek" Thomson.

From here continue north to St. Vincent Street and turn right to reach Nelson Mandela Place, also called St. George's Place. Here is the **Scottish Stock Exchange** ⑬, worthwhile for the ornate "French Venetian"–style exterior alone. George Square, your starting point, is just along West George Street.

TIMING

This walk can be accomplished comfortably in a day, which will allow time to browse in the People's Palace and the Gallery of Modern Art. Aim to start after the end of the morning rush hour, say at 10 AM, and to finish before the evening rush starts, about 4 PM, in order to avoid the worst of the traffic fumes and hurrying commuters. Remember that The Barras is only open on weekends, and the City Chambers only on weekdays.

Sights to See

❼ The Barras. Scotland's largest indoor market, named for the "barrows," or pushcarts formerly used by the stallholders, is a mecca for those addicted to searching through piles of junk for bargains. Open only on weekends, this is probably the nearest Scotland gets to a flea market. The atmosphere is always good humored, and you can find just about anything here, in any condition, from old model railroads to cheese rolls. ⊠ *A quarter of a mile east of Glasgow Cross,* ☎ *0141/552–7258.* ☞ *Free.* ⊗ *Weekends 9–5.*

★ ❷ City Chambers. Dominating the east side of George Square, this splendidly exhuberant expression of Victorian confidence was opened by Queen Victoria herself in 1888. Among the outstanding features of the interior are the vaulted ceiling of the entrance hall, marble and alabaster staircases, and the banqueting hall, as well as a number of the smaller suites, each furnished in different woods. ⊠ *George Sq.,* ☎ *0141/227–4017. Free guided tours weekdays at 10:30 and 2:30 (may be closed for occasional civic functions).*

❶ George Square. The focal point of Glasgow's business district is lined with an impressive array of statues of worthies from days gone by: Queen Victoria; Scotland's national poet Robert Burns; the inventor and developer of the steam engine, James Watt; Prime Minister William Gladstone; and towering above them all, Scotland's foremost writer, Sir Walter Scott. The column was intended for George III, after whom the square is named, but his statue was not erected after he was found to be insane toward the end of his reign. On the east side of the square stands the magnificent Italian Renaissance–style **City Chambers** (☞ *above*), and the handsome **Merchants' House** (☞ *below*) fills the corner with West George Street.

★ ❸ Glasgow Cathedral. An unusual double church, one above the other, and dedicated to St. Mungo, Glasgow's patron saint, the cathedral was begun in the 12th century and completed about 300 years later. It was spared the ravages of the Reformation, which destroyed so many of Scotland's medieval churches, because the trade guilds of Glasgow regarded it as their own church and defended it. In the lower church is the splendid crypt of St. Mungo, who is sometimes also called St. Kentigern. (Kentigern means "chief word," while Mungo is perhaps a nickname meaning "dear name.") The site of the tomb has been revered since the 6th century, when St. Mungo founded a church here. ⊠ *Cathedral St.,* ☎ *0131/668–8600.* ☑ *Free.* ⊙ *Apr.–Sept., Mon.–Sat. 9:30–6, Sun. 2–5; Oct.–Mar., Mon.–Sat. 9:30–4, Sun. 2–4, and for services.*

⑥ Glasgow Cross. This was the very center of the medieval city. The Mercat Cross (*mercat* means market), topped by a unicorn, marked the spot where merchants met, where the market was held, and where criminals were executed. Here, too, was the *tron,* or weigh beam, used to check merchants' weights, installed in 1491. The Tolbooth Steeple dates from 1626 and served as the civic center and place where travelers entering the city paid tolls.

⑫ Glasgow Gallery of Modern Art. Opened in 1996, the newest of Glasgow's many excellent galleries occupies the former **Royal Exchange** building. Designed by David Hamilton and finished in 1829, the Exchange was a meeting place for merchants and traders. It later became Stirling's Library. It incorporates the mansion built in 1780 by William Cunninghame, one of the wealthiest of the "tobacco lords." The modern art, craft, and design collections contained within this handsome building include a strong gathering of Scottish figurative art, works by Scottish artists such as Peter Howson and John Bellany, and also paintings and sculpture from elsewhere in the world, including Papua New Guinea, Ethiopia, and Mexico. The display scheme is designed to reflect, on each floor, one of the four elements—earth, air, fire, and water—which creates some unexpected juxtapositions and also allows for the incorporation of various interactive exhibits. ⊠ *Queen St.,* ☎ *0141/287–2000.* ☑ *Free.* ⊙ *Mon.–Sat. 10–5, Sun. 11–5.*

⑧ Glasgow Green. Glasgow's oldest park, by the River Clyde, has a long history as a favorite spot for public recreation and political demonstrations. Note the Nelson Column, erected long before London's; the Arch, now the finish line for the thousands of runners of the Glasgow Half Marathon; and the Templeton Business Centre, once a carpet factory, built in the late 19th century in the style of the Doge's Palace in Venice. The most significant building in the park is the **People's Palace** (☞ *below*).

★ ⑩ Hutcheson's Hall. Now a visitor center, shop, and regional office for the National Trust for Scotland, this elegant neoclassical building was designed by David Hamilton in 1802. The hall was originally a hospice founded by two brothers, George and Thomas Hutcheson; you can see their statues in niches in the facade. ⊠ *158 Ingram St.,* ☎ *0141/552–8391.* ☑ *Free.* ⊙ *Mon.–Sat. 9:30–5 (hall may be closed for occasional civic functions).*

The Merchant City. This once run-down area around Hutcheson Street is now renovated. Among the preserved Georgian and Victorian buildings are elegant designer boutiques. The **City and County Buildings** were built in 1842 to house civil servants; note the impressive arrangement of bays and Corinthian columns.

Merchants' House. On the corner of West George Street and George Square is a handsome building of 1874, topped by a golden sailing ship against the sky, a reminder of the importance of trade to Glasgow's prosperity: It is the home of Glasgow's Chamber of Commerce. Inside is a fine Merchants' Hall, embellished with stained-glass windows and many portraits. ⊠ *West side of George Sq.,* ☎ *0141/221–8272.* ☞ *Free.* ⊘ *Hall and anterooms may be seen by appointment, or from 2–4 on weekdays unless closed for meetings.*

❹ Necropolis. A burying ground since the beginning of recorded history, the Necropolis contains some extraordinarily elaborate Victorian graves, watched over by a statue of John Knox. It includes the tomb of 19th-century Glasgow merchant William Miller, author of the "Wee Willie Winkie" nursery rhyme. ⊠ *Behind Glasgow Cathedral,* ☎ *0141/333–0800.*

★ ❾ People's Palace. An impressive Victorian red sandstone building houses an intriguing museum dedicated to the city's social history; included among the exhibits is one devoted to the ordinary folk of Glasgow, called "The People's Story." Also on show are the writing desk of John McLean, the "Red Clydeside" political activist who came to Lenin's notice, and the famous "banana boots" worn on stage by Billy Connolly. Behind the museum are the well-restored Winter Gardens, a relatively sheltered spot favored by visitors who want to escape the often chilly winds whistling across the green. ⊠ *Glasgow Green,* ☎ *0141/554–0223.* ☞ *Free.* ⊘ *Mon.–Sat. 10–5, Sun. 11–5.*

❺ Provand's Lordship. Glasgow's oldest house was built in 1471 by Bishop Andrew Muirhead as a residence for churchmen. Mary, Queen of Scots, is said to have stayed here. After her day, however, the house fell into decline and was used alternately as a sweet shop, a soft-drink factory, the home of the city hangman, and a junk shop. It was eventually rescued by the city and turned into a museum. Exhibits show the house as it might have looked in its heyday. ⊠ *Castle St.,* ☎ *0141/552–8819.* ☞ *Free.* ⊘ *Mon.–Sat. 10–5, Sun. 11–5.*

St. Mungo Museum and Cathedral Visitor Center. An outstanding collection of artifacts covering the many religious groups who've settled throughout the centuries in Glasgow and the west of Scotland is on display here. The centerpiece is Salvador Dali's magnificent painting, *Christ of St. John of the Cross.* Inside there's a gift shop and a café. ⊠ *2 Castle St.,* ☎ *0141/553–2557.* ☞ *Free.* ⊘ *Mon.–Sat. 10–5, Sun. 11–5. Closed Dec. 25, Jan 1.*

⓭ Scottish Stock Exchange. Scotland's hub of commerce was built in 1877 by John Burnet, who was inspired by London's Law Courts in the Strand, designed by William Burgess. Burgess is said to have been flattered rather than perturbed by Burnet's close imitation. ⊠ *7 Nelson Mandela Place,* ☎ *0141/221–7060. Not open to the public.*

⓫ Virginia Court. Somewhat faded now, Virginia Court is a reminder of the long-gone days of the tobacco merchants who traded with the Americas. Peer through the bars of the gates and note the wagon-wheel ruts still visible in the roadway. Nearby are antiques shops, notably the Virginia Galleries with its pleasant indoor café. ⊠ *Virginia St.*

The West End

Glasgow's West End offers a stellar mix of education, culture, art, and parkland. The neighborhood is dominated by the University of Glasgow, founded in 1451, making it the third-oldest in Scotland after St. Andrews and Aberdeen, and at least 130 years ahead of the University of Edinburgh. It has thrived as a center of educational excellence, particularly in the sciences. The university buildings are set in parkland, reminding the visitor that Glasgow is a city with more green space per citizen than any other in Europe. It is also a city of museums and art galleries, having benefited from the generosity of industrial and commercial philanthropists and from the deep-seated desire of the city fathers to place Glasgow at the forefront of British cities.

A Good Walk

A good place to start is at the city's main art gallery and museum, **Kelvingrove** ⑭ in Kelvingrove Park, west of the M8 beltway, at the junction of Sauchiehall (pronounced *socky*-hall) and Argyle streets. There are parking facilities, and plenty of buses go there from downtown. Across Argyle Street in the Old Kelvin Hall exhibition center is the **Museum of Transport** ⑮.

As you walk up Kelvin Way through the trees, the skyline to your left is dominated by the Gilbert Scott building, the **University of Glasgow**'s main edifice. Turn left up University Avenue, past the Memorial Gates, which were erected in 1951 to celebrate the university's 500th birthday. On either side of the road are two important galleries, both maintained by the university. On the south side of University Avenue, in the Victorian part of the university, is the **Hunterian Museum** ⑯. Even more interesting is the **Hunterian Art Gallery** ⑰, in an unremarkable building from the 1970s across the road.

At this point you can either make a small detour to the Botanic Gardens and return along the banks of the River Kelvin to Kelvingrove Park or go directly through some of Glasgow's elegant 19th-century districts to the extreme northwest of the downtown area, where the rest of the tour resumes. The walk from the university to the **Botanic Gardens** ⑱ is unfortunately not very exciting, but it's worth the effort. Continue along University Avenue and turn right at Byres Road, going as far as Great Western Road and the Grosvenor Hotel. The 40 acres of gardens are across the busy Great Western Road.

After leaving the Botanic Gardens, cross the River Kelvin on St. Margaret Drive just past the BBC Scotland building. Turn right, then right again down the steps to the Kelvin Walkway on the north bank of the river. (Farther upstream the Kelvin Walkway connects with the West Highland Way, an official long-distance footpath leading to Fort William, approximately 100 miles away.) The walkway headed downstream back toward the city center first crosses a footbridge, then passes old mill buildings and goes under Belmont Street and the Great Western Road at Kelvinbridge. At this point it passes Kelvinbridge underground station and goes under the Gibson Street bridge, then back into Kelvingrove Park.

At this point, you can choose to take one of the paths up the hill and explore the stately Victorian crescents and streets of the park area or you can take the lower road past the fountain and head directly back to Sauchiehall Street. Whichever way you choose, you should end up, having walked eastward, at the point where Sauchiehall Street crosses the M8 motorway. Down North Street to your right (southward) you'll see the front of **Mitchell Library** ⑲, the largest public reference library in Europe. Cross the M8 motorway and continue down Sauchiehall Street to the **Regimental Museum of the Royal Highland Fusiliers** ⑳. Turn up Garnet Street and go to the top, then right on Buccleuch (pronounced buck-*loo*) Street. On the left is the **Tenement House** ㉑, a special find tucked away from normal tourist routes. Coming out of the Tenement House, turn east on Buccleuch Street to Scott Street. As you turn south on Scott Street, notice the mural that reflects the name of the area, Garnethill, then turn left onto Renfrew Street to reach Charles Rennie Mackintosh's masterpiece, the **Glasgow School of Art** ㉒. To return to the city center either continue down Scott Street, then east on

Sauchiehall Street or turn south down Blythswood Street, noting the elegant Blythswood Square (1823–29).

TIMING

At least a day is needed for this walk, and even then you will not manage to see all you want to at the Kelvingrove and Hunterian museums; if you anticipate lingering at the museums and galleries, each of which could take up an enjoyable day in itself, plan to allow two days. The Tenement House is only open in the afternoon.

Sights to See

⑱ Botanic Gardens. Begun by the Royal Botanical Institute of Glasgow in 1842, the displays here include an herb garden, a wide range of tropical plants, and a world-famous collection of orchids. The most spectacular building in the complex is the **Kibble Palace,** built in 1873; it was originally the conservatory of a Victorian eccentric named John Kibble. Its domed, interlinked greenhouses contain tree ferns, palm trees, temperate plants, and the Tropicarium, where you can experience the lushness of a tropical rain forest. Elsewhere on the grounds are more conventional greenhouses, as well as well-maintained lawns and colorful flower beds. ⊠ *Great Western Rd.,* ☎ *0141/334–2422.* ⊠ *Free. Gardens:* ☉ *daily 7–dusk; Kibble Palace:* ☉ *Mon.–Sat. 10–4:45, Sun. 12–4:45; other greenhouses:* ☉ *weekdays 10–12 and 1–4:45 (all close at 4:15 in winter).*

★ **㉒ Glasgow School of Art.** This building—exterior and interior, structure, furnishings, and decoration—forms a unified whole, reflecting the inventive genius of Charles Rennie Mackintosh, who was only 28 years old when he won the competition for its design. Architects and designers from all over the world come to admire it, but because it is a working school of art, general visitor access is sometimes limited. Conducted tours are available, and there is always the chance that you can have a quick look inside. It's best to call ahead for more information. ⊠ *167 Renfrew St.,* ☎ *0141/353–4500.*

NEED A   The **Willow Tearoom** (⊠ 217 Sauchiehall St., ☎ 0141/332–0521) has
BREAK?   been restored to its original, archtypal Charles Rennie Mackintosh Art
             Nouveau design, right down to the decorated tables and chairs. The
             building was designed by Mackintosh in 1903 for Miss Kate Cranston,
             who ran a chain of tearooms. The tree motifs are echoed in the street
             address, since *sauchie* is an old Scots word for *willow.*

★ **⑰ Hunterian Art Gallery.** This gallery, part of the University of Glasgow, houses William Hunter's collection of paintings (his antiquarian collection is housed in the Hunterian Museum nearby), together with prints and drawings by Reynolds, Rodin, Rembrandt, and Tintoretto, as well as a major collection of paintings by James McNeill Whistler, who had a great affection for the city that bought one of his earliest paintings. Also in the gallery is a replica of Charles Rennie Mackintosh's town house, which used to stand nearby. The rooms are all furnished with Mackintosh's distinctive Art Nouveau chairs, tables, beds, and cupboards, and the walls are decorated in the equally distinctive style devised by him and his wife, Margaret. ⊠ *Glasgow University, Hillhead St.,* ☎ *0141/330–5431.* ⊠ *Free.* ☉ *Mon.–Sat. 9:30–5. Mackintosh House closed for lunch 12:30–1:30.*

⑯ Hunterian Museum. The city's oldest museum (1807) and part of the University of Glasgow, the Hunterian houses part of the collections of William Hunter, an 18th-century Glasgow doctor who assembled a staggering quantity of extremely valuable material. (The doctor's art treasures are housed in the Hunterian Art Gallery nearby.) The museum displays Hunter's hoards of coins, manuscripts, scientific instruments, and archaeological artifacts in a striking Gothic building. ⊠ *Glasgow University,* ☎ *0141/330–4221.* ⌑ *Free.* ☉ *Mon.–Sat. 9:30–5.*

★ ⑭ **Kelvingrove.** Looking like a combination of cathedral and castle, a magnificently ornamented red sandstone edifice dating from the early part of this century contains Glasgow's main museum and art gallery. There has always been debate as to which facade is the front and which is the back. However you enter, Kelvingrove houses what is claimed to be Britain's finest civic collection of British and Continental paintings, with 17th-century Dutch art, a selection from the French Barbizon school, French Impressionism, Scottish art from the 17th century to the present, silver, ceramics, European armor, and even Egyptian archaeological finds. ⊠ *Kelvingrove Park,* ☎ *0141/287–2000,* ⌑ *Free.* ☉ *Mon.–Sat. 10–5, Sun. 11–5.*

Kelvingrove Park. Taking its name from the River Kelvin, which flows through it, the land for this park was purchased by the city in 1852. Apart from the abundance of statues of prominent Glaswegians, including Lord Kelvin, the scientist who pioneered a great deal of work in electricity, the park is graced by a massive fountain commemorating a Lord Provost of Glasgow from the 1850s, a duck pond, a play area, a small open-air theater, and lots of exotic trees. It can be a charming retreat from the noise and bustle of the city.

⑲ **Mitchell Library.** The largest public reference library in Europe houses over a million volumes, including what is claimed to be the largest collection on Robert Burns in the world. The library's founder, Stephen Mitchell, who died in 1874 (the same year the library was founded), is commemorated by a bust in the entrance hall. Minerva, goddess of wisdom, looks down from the library's dome, encouraging the library's users and frowning at the drivers thundering along the motorway just in front of her. The western facade (at the back) is particularly beautiful. ⊠ *North St.,* ☎ *0141/287–2931.* ⌑ *Free.* ☉ *Weekdays 9–9, Sat. 9–5.*

★ ⑮ **Museum of Transport.** Here Glasgow's history of locomotive building is dramatically displayed with full-size exhibits. The collection of Clyde-built ship models is world famous. Anyone who remembers Britain in the 1950s will be able to wallow in nostalgia at the re-created street scene from that era. ⊠ *Kelvin Hall, 1 Bunhouse Rd.,* ☎ *0141/287–2000.* ⌑ *Free.* ☉ *Mon.–Sat. 10–5, Sun. 11–5.*

⑳ **Regimental Museum of the Royal Highland Fusiliers.** This museum displays the history of a famous regiment and the men who served in it. Exhibits include medals, badges, and uniforms. ⊠ *518 Sauchiehall St.,* ☎ *0141/332–0961.* ⌑ *Free.* ☉ *Mon.–Thurs. 9–4:30, Fri. 9–4, weekends by appointment only.*

★ ㉑ **The Tenement House.** This ordinary, simple city-center apartment is anything but ordinary inside: It was occupied from 1911 to 1965 by the same woman, Miss Agnes Toward, who seems never to have thrown anything away. What is left is a fascinating time capsule, painstakingly preserved with her everyday furniture and belongings. The red sandstone tenement building itself dates from 1892. ⊠ *145 Buccleuch St.,* ☎ *0141/333–0183.* ⌑ *£2.60.* ☉ *Mar.–Oct., daily 2–5 (last admission 4:30).*

University of Glasgow. The Gilbert Scott Building, the University of Glasgow's main edifice, was built just over a century ago and is a good example of the Gothic Revival style. The **University of Glasgow Visitor Centre** has exhibits on the university, a coffee bar, and a gift shop, and is the starting point for walking tours of the campus. ⊠ *Univer-*

sity Ave., ☎ 0141/330–5511. 🎟 *Free.* ⏰ *Mon.–Sat. 9:30–5; also Sun. 2–5 from May–Sept.*

DINING

See Pleasures and Pastimes, *above,* for an overview of Glasgow dining.

WHAT TO WEAR

In the majority of Glasgow's restaurants, almost anything goes—T-shirts and jeans included. However, a few upmarket establishments encourage more formal attire (jacket, or jacket and tie), and this is noted.

CATEGORY	COST*
$$$$	over £40
$$$	£30–£40
$$	£15–£30
$	under £15

*per person for a three-course meal, including VAT and excluding drinks and service

$$$ ★ ✕ **Rogano.** This restaurant's art deco interior, modeled after the style of the *Queen Mary* liner—bird's eye maple paneling, chrome trim, and dramatic ocean murals—is enough to recommend it; the excellent food in the sumptuous main restaurant, the lively downstairs **Café Rogano** diner, and the oyster bar near the entrance are bonuses. Portions are generous in the main restaurant, where specialties include game terrine and classic seafood dishes that are impeccably prepared. Downstairs, where the menu changes monthly, the brasserie-style food is more modern and imaginative; the menu might list clam chowder or Mediterranean grilled swordfish. The theater menu provides early-evening and late-night bargains, and the fixed-price lunch menu is popular upstairs. Rogano is patronized by the Glasgow establishment and visiting glitterati, who appreciate, as you will, the extremely good service. ✉ *11 Exchange Pl.,* ☎ *0141/248–4055. Jacket and tie. AE, DC, MC, V. Closed bank holidays.*

$$–$$$ ★ ✕ **Buttery.** This restaurant's exquisite Victorian–Edwardian surroundings are echoed by the staff's period uniforms. The best Scottish fish, beef, and game is on the menu, as well as excellent vegetarian dishes. Try the grilled fillet of brill with peppercorn butter. Service is friendly and the ambience relaxed. ✉ *652 Argyle St.,* ☎ *0141/221–8188. AE, DC, MC, V. Closed Sun. No lunch Sat.*

$$ ✕ **Drum and Monkey.** This spectacular bar-restaurant in relaxed Victorian surroundings is a popular lunch and after-work meeting place. Snacks and bar meals are appetizing, and the bistro serves exceptional Scottish–French cuisine; try the lamb cutlets, pan-fried with herbs, and the carrot and orange soup. ✉ *93–95 St. Vincent St.,* ☎ *0141/221–6636. AE, DC, MC, V.*

$$ ✕ **Loon Fung.** There is plenty of space in this popular Cantonese restaurant, which was once a cinema and now seats 200. The pleasant and efficient staff guides you enthusiastically through the house specialties, including the famed dim sum. If you like seafood, try the deep-fried won ton with prawns, crispy stuffed crab claws, or lobster in garlic and cheese sauce. The business lunch and fixed-price dinner are reasonably priced. ✉ *417 Sauchiehall St.,* ☎ *0141/332–1240. AE, MC, V.*

$$ ✕ **Malmaison Café Bar and Brasserie.** A hotel basement (☞ Lodging, *below*) fitted with wooden booths provides a quiet, relaxed environment to appreciate a varied British–Continental menu. Traditional favorites like grilled liver and bacon with caramelized onion, or Cumberland sausage and mash, appear alongside classic French coq au vin. For dessert

try the creamed rice pudding with Armagnac prunes. ✉ *278 W. George St.,* ☎ *0141/221–6401. Reservations essential. AE, DC, MC, V.*

$$ ✗ **Two Fat Ladies.** It's easy to mistake this restaurant for an all-night grocery because the kitchen can be seen through the window. The dining room has no ornamentation of any sort, just varnished wooden tables, nicotine-yellow walls, and a wooden floor. The cooking, however, compensates for the austere decor. Fish predominates—fresh and prepared with imagination and skill. Squad lobster, turbot, John Dory, and monkfish are a typical selection. Portions are generous; the salads, colossal. Desserts are less interesting—*tiramisù* (ladyfingers with mascarpone, chocolate, and espresso), apple tart, and chocolate mousse—and the wine list is, like the decor, minimalist. Unforgettable, nevertheless. ✉ *88 Dumbarton Rd.,* ☎ *0141/339–1944. MC, V. Closed Sun., Mon., and 2 wks in early Jan. No lunch Fri. and Sat.*

$$ ✗ **The Ubiquitous Chip.** Set in a courtyard inside a Victorian mews (once used for stables) with a fountain and lots of plants, this is one of the most interesting locales in which to relax over a meal. The menu changes daily but usually includes seafood from the West Coast, roedeer steaks, and lamb. For traditionalists there is braised venison and silverside, and for the more adventurous, pigeon with wild mushroom sauce or turbot with a crust of pine nuts. The cellar here is the best in the city, with a comprehensive wine list and a huge selection of single malts. Lunches are informal; a large variety of salads and one or two hot dishes are served. The clientele is steady—executives from the nearby BBC headquarters and academics from Glasgow University. ✉ *12 Ashton La.,* ☎ *0141/334–5007. AE, DC, MC, V.*

$–$$ ✗ **Café Gandolfi.** Once a Victorian pub, this café's location and decor reflect its trend-setting aspirations. On the edge of the Merchant City, it is now a haven for the design-conscious under-thirty crowd. Wooden tables and chairs carved by Scottish artist Tim Stead are so fluidly shaped it is hard to believe they're inanimate. The café opens early for breakfast, serving croissants, eggs *en cocotte* (casserole-style), and espresso. The rest of the day is filled with interesting soups, salads, local specialties, and Mediterranean favorites. Don't miss the smoked venison or the finnan haddie. Homemade ice cream and good pastries ensure busy afternoons, and evenings are livened up with good beers but less compelling wines. ✉ *64 Albion St.,* ☎ *0141/552–6813. MC, V.*

$–$$ ✗ **Cottier's.** A converted Victorian church with interior decor by Glasgow artist Daniel Cottier is the unusual setting for this theater bar and restaurant (the Arts Theatre is attached). Red walls warm the downstairs bar with its beamed ceilings. Chicken in pumpkin-seed sauce or Colombian beef and dried fruit stew might be among the South American dishes on the menu. ✉ *93 Hyndland St.,* ☎ *0141/357–5825. AE, DC, MC, V. Closed Dec. 25, Jan. 1.*

$–$$ ✗ **Janssens Café Restaurant.** Described as "Amsterdam in Glasgow," this restaurant has spare but pleasantly relaxing surroundings in which to enjoy a Continental menu served by a friendly Dutch staff. Pita bread filled with grilled lamb, or gratinéed mussels are typical of the dishes served, and there are lots of fresh salads. ✉ *1355 Argyle St.,* ☎ *0141/ 334–9682. MC, V.*

$ ✗ **Ali Baba's Balti Bar.** Balti—a kind of Indian stir-fry served in the pan in which it is cooked—has become very popular in Glasgow in recent years; this was the first Balti restaurant in the city. There's a comfortable sofa to sprawl in for pre-dinner drinks, and spacious dining areas decorated à la "Arabian Nights." Try the *pakora* (spicy fritters), lamb *kofta* (simmered meatballs), or delicious *aloo sag* (potato and spinach) balti. The service is fast and efficient. ✉ *54 W. Regent St.,* ☎ *0141/332–6289. AE, MC, V.*

Glasgow Dining and Lodging

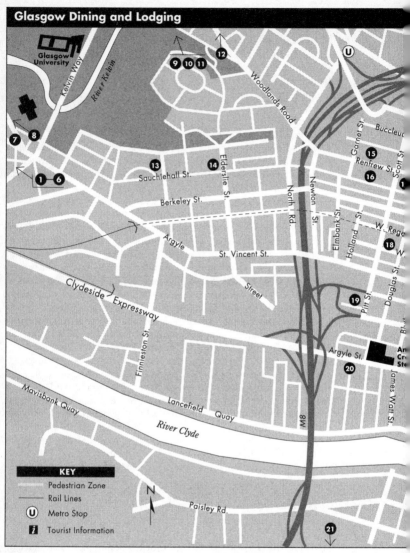

KEY
- Pedestrian Zone
- Rail Lines
- Ⓤ Metro Stop
- 𝒊 Tourist Information

Dining

Ali Baba's
Balti Bar, **23**

Ashoka West
End, **4**

The Bay Tree, **12**

Buttery, **20**

Café Gandolfi, **27**

CCA Café/Bar, **17**

Cottier's, **8**

Drum and Monkey, **24**

Fazzi Café Bar, **22**

Janssens
Café Restaurant, **7**

Loon Fung, **16**

Malmaison Café Bar
and Brasserie, **18**

Rogano, **25**

Two Fat Ladies, **5**

The Ubiquitous
Chip, **2**

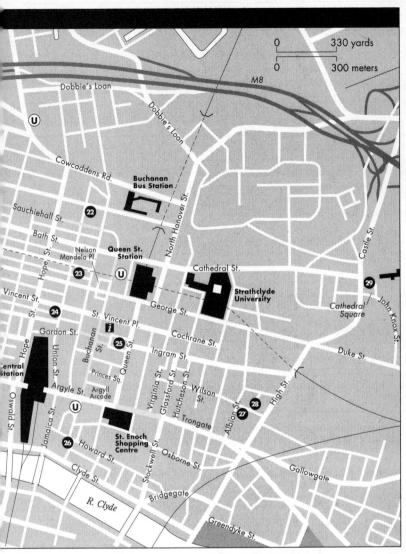

Lodging
Angus, **13**
Babbity Bowster's, **28**
Cathedral House, **29**
Devonshire Hotel, **6**
Glasgow Hilton, **19**
Kirklee Hotel, **9**

The Malmaison
Glasgow, **18**
One Devonshire
Gardens, **1**
The Sandyford, **14**
Sherbrooke Castle
Hotel, **21**

St. Enoch Hotel, **26**
The Town House, **11**
The Victorian
House, **15**
The White House, **10**
Wickets, **3**

$ ✕ **Ashoka West End.** This Punjabi restaurant consistently outperforms its many competitors in quality, range, and taste. Its extensive menu is split into popular and gourmet sections, but all portions are large enough to please the ravenous. There is nothing heavy-handed about the cooking here: Vegetable *samosas* (stuffed savory deep-fried pastries) are crisp and light; the spicing for the lamb, chicken, and prawn dishes is fresh and fragrant; and the milder *kormas* (curried, stewed meat) are pleasantly creamy. The selection of breads is superb. The eclectic Eastern decor, involving a bizarre mixture of plants, murals, rugs, and brass lamps, and inappropriate Western music simply emphasize the Ashoka's idiosyncracy. ☒ *1284 Argyle St.,* ☎ *0141/339–0936. AE, DC, MC, V. No lunch.*

$ ✕ **The Bay Tree.** A small vegetarian haven in the university area, this no-smoking café serves hearty fare such as peanut and paprika soup or vegetable and bean hotchpotch. The modern paintings on the walls are often for sale. ☒ *403 Great Western Rd.,* ☎ *0141/334–5898. Reservations not accepted. No credit cards. Closed Dec. 25, Jan. 1.*

$ ✕ **CCA Café/Bar.** Attached to the Centre for the Contemporary Arts, this warehouse-style café with oilcloths on the tables, bentwood chairs, and plants and posters galore offers a particularly good choice of vegetarian dishes, although meat and fish entrées are also served. Try the spinach dumplings with tomato sauce and cheese-and-chive topping, or the wild mushroom loaf with apple-and-ginger chutney. There's a good wine and beer list chalked up on the blackboard (and a minumum charge of £7). ☒ *350 Sauchiehall St.,* ☎ *0141/332–7864. AE, DC, MC, V. Closed Dec. 25, Jan. 1.*

$ ✕ **Fazzi Café Bar.** This inexpensive Italian café-bar (with a delicatessen at one end), with its red-and-white checked tablecloths and bentwood chairs set on a tiled floor, is a cheerful place for a quick plateful of gnocchi *a la pomarda* (with tomato sauce), or spinach and ricotta ravioli. ☒ *65–67 Cambridge St.,* ☎ *0141/332–0941. AE, MC, V.*

LODGING

See Pleasures and Pastimes, *above,* for an overview of Glasgow lodging.

CATEGORY	COST*
$$$$	over £110
$$$	£80–£110
$$	£45–£80
$	under £45

All prices are for a standard double room, including service, breakfast, and VAT.

$$$$ 🛏 **Devonshire Hotel.** This upscale hotel occupies an elegant terraced mansion, and the native Glasgow hospitality and friendliness contrast sharply with the formality of the sumptuous decor—elegant drapes, marbled pillars, stained glass, and four-poster beds. Frequented by stars when they're in town (Whitney Houston and Bruce Springsteen among them), the hotel strives for excellence in every department, including the modern British cuisine that makes the most of Scotland's fish and game. ☒ *5 Devonshire Gardens, G12 0UX,* ☎ *0141/339–7878,* 📠 *0141/339–3980. 16 rooms with bath and shower. Restaurant. AE, DC, MC, V.*

$$$$ 🛏 **Glasgow Hilton.** You'll be struck by the professionalism at this typical international hotel; Glasgow friendliness permeates the very upscale image. Two themed restaurants, **Cameron's,** a Highland shooting lodge, and **Minsky's,** a New York–style deli and carvery; and **Raffles,** a colonial-themed bar, serve superb food. ☒ *1 William St., G3 8HT,* ☎ *0141/204–5555,* 📠 *0141/204–5004. 319 rooms with bath. 2* *restaurants (jacket and tie in Cameron's), 2 bars, beauty salon, health club, meeting rooms. AE, DC, MC, V.*

$$$$ ⊞ **One Devonshire Gardens.** This hotel comprises a group of Victo-
★   rian houses on a sloping tree-lined street 10 minutes west of the city center. Celebrities such as Luciano Pavarotti and Elizabeth Taylor name it as their favorite. Each individually decorated bedroom has rich wallpaper, heavy drapes, and French mahogany furniture; nine rooms have four-poster beds. The restaurant is equally stylish with a menu that changes daily and specialties that include fillet of venison with potato and turnip gratin, and terrine of chicken and bacon with Cumberland sauce. The wine list is commanding, as are the prices. ⊠ *1 Devonshire Gardens, G12 0UX,* ☎ *0141/339–2001,* ℻ *0141/337–1663. 27 rooms with bath or shower. Restaurant (reservations essential). AE, DC, MC, V.*

$$–$$$$ ⊞ **Sherbrooke Castle Hotel.** Come to the Sherbrooke for a flight of Gothic fantasy. Its cavernous rooms hark back to grander times when the south side of Glasgow was home to the immensely wealthy tobacco barons, whose homes were built with turrets and towers. The spacious grounds are far from the noise and bustle of the city, yet only 10 minutes' drive from the city center. Like the tobacco barons, the hotel's proprietor insists on tasteful decor and good traditional cooking. The busy bar is well patronized by locals. ⊠ *11 Sherbrook Ave., Pollokshields, G41 4PG,* ☎ *0141/427–4227,* ℻ *0141/427–5685. 25 rooms with bath or shower. Restaurant, bar. AE, DC, MC, V.*

$$$ ⊞ **The Malmaison Glasgow.** Set in a converted church, the Malmaison prides itself on being a "small, personal service hotel. " The modern decor is plain, but there's a splendid staircase with a wrought-iron balustade illustrating Napoléon's exploits (the hotel takes its name from the French emperor's home). In the basement is a café-bar serving delicious traditional British–Continental favorites (☞ Dining, *above*). ⊠ *278 W. George St., G2 4LL,* ☎ *0141/221–6400,* ℻ *0141/221–6411. 21 rooms with bath. AE, DC, MC, V.*

$$$ ⊞ **The White House.** This is an unusual Glasgow hotel insofar as it has no dining room. All accommodations at the White House are in self-contained suites, and guests can either cook their own food in the fully appointed kitchen, or eat out. The larger suites comprise several linked rooms, and the less expensive have a kitchen area in the sitting room. Stays can be as short as one night or as long as one year. ⊠ *11–13 Clevedon Crescent, G12 0PA,* ☎ *0141/339–9375,* ℻ *0141/337–1430. 31 suites. AE, DC, MC, V.*

$$–$$$ ⊞ **Babbity Bowster's.** There's a lively atmosphere at this small, intimate hotel in a restored 18th-century town house designed by Robert Adam. In addition to a gallery on the first floor that features many works by Glaswegian artists, the hotel offers a bar, restaurant, and café. ⊠ *16–18 Blackfriars St., G1 1PE,* ☎ *0141/552–5055,* ℻ *0141/552–7774. 6 rooms with shower. Restaurant, bar, café, lighted boules court. AE, MC, V.*

$$–$$$ ⊞ **Wickets.** In the heart of Billy Connolly's neighborhood, Partick, this hotel dominates one of the area's few green spaces—the West of Scotland cricket ground. It is a handsome white mansion house with an airy, Continental feel. Its glass-fronted restaurant looking onto an extensive garden is a rare pleasure in the city. The bar areas are split between the traditional and the artfully Parisienne. Since cricket is not Glasgow's premier sport, Wickets enjoys a tranquil, leafy setting. The rooms are furnished with a cheerful bravado. ⊠ *52 Fortrose St., G11 5LP,* ☎ ℻ *0141/334–9334. 10 rooms, 8 with bath, 2 with shower. AE, MC, V.*

\$\$ **Angus.** Another privately run city-center hotel on Sauchiehall Street, the Angus is intimate yet spacious. Its biggest pluses are the friendly staff and their eye for detail. All rooms have been tastefully decorated creating a Victorian ambience. ⊠ *966 Sauchiehall St., G3 7TQ,* ☎ *0141/ 357–5155,* FAX *0141/339–9469. 17 rooms with bath or shower. AE, DC, MC, V.*

\$\$ **Cathedral House.** In the heart of old Glasgow, near the cathedral, this small, friendly, freshly decorated hotel is convenient for sight-seeing. The café–bar offers a fixed-price lunch, and there's also a restaurant with an à la carte menu that lists interesting Icelandic dishes among more usual fare. ⊠ *28–32 Cathedral Sq., G4 0XA,* ☎ *0141/552–3519,* FAX *0141/552–2444. 7 rooms with bath. Restaurant, bar. AE, DC, MC, V.*

\$\$ **Kirklee Hotel.** In a quiet district of Glasgow near the university, this
★   hotel is small and cozy. Its owners take pride in being friendly and help-ful and in keeping the hotel spotless and comfortable. ⊠ *11 Kensing-ton Gate, G12 9LG,* ☎ *0141/334–5555,* FAX *0141/339–3828. 9 rooms with bath and shower. AE, MC, V.*

\$\$ **The Town House.** A handsome old terraced house in a quiet cul-de-sac, the Town House thrives on repeat business from satisfied guests. The owners are particularly welcoming. The high ceilings, plaster-work, and other original architectural features of the house are com-plemented by restrained cream-and-pastel–striped decor, stripped pine doors, and plain fabrics. Evening meals are served on request. There is a comfortable sitting room with books and informative leaflets to browse through. ⊠ *4 Hughenden Terrace, G12 9XR,* ☎ *0141/357–0862,* FAX *0141/339–9605. 10 rooms with shower. MC, V.*

\$–\$\$ **St. Enoch Hotel.** A location right in the city center makes this hotel a good base for sight-seeing. Completely refurbished in 1995, the hotel is decorated throughout in an unimaginative modern style with few pretensions, but the low room rates compensate for the lack of atmo-sphere. There is a café–bar serving inexpensive, quick meals. ⊠ *St. Enoch Sq., 44 Howard St., G1 4EE,* ☎ FAX *0141/221–2400. 43 rooms with shower. AE, MC, V.*

\$ **The Sandyford.** With a fine Victorian exterior, this hotel on the west end of famous Sauchiehall Street is convenient to all city-center facil-ities, including the Scottish Exhibition Centre and many art galleries. The Sandyford is more an upscale bed-and-breakfast than a hotel, al-though its rooms are somewhat spartan, with stark white interiors and pine furniture. ⊠ *904 Sauchiehall St., G3 7TF,* ☎ *0141/334–0000,* FAX *0141/337–1812. 41 rooms, 3 with bath, 33 with shower. MC, V.*

\$ **The Victorian House.** This "overgrown bed-and-breakfast" on a quite residential street is only one block away from the Charles Ren-nie Mackintosh–designed Glasgow School of Art. The plain bedrooms are rather disappointing after the dramatic, dark red decor of the en-trance hall and reception area. The staff is welcoming. No meals are served other than breakfast, but there are plenty of restaurants on nearby Sauchiehall Street. ⊠ *212 Renfrew St., G3 6TX,* ☎ *0141/332–0129,* FAX *0141/353–3155. 45 rooms, 1 with bath, 36 with shower. MC, V.*

NIGHTLIFE AND THE ARTS

Glasgow was the 1990 European City of Culture, the first British city to be so designated, and is to be the UK City of Architecture and De-sign in 1999. It's clear just how strong Glasgow's international repu-tation is when it comes to cultural events. That reputation has grown from the strong base developed by the city authorities in the 19th cen-tury and has continued in the remarkable renaissance the city has en-joyed in the past 10 years. The second-largest arts festival in Scotland is now **Mayfest,** held in Glasgow during virtually all of May. For details, ☎ 0141/552–8000.

The Arts

Concerts

Glasgow's **Royal Concert Hall** (✉ 2 Sauchiehall St., ☎ 0141/227–5511) was opened for the City of Culture celebrations in 1990. It has 2,500 seats and is the permanent home of the Royal Scottish Orchestra, which performs a winter series of concerts and a summer proms series. **City Halls** (✉ Candleriggs, ☎ 0141/227–5511) house a wide variety of musical events. The **Henry Wood Hall** (✉ Claremont St., ☎ 0141/221–4030), a former church, is now used for classical concerts. The **Scottish Exhibition and Conference Centre** (✉ Finnieston, ☎ 0141/ 248–3000) is a regular venue for pop concerts.

Film

The **Glasgow Film Theatre** (✉ Rose St., ☎ 0141/332–6535) is an independent public cinema screening the best nonmainstream films from all over the world. The **MGM Film Centre** (✉ Sauchiehall St., ☎ 0141/332–9513), the **Grosvenor** (✉ West End, ☎ 0141/339–4298), and the **Odeon Film Centre** (✉ Renfield St., ☎ 01426/933413) show all the latest releases. For details of programs, consult the daily newspapers.

Opera and Ballet

Glasgow is home to the Scottish Opera and Scottish Ballet, both of which perform at the **Theatre Royal** (✉ Hope St., ☎ 0141/332–9000). Visiting dance companies from many countries perform here also.

Theater

Glasgow offers a plethora of live theater. One of the most exciting is the internationally renowned **Citizen's Theatre** (✉ 119 Gorbals St., ☎ 0141/429–0022), where productions, and their sets, are often of hairraising originality. More contemporary works are staged at **Cottier's Arts Theatre** (✉ 93 Hyndland St., ☎ 0141/339–5868), in a converted church. The **Centre for the Contemporary Arts** (✉ 350 Sauchiehall St., ☎ 0141/332–7521) not only stages modern plays, but also has exhibitions, films, and musical performances. The **King's Theatre** (✉ Bath St., ☎ 0141/227–5511) stages drama, light entertainment, variety shows, musicals, and amateur productions. The **Mitchell** (✉ Mitchell Library, North St., ☎ 0141/227–5511) mostly accommodates amateur productions, but also hosts lectures and meetings. The **Pavilion** (✉ Renfield St., ☎ 0141/332–1846) offers family variety entertainment along with rock and pop concerts. The **Royal Scottish Academy of Music and Drama** (✉ 100 Renfrew St., ☎ 0141/332–5057) stages a variety of international and student performances. The **Tramway** (✉ 25 Albert Dr., ☎ 0141/227–5511), the city's old museum of transport, is now an exciting venue for opera, drama, and dance. The **Tron** (✉ 63 Trongate, ☎ 0141/552–4267) houses Scottish and international contemporary theater. The **Arches** (✉ Midland St., ☎ 0141/221–9736) stages serious and controversial drama from around the world. **Theatre Royal** (✉ Hope St., ☎ 0141/332–9000) has performances of major drama, including an occasional season of plays by international touring companies.

Tickets for performances can be purchased at theater box offices or at the **Ticket Center** (✉ Candleriggs, ☎ 0141/227–5511).

Nightlife

Dancing

Among the city's large number of dancing hot spots is **Volcano** (✉ Benalder St., off corner of Dumbarton and Byres Rds., ☎ 0141/334–8292. ⏲ 11 PM–2:30 AM. 💳 £3–£6), dark and spartan, with a different mood and music nightly. **Cleopatra's** (✉ 508 Great Western Rd., ☎ 0141/334–0560. ⏲ 11 PM–1 or 3 AM. 💳 £5), is favored by Glasgow University students as well as trendy young professionals. **The Tunnel** (✉ 84 Mitchell St., ☎ 0141/204–1000. ⏲ 10:30 PM–3 AM. 💳 £5–£7), is unpredictable yet fashionable.

Pubs

Glasgow's pubs were once famous for hard drinkers who demanded few comforts. Times have changed and many pubs have been turned into smart wine bars. For a taste of an authentic Glasgow pub with some traditional folk music occasionally thrown in, go to the **Stockwell Street** area and search out Scotia Bar, The Victoria Bar, or Clutha Vaults. Real ale enthusiasts should visit the **Brewery Tap** (✉ 1055 Sauchiehall St., ☎ 0141/339–8866) or the **Bon Accord** (✉ 153 North St., ☎ 0141/248–4427). If you visit only one pub in Glasgow, make it the **Horseshoe Bar** (✉ 17–21 Drury St., ☎ 0141/221–3051), which offers a sepia-tinted sentimental glimpse of all the friendlier Glasgow myths, and serves that cheerful distillation over what is purported to be the world's longest bar. Refurbishment would be a curse on its original tiling, stained glass, and deeply polished woodwork. Almost as intriguing as the decor is the clientele—a complete cross section of the city's populace. The upstairs lounge serves the steak pie Britain became famous for, and the waitress will ask some pretty stiff questions if you don't finish.

In the center of town try the **Drum and Monkey** (✉ 93 St. Vincent St.), a trendy pub with a classic Victorian look and live music during the week. **Nico's** (✉ 375 Sauchiehall St.), designed along the lines of a Paris café, is a favorite with the nearby art school students and young Glaswegian professionals. The best Gaelic pub is **Uisge Beatha** (pronounced *oos*-ki *bee*-ha; ✉ 232–246 Woodlands Rd., ☎ 0141/332–0473), which means "water of life"—a euphemism for scotch. It serves beer from its own Glaschu Brewery, nearby; try the Fraoch (heather beer) in season. There is good live music in the **Halt** (✉ 106 Woodlands Rd., ☎ 0141/332–1210), which has a mixed-age clientele. In the city center, close to the River Clyde, the **Riverside Club** (✉ Fox St., off Clyde St., ☎ 0141/248–3144) features traditional ceilidh bands on Friday and Saturday evenings; arrive early—it's very popular.

Any tourist office (☞ Glasgow A to Z, *below*) provides up-to-date listings, as does the fortnightly magazine, *The List*.

OUTDOOR ACTIVITIES AND SPORTS

Bicycling and Jogging

The tourist board (☞ Glasgow A to Z, *below*) can provide a list of cycle paths and of the many parks and gardens in Glasgow with facilities for these sports; many of the parks also have tennis courts and/or bowling greens.

Fishing

With loch, river, and sea fishing available, the area is a mecca for fishermen. Details of fishing permits and locations are available from the tourist board.

Golf

Municipal courses are operated within Glasgow proper by the local authorities. Bookings are relatively inexpensive, and should be made 24 hours in advance direct to the course. Telephone early (courses open at 7 AM) to ensure prime tee times. A comprehensive list of contacts, facilities, and charges of the 30 or so other courses nearby the city is available from the Greater Glasgow Tourist Board.

King's Park (✉ Croftfoot, ☎ 0141/637–1066). 9 holes, 2,103 yards, SSS 32.

Lethamhill (✉ Cumbernauld Rd., ☎ 0141/770–6220). 18 holes, 6,081 yards, SSS 69.

Linn Park (✉ Simshill Rd., ☎ 0141/637–5871). 18 holes, 4,814 yards, SSS 64.

Littlehill (✉ Auchinairn Rd., ☎ 0141/772–1916). 18 holes, 6,199 yards, SSS 69.

Ruchill (✉ Brassey St., ☎ 0141/946–9728). 9 holes, 2,208 yards, SSS 32.

Health and Fitness Clubs

There are some 40 clubs throughout the city. Most include a swimming pool and gymnasium, and some have squash, karate, horseback riding, shooting, badminton, or sailing facilities. See the brochure available from the tourist board for details. The larger hotels in the city also offer a variety of sports and leisure facilities, usually free of charge, to their guests. Currently, the following hotels have at least a pool and gym: **Central** (☎ 0141/221–9680), **Moat House** (☎ 0141/306–9988), **Marriott** (☎ 0141/226–5577), **Jury Glasgow** (☎ 0141/334–8161), **Hilton** (☎ 0141/204–5555), and **Swallow** (☎ 0141/427–3146).

Sailing and Water Sports

The Firth of Clyde and Loch Lomond both offer water-sports facilities with full equipment rental. Details are available from the tourist board.

Soccer

The city has been sports-mad, especially for football (soccer), for more than 100 years, and the rivalry between its two main clubs, Rangers and Celtic, is legendary. Rangers wear blue, are predominantly Protestant, and play at **Ibrox** (pronounced *eye*-brox; ☎ 0141/427–8500) to the west of the city. Celtic wear green, are predominantly Roman Catholic, and play in the east at **Parkhead** (☎ 0141/552–8591). Matches are played usually on a Saturday in winter, and Glasgow has in total nine different teams playing in the Scottish Leagues. Admission prices start at about £12. Do not go looking for the family-day-out atmosphere of many American football games; soccer remains a man's game played in relatively primitive surroundings, though Ibrox is an exception to this.

SHOPPING

Department Stores

The main department stores are **Debenham's** (☞ Argyle Street, *below*) and **Frasers** (☞ Buchanan Street, *below*); other names—**Littlewoods** (✉ 56 Argyle St., ☎ 0141/248–3713), **British Home Stores** (✉ 67–81 Sauchiehall St., ☎ 0141/332–0401), **C&A** (✉ 218 Sauchiehall St., ☎ 0141/333–9441), and **Marks and Spencer** (✉ 2–12 Argyle St., ☎ 0141/552–4546)—are also represented. Frasers is the store most worth visiting, not only for its exceptional interior and display, but also for its variety of designer names and helpful, friendly staff.

Shopping Districts

Argyle Street/St. Enoch Square

Start at St. Enoch Square (which is also the main underground station); it houses the St. Enoch Shopping Centre. Walk east toward the main pedestrian area of Argyle Street and you will find all the usual High Street chain stores. **Debenham's** (✉ 97 Argyle St., ☎ 0141/221–0088) department store's stock includes china and crystal as well as women's and men's clothing (it can also be entered from the St. Enoch Centre). The pedestrian zone on Argyle Street is invariably overcrowded, especially on Saturday, and is certainly not for the impatient shopper. An interesting diversion off Argyle Street is **Argyll Arcade,** a covered street which has the largest collection of jewelers under one roof in Scotland. This L-shape arcade, built in 1904, houses several locally based jewelers and a few shops specializing in antique jewelry. The other end of the Argyll Arcade leads to Buchanan Street.

Buchanan Street

This is probably Glasgow's premier shopping street and is almost totally pedestrianized. Buchanan Street runs perpendicular to Argyle Street. At one end are Buchanan Street underground and Scotrail Queen Street stations.

Immediately opposite the exit of the Argyll Arcade is **Frasers** (✉ 21–45 Buchanan St., ☎ 0141/221–3880), Glasgow's largest and most interesting department store. Frasers is a Glasgow institution, and its wares reflect much of Glasgow's new and traditional images—leading European designer clothes and fabrics combining with home-produced articles, such as tweeds, tartans, glass, and ceramics. The magnificent interior is itself worth a visit, set off by the grand staircase rising to various floors and balconies.

In addition to household names like Laura Ashley, Burberry's, Liberty, Jaeger, and Roland Cartier, there are other Buchanan Street shops to look out for. **R. G. Lawrie Ltd.** (✉ 110 Buchanan St., ☎ 0141/221–0217) specializes in Highland outfitting, Scottish gifts, woolens, and cashmere. **Henry Burton** (✉ 111 Buchanan St., ☎ 0141/221–7380) is a traditional gentleman's outfitter offering both off-the-peg items and a made-to-measure service. You will find excellent outerwear at **Tiso Sports** (✉ 129 Buchanan St., ☎ 0141/248–4877), if you are planning some walking in the Highlands during your trip. Buchanan Street also sports the entrances to the excellent **Princes Square** (✉ 48 Buchanan St., ☎ 0141/221–0324) shopping mall. Elegant and stylish, this houses many of the finest specialty stores.

For another shop worthy of mention, follow Buchanan Street to St. Vincent Street, turn to your left, and you will find **Robert Graham** (✉ 71 St. Vincent St., ☎ 0141/221–6588), tobacconist. This shop has a tremendous variety of tobaccos and pipes. Much of Glasgow's wealth was generated by the Tobacco Lords during the 17th and 18th centuries; at Graham's you will experience a little of that colorful history. Also on St. Vincent Street is **John Smith & Son (Glasgow) Ltd.** (✉ 57 St. Vincent St., ☎ 0141/221–7472), founded in the mid-18th century, which prides itself on being a thoroughly Scottish bookshop, with an excellent selection of books about Scotland.

Merchant City

This area on the edge of the city center is a recent upscale development consisting of some new buildings and old warehouses converted into living space. It is home to many of Glasgow's young and upwardly mobile. Shopping here is expensive, but the area is certainly worth visiting for those who are seeking the young Glasgow style. The Merchant

City is close to ScotRail's High Street station or can be easily reached by walking eastward from ScotRail's Argyle Street station.

Ichi Ni San (⊠ 26 Bell St., ☎ 0141/552–2545) is a glitzy fashion shrine with the latest looks from the hottest designers. **Alexandra Stewart Interiors** (⊠ 54 Wilson St., ☎ 0141/552–2002) is an interior design store full of tempting furnishings and decorative knickknacks. Also worth a visit is **In House** (⊠ 24–26 Wilson St., ☎ 0141/552–5902), with its top-quality designer Italian furniture as well as glassware, china, and textiles. **Casa Fina** (⊠ 1 Wilson St., ☎ 0141/552–6791) stocks stylish and modern furniture and giftware. Wander around **Stockwell China Bazaar** (⊠ 67–77 Glassford St., ☎ 0141/552–5781) for a huge array of fine china and earthenware, glass, and ornaments. Items will be packed and sent overseas for you, if required. While in this area you will also find the **National Trust for Scotland**'s shop (⊠ Hutcheson's Hall, 158 Ingram St., ☎ 0141/552–8391). Many items for sale are designed exclusively for National Trust properties and are generally handmade.

The Barras

This is Glasgow's famous weekend street market and should certainly not be missed during your visit. Apart from the excellent opportunity to pick up a bargain while you browse among the stalls, you will enjoy the lively and colorful surroundings. Stalls sell antique (and not-so-antique) furniture, bric-a-brac, student-designed jewelry and textiles—you name it, it's here. The Barras (☎ 0141/552–7258, ☉ Weekends 9–5) is approximately 80 years old and is made up of nine markets—the largest indoor market in Europe. It prides itself on selling everything "from a needle to an anchor."

You can reach the Barras by walking from Scotrail's Argyle Street station, or take any of the various buses to Glasgow Cross at the foot of the Gallowgate.

West Regent Street/Blythswood Square

West Regent Street can be reached by walking from Renfield Street (parallel to Buchanan St.); most buses from the West End coming into town travel along this street or one running parallel to it. Renfrew Street can be reached by walking to the right along Pitt Street at the end of West Regent Street.

For antiques connoisseurs and art lovers, a walk along West Regent Street is highly recommended. Your first stop should be the **Victorian Village** (⊠ 57 West Regent St.), a complex of small antiques shops. Of particular interest among the jewelry, coins, and bric-a-brac are stores specializing in antiquarian books, army memorabilia, 1920s clothing, and Victorian pastimes. Farther along West Regent Street are various galleries and antiques shops, some specializing in Scottish antiques and paintings. **Cyril Gerber Fine Art** (⊠ 148 West Regent St., ☎ 0141/221–3095 or 0141/204–0276, FAX 0141/248–1322), specialists in 20th-century British paintings, will export, as will most galleries. The **Compass Gallery** (⊠ 178 West Regent St., ☎ 0141/221–6370) usually has interesting exhibitions on view.

In this area you are not far from **Glasgow School of Art** (⊠ 167 Renfrew St., ☎ 0141/353–4526), which has a shop selling various books, cards, jewelry, and ceramics. Students often sell their work, if you are lucky enough to be visiting during the degree shows in June.

The West End/Byres Road

This part of the city is dominated by the university, and the shops cater to local and student needs. One place of interest is **De Courcey's** antiques and crafts arcade (⊠ 5–21 Cresswell La.). There are quite a few shops to visit, and a variety of goods, including paintings and jewelry, are regularly auctioned here. De Courcey's is in one of the cobblestone lanes to the rear of Byres Road. **Peckham's Delicatessen** (⊠ 100 Byres Rd., ☎ 0141/357–1454; ⊠ 43 Clarence Dr., ☎ 0141/357–2909; ⊠ Central Station, ☎ 0141/248–4012) is a Glasgow institution for Continental sausages, cheeses, and everything for a delicious picnic. **The Californian Gourmet** (⊠ 293 Byres Rd., ☎ 0141/337–1642) has everything edible for homesick Americans: bagels, pecan pie, and Ben & Jerry's ice cream. **Papyrus** (⊠ 374 Byres Rd., ☎ 0141/334–6514; ⊠ 296–298 Sauchiehall St., ☎ 0141/353–2182) has a wide range of designer cards, small gifts, and a good selection of books.

Byres Road is reached on the underground system: Get off at Hillhead station. By bus from the city center, numbers 44 and 59 pass by the university and cross over Byres Road (get off at the first stop on Highburgh Rd. and walk back).

Arcades and Shopping Centers

As in many other major cities and towns, various centers can be found in and around the city. **St. Enoch's Shopping Centre** (⊠ 55 St. Enoch Sq., ☎ 0141/204–3900) is eye-catching if not especially pleasing. It houses various stores, but most could be found elsewhere. There is, however, an indoor ice-skating rink where equipment can be rented, an interesting diversion during a day's shopping. By far the best complex is **Princes Square** (⊠ 48 Buchanan St.); high-quality shops in an art-nouveau setting, with cafés and restaurants. Look particularly for the Scottish Craft Centre, which has an outstanding collection of work created by some of the best craftspeople in Scotland.

Specialty Stores

Clothing

Glasgow has a very fashion-conscious image in Scotland, and a variety of both local and international fashion houses can be visited. The Merchant City area (☞ *above*) is popular with young people. At Princes Square there are famous designer names like **Katherine Hamnett** (⊠ Unit 38 Princes Sq., ☎ 0141/248–3826), selling pricey women's and men's clothing in classic and modern styles. **Ted Baker** (⊠ Unit 25 Princes Sq., ☎ 0141/221–9664) sells men's designer clothing—lots of shirts, ties, and accessories, but no suits—at designer prices. The West End has a number of shops where you may find items of local design. Worth a special mention is **Strawberry Fields** (⊠ 517 Great Western Rd., ☎ 0141/339–1121), housing a colorful array of children's wear.

Gifts

All the usual Scottish-theme gifts can be found in various locations in Glasgow. Gift items here tend to be a little more interesting and of a higher quality than those found in other, more tourist-oriented areas of the country.

MacDonald MacKay Ltd (⊠ 105 Hope St., ☎ 0141/204–3930) makes and sells Highland dress and accessories, ladies' kilts, and skirts made to measure and offers an export service.

Glasgow has a definite place in the history of art and design, being most famous for its association with Charles Rennie Mackintosh. For high-quality giftware in his style, **Catherine Shaw** (⊠ 24 Gordon St., ☎ 0141/204–4762; ⊠ 32 Argyll Arcade, ☎ 0141/221–9038) offers a unique selection.

SIDE TRIPS

Glasgow is also well placed as a touring base for excursions south to the fertile farmlands of **Ayrshire,** with its Robert Burns connections, and **the Clyde Valley,** two one-day itineraries for which are given below. You could do them by car or, in a modified form, by public transportation.

Closer to the city, **Pollok Country Park** provides a peaceful green oasis on the south side of the River Clyde, just a few miles southwest of central Glasgow. The key attraction here is the **Burrell Collection,** Scotland's finest art collection, and not to be missed. Allow at least a half-day to enjoy the collections.

The town of **Paisley** was once a distinct burgh in its own right, but is now part of the Greater Glasgow suburban area. If your taste runs toward the urban rather than the rural, this town offers plenty of gritty character, largely because of vestiges of its industrial heritage: It was once famous for its shawl manufacturing and its museum has a fine shawl collection.

Pollok Country Park

The Burrell Collection

23 Set in Pollock Country Park (*see* Exploring Glasgow map) a custom-built, ultramodern yet elegant building houses 8,000 exhibits of all descriptions, from ancient Egyptian, Greek, and Roman artifacts to Chinese ceramics, bronzes, and jade, to medieval tapestries, stained glass, Rodin sculptures, and exquisite French Impressionist paintings—all from the magpie collection of an eccentric millionaire, Sir William Burrell, who donated his treasures to the city in 1944. The building was designed with large glass walls so that the items on display could relate to their surroundings: art and nature, supposedly in perfect harmony. It does, however, seem an incongruous setting for Chinese porcelain and the reconstruction of medieval castle rooms. ☎ *0141/649–7151.* 🎫 *Free.* ⊘ *Mon.–Sat. 10–5, Sun. 11–5.*

Pollok House

Dating from the mid-1700s, Pollok House contains the Stirling Maxwell Collection of paintings, including works by El Greco, Murillo, Goya, Signorelli, and William Blake. Fine 18th- and early 19th-century furniture, silver, glass, and porcelain are also on display. The house has fine gardens and looks over the White Cart River and Pollok Park, where, amid mature trees and abundant wildlife, the City of Glasgow's own highland cattle peacefully graze. ☎ *0141/632–0274.* 🎫 *Free.* ⊘ *Mon.–Sat. 10–5, Sun. 11–5.*

Pollok Country Park A to Z

ARRIVING AND DEPARTING

Pollok Country Park is off Paisley Road, just 3 miles southwest of the city center. You can get there by taxi or car, by city bus, or by a train from Glasgow Central Station to Pollokshaws West Station. Contact the St. Enoch Square Travel Centre (☎ 0141/226–4826) for details of all public transport options.

Ayrshire and the Clyde Coast

Robert Burns is Scotland's national and well-loved poet. His birthday is celebrated with speeches and dinners, drinking and dancing (Burns Suppers) on January 25, in a way in which few other countries celebrate a poet. He was born in Alloway, beside Ayr just an hour or so to the south of Glasgow, and the towns and villages where he lived and loved make an interesting day out from the city.

On your way there, you will travel beside the great River Clyde and be able to and look across to Dumbarton and its Rock, a nostalgic farewell point for emigrants leaving Glasgow. The river is surprisingly narrow here, when you remember that the *Queen Elizabeth 2* and the other *Queens* and great ocean liners sailed these waters from the place of their birth. Further along the coast, the views north and west to Loch Long, the Holy Loch, and the Argyll Forest Park are outstanding on a clear day. Two high points of the trip, in addition to the Burns connections, are Mount Stuart House, on the island of Bute, and, below Ayr, Culzean Castle, flagship of the National Trust for Scotland.

Wemyss Bay

㉔ From the old Victorian village of **Wemyss Bay** there is a ferry service to the Isle of Bute, a favorite holiday spot for Glaswegians earlier this century. The many handsome buildings, especially the station and its covered walkway between platform and steamer pier, with its exuberant wrought-ironwork, are a reminder of the grandeur and style of the Victorian era and the generations of visitors who used trains and ferries for their summer holidays. (South of Wemyss Bay, you can also look across to the island of Arran, another Victorian holiday favorite, and then the island of Great Cumbrae, a weighty name for a tiny island.)

Isle of Bute

㉕ The **Isle of Bute** offers a host of relaxing walks and scenic vistas. **Rothesay,** a faded but appealing resort, is the main town. Bute's main at-
★ traction is spectacular **Mount Stuart,** ancestral home of the marquesses of Bute and located close to Rothesay. A massive Victorian Gothic palace built in red sandstone, its mind-blowingly ornate interiors include the Marble Hall, with star-studded vault, stained glass, arcaded galleries, and magnificent tapestries woven in Edinburgh in the early 20th century. The collection of paintings and the furniture throughout the house are equally outstanding. ⊠ *Isle of Bute, PA20 9LR,* ☎ *01700/503877,* ℻ *01700/505313.* ☞ *Combined ticket, house and gardens: £5.50; gardens only: £3.* ☉ *May–Sep., Mon., Wed., Fri.–Sun. 10–5 (gardens), 11–5 (house); last admission 4:30.*

DINING AND LODGING

$$ ✕▥ **Ardmory House Hotel.** Outstanding views over Rothesay Bay and the Firth of Clyde are a feature of this attractive little hotel, set in large gardens in a peaceful residential area. The atmosphere is "home away from home" rather than elegant, with beamed ceilings and a cozy bar with an open fire downstairs, and plainly furnished but comfortable bedrooms in muted colors. The staff are exceptionally friendly and attentive. Standard bar meals such as homemade soup, lasagna, or chili are offered at lunchtime and in the evening, while the restaurant serves slightly more elaborate dishes such as poached salmon with cucumber and dill mayonnaise, or medallions of venison in blackberry sauce. ⊠ *Ardmory Road, Ardbeg, Rothesay, Bute, PA20 0PG,* ☎ ℻ *01700/502346. 5 rooms, 2 with bath, 3 with shower. Restaurant, bar. AE, DC, MC, V.*

Largs

㉖ At the coastal resort of **Largs,** the community makes the most of the town's Viking history. It was the site in 1263 of a major battle which finally broke the power of the Vikings in Scotland, and every September a commemorative Viking Festival is held. All year round, **Vikingar, the Viking Heritage Centre,** tells the story of the Viking influence in Scotland by way of film, tableaux, and displays. ⊠ *Barrfields, Greenock Rd., KA30 8QL,* ☎ *01475/689777,* ℻ *01475/689444.* ☞ *£3.50.* ☉ *Apr.–Sep. daily 9–6; Oct.–Mar., daily 10–4.*

If you are in Largs on a summer's afternoon, take time to look into the **Clark Memorial Church** on the seafront, which has a particularly splendid array of Glaswegian Arts & Crafts stained glass of the 1890s in its windows. Among the studios involved in their design were those of Steven Adam and Christopher Wall. ☎ *01475/672370.*

Just south of Largs is **Kelburn Castle and Country Park,** the historic estate of the Earl of Glasgow. There are walks and trails through the mature woodlands, including the mazelike Secret Forest, which leads deep into the thickets. The visitor center explains it all, and the adventure center and commando-assault course will wear out overexcited children. (They tell a tale here of rescuing an elderly lady from halfway around the assault course, who commented, "Well, I did think it was rather a *hard* nature trail." Make sure you read the signposts.) ⊠ *Fairlie, Ayrshire, KA2Q ORE,* ☎ *01475/568685.* ☜ *£4.* ⊙ *Late Mar.–late Oct., daily 10–6; grounds only, Nov.–Mar., daily 11–5.*

Irvine

Robert Burns puts in an appearance at **Irvine**: the Irvine Burns Club is possibly the oldest in the world. He came here to learn to dress flax (the raw material for linen), and the heckling (flax-dressing) shed where he worked and the house where he lived are museums. ⊠ *4 and 10 Glasgow Vennel,* ☎ *01294/275059.* ☜ *Free.* ⊙ *June–Sept., Mon., Tues., Thurs.–Sat. 10–1 and 2–5, Sun. 2–5; Oct.–May, Tues., Thurs.–Sat. 10–1 and 2–5.*

Troon

The small coastal town of **Troon** is famous for its international golf course, Royal Troon. You can easily see why golf is so popular here. At times, the whole Ayrshire coast, 60 miles long, seems one endless golf course.

GOLF

Royal Troon (⊠ Troon, Ayrshire, ☎ 01292/311555), a club founded in 1878, has two 18-hole courses: the Old, 6,649 yds., and the Portland, 6,274 yds. Access for visitors is limited—call for details.

LODGING

$$$ ⛾ **Piersland House Hotel.** This is located in a late Victorian mansion, formerly the home of a whisky magnate. Oak paneling and log fires in the restaurant provide a warm backdrop for specialties such as beef medallions in pickled walnut sauce. All the bedrooms are individually designed and furnished in traditional style. ⊠ *15 Craigend Rd. (just north of Ayr), KA10 6HD,* ☎ *01292/314747,* FAX *01292/315613. 23 rooms, 17 with bath, 6 with shower. Restaurant (reservations essential). AE, DC, MC, V.*

SHOPPING

Many Glaswegians frequent **Regalia** (⊠ 44–48 Church St., ☎ 01292/312162) for its unusual collection of designer outfits for women.

Ayr

The commercial port of **Ayr** is Ayrshire's chief town, a peaceful and elegant place with an air of prosperity and some good shops. Burns was baptized in the Auld Kirk (Old Church) in the town and wrote a humorous poem about the Twa Brigs (two bridges) that cross the river nearby. He described Ayr as a town unsurpassed "for honest men and bonny lasses."

If you are on the Robert Burns trail, head for **Alloway,** on B7024 in Ayr's southern suburbs. Here, among the many middle-class residences, you will find the one-room thatched **Burns Cottage,** where Scot-

Glasgow Excursions: Ayrshire and the Clyde Valley

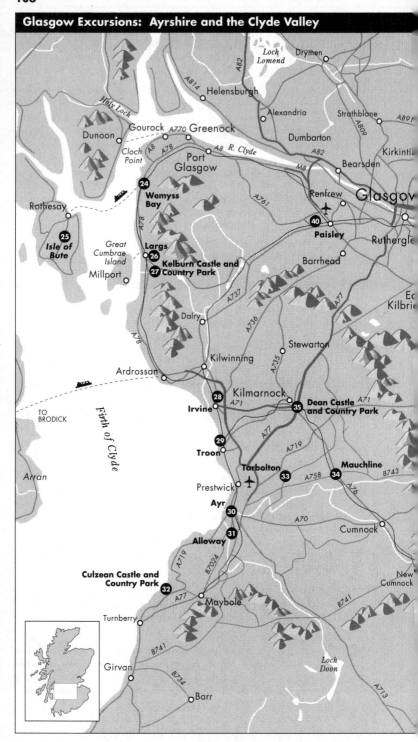

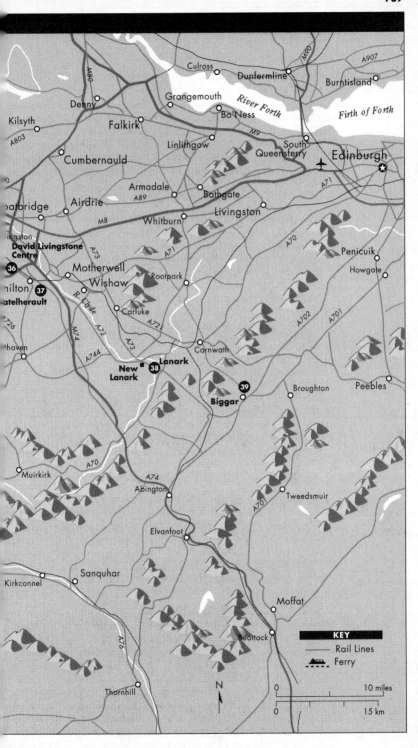

KEY

—— Rail Lines

🚂 Ferry

0   10 miles

0   15 km

N

land's national poet was born in 1759 and which his father built. There is a museum of Burnsiana next door. ☎ *01292/441215.* 🖭 *£2.50 (includes admission to Burns Monument, and allows discounted admission to the Tam o' Shanter Experience).* ⊙ *June–Aug., Mon.–Sat. 9–6, Sun. 10–6; Apr., May, Sept., Oct., Mon.–Sat. 10–5, Sun. 1–5; Nov.–Mar., Mon.–Sat. 10–4, Sun. 12–4.*

Find out all about Burns at the **Tam o' Shanter Experience.** Here you can first enjoy a 10-minute audiovisual journey through the life and times of the poet himself, then watch as one of Burns's most famous poems, "Tam o' Shanter," is "brought to life" on a three-screen theatrical set. It is down the road from Burns Cottage and around the corner from Alloway's ruined church. ☎ *01292/443700.* 🖭 *£2.50 (includes admission to the Burns Monument, and allows discounted admission to Burns Cottage and museum).* ⊙ *Daily 9–6 (closed Dec. 25, Jan.1).*

Other sites associated with Burns can be found nearby. **Auld Alloway Kirk** is where Tam o' Shanter unluckily passed a witches' revel—with Old Nick himself playing the bagpipes—on his way home from a night of drinking. Tam, in flight from the witches, managed to cross the **Brig o' Doon** (brig is Scots for bridge) just in time. His gray mare, Meg, lost her tail to the closest witch. (Any resident of Ayr will tell you that witches cannot cross running water.) The **Burns Monument** (entrance fee included in charge for Burns Cottage and for Tam o'Shanter Experience) overlooks the Brig o' Doon.

DINING

$$ ✕ **Fouter's Bistro.** Fouter's is in a long and narrow cellar, yet its white walls and decorative stenciling create a light ambience. The cuisine is also light and skillful—no heavy sauces here. Try the roast Ayrshire lamb with pan juices and red wine and mint, or sample the "Taste of Scotland" appetizer, nibbling on smoked salmon, trout, and other goodies. This is modern Scottish cooking at its best, all in a friendly setting. ✉ *2A Academy St.,* ☎ *01292/261391. AE, DC, MC, V.*

SHOPPING

Ayr has a good mixture of traditional and new shops. Queen's Court, Sandgate, combines small crafts and gift shops. The **Diamond Factory** (✉ 27 Queen's Ct., ☎ 01292/280476) is a jewelry workshop where visitors are invited to view craftsmen at work. All jewelry is designed and made on the premises. Ask about rings that can be engraved with a family crest and about seal engraving. The store will export your purchases if you do not have time to wait for completion of the work. The **Mill Shop, Begg of Ayr** (✉ Viewfield Rd., ☎ 01292/267615) has a good selection of scarves, stoles, plaids, and travel rugs that are handmade on the premises.

Culzean Castle and Country Park

★ ㉜ **Culzean** (pronounced ku-*lain*) **Castle and Country Park** is the National Trust for Scotland's most popular property. The castle, complete with walled garden, is a superb neoclassical mansion designed by Robert Adam in 1777 on a dramatic cliff-top site. The country park welcomes 200,000 visitors a year, yet remains unspoiled. In addition to its marvelous interiors, the castle contains the National Guest Flat, given by the people of Scotland in appreciation of General Eisenhower's services during World War II. As president he stayed once or twice at Culzean and his relations still do occasionally. Between visits it is used by the N.T.S. for official entertaining. Approach is by way of rooms evoking the atmosphere of World War II: Mementos of Glenn Miller, Winston Churchill, Vera Lynn, and other personalities of the era all help create a suitably 1940s mood. ☎ *01655/760269.* 🖭 *Country park and cas-*

tle £5.50; castle £3.50; country park £3. ⊙ *Castle: Apr.–Oct., daily 10:30–5:30 (last admission 5 PM); country park: daily 9:30–sunset.*

Tarbolton

㉝ At **Tarbolton** you will find the **Bachelors' Club,** a 17th-century house where Robert Burns learned to dance, founded a debating and literary society, and became a Freemason. ☎ *01292/541940.* 🖾 *£1.60.* ⊙ *Easter and May–Sept., daily 1:30–5:30; Oct., weekends 1:30–5:30.*

Mauchline

㉞ **Mauchline** also has strong connections with the poet Robert Burns. There is a Burns House here; four of his daughters are buried in the churchyard; and Poosie Nansie's pub, where he used to drink, is still in use today. The village is also famous for making curling stones.

Kilmarnock

This industrial town, home of Johnny Walker whisky, has more enjoyment for Burns enthusiasts: the Burns Museum and the Dick Institute.

㉟ But if you are looking for something different by now, go to **Dean Castle and Country Park** to enjoy a 14th-century castle with a wonderful collection of medieval arms and armor. Burns also inevitably gets a mention. ✉ *Off Glasgow Road,* ☎ *01563/522702.* 🖾 *£2.* ⊙ *Daily noon–5. Closed Dec. 25, Jan 1.*

Ayrshire and the Clyde Coast A to Z

ARRIVING AND DEPARTING

By Bus or Train. Take the bus or train to Largs for Cumbrae; Ardrossan for Arran; Ayr and Kilmarnock for the Burns Heritage Trail; and Troon, Prestwick, and Ayr to play golf. Bus companies also operate one-day guided excursions to this area; for details, contact the tourist information center in Glasgow. Buchanan Street Bus Station, ☎ 0141/332–7133; Glasgow train inquiry line, ☎ 0141/204–2844.

By Car. Begin your trip from Glasgow city center westbound on the M8, signposted for Glasgow Airport and Greenock. Join the A8 and follow it from Greenock to Gourock and around the coast past the Cloch lighthouse. Head south on the A78 to the old Victorian village of Wemyss Bay, and take the ferry over to Bute to see Mount Stuart (leave your car behind: a bus service takes you to the house from the ferry). Then continue down the A78 through Largs, Irvine, Troon and so to Ayr and Alloway. Travel on to Culzean Castle, then return to Ayr and turn eastward on the B743, the Mauchline Road, but before you get there, turn left on a little road to Tarbolton. Return to the B743, visit Mauchline, then head north on A76 to Kilmarnock. Glasgow is only half an hour away on the fast A77.

VISITOR INFORMATION

There are tourist information centers at:

Ayr (✉ Burns House, 16 Burns Statue Square, ☎ 01292/288688).
Irvine (✉ New St., ☎ 01294/313886).
Kilmarnock (✉ 62 Bank St., ☎ 01563/539090).
Largs (✉ Promenade, ☎ 01475/673765).
Mauchline (✉ National Burns Memorial Tower, Kilmarnock Rd., ☎ 01290/551916).
Troon (✉ Municipal Buildings, South Beach, ☎ 01292/317696. ⊙ Easter–Sept.)

The Clyde Valley

The River Clyde is (or certainly was) famous for its shipbuilding and heavy industries, yet its upper reaches flow through some of Scotland's most fertile farmlands, which concentrate on growing tomatoes. It is an interesting area, with ancient castles as well as industrial and social museums that tell the story of manufacturing and mining prosperity.

Blantyre

36 In the not-very-pretty town of Blantyre, look for signs to the **David Livingstone Centre,** a park area around the tiny (tenement) apartment where the great explorer of Africa was born in 1813. Displays tell of his journeys, of his meeting with Stanley ("Doctor Livingstone, I presume"), of Africa, and of the industrial heritage of the area. ☎ 01698/823140. ⌨ £2.70. ⊙ Mar.–Oct. Mon.–Sat. 10–5, Sun. 12:30–5; visiting in the winter season may be possible, please call for details.

Close by is **Bothwell Castle,** dating from the 13th century. Its walls are well preserved and stand above the River Clyde. ☎ 0131/668–8600. ⌨ £1.50. ⊙ Apr.–Sept., Mon.–Sat. 9:30–6, Sun. 2–6, Oct.–Mar., Mon.–Wed. and Sat. 9:30–4, Sun. 2–4, Thurs. 9:30–12.

Hamilton

The Hamilton Mausoleum, in Strathclyde Country Park near the industrial town of Hamilton, was built in the 1840s as an extraordinary monument to the lavish eccentricities of the dukes of Hamilton (who
37 had more money than sense). Also nearby is **Chatelherault** (pronounced *Shat*-lerro), a unique one-room-deep facade, part shooting lodge, part glorified dog kennel, designed in elegant Georgian style by William Adam, also for the dukes of Hamilton. Within Chatelherault is an exhibition describing life on the estate in all its former glory. ☎ 01698/426213. ⌨ Free. ⊙ Apr.–Sept., Mon.–Sat. 10–5, Sun. 12-5:30; Oct.–Mar., Mon.–Sat. 10–5, Sun. 12–5; lodge closed Fri. year-round; occasionally closed for functions.

Lanark

38 Set in pleasing, rolling countryside, **Lanark** is an old established typical Scottish town. It is now most often associated with its unique neighbor **New Lanark,** a nominated World Heritage Site. New Lanark is distinguished because it was the site of a social experiment. The River Clyde powers its way through a beautiful wooded gorge and its waters were harnessed to drive textile mill machinery before the end of the 18th century. The owner, David Dale, unusual for that era, was noted for his caring attitude to the workers. Later, his son-in-law, Robert Owen, took these social experiments further, founding a benevolent doctrine known as "Owenism," and eventually crossing the Atlantic to become involved in a similar project in Indiana, called New Harmony which, unlike New Lanark, failed. (Robert Owen's son Robert Dale Owen helped found the Smithsonian Institution.)

After many changes of fortune the mills eventually closed, but the site has been saved and has a new lease on life with renovated housing. The refurbishment was excellent, and those who bought the houses seem able to lead normal lives despite having tourists peering in all day. One of the mills has been converted into an interpretative center, which tells the story of this brave social experiment. Upstream, the Clyde flows through some of the very finest river scenery anywhere in Lowland Scotland, with woods and spectacular waterfalls. *Visitor Centre,* ☎ 01555/665876. ⌨ £3.45. ⊙ Daily 11–5. Closed Dec. 25, Jan. 1–2.

SHOPPING

Lanark offers an interesting selection of shops within walking distance of each other. **McKellar's the Jewellers** (✉ 41 High St., ☎ 01555/661312) has a good range of Charles Rennie Mackintosh–inspired designs in gold and silver. **Strands** (✉ 2 Broomgate, ☎ 01555/665757) carries a wide variety of yarns and knitwear, including Aran designs and one-of-a-kind creations by Scottish designers. **Hop Skip n' Jump** (✉ 8 Broomgate, ☎ 01555/665655) is an excellent children's clothes boutique, stocking British and Continental items. **The Lanark Gallery** (✉ 116–118 North Vennel, ☎ 01555/662565) displays paintings, pottery and ceramics, and sculptures all by Scottish artists.

Biggar

③⑨ A pleasant stone-built town, **Biggar** is a rewarding place to spend an hour or two, out of all proportion to its size. **Gladstone Court Museum** offers a fascinating portrayal of life in the town, with reconstructed Victorian shops, a bank, a telephone exchange, and a school. ✉ *Gladstone Ct., Biggar,* ☎ *01899/221050.* ⊡ *£1.50.* ☉ *Apr.–Oct., Mon.–Sat. 10–12:30 and 2–5, Sun. 2–5.*

For the town's geology and prehistory, plus an excellent embroidery collection (including samplers and fine patchwork coverlets), visit the **Moat Park Heritage Centre,** also in the town center, in a former church. ☎ *01899/221050.* ⊡ *£2.* ☉ *Easter–early Oct., Mon.–Sat. 10–5, Sun. 2–5.*

Just down the street is the **Gasworks,** built in 1839, a fascinating reminder of the efforts once needed to produce gas for light and heat. *National Museums of Scotland,* ☎ *0131/225–7534.* ⊡ *Free.* ☉ *June–Sept., daily 2–5.*

On the outskirts of the town is the **Greenhill Covenanters' House,** a farmhouse with Covenanting relics, 17th-century furnishings, costume dolls, and rare farm breeds. ☎ *01899/221050.* ⊡ *80p.* ☉ *Easter–early Oct., daily 2–5.*

☺ **Biggar Puppet Theatre** regularly presents performances by Purves Puppets. Between performances, two hands-on, half-hour tours are available, led by the puppeteers. One tour goes backstage with the puppets being demonstrated on stage, the other is of the puppet museum. The theater also has games and a picnic area. ✉ *B7016, east of Biggar,* ☎ *01899/220631.* ⊡ *Performances: £4.40.* ☉ *Mon., Tues., and Thurs.–Sat 10–5; also Easter–Sept., Sun. 2–5. (Call for additional opening times and details.)*

At Biggar, you are near the headwaters of the Clyde, on the moors in the center of southern Scotland. The Clyde flows west toward Glasgow and the Atlantic Ocean, while the Tweed, only a few miles away, flows eastward toward the North Sea. There are fine views around Biggar: to Culter Fell and to the Border Hills in the south.

DINING AND LODGING

$$$ ✕🏠 **Shieldhill.** This foursquare Norman manor has stood on this spot since 1199 (though it was greatly enlarged in 1560). It is in an ideal location for touring the Borders—just 27 miles from Edinburgh and 31 from Glasgow. The rooms are named after great Scottish battles—Culloden, Glencoe, Bannockburn—and are furnished with great comfort (miles of Laura Ashley fabrics and wallpaper). ✉ *Quothquan, near Biggar, ML12 6NA,* ☎ *01899/220035,* ℻ *01899/221092. 11 rooms with bath or shower. Restaurant. AE, DC, MC, V.*

The Clyde Valley A to Z

ARRIVING AND DEPARTING

By Bus. Bus services run out of Glasgow to Hamilton, Lanark and Biggar. Inquire at the Buchanan Street Bus Station (☎ 0141/332–7133) for details.

By Car. Take A724 out of Glasgow, south of the river through Rutherglen toward Hamilton. It is not a very pretty road, but in Blantyre look for signs to the David Livingstone Centre. From Blantyre, take the main road to Hamilton. Then travel on the A72 past Chatelherault toward Lanark, a pleasant agricultural town. You pass the ruins of medieval Craignethan Castle, lots of greenhouses for tomatoes, plant nurseries, and gnarled old orchards running down to the Clyde. Before reaching Lanark, follow the signs down a long winding hill, to New Lanark. A72 continues south of Lanark to join A702 near Biggar. At the end of a full day of touring you can return to Glasgow the quick way by joining the M74 from the A744 west of Lanark (the Strathaven road). Or take a more scenic route through Strathaven (pronounced *stra*-ven) itself, A726 to East Kilbride, and enter Glasgow from south of the river.

By Train. Services run from Glasgow Central Station (☎ 0141/204–2844) to Hamilton and Lanark. There are no trains to Biggar, but there is a connecting bus service from Hamilton to Biggar.

VISITOR INFORMATION

There are tourist information centers at:

Biggar (⊠ 155 High St., ☎ 01899/221066).
Hamilton (⊠ Road Chef Services, M74 Northbound, ☎ 01698/285590).
Lanark (⊠ Horsemarket, Ladyacre Rd., ☎ 01555/661661).

Paisley

 The industrial prosperity of **Paisley** came from textiles and, in particular, from the woolen Paisley shawl. The internationally recognized Paisley pattern is based on the shape of a palm shoot, an ancient Babylonian fertility symbol brought to Britain by way of Kashmir. The full story of the pattern and of the innovative weaving techniques introduced in Paisley is told in the **Paisley Museum and Art Gallery,** which has a world-famous shawl collection. ⊠ *High St.,* ☎ *0141/889–3151.* ☞ *Free.* ◷ *Mon.–Sat. 10–5. Closed public holidays.*

The life of the workers in the textile industry is brought to life in **Sma' Shot Cottages,** re-creations of mill workers' houses with displays of linen, lace, and Paisley shawls. An 18th-century weaver's cottage is also open to visitors. ⊠ *11/17 George Pl.,* ☎ *0141/889–1708.* ☞ *Free.* ◷ *Apr.–Sept., Wed. and Sat. 1–5 or by appointment.*

Paisley's 12th-century Cluniac **Abbey** dominates the town center. Almost completely destroyed in 1307 and then rebuilt after the Battle of Bannockburn, the abbey is traditionally associated with Walter Fitzallan, the High Steward of Scotland, who gave his name to the Stewart monarchs of Scotland. Outstanding features include the fine stone-vaulted roof and stained glass of the choir. Paisley Abbey is today a busy parish church. ☎ *0141/889–7654.* ☞ *Free; group visits by arrangement.* ◷ *Mon.–Sat. 10–3:30, and for Sunday services at 11, 12:15, and 6:30.*

Paisley A to Z

ARRIVING AND DEPARTING

By Bus. There are regular services to Paisley from Buchanan Street Bus Station (☎ 0141/332–7133).

By Car. Take the M8 westbound and then the A737 clearly signed to Paisley.

By Train. Services run every 5–10 minutes throughout the day from Glasgow Central Station (☎ 0141/204–2844).

VISITOR INFORMATION

Town trail leaflets are available from the tourist information center. ⊠ *Town Hall, Abbey Close,* ☎ *0141/889–0711,* ⊘ *Apr.–Nov.*

GLASGOW A TO Z

Arriving and Departing

By Bus

Glasgow's bus station is at **Buchanan Street** (☎ 0141/332–7133). The main inter-town operator is **National Express/Scottish Citylink** (☎ 0990/505050), which serves a wide variety of towns and cities in Scotland, Wales, and England, including London (journey time from London is approximately 8½–9 hours); it also has services to Edinburgh. Buchanan Street is close to the underground station of the same name and to Queen Street station.

By Car

Visitors who come to Glasgow from England and the south of Scotland will probably approach the city from the M6, M74, and A74. The city center is clearly marked from these roads. From Edinburgh the M8 leads to the city center and is the motorway that cuts straight across the city center and into which all other roads feed. From the north either the A82 from Fort William or the A/M80 from Stirling also feed into the M8 in Glasgow city center. From then on, you only have to know your exit: Exit 16 serves the north of the city center, exit 17/18 leads to the northwest and Great Western Road, and exit 18/19 takes you to the hotels of Sauchiehall Street, the Scottish Exhibition Centre, and the Anderston Centre.

By Plane

Glasgow Airport, about 7 miles west of the city center on the M8 to Greenock, offers internal Scottish and British services, European and transatlantic scheduled services, and vacation-charter traffic. Most major European carriers fly into Glasgow, offering frequent and convenient connections (some via airports in England) to Amsterdam, Brussels, Copenhagen, Frankfurt, Munich, and Reykjavík. There are frequent shuttle services from London, as well as regular flights from Birmingham, Bristol, East Midlands, Leeds/Bradford, Manchester, Southhampton, Isle of Man, and Jersey. There are also flights from Wales (Cardiff) and Ireland (Belfast, Carrickfinn, Dublin, and Londonderry).

Local Scottish connections can be made to Aberdeen, Barra, Benbecula, Campbeltown, Edinburgh, Inverness, Islay, Kirkwall, Shetland (Sumburgh), Stornoway, and Tiree. There is an airport information desk (☎ 0141/887–1111) and a tourist information desk and accommodations-booking service (☎ 0141/848–4440).

Airlines operating through Glasgow Airport to Europe and the rest of the United Kingdom include **Aer Lingus** (☎ 0645/737747), **Air Malta** (☎ 0181/785–3177), **Air UK** (☎ 0345/666777), **British Airways** and **British Airways Express** (☎ 0345/222111), **British Midland** (☎ 0345/554554), **Business Air** (☎ 0500/340146), **Easyjet** (☎ 01582/445566), **Icelandair** (☎ 0181/388–5599), **Lufthansa** (☎ 0345/737747) **Manx** (☎ 0345/256256), **Sabena** (☎ 0181/780–1444) and **SAS** (☎ 0171/706–8832).

Scheduled services to and from North America are provided by **Air Canada** (☎ 0990/247226) and **British Airways** (☎ 0345/222111).

Though there is a railway station (Paisley Gilmour St.) about 2 miles from Glasgow Airport, most people travel the short distance to the city center by bus or taxi. Journey time is about 20 minutes except at rush hour.

By Bus: Express buses run from Glasgow Airport to near the Central railway station (☎ 0141/204–2844) and to the Buchanan Street bus station (☎ 0141/332–7133). There is service every 15 minutes throughout the day. The fare is about £2.

By Limousine: Most of the companies that provide chauffeur-driven cars and tours will also do limousine airport transfers. Companies that are currently members of the Greater Glasgow Tourist Board are **Charlton** (☎ 0141/427–1155), **Charter** (☎ 0141/942–4228), **Kingston** (☎ 0141/554–6066), **Little's** (☎ 0141/883–2111), **Peter Holmes** (☎ 0141/954–4455), and **Robert Neil** (☎ 0141/641–2125).

By Rental Car: All the usual rental companies, including **Alamo** (☎ 0141/848–1166), **Avis** (☎ 0141/887–2261), **Budget Rent-a-Car** (☎ 0141/887–0501), **Eurodollar** (☎ 0141/887–7915), **Europcar** (☎ 0141/887–0414), and **Hertz** (☎ 0141/887–2451) have offices within the terminal building. Costs vary according to the size of the cars, but average about £20–£30 per day.

By Taxi: Metered taxis are available at the terminal building. The fare should be about £12.

The drive from Glasgow Airport into the city center is normally quite easy even for visitors who are used to driving on the right. The M8 motorway runs beside the airport (junction 29) and takes you straight into Glasgow city center (and offers excellent views of the city and the River Clyde). Thereafter Glasgow's streets follow a grid pattern, at least in the city center, but a map is useful and can be supplied by the rental company.

Prestwick Airport (☎ 01292/479822), on the Ayrshire coast about 30 miles southwest of Glasgow and for some years eclipsed by Glasgow Airport, is beginning to come back into the reckoning, not least because of the activities of **Ryanair** (☎ 0171/435–7101), a company which has sparked off a major price war on the Anglo-Scottish routes (e.g., between London and Glasgow/Edinburgh). At press time (spring 1996), it offered unbeatable, no-frills, rock-bottom air fares between London Stansted and Prestwick.

By Bus: An hourly coach service operates to Glasgow, but takes much longer than the excellent train service.

By Car: **Europcar** (☎ 01292/678198) and **Avis** (☎ 01292/477218) have rental desks at the airport. The city center is reached via the fast A77 in about 40 minutes (longer in the rush hour).

By Taxi: Metered taxi cabs are available at the airport. The fare to Glasgow is about £25.

By Train: There is an excellent, rapid half-hourly train service (hourly on Sundays) direct from the terminal building.

By Train

Glasgow has two main rail stations: **Central** and **Queen Street**. Central is the arrival and departure point for trains from London Euston (journey time is approximately 5 hours), which come via Crewe and

Carlisle in England, as well as via Edinburgh from Kings Cross. It also serves other cities in the northwest of England and towns and ports in the southwest of Scotland. These include Kilmarnock, Dumfries, Ardrossan (for the island of Arran), Gourock (for Dunoon), Wemyss Bay (for the island of Rothesay), and Stranraer (for Ireland). Queen Street Station has connections to Edinburgh (journey time 50 minutes) and onward on the east coast route to Aberdeen or south via Edinburgh to Newcastle, York, and London Kings Cross. Other services from Queen Street go to Stirling, Perth, and Dundee; northward to Inverness, Kyle of Lochalsh, Wick, and Thurso; along the Clyde to Dumbarton and Balloch (for Loch Lomond); and on the scenic West Highland line to Oban, Fort William, and Mallaig. Oban and Mallaig have island ferry connections. The passenger-information line (☎ 0141/204–2844) for both Central and Queen Street stations operates 24 hours.

A regular bus service links Queen Street and Central stations. Both of these are close to stations on the Glasgow Underground. At Queen Street go to Buchanan Street, and at Central go to St. Enoch. Black city taxis are available at both stations.

Getting Around

Glasgow city center—the area defined by the M8 motorway to the north and west, the River Clyde to the south, and Glasgow Cathedral to the east—is relatively compact, and visitors who are staying in this area should make some of their excursions on foot. Glaswegians themselves walk a good deal and the streets are designed for pedestrians (some are for pedestrians only). The streets are relatively safe even at night (but you should be sensible), and good street maps are available from bookstores and the excellent tourist-information center (☞ Visitor Information, *below*). Most of the streets follow a grid plan; if you get lost, though, just ask a local—they are famous for being friendly.

To go farther afield, to the West End (the university, the Transport Museum, Kelvingrove Museum and Art Gallery, or the Hunterian Museum) or to the south (for example, the Burrell Collection), some form of transportation is required. Glasgow is unusual among British cities in having an integrated transport network, and information about all options is available from Strathclyde Passenger Transport Executive (PTE) Travel Centre, St. Enoch Square (☎ 0141/226–4826).

By Bus
The many different bus companies cooperate with the underground and ScotRail to produce the Family Day Tripper Ticket (£12), which is an excellent way to get around the whole area from Loch Lomond to Ayrshire. Tickets are a good value and are available from the Strathclyde Passenger Transport Executive (PTE) Travel Centre, St. Enoch Square (☎ 0141/226–4826) and at main railway and bus stations.

By Car
A car is not necessary in the city center. Though most of the newer hotels have their own parking lots, parking in the city center can be very trying. More convenient are the park-and-ride schemes at underground stations (Kelvinbridge, Bridge St., and Shields Rd.) that will bring you into the city center in a few minutes. The West End museums and galleries have their own parking lots, as does the Burrell, so there are no problems there. Remember, parking wardens are constantly on patrol, and you will be fined if you park illegally. Multistory parking garages are open 24 hours a day at the following locations: Anderston Centre, George Street, Waterloo Place, Mitchell Street, Cambridge Street,

and Buchanan Street. Rates at the individual garages vary between £1 and £2 per hour.

By Subway

As befits the Second City of the Empire, Glasgow is the only city in Scotland that has a subway, or underground, as it's called here. It was built at the end of the last century and takes the simple form of two circular routes, one going clockwise and the other counterclockwise. All trains will eventually bring you back to where you started, and the complete circle takes 24 minutes. This extremely simple and effective system operated relatively unchanged in ancient carriages (cars) until the 1970s when it was entirely modernized. The tunnels are relatively small, so the trains themselves are tiny (by London standards) and this, together with the affection in which the system is held and the bright orange paintwork of the trains, gives it the nickname the Clockwork Orange.

Flat fares (60p) and the **Heritage Trail** one-day pass (£1.80) are available. Trains run regularly Monday to Saturday, with a limited Sunday service, and connect the city center with the West End (for the university) and the city south of the River Clyde. Look for the orange "U" signs marking the 15 stations. Further information is available from the Strathclyde Passenger Transport Executive Travel Centre, St. Enoch Square (☎ 0141/226–4826).

By Taxi

Metered taxis (usually black and of the London type) can be found at taxi ranks all over the city center. Most have radio dispatch, so they can be called very easily. Some have also been specially adapted to take wheelchairs. In the street, a taxi can be hailed if it is displaying its illuminated FOR HIRE sign.

By Train

In addition to the underground, the Glasgow area has an extensive network of suburban railway services. They are still called the Blue Trains by local people, even though most of them are now orange. Look for signs to LOW LEVEL TRAINS at Queen Street and Central stations. For further information and a free map, call Strathclyde PTE (☎ 0141/226–4826) or ScotRail (☎ 0141/204–2844). Details are also available from the tourist board.

Contacts and Resources

Car Rentals

Avis, ✉ 161 North St., ☎ 0141/221–2827; **Budget Rent-a-Car,** ✉ 101 Waterloo Street, ☎ 0141/226–4141; **Eurodollar,** ✉ 76 Lancefield Quay, ☎ 0141/204–1051; **Europcar,** ✉ Pollokshaws Rd., ☎ 0141/423–5661; **Hertz,** ✉ 106 Waterloo St., ☎ 0141/248–7736.

Discount Admission Tickets

The **Historic Scotland Explorer Ticket,** available from any staffed Historic Scotland property, and many tourist information centers, allows visits to HS properties over a 7- or 14-day period. The **Touring Ticket** issued by the National Trust for Scotland (☎ 0131/226–5922) is also available for 7 or 14 days and allows access to all NTS properties. It is available from the NTS or main tourist information centers (*see below*).

Doctors and Dentists

Your hotel receptionist or bed-and-breakfast landlady will be the best person to ask for the names of local doctors who will treat visitors. Most dentists will treat visitors by appointment. A full list can be found in the Yellow Pages telephone directory. Emergency dental treatment can be obtained from the **Glasgow Dental Hospital** (378 Sauchiehall St., ☎ 0141/211–9600 weekdays from 9–3).

Emergencies

Dial **999** from any telephone (no coins are needed for emergency calls from public telephones) to obtain assistance from the police, ambulance, fire brigade, mountain rescue, or coastguard.

Guided Tours

BOAT TOURS

Cruises are available on Loch Lomond and to the islands in the Firth of Clyde; details are available from the tourist board.

HELICOPTER TOURS

Clyde Helicopters (☎ 0141/226–4261) swoop over downtown Glasgow and the immediate environs as far as Loch Lomond, taking off from the helipad at the Scottish Exhibition Centre. Trips normally last 10 to 30 minutes and cost between £35 and £90.

ORIENTATION TOURS

Discovering Glasgow bus tours leave daily in summer from the west side of George Square. The Greater Glasgow Tourist Board (☞ Visitor Information, *below*) can give further information and arrange reservations. Details of longer tours northward to the Highlands and Islands can be obtained from the tourist board or the Strathclyde PTE (☞ Getting Around, *above*).

PERSONAL GUIDES AND WALKING TOURS

In each case your first contact should be the tourist board, where you can find out about special walks on a given day. The **Scottish Tourist Guides Association** (☎ FAX 0141/776–1052) also offers an all-around service.

SPECIAL-INTEREST

The Scottish Tourist Guides Association (☎ FAX 0141/776–1052) can tailor a tour to suit you. Standard fixed fees apply. **Classique Sun Saloon Luxury Coaches** (☎ 0141/889–4050) operates restored coaches from the '50s, '60s, and '70s on tours to the north and west. The following Glasgow companies run regular bus tours around the region: **Scott Guide Coaches,** ☎ 0141/204–0444; **Southern Coaches,** ☎ 0141/876–1147; and **Weirs Tours Ltd.,** ☎ 0141/941–2843. **Little's Chauffeur Drive** (Glasgow, ☎ 0141/883–2111) also offers personally tailored car-and-driver tours.

Several chauffeur-driven limousine companies (☞ Between the Airport and City Center, *above*) also provide tours of the city center and beyond.

Taxi firms also arrange tours of the city. They vary from one to three hours, usually at a fixed price of about £12 per hour. They can be booked in advance, and you can be picked up and dropped off where you like. Contact the **Taxi Owners Association** (☎ 0141/332–7070) or the **Taxi Cab Association** (☎ 0141/332–6666).

Hospitals

Twenty-four-hour accident and emergency services are provided at **Glasgow Royal Infirmary** (Castle St., ☎ 0141/552–3535). The hospital is by the cathedral. Accident and emergency facilities are also available at **Glasgow Western Infirmary** (Dumbarton Rd., ☎ 0141/211–2000), near the university.

Late-Night Pharmacies

Pharmacies in Glasgow operate on a rotating basis for late-night opening (hours are posted in storefront windows). **Sinclair Pharmacy** (693 Great Western Rd., ☎ 0141/339–0012) is open daily 9–9.

Post Office

The **head post office** is at St. Vincent St., (☎ 0141/204–3688); there are many smaller post offices around the city.

Travel Agencies

American Express: ✉ 115 Hope St., ☎ 0141/221–4366.

Thomas Cook: ✉ 15–17 Gordon St., ☎ 0141/221–6611.

Visitor Information

The **Greater Glasgow Tourist Board** (☎ 0141/204–4400) offers an excellent tourist information service from its headquarters at 35 St. Vincent Place, which is just around the corner from George Square and Queen Street Station. At this location there is also an accommodations-booking service, bureau de change, and ticket office for the theater, city bus tours, guided walks, boat trips, and extended coach tours around Scotland. Books, maps, and souvenirs are sold. The office is open Monday–Saturday 9–6 and, in summer, Monday–Saturday 9–8 and Sunday 10–6. The tourist board's branch office at the airport is open daily 7:30–6.

Information about goings-on around town can be found in the Greater Glasgow Tourist Board's own publications, as well as in *The List* and the *Herald* and *Evening Times* newspapers.

5 The Borders and the Southwest

Dumfries, Galloway

The Borders area comprises the great rolling hills, moors, wooded river valleys, and farmland that stretch south from Lothian, the region crowned by Edinburgh, to England. The Dumfries and Galloway region south of Glasgow is a hilly and sparsely populated area, divided from England by the Solway Firth; it's a region of somber forests and radiant gardens, where the palm, in places, is as much at home as the pine.

By Gilbert
Summers

I F YOU ARE COMING TO SCOTLAND from any point south of the border with England, then the Borders is the first region you will encounter. Let it be said straightaway that although the border has no checkpoints or customs outposts, the Scottish tourist authorities firmly promulgate the message that it is indeed Scottish land you are on once you cross the border. All the idiosyncrasies that distinguish Scotland—from the myriad names for beer, to the seemingly unpredictable Monday local holidays—start as soon as one reaches the first Scottish signs by the main roads north.

Although most visitors inevitably pass this way, the Borders and especially Galloway to the west are unfortunately overlooked. So strong is the tartan-ribboned call of the Highlands that many visitors rush past, pause for breath at Edinburgh, then plunge northward, thus missing a scenic portion of upland Scotland.

The Borders and the Dumfries and Galloway regions have as broad a selection of stately homes and fortified castles as you will encounter in Scotland (with the possible exception of Grampian). Galloway, west of Dumfries, has the advantage of a coastline facing south, made even more appealing by the North Atlantic Drift (Scotland's part of the Gulf Stream), which bathes the coastal lands with warmer water. With its coastal farmlands giving way to woodlands, high moors, and some craggy hills, Galloway may not be the Highlands, but it gives a convincing impression to those seeking the authentic Scotland.

Pleasures and Pastimes

Bicycling

This essentially is a rural farming area with some upland stretches but with a wide choice of quiet side roads to avoid the heavy traffic on "A" routes. The Craik Forest is typical of Forestry Commission properties with mountain bike routes and trails in the network of forestry access roads.

Dining

The Borders are reasonably well served by hotels ranging from the budget to the luxury categories, and most good restaurants are, with a very few exceptions, found within hotels rather than as independent establishments. Despite being slightly off the beaten tourist path, Dumfries and Galloway offer a good selection of relatively inexpensive options for dining, though once again most are within hotels.

WHAT TO WEAR

Dress in this region is more conservative than in Glasgow. But although jeans, shorts, and T-shirts would be frowned upon in any even vaguely upmarket hotel restaurant, smaller cafés and restaurants accept almost anything—except swimwear.

CATEGORY	COST*
$$$$	over £40
$$$	£30–£40
$$	£15–£30
$	under £15

*per person for a three-course meal, including VAT and excluding drinks and service.

Fishing

This region is a fisherman's paradise. The Solway Firth is noted for sea angling, notably at Isle of Whithorn, Port William, Portpatrick, Stranraer, and Loch Ryan. The wide range of game fishing opportunities extends from the expensive salmon beats of the River Tweed, sometimes called the Queen of Scottish Rivers, to undiscovered hill lochans.

Lodging

The Borders offer a wide range of price categories, from top-class hotels to top-quality bed-and-breakfasts. Dumfries and Galloway tends to be a little cheaper for each category of accommodation. In this area, a farmhouse bed-and-breakfast is a good option: You're likely to get a hearty farm breakfast, but keep in mind that many of these B&Bs are *working* farms, where early morning activity and the presence of animals are an inescapable part of the scene.

CATEGORY	COST*
$$$$	over £110
$$$	£80–£110
$$	£45–£80
$	under £45

*Prices are for a standard double room, including service, breakfast, and VAT.

Shopping

As with other, more rural areas of Scotland away from the Central Belt, shopping in the Borders and Dumfries and Galloway area centers on the larger towns; stores in the smaller towns and villages usually fulfill only day-to-day requirements. The Borders is well-known for its knitwear industry, and mill shops are in abundance. Throughout the Borders region also look for the specialty sweets indigenous to the area— Jethart Snails, Hawick Balls, Berwick Cockles, and Soor Plums— which, with tablet (a solid caramellike candy) and fudge, are available from most local confectioners.

The Borders in particular has a fairly affluent population, which is reflected in the variety of upscale shops in Peebles, for example, where there are more deluxe stores than might be expected. If you want to spend a morning shopping, Peebles is the place to do it.

Exploring the Borders and the Southwest

The best way to explore the region is to get off the main arterial roads—the A1, A697, A68, A7, M74/A74, and A75—onto the little back roads. You may occasionally be delayed by a herd of cows on their way to the milking parlor, but this is often far more pleasant than, for example, tussling on the A75 with heavy-goods vehicles rushing to make the Irish ferries.

The Scottish Borders are largely characterized by upland moors and hills, with fertile, farmed, and forested river valleys. The textile towns of the Borders have plenty of personality—Border folk are sure of their own identity and are fiercely partisan toward their own native towns. The Southwest, often known as Galloway, shares the upland characteristics and, if anything, has a slightly wilder air (the highest hill in the Southwest is The Merrick, 2765 feet). Towns are very attractive, in the main, with wide streets and colorful frontages; essentially, the area is easygoing and peaceful.

Great Itineraries

To visit all the places described in the Borders would certainly take more than one day. To travel in a leisurely way and spend time at some of the grand mansions noted, one could easily allow three days, although the total driving distance between each town is not great: In the Borders there are several points of interest quite close to one another.

Owing to the high ground and forests at the heart of Dumfries and Galloway, a linear itinerary that keeps largely to the coast might be best. Once again, distances between towns are not large, but traveling on narrow country roads can take a little longer than you might expect. If you particularly enjoy sketching or taking photographs, this is not an area to be rushed, in which case three days is the minimum time to allow to sample an abbey or two and see the settings of the Southwest towns.

IF YOU HAVE 2 DAYS

Numbers in the text correspond to numbers in the margin and on the Borders and Dumfries and Galloway maps.

Jedburgh ① is the best orientation place to get an idea of how important the Border abbeys were. If you cross the border to the west, then head for somewhere like **Kirkcudbright** ㉜ for a flavor of the Southwest. In short, if you only have two days, then you will have to choose between the Borders and the Southwest.

IF YOU HAVE 5 DAYS

Plan to divide your time between the Borders (three days) and the Southwest (two days); this schedule will give you time to visit all of the towns outlined in the tour, although you will need to be selective about which abbeys and stately homes to make more than a quick visit to. Jedburgh Abbey in **Jedburgh** ① is a must-see, as is Melrose Abbey in **Melrose** ⑫. Melrose Abbey also has gardens to enjoy, several museums, and famous stately homes nearby, including **Abbotsford House** ⑬, home of Sir Walter Scott. Finish up at **Peebles** ⑳, where you should allow plenty of time to shop.

In the Southwest, two days will give you time to visit **Sweetheart Abbey** ㉗ in New Abbey, then **Arbigland Gardens** ㉘ in Kirkbean, an excellent example of the lush gardens for which the area is famous. Try to fit in Castle Douglas and **Threave Garden** ㉛, with gaunt Threave Castle nearby, on a river island and reached by boat, to provide a gritty contrast. **Kirkcudbright** ㉜ is also worth even a quick visit, for its artistic connections.

IF YOU HAVE 10 DAYS

Five days in the Borders will allow you to visit any of the places mentioned in the recommended excursions. Such jewels as **Floors Castle** ⑤, **Mellerstain House** ⑦, and **Paxton House** ⑩ can all be enjoyed (though you may get stately home indigestion), and you will also have time to admire the views and soak up the historic atmosphere at **Smailholm Tower** ⑧ or **Dryburgh Abbey** ⑭. One of the most unlikely attractions, Robert Smail's Printing Works at **Innerleithen** ⑲ is also one of the most historically interesting, and it is close to Traquair House, said to be the oldest continually inhabited house in Scotland. You will also have time for an essential shopping visit to **Peebles** ⑳.

Five days in the Southwest will also minimize the problem of choosing what to see—you'll have time for nearly everything on the excursions. Still, at the top of your list should be **Kirkcudbright** ㉜, **Threave Garden** ㉛, and the castle. You should spend some time exploring the hills above Gatehouse of Fleet, with its **Cardoness Castle** ㉝ and heritage center, meander around the southern coastline, penetrate into the wild and wooded **Glen Trool** ㊱, and travel deep into the Machars to **Whithorn** ㊳, a site of immense early religious importance. You will even be able to see **Castle Kennedy Gardens** ㊵ and **Logan Botanic Gardens** ㊷ to complete your Galloway gardens experience.

When to Tour the Borders and the Southwest

Because many properties are privately owned and close from early autumn until early April, the area is rather less well suited to off-season

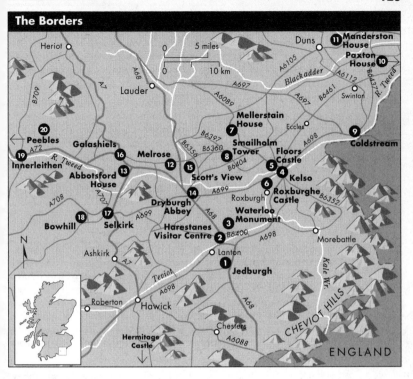

The Borders

touring than some other parts of Scotland, though the entire area can look magnificent in autumn, especially along the Borders's wooded river valleys. Late spring is the time to see the rhododendrons of the gardens in the Southwest.

THE BORDERS
Towns, Towers, and Countryside

This area never possessed the high romance of the Gaelic-speaking clans in the Highlands to the north, but it did have (and still has) powerful Border families, whose ancestry is soaked in the bloodshed that occurred along this once very real frontier between Scotland and her more opportunist neighbor to the south.

The Borders folk take great pride in the region's heritage as Scotland's main woolen-goods manufacturing area. To this day the residents possess a marked determination to defend their towns and communities. We can all be thankful, however, that the changing times have allowed them to reposition their priorities: Instead of guarding against southern raiders, they now concentrate on maintaining a fiercely competitive rugby team for the popular intertown rugby matches. The Borders are a stronghold of this European counterpart to American football.

Border communities are also re-establishing their identities through the curious affairs known as the Common Ridings. Long ago it was essential that each town be able to defend its area, and over the centuries this need has become formalized in mounted gatherings to "ride the boundaries." The observance of the tradition lapsed in certain places but has been revived. Leaders and attendants are solemnly elected each year, and Borderers who now live away from home make a point of attending their town's event. (You are welcome to watch and enjoy the excitement of clattering hooves and banners proudly displayed, but this is essentially a time for the native Borderers.) The Common Ridings possess at least as much authenticity and historic significance as the concocted Highland Games, so often taken to be the essence of Scotland. The little town of Selkirk, in fact, claims its Common Riding to be the largest mounted gathering anywhere in Europe.

The towns described below cluster around and between the two great Borders rivers, the Tweed and the Teviot. They encompass all four of the great ruined Border abbeys. The monks in these long-abandoned religious foundations were the first to work the fleeces of their sheep flocks, hence laying the foundation for what is still the area's main industry.

Jedburgh

➊ *50 mi south of Edinburgh, 95 mi southeast of Glasgow.*

The town of Jedburgh (*-burgh* is always pronounced *burra* in Scots) was for centuries the first major Scottish target of invading English armies. In more peaceful times it developed textile mills, most of which have since perished. The large landscaped area around the town's tourist information center was once a mill but now provides an encampment for the modern armies of tourists. The past still clings to this little town, however. The ruined abbey dominates the skyline and is compulsory visiting for anyone interested in acquiring a feeling of the former role of the Border abbeys.

★ Still impressive, though it is now only a roofless shell, **Jedburgh Abbey** was destroyed by the English earl of Hertford's forces in 1544–45, during the destructive time known as "the Rough Wooing." This was the English king Henry VIII's armed attempt to persuade the Scots that it was a good idea to unite the kingdoms by the marriage of his young son to the infant Mary, Queen of Scots. (The Scots disagreed and sent Mary to France instead.) The full story is explained in vivid detail at the **Jedburgh Abbey Visitor Centre,** which provides information on interpreting the ruins. Only ground patterns and foundations remain of the once-powerful religious complex. ⊠ *High St.,* ☎ *0131/668–8600.* ⍐ *£2.50.* ◷ *Apr.–Sept., Mon.–Sat. 9:30–6, Sun. 2–6; Oct.–Mar., Mon.–Sat. 9:30–4, Sun. 2–4.*

There is much else to see in Jedburgh, including **Mary, Queen of Scots House.** This *bastel* (from the French *bastille*) was the fortified town house in which, some say, Mary stayed before embarking on her famous 20-mile ride to visit her wounded lover, the earl of Bothwell, at **Hermitage Castle** (☞ *Off the Beaten Path, below*). An interpretative center in the building relates the tale. ⊠ *Queen St.,* ☎ *01835/863331.* ⍐ *£1.50.* ◷ *Mar.–mid Nov., daily 10–5.*

➋ Just a few miles north of Jedburgh, the **Harestanes Visitor Centre** describes the role that the Borders estates—major landholdings with woodland and tenanted farms—played in shaping the Borders landscapes. The center is on the estate of the marquis of Lothian and conveys life in the Borders through a custom-built interpretative center which contains audiovisuals and displays on the themes of the countryside and wildlife. Outside there is a play area and nature trail. ⊠ *Monteviot, at the junction of A68 and B6400,* ☎ *01835/830306.* ⍐ *Free.* ◷ *Apr.–Oct., daily 10–5.*

➌ In view on the skyline is the **Waterloo Monument,** a pencil-thin tower that is another reminder of the whims and power of the landowning gentry: A marquis of Lothian built the monument in 1815, with the help of his tenants, in celebration of the victory of Wellington at Waterloo. If you have time, you can walk to the tower from the Harestanes Visitor Centre. ⊠ *Off B6400, 5 mi north of Jedburgh.*

OFF THE
BEATEN PATH

HERMITAGE CASTLE – If you have the time, and wish to appreciate Mary Queen of Scots's famous 20-mile ride to visit her wounded lover, the earl of Bothwell, travel southwest from Jedburgh to this, the most complete remaining example of the gaunt and grim medieval border castles, full of gloom and foreboding. Restored in the early 19th century, it was built in the 14th century (replacing an earlier structure) to guard what was at the time one of the important routes from England into Scotland. The original owner, Lord Soulis, notorious for diabolical excess, was captured by the local populace, who wrapped him in lead and boiled him in a cauldron, or so the tale goes. The castle lies on an unclassified road between the A7 and B6399, about 10 miles south of Hawick, in the desolate Borders hills. ⊠ *Liddesdale,* ☎ *0131/668–8600.* 🎫 *£1.20.* ⊙ *Apr.–Sept., Mon.–Sat. 9:30–6, Sun. 2–6; Oct.–Mar., Sat. 9:30–4:30, Sun. 2–4.*

Lodging

$–$$ 🏠 **Larkhall Burn.** Your accommodations in this new development will
★   be in one of a series of modern, terraced cottages set on a sunny hillside high above the rooftops of the attractive town of Jedburgh. The interiors of these units are decorated in pastel shades and floral fabrics. You can order your meals to be delivered from a restaurant in town, or utilize the well-equipped kitchen. You also have the option of maid service. Larkhall Burn provides more comfort than many hotels, and at a competitive price. The minimum stay is two nights. Prices include everything except phone charges. ⊠ *Larkhall Burn, Jedburgh, Roxburghshire TD8 6AX,* ☎ 🆁🆇 *01835/862313. 4 2-bedroom and 2 3-bedroom cottages available at press time (spring 1996). MC, V.*

$ 🏠 **Spinney Guest House.** Made up of unpretentiously converted and modernized farm cottages, this bed-and-breakfast offers the highest standards for the price. ⊠ *Langlee, TD8 6PB,* ☎ 🆁🆇 *01835/863525. 3 rooms with bath or shower. No credit cards. Closed Dec.–Feb.*

Kelso

④ *12 mi northeast of Jedburgh.*

One of the most attractive Borders burghs, Kelso is often described as having a Continental flavor—some visitors think it resembles a Belgian market town. The town has a broad, paved square and attractive examples of Scots town architecture.

Kelso Abbey is the least intact ruin of the four great Border abbeys—just a gaunt fragment of what was once the largest of the group. On a main invasion route, the abbey was burned three times in the 1540s alone, on the last occasion by the English Earl of Hertford's forces in 1545 when the garrison of 100 men and 12 monks were butchered and the structure all but destroyed. ⊠ *Bridge St.,* ☎ *0131/668–8600.* 🎫 *Free.* ⊙ *Apr.–Sept., Mon.–Sat. 9:30–6, Sun. 2–6; Oct.–Mar., Mon.–Sat. 9:30–4, Sun. 2–4.*

Just across the road from the abbey is **Kelso Museum and the Turret Gallery.** Housed in one of the town's oldest buildings, this museum includes displays of a Victorian schoolroom, a 19th-century marketplace, a reconstructed skinner's workshop, and an interpretation of Kelso Abbey and its importance, as well as an arts-and-crafts gallery. ⊠ *Abbey Court,* ☎ *01573/225470.* 🎫 *£1.* ⊙ *Easter–late Oct., Mon.–Sat. 10–noon and 1–5, Sun. 2–5.*

★ ❺   On the bank of the River Tweed, just 2 miles northwest of Kelso, stands the palatial mansion of **Floors Castle.** Ancestral home of the duke of Roxburghe, the castle was built by William Adam in 1721 and modified with mock-Tudor touches by William Playfair in the 1840s. A holly tree in the deer park marks the place where King James II was killed in 1460 by cannon-shot. ⊠ *A6089,* ☎ *01573/223333.* ⊡ *£3.90; grounds £2.* ☉ *Easter–Sept., daily 10–4.*

❻   Do not confuse the comparatively youthful Floors Castle with **Roxburghe Castle,** nearby. Only traces of rubble and earthworks remain of this ancient pile. The modern-day village of **Roxburgh** is young; the original Roxburgh, one of the oldest burghs in Scotland, has virtually disappeared, though its name lives on in the duke's title and in the name of the old county of Roxburghshire. ⊠ *Off the A699.*

❼   Devotees of ornate country houses are well served in the Borders. Begun in the 1720s, **Mellerstain House** was finished in the 1770s by Robert Adam and is considered to be one of his finest creations. Sumptuous plasterwork covers almost all interior surfaces, and there are outstanding examples of 18th-century furnishings. The beautiful terraced gardens are as renowned as the house. The house is 7 miles northwest of Kelso. ⊠ *Off A6089,* ☎ *01573/410225.* ⊡ *£4.* ☉ *Easter, May–Sept., Sun.–Fri. 12:30–5.*

★ ❽   In the hills south of Mellerstain sits a characteristic Borders structure that certainly contrasts with the luxury of Mellerstain House. **Smailholm Tower** stands uncompromisingly on top of a barren, rocky ridge. Built solely for defense, this 16th-century Border *peel* (small fortified towers common to this region) offers memorable views. If you let your imagination wander in this windy spot, you can almost see the flapping pennants and rising dust of an advancing raiding party and hear the anxious securing of doors and bolts. Sir Walter Scott found this an inspiring spot. His grandfather lived at nearby Sandyknowe Farm (not open to the public), and the young Scott visited the tower often during his childhood. ⊠ *Off B6404,* ☎ *0131/668–8600.* ⊡ *£1.50.* ☉ *Apr.–Sept., Mon.–Sat. 9:30–6, Sun. 2–6.*

Dining and Lodging

$$–$$$
★   ╳🗔 **Ednam House Hotel.** This large, attractive hotel is on the banks of the River Tweed, close to Kelso's grand abbey and the many fine Georgian and early Victorian buildings in the old Market Square. Ninety percent of the guests are return visitors; the open fire in the hall, sporting paintings, and cozy armchairs give the place a homey feeling. The restaurant's three glass walls afford views of the garden and river; the fare here includes fresh local vegetables, salmon from the River Tweed, Aberdeen Angus beef, and homemade ice cream and traditional puddings. ⊠ *Bridge St., TD5 7HT,* ☎ *01573/224168,* 🆉🆇 *01573/226319. 32 rooms with bath or shower. Restaurant, golf privileges, horseback riding, fishing. MC, V. Closed Christmas–early Jan.*

Coldstream

❾   *9 mi east of Kelso on A698.*

Three miles west of Coldstream, the England-Scotland border comes down from the hills and runs beside the Tweed for the rest of its journey to the sea. Coldstream itself, like Gretna, was once a marriage place for runaway couples from the south at a time when the marriage laws of Scotland were more lenient than those of England (a plaque on the former bridge tollhouse recalls this fact). It is also celebrated in military history: In 1659, General Monck raised a regiment of foot guards here on behalf of his exiled monarch Charles II. Known as the Coldstream Guards, the successors to this regiment have become an elite corps in the British army.

The **Coldstream Museum,** situated in the Coldstream Guards' former headquarters, investigates the history of the community of Coldstream, past and present. A special exhibition recalls the history of the Coldstream Guards. ⊠ *Market Sq.,* ☎ *01890/882630.* ▣ *£1.* ☉ *Easter–Oct., Mon.–Thur., and Sat. 10–5, Sun. 2–5.*

The stretch of the Tweed near Coldstream is lined with dignified houses and gardens, the best known of which is **The Hirsel,** the estate of the former British prime minister the late Sir Alec Douglas Home (Lord Home of The Hirsel). A complex of farmyard buildings now serves as a crafts center and museum, and there are interesting walks in the extensive grounds. It's a favorite spot for bird-watchers, and superb rhododendrons bloom here in late spring. The house itself is not open to the public. ⊠ *A697, immediately west of Coldstream,* ☎ *01890/882834.* ▣ *Free (£2 parking charge in summer, £1 in winter). Grounds:* ☉ *Daily, sunrise–sunset. Museum and crafts center:* ☉ *Weekdays 9–5, weekends noon–5.*

⑩ If you are spending a lot of time in the area, you could tour northeast from Coldstream to see more stately mansions. **Paxton House** is a handsome Palladian mansion with interiors designed by Adam, and Chippendale and Trotter furniture. The splendid Regency picture gallery is an outstation of the National Galleries of Scotland and contains a magnificent collection of paintings. The house lies to the west of Berwick-upon-Tweed, and can be reached from Coldstream via the A6112 and B6461. ⊠ *Paxton,* ☎ *01289/386291.* ▣ *£4. Garden only: £1.75.* ☉ *Easter–Oct., daily noon–5. Tearoom open daily 10–5.*

⑪ **Manderston House** is a good example of the grand, no-expense-spared Edwardian country house. The family who built it made their fortune selling herring to Russia. An original 1790s Georgian house on the site was completely rebuilt to the specifications of John Kinross. The staircase is silver plated (thought to be unique) and was modeled after the Petit Trianon at Versailles. There is also much to see downstairs in the kitchens, and outdoors, among a cluster of other buildings, is the one-of-a-kind marble dairy. The house is reached by traveling farther along the A6112 to Duns, then taking the A6105 east. ⊠ *2 mi east of Duns,* ☎ *01361/882636.* ▣ *House and grounds, £5; grounds only, £2.50.* ☉ *Mid-May–Sept., Thurs. and Sun. 2–5:30.*

Dining and Lodging

$$ ✕▥ **Wheatsheaf Hotel and Restaurant.** A country inn on the main street of Swinton, midway between Coldstream and Duns, the Wheatsheaf offers outstanding food in both the black-beamed bar and the restaurant. The sheer class of the cuisine, whether the meal is beef, salmon, or venison, has won widespread praise, yet neither the food nor the small but carefully chosen wine list is overpriced. If you do not want to leave after your meal, stay in one of the four attractive bedrooms decorated in country style. ⊠ *Wheatsheaf Hotel, Swinton,* ☎ 🅵🅰🆇 *01890/860257. 4 rooms, 3 with bath or shower. Restaurant (reservations essential). MC, V. Closed last 2 wks in Feb. and last wk in Oct.*

Melrose

⑫ *15 mi west of Coldstream.*

In the center of the handsome community of Melrose sits **Melrose Abbey,** another of the four Borders abbeys. "If thou would'st view fair Melrose aright, go visit it in the pale moonlight," wrote Scott in *The Lay* *of the Last Minstrel,* and so many of his fans took the advice literally that a sleepless custodian begged him to rewrite the lines. Today the abbey is still impressive: a red sandstone shell with slender windows in the Perpendicular style and some delicate tracery and carved capitals, carefully maintained. Among the carvings high on the roof is one of a bagpipe-playing pig. ⊠ *Main Sq., Melrose,* ☎ *0131/668–8600.* 🖃 *£2.50.* ⊙ *Apr.–Sept., Mon.–Sat. 9:30–6, Sun. 2–6; Oct.–Mar., Mon.–Sat. 9:30–4, Sun. 2–4.*

Next to Melrose Abbey is the National Trust for Scotland's **Priorwood Gardens,** which specializes in flowers for drying. There is also an orchard adjacent to the gardens with a variety of old apple species. ⊠ *Main Square.* 🖃 *£1.* ⊙ *Apr.–June and Sept., Mon.–Sat. 10–5:30, Sun. 1:30–5:30; July–Aug., Mon.–Sat. 10–6:30, Sun. 1:30–6:30; Oct.–Dec., Mon.–Sat. 10–4, Sun. 1:30–4.*

The renovated **Melrose Station,** a poignant survivor of the old **Waverley Route,** a railroad which until 1969 ran between Edinburgh and Carlisle, is now used as offices, with a restaurant on the ground floor.

NEED A
BREAK?

The **Melrose Station Restaurant** (☎ 01896/822546) serves morning coffee and light lunches as well as complete evening meals.

In the center of Melrose at the Ormiston Institute is the **Trimontium Exhibition,** which reveals the fact that the largest Roman settlement in Scotland was at nearby Newstead and displays artifacts discovered there. Tools and weapons, a blacksmith's shop, pottery, and scale models of the fort are included in the display. ☎ *01896/822463.* 🖃 *£1.25.* ⊙ *Apr.–Oct., daily 10:30–4:30.*

Other attractions in Melrose include **Teddy Melrose,** a teddy bear museum, which tells the story of British teddy bears from the early 1900s. There's a collector's bear shop. ⊠ *High St.,* ☎ *01896/822464.* 🖃 *£1.50.* ⊙ *Mon.–Sat. 10–5, Sun. 11–5.*

Melrose Motor Museum is the place for automotive historians to view early products of Scottish manufacture, including a 1909 Albion and an Arrol Johnston from 1926. ⊠ *Annay Rd.,* ☎ *01896/822624 or 01835/822356.* 🖃 *£2.* ⊙ *May–Oct., daily 10:30–5:30.*

★ ⑬ Two miles west of Melrose stands one of the Borders' most visited attractions, **Abbotsford House,** home of Sir Walter Scott. In 1811, already an established writer, Scott bought a farm on this site named Cartleyhole, which was a euphemism for the real name, Clartyhole (*clarty* means muddy or sticky in Scots). The name was surely not romantic enough for Scott, who renamed the property and eventually had it entirely rebuilt in the Romantic style, emulating several other Scottish properties. The resulting pseudo-monastic, pseudo-baronial mansion became the repository for the writer's collection of Scottish memorabilia and historic artifacts. The library holds some 9,000 volumes. Scott died here in 1832. Today the house is owned by his descendants. ⊠ *B6360,* ☎ *01896/752043.* 🖃 *£3.* ⊙ *Mid-Mar.–Oct., Mon.–Sat. 10–5, Sun. 2–5.*

★ ⑭ Sir Walter's final resting place, **Dryburgh Abbey,** is situated on gentle parkland in a loop of the Tweed, southeast of Melrose. Dryburgh is certainly the most peaceful and secluded of the Border abbeys. The abbey suffered from English raids until, like Melrose, it was abandoned in 1544. The style is Transitional, a mingling of rounded Romanesque and pointed early English. The side chapel, where the Haig and Scott families lie buried, is lofty and pillared, detached from the main buildings. ⊠ *Off A68,* ☎ *0131/668–8600.* 🖃 *£2.* ⊙ *Apr.–Sept., Mon.–Sat. 9:30–6, Sun. 2–6; Oct.–Mar., Mon.–Sat. 9:30–4, Sun. 2–4.*

★ **⑮** There is no escaping Sir Walter in this part of the country: Four miles north of Dryburgh is **Scott's View,** possibly the most photographed rural view in the south of Scotland. (Perhaps the only view that is more often used to summon a particular interpretation of Scotland is Eilean Donan Castle, far to the north.) You arrive at this peerless vista by taking the B6356 north from Dryburgh. A poignant tale is told of the horses of Scott's funeral cortege: On their way to Dryburgh Abbey they stopped here out of habit as they had so often in the past. The sinuous curve of the River Tweed, the gentle landscape unfolding to the triple peaks of the **Eildons,** then rolling out into shadows beyond, is certainly worth seeking—and costs nothing to enjoy.

OFF THE
BEATEN PATH

THIRLESTANE CASTLE – At the children's nursery in this 17th-century castle, children are allowed to play with Victorian-style toys and masks and to dress up in costumes. Thirlestane is on the A68 10 miles north of Melrose. ⊠ *Lauder,* ☎ *01578/722430.* 🖃 *£4; grounds only, £1.* ☉ *Easter week, May, June, and Sept., Mon., Wed., Thurs., and Sun. 2–5; July–Aug., Sun.–Fri. 2–5 (grounds open noon–6). Last admission to house and grounds 4:30.*

Dining and Lodging

$ ★ ✕ **Marmion's Brasserie.** This cozy restaurant has outstanding country-style cuisine. It is a great place to stop for lunch after a visit to nearby Abbotsford or Dryburgh Abbey. Try the honey-and-orange lamb, or the Stilton-stuffed mushrooms. ⊠ *Buccleuch St.,* ☎ *01896/822245. MC, V. Closed Sun.*

$$$–$$$$ ✕🏨 **Dryburgh Abbey Hotel.** Right next to the abbey ruins, this civilized hotel is surrounded by beautiful scenery and has a restaurant (no smoking) specializing in traditional Scottish fare. The restrained decor and earthy, muted colors throughout create a peaceful atmosphere in keeping with the location. ⊠ *St. Boswells, TD6 0RQ,* ☎ *01835/822261,* ℻ *01835/823945. 26 rooms with bath. Restaurant (jacket and tie), golf privileges. AE, MC, V.*

$$ ✕🏨 **Burts Hotel.** Built in 1772, this quiet hotel in the center of Melrose retains a considerable amount of its period style, updated with modern conveniences. It has a particularly welcoming bar, with a cheerful open fire and a wide selection of fine malt whiskies, ideal for a quiet dram before or after a meal in the elegant dining room, which has dark-green striped wallpaper, high-back upholstered chairs, and white linen tablecloths. Saddle of venison and roast duck terrine are typical entrées. The bedrooms and public areas are individually decorated with reproduction antiques and floral pastels. Shooting and fishing can be arranged. ⊠ *Market Sq., Melrose, TD6 9PN,* ☎ *01896/822285,* ℻ *01896/822870. 21 rooms with bath or shower. Restaurant. AE, DC, MC, V. Closed Dec. 24–26.*

Galashiels

⑯ *5 mi northwest of Melrose.*

A gray and busy Borders town, Galashiels is still active with textile mills and knitwear shops. At the **Peter Anderson Woollen Mill** is a museum of the town's history and industry; visitors can go on a mill tour and learn about the manufacture of tartans and tweeds. ⊠ *Nether Mill, Galashiels,* ☎ *01896/752091.* 🖃 *£1.75.* ☉ *Year-round, Mon.–Sat. 9–5; June–Sept., also Sun. 12–5. Guided tours Mon.–Thurs. 10:30, 11:30, 1:30, 2:30; Fri. 10:30 and 11:30.*

Dating from 1583, **Old Gala House,** a short walk from the town center, is the former home of the lairds of Galashiels. It is now a museum with displays on the building's history and the town of Galashiels, and also a contemporary art gallery and exhibition space. ⊠ *Scott Crescent,* ☎ *01750/20096.* ⌑ *Free.* ◔ *Tues.–Sat. 10–4, Sun. 2–4.*

Dining and Lodging

$$ ✕⌑ **Woodlands House Hotel.** This Gothic revival–style hotel, chintz-hung and traditionally furnished, has stunning views over Tweeddale (the tree-lined, lush green valley of the River Tweed). The main restaurant specializes in fresh seafood and hearty Scottish cuisine, while Sanderson's Steakhouse is named after a former owner of the house whose portrait gazes down on diners. ⊠ *Windyknowe Rd., TD1 1RG,* ☎ ⅜ *01896/754722. 9 rooms with bath. 2 restaurants, golf privileges, horseback riding, fishing. MC, V.*

Shopping

Peter Anderson Woollen Mill (⊠ Nether Mill, Galashiels, ☎ 01896/ 752091) has a wide selection of woolens and tweeds.

Selkirk

⓱ *7 mi south of Galashiels via A7.*

Selkirk is a hilly outpost with a smattering of antiques shops and an assortment of bakers selling the Selkirk Bannock and other cakes—evidence of Scotland's incurable sweet tooth. Sir Walter Scott was sheriff (county judge) of Selkirkshire from 1800 until his death in 1832, and his statue stands in Market Place. **Sir Walter Scott's Courtroom,** where he presided, contains a display examining Scott's life, his writings, and his time as sheriff, and includes an audiovisual presentation. ⊠ *Market Place,* ☎ *01750/20096.* ⌑ *Free.* ◔ *Apr.–Oct., Mon., Wed.–Sat. 10–4, Sun. 2–4.*

Halliwell's House Museum is tucked off the main square in Selkirk. The building was once an ironmonger's shop, now re-created downstairs, while an exhibit upstairs tells the story of the town. (There is useful background information on the Common Ridings, with an audiovisual presentation.) ⊠ *Market St.,* ☎ *01750/20096.* ⌑ *Free.* ◔ *Apr.–June and Sept.–Oct, Mon.–Sat. 10–5, Sun. 2–4; July–Aug., daily 10–6.*

⓲ Another of the stately homes in the Borders, **Bowhill** stands close to Selkirk. It is a 19th-century building that houses an outstanding collection of works by Gainsborough, Van Dyck, Canaletto, Reynolds, and Raeburn, as well as porcelain and period furniture. ⊠ *Off A708, 3 mi west of Selkirk,* ☎ *01750/20732. House:* ⌑ *£4.* ◔ *July, daily 1–4:30. Grounds and playground:* ⌑ *£1.* ◔ *May–June, Aug., Sat.–Thurs. noon–5; July, daily noon–5.*

Dining and Lodging

$$$ ✕⌑ **Philipburn House.** An 18th-century house set on 4 acres of gardens, Philipburn is an ideal place for families, though it is well-worn in many areas. Bedrooms and the dining room have an Austrian feeling, all pine and floral prints. Poolside suites and a pine lodge are also available. Venison, Borders lamb, and, of course, salmon and trout from the nearby River Tweed are featured on Philipburn's imaginative menu, which is also enlivened with Alpine specialties such as *rösti* (a Swiss dish of grated, pan-fried potatoes often prepared with onions or cheese). ⊠ *Linglie Rd., Selkirk, TD7 5LS,* ☎ *01750/20747,* ⅜ *01750/21690. 16 rooms with bath or shower. Restaurant, pool. AE, MC, V.*

Innerleithen

⑲ *15 mi northwest of Selkirk.*

The main attraction in the linear community of Innerleithen is **Robert Smail's Printing Works,** a fully operational restored print shop with reconstructed waterwheel, which will fascinate adults and older children, who can try their hand at typesetting. ⊠ *7/9 High St., Innerleithen,* ☎ *01896/830206.* ☜ *£2.10.* ☺ *May–Sept., Mon.–Sat. 10–1 and 2–5, Sun. 2–5; Oct., Sat. 10–1 and 2–5, Sun. 2–5 (last admission 45 min before closing).*

Near the town is **Traquair House,** said to be the oldest continually occupied house in Scotland; ale is still brewed in the 18th-century brewhouse here, and is recommended! ⊠ *Traquair, near Innerleithen,* ☎ *01896/830323.* ☜ *£3.80.* ☺ *Apr., May, Sept., daily 12:30–5:30; June–Aug., daily 10:30–5:30 (last admission 5 PM); Oct., Fri.–Sun. 2–5 (last admission 4:30.*

Shopping

The **Scottish Museum of Woollen Textiles** (⊠ Walkerburn, 2 mi east of Innerleithen, ☎ 01896/870619) has a large mill shop offering a wealth of styles.

Peebles

⑳ *6 mi west of Innerleithen.*

Peebles gives the impression of catering primarily to well-to-do, leisured country gentlefolk. Architecturally the town is nothing out of the ordinary, a very pleasant Borders burgh (do not miss the splendid dolphins ornamenting the bridge crossing the River Tweed): The main reason for inclusion here is its excellent, though pricey, shopping.

Dining and Lodging

$$$–$$$$ ✕🏠 **Peebles Hydro.** Not only does it have something for everyone, but
★ it has it in abundance: Archery, snooker, pony trekking, squash, a whirlpool, and a sauna are just a few of the diversions the hotel offers. The elegant Edwardian building, reminiscent of a French château, is set on 30 acres. Bedrooms are comfortably furnished, though inevitably in a hotel of this size, room sizes and decorative standards can vary. The high-ceilinged public areas have an airy, spacious ambience. The restaurant features a Scottish menu with local salmon, lamb, and beef. ⊠ *Peebles,* ☎ *01721/720602,* FAX *01721/722999. 137 rooms with bath. Restaurant (jacket and tie), pool, tennis court, health club, bicycles, baby-sitting, children's programs (ages 0–16), playground, laundry service. AE, DC, MC, V.*

$$$ ✕🏠 **Cringletie House.** Surrounded by grounds that include an old-fash-
★ ioned walled garden whose produce is used in the restaurant, this privately owned property, personally supervised by the owners and their family, is well worth seeking out. There are turrets and crow-step gables in traditional Scottish baronial style, and the spacious first-floor drawing room has an elaborate ceiling and pretty views of the valley. The simple yet comfortably furnished bedrooms are a prelude to the hotel's major achievement: its food. The restaurant is popular with locals (especially for Sunday lunch) for its straightforward, delicious home-cooked meals, such as roast duckling with red currant-and-Cassis sauce. Afternoon tea served in the conservatory is especially recommended. ⊠ *Eddleston, by Peebles, EH45 8PL* ☎ *01721/730233,* FAX *01721/730244. 13 rooms with bath. Restaurant, putting green, tennis court, croquet. AE, MC, V. Closed Jan.–early Mar.*

\$\$–\$\$\$ ✕⛢ **Park Hotel.** This hotel, on the banks of the River Tweed at the northern tip of the Ettrick Forest, offers comfort and tranquility. Rooms have striped or floral wallpaper and pastel fabrics. The restaurant serves superior Scottish cuisine, many of the dishes based on local salmon and trout. ✉ *Innerleithen Rd., EH45 8BA,* ☎ *01721/720451,* ☎ *01721/723510. 24 rooms with bath. Restaurant. AE, DC, MC, V.*

\$ ⛢ **Drummore.** This hillside bed-and-breakfast, set in an acre of wild gardens full of bird life, is well-positioned both for touring the Borders and for visiting Edinburgh. The house is modern and clean, and the guest lounge has a vast picture window which overlooks the River Tweed. ✉ *Venlaw High Rd., EH45 8RL,* ☎ *01721/720336,* ☎ *01721/723004. 2 rooms. No credit cards.* ☽ *Apr.–Oct.*

Outdoor Activities and Sports
BICYCLING
Bicycles may be hired from **Glentress Bike Centre** (Glentress, Peebles, ☎ 01721/722934).

Shopping
You can easily spend a day browsing on Peebles High Street and in the courts and side streets leading off it, temptations awaiting at every turn. **Scott's Hardware Store** (✉ 48 High St., ☎ 01721/720262) has every kind of tool, implement, fixture, fitting, and garden requirement (and mousetraps) spread in glorious array over floors and walls—and even hanging from the ceiling. **Head to Toe** (✉ 43 High St., ☎ 01721/722752) stocks natural beauty products of all descriptions, together with an attractive stock of linens—everything from lace doilies to patchwork quilts; dried flowers and porcelain display dishes are also available. Craftspeople and jewelers are also well represented on the street. **Keith Walter** (✉ 28 High St., ☎ 01721/720650) is a gold- and silversmith who makes items on the premises and and stocks jewelry made by other local designers. **The Country Shop** (✉ 56 High St., ☎ 01721/720630) is an upscale gift store with plenty of souvenirs; if you need a rest after all that shopping, The Country Shop has a coffee shop upstairs, with views over the town and bustling High Street.

THE GALLOWAY HIGHLANDS

Galloway is the name given to the southwest portion of Scotland, west of the main town of Dumfries. The area's scenery is diverse—from its gentle coastline and breezy uplands to places that are gradually disappearing below blankets of conifers. Use caution when negotiating the A75: Although this main trunk road has been improved in recent years, dawdling visitors are liable to find aggressive trucks tailgating them as these commercial vehicles race for the Irish ferries at Stranraer and Cairnryan. (Anything as environmentally sensible as a direct east–west railway link was closed years ago.) Trucks notwithstanding, once you are off the main roads Galloway offers some of the most pleasant touring roads in Scotland. The towns here were chosen in part because they are on rural routes and away from the traffic (though herds of cows on the way to be milked are occasionally a potential hazard).

Gretna

㉑ *10 mi north of Carlisle, 87 mi south of Glasgow, 92 mi southwest of Edinburgh.*

Gretna and **Gretna Green** are, quite simply, an embarrassment to native Scots. What else can you say about a place that advertises "amusing joke weddings," as does one of the visitor centers here? The reason for all these strange goings-on is tied to the reputation the community received as a refuge for runaway couples from England, who once came north to take advantage of Scotland's less strict marriage laws. This was the first place they reached on crossing the border. At one time anyone could perform a legal marriage in Scotland. Often the village blacksmith did the honors, presumably because he was conveniently situated near the main road.

Ruthwell

21 mi west of Gretna via B721 and B724, 83 mi south of Glasgow, 88 mi southwest of Edinburgh.

The landscape is not very impressive around the flat fields of the **Upper Solway Firth,** but as you progress west you'll find more of interest. Inside **Ruthwell Parish Church** is the 8th-century **Ruthwell Cross,** a Christian sculpture admired for the quality of its carving. Considered an idolatrous monument, it was destroyed by the Scottish authorities in 1640 but was later reassembled. Near the church is the **Savings Bank Museum,** which tells the story of the savings-bank movement, founded by the Reverend Doctor Henry Duncan in 1810. ⊠ *Ruthwell, 6½ mi west of Annan,* ☎ *01387/870640.* ⊡ *Free.* ⊙ *Daily 10–1 and 2–5; closed Sun. and Mon. Oct.–Mar.*

At nearby Clarencefield, **Comlongon,** a more recent mansion house, adjoins a well-preserved 15th-century border keep. Visitors can also enjoy the accommodations of a bed-and-breakfast at the castle. ⊠ *B724, midway between Dumfries and Annan,* ☎ *01387/870283,* FAX *01387/870266.* ⊡ *£3.* ⊙ *Mar.–Nov., Sun. 10–6.*

★ ❷❹ Built in a triangular design unique in Britain, moated **Caerlaverock Castle** stands overlooking a nature reserve on a coastal loop of the B725 west of Ruthwell. This 13th-century fortress has solid-sandstone masonry and an imposing double-tower gatehouse. King Edward of England besieged the castle in 1300, when his forces occupied much of Scotland as the Wars of Independence commenced. The castle suffered many times in Anglo-Scottish skirmishes. ⊠ *Off B725,* ☎ *0131/668–8600.* ⊡ *£2.* ⊙ *Apr.–Sept., Mon.–Sat. 9:30–6, Sun. 2–6; Oct.–Mar., Mon.–Sat. 9:30–4, Sun. 2–4.*

The **Caerlaverock National Nature Reserve** is a treat for bird-watchers, who can observe wintering wildfowl from blinds and a visitor center. ⊠ *B725, by Caerlaverock Castle,* ☎ *01387/770275.* ⊡ *Free.* ⊙ *Year-round.*

Dumfries

❷❻ *15 mi northwest of Ruthwell via B725, 76 mi south of Glasgow, 81 mi southwest of Edinburgh.*

The town of Dumfries, where Robert Burns spent the last years of his short life, is a no-nonsense, red-sandstone community. The **River Nith** meanders through Dumfries, and the pedestrian-only town center makes shopping a pleasure (the A75 now bypasses the town). The town also contains Robert Burns's favorite pub (the Globe Inn), the house he lived in, and his mausoleum.

Not surprisingly, in view of its close association to the poet, Dumfries has a **Robert Burns Centre,** housed in a sturdy former mill overlooking the river. The center has an audiovisual program and an extensive exhibit on the life of the poet. ⊠ *Mill Rd.,* ☎ *01387/264808.* ⊡ *Free (small charge for audiovisual show).* ⊙ *Apr.–Sept., Mon.–Sat. 10–8, Sun. 10–5; Oct.–Mar., Tues.–Sat. 10–1 and 2–5.*

Dumfries and Galloway

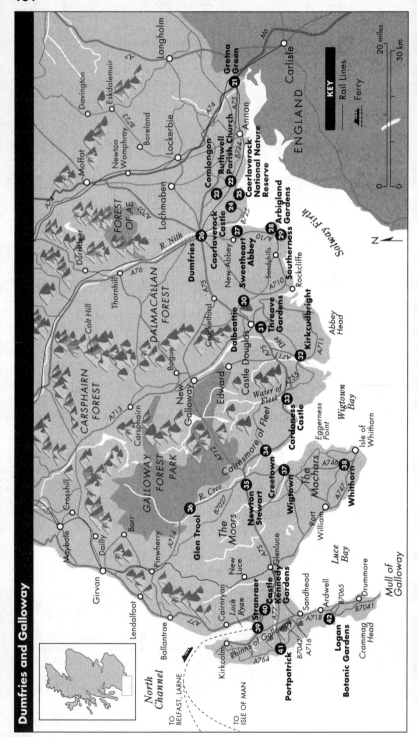

DRUMLANRIG CASTLE – This ornate red-sandstone structure was built on the site of an earlier Douglas stronghold in Nithsdale. The 17th-century castle contains Louis XIV furniture and a valuable collection of paintings by Leonardo da Vinci, Holbein, Rembrandt, and others. There's also a bird of prey center with falconry displays, crafts workshops, and a visitor center on the grounds. The castle is about 15 miles northwest of Dumfries off the A76. ⊠ *Near Thornhill,* ☎ *01848/330248.* ⚏ *£4; park only, £2. Castle:* ⊙ *May–Aug., Fri.–Wed. 11–5; last entry 4.*

MUSEUM OF SCOTTISH LEAD MINING – Reached by taking the Mennock Pass through rounded moorland hills, this museum is at Wanlockhead, a fairly bleak spot and Scotland's highest elevated village. The museum tells the story of one of Scotland's lesser-known industries. There are underground trips for the stout-hearted. The Miners' Library not only shows how the miners educated themselves, but offers a genealogical computer database. ⊠ *Goldscaur Rd., Wanlockhead, on B797 northeast of Sanquhar, 27 mi northwest of Dumfries.* ☎ *01659/74387.* ⚏ *£3.50.* ⊙ *Apr.–Oct., daily 11–4:30 (last guided tour at 4); in winter by appointment only.*

The Arts

Gracefield Arts Centre (⊠ Edinburgh Rd., ☎ 01387/262084) has public art galleries and studios with a constantly changing exhibition program. **The Dumfries and Galloway Arts Festival** is usually held at the end of May, at several venues throughout the region.

The **Robert Burns Centre Film Theatre** (⊠ Mill Rd., ☎ 01387/264808) features special-interest, foreign, and other films that are not widely released.

Outdoor Activities and Sports

BICYCLING

Cycles can be rented from **Greirson and Graham** (⊠ 10 Academy St., ☎ 01387/259483).

Shopping

Dumfries is the main shopping center for the region, with all the big-name chain stores as well as specialty shops. **Greyfriars Crafts** (⊠ 56 Buccleuch St., ☎ 01387/264050) has mainly Scottish goods, including Stuart Crystal, Caithness Glass, and Ettrick Valley textiles. For a souvenir that's easier to pack, try **David Hastings** (⊠ Marying, Shield-hill, Amisfield, Dumfries, ☎ 01387/710451; visitors by appointment; negative-option direct mail service offered), which has more than 80,000 old postcards.

If you are visiting Drumlanrig Castle (☞ Off the Beaten Path, *above*), do not miss the **crafts center** (☎ 01848/331555, ⊙ May–Aug., Fri.–Wed. 11–5) in the stable block, chock full of all types of crafts work, including leathercraft, blown-glass pieces, landscape and portrait artists, stainless steel jewelry and cutlery, and knitted crafts.

New Abbey

7 mi south of Dumfries via A710, 83 mi south of Glasgow, 88 mi southwest of Edinburgh.

27 The village of New Abbey has at its center **Sweetheart Abbey,** which provides a mellowed red and roofless backdrop to the village. It was founded in 1273 by Devorgilla Balliol, in memory of her husband, John. The couple's son, also named John, was the puppet king installed in Scotland by Edward of England, when the latter claimed sovereignty over Scotland. After John's appointment the Scots gave him a scathing nickname that would stay with him for the rest of his life: *Toom*

Tabard, meaning "Empty Shirt." ⊠ *A710 at New Abbey,* ☎ *0131/668–8600.* ⚑ *£1.* ⊙ *Apr.–Sept., Mon.–Sat. 9:30–6, Sun. 2–6; Oct.–Mar., Mon.–Wed. and Sat. 9:30–4, Thurs. 9:30–noon, Sun. 2–4.*

Kirkbean

5 mi south of New Abbey via A710, 88 mi south of Glasgow, 94 mi southwest of Edinburgh.

㉘ A little community (blink and you've missed it) set in a bright green landscape is the location of **Arbigland Gardens;** follow signs from the village. Here pops up another of Galloway's curious tales: The son of a former gardener of Arbigland, whose name was John Paul, left Scotland and became the founder of the U.S. Navy. This seafaring son, John Paul Jones, returned to his native coast in a series of daring raids in 1778. A museum here tells the story. The gardens tended by Jones's father are typical of the area: lush and sheltered, with blue water visible through the protecting trees. You are only moments from the coast. ⊠ *Off A710, by Kirkbean,* ☎ *01387/880283.* ⚑ *£2.* ⊙ *May–Sept., Tues.–Sun. and bank holidays, 2–6.*

Southerness

㉙ *3 mi south of Kirkbean via A710, 91 mi south of Glasgow, 97 mi southwest of Edinburgh.*

The road to Southerness ends in a welter of recreational vehicles and trailer homes in the shadow of one of Scotland's earliest lighthouses, built in 1749 by the port authorities of Dumfries who were anxious to make the treacherous River Nith approaches safer.

En Route The road turns west and becomes faintly Riviera-like. You can take a brisk walk from Sandyhills to Rockcliffe, two of the sleepy coastal communities overlooking the creeping tides and endless shallows of the Solway coast.

Dalbeattie

㉚ *12 mi northwest of Southerness via A710, 89 mi south of Glasgow, 95 mi southwest of Edinburgh.*

Like the much larger Aberdeen far to the northeast, Dalbeattie's buildings were constructed with local grey granite from the town's quarry. The predominance of granite, with its well-scrubbed gray glitter, makes Dalbeattie atypical of Galloway towns, whose house fronts are predominantly painted in pastels.

Lodging

$$ ⊞ **Auchenskeoch Lodge.** This quaint and informal Victorian shooting
★ lodge, now a country-house hotel, has three bedrooms and delicious food (for residents only). Many of the vegetables and herbs used in the kitchen are grown on the 20 acres of gardens and woodland surrounding the house; guests are urged to help themselves to delectable puddings. The furnishings, decorated with chintz, have a comfortable, faded elegance; there is a full-size billiards table in the games room. The sitting room offers crammed bookshelves and an open fire. A private loch, turf and gravel maze, and croquet lawn provide outdoor entertainment. ⊠ *Auchenskeoch, by Dalbeattie, DG5 4PG,* ☎ *01387/780277. 3 rooms with bath or shower. MC, V. Closed Dec. 25, Jan. 1.*

Outdoor Activities and Sports

HORSEBACK RIDING

Barend Properties Riding School and Trekking Centre (✉ Sandyhills, by Dalbeattie, Kirkcudbright, ☎ 01387/780663) helps you to a "horse-high" view of the beautiful coast and countryside of this region.

Castle Douglas

6 mi west of Dalbeattie, 94 mi south of Glasgow, 99 mi southwest of Edinburgh.

Although it is a pleasant town with a long main street where the home bakeries vie for business, Castle Douglas's main attraction is its proximity to **Threave Garden.** As Scotland's best-known charitable conservation agency, the National Trust for Scotland cares for several garden properties. This horticultural undertaking demands the employment of many gardeners—and it is at Threave that the gardeners train, thus ensuring there is always some fresh development or experimental planting here. This gives lots of vigor and interest to the sloping parkland around the mansion house of Threave. There is a good visitor center as well. ✉ *South of A75, 1 mi west of Castle Douglas,* ☎ *01556/502575.* ✍ *£3.60. Gardens:* ☉ *Daily 9:30–sunset; walled garden and greenhouses:* ☉ *Daily 9:30–5. Visitor center and shop:* ☉ *Apr.–Oct., daily 9:30–5:30.*

Threave Castle (not to be confused with the mansion house in Threave Garden) is a few minutes away by car and is signposted from the main road. To get there you must leave your car in a farmyard (trying to pretend you don't have the feeling you're intruding) and walk the rest of the way. Reassured by the Historic Scotland signs (because Threave is being cared for by the national government), you make your way down to the reeds by the river on an occasionally muddy path. At the edge of the river you can then ring a bell, and, rather romantically, a boatman will come to ferry you across to the great, gaunt tower looming from a marshy island in the river. Threave was an early home of the Black Douglases, the earls of Nithsdale, and lords of Galloway. The castle was dismantled in the religious wars of the mid-17th century, though enough of it remains to have housed prisoners from the Napoleonic Wars of the 19th century. ✉ *North of A75, 3 mi west of Castle Douglas,* ☎ *0131/668–8600.* ✍ *£1.50 (includes ferry).* ☉ *Apr.–Sept., Mon.–Sat. 9:30–6, Sun. 2–6.*

Castle Douglas's **Blowplain Open Farm** provides guided tours showing the area's daily life on a small hill farm. ✉ *Balmaclellan, Castle Douglas,* ☎ *01644/420206.* ✍ *£2.* ☉ *Easter–Oct., weekdays, tour at 2 PM (lasts 2 hrs).*

Outdoor Activities and Sports

BICYCLING

You can rent cycles from **Ace Cycles** (✉ Church St., Castle Douglas, ☎ 01556/504542).

WATER SPORTS

The **Galloway Sailing Centre** (✉ Loch Ken, ☎ 01644/420626) rents dinghies, windsurfing equipment, and canoes, and runs sailing courses.

Shopping

The Posthorn (✉ 26–30 St. Andrew St., ☎ 01556/502531) consists of two shops specializing in gift items, including the figurines made by Border Fine Art; export facilities are provided. **Galloway Gems** (✉ 130–132 King St., ☎ 01556/503254) not only has gold and silver jewelry, but also stocks mineral specimens and polished stone slices.

It is well worth the short drive north from Castle Douglas (A75 then B794) to visit **Benny Gillies Books, Maps and Prints** (⊠ 31 Victoria St., Kirkpatrick Durham, ☎ 01556/650412), which stocks an outstanding selection of hand-colored antique maps and prints featuring areas throughout Scotland.

Kirkcudbright

㉜ *11 mi southwest of Castle Douglas via B736 and B727, 103 mi south of Glasgow, 109 mi southwest of Edinburgh.*

Kirkcudbright is an 18th-century town of unpretentious houses, some of them color washed in pastel shades and roofed with the blue slates of the district. For much of this century it has been known as an artists' town, and its L-shaped main street is full of crafts and antiques shops. Conspicuous in the town center is **MacLellan's Castle,** the shell of a once-elaborate castellated mansion dating from the early 16th century. ⊠ *Off High St.,* ☎ *0131/668–8600.* ☞ *£1.20.* ⊗ *Apr.–Sept., Mon.–Sat. 9:30–6, Sun. 2–6; Oct.–Mar., Sat. 9:30–4, Sun. 2–4.*

The 17th-century **Broughton House** was once the home of the artist E. A. Hornel (he was one of the "Glasgow Boys" of the early 20th century). Many of his paintings hang in the house, which is furnished in period style and contains an extensive library specializing in local history. There is also a Japanese garden. ⊠ *12 High St.,* ☎ *01557/330437.* ☞ *£2.10.* ⊗ *Apr.–Oct., daily 1–5:30 (last admission 4:45).*

The delightfully old-fashioned **Stewartry Museum,** stuffed with all manner of local paraphernalia, allows you to putter and absorb as much or as little as takes your interest in the display cases. ⊠ *St. Mary St.,* ☎ *01557/331643.* ☞ *£1.50.* ⊗ *Mar.–Apr. and Oct., Mon.–Sat. 11–4; May, Mon.–Sat. 11–5; June and Sept., Mon.–Sat. 11–5, Sun. 2–5; July–Aug., Mon.–Sat. 10–6, Sun. 2–5; Nov.–Feb., Sat. 11–4.*

The **Tolbooth Arts Centre,** in the old tolbooth, gives a history of the town's artists' colony and its leaders E. A. Hornel, Jessie King, and Charles Oppenheimer, and displays some of their paintings as well as work by modern artists and craftspeople. ⊠ *High St.,* ☎ *01557/331556.* ⊗ *Mar.–Apr. and Oct., Mon.–Sat. 11–4; May, Mon.–Sat. 11–5; June and Sept., Mon.–Sat. 11–5, Sun. 2–5; July and Aug., Mon.–Sat. 10–6, Sun. 2–5; Nov.–Feb., Sat. 11–4.*

Gatehouse of Fleet

9 mi west of Kirkcudbright via A755 and B727, 108 mi southwest of Glasgow, 114 mi southwest of Edinburgh.

A peaceful, pleasant backwoods sort of place, Gatehouse of Fleet has a castle guarding its southern approach from the A75. **Cardoness Castle** is a typical Scottish tower house, severe and uncompromising. The 15th-century structure once was the home of the McCullochs of Galloway, then later the Gordons. ⊠ *A75, 1 mi southwest of Gatehouse of Fleet,* ☎ *0131/668–8600.* ☞ *£1.20.* ⊗ *Apr.–Sept., Mon.–Sat. 9:30–6, Sun. 2–6; Oct.–Mar., Sat. 9:30–4, Sun. 2–4.*

The **Mill on the Fleet** heritage center is a converted cotton mill in which you can learn the story of this pretty little town's involvement in this industry. As you go around, you wear a hard hat with earphones which pick up individual room commentaries—a little disconcerting at first. There is also a tearoom serving light lunches and delicious home-baked goods. ⊠ *High St.,* ☎ *01557/814099. Call for details of opening times and charges.*

Dining and Lodging

$$$ ✕🏠 **Cally Palace.** This hotel was once a private mansion (built in 1759). Many of the public rooms in the Georgian building retain their original grandeur, which includes elaborate plaster ceilings and marble fireplaces. The bedrooms are individually decorated and well equipped. The house is surrounded by 150 acres of gardens, loch, and parkland, including an 18-hole golf course, and has an indoor leisure center with pool, solarium, and sauna. Scottish produce stars in the French-influenced restaurant in such dishes as poached salmon with hollandaise sauce. The staff is exceptionally friendly and prepared to spoil you. ⊠ *Gatehouse of Fleet, Galloway, DG7 2DL,* ☎ *01557/814341,* FAX *01557/814522. 56 rooms with bath. Restaurant, bar, indoor pool, hot tub, sauna, 18-hole golf course, putting green, tennis court, croquet, fishing. MC, V. Closed Jan. and Feb.*

$ 🏠 **High Auchenlarie Farmhouse.** This working beef farm, set high on a hillside overlooking Wigtown Bay, offers bed-and-breakfast and, for a small additional charge, evening meals. It's an excellent place to come to enjoy the throaty call of moo-cows. ⊠ *Gatehouse of Fleet, DG7 2DW,* ☎ *01557/840231. 3 rooms with bath or shower. No credit cards.* ☼ *Mar.–Oct.*

Shopping

There is a well-stocked gift and crafts shop at the **Mill on the Fleet** heritage center (⊠ High St., ☎ 01557/814099). **Galloway Lodge Preserves** (⊠ 24–28 High St., ☎ 01557/814357) has a marmalade, mustard, and merchandise shop which stocks the complete line of the company's locally made produce, plus Scottish pottery.

En Route If you single-mindedly pursue the suggested policy of avoiding the A75, then your route will loop to the northwest. Take a right by the Anwoth Hotel in Gatehouse of Fleet, where the signpost points to Gatehouse Station. This route will provide you with a taste of the Galloway hinterland. Beyond the wooded valley where the Water of Fleet runs (local rivers are often referred to as "Water of . . ."), dark hills and conifer plantings lend a brooding, empty air to this lonely stretch.

Creetown

34 *12 mi west of Gatehouse of Fleet, 95 mi southwest of Glasgow, 112 mi southwest of Edinburgh.*

The low-ground community of Creetown is noted for its **Gem Rock Museum.** The museum has an eclectic mineral collection, a dinosaur egg, and an entertaining demonstration of the various colors with which some rocks fluoresce. ⊠ *A75,* ☎ *01671/820357.* 🎫 *£2.50.* ☼ *Easter–Sept., daily 9:30–6; Oct.–Dec. 25, daily 10–4; mid-Jan.–Feb., weekends 10–4; Mar.–Easter, daily 10–4 (last admission 30 min before closing); and by appointment.*

Shopping

The **Creetown Gem Rock Museum** (⊠ Creetown, ☎ 01671/820357) sells extraordinary mineral and gemstone crystals in its gift shop—both loose and in settings.

Newton Stewart

35 *8 mi northwest of Creetown, 89 mi southwest of Glasgow, 108 mi southwest of Edinburgh.*

The solid and bustling little town of Newton Stewart makes a good touring base for the western region of Galloway.

★ ③⑥ One possible excursion to the north from Newton Stewart takes you to the **Galloway Forest Park** (☉ At all times; ✉ Free). Take the A714 north from town along the wooded valley of the **River Cree** (there is a nature reserve, the Wood of Cree, on the far bank). After about 10 miles turn right at the signpost for **Glen Trool.** This road leads you toward the hills that have thus far been the backdrop for the woodlands. Watch for another sign for Glen Trool. Follow this little road through increasingly wild woodland scenery to its terminus at a parking lot. Only after you have left the car and climbed for a few minutes onto a heathery knoll does the full, rugged panorama become apparent. With high purple-and-green hilltops shorn rock-bare by glaciers, a dark, winding loch, and thickets of birch trees sounding with birdcalls, the setting almost looks more highland than the real Highlands to the north. Glen Trool is one of Scotland's best-kept secrets. Note **Bruce's Stone,** just above the car park, marking the site where Scotland's champion Robert the Bruce (King Robert I) won his first victory, in 1307, in the Scottish Wars of Independence.

En Route   The **Machars** is the name given to the triangular promontory south of Newton Stewart. This is an area of gently rolling farmlands, yellow gorse hedgerows, rich grazings for dairy cattle, and a number of stony prehistoric sites. Most of the glossy, green expanse is used for dairy farming. Fields are bordered by dry stane dykes (dry walling) of sharp-edge stones; and small hills and hummocks give the area its characteristic frozen-wave look, a reminder of the glacial activity that shaped the landscape.

Wigtown

③⑦ *8 mi south of Newton Stewart, 96 mi southwest of Glasgow, 114 mi southwest of Edinburgh.*

The sleepy hamlet of Wigtown has a broad main street and colorful housefronts. Down by the muddy shores of Wigtown Bay there's a monument to the Wigtown Martyrs, two women who were tied to a stake and left to drown in the incoming tide during the anti-Covenant witch-hunts of 1685. Much of Galloway's history is linked with Border feuds, but even more with the ferocity of the so-called Killing Times, when the Covenanters were persecuted for their belief that the king should be second to the church, and not vice versa. Wigtown, like several other places in the region, is dominated by a hilltop Covenanters' Monument, a reminder of the old persecutions.

Whithorn

③⑧ *11 mi south of Wigtown, 107 mi southwest of Glasgow, 125 mi southwest of Edinburgh.*

The Machars are well known for their early Christian sites. The road that is now the A746 was a pilgrim's way and a royal route that ended at **Isle of Whithorn** (which is not, in fact, quite an island), a place that early Scottish kings and barons sought to visit at least once in their lives. The pilgrimage was often prescribed as a penance, but these pleasant shores impose no penance today. The goal was St. Ninian's chapel, the 4th-century cell of Scotland's premier saint. Some pilgrims made for Whithorn village and others for the sandspit "isle." Both places claimed to be the site of the original "Candida Casa" of the saint. As you approach Whithorn's 12th-century priory, observe the royal arms of pre-1707 Scotland (that is, Scotland before the Union with England) carved and painted above the arch of the Pend (covered way).

The **Whithorn Dig and Visitor Centre** explains the significance of what is claimed to be the site of the earliest Christian community in Scotland. The museum includes a collection of early Christian crosses. The dig site itself is overlooked by the shell of the priory. ⊠ *Main St., Whithorn,* ☎ *01988/500508.* ⌑ *£2.70.* ⊙ *Apr.–Oct., daily 10:30–5 (last tour 4:30).*

Dining and Lodging

$$$ ✕⊡ **Corsemalzie House.** This attractive 19th-century mansion is set on 40 acres of peaceful grounds behind the fishing village of Port William, west of Whithorn. Sporting pursuits are the hotel's main attraction, with shooting, sea and game fishing, and golf on tap. The restaurant features a "Taste of Scotland" menu, and the public rooms and bedrooms are in keeping with the country-house style of the hotel. ⊠ *Corsemalzie, Port William, Newton Stewart, Wigtownshire, DG8 9RL,* ☎ *01988/860254,* FAX *01988/860213. 15 rooms with bath. Golf privileges, fishing. AE, MC, V. Closed late-Jan.–Feb.*

Stranraer

39 *34 mi northwest of Whithorn via A747 and A75, 89 mi southwest of Glasgow via A77, 133 mi southwest of Edinburgh.*

Stranraer is the main ferry port (if you happen to make a purchase in one of its shops, you may wind up with some Irish coins in your change). It is not a very scenic place itself, but nearby is a high point
★ **40** of this region. **Castle Kennedy Gardens** surround the gaunt shell of the original Castle Kennedy, which was burned out in 1716. The present property owners, the Earl and Countess of Stair, live on the grounds, at Lochinch Castle, built in 1864 (not open to the public). Pleasure grounds dispersed throughout the property were built by the second earl of Stair in 1733. The Earl was a field marshal and used his soldiers to help with the heavy work of constructing banks, ponds, and other major landscape features. When the rhododendrons are in bloom, the effect is kaleidoscopic. ⊠ *North of A75, 3 mi east of Stranraer,* ☎ *01776/702024.* ⌑ *£2.* ⊙ *Apr.–Sept., daily 10–5.*

NEED A
BREAK? There is a pleasant **tearoom** at the Castle Kennedy Gardens, but if a more substantial meal is required, try the **Eynhallow Hotel** (☎ 01581/ 400256) nearby, for its homecooked bar lunches (noon–2:30), afternoon teas (2–5) or bar suppers (6–late).

Portpatrick

41 *8 mi southwest of Stranraer via A77, 97 mi southwest of Glasgow, 143 mi southwest of Edinburgh.*

The holiday town of Portpatrick lies across the Rhinns of Galloway from Stranraer. Once an Irish ferry port, Portpatrick's exposed harbor eventually proved too risky for larger vessels. Today the village is the starting point for Scotland's longest official long-distance footpath, the **Southern Upland Way,** which runs a switchback course for 212 miles to Cockburnspath, on the eastern side of the Borders. Just south of Portpatrick are the lichen-yellow ruins of 16th-century **Dunskey Castle,** accessible by a clifftop path.

The southern half of the **Rhinns of Galloway** has a number of interesting places to visit, all easily reached from Portpatrick. **Ardwell House Gardens** is a pleasant garden on a domestic scale. ⊠ *Ardwell,* ☎ *01776/860227.* ⌑ *£1.50.* ⊙ *Apr.–Sept., daily 10–6 (walled garden 10–5).*

★ Spectacular for garden lovers and close to Ardwell are the **Logan Botanic Gardens,** a specialist garden of Edinburgh's **Royal Botanic Garden.** The Logan Gardens feature plants that enjoy the prevailing mild climate, especially tree ferns, cabbage palms, and other Southern Hemisphere exotica. ⊠ *Off B7065 at Port Logan,* ☎ *01776/860231,* ℻ *01776/860333.* ▭ *£2.* ☉ *Mar. 15–Oct., daily 10–6.*

If you wish visit the southern tip of the Rhinns of Galloway, called the **Mull of Galloway,** follow the B7065/B7041 until you run out of land. The cliffs and seascapes here are rugged, and there is a lighthouse and a bird reserve.

THE BORDERS AND THE SOUTHWEST A TO Z

Arriving and Departing

By Bus
From the south the main bus services use the M6 or A1, with appropriate feeder services into the hinterland; contact **Scottish Citylink/National Express** (☎ 0990/808080). There are also bus links from Edinburgh and Glasgow. Contact **Lowland Omnibuses** (☎ 01896/752237) or **Stagecoach Western Scottish** (☎ 01563/525192, 01387/253496, or 01776/704484).

By Car
The main route into both the Borders and Galloway from the south is the M6, which deteriorates into the less well-maintained A74 north of the Border (it is currently being upgraded). This road gives the choice of the leisurely A7 (signed off from the A74) northeastward through Hawick toward Edinburgh or the A75 and other parallel routes westward into Galloway and to the ferry ports of Stranraer and Cairnryan.

There are, however, a number of alternative routes: Starting from the east, the A1 brings you from the English city of Newcastle to the border in about an hour. The A1 has the added attraction of Berwick-Upon-Tweed, on the English side of the border. Moving west, the A697, which leaves the A1 beside Alnwick (in England) and crosses the border at Coldstream, is a leisurely back-road option with an attractive view of the countryside. The A68 offers probably the most scenic route to Scotland: after climbing to Carter Bar, it reveals a view of the rolling blue Border hills and windy skies before dropping into the ancient town of Jedburgh, with its ruined abbey.

By Ferry
P&O European Ferries runs a service from Larne in Northern Ireland to Cairnryan several times daily, with a crossing time of 2 hours, 15 minutes. Details are available from P&O at Cairnryan, Stranraer, Dumfries, and Galloway, DG9 8RF, ☎ 01581/200276. **Seacat** operates a fast-speed catamaran service four times a day, taking only 90 minutes to cross from Belfast to Stranraer. For details and bookings, ☎ 0345/523523.

By Plane
The nearest Scottish airports are at **Edinburgh** and **Glasgow.** ☞ Chapters 3 and 4 for details.

By Train
The Borders are not well served by rail. Visitors can use services from **London Euston,** in England, to **Glasgow;** these trains stop at **Carlisle,** just south of the border, and some stop at **Lockerbie.** There are also direct trains from Carlisle to **Dumfries,** stopping at **Gretna Green.** On

the east coast some services stop at **Berwick-Upon-Tweed,** just south of the border. For more information, call Glasgow's Central Station (☎ 0141/204–2844).

Getting Around

By Bus

Bus services in the area include **Stagecoach Western Scottish** (☎ 01563/525192, 01387/253496, or 01776/704484), which serves towns and villages in Dumfries and Galloway, and **Lowland Omnibuses** (☎ 01896/752237), which offers Reiver Rover (£24 weekly, £6.50 daily, children half-price) and Waverley Wanderer (£28 weekly, £9.50 daily, children half-price) flexible tickets that provide considerable savings for travel in the Borders.

By Car

A solid network of rural roads allows you to avoid the A1 in the eastern Borders, as well as the A75, which runs along the Solway coast east to west linking Dumfries and Stranraer. Both roads carry heavy traffic, partly because of the poor rail connections.

By Train

Train travel is not very practical in the Borders. In fact the **Scottish Borders Rail Link** is nothing of the kind: It's actually a bus service linking **Hawick, Selkirk,** and **Galashiels** with rail services at **Carlisle.** In Dumfries and Galloway there are connecting trains from Carlisle to **Stranraer,** which also has a direct link to Ayr and Glasgow. There is also a direct service twice daily between **Dumfries** and Stranraer. (Both the Borders and Dumfries and Galloway suffered badly in the shortsighted contraction of Britain's rail network in the 1960s.) Contact **National Rail Enquiries** (☎ 01228/44711) for further details.

Contacts and Resources

Emergencies

For **police, fire,** or **ambulance,** dial 999 from any telephone. No coins are needed for emergency calls from public telephone booths.

Fishing

A Comprehensive Guide to Scottish Borders Angling is the only way to find your way around the many Borders waterways. The *Castabout Anglers Guide to Dumfries and Galloway* covers the southwest. The tourist boards for Dumfries and Galloway and the Borders (☞ Visitor Information, *below*) carry these and other publications (including a comprehensive information pack). In short, finding suitable water in this area is quite easy.

Golf

There are 29 courses in Dumfries and Galloway and 18 in the Borders. The Freedom of the Fairways Pass (5-day, £66; 3-day, £43) allows play on all 18 Borders courses, and is available from the Scottish Borders Tourist Board. All tourist boards (☞ Visitor Information, *below*) supply comprehensive leaflets.

Guided Tours

ORIENTATION

The bus companies mentioned above also run a variety of orientation tours in the area. In addition, tours are run by **Galloway Heritage Tours** (✉ Rosemount Guest House, Kippford, ☎ 01556/620214).

SPECIAL-INTEREST

The area is primarily covered through Edinburgh- or Glasgow-based companies (☞ Chapters 3 and 4 for details). **James French** (✉ French's

Garage, Coldingham, ☎ 01890/771283) runs coach tours in the summer season. **Ramtrad Holidays** (✉ 54 Edinburgh Rd., Peebles, ☎ 01721/720845) offer chauffeur-driven tours tailored to customers' requirements, and also golf and fishing packages.

Late-Night Pharmacies

All towns in the region have at least one pharmacy. Pharmacies are not found in rural areas, where general practitioners often dispense medicines. The police will provide assistance in locating a pharmacist in an emergency.

Visitor Information

Dumfries (✉ Whitesands, ☎ 01387/253862). **Gretna Gateway** (✉ off the M74 northbound at Gretna (☎ 01461/338500). **Hawick** (✉ Drumlanrig's Tower, High Street,☎ 01450/372547). **Jedburgh** (✉ Murray's Green,☎ 01835/863435).

Seasonal information centers are at Castle Douglas, Coldstream, Dalbeattie, Eyemouth, Galashiels, Gatehouse of Fleet, Gretna Green, Kelso, Kirkcudbright, Langholm, Melrose, Moffat, Newton Stewart, Peebles, Sanquhar, Selkirk, and Stranraer.

6 Fife and Angus

St. Andrews, Dundee

Fife has the distinction of being the sunniest and driest part of Scotland. It is an area of sandy beaches, fishing villages, and windswept cliffs, hills, and glens. The east coast is home to the ancient university and golf town of St. Andrews, with its romantic stone houses and seaside ruins. North of Fife, Angus is the hinterland of Scotland's fourth-largest city Dundee. Angus glens provide scenic hikes by way of secluded and out-of-the-way hill passes that penetrate the massif and lead to high, empty and wild places.

THE REGIONS OF FIFE AND ANGUS sandwich Scotland's fourth-largest—and often overlooked—city,
Dundee. This is typical eastern-seaboard country:
open beaches, fishing villages, and breezy cliff-top walkways. Scotland's
east coast has only light rainfall throughout the year; northeastern Fife,
in particular, may claim the record for the most sunshine and the least
rainfall in all Scotland, which all adds to the enjoyment when you're
touring the East Neuk (*neuk,* pronounced nyook, is Scots for corner)
or exploring St. Andrews' nooks and crannies.

By Gilbert
Summers

The particular charm of Angus is its variety: In addition to its seacoast
and pleasant Lowland market centers, there's also a hinterland of
lonely rounded hills with long glens running into the typical Grampian
Highland scenery beyond. One of Angus's interesting features, which
it shares with the eastern Lowland edge of Perthshire, is its fruit-growing industry. Seen from roadside or railway, what at first sight appear
to be sturdy grapevines on field-length wires turn out to be soft-fruit
plants, mainly raspberries. The chief fruit-growing area is Strathmore,
the broad vale between the northwesterly Grampian mountains and
the small coastal hills of the Sidlaws behind Dundee. Striking out from
this valley—the heart of the Angus region—visitors can make a number of day trips to uplands or seacoast.

Pleasures and Pastimes

Dining

With its affluent population, St. Andrews supports several upmarket
hotel restaurants. Since it is also a university town and popular tourist
destination, there are also many good-value cafes and bistro-style
restaurants. Not far away at Peat Inn is a restaurant that many would
claim to be one of the very best in Scotland. The coastal communities
can also serve up excellent seafood, in particular at Anstruther. In some
of the West Fife towns, such as Kirkcaldy and Dunfermline, and in
Dundee, you will find restaurants serving not only traditional Scottish
fare, but also ethnic food (Italian, Indian, and Chinese are popular),
in addition to numerous small cafés of all kinds. Bar lunches are becoming the rule in large and small hotels throughout the region, and
in seaside places the "carry oot" (to go) meal is an old tradition. A feature of this area is that relatively isolated small communities manage
to support high-quality restaurants, because people are prepared to travel
out of the cities.

WHAT TO WEAR

Dress is, for the most part, casual; that said, some center city establishments might prefer more formal dinner attire, and this is noted.

CATEGORY	COST*
$$$$	over £30
$$$	£20–£30
$$	£10–£20
$	under £10

*per person for a three-course meal, including VAT and excluding drinks and
service

Golf

Every golfer's ambition is to play at St. Andrews, and once you are in
Fife the ambition is easily realized. Five St. Andrews courses are open
to visitors (all are part of the St. Andrews Club). There are more than
40 other courses in the region. Most offer golf to the visitor by the round

or the day. Many of the area's hotels offer golfing packages or will arrange a day of golf.

Lodging

If you're staying in Fife, the obvious base is St. Andrews, where you will find ample accommodations of all kinds. Other towns also offer a reasonable selection, and you will find good hotels and guest houses at Dunfermline and Kirkcaldy. Along the coastal strip and in the Howe of Fife between Strathmiglo and Cupar there are some superior country-house hotels, many with their own restaurants.

CATEGORY	COST*
$$$$	over £110
$$$	£80–£110
$$	£45–£80
$	under £45

All prices are for a standard double room, including service, breakfast, and VAT.

Shopping

Shopping in this mainly rural region is inevitably concentrated in the larger towns. St. Andrews, with its university and its world-renowned golfing facilities, attracts enough affluent people to sustain some smaller specialty shops. Dundee, as Scotland's fourth-largest city, is an important retail shopping center for the northern part of Angus, but the choices for shoppers here are similar to those found in most large towns (department stores, such as Marks and Spencer, predominate).

Exploring Fife and Angus

Fife lies north of the Firth of Forth, stretching far up the Forth Valley (which is west and a little north of Edinburgh), with St. Andrews on its eastern coast. Northwest of Fife, the city of Dundee and its rural hinterland, Angus, stretch still farther north and west towards the foothills of the Grampian mountains. Each of these regions is described in its own section, below.

Great Itineraries

This is not a huge area, so getting around is straightforward. Treat it as a series of excursions off the main north-south artery, the A90, which leads from Edinburgh to Aberdeen. Fife has a pleasant but not spectacular rural hinterland—in fact, it feels a long way from the hills. Angus is different, with a strong sense of a looming massif always to the north. To explore it, take your pick of the Angus Glens—especially Glens Prosen or Clova or—farthest north—Esk; all beautifully out of the way. They represent probably one of the most overlooked corners of Scotland.

IF YOU HAVE 2 DAYS

Numbers in the text correspond to numbers in the margin and on the Fife Area, St. Andrews, and Angus Area maps.

Two days allows you to sample the extremes of the area in every sense. Make your way to ⊞ **St. Andrews** ① to take in this most attractive of Scottish east coast Lowland towns. Next day travel north of ⊞ **Dundee** ⑱ to visit **Kirriemuir** ㉖, a typical Angus town with "Peter Pan" connections, and **Glamis** ㉘, for its castle—and perhaps penetrate the hills via the Glens of Angus west of Kirriemuir.

IF YOU HAVE 4 DAYS

This allows plenty of time to spend two or three days sampling not just **St. Andrews** ① but also the rest of the East Neuk, the easternmost corner with its characteristic pantile-roofed fishing villages—**Crail** ⑧, Anstruther with its **Scottish Fisheries Museum** ⑨, **Pittenweem** ⑩ and, just inland, **Kellie Castle** ⑪—strung along the south-facing coast. If you golf, then you could allocate a day on a golf course as well. Likewise, in Angus, you could first travel along the breezy coast towards **Arbroath** ㉑ and **Montrose** ㉒, where the sharply contrasting Adam-designed **House of Dun** ㉓ and ancient **Edzell Castle** ㉕ lie within easy reach. Staying overnight near 🏨 **Forfar** ㉗ would bring the inland communities of Kirriemuir, Glamis, and Meigle, with its outstanding collection of early medieval sculpture, within easy reach the next day.

IF YOU HAVE 7 DAYS

You can cover not only Fife and Angus, but also add to the itinerary suggested for four days the inland communities of **Falkland** (its **palace** ⑬ was once a royal hunting lodge), **Cupar** ⑮, close to **Hill of Tarvit House** ⑯, and the **Fife Folk Museum** ⑰ at **Ceres** (for a real treat, have a meal and stay overnight at the Peat Inn). Also spend as much time in the city of Dundee as you wish—though in a week your explorations should take you beyond the strict boundaries of the area, as Perth, Stirling, Royal Deeside, and Aberdeen are all within easy reach.

When to Tour Fife and Angus

Spring in the Angus glens can be quite attractive, with the high tops still snow-covered. Similarly, the moorland colors of autumn are appealing. (In autumn and winter, some hotels in rural Angus get quite busy with foreign sportsmen intent on marauding the local wildfowl.) However, it has to be said that Fife and Angus are really spring and summer destinations—unless you simply like wandering about enjoying scenery.

AROUND FIFE

In its western parts, Fife still bears the scars of heavy industry, especially coal mining. Yet these signs are less evident as you move farther east: Northeastern Fife, around the university-and-golf town of St. Andrews, seems to have played no part in the industrial revolution; the residents instead earned a livelihood from the grain fields or from the sea. Fishing has been a major industry, and in the past a string of Fife ports traded across the North Sea. Today the legacy of Dutch-influenced architecture—crow-step gables and distinctive town houses, for example—is still plain to see and gives these East Neuk villages a distinctive charm.

St. Andrews is unlike any other Scottish town. Once Scotland's most powerful ecclesiastical center, seat also of the country's oldest university, and then, much later, the very symbol and spiritual home of golf, the town has a comfortable, well-groomed air, sitting almost smugly apart from the rest of Scotland.

St. Andrews

❶ *52 mi northeast of Edinburgh, 83 mi northeast of Glasgow.*

Scotland's golf mecca, St. Andrews is, after Edinburgh, one of the most visited places in Scotland. The center of this compact town retains its original medieval street plan of three roughly parallel streets—North Street, Market Street, and South Street—leading away from the city's earliest religious site, near the cathedral.

The local legend regarding the founding of St. Andrews has it that a certain St. Regulus, or Rule, acting under divine guidance, carried relics of St. Andrew by sea from Patras in Greece. He was shipwrecked on this Fife headland and founded a church. The holy man's name survives in the square-shaped **St. Rule's Tower,** consecrated in 1126 and ❷ the oldest surviving building in St. Andrews. Nearby is the city **cathe-** ❸

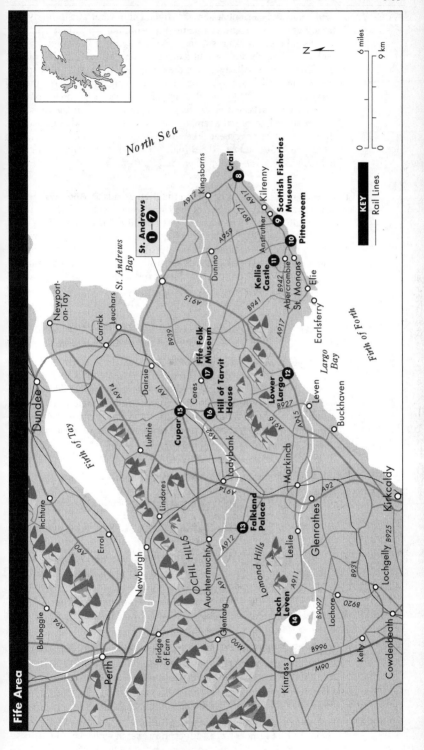

Fife Area

North Sea

St. Andrews 1–7

Crail 8
Kilrenny
Scottish Fisheries Museum 9
Pittenweem 10
Anstruther
Kellie Castle 11
St. Monans
Abercrombie
Elie
Earlsferry

Kingsbarns
Dunino
Newport-on-Tay
Leuchars
Carrick

Firth of Forth

Largo Bay
Leven
Buchhaven
Lower Largo 12
Hill of Tarvit House 16
Fife Folk Museum 17
Ceres
Cupar 15
Dairsie
Luthrie
Lindores
Ladybank
Markinch
Glenrothes
Kirkcaldy

Firth of Tay
Dundee

Inchture
Errol
Balbeggie
Newburgh
Auchtermuchty
Strathmiglo
OCHIL HILLS
Falkland Palace 13
Leslie
Lomond Hills
Loch Leven 14
Lochgelly
Lochore
Kinross
Kelty
Cowdenbeath

Bridge of Earn
Glenfarg
Perth

St. Andrews Bay

KEY
— Rail Lines

6 miles
9 km

N

dral, today only a ruined, poignant fragment of what was formerly the largest and most magnificent church in Scotland. Work on it began in 1160, and consecration was finally celebrated in 1318, after several setbacks. The cathedral was subsequently damaged by fire and repaired, but finally fell into decay during the Reformation, in the 16th century. Only ruined gables, parts of the nave south wall, and other fragments survive, although you can still enjoy dizzying views of town from St. Rule's Tower, accessed via a steep set of stairs. The on-site museum helps visitors interpret the remains and gives a sense of what the cathedral must once have been like. *Museum and St. Rule's Tower,* ☎ *0131/668–8600.* ✆ *£1.50.* ✉ *Joint ticket to cathedral and castle (☞ below): £3.* ☉ *Apr.–Sept., Mon.–Sat. 9:30–6, Sun. 2–6; Oct.–Mar., Mon.–Sat. 9:30–4, Sun. 2–4.*

❹ Directly north of the cathedral on the shore stands **St. Andrews Castle,** which was started at the end of the 13th century. Although now a ruin, the remains include a rare example of a bottle dungeon, cold and gruesome, in which many prisoners spent their last hours. Even more atmospheric is the castle's mine and countermine. The former was a tunnel dug by besieging forces in the 16th century; the latter, a tunnel dug by castle defenders in order to meet and wage battle below ground. You can stoop and crawl into this narrow passageway—an eerie experience, despite the addition of electric light. The visitor center has a good audiovisual presentation on the castle's history. ☎ *0131/668–8600.* ✆ *£2.* ✉ *Joint ticket to cathedral and castle: £3.* ☉ *Apr.–Sept., Mon.–Sat. 9:30–6, Sun. 2–6; Oct.–Mar., Mon.–Sat. 9:30–4, Sun. 2–4.*

❺ The **Royal & Ancient Golf Club of St. Andrews** on The Scores, the ruling house of golf worldwide, is the spiritual home of all who play or follow the game. Its clubhouse on the dunes—a dignified building, more like a town hall than a clubhouse and open to club members only—is adjacent to St. Andrews's famous **Old Course.** The town of St. Andrews prospers on golf, golf schools, and golf equipment (the manufacture of golf balls has been a local industry for more than 100 years), and the Old Course is associated with the greatest players of the game.

❻ Just opposite the Royal & Ancient Golf Club is the **British Golf Museum,** which explores the centuries-old relationship between St. Andrews and golf and displays a variety of golf memorabilia. ✉ *Golf Pl.,* ☎ *01334/478880.* ✆ *£3.75.* ☉ *Mid-Apr.–mid-Oct., daily 10–5:30; mid-Oct.–mid-Apr., Thurs.–Mon. 11–3. Closed Dec. 25, Jan. 1.*

❼ St. Andrews is also the home of Scotland's oldest university. Founded in 1411, **St. Andrew's University** now consists of two stately old colleges in the middle of town and some attractive modern buildings on the outskirts. A third weather-worn college, originally built in 1512, has become a girls' school. The handsome university buildings can be explored on guided walks, sometimes led by students in scarlet gowns. ☎ *01334/462110.* ☉ *Tours twice daily in July and Aug.*

☝ At the **Sea Life Centre** sea lions, penguins, and many other forms of marine life are displayed in settings designed to simulate their natural environments. The exhibits include numerous aquariums and pool gardens. ✉ *The Scores, West Sands, St. Andrews,* ☎ *01334/474786.* ✆ *£3.95.* ☉ *Daily 10–6 (extended hours in July and Aug.).*

Only a few minutes northwest of St. Andrews's famous Old Course on the A919, **Leuchars** has a 12th-century church with some of the finest Norman architectural features to be seen anywhere in Scotland. Note in particular the blind arcading (arch shapes on the wall) and the beautifully decorated chancel and apse.

St. Andrews

151

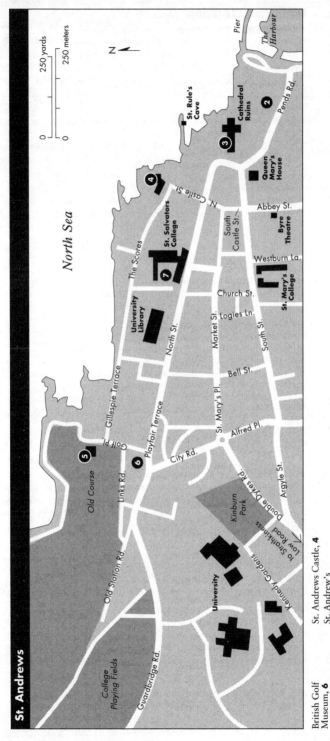

North Sea

The Harbour
Pier
St. Rule's Cave
Cathedral Ruins
Queen Mary's House
Pends Rd.
N. Castle St.
Abbey St.
St. Salvators College
Byre Theatre
South Castle St.
Westburn La.
The Scores
Church St.
St. Mary's College
University Library
North St.
Market St.
Logies Ln.
South St.
Gillespie Terrace
Bell St.
Golf Pl.
Playfair Terrace
St. Mary's Pl.
Alfred Pl.
City Rd.
Argyle St.
Links Rd.
Old Course
Kinburn Park
Double Dykes Rd.
Low Road
to Strathkiness
Old Station Rd.
University
Kennedy Gardens
College Playing Fields
Guardbridge Rd.

250 yards
250 meters

British Golf Museum, **6**
Cathedral, **3**
Royal & Ancient Golf Club of St. Andrews, **5**

St. Andrews Castle, **4**
St. Andrew's University, **7**
St. Rule's Tower, **2**

Dining and Lodging

$$ ✕ **The Grange Inn.** On a breezy hilltop overlooking St. Andrews, the Grange Inn offers an attractive blend of old-fashioned charm with polished brass, low lights, and open fires. The three dining areas include two (non-smoking) with superb views over St. Andrews. The delicious specials might include monkfish with pesto, braised duck with red cabbage, or gravlax with sweet dill mustard. There is also an extensive wine list. ⊠ *Grange Rd., St. Andrews, Fife, KY16 8LJ,* ☎ *01334/472670. AE, DC, MC, V. Closed Mon. and Tues. Nov.–Mar.*

$$$–$$$$ ✕⊞ **Rufflets Country House Hotel.** This ivy-bedecked country house just outside St. Andrews is surrounded by 10 acres of formal and informal gardens. All the rooms are attractively decorated and comfortable, with all the amenities one would expect of a top-class hotel, but at a moderate price. Dinner is served in the roomy Garden Restaurant, famous for its use of local produce to create memorable Scottish dishes. Recommended are the Tay salmon and fillet of Aberdeen Angus beef. ⊠ *Strathkinness Low Rd., St. Andrews, Fife, KY16 9TX,* ☎ *01334/472594. 26 rooms with bath or shower. Restaurant, bar. AE, DC, MC, V.*

$ ⊞ **University of St. Andrews.** For accommodation within walking distance of all the town's attractions, it's hard to better the university for value and convenience. Room sizes—mainly singles—vary from adequate in the new building to happily spacious in the old building. The newer rooms have private bathrooms (all rooms come equipped with sinks), and all have access to a restaurant, bar, lounge, TV room, and laundry facilities. ⊠ *79 North St.,* ☎ *01334/462000,* FAX *01334/462500. 153 rooms, 72 with shower. Restaurant, bar, coin laundry. MC, V. Closed early Sept.–May.*

Nightlife and the Arts

PUBS

Bert's Bar (⊠ South St.) is a spartan, no-nonsense drinking den where leathery old men like to swill pints and swap stories. The crowd is quite friendly, and the decor—even down to the black-and-white television and pickled eggs—is decidedly Scottish. **Chariots** (⊠ The Scores), located inside the Scores Hotel, is popular with locals in their thirties and forties. With open fires and dark wood paneling, the **Grange Inn** (☞ Dining and Lodging, *above*) has a pleasant old-style, traditional feel, not to mention its excellent menu.

THEATER

Byre Theatre (⊠ Abbey St., ☎ 01334/476288) has a resident repertory company that performs during the summer months.

Outdoor Activities and Sports

GOLF

The following five St. Andrews courses are open to visitors (all are part of the St. Andrews Club). For details of availability—there is usually a waiting list—contact the Reservations Department, Links Management Committee, Pilmour Cottage, St. Andrews, KY16 9SF (☎ 01334/475757).

Old Course (15th century). 18 holes, 6,578 yards, SSS 72, handicap certificate required.
New Course (1894). 18 holes, 6,604 yards, SSS 72.
Jubilee Course (1899). 18 holes, 6,284 yards, SSS 72.
Eden Course (1913). 18 holes, 5,971 yards, SSS 69.
Strathyrum Course (1993). 18 holes, 5,195 yards, SSS 69.

Shopping

Among the worthwhile specialty shops you'll find in St. Andrews is **Graeme Renton** (⊠ 72 South St., ☎ 01334/476334), the best place in the region, if not in all Scotland, for Oriental rugs and carpets of all colors, patterns, and sizes—many of them antiques. **Church Square Ceramics and Workshops** (⊠ Church Sq., between South St. and Market St., ☎ 01334/477744) offers decorative and domestic stoneware, ceramic, and enameled jewelry. **Bonkers** (⊠ 80 Market St., ☎ 01334/473919) has a huge selection of clothing, clocks, books, cards, pottery, and gift items. **St. Andrews Fine Art** (⊠ 84A Market St., ☎ 01334/474080) is the place to go for Scottish paintings from 1800 to the present (oils, watercolors, drawings, and prints are available).

Crail

★ **8** *10 mi south of St. Andrews via A917.*

One of numerous East Neuk fishing communities along the Fife coast, the town of Crail has a picturesque Dutch-influenced town house, or tolbooth, which contains the oldest bell in Fife, cast in Holland in 1520. Full details on the heritage and former trading links of this tiny port can be found in the **Crail Museum and Heritage Center.** ⊠ *62 Marketgate, Crail,* ☎ *01333/450869.* ◻ *Free.* ۞ *Easter wk and June–Sept., Mon.–Sat. 10–1 and 2–5, Sun. 2–5; after Easter wk until the end of May, weekends and public holidays 2–5.*

Anstruther

4 mi southwest of Crail.

Anstruther boasts an attractive waterfront (larger than Crail's) with a few shops brightly festooned with children's pails and shovels as a gesture to seaside vacationers. Facing Anstruther harbor is the **Scottish Fisheries Museum,** housed in a colorful cluster of buildings, the earliest of which dates from the 16th century. This museum illustrates the difficult life of Scottish fishermen, past and present, through documents, artifacts, paintings, and tableaux. (These displays, complete with the reek of tarred rope and net, have been known to induce nostalgic tears in not a few old deckhands.) There are also floating exhibits at the quayside. ⊠ *Anstruther harbor,* ☎ *01333/310628.* ◻ *£3.* ۞ *Apr.–Oct., Mon.–Sat. 10–5:30, Sun. 11–5; Nov.–Mar., Mon.–Sat. 10–4:30, Sun. 2–4:30.*

Dining

$$$ ✕ **The Cellar.** Specializing in fish, but offering a selection of Scottish
★ beef and lamb as well, the Cellar is devoted to serving top-quality ingredients cooked simply to preserve all the natural flavor. The crayfish-and-mussel bisque is famous, and the wine list reflects high standards. Entered through a small courtyard, the restaurant is charmingly furnished in an unpretentious, old-fashioned style. It is popular with the locals, but its fame is more widespread. ⊠ *24 E. Green St., Anstruther, Fife,* ☎ *01333/310378. AE, MC, V.*

Nightlife

The **Dreel Tavern** (⊠ 16 High St., ☎ 01333/310727) is a 16th-century coaching inn famous for its hand-drawn ales.

Outdoor Activities and Sports

BICYCLING

The back roads of Fife make pleasant bicycling terrain. Cycles can be rented from **East Neuk Outdoors** (⊠ Cellardyke Park, Anstruther, ☎ 01333/311929),which also offers archery, rappelling, and canoeing packages.

Pittenweem

➓ *1½ mi southwest of Anstruther.*

The working harbor at Pittenweem is backed by many examples of East Neuk architecture. Look for the crow-step gables (the stepped effect on the ends of the roofs), the white *harling* (Scots for rough-casting, the rough mortar finish on walls), and the red pantiles (S-shaped in profile). The "weem" part of the town's name comes from the Gaelic *uaime,* or cave. This town's particular cave is at Cove Wynd up a close (alleyway) behind the waterfront. St. Fillan's Cave contains the shrine of St. Fillan, a 6th-century hermit who lived therein. ⊠ *Cove Wynd, near harbor,* ☎ *01333/311495 (St. John's Episcopal Church).* 🏷 *40p.* ☉ *Tues.–Sat. 10–5, Sun. noon–5.*

➕ For a break from this nautical atmosphere follow B942 inland to **Kellie Castle.** Dating from the 16th and 17th centuries and restored in Victorian times, the castle stands among the grain fields and woodlands of northeastern Fife. The castle is surrounded by 4 acres of attractive gardens. ⊠ *B9171 (3 mi northwest of Pittenweem),* ☎ *01333/720271.* 🏷 *Castle and gardens, £3.10; gardens only, £1.* ☉ *Castle: Easter and May–Sept., daily 1:30–5:30; Oct., weekends 1:30–5:30 (last admission 4:45). Garden and grounds: Apr.–Oct., daily 9:30–7; Nov.–Mar., daily 9:30–4.*

Lower Largo

➓ *10 mi west of Pittenweem.*

The main claim to fame of Lower Largo is that it was the birthplace of Alexander Selkirk, the Scottish sailor who was the inspiration for Daniel Defoe's Robinson Crusoe. His statue can be seen above the doorway of the house where he was born in Main Street.

Shopping

At nearby Upper Largo, in a converted barn, **Scotland's Larder** (⊠ Upper Largo, KY8 6EA, ☎ 01333/360414) is a shop (and restaurant) that sells a huge assortment of Scottish preserves, baked goods, and seasonal produce—anything from shortbread to smoked salmon, Dundee cakes to oysters. It also offers tastings, talks, and cooking demonstrations, all of which show off the excellent foods of Scotland.

Glenrothes

9 mi west of Lower Largo.

A modern planned town, Glenrothes is notable for its public murals and sculptures.

Shopping

The **Balbirnie Craft Centre** (⊠ near Balbirnie House, Glenrothes ☎ 01592/758759), in an 18th-century stable mews, is a peaceful setting in which to buy items made by craftspeople who live on the premises: Their work includes furniture, silver, jewelry, paintings and picture framing, glassblowing, sculpture, and leather goods.

Falkland

5 mi north of Glenrothes via A92 and A912.

One of the most attractive communities in all Fife, Falkland is a royal burgh of twisting streets and crooked stone houses. The town is dominated by **Falkland Palace,** a former hunting lodge of the Stuart monarchs and one of the earliest examples in Britain of the French Renaissance

★ inated by

style. Overlooking the main street is the palace's most attractive feature—the south range of walls and chambers, rich with Renaissance buttresses and stone medallions, built for James V in the 1530s by French masons. He died here in 1542, and the palace was a favorite resort of his daughter, Mary, Queen of Scots. Behind the palace are gardens that contain a most unusual survivor: a "royal" tennis court (not at all like its modern counterpart) built in 1539 and still in use. ⊠ *Falkland,* ☎ *01337/857397.* 🎫 *£4.10; gardens only, £2.10.* ☉ *Apr.–Oct., Mon.–Sat. 11–5:30, Sun. 1:30–5:30 (last admission to palace 4:30, to garden 5).*

Loch Leven

⑭ *10 mi southwest of Falkland via A911.*

Scotland's largest Lowland loch, Loch Leven is famed for its fighting trout. The area is also noted for its birdlife, particularly its wintering wildfowl. On the southern shore overlooking the loch, **Vane Farm Nature Reserve,** a visitor center run by the Royal Society for the Protection of Birds, is informative about Loch Leven's ecology. ⊠ *Vane Farm, Rte. B9097, just off M90 and B996,* ☎ *01577/862355.* 🎫 *£2.* ☉ *Apr.–Dec., daily 10–5; Jan.–Mar., daily 10–4.*

Cupar

⑮ *21 mi northwest of Loch Leven via M90 and A91.*

⑯ Cupar is a busy market town with a variety of shops. On rising ground near the town is the National Trust for Scotland's **Hill of Tarvit House.** A 17th-century mansion, the house was later altered in the high-Edwardian style at the turn of the 20th century by the Scottish architect Sir Robert Lorimer. Inside the house are fine collections of antique furniture, Chinese porcelain, bronzes, tapestries, and Dutch paintings. You will find the house two miles south of town off A916. ☎ *01334/653127.* 🎫 *£3.10; gardens only, £1.* ☉ *House: Easter and May–Sept., daily 1:30– 5:30; Oct., weekends 1:30–5:30 (last admission 4:45). Garden and grounds: Apr.–Oct. daily 9:30–7; Nov.–Mar., daily 9:30–4.*

NEED A BREAK?

In summer the National Trust operates a **tearoom** inside Hill of Tarvit House. It is always stocked with tasty homemade Scottish baked goods. ☉ *Same dates as house, but opens at 12:30.*

☖ Just outside Cupar at the **Scottish Deer Centre** red deer can be seen at close quarters on ranger-guided tours. There are also nature trails, a winery, falconry displays, an adventure playground (a wood and tire fortress not suited for young children), a shop, and a restaurant. ⊠ *A91, near Rankelour Farm,* ☎ *01337/810391.* 🎫 *£2.50.* ☉ *daily 9:30–6.*

OFF THE BEATEN PATH

DAIRSIE BRIDGE – A few minutes east of Cupar at Dairsie, an unclassified road goes off to the right from the A91 and soon runs by the River Eden. Dairsie Bridge over the river is 450 years old and has three arches. Above the trees rises the spire of Dairsie Church, dating from the 17th century, and the stark ruin of Dairsie Castle, often overlooked, stands gloomily over the river nearby. With wild-rose hedges, grazing cattle, and pheasants calling from the woody thickets, this is the very essence of rural, Lowland Fife, yet it's only about 15 minutes from the Old Course.

Outdoor Activities and Sports

HEALTH AND FITNESS CLUB

Cupar Sports Centre (⊠ Carselogie Rd., Cupar, ☎ 01334/654793) has a swimming pool, sports hall, fitness rooms, squash, steam bath, and tanning beds.

Shopping

Margaret Urquhart (⊠ 13–17 Lady Wynd, ☎ 01334/652205) attracts customers from as far away as Edinburgh and Glasgow and stocks a wide range of British and international designer names.

Ceres

3 mi southeast of Cupar via A916 and B939, 9 mi southwest of St. Andrews.

⑰ To learn more about the history and culture of rural Fife, visit the **Fife Folk Museum** at Ceres. The life of local rural communities is reflected in artifacts and documents, all housed in suitably authentic buildings that include a former weigh house and adjoining weavers' cottages. ☎ *01334/828250.* ☜ *£1.60.* ⊙ *Easter and May–Oct., Sat.–Thurs. 2–5.*

Dining and Lodging

$$$–$$$$ ✕☗ **The Peat Inn.** This popular inn and eatery is best known for its
★   outstanding restaurant, generally considered one of the finest in Scotland. Mouthwatering entrées like ragout of scallops, monkfish, and pork, or roast saddle of venison with lentils and smoked bacon justify the high prices charged for dinner; lunch is slightly cheaper, but for either you may have to book well in advance. In a detached building there are eight comfortable double suites, making this a French-style restaurant with rooms. ⊠ *Junction of B940 and B941, 5 mi southwest of St. Andrews,* ☎ *01334/840206,* ☒ *01334/840530. 8 rooms with bath. Restaurant, bar. AE, DC, MC, V. Closed Sun. and Mon.*

DUNDEE AND ANGUS

The industrial city of Dundee, famed historically for its economic reliance on "jute, jam, and journalism," contrasts dramatically with the farmlands and glens of its rural hinterland and the coastal links northward. Peaceful back roads in this area are uncluttered; the main road from Perth/Dundee to Aberdeen—the A90—requires special care, with its mix of fast cars, lorries, and unexpectedly slow farm traffic.

Dundee

⑱ *14 mi northwest of St. Andrews, 58 mi north of Edinburgh, 79 mi northeast of Glasgow.*

Dundee's urban renewal program—its determination to shake off its grimy industrial past—was motivated in part by the arrival of the **RRS (Royal Research Ship)** *Discovery,* the vessel used by Captain Robert Scott on his polar explorations. The steamer was originally built and launched in Dundee; now it's a permanent tourist exhibit. A visitor center and onboard exhibition allow visitors to sample life as it was aboard the intrepid *Discovery.* ⊠ *Discovery Point, Discovery Quay,* ☎ *01382/201245.* ☜ *£4.* ⊙ *Mon.–Sat. 10–5, Sun. 11–5; Nov.–Mar., daily until 4.*

At Victoria Dock, the frigate *Unicorn,* a 46-gun wooden warship, lies berthed. The *Unicorn* has the distinction of being the oldest British-built warship afloat (the fourth-oldest in the world), having been launched at Chatham, England, in 1824. Onboard models and displays offer a glimpse into the history of the Royal Navy. ⊠ *Victoria Dock (just east of Tay Rd. Bridge),* ☎ *01382/200900.* ☜ *£2.* ⊙ *Mid-Mar.–Oct. daily 10–5 (call for winter opening hours).*

Dundee's principal museum and art gallery is **The McManus Galleries,** which has displays—many of them new—on a range of subjects, in-

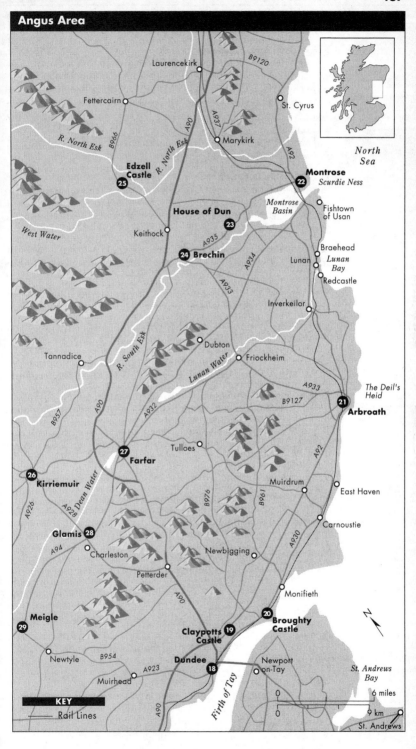

Angus Area

Laurencekirk

B9120

Fettercairn

St. Cyrus

R. North Esk

B966

A937

A90

Marykirk

North Sea

A92

Edzell Castle 25

R. North Esk

Montrose 22
Scurdie Ness

House of Dun 23

Montrose Basin

Fishtown of Usan

A935

Keithock

24 **Brechin**

Braehead
Lunan Bay

Lunan

A934

Redcastle

A933

Inverkeilor

R. South Esk

Dubton

Friockheim

Tannadice

Lunan Water

A933

The Deil's Heid

B9127

21

Arbroath

A90

B957

A932

27 **Farfar**

Tulloes

A92

26

Kirriemuir

Muirdrum

Dean Water

East Haven

A926

A928

B976

B961

Carnoustie

Glamis 28

A94

Charleston

Newbigging

A930

Petterder

Monifieth

Meigle

29

Newtyle

B954

A90

Newbigging

20 **Broughty Castle**

Claypotts Castle 19

Muirhead

A923

Dundee 18

Newport on-Tay

St. Andrews Bay

Firth of Tay

N

0   6 miles
0   9 km

St. Andrews

KEY

—— Rail Lines

cluding local history, trade, and industry. ⊠ *Albert Sq.,* ☎ *01382/ 223141.* 🖾 *Free.* ☉ *Mon. 11–5, Tues.–Sat. 10–5.*

The **Barrack Street Museum** specializes in natural history, with exhibitions on the wildlife and geology of Angus and the Highlands. The museum also displays the skeleton of the famous Tay Whale, immortalized by Scotland's worst poet, William MacGonagall, born in Dundee in 1830. His consistently dire poems caused him to be lionized by Edinburgh's legal and student fraternity. The stranding of a whale locally was one of many incidents that moved him to verse. ⊠ *Barrack St. and Meadowside,* ☎ *01382/223141, ext. 65152.* 🖾 *Free.* ☉ *Mon. 11– 5, Tues.–Sat. 10–5.*

The **University Botanic Gardens** are a well-landscaped collection of native and exotic plants. Also on the premises are tropical and temperate greenhouses and a visitor center. ⊠ *Riverside Dr.,* ☎ *01382/566939.* 🖾 *£1.* ☉ *Mar.–Oct., Mon.–Sat. 10–4:30, Sun. 11–4; Nov.–Feb., Mon.–Sat. 10–3, Sun. 11–3.*

In the eastern suburbs of Dundee, away from the surviving Victorian architecture of the city center, are two castles of interest. **Claypotts Castle** is a well-preserved 16th-century tower house laid out on a Z-plan. ⊠ *South of A92 (3 mi east of city center),* ☎ *0131/668–8600. Call for opening times and charges.*

Built to guard the Tay estuary, **Broughty Castle** is now a museum with displays on fishing, ferries, and the history of the town's whaling industry. There is also a display of arms and armor. ⊠ *Broughty Ferry (4 mi east of city center),* ☎ *01382/776121.* 🖾 *Free.* ☉ *Mon. 11–1 and 2–5; Tues.–Thurs. and Sat. 10–1 and 2–5; also Sun. 2–5 July–Sept.*

Dundee is ringed by country parks that offer ample sports and leisure activities. **Crombie Country Park** has a reservoir with extensive woodlands in 250 acres, as well as wildlife blinds, nature trails, a children's play park, picnic areas, and a display-and-interpretation center staffed by a ranger. ⊠ *Off Rte. B961 (7 mi from Newbigging),* ☎ *01241/ 860360.* 🖾 *Free.* ☉ *Daily 10–dusk.*

Dining and Lodging

$$–$$$ ✗🏨 **Angus Thistle Hotel.** In the center of Dundee, this hotel offers pleasant views, especially from rooms on the higher floors. Some suites have four-poster beds, whirlpool baths, and private sitting rooms. The decor is modern throughout. The hotel's restaurant serves adequate meals, drawn mostly from the beef and fish categories. ⊠ *101 Marketgait, Dundee, DD1 1QT,* ☎ *01382/226874,* 🖷 *01382/322564. 58 rooms with bath. Restaurant, bar. AE, DC, MC, V.*

Nightlife and the Arts

DISCOS

Dundee has several discos: **De Sthils** (⊠ S. Ward Rd., ☎ 01382/200066), **Fat Sam's Disco** (⊠ 31 S. Ward Rd., ☎ 01382/228181), **Arthur's** (⊠ St. Andrews St., ☎ 01382/221061), and **Oscar's** (⊠ Brown St., ☎ 01382/ 221176).

FILM

Cannon Film Centre (⊠ Seagate, ☎ 01382/225247 or 226865) screens mainstream films.
Odeon Multiplex (⊠ Stack Leisure Park, ☎ 01382/400855) shows recent releases.
Steps Film Theatre (⊠ Wellgate Centre, ☎ 01382/434037) screens less-mainstream films, as well as current releases.

MUSIC

Bonar Hall (⊠ Park Pl., ☎ 01382/229450) hosts classical, jazz, and rock concerts, as well as chamber music.

Caird Hall (⊠ City Sq., ☎ 01382/434940 or 434941) is one of Scotland's finest concert halls, staging a wide range of music.

West Port Bar (⊠ Henderson's Wynd, ☎ 01382/200993) offers folk music on most Mondays—call to confirm.

THEATER

Dundee Repertory Theatre (⊠ Tay Sq., ☎ 01382/223530) is in an award-winning complex that includes an exhibition gallery, and is home to a resident theater group as well as a dance company. Both offer diverse programs.

Little Theatre (⊠ Victoria Rd., ☎ 01382/225835) presents a wide variety of performances, especially modern theatrical works by local and visiting groups.

Whitehall Theatre (⊠ Bellfield St., ☎ 01382/322684) offers a variety of choices, including Scottish shows, light opera, and variety and musical entertainments.

Outdoor Activities and Sports

HEALTH AND FITNESS CLUB

Dundee Olympia Leisure Centre (⊠ Earl Grey Pl., ☎ 01382/223141, ext. 4187) has four swimming pools, a diving pool, sauna, water slides, exercise equipment, and a restaurant.

Shopping

The modern covered shopping mall in Dundee—the **Wellgate Shopping Centre** (⊠ off Panmure Street, ☎ 01382/225454)—is the place to visit if you're looking for the major retail chains. But if you search around a little, you'll find a scattering of smaller shops that have more character and unusual selections. **The Cookshop** (⊠ 27 Wellgate Centre, ☎ 01382/221256) stocks an enormous variety of cooking equipment and other kitchenware. **J. Allan Braithwaite** (⊠ 6 Castle St., ☎ 01382/322693) offers 13 freshly roasted coffees and over 30 blended teas, including mango and apricot (remember that such specialty teas can usually be taken home without import restriction if you purchase them as gifts). There are also several good jewelers in Dundee. **Rattrays** (⊠ 32 Nethergate, ☎ 01382/ 227258) has been in business for more than 140 years. **Stephen Henderson the Jeweller** (⊠ 1 Union St., ☎ 01382/221339) has a good selection of silver and pewter Ortak jewelry from Orkney, *skean dhus* (ornamental Highlander daggers), and *quaichs,* a small dish with handles traditionally used for whisky tasting.

Arbroath

㉑ *15 mi north of Dundee via A92.*

In the holiday resort and fishing town of Arbroath traditional boat-building can still be seen. Arbroath has several small curers and processors, with shops offering the town's most famous delicacy, "Arbroath smokie"—whole haddock gutted and lightly smoked.

Arbroath Abbey, founded in 1178, in the center of town, is unmistakable and seems to straddle whole streets, as if the town were simply ignoring the redstone ruin in its midst. Surviving today are remains of the church, as well as one of the most complete examples in existence of an abbot's residence. From here in 1320, a passionate plea was sent by King Robert the Bruce and the Scottish church to Pope John XXII in far-off Rome. The pope had until then sided with the English kings, who adamantly refused to acknowledge Scottish independence. The Declaration of Arbroath stated firmly, "For as long as but a hundred of us remain alive, never will we on any conditions be brought under English rule. It is in truth not for glory, nor riches, nor honours that we are fighting, but for freedom—for that alone, which no honest man gives up but with life itself." Some historians describe this plea (originally drafted in Latin) as the single most important document in Scottish history. The pope advised English King Edward to make peace, but warfare was to break out along the border from time to time for the next 200 years. ✉ *Arbroath town center,* ☎ *0131/668–8600.* ✏ *£1.50.* ☻ *Apr.–Sept., Mon.–Sat. 9:30–6, Sun. 2–6; Oct.–Mar., Mon.–Sat. 9:30–4, Sun. 2–4.*

Also notable in Arbroath is the **Signal Tower Museum.** Arbroath was the shore base for the construction of the Bell Rock lighthouse, on a treacherous, barely exposed offshore rock in the early 19th century. This signal tower was built to facilitate communication between the mainland and the builders working offshore. The museum in the tower now tells the story of the lighthouse, built by Robert Stevenson in 1811. (The name Stevenson is strongly associated with the building of lighthouses throughout Scotland, though the most famous son of that family is remembered for another talent. In fact, Robert Louis Stevenson gravely disappointed his family by choosing to become a writer instead of an engineer.) The museum also houses a collection of items related to the history of the town, its folk life, and the local fishing industry. ✉ *Ladyloan (west of harbor),* ☎ *01674/673232.* ✏ *Free.* ☻ *Mon.–Sat. 10–5; also Sun. 2–5 in July and Aug.*

Dining

$ ✕ **Byre Farm Restaurant.** Amid the farms and woods of Angus's cozy hinterland, you may stumble upon this unpretentious little establishment on the edge of a tiny village and wonder how it survives. The answer: its good plain Scottish cooking, and its proximity to the city of Dundee. You'll eat in a long, low room—a barn conversion—at unfussy pine tables. Try the salmon cutlets braised in butter, the pan-fried lamb chops, or the roast beef with roasted potatoes. There's also a Scottish traditional high tea here, a substantial meal served in the late afternoon. ✉ *Redford, Carmyllie, Arbroath, Angus,* ☎ *01241/860245. MC, V. Closed Mon. Nov.–Feb., closed Tues. Mar.–Oct.*

Nightlife

DISCO

Arbroath dances at **Club Metro** (✉ Queen's Dr., ☎ 01241/872338).

PUBS

Seek out the **Foundry Bar** (✉ E. Mary St., ☎ 01241/872524), a spartan bar frequented by locals, which is enlivened by impromptu music sessions—customers often bring along their fiddles and accordions, and all join in.

Outdoor Activities and Sports

HEALTH AND FITNESS CLUBS

Arbroath Sports Centre (✉ Keptie Rd., ☎ 01241/872999) has a swimming pool, squash courts, games hall, and a gymnasium.

The **Saltire Centre** (✉ Montrose Rd., ☎ 01241/431060) has fitness rooms, sauna, and exercise equipment.

Montrose

㉒ *14 mi north of Arbroath via A92.*

A handsome, unpretentious town with a museum and a selection of shops, Montrose is also noted for its attractive beach. Behind Montrose the River Esk forms a wide estuary known as the Montrose

Basin. The Scottish Wildlife Trust operates a nature reserve here, with a good number of geese, ducks, and swans.

★ ㉓ The National Trust for Scotland's leading attraction in this area, the **House of Dun,** overlooks the Montrose Basin. This 1730s mansion, built by architect William Adam, is particularly noted for its ornate plasterwork. ⊠ *A935 (4 mi west of Montrose),* ☎ *01674/810264.* ⊡ *£3.10; garden only, £1.* ☉ *House: Easter and May–Sept., daily 1:30–5:30; Oct., weekends 1:30–5:30 (last admission 5). Garden and grounds, daily 9:30–sunset.*

Outdoor Activities and Sports
HEALTH AND FITNESS CLUB
Montrose Sports Centre (⊠ Marine Ave., ☎ 01674/676211) is an indoor sports center with a gymnasium.

Brechin

㉔ *10 mi west of Montrose.*

The small market town Brechin, in Strathmore, has a cathedral founded about 1200 which contains an interesting selection of antiquities. The town's 10th-century **Round Tower** is one of only two on mainland Scotland (they are more frequently found in Ireland). It was originally built for the local Culdee monks.

Nightlife
Brechin dances at **Flicks** (⊠ High St., ☎ 01356/624313), which has a mix of live bands and DJs, and attracts young people (over 18) from a wide area.

Edzell

6 mi north of Brechin via B966.

★ ㉕ Most Scots now associate the little community of Edzell with the U.S.-run military listening post nearby. **Edzell Castle,** an impressive ruin from the 16th century, is nestled among the Grampian foothills. This structure was originally a typical Scottish fortified tower, but was later transformed into a house that gave some degree of domestic comfort as well as protection from the elements. The simple "L" shape of the original building was extended, and a pleasance, or walled garden, was added in 1604. This formal garden, along with unique heraldic and symbolic sculptures, survives today. ⊠ *Off B966,* ☎ *0131/668–8600.* ⊡ *£2.* ☉ *Apr.–Sept., Mon.–Sat. 9:30–6, Sun. 2–6; Oct.–Mar., Mon.–Wed. and Sat. 9:30–4, Thurs. 9:30–noon, Sun. 2–4.*

OFF THE BEATEN PATH
WHITE AND BROWN CATERTHUNS – The remains of Iron Age hill forts crown two rounded hills to the west and south of Edzell Castle. Lovers of wild places will enjoy the drive to the Caterthuns from Edzell (if in doubt at junctions, turn left), especially the climb up the narrow road (from Balrownie to Pitmudie) that passes between the two hills; along the way there are magnificent views southward to the patterned fields of Strathmore. Marked paths run up to each fort (both are now officially protected sites) from the main road. The White Caterthun, so called because of the pale quartzite rock that was used to build its now-tumbled ramparts, is the better preserved of the two.

En Route You can rejoin the hurly-burly of the A90 for the journey back southward, though the more pleasant route leads southwestward using minor roads (there are several options) along the face of the Grampians, following the fault line that separates Highland and Lowland at this point. The **Glens of Angus** extend north from various points on Route A90. Known individually as the glens of Isla, Prosen, Clova, and Esk, these long valleys run into the high hills of the Grampians and offer a choice of clearly marked walking routes (those in Glen Clova are especially appealing).

Kirriemuir

㉖ *20 mi southwest of Edzell.*

Kirriemuir stands at the heart of Angus's red sandstone countryside and was the birthplace of the writer and dramatist Sir James Barrie (1860–1937), most well known abroad as the author of *Peter Pan.* Barrie's house, now in the care of the National Trust for Scotland, has upper floors furnished as they might have been in Barrie's time, with manuscripts and personal mementoes displayed. The outside washhouse is said to have been Barrie's first theater. Next door, at 11 Brechin Road, is an exhibition on "The Genius of J. M. Barrie" that gives literary and theatrical background. ⊠ *9 Brechin Rd.,* ☎ *01575/572646 or 01575/572353.* 🖃 *£1.60.* ◷ *Easter and May–Sept., Mon.–Sat. 11–5:30, Sun. 1:30–5:30; Oct., Sat. 11–5:30, Sun. 1:30–5:30 (last admission 5).*

Dining

$ ✕ **Drovers Inn.** Set in the heart of the Angus farmlands, the Drovers
★ is a rare find in Scotland, having more of the feeling of an English country pub. Plain but friendly surroundings, decorated with old farm implements and historic photographs, are the setting for simple bar food, homemade pies, and nourishing soups. It's a popular place with locals; on weekends it's best to make reservations, even for bar meals. ⊠ *Memus, near Kirriemuir,* ☎ *01307/860322. MC, V.*

Forfar

㉗ *7 mi east of Kirriemuir.*

Forfar goes about its business of being the center for a farming hinterland, without being preoccupied about tourism. This means it is an everyday, friendly, pleasant enough Scottish town, bypassed by the A90 on its way north.

Dining and Lodging

$$ ✕🖸 **Royal Hotel.** In the center of Forfar, this former coaching inn has been fully modernized; it has a leisure complex with swimming pool, gymnasium, and roof garden. The bedrooms are well equipped, though some in the most modern part of the hotel are rather small. All are decorated in an attractive green-and-peach color scheme, with stained wood finishes and floral fabrics. The public rooms have retained their 19th-century charm. This hotel provides an attractive base for exploring or golfing. The restaurant provides well-cooked, standard fare—fish and chips, lasagna—served by a friendly staff. ⊠ *Castle St., Forfar, Angus, DD8 3AE,* ☎ 🖷 *01307/462691. 19 rooms with bath or shower. Restaurant, indoor pool, sauna. AE, DC, MC, V. Closed Dec.26.*

$ 🖸 **Quarrybank Cottage.** Once a Victorian quarryman's cottage, this property is now an immaculately kept bed-and-breakfast establishment, set among the green fields of Angus just a few minutes' drive from Forfar. The freshly decorated rooms are enlivened with items from all over the world. Evening meals can be provided on request. ⊠ *Balgavies, by Forfar, DD8 2TF,* ☎ *01307/830303,* 🖷 *01307/830414. 3 rooms with bath or shower. AE. Closed Nov.–Feb.*

$ ★ 🖫 **Redroofs.** This former cottage hospital, now an attractive private home, offers excellent bed-and-breakfast accommodation in spacious surroundings, set among trees. Guests can also use a characterful sitting room decorated with curios collected by the owners on their travels. ✉ *Balgavies, by Forfar, DD8 2TN,* ☎ ⅎⁱⁱ *01307/830268. 3 rooms, 1 with shower en suite. No credit cards.*

Glamis

★ ㉘ *5 mi southwest of Forfar, 6 mi south of Kirriemuir via A928.*

Set in pleasantly rolling countryside is the village of Glamis, site of the **Angus Folk Museum.** This museum village is made up of a row of 19th-century cottages with unusual stone-slab roofs; exhibits focus on the crafts and tools of domestic and agricultural life in the region over the past 200 years. ✉ *Off A94,* ☎ *01307/840288.* ⌦ *£2.10.* ☉ *Easter and May–Sept., daily 11–5; Oct., weekends 11–5 (last admission 4:30).*

★ One of Scotland's best-known castles, because of its association with the present Royal Family, is **Glamis Castle.** This was the childhood home of the current Queen Mother and the birthplace of Princess Margaret. The property of the earls of Strathmore and Kinghorne since 1372, the castle was largely reconstructed in the late 17th century; the original keep, which is much older, is still intact. One of the most famous rooms in the castle is Duncan's Hall, the legendary setting for Shakespeare's *Macbeth.* Guided tours offer visitors a look at fine collections of china, tapestries, and furniture. Other visitor facilities include shops, a produce stall, and a licensed restaurant. The castle is approximately 1 mile southwest of Glamis village. ✉ *A94,* ☎ *01307/840242.* ⌦ *£4.70; grounds only, £2.20.* ☉ *Apr.–late Oct, daily 10:30–5:30 (last tour at 4:45).*

Meigle

㉙ *7 mi southwest of Glamis, 15 mi west of Dundee.*

The local museum at Meigle, in the wide swathe of Strathmore, has a magnificent collection of some 25 sculptured monuments from the Celtic Christian period (8th to 10th centuries), nearly all of which were found in or around the local churchyard. This is one of the most notable collections of medieval work in Western Europe. ✉ *A94,* ☎ *0131/668–8600.* ⌦ *£1.20.* ☉ *Apr.–Sept., Mon.–Sat. 9:30–6, Sun. 2–6.*

FIFE AND ANGUS A TO Z

Arriving and Departing

By Bus
Travel into Edinburgh from Edinburgh Airport (☞ Chapter 3). From St. Andrew Square Bus Station in Edinburgh city center, services run into Fife and Angus. There is an hourly service to Dundee operated by **Scottish Citylink** (☎ 0990/505050). **Stagecoach/Fife Scottish** (☎ 01383/621249) serves Fife and St. Andrews.

By Car
The M90 motorway from Edinburgh takes visitors to within a half hour of St. Andrews and Dundee. Travelers coming from Fife can use the A91 and the A914, then cross the Tay Bridge to reach Dundee, though the quickest way is to use the M90/A90. Travel time from Edinburgh to Dundee is about one hour, from Edinburgh to St. Andrews, 1½ hours.

By Plane

Glasgow Airport (☞ Chapter 4), 50 miles west of Edinburgh, is now a major point of entry for international flights. Passengers landing in Glasgow have easy access to Edinburgh and Fife and Angus. **Edinburgh Airport** (☞ Chapter 3), 7 miles west of downtown Edinburgh, offers connections throughout the United Kingdom, as well as with a number of cities on the Continent.

By Train

ScotRail (☎ 0131/556–2451) stops at Kirkcaldy, Markinch (for Glenrothes), Cupar, Leuchars (for St. Andrews), Dundee, Arbroath, and Montrose.

Getting Around

By Bus

A local network provides service from St. Andrews and Dundee to many of the smaller towns throughout Fife and Dundee. The fare for the Kirkcaldy–St. Andrews run is £2.60; St. Andrews–Dundee, £1.65; Perth–Montrose, £5.90. For information about routes and fares call **Fife Scottish** (☎ 01592/642394), **Scottish Citylink** (☎ 0990/505050) or **Strathtay Scottish** (☎ 01382/228345).

By Car

Fife is an easy area to get around and presents no major obstacles to the traveler. Most of the roads are quiet and uncongested. The most interesting sights are in the east, which is served by a network of cross-country roads. Angus is likewise an easy region to explore, being serviced by a main fast road—the A90—which travels through the middle of the Strathmore valley and then on to Aberdeen; another, gentler road—the A92—that runs to the east near the coast; and a network of rural roads between the Grampians and Route A90.

By Train

See Arriving and Departing, *above,* for the main towns with stations in this area.

Contacts and Resources

Doctors and Dentists

Consult your hotel, a tourist information center, or the yellow pages of the telephone directory for listings of local doctors and dentists.

Emergencies

For **police, fire,** or **ambulance,** dial 999 from any telephone. No coins are needed for emergency calls made from public telephone booths.

Fishing

As in most of the rest of Scotland, there is a wide choice of fishing in sea, loch, and river. Leaflets giving detailed information are available at tourist information centers (☞ Visitor Information, *below*).

Golf

Details about locations of courses and opening hours are available from tourist information centers (☞ Visitor Information, *below*). Many of the area's hotels offer golfing packages or will arrange a day's golf.

Guided Tours

ORIENTATION

Tayside Greyhound (✉ Commercial St., Dundee, ☎ 01382/201121) offers a variety of general orientation tours of the main cities and the region from late July to early August. **Fisher Tours** (✉ West Port,

Dundee, ☎ 01382/227290) has tours all year both within and outside the region; one of their most popular tours is "Lochs and Glens."

SPECIAL-INTEREST
Links Golf Tours (✉ 7 Pilmour Links, St. Andrews, ☎ 01334/478639, FAX 01334/474086) offers tours tailored to individual requirements.

Late-Night Pharmacies
Late-night pharmacies are not found outside the larger cities. In St. Andrews, Dundee, and other larger centers, pharmacies use a rotating system for off-hours and Sunday prescription service. Consult the listings displayed on pharmacy doors for the names and addresses of pharmacies that provide service outside regular hours. In an emergency the police can help you contact a pharmacist. Note that in rural areas general practitioners may also dispense medicine.

Visitor Information
Arbroath (✉ Market Pl., ☎ 01241/872609). **Dundee** (✉ 4 City Sq., ☎ 01382/227723). **Glenrothes** (✉ Rothes Halls, Rothes Square, ☎ 01592/754954). **Kirkcaldy** (✉ 19 Whytescauseway). **Leven** (✉ The Beehive, Durie St., ☎ 01333/429464). **St. Andrews** (✉ 70 Market St., ☎ 01334/472021).

Smaller tourist information centers operate seasonally in the following towns: Anstruther, Brechin, Carnoustie, Crail, Cupar, Forfar, Kirriemuir, and Montrose.

7 The Central Highlands

Stirling, Loch Lomond and the Trossachs, Perthshire

The main towns of Perth and Stirling are easily accessible gateways to the Central Highlands, the rugged and spectacular terrain stretching north from Glasgow. This may not be the famed Highlands of the north, but there's plenty of wild country; here you'll find lush, green woodlands and many lochs. In the Trossachs and also to the west, deep lochs—including Loch Lomond—shimmer at the foot of hills covered in birch, oak, and pine.

By Gilbert
Summers

THE CENTRAL HIGHLANDS CONSIST of what were once the counties of Perthshire and Stirlingshire. Today the old county seats of Perth and Stirling, respectively, still play important roles as the primary administrative centers in the region. Both lie on the edge of a Highland area that offers reliable road and rail connections to the central belt of Scotland. Just how near the area is to the well-populated Midland Valley can be judged by the visitor who looks out from the ramparts of Edinburgh Castle: the Highland hills—which meander around the Trossachs and above Callander—are clearly visible. Similarly, the high-tower blocks of some of Glasgow's peripheral housing developments are noticeable from many of the higher peaks, notably Ben Lomond.

In fact, the Lowland/Highland contrast is pronounced in this region. Geologists have designated a prominent boundary between the two distinct landscapes as the Highland Boundary Fault. This geological divide also marked the boundary between Scotland's two languages and cultures, Gaelic and Scots, with the Gaels ensconced behind the mountain barrier. In the Central Highlands the fault line runs through Loch Lomond, close to Callander, to the northeast above Perth, and into the old county of Angus.

As early as 1794 the local minister in Callander, on the very edge of the Highlands, wrote: "The Trossachs are often visited by persons of taste, who are desirous of seeing nature in her rudest and unpolished state." What these early visitors came to see was a series of lochs and hills, whose crags and slopes were hung harmoniously with shaggy birch, oak, and pinewoods. The tops of the hills are high but not too wild (real wilderness would have been too much for these fledgling nature lovers). The Romantic poets, especially William Wordsworth, sang the praises of such locales. Though Wordsworth is most closely associated with the Lake District in England, his travels through Scotland and the Trossachs inspired several poems. But it was Sir Walter Scott who definitively put this Highland-edge area on the tourist map by setting his dramatic verse narrative, *The Lady of the Lake,* written in 1810, firmly in the physical landscape of the Trossachs. Scott's verse was an immediate and huge success, and visitors flooded in to trace the events of the poem across the region. Today visitors continue to flock here, though few can quote a line of his poem.

If the Trossachs have long attracted those with discriminating tastes, then much of the same sentimental aura has attached itself to Loch Lomond. This is Scotland's largest loch in terms of surface area. By looking at the map, you will see that the loch is narrow to the north and broad in the south. The hard rocks to the north confine it to a long thin ribbon, and the more yielding Lowland structures allow it to spread out and assume a softer, wider form. Thus Lowland fields and lush hedgerows quickly give way to dark woods and crags (all this just a half hour's drive from the center of Glasgow). The song, "The Banks of Loch Lomond," said to have been written by a Jacobite prisoner incarcerated in Carlisle, England, seems to capture a particular style of Scottish sentimentality, resulting in the popularity of the "bonnie, bonnie banks" around the world, wherever Scots are to be found.

The main towns of Perth and Stirling serve as roadway hubs for the area, but there are also many smaller towns, such as Callander, Crieff, Pitlochry, Dunkeld, and Aberfeldy. A string of small but embracing villages—Killin, Crianlarich, Lochearnhead, Kenmore, and Kinloch Rannoch—are tucked into the hills and described below.

Finally, remember that even though the Central Highlands are easily accessible, there is still much high, wild country in the region. Ben Lawers, near Killin, is the ninth-highest peak in Scotland, and the moor of Rannoch is as bleak and empty a stretch as can be seen anywhere in the northlands. But if the glens and lochs prove to be too lonely or intimidating, it's a short journey to the softer and less harsh Lowlands.

Pleasures and Pastimes

Bicycling

The big attraction for cyclists is the dedicated Glasgow–Killin cycleway. This takes advantage of former railroad track-beds, as well as otherwise private roads, plus some quiet minor ones, to get well into the Central Highlands by way of the Trossachs and Callander. Away from the cycleway, the main roads can be busy with holiday traffic.

Dining

The restaurants of this region have been continually improving over the past several years. Regional country delicacies—loch trout, river salmon, mutton, and venison—are now found regularly on even modest menus; this was extremely rare 20 years ago. The urban areas south and southwest of Stirling, in contrast, lack refinement in matters of eating and drinking. There you will find simple low-built pubs, often crowded and noisy, but serving substantial food at lunchtime (eaten balanced on your knee, perhaps, or at a shared table). Three heavy courses at one of these pubs will cost you about £10.

WHAT TO WEAR

Dress in the Central Highlands is casual, but you should err on the smart side. Most country house hotels prefer jacket and tie.

CATEGORY	COST*
$$$$	over £40
$$$	£30–£40
$$	£15–£30
$	under £15

*per person for a 3-course meal, including VAT and excluding drinks and service

Lodging

In Stirling and Callander, as well as in the small towns and villages throughout the region, you will find a selection of tourist accommodations out of all proportion to the size of the communities. (The industrial towns are the exceptions). Standards of less-expensive establishments have improved in recent years and are still improving. The grand hotels, though few, were brought into existence by the carriage trade of the 19th century, when travel in Scotland was the fashion. The level of service at these places has, by and large, not slipped. You will also find many country hotels, however, that match the grand hotels in comfort.

CATEGORY	COST*
$$$$	over £110
$$$	£80–£110
$$	£45–£80
$	under £45

*Prices are for a standard double room, including service, breakfast, and VAT.

Nightlife

The nightlife in the area tends toward *ceilidhs* (participatory song, music, dance) and Scottish concerts. Folk evenings in a number of hotels are also popular. In general, local pubs are friendly and down-to-earth, with patrons who don't mind talking to visitors about what to see and do.

Shopping

The Central Highlands presents an interesting assortment of shopping choices, ranging from the larger population centers of Perth (known, since Roman times, for its freshwater Scottish pearls) and Stirling, where High Street stores compete with long-established local firms, to the smaller towns and villages, where the selection is more limited but the relaxed pace makes for pleasant shopping.

Exploring the Central Highlands

The main towns of Stirling and Perth are at the junction of many routes, making both places natural starting points for Highland tours. Stirling itself is worth covering in some detail on foot. The successive waves of development of this important town can easily be traced—from castle and Old Town architecture to Victorian developments and urban and industrial sprawl.

The Trossachs are a short distance from Stirling, and visitors usually cover them in a loop. Those visiting Loch Lomond can get there from either Glasgow or Stirling, and there are two other routes available as well. The main road up the west bank (A82) is not recommended for leisurely touring. Do use this road, however, if you are on your way to Oban, Kintyre, or Argyll. Loch Lomond is best seen from one of two cul-de-sac roads: by way of Drymen at the south end, up to Rowardennan or, if you are pressed for time, west from Aberfoyle to reach Loch Lomond near its northern end, at Inversnaid. Visitors should note that in the Trossachs, the road that some maps show going all the way around Loch Katrine is a private road belonging to the Strathclyde Water Board and is open only to walkers and cyclists.

Getting around Perthshire is made interesting by the series of looped tours accessible from the A9, a fast main artery. Exercise caution while driving the A9 itself, however: There have been many auto accidents in this area. Although the entire suggested route can be completed in a single day, travelers with some time on their hands who seek a little spontaneity can choose from a variety of accommodations in villages along the way.

Great Itineraries

This is excellent touring country. The glens, in some places, run parallel to the lochs, including those along Lochs Earn, Tay, and Rannoch, making for satisfying loops and round trips.

IF YOU HAVE 2 DAYS
Numbers in the text correspond to numbers in the margin and on the Central Highlands and Stirling maps.

There is enough to see in ⊞ **Stirling** ① to take up at least a day, leaving the **Trossachs** ㉑ loop for the second day.

IF YOU HAVE 5 DAYS
See ⊞ **Stirling** ① and the **Trossachs** ㉑, sampling **Loch Lomond** ㉕ from **Drymen** ㉔. Take in ⊞ **Perth** ㉖ and the Highland resort towns such as **Dunkeld** ㉚, **Pitlochry** ㉛, **Aberfeldy** ㊱, and **Crieff** ㊶. You should also have time for a day's walking, say, around the Trossachs.

IF YOU HAVE 7 DAYS
Start your visit by spending a couple of days in ⊞ **Stirling** ①. (Don't overlook the Mill Trail country, east of Stirling, if you are shopping for Scottish woolens.) Then cover the route suggested for the **Trossachs** ㉑

The Central Highlands

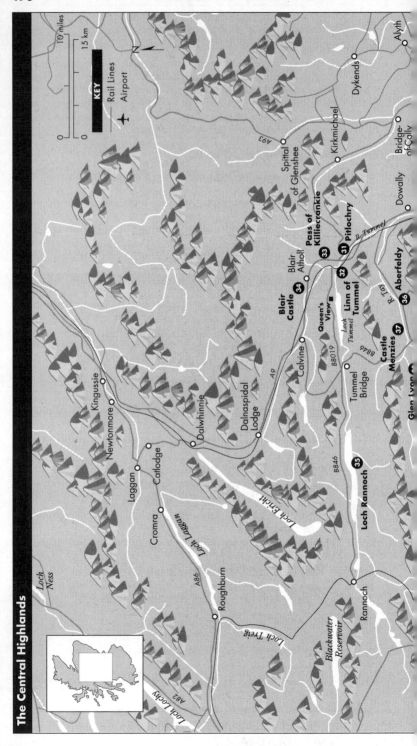

KEY
— Rail Lines
✈ Airport

10 miles
15 km

N

Alyth
Dykends
Bridge of Cally
Kirkmichael
Dowally
Spittal of Glenshee
A93
Pass of Killiecrankie
Pitlochry
R. Tummel
31
33
Blair Atholl
32
Aberfeldy
36
Blair Castle
34
Queen's View
Linn of Tummel
Loch Tummel
Castle Menzies
37
B8019
R. Tay
Calvine
B846
Glen Lyon
A9
Dalnaspidal Lodge
Tummel Bridge
Dalwhinnie
Kingussie
Newtonmore
Catlodge
B846
35
Laggan
Loch Ericht
Loch Rannoch
Cromra
Loch Ness
Loch Laggan
A86
Roughburn
Rannoch
Blackwater Reservoir
Loch Treig
Loch Lochy
A82

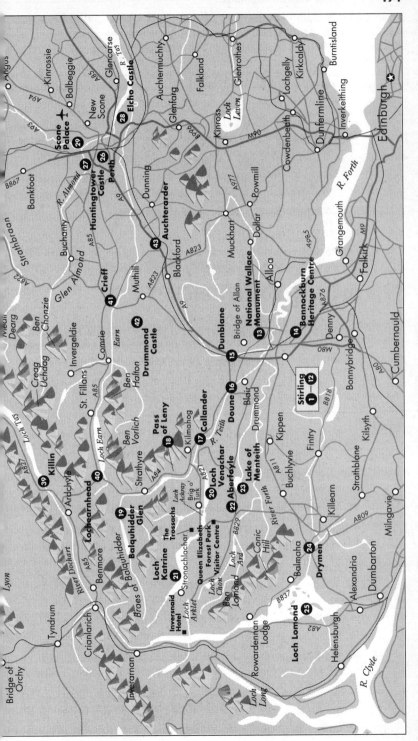

and **Loch Lomond** ㉕: Visit the historic towns of **Dunblane** ⑮ and **Doune** ⑯, staying overnight at ⊞ **Callander** ⑰ in order to explore the fine country northward toward **Balquhidder Glen** ⑲. Spend a day in the Trossachs around **Loch Venachar** ⑳ and **Loch Katrine** ㉑, and take a boat ride to see the landscape at its best. The next day, travel to **Drymen** ㉔ for a morning around Loch Lomond before driving into Perthshire. Spend a night at ⊞ **Auchterarder** ㊸ with its antiques shops, or travel straight to Perth, where you should base yourself for two or three days while exploring Perthshire. Go west for **Crieff** ㊶ and **Drummond Castle** ㊷, or north for Highland resort towns such as **Dunkeld** ㉚, with its cathedral; **Pitlochry** ㉛, close to the historic **Pass of Killiecrankie** ㉝ and impressive **Blair Castle** ㉞; and **Aberfeldy** ㊱. Between Pitlochry and Aberfeldy, make time for the wild landscapes of **Loch Rannoch** ㉟—a great contrast to the generally pastoral Perthshire countryside.

When to Tour The Central Highlands

The Trossachs and Loch Lomond can get quite busy in high summer. This area is also a good choice for off-season touring. You are near enough to the Lowland edge to take advantage of any good weather in winter to enjoy the dramatic Highland light; fall colors are also spectacular.

STIRLING AND ENVIRONS

In some ways, Stirling is like a smaller version of Edinburgh. Its castle, built on a steep-sided plug of rock, dominates the landscape, and its Esplanade offers views of the surrounding valley-plain of the River Forth. To take advantage of its historical heritage (the Stewart monarchs held court here from time to time, as they did in Edinburgh), Stirling maintains a busy tourism calendar that includes a summer program of open-air historical tableaux.

Stirling

❶ *26 mi northeast of Glasgow, 36 mi northwest of Edinburgh.*

Stirling is one of Britain's great historic towns. An impressive proportion of the **old town walls** remain and can be seen from Dumbarton Road, as soon as you step outside the tourist information center to start exploring. On Corn Exchange Road there is a modern statue of **Rob Roy MacGregor,** notorious cattle dealer and drover, part-time thief and outlaw, and Jacobite (most of the time). In 1995 Hollywood discovered this local folk hero with the film *Rob Roy,* starring Liam Neeson. Rob is practically inescapable if you visit Callander and the Trossachs, where he had his home. Along Dumbarton Road to the west is the **Smith Art Gallery and Museum,** founded in 1874 with the bequest of a local

❷ collector. It's a good example of a community art gallery that offers a varied exhibit program. ☎ *01786/471917.* ▣ *Free.* ☉ *Tues.–Sat. 10:30–5, Sun. 2–5.*

Near Rob Roy's statue, a gentle but relentless uphill path known as the **Back Walk** eventually leads to the town's most famous and worth-

❸ while sight—**Stirling Castle.** The Back Walk will take you along the outside of the city's walls, past a watchtower and the grimly named Hangman's entry, carved out of the great whinstone boulders that once marked the outer defenses of the town.

On Academy Road is the **Old High School,** built in 1854 on the site of the former Greyfriars Monastery and now the Stirling Highland Hotel (☞ Dining and Lodging, *below*). A fine example of Scottish domestic

❹ architecture now used for private housing, **Darrow House** dates from the 17th century. Look for the characteristic crow-step gables, dormer

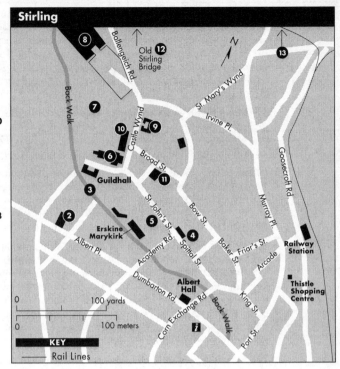

windows, and a projecting turn-pike stair. The adjacent **Spittal House** has been restored to match its handsome partner. They both stand near the junction of Academy Road and Spittal Street.

5 Another typical town house stands on St. John's Street, uphill from Darrow House. Sometimes known as **Bothwell Ha** (Hall), it is said to have been owned by the Earl of Bothwell, Mary, Queen of Scots' third husband. The former military detention barracks behind Bothwell Ha is now known as the **Old Town Jail** and tells the story of life in a 19th-century Scottish prison. Bringing the past to life are people dressed as prisoners, wardens, and prison reformers, all in appropriate costume; furnished cells; models; and exhibitions. ✉ *St. John's St. Opening times and admission charges not available at press time (spring 1996); inquire at local tourist information center.*

Adjacent to the Old Town Jail is **Erskine Marykirk,** a neoclassical church built in 1824 that now houses a youth hostel (☞ Dining and Lodging, *below*).

6 At the top of St. John's Street, in the **Church of the Holy Rude,** is a nave that survives from the 15th century. A portion of the original medieval timber roof can also be seen. The church has the distinction of being the only church in Scotland still in use that witnessed the coronation of a Scottish monarch: James VI in 1567.

The **Guildhall,** built as Cowane's Hospital in 1639 for *decayed breithers* (unsuccessful merchants), is now the setting for summer concerts and ceilidhs. Above the entrance is a small, cheery statue of the founder himself, John Cowane, that is said to come alive on Hogmanay Night (December 31) to walk the streets with the locals and join in their New Year's revelry. ✉ *St. John's St.* ✉ *Free.* ☉ *Weekdays 9–5 (except when functions are being held).*

❼ Within the **cemetery** beyond the Church of the Holy Rude are some unusual monuments. The most notable are the **Star Pyramid** of 1858 and the macabre, glass-walled **Martyrs Monument,** erected in memory of two Wigtownshire girls who were drowned in 1685 for their Covenanting faith. At this point, you can't help but see the castle, which dominates the foreground. From **Ladies' Rock,** a high perch within the cemetery, there are excellent views of the looming fortress.

The **Royal Burgh of Stirling Visitor Centre** stands beside Stirling Castle Esplanade. It houses a shop and exhibition hall with an audiovisual production on the town and surrounding area. ☎ *01786/462517.* ✉ *Free.* ☉ *Apr.–Sept., daily 9:30–5:15; Oct.–Mar., daily 9:30-4:15.*

★ ❽ **Stirling Castle**'s strategic position made it the grandest prize in the Scots Wars of Independence in the late 13th and early 14th centuries. The Battle of Bannockburn in 1314 was fought within sight of its walls, and the victory by Robert the Bruce (King Robert I) yielded both the castle and freedom from English subjugation for almost four centuries.

King Robert's daughter, Marjory, married Walter, the High Steward of Scotland. Their descendants included the Stewart dynasty of Scottish monarchs (Mary, Queen of Scots, was a Stewart, though she preferred the French spelling, *Stuart*). The Stewarts were mainly responsible for many of the works that survive within the castle walls today. They made Stirling Castle their court and power base, creating fine Renaissance-style buildings that were not completely obliterated, despite subsequent reconstruction for military purposes.

The castle is entered through its outer defenses, which consist of a great curtain wall and batteries that date from 1708, built to bulwark earlier defenses by the main gatehouse. From this lower square the most conspicuous feature is the **palace,** built by King James V between 1538 and 1542. This edifice shows the influence of French masons in the decorative figures festooning the ornately worked outer walls. Overlooking the upper courtyard is the **Great Hall,** built by King James IV in 1503. Before the Union of Parliaments in 1707, when the Scottish aristocracy sold out to England, this building had been used as one of the seats of the Scottish Parliament. After 1707 it sank into decline, becoming a riding school, then a barracks. Today, a slow restoration is underway.

Among the later works built for regiments stationed here, the **King's Old Building** stands out; it is a 19th-century baronial revival on the site of an earlier building. The oldest building on the site is the **Mint,** or **Coonzie Hoose,** perhaps dating from as far back as the 14th century. Below is an arched passageway leading to the westernmost section of the ramparts, the **Nether Bailey.** You'll have the distinct feeling here that you are in the bow of a warship sailing up the *carselands* (valley-plain) of the Forth Valley, which fans out before the great superstructure of the castle. Among the gun platforms and the crenellations of the ramparts, this is the place to ponder the strategic significance of Stirling. To the south lies the hump of the Touch and the Gargunnock Hills (part of the Campsie Hills), diverting would-be direct routes from Glasgow and the south. For centuries all roads into the Highlands across the narrow waist of Scotland led to Stirling. If you look carefully northward, you can still see the Old Stirling Bridge, once the lowest and most convenient place to cross the river. For all these geographic reasons, the castle here was perhaps the single most important fortress in Scotland. ✉ *Central Stirling,* ☎ *0131/668–8600.* ✉ *£3.50.* ☉ *Apr.–Sept., daily 9:30–5:15; Oct.–Mar., daily 9:30–4:15.*

Immediately below the Castle Esplanade is the heart of the old town of Stirling, recently the subject of a massive renovation program. Along
9 Castle Wynd is a series of interesting buildings: **Argyll's Ludging** ("ludging" was "lodging," a nobleman's town house), was built in three phases from the 16th century onward. The building is actually older than the name it bears—that of Archibald, ninth Earl of Argyll, who bought it in 1666. It was for many years a military hospital, then a youth hostel. It is currently being refurbished to show how nobility lived in 17th-century Stirling; specially commissioned reproduction furniture and fittings are based on the original inventory of the house's contents at that time. ⊠ *Castle Wynd. Opening times and admission charges not available at press time (spring 1996); inquire at local tourist information center.*

10 The long and ornate facade of **Mar's Wark** (work or building), windowless and roofless, is constructed in a distinctive Renaissance style. Look for the armorial carved panels, the gargoyles, and the turrets flanking a railed-off *pend* (archway). This ruin is the stark remains of a palace built in 1570 by Lord Erskine, Earl of Mar, as well as Stirling Castle governor. Mar's Wark was sieged and severely damaged during the 1745 Jacobite rebellion, but its admirably worn shell survives. ⊠ *Castle Wynd,* ☎ *0131/668–8600. View from outside only.*

When you stand in front of Mar's Wark and look downhill, you gaze into the heart of the old town. One of its most notable structures is
11 the **Tolbooth** of 1705, which has a traditional Scottish steeple and gilded weathercock. For centuries the Burgh Court handed down sentences here. The **Mercat Cross,** where proclamations were made, stands on Broad Street, as does the Tolbooth.

The **Cornerstone Gallery** occupies Mar Place House, a Georgian town house saved from dereliction and painstakingly restored. The complex, in three parts, comprises a gallery with changing exhibitions of Scottish contemporary work and displays of quality Scottish prints; a shop with upscale Scottish gifts (☞ *Shopping, below*); and a conservatory tearoom. ⊠ *Mar Place,* ☎ *01786/474444.* 🎟 *Free.* ☉ *Apr.–Oct., daily 10–6 (till later at height of summer season); Nov.–Mar., daily 10:30–6.*

NEED A BREAK?   The tearoom at the **Cornerstone Gallery** (☞ above) offers fresh coffee and homemade cakes, light lunches, and delicious afternoon teas in an airy conservatory that extends out into the garden.

---

12 North of Stirling Castle, on the edge of town, is **Old Stirling Bridge,** by the A9. Dating from the 15th century, the bridge can still be crossed on foot. It was near Old Stirling Bridge that the Scottish freedom fighter William Wallace and a ragged army of Scots won a major victory in 1297. The 1995 movie *Braveheart,* starring Mel Gibson, was based on Wallace's life. A more accurate version is told in an exhibition and audio-
13 visual presentation at the pencil-thin **National Wallace Monument** on the Abbey Craig. Visitor numbers here have soared as a result of the film. Up close, this Victorian shrine to William Wallace, built between 1856 and 1869, becomes less slim and soaring, revealing itself to be a substantial square tower with a creepy spiral stairway. There are superb views from the top of the tower. To reach the monument, follow Bridge of Allan signs (A9) northward, crossing the River Forth by Robert Stephenson's New Bridge of 1832, next to the historic old one. The National Wallace Monument is signposted at the next traffic circle. ⊠ *Abbey Craig,* ☎ *01786/472140.* 🎟 *£2.50.* ☉ *Mar.–May and Oct., daily 10–5; June and Sept., daily 10–6; July–Aug., daily 9:30–6:30; Feb. and Nov., weekends 10–4; closed Dec.–Jan.*

On the south side of the Abbey Craig, the scanty remains of 13th-century **Cambuskenneth Abbey** lie in a sweeping bend of the River Forth, with the dramatic outline of Stirling Castle as a backdrop. Important meetings of the Scottish Parliament were once held here, and King Edward I of England visited in 1304. The abbey was looted and damaged during the Scots Wars of Independence (1307–14). The reconstructed tomb of King James III (who died in 1488) can be seen near the outline of the high altar.

★ ⑭ In 1298, the year after William Wallace's victory, Robert the Bruce materialized as the nation's champion, and the last bloody phase of the Wars of Independence began. Bruce's rise resulted from the uncertainties and timidity of the great lords of Scotland (ever unsure of which way to jump and whether to bow to England's demands). This tale is recounted at the **Bannockburn Heritage Centre,** hidden among the sprawl of housing and commercial developments on the southern edge of Stirling. This was the site of the famed Battle of Bannockburn in 1314. In Bruce's day, the Forth had a shelved and partly wooded floodplain. He chose the site cunningly, noting the boggy ground on the lower reaches in which the heavy horses of the English would founder. The atmosphere has been re-created within the center by means of an audiovisual presentation, models, and costumed figures, and an arresting mural depicting the battle in detail (look closely for some particularly unsavory goings-on). ⊠ *Off M80,* ☎ *01786/812664.* ☞ *£2.10.* ⊙ *Mar., mid-Nov.–Dec. 23, daily 11–3; Apr.–Oct., daily 10–5:30.*

Dining and Lodging

$$–$$$ ✕ **Heritage.** This elegant 18th-century establishment is run by a French family. The decor is all fanlights and candles; the menu features French and Scottish classics. ⊠ *16 Allan Park,* ☎ *01786/473660. MC, V. Closed Dec. 25, Jan. 1.*

$–$$ ✕ **Cross Keys Hotel.** A stone-walled dining room adds atmosphere to this restaurant's varied, traditionally Scottish menu. ⊠ *Main St., Kippen (A811, west of Stirling),* ☎ *01786/870293. MC, V.*

$$$$ ✕🏠 **Stirling Highland Hotel.** The handsome and historic building that this hotel occupies was once the Old High School. Many original architectural features were retained and add to the historic atmosphere. Furnishings are old-fashioned, with solid wood, tartan, florals, and low-key, neutral color schemes. Menus in the restaurants are French-influenced, assembled from the best Scottish ingredients; the seafood is particularly outstanding. ⊠ *Spittal St., FK8 1DU,* ☎ *01786/475444,* FAX *01786/462929. 76 rooms with bath, 4 suites. 2 restaurants, piano bar. AE, DC, MC, V.*

$$$ 🏠 **Terraces Hotel.** This centrally located hotel with plenty of parking space is a good base for exploring Stirling and the region. A comfortable Georgian town house, it is comparatively small, with friendly and attentive service. ⊠ *4 Melville Terr., FK8 2ND,* ☎ *01786/472268,* FAX *01786/450314. 18 rooms with bath or shower. Restaurant. AE, DC, MC, V.*

$ ★ 🏠 **Castlecroft.** Tucked beneath Stirling Castle, with fine views over the plain of the River Forth toward the Highland hills, this warm and comfortable modern house has a particularly helpful host who is full of local information. ⊠ *Ballengeich Rd., Stirling, FK8 1TN,* ☎ *01786/474933. 6 rooms with bath or shower. No credit cards.*

$ 🏠 **Lochend Farm.** Extensive views, wholesome farm cooking, and a pleasantly relaxing pace are the hallmarks of this peaceful working farm. Only 5 miles from the M9/M80, southwest of Stirling, it also makes a good touring base. The traditionally furnished (and very comfortable) bedrooms have washbasins and share a bathroom. ⊠ *Carronbridge, Denny, Stirlingshire, FK6 5JJ*, ☎ *01324/822778. 2 rooms. No credit cards.*

$ 🏠 **Stirling Youth Hostel.** Built within the shell of a former church, the hostel offers high-grade four- and six-bed rooms (and a few doubles) with en suite facilities. Use of the television room, the dining room, and the self-catering, fully equipped kitchen is included in the bargain price of £10.15 per person, including breakfast. ⊠ *Erskine Marykirk, St. John's St., FK8 1DU*, ☎ *01786/473442*, FAX *01786/445715. 128 beds. MC, V.*

$ 🏠 **West Plean.** This handsome house is part of a working farm. It has a walled garden and woodland walks. Well-cooked food and spacious rooms make this bed-and-breakfast an excellent bargain. ⊠ *Denny Rd., FK7 8HA*, ☎ *01786/812208. 3 rooms with bath or shower. No credit cards.*

Nightlife and the Arts
The **Macrobert Arts Centre** (⊠ Stirling University, ☎ 01786/461081) has a theater, an art gallery, and a studio with programs that range from films to pantomime.

Shopping
In the Old Town, **McCutcheons** (⊠ 30 Spittal St., ☎ 01786/461771) will keep lovers of antiquarian books happy for an hour or two, with its huge range of titles, including books on every aspect of Scotland. The **Cornerstone Gallery** (⊠ Mar Place, ☎ 01786/474444) includes a shop with traditional but exceptionally high-quality Scottish and other British gifts, including tartan items, heraldic crests and collectors' chess sets. **R. R. Henderson Ltd.** (⊠ 6–8 Friars St., ☎ 01786/473681) is a "Highland outfitters," selling tartans, woolens, and accessories and offering a made-to-measure kilt service. **The Thistle Centre** is an attractive shopping arcade just off the main street.

South of Stirling, at Larbert, don't miss **Barbara Davidson's pottery studio** (⊠ Muirhall Farm, Larbert, ☎ 01324/554430) in an 18th-century farm setting. Here's an opportunity to buy a souvenir from one of the best-known potters in Scotland; in July and August you can even try throwing your own pot (for a small fee).

East of Stirling is **Mill Trail** country, along the foot of the Ochil Hills. A leaflet from a tourist information center will lead you to the delights of a real mill shop and low mill prices—even on cashmere—at **Tillicoultry, Alva,** and **Alloa.**

THE TROSSACHS AND LOCH LOMOND

Inspired by the views of mountainous terrain seen from the ramparts of Stirling Castle, visitors use this route to explore areas west and north to the Highland line. Distances are not great if you go by car. If you travel the classic Trossachs loop, you will share the route with plenty of day-trippers from the central belt.

Dunblane

★ ⑮ *7 mi north of Stirling.*

The oldest part of Dunblane—with its twisting streets and mellow town houses—huddles around the square and churchyard where the partly restored ruins of **Dunblane Cathedral** stand. King David built the existing structure in the 13th century on the site of St. Blane's tiny 8th-century cell. It is contemporary with the Border abbeys (☞ Chapter 5), but more mixed in its architecture—part Early English and part Norman. Dunblane ceased to be a cathedral, as did most others in Scotland, at the time of the Reformation in the mid-16th century. ☎ *0131/668–8600.* ☜ *Free.* ☉ *Apr.–Sept., Mon.–Sat. 9:30–6, Sun. 2– 6; Oct.–Mar., Mon.–Sat. 9:30–4, Sun. 2–4; and for services.*

Dining and Lodging

$$$$ ✕ ⊞ **Cromlix House Hotel.** This Victorian hunting lodge's period atmosphere is enhanced by cherished furniture and paintings, the original conservatory, and the library. The restaurant offers country-house decor and a choice of two elegant dining rooms. Specialties include game and lamb from the hotel estate. Try the delicious cheese and potato terrine as a starter, followed by beef with pickled walnuts. ⊠ *Kinbuck, on B8033, 3 mi northeast of Dunblane, 10 mi northeast of Stirling, FK15 9JT,* ☎ *01786/822125,* ☒ *01786/825450. 14 rooms with bath. Restaurant, tennis court, fishing. AE, DC, MC, V. Closed late Jan.–early Feb.*

Doune

★ **⑯** *5 mi west of Dunblane via A820.*

The Highland-edge community of Doune was once a center for pistol making. No Highland chief's attire was complete without a prestigious and ornate pair of pistols. Today, Doune is more widely known as the site of one of the best-preserved medieval castles in Scotland. **Doune Castle** looks like an early castle is supposed to look: grim and high-walled, with echoing stone vaults and numerous drafts. Construction of the fortress began in the early 15th century on a now-peaceful riparian tract. The best place to photograph this squat, great-walled fort is from the bridge, a little way upstream, which carries the A84 west. The castle is signposted left as you enter the town from the Dunblane road. ⊠ *Off A84,* ☎ *0131/668–8600.* ☜ *£2.* ☉ *Apr.–Sept., Mon.–Sat. 9:30–6, Sun. 2–6; Oct.–Mar., Mon.–Wed. and Sat. 9:30–4, Thurs. 9:30– noon, Sun. 2–4.*

Callander

⑰ *8 mi northwest of Doune via A84.*

A traditional Highland-edge resort, Callander bustles throughout the year—even on Sunday during off-peak times—simply because it is a gateway to Highland scenery within easy reach of Edinburgh and Glasgow. As a result, there is plenty of window-shopping here, plus nightlife in pubs and a good choice of accommodations.

Callander's **Rob Roy and Trossachs Visitor Centre,** housed in the former St. Kessog's Church, provides another encounter with the famed Rob Roy MacGregor. As defender of the downtrodden and scourge of the authorities, MacGregor is known as a tartan Robin Hood. A much revered Highland hero, he died peacefully at his home in 1734. You can learn more about his high jinks in a high-tech account—replete with displays and tableaux—in the modern visitor center. ⊠ *Ancaster Sq.,* ☎ *01877/330342.* ☜ *£2.* ☉ *Feb.,weekends 10–4; Mar.–Dec., daily 10–5.*

NEED A BREAK?	**Pip's Coffee House** (☎ 01877/330470; closed Wed. Oct.–Mar.), just off the main street, is a cheerful little place that offers light meals, soups, and salads, as well as Scottish home-baking, and more substantial three-course meals in the evenings (Apr.–Oct.). There is also a small picture gallery with plenty of Scottish material to browse through.

Callander's other attractions, away from the bustle of the main street, are mostly rural. A walk is signposted from the east end of the main street to the **Bracklinn Falls,** over whose lip Sir Walter Scott once rode

In case you want to see the world.

At American Express, we're here to make your journey a smooth one. So we have over 1,700 travel service locations in over 120 countries ready to help. What else would you expect from the world's largest travel agency?

do more®

http://www.americanexpress.com/travel

Travel

In case you want to be welcomed there.

We're here to see that you're always welcomed at establishments everywhere. That's why millions of people carry the American Express® Card – for peace of mind, confidence, and security, around the world or just around the corner.

do more®

Cards

In case you're running low.

We're here to help with more than 118,000 Express Cash locations around the world. In order to enroll, just call American Express before you start your vacation.

do more

Express Cash

And just in case.

We're here with American Express® Travelers Cheques and Cheques *for Two*.® They're the safest way to carry money on your vacation and the surest way to get a refund, practically anywhere, anytime.

Another way we help you...

do more ®

Travelers Cheques

a pony to win a bet. Another walk goes through the woods up to the **Callander Crags,** with views of the Lowlands as far as the Pentland Hills behind Edinburgh. (This walk is for the fit and well-shod only.)

Callander is the gateway to the Trossachs, but since it is on the main road, the A84, it also attracts overnight visitors on their way to Oban, Fort William, and beyond. All this traffic enters the proper Highlands just north of Callander, where the thickly clad slopes squeeze both the (18) road and rocky river into the narrow **Pass of Leny.** An abandoned railway—now a pleasant walking or bicycling path—also goes through the pass, past **Ben Ledi mountain** and **Loch Lubnaig.**

Through the Pass of Leny and beyond Strathyre, with its extensive forestry-commission plantings, within a 20-minute drive of Callander, (19) is **Balquhidder Glen** (pronounced *bal*-whidd-*er*), a typical Highland glen that runs westward. Note its characteristics, seen throughout the north: a flat-bottomed, U-shape profile formed by prehistoric glaciers; extensive forestry plantings replacing much of the natural woodlands above; a sprinkling of farms; and farther up the glen, new hill roads bulldozed into the slopes to provide access for shepherds and foresters. Note also the boarded-up look of some of the houses, many of which are second homes for affluent residents of the south. The glen is also where **Lochs Voil** and **Doune** spread out, adding to the stunning vistas. This area is often known as the Braes (Slopes) of Balquhidder and was once the home of the MacLarens and the MacGregors. Rob Roy MacGregor's grave is signposted beside Balquhidder village itself. The site of his house, now a private farm, is beyond the car park at the end of the road up the glen.

The glen has no through road, although in earlier times local residents were familiar with hill passes to the north and south. There still exists, for example, a right of way from the churchyard where Rob Roy is buried, through the plantings in Kirkton Glen and then on to open windy grasslands and a blue *lochan* (little lake). This path eventually drops into the next valley, Glen Dochart, and rejoins the A84.

Dining and Lodging

$$$$
★ ✕🏨 **Roman Camp.** This former hunting lodge, dating from 1625, has 20 acres of gardens with river frontage, yet is within easy walking distance of Callander's town center. Private fishing on the River Teith is another attraction, as are the sitting rooms and the library, which, with their numerous antiques, are more reminiscent of a stately family home than a hotel. The restaurant has high standards, with a good reputation for its salmon, trout, and other seafood, cooked in an imaginative, modern Scottish style by a chef who won't serve the same main course twice. ✉ *Callander, Perthshire, FK17 8BG,* ☎ *01877/330003,* FAX *01877/331533. 14 rooms with bath or shower. Restaurant (jacket and tie). AE, DC, MC, V.*

Outdoor Activities and Sports

BICYCLING
You can rent bicycles from **Wheels** (✉ Manse La., ☎ 01877/331100, FAX 01877/331510).

GOLF
The golf course at Callander (✉ Aveland Rd., ☎ 01877/330090, 18 holes, 5,125 yards, par 66) was designed by Tom Morris and has a scenic, upland feel, with fine views and a tricky moorland layout.

Shopping

A vast selection of woolens is on display at three mill shops in and near Callander. All the stores, which are part of the Edinburgh Woollen Mill Group, offer overseas mailing and tax-free shopping: **Kilmahog Woollen**

Mill (☎ 01877/330268), **Trossachs Woollen Mill** (✉ north of town at Trossachs turning, ☎ 01877/330178), and **Callander Woollen Mill** (✉ Main St., ☎ 01877/330273).

Uniquely Scottish is the stoneware of **Mounter Pottery** (✉ Ancaster Square La., ☎ 01877/331052), which you can see being made.

The Trossachs

10 mi west of Callander via A84 and A821 (to the Trossachs car park at Loch Katrine, taken to be the center of the Trossachs).

With their harmonious scenery of hill, loch, and wooded slopes, the Trossachs have been a tourist mecca since the late 18th century, at the dawn of the age of the romantic poets. Influenced by the writings of Sir Walter Scott, early visitors who strayed into the Highlands from the central belt of Scotland admired this as the first "wild" part of Scotland they encountered. The Trossachs represent the very essence of what the Highlands are supposed to be: birchwood and pine forests; vistas down lochs where the woods creep right to the water's edge; and in the background, peaks that rise high enough to be called mountains, though they're not as high as those to the north and west. The Trossachs are almost, but not quite, a Scottish visual cliché. They're popular right through the year, drawing not only first-time visitors from all around the world, but also Edinburghers and Glaswegians out for a Sunday drive.

② The A821 runs west along with the first and gentlest of the Trossachs lochs: **Loch Venachar.** The sturdy gray stone buildings, with a small dam at the Callander end, control the water fed into the River Teith (and, hence, into the Forth) to compensate for the Victorian tinkerings with the water supply. Within a few minutes the road becomes muffled in woodlands, and twists gradually down to **Brig o' Turk.** (*Turk* is Gaelic for the Scots *tuirc,* meaning wild boar, a species that has been extinct in this region since about the 16th century).

West of Brig o' Turk stretches **Loch Achray,** dutifully fulfilling expectations of what a verdant Trossachs loch should be: small, green, reedy meadows backed by dark plantations, rhododendron thickets, and lumpy, thickly covered hills. The car park by Loch Achray is where walkers begin their ascent of the steep, heathery **Ben An.** To enjoy the best Trossachs' views, you will need a couple of hours, and good lungs.

★ **②** At end of Loch Achray, a side road turns right into a narrow pass, leading to **Loch Katrine,** the heart of the Trossachs. During the time of Sir Walter Scott, the road here was narrow and almost hidden by the overhanging crags and mossy oaks and birches. Today it ends at a slightly anticlimactic parking lot with a shop, café, and visitor center. To see the finest of the Trossachs lochs properly, you must—even for just a few minutes—go westward on foot. The road beyond the parking lot (open only to Strathclyde Water Board vehicles) is well-paved and level. Loch Katrine's water is taken by aqueduct and tunnel to Glasgow—a Victorian feat of engineering that has ensured the purity of the supply to Scotland's largest city for more than a hundred years. Not readily visible from the parking lot, the steamer **SS** *Sir Walter Scott* embarks on cruises of Loch Katrine every summer. Take the cruise if time permits, as the shores of Katrine remain undeveloped and impressive. This loch is the setting of Scott's narrative poem, "The Lady of the Lake," and Ellen's Isle is named after his heroine. ✉ *Trossachs Pier,* ☎ *0141/ 955–0128.* 🎫 *£3.50.* ☼ *Cruises run Apr.–late Oct., Sun.–Fri. at 11, 1:45 and 3:15, Sat. at 2 and 3:30.*

Dining and Lodging

\$–\$\$ ✕ **Byre Restaurant.** Adjoining Dundarroch Country House (☞ *below*), this is a well-run pub and restaurant just beyond Brig o' Turk, with dark beams and loosely defined Victorian decor, as well as attentive, friendly service. It's a lunchtime haven, particularly on a wet day in the woodlands, but also offers a full evening menu. Savory Scottish offerings include poached Tay salmon with hollandaise sauce. Call ahead in winter, when hours are limited. ⊠ *Brig o' Turk,* ☎ *01877/376292. MC, V.*

\$\$ ▦ **Dundarroch Country House.** This Victorian country house, set on 14 acres, offers first-class accommodations furnished with antiques, paintings, and tapestries, in a warm, relaxing atmosphere. The mountain views from the guest rooms are stunning. ⊠ *Brig o' Turk, Trossachs, Perthshire, FK17 8HT,* ☎ *01877/376200,* 𝔽𝔸𝕏 *01877/376202. 3 rooms with bath or shower. MC, V. Closed Nov.–Mar.*

Outdoor Activities and Sports

WALKING

The Highland Boundary Fault Walk runs along the Highland boundary fault edge, offering superb views of both the Highlands and Lowlands, 6 miles south of the Trossachs on A821. ⊠ *Forestry Commission, Aberfoyle, Stirlingshire, FK8 3UX,* ☎ *01877/382383.*

En Route After going back through the pass to the main A821, turn right and head south, to higher moorland blanketed with conifer plantations (some of which have near-mature timber planted about 60 years ago by the Forestry Commission). The conifers hem in the views of Ben Ledi and Ben Venue, which can be seen over the spiky green waves of trees as the road snakes around heathery knolls and hummocks. There is another viewpoint at the highest point here, indicated by a small car park on the right. Soon the road swoops off the Highland edge and leads downhill. Near the start of the descent, the **Queen Elizabeth Forest Park Visitor Centre** can be seen on the left. The center features displays on the life of the forest, a summer-only café, some fine views over the Lowlands to the south, and a network of footpaths. The Trossachs end here.

Aberfoyle

㉒ *11 mi south of Loch Katrine.*

You are unlikely to want to linger in the small resort town of Aberfoyle, with its range of souvenir shops, unless you have children with
Ⓒ you. The **Scottish Wool Centre** tells the story of Scottish wool "from the sheep's back to your back." The Sheep Amphitheatre has live specimens of the main breeds, while in the Textile Display Area, you can try spinning and weaving. There is also a Kids' Farm (with lambs and kids) and Sheepdog Training School. The shop stocks a huge selection of woolen garments and knitwear. ⊠ *off Main Street, Aberfoyle, Stirlingshire,* ☎ *01877/382850.* ▣ *£2.50.* ☉ *Apr.–Sept., daily 9:30–6; Oct.–Mar., daily 10–5 (live sheep shows in summer).*

㉓ A short distance to the east of Aberfoyle is the **Lake of Menteith.** The tiny island of **Inchmahom** on the loch was a place of refuge for the young Mary, Queen of Scots in 1547.

From Aberfoyle, you can take a trip to see the more enclosed northern portion of **Loch Lomond,** (☞ Loch Lomond, *below*). During the off-season, the route has a wild and windswept air when it extends beyond the shelter of trees. Take the B829 (signposted Inversnaid and Stronachlachar), which runs west from Aberfoyle and offers outstanding views of **Ben Lomond,** especially in the vicinity of **Loch Ard.** The next loch, where the road narrows and bends, is **Loch Chon,** dark and forbidding. Its ominous reputation is further enhanced by the local legend: the presence of a dog-headed monster prone to swallowing passersby. Beyond Loch Chon, the road climbs gently from the plantings to open moor with a breathtaking vista over **Loch Arklet** to the **Arrochar Alps,** the name given to the high hills west of Loch Lomond. Hidden from sight in a deep trench, Loch Arklet is dammed to feed Loch Katrine. Go left at a road junction (a right will take you to Stronachlachar) and take the open road along Loch Arklet. These deserted green hills were once the rallying grounds of the Clan Gregor. Near the dam on Loch Arklet, on your right, **Garrison Cottage** recalls the days when the government had to billet troops here to keep the MacGregors in order. From Loch Arklet, the road zigzags down to **Inversnaid,** where you will see a hotel, a house, and a car park, with Loch Lomond stretching out of sight above and below. The only return to Aberfoyle is by retracing the same route.

Outdoor Activities and Sports

BICYCLING

Rent bicycles from **Trossachs Cycle Hire** (✉ Trossachs Holiday Park, ☎ 01877/382614).

WALKING

The long-distance walkers' route, the **West Highland Way,** which runs 95 miles from Glasgow to Fort William, follows the bank of Loch Lomond at Inversnaid. Take a brief stroll up the path, particularly if you are visiting during the spring, when the oak-tree canopy is filled with birdsong. You may get an inkling why Scots get so romantic about their bonny, bonny banks.

Drymen

㉔ *11 mi southwest of Aberfoyle via A81 and A811.*

Drymen is a respectable and cozy town in the Lowland fields, with shops and pubs catering to the well-to-do Scots who have moved here from Glasgow.

For the most outstanding Loch Lomond view from the south end, drive west from Drymen and take just a few minutes to clamber up bracken-covered **Duncryne Hill.** You may be rewarded by a spectacular sunset. You can't miss this unmistakable dumpling-shaped hill, behind Gartocharn on the Drymen–Balloch road, the A811.

NEED A   Drymen has a handful of pubs and tea shops. Try the **Clachan Inn**
BREAK?   (☎ 01360/660824), which serves appetizing bar meals.

Shopping

The Rowan Gallery (✉ 36 Main St., ☎ 01360/660996) shows original paintings and prints, specializing in Scottish scenes, but also has a fine selection of Scottish crafts, cards, books, and jewelry.

Loch Lomond

㉕ *3 mi west of Drymen via B837 signposted Rowardennan and Balmaha, 14 mi west of Aberfoyle.*

At the little settlement of **Balmaha,** the versatile recreational role filled by Loch Lomond is clear: Cruising craft are at the ready, hikers appear out of woodlands on the West Highland Way, and day-trippers stroll at the loch's edge. The heavily wooded offshore islands look alluringly near. One of the best ways to explore them is to take a cruise or rent a boat (☞ *below*). The island of **Inchcailloch** (*inch* is *innis,* Gaelic for island), just offshore, can be explored in an hour or two. There are pleasant pathways through oak woods planted in the 18th century, when the bark was used by the tanning industry.

Behind Balmaha is **Conic Hill,** a wavy ridge of bald heathery domes above the pine trees. You can note from your map how Inchcailloch and the other islands line up with it. This geographic line is indicative of the Highland Boundary Fault, which runs through Loch Lomond and the hill.

If you want to take in even more of Loch Lomond, a road that will end in a cul-de-sac continues northwest to **Rowardennan,** with the loch seldom more than a narrow field's length away. Where the drivable road ends, in a car park crunchy with pinecones, you can ramble along one of the marked loch-side footpaths, or make your way toward not-so-nearby Ben Lomond.

Dining and Lodging

$$$$
★

✕🖬 **Cameron House.** This luxury hotel offers a mix of top-quality hotel and country-club facilities (including swimming pools, a gymnasium, and squash courts) on the shores of Loch Lomond. Award-winning chef Jef Bland (formerly of the Caledonian Hotel in Edinburgh) oversees Scottish-French cuisine of the highest order, served in rich Victorian surroundings. Bedrooms are decorated in modern pastel shades with high-quality reproductions of antique furniture. ✉ *Loch Lomond, Alexandria, Dumbartonshire, G83 8QZ,* ☎ *01389/755565,* 𝔽𝔸𝕏 *01389/759522. 68 rooms with bath. Restaurant, bar, 2 pools, golf privileges, health club, fishing. AE, DC, MC, V.*

Outdoor Activities and Sports

BICYCLING

You can rent bicycles from **Lochside Mountain Bike Hire** (✉ Lochside Guest House, Arrochar, ☎ 01301/702467), on the west side of Loch Lomond, slightly less than 1 mile from Tarbet.

CRUISES AND BOAT RENTALS

MacFarlane and Son (✉ Boatyard, Balmaha, Loch Lomond, ☎ 01360/870214) run cruises on Loch Lomond. They also operate the mail boat to the islands (all year, Mon.–Sat. 10:50 AM in winter, 11:30 AM Apr.–Oct.) which takes passengers. You can even rent a rowboat from MacFarlane's if you prefer to do your own exploration. From Tarbet on the western shore, **Cruise Loch Lomond** (✉ Shore Cottage, Tarbet, ☎ 01301/702356) runs tours. From Balloch there are the **Lomond Duchess** and **Lomond Maid** (✉ Balloch Marina, Riverside, ☎ 01389/751481).

Shopping

The **Thistle Bagpipe Works** (✉ Luss, ☎ 01436/860250), on the western shore of Loch Lomond, will let you commission your own made-to-order bagpipe. You can also order a complete Highland outfit: kilt, jacket, etc.

PERTHSHIRE

Although Perth has an ancient history, it has been rebuilt and recast innumerable times and, sadly, no trace remains of the pre-Reformation monasteries that once dominated the skyline. In fact, modern Perth has swept much of its colorful history under a grid of bustling shopping streets. The town serves a wide rural hinterland and has a well-to-do air, making it one of the most interesting shopping towns, aside from Edinburgh and Glasgow.

Perth's rural hinterland is grand in several senses. On the Highland edge, prosperous-looking farms are scattered across well-wooded countryside, while even larger properties are screened by trees and parkland. All this changes as the mountain barrier is penetrated, with grouse moors and deer forest (where forest is used in the Scots sense of, paradoxically, open hill). Parts of Perthshire are quite wild without ever losing their cozy feel.

Perth

26 *36 mi northeast of Stirling, 43 mi north of Edinburgh, 61 mi northeast of Glasgow.*

Some say Perth took its name from a Roman camp, Bertha, on the shores of the Tay. Whatever the truth, this strategic site has been occupied continuously for centuries, even prior to its becoming a Royal Burgh in 1210. Perth has long been a focal point in Scottish history, and several critical events took place here, including the assassination of King James I in 1437 and John Knox's preaching in St. John's Kirk in 1559. (Knox's sermon undoubtedly stirred his congregation: Afterward, they went rampaging through the town, igniting the Reformation in Scotland.) Later, the 17th-century religious wars in Scotland saw the town occupied, first by the marquis of Montrose, then later by Oliver Cromwell's forces. Perth was also occupied by the Jacobites in the 1715 and 1745 rebellions. Perth's attractions—with the exception of the shops—are scattered and take time to reach on foot. Some, in fact, are far enough away to necessitate the use of a car, bus, or taxi.

St. John's Kirk (⊠ St. John St., ☎ 01738/626159) dating from the 15th century, escaped the worst excesses of the Reformation mob and is now restored. **Perth Art Gallery and Museum** (⊠ George St., ☎ 01738/632488) has a wide-ranging collection of local history and archaeology, plus a rotating exhibit program.

On the North Inch of Perth, look for **Balhousie Castle** and the **Regimental Museum of the Black Watch.** Some will tell you the Black Watch was a Scottish regiment whose name is a reference to the color of its tartan. An equally plausible explanation, however, is that the regiment was established to keep an undercover watch on rebellious Jacobites. *Black* is the Gaelic word *dubh,* meaning, in this case, hidden or covert, used in the same way as the word blackmail. ⊠ *Facing North Inch Park (entrance from Hay St.),* ☎ *01738/621281, ext. 8530.* ▣ *Free.* ⊙ *Weekdays 10–4:30 (3:30 in winter). Closed Dec. 23–Jan 3.*

The nearby Round House is home to the **Fergusson Gallery,** displaying a selection of 6,000 works—paintings, drawings, prints—by the Scottish artist J. D. Fergusson. ⊠ *Marshall Pl.,* ☎ *01738/441944.* ▣ *Free.* ⊙ *Mon.–Sat. 10–5.*

Off the A9 west of town, is **Caithness Glass,** where, from the viewing gallery, you can watch glassworkers creating smoky-smooth bowls, vases, and other glassware. There is also a small museum, restaurant, and shop. ⊠ *Inveralmond, Perth,* ☎ *01738/637373.* ▣ *Free.* ⊙ *Factory: weekdays 9–4:30. Shop: Easter–Oct., Mon.–Sat. 9–5, Sun. 10–5; Oct.–Easter, Mon.–Sat. 9–5, Sun. noon–5.*

27 A modest selection of castles is within easy reach of Perth. **Huntingtower Castle,** a curious double tower that dates from the 15th century, is associated with an attempt to wrest power from the young James VI in 1582. Some early painted ceilings survive, offering the vaguest hint of the sumptuous decor once found in many such ancient castles that are now reduced to bare and drafty rooms. ⊠ *Off A85,* ☎ *0131/*

668–8600. ⊠ £1.50. ◷ Apr.–Sept., Mon.–Sat. 9:30–6, Sun. 2–6; Oct.–Mar., Mon.–Wed. and Sat. 9:30–4, Thurs. 9–12, Sun. 2–4.

㉘ Elcho Castle is a fortified mansion on the east side of Perth. It is the abandoned 15th-century seat of the earls of Wemyss, and now only a shell. ⊠ *On River Tay,* ☎ *0131/668–8600. View from outside only.*

★ **㉙ Scone Palace** is much more cheerful and vibrant than Perth's other castles. The palace is the present home of the Earl of Mansfield and is open to visitors. Although it incorporates various earlier works, the palace today consists mainly of a 19th-century theme, featuring mock castellations that were fashionable at the time. There is plenty to see for the visitor with an interest in the acquisitions of an aristocratic Scottish family: magnificent porcelain, furniture, ivory, clocks, and 16th-century needlework. Visitor facilities also include a coffee shop, restaurant, gift shop, and play area, as well as extensive grounds that include a pinetum. The palace has its own chapel nearby, on the site of a long-gone abbey. The chapel stands by **Moot Hill**, the ancient coronation place of the Scottish kings. To be crowned, they sat upon the Stone of Scone, which was seized in 1296 by Edward I of England, Scotland's greatest enemy, and placed in the coronation chair at Westminster Abbey in London, where it is still on view. Some Scots hint darkly that Edward was fooled by a substitution, and that the real stone is hidden north of the border, waiting for Scotland to regain its independence. ⊠ *Braemar Rd.,* ☎ *01738/552308.* ⊠ *£4.70.* ◷ *Easter–Oct., daily 9:30–5.*

♻ Near Perth, **Fairways Heavy Horse Centre** offers Clydesdale horses for day rides. For £2 (£1 children) you can tour the center's stables and exercise fields. ⊠ *Glencarse Village,* ☎ *01738/632561.* ◷ *daily 10–5.*

Dining and Lodging

$$$ ✕▥ **Parklands.** A smart Georgian town house overlooking lush woodland—an ideal setting for this top-quality hotel—Parklands is perhaps best known for its cuisine, featuring Scottish fish, game, and beef. The restrained decor and modern furniture are in keeping with the subdued but elegant ambience. ⊠ *2 St. Leonard's Bank, PH2 8ER,* ☎ *01738/622451,* ℻ *01738/622046. 14 rooms with bath. Restaurant. AE, DC, MC, V.*

$$–$$$ ✕▥ **Sunbank House Hotel.** You'll find this early Victorian gray stone ★ mansion in a fine residential area near Perth's Branklyn Gardens. Recently redecorated in traditional style, it offers solid, unpretentious comforts along with great views over the River Tay and the city. The restaurant specializes in local produce, imaginatively cooked Continental style with some Scottish overtones. ⊠ *50 Dundee Rd., PH2 7BA,* ☎ *01738/624882,* ℻ *01738/442515. 10 rooms with bath or shower. Restaurant. MC, V.*

Nightlife and the Arts

The **Perth Repertory Theatre** (⊠ High St., Perth, ☎ 01738/621031) is a Victorian theater offering a variety of plays and musicals. In the summer it is the main venue for the Perth Festival of the Arts. **Perth City Hall** (☎ 01738/624055) is the main venue for musical performances of all types.

Shopping

Perth proffers an unusual buy: Scottish freshwater pearls from the River Tay, in delicate settings that take their theme from Scottish flowers. The Romans coveted these pearls. If you do, too, then you can make your choice at **Cairncross Ltd., Goldsmiths** (⊠ 18 St. John's St., ☎ 01738/624367), where you can also admire a display of some of the more unusual shapes and colors of pearls found. Antique Scottish jewelry and silver can be found at **Timothy Hardie** (⊠ 25 St. John's St.,

☎ 01738/633127). **Whispers of the Past** (✉ 15 George St., ☎ 01738/ 635472) has a collection of linens, old pine, and jewelry. A comprehensive selection of sheepskins, leather jackets, and hand-knit Aran sweaters are sold at **C & C Proudfoot** (✉ 104 South St., ☎ 01738/ 632483). Perth is an especially popular hunting ground for china and glass: **William Watson & Sons** (✉ 163–167 High St., ☎ 01738/639861) has sold exquisite bone china and cut crystal since 1900 and can pack your purchase safely for shipment overseas. **The Perthshire Shop** (✉ Lower City Mills, W. Mill St., ☎ 01738/627958) sells giftware, including rugs, scarves, handbags, and mugs in Perthshire's own tartan. At **Caithness Glass** (✉ Inveralmond, off the A9 at the northern town boundary, ☎ 01738/637373), you can buy all types of glassware in the factory shop.

Dunkeld

 14 mi north of Perth.

At Dunkeld, Thomas Telford's handsome river bridge of 1809 carries the road into town. In Dunkeld you will find that the National Trust for Scotland not only cares for grand mansions and wildlands but also actively restores smaller properties. The work completed under its "Little Houses" project can be seen in the square off the main street, opposite the fish-and-chips shop. All the houses in the square were rebuilt after the 1689 Battle of Killiecrankie (☞ *below*) when, after its victory, the Jacobite army marched south and was defeated here.

The ospreys that frequent Speyside's Loch Garten in summer get so much attention from conservation societies that they sometimes overshadow **Loch of the Lowes,** a Scottish Wildlife Trust reserve behind Dunkeld. Here the domestic routines of the osprey, one of Scotland's conservation success stories, can be observed in relative comfort. The reserve is off the A923 northeast of Dunkeld. ☎ *01350/727337.* ⏲ *Visitor center, Apr.–Sept., daily 10–5. Observation blind open at all times.*

Shopping
Dunkeld Antiques (✉ Tay Terrace, ☎ 01350/728832), facing the river just as you cross the bridge, is well worth a browse, stocking everything from large items of furniture down to ornaments and jewelry, books, and prints. At the **Highland Horn and Deerskin Centre** (✉ City Hall, Atholl St., ☎ 01350/727569), you can purchase stag antlers and cow horns shaped into horn-handled walking sticks, cutlery, and tableware. Deerskin shoes and moccasins are also sold. The center offers a worldwide postal service and a tax-free shop.

Pitlochry

 15 mi north of Dunkeld.

A typical central Highland resort, always full of leisurely hustle and bustle, Pitlochry has wall-to-wall souvenir and gift shops, large hotels recalling even more laid-back days, and a mountainous golf course. One popular attraction is the **Pitlochry Dam and Fish Ladder,** just behind the main street. Most Scottish dams have salmon passes or ladders of some kind, enabling the fish to swim upstream to their spawning grounds. In Pitlochry, the fish ladder leads into a glass-paneled pipe so that the fish can observe the visitors.

For those with a whisky-tasting bent, Pitlochry also is home to **Edradour Distillery,** which claims to be the smallest single-malt distillery in Scotland (but then, so do others). ✉ *2½ mi east of Pitlochry,* ☎ *01796/*

472095. ⊠ *Free.* ⊙ *For tours and tastings, Mar.–Oct., Mon.–Sat. 9:30–5, Sun. noon–5; shop also open Nov.–Feb., Mon.–Sat. 10–4.*

㉜ The **Linn of Tummel,** a series of marked walks along the river and through tall, mature woodlands, is a little north of Pitlochry. Above the Linn, the new A9 is raised on stilts and gives an exciting view of the valley.

★ **㉝** The **Pass of Killiecrankie,** set among the oak woods and rocky river just north of the Linn of Tummel, was a key strategic point in the Central Highlands: A famous battle was won here in the Jacobite rebellion of 1689. The National Trust for Scotland's **visitor center** at Killiecrankie explains the significance of this, the first attempt to restore the Stewart monarchy. The battle was noted for the death of the Jacobite leader, James Graham of Claverhouse, also known as Bonnie Dundee, who was hit by a stray bullet; the rebellion fizzled out after that. To reach Killiecrankie from Pitlochry, stay on the old A9, heading north. ⊠ *Off A9,* ☎ *01796/473233.* ⊠ *£1.* ⊙ *Visitor center: Apr.–Oct., daily 10–5:30. Site open year round.*

★ **㉞** Only a few minutes farther north from the Pass of Killiecrankie sits **Blair Castle.** Because of its historic contents and its war-torn past, this is one of Scotland's most highly rated castles. White painted and turreted, Blair Castle was home to successive dukes of Atholl and their family, the Murrays, until the recent death of the 10th duke. Its ownership and care has now passed to a charitable trust. One of the many fascinating details in the interior is a preserved piece of flooring that still bears marks of the red-hot shot fired through the roof during the 1745 Jacobite rebellion—the last occasion in Scottish history that a castle was besieged. The castle holds not only military artifacts—historically, the duke was allowed to keep a private army, the Atholl Highlanders—but also a fine collection of furniture and paintings. Outside, a Victorian walled garden has been restored, and there are extensive parklands backed by high rounded hills. To reach the castle from Pitlochry, take the A9 to Blair Atholl, where the castle is clearly signposted. ☎ *01796/481207.* ⊠ *£5.* ⊙ *Apr.–late Oct., daily 10–6 (last admission at 5).*

㉟ Also easily reached from Pitlochry is **Loch Rannoch,** which, with its shoreline birch trees framed by dark pines, is the quintessential Highland loch. The road ends at Rannoch, where you meet the West Highland railroad line on its way across Rannoch Moor to Fort William. Fans of Robert Louis Stevenson, especially of *Kidnapped,* will not want to miss the last, lonely section of road. Stevenson describes the setting: *The mist rose and died away, and showed us that country lying as waste as the sea; only the moorfowl and the peewees crying upon it, and far over to the east a herd of deer, moving like dots. Much of it was red with heather, much of the rest broken up with bogs and hags and peaty pools . . . .*

Apart from the blocks of alien conifer plantings in certain places, little here has changed. To reach this atmospheric locale, take the B8019 at the Linn of Tummel north of Pitlochry, then the B846 at Tummel Bridge.

Lodging

$$ 🏨 **Cuilmore Cottage.** This 18th-century croft halfway to Rannoch Moor has been carefully modernized to a very high standard, but it is the superb food (included in the room rate) which is most memorable: The hostess, Mrs. Steffan, has been awarded a special prize by the Taste of Scotland organization for her homegrown fruit and vegetables, and for her home baking. Try the loin of lamb with red currant jelly or saddle of rabbit with herb dumplings. ⊠ *Kinloch Rannoch, Perthshire, PH16 5QB,* ☎ FAX *01882/632218. 2 rooms with bath. MC, V.*

Nightlife and the Arts

Pitlochry Festival Theatre (✉ Pitlochry, ☎ 01796/472680 or 473054) presents seven plays each season and features concerts on some Sundays. The theater is open from May to early October.

Aberfeldy

㊱ *15 mi southwest of Pitlochry.*

Aberfeldy is a sleepy town that is popular as a tourist base. Aberfeldy Bridge (1733), with five arches and a humpback, was designed by William Adam.

㊲ West of Aberfeldy, on the opposite bank of the River Tay, stands **Castle Menzies.** This Z-plan 16th-century fortified tower/house is now the setting for the **Clan Menzies' Museum.** ☎ 01887/820982. ✒ £2.50. ☉ *Apr.–mid-Oct., Mon.–Sat. 10:30–5, Sun. 2–5 (last admission at 4:30).*

㊳ **Glen Lyon** is one of central Scotland's most attractive glens; it comprises a rushing river, forests, high hills on both sides, prehistoric sites complete with legendary tales, and the typical *big hoose* (big house) hidden on private grounds. There is even a dam at the head of the loch, as a reminder that little of Scotland's scenic beauty is unadulterated. You can reach the glen by a high road from Loch Tay: Take the A827 to Fearnan, then turn north to Fortingall. The **Fortingall yew,** in the churchyard near the Fortingall Hotel, wearily rests its great limbs on the ground. This tree is thought to be more than 3,000 years old. Legend has it that Pontius Pilate was born beside it, while his father served as a Roman legionnaire in Scotland. After viewing the yew, turn west into Glen Lyon.

Outdoor Activities and Sports

WATER SPORTS

Loch Tay Boating Centre (✉ Carlin and Brett, Pier Rd., Kenmore, ☎ 01887/830291) has cabin cruisers and canoes from April to October.

En Route   Between Aberfeldy and Killin, take the north-bank road by Loch Tay, the A827, which offers fine views west along Loch Tay toward Ben More and Stobinian, and north to Ben Lawers.

Killin

㊴ *24 mi southwest of Aberfeldy, 39 mi north of Stirling, 45 mi west of Perth.*

A village with an almost alpine flavor, known for its modest but surprisingly diverse selection of crafts and woolen wares, Killin is also noted for its scenery. The **Falls of Dochart,** white-water rapids overlooked by a pine-clad islet, are at the west end of the village. By the Falls of Dochart you will find the **Breadalbane Folklore Centre,** with its canter through the heritage and folk tales of the area. The most curious of these are the "healing stones of St Fillan"—water-worn stones, on view, which have been looked after lovingly for centuries for their supposed curative powers. ✉ *Killin,* ☎ 01567/820254. ✒ £1. ☉ *Mar.–Apr. and Sept.–Oct., daily 10–5; June–Aug., daily 9–6; Nov.–Dec. and Feb., weekends 10–4; closed Jan.*

Across the River Dochart and near the golf course sit the ruins of **Finlarig Castle,** built by Black Duncan of the Cowl, a notorious Campbell laird. The castle can be visited at any time.

Dining and Lodging

$–$$ ✕🏠 **The Lodge House.** Few other guest houses in Scotland can match the mountain views from this 100-year-old property; it's certainly worth the short drive west from Killin to Crianlarich to reach it. Informal and cozy, the hotel is successful thanks to what the Scots call "the crack"—conviviality between host and guests. The food is good Scots fare: haggis, salmon, and oatcakes. The bedrooms are plain and unfussy, but more than adequate. You may wish to walk along the riverbank after dinner, or have a wee dram in the tiny bar instead. ⊠ *Lodge House, Crianlarich, Perthshire, FK20 8RU,* ☎ *01838/300276. 6 rooms with bath or shower. Restaurant. MC, V.*

Outdoor Activities and Sports

BICYCLING

If you want to explore the northern end of the Glasgow–Killin cycleway, rent a bicycle from **Killin Outdoor Centre and Mountain Shop** (⊠ Main St., Killin, ☎ FAX 01567/820652).

En Route Southwest of Killin the A827 joins the main A85. By turning south over the watershed, you will see fine views of the hill ridges behind Killin. The road leads into Glen Ogle, "amid the wildest and finest scenery we had yet seen . . . putting one in mind of prints of the Khyber Pass," as Queen Victoria recorded in her diary when she passed this way in 1842.

Lochearnhead

40 *8 mi south of Killin, 37 mi west of Perth, 31 mi northwest of Stirling.*

The settlement of Lochearnhead is set, as its name suggests, on the shore of **Loch Earn.** To the east are good views of the long, gray screes of Ben Vorlich southward across the loch.

Outdoor Activities and Sports

WATER SPORTS

Lochearnhead Water Sports Centre (⊠ Loch Earn, ☎ 01567/830330) rents sailboats, canoes, and sailboards for wind surfing, and offers instruction for water-sports enthusiasts, from novices to experts.

En Route Between Lochearnhead and Crieff, the road passes through lush Perthshire estates and farmlands, reminiscent of the Lowlands. The little communities of St. Fillans and Comrie punctuate the route; the higher hills can always be seen to the north.

Crieff

41 *19 mi east of Lochearnhead.*

The hilly town of Crieff offers walks with Highland views from **Knock Hill** above the town. Tours of the **Glenturret Distillery** can be undertaken if you have not already discovered the delights of whisky-distilling. It is signposted on the west side of the town. ☎ *01764/656565.* ☞ *£2.90.* ☉ *Mar.–Dec., Mon.–Sat. 9:30–4:30, Sun. 12–4:30; Jan.–Feb., weekdays 11:30–2:30.*

NEED A BREAK? **Glenturret Distillery Visitor Centre** (☞ *above*) offers a choice of restaurants that serve award-winning "Taste of Scotland" menus.

Just south of Crieff is a paperweight manufacturer, part of a complex called the **Crieff Visitors Centre.** Adjacent to the complex is a small pottery factory and a restaurant. During the week there are surprisingly interesting tours of the factory grounds, where you can see Thistle hand-painted pottery, intricate millefiori glass, and lamp-work Perthshire paperweights being made. ⊠ *A822, south of Crieff,* ☎ *01764/654014.* ☞ *Free (small charge for pottery factory tour).* ☉ *Daily 9–6 (restricted hours in winter; call ahead).*

㊷ **Drummond Castle,** southwest of the town, has an unusual formal Italian garden. ⊠ *Off Crieff–Muthill road,* ☎ *01764/681257.* ✑ *Gardens: £3.* ⊙ *May–Oct., daily 2–6 (last admission at 5).*

Shopping

Crieff is a center for china and glassware. **Stuart Crystal** (⊠ Muthill Rd., ☎ 01764/654004), a factory shop, sells Stuart crystal, but also Waterford and Wedgwood wares. Also visit the **Crieff Visitors Centre** (☞ *above*).

Auchterarder

㊸ *11 mi southeast of Crieff, 15 mi southwest of Perth, 21 mi northeast of Stirling.*

Famous for the **Gleneagles Hotel** (☞ Dining and Lodging, *below*), Auchterarder also has a flock of antiques shops.

Dining and Lodging

$$$$ ✕▥ **Auchterarder House Hotel.** Secluded and superbly atmospheric,
★ this is a wood-paneled, richly furnished, Victorian country mansion. The staff is particularly friendly and attentive in this family home. The plush, exuberantly styled dining room, filled with glittering glassware, is an appropriate setting for the unusual and creative use of many locally produced foods. ⊠ *On B8062, at Auchterarder, 15 mi southwest of Perth, PH3 1DZ,* ☎ *01764/663646,* ℻ *01764/662939. 15 rooms with bath. Restaurant (reservations essential), golf privileges, croquet. AE, DC, MC, V.*

$$$$ ✕▥ **Gleneagles Hotel.** One of Britain's most famous hotels, Gleneagles is the very image of modern grandeur. Like a vast, secret palace, it stands hidden in breathtaking countryside amid world-famous golf courses. Recreation facilities are nearly endless, and there are three restaurants: the **Strathearn,** for à la carte and table d'hôte; the **Clubhouse Grill** (at the 18th hole of the King's Course), for à la carte; and the **Gallery Brasserie,** by the swimming pool. All this, plus a shopping arcade, Champneys Health Spa, the Gleneagles Mark Phillips Equestrian Centre, the British School of Falconry, Gleneagles Jackie Stewart Shooting School, the Golf Academy, and the Off-road at Gleneagles driving school, make a stay here a luxurious and unforgettable experience. ⊠ *Auchterarder, near Perth, PH3 1NF,* ☎ *01764/662231,* ℻ *01764/662134. 236 rooms with bath. 3 restaurants (reservations essential), sauna, golf privileges, tennis court, exercise room. AE, DC, MC, V.*

THE CENTRAL HIGHLANDS A TO Z

Arriving and Departing

By Bus

There is a good network of buses connecting with the central belt via Edinburgh and Glasgow. Express services also link the larger towns in the Central Highlands with all main towns and cities in England. Contact **National Express/Scottish Citylink** (☎ 0990/505050), or **Stagecoach** (⊠ Ruthvenfield Rd., Inveralmond Industrial Estate, Perth, ☎ 01738/629339).

By Car

Visitors will find easy access to the area from the central belt of Scotland via the motorway network. The M9 runs within sight of the walls of Stirling Castle, and Perth can be reached via the M90 over the Forth Bridge.

By Plane

Perth and Stirling can be reached easily from **Edinburgh** and **Glasgow** airports (☞ Chapters 3 and 4) by train, car, or bus.

By Train

The Central Highlands are linked to Edinburgh and Glasgow by rail, with through routes to England (some direct-service routes from London take fewer than five hours). A variety of "Savers" ticket options are available, although in some cases on the ScotRail system, the discount fares must be purchased before your arrival in the United Kingdom. Contact **ScotRail** (☎ 01738/637117) for details.

Getting Around

By Bus

The following companies offer reliable service on a number of convenient routes.

Scottish Citylink-National Express (✉ Leonard St., bus station, Perth, ☎ 01738/626848).
Midland Bluebird Bus Services (✉ Goosecroft Rd. bus station, Stirling, ☎ 01786/473763).
Stagecoach (✉ Ruthvenfield Rd., Inveralmond Industrial Estate, Perth, ☎ 01738/629339).

By Car

There is an adequate network of roads, and the area's proximity to the central belt speeds road communications. The Scottish Tourist Board's touring map is useful.

By Train

The **West Highland Line** runs through the western portion of the area. Services also run to Stirling, Dunblane, Perth, and Gleneagles; destinations on the Inverness–Perth line include Dunkeld, Pitlochry, and Blair Atholl. Contact **ScotRail** (☎ 01738/637117) for details.

Contacts and Resources

Doctors and Dentists

Local practitioners will usually treat visitors. Information is available from tourist information centers, or from your hotel receptionist or bed-and-breakfast host. Names of doctors can also be found in the Yellow Pages telephone directory.

Emergencies

For **police, fire,** or **ambulance,** dial 999 from any telephone. No coins are needed for emergency calls from telephone booths.

The main hospital emergency rooms in the region are **Perth Royal Infirmary** (✉ Tullylumb, Perth, ☎ 01738/623311), **Stirling Royal Infirmary** (✉ Livilands Gate, Stirling, ☎ 01786/434000), and **Vale of Leven Hospital** (✉ Main St., Alexandria, ☎ 01389/754121).

Fishing

There are several fishing options in the area, including course and game fishing, loch and river fishing, and sea angling. Tourist information centers have publications, updated annually, that show the best locations.

Golf

There are many excellent courses in the region (☞ Chapter 2). Tourist information centers can supply details of local courses.

Guided Tours

ORIENTATION

The bus companies listed in Getting Around By Bus (☞ *above*) offer a number of general orientation tours. Inquire at the nearest tourist information center, where tour reservations can usually be booked.

SPECIAL-INTEREST

There are many taxi and chauffeur companies offering tailor-made tours by the day or week; the nearest tourist information center is your best source for detailed, up-to-date information.

Do not miss the opportunity to take a boat trip on a Scottish loch. Details of cruise operators are given in the Trossachs (for Loch Katrine) and Loch Lomond entries (☞ *above*), or consult a tourist information center.

Hiking

Tourist information centers carry information on a variety of local routes. The publications *Walk Loch Lomond and the Trossachs* or *Walk Perthshire* are invaluable for hikers and trekkers and are available at bookshops or tourist information centers.

Late-Night Pharmacies

Late-night pharmacies are found only in the larger towns and cities. In an emergency, the police will help you find a pharmacist. In rural areas, general practitioners may also dispense medicine.

Visitor Information

Local tourist information centers can be found throughout the region:

Aberfeldy (⊠ The Square, ☎ 01887/820276). **Alva** (⊠ Glentana Mills, West Stirling St., ☎ 01259/769696). **Auchterarder** (⊠ 90 High St., ☎ 01764/664235). **Blairgowrie** (⊠ 26 Wellmeadow, ☎ 01250/872960). **Crieff** (⊠ Town Hall, High St., ☎ 01764/652578). **Drymen** (⊠ The Square, ☎ 01360/660068). **Kinross** (⊠ Service Area Junction 6 M90, ☎ 01577/863680). **Perth** (⊠ 45 High St., ☎ 01738/638353). **Pitlochry** (⊠ 22 Atholl Rd., ☎ 01796/472215). **Stirling** (⊠ 41 Dumbarton Rd., ☎ 01786/475019).

Seasonal tourist information centers are also open (generally Apr.–Oct.) in the following towns: Aberfoyle, Balloch, Callander, Dumbarton, Dunblane, Dunkeld, Helensburgh, Inveralmond, Killin, Pirnhall, Pitlochry, Tarbert, and Tyndrum. All are clearly marked with the standard I sign in white on a blue background.

8 Aberdeen and the Northeast

Aberdeen, Scotland's third-largest city, is built largely of glittering granite, and is a main port of North Sea oil operations. The Grampian region spreads to the west, the terrain changing from coastline—some of the U.K.'s wildest shorelines of high cliffs and sandy beaches—to farmland, to forests, to hills. The Grampian mountains and the Cairngorms, regions of heather and forest, granite peaks and deep glens, are popular for hill walking and skiing. The Northeast is also known for its wealth of castles and whisky distilleries.

By Gilbert
Summers

BECAUSE OF ITS GEOGRAPHIC ISOLATION, the granite city of Aberdeen has, throughout its history, been a fairly autonomous place. Even now, it is still perceived by many inhabitants of the United Kingdom as lying almost out of reach in the north. In reality, this northeastern locale is only 90 minutes flying time from London or—thanks to recent road improvements—a little more than two hours by car from Edinburgh. Its magnificent, confident 18th- and early 19th-century city center amply rewards exploration, and there are also many surviving buildings from earlier centuries to seek out.

Yet even if Aberdeen, the country's third-largest city after Glasgow and Edinburgh, vanished from the map of Scotland, an extensive portion of the Northeast would still be worth exploring. The area's chief scenic attraction lies in the gradual transition from high mountain plateau— by a series of gentle steps through hill, forest, and farmland—to the Moray Firth and North Sea coastline where the word *unadulterated* truly applies. The coastline includes some of the United Kingdom's most perfect wild shorelines, both sandy and high cliff. The Grampian Mountains to the west contain some of the highest ground in the United Kingdom, in the area of the Cairngorms. But the Grampian hills have also shaped the character of the folk who live in the Northeast. In earlier times, the massif made communication with the south somewhat difficult. As a result, native Northeasterners still speak the richest Lowland Scottish (*not* Gaelic, which is an entirely different language).

Nowhere else in Scotland is there such an eclectic selection of castles, offering visitors an opportunity to touch the fabric of Scotland's story. There are so many that in one part of the region a Castle Trail has been assembled, leading you to fortresses like the ruined medieval Kildrummy Castle, which once controlled the strategic routes through the valley of the River Don. Later work, such as Craigievar, a narrow-turreted castle resembling an illustration from a fairy-tale book, reflects the changing times of the 17th century, when defense became less of a priority. Later still, grand mansions, such as Haddo House, with its symmetrical facade and elegant interiors, surrender any defensive need entirely and instead make statements about their owner's status and power.

As a visitor to Scotland, you can be sure of one thing: No matter where you are, a whisky distillery can't be far off; Morayshire, in the northwestern part of this region, where the distilling is centered in the valley of the River Spey and its tributaries, is no exception. Just as the Loire in France has famous vineyards clustered around it, the Spey has famous single-malt distilleries. Instead of Muscadet, Chinon, Vouvray or Pouilly-sur-Loire, there's Glenfiddich, Glen Grant, Tamdhu, or Tamnavulin. As well as being sweeter and less peaty than some of the island malts, eastern or Speyside malts have the further advantage of having generally easier-to-pronounce brand names.

Pleasures and Pastimes

Bicycling

Northeast Scotland is excellent biking country, with networks of minor roads and farm roads crisscrossing rolling fields. It's also now possible to bicycle on a variety of train-to-trails routes—former railway track beds converted to bicycle and pedestrian pathways. The Buchan line, from Aberdeen to Fraserburgh and Peterhead, is a good route.

Dining

Partly in response to the demands of spendthrift oilmen, the number of restaurants in Aberdeen has grown over the past several years, and the quality of the food has improved. Elsewhere in the region you are never far from a good pub lunch or a hotel high tea or dinner.

WHAT TO WEAR

In Aberdeen, people tend to dress up when dining out; the same is true at more expensive restaurants outside Aberdeen. Otherwise, casual but smart dress is preferred.

CATEGORY	COST*
$$$$	over £40
$$$	£30–£40
$$	£15–£30
$	under £15

*per person for a three-course meal, including VAT and excluding drinks and service

Fishing and Water Sports

With major rivers such as the Dee, Don, Deveron, and Ythan as well as popular smaller rivers times such as the Ugie, plus loch and estuary fishing, this is one of Scotland's leading game-fishing areas.

Only in 1997, on July 12–15, the Cutty Sark Tall Ships Race—which moves annually around Europe's major ports—comes to Aberdeen. A weekend of revelries precedes the actual race, which will take the ships from Aberdeen to the finish line at Trondheim, Norway.

Lodging

The Northeast has some splendid country hotels with log fires and rich furnishings, where you can also be sure of eating well if you have time for a leisurely meal. Note that in Aberdeen, many hotels offer very competitive room rates on weekends.

CATEGORY	COST*
$$$$	over £110
$$$	£80–£110
$$	£45–£80
$	under £45

*All prices are for a standard double room, including service, breakfast, and VAT.

Shopping

Aberdeen, serving a large and fairly prosperous hinterland, has the widest choice of shopping in the region. Elgin, a smaller center, also has some shops of interest. Because of the fishing and farming prosperity, plus new money from oil and even newer money from people moving from the south, there are a few shopping surprises in some of the smaller towns as well.

Exploring Aberdeen and the Northeast

Once you have spent time in Aberdeen, you may be inclined to venture west up Deeside, with its Royal connections and looming mountain backdrop, and then pass over the hills into the "castle country" to the north. Then you might head farther west to touch on Speyside and "whisky country," before meandering back east and south along the pristine coastline at the northeasternmost tip of Scotland.

Union Street is the center of Aberdeen, and through traffic from the north and northwest is signposted through Aberdeen beyond its east end and to the harbor. Through traffic from the south is signposted around Anderson Drive, from where all the main routes into the Grampian hinterland are also signposted: for example, the Deeside and Donside routes, the main Inverness A96, as well as coastal routes to the north. Outside Aberdeen, the Castle and Whisky trails are generally well marked.

Great Itineraries

Remember that Grampian is not a huge area, though one with great variety. Overall, to get a real flavor of this most authentic of Scottish regions, make sure you sample both the coastline and the mountains.

IF YOU HAVE 2 DAYS

Numbers in the text correspond to numbers in the margin and on the Aberdeen, Royal Deeside, and The Northeast maps.

Spend a day touring in Royal Deeside and take in a castle. Balmoral may not be your best bet, as there are more worthwhile castle experiences to enjoy, such as **Drum** ⑲, **Crathes** ⑳ and **Braemar** ㉗. Stay overnight in **Aberdeen** ①, then the following day, look at the coastline north from Aberdeen toward **Fraserburgh** ㊾, with its memorable Lighthouse Museum, and west toward **Banff** ㊼, where there is a splendid collection of pictures at Duff House.

IF YOU HAVE 4 DAYS

Downtown **Aberdeen's** ① silver granite certainly deserves a little time. Then travel from Aberdeen into Speyside for its distilleries: **Dufftown** ㉞, and north via **Craigellachie** ㉟ and **Aberlour** ㊱ to **Elgin** ㊲. Spend a morning exploring Elgin before moving east along the coast to stay overnight in **Fordyce** ㊺ or **Banff** ㊼. Visit the magnificent Duff House gallery in Banff itself, before travelling on east along a spectacular coastline (take the B9031 from Macduff) to **Fraserburgh** ㊾ for Scotland's Lighthouse Museum; return to Aberdeen. If you have time on the last day, travel into Deeside to see a castle or two: **Drum** ⑲ or **Crathes** ⑳, and the beautiful birch woodlands beside the River Dee beyond **Banchory** ⑱.

IF YOU HAVE 7 DAYS

Plan to cover the same ground as the four day route, but take time to look at some of the smaller northeast coastal places such as **Cullen** ㊹ or **Pennan** ㊽. Traveling southward from Fraserburgh, spend a night near **Mintlaw** ㊿ or **Ellon** (51) to take in one or two of the area's Castle Trail properties: **Pitmedden Garden** (52), **Haddo House** (53) or **Fyvie Castle** (54). In Royal Deeside, you will have time to stay overnight at **Ballater** ㉔ and, after visiting Braemar, to loop north and east for yet more memorable castles: **Corgarff** ㉙, the ruined castle at **Kildrummy** ㉚, fairy-tale **Craigievar** ㉜, and **Castle Fraser** ㉝.

When to Tour Aberdeen and the Northeast

Because the National Trust for Scotland tends to close its properties in the winter, many of the Northeast's castles are not suitable for off-season travel, though you can always see them from the outside. However, with the Lighthouse Museum, Duff House, and some of the distilleries open much of the year, Grampian certainly does not shut down entirely. May and June are probably the best times here.

ABERDEEN—THE SILVER CITY

In the 18th century, local granite quarrying produced a durable silver stone that would be used to build the Aberdonian structures of the Victorian era. Thus granite was used boldly—in glittering blocks, spires, columns, and parapets—to build downtown Aberdeen, which remains one of the United Kingdom's most distinctive urban environments, although some would say it depends on the weather and the brightness of the day. The mica chips embedded in the rock are a million mirrors in sunshine. In rain and heavy clouds, however, their sparkle is snuffed out.

The North Sea has always been an important feature of Aberdeen: In the 1850s, the city was famed for its fast clippers, sleek sailing ships that raced to India for cargoes of tea. In the late 1960s, the course of Aberdeen's history was unequivocally altered when oil and gas were discovered in the North Sea. Aberdeen at first seemed destined to become an oil-rich boomtown, and throughout the 1970s the city was overcome by new shops, new office blocks, new hotels, new industries, and new attitudes. Fortunately, some innate local caution has helped the city to retain a sense of perspective and prevented it from selling out entirely.

Aberdeen

1 *131 mi north of Edinburgh, 152 mi northeast of Glasgow.*

What Princes Street is to Edinburgh, **Union Street** is to Aberdeen: the central pivot of the city plan and the product of a wave of enthusiasm to rebuild the city in a contemporary style in the early 19th century. Some hints of an older Aberdeen have survived and add to the city's charm. Conversely, today's plans are also changing the face of Aberdeen, but it is still a city of handsome granite buildings that give it a silvery complexion.

★ **2** **Marischal College,** dominating Broad Street, was founded in 1593 by the Earl Marischal as a Protestant alternative to the Catholic King's College in Old Aberdeen (☞ *below*), though the two combined to form Aberdeen University in 1860. (The earls Marischal held hereditary office as keepers of the king's mares.) The original university buildings on this site have undergone extensive renovations. What you see in front of you is a facade built in 1891. The spectacularly ornate work is set off by the gilded flags, and this turn-of-the-century creation is still the second-largest granite building in the world. Only the Escorial in Madrid is larger. The main part of the building, no longer needed by the university, is at present the subject of various plans, one to turn it into a hotel. The **Marischal Museum** exhibits artifacts and photographs relating to the heritage of the Northeast. ⊠ *Broad St.,* ☎ *01224/632727.* ☞ *Free.* ☼ *Museum weekdays 10–5, Sun. 2–5.*

A survivor from an earlier Aberdeen can be found beyond the concrete supports of St. Nicholas House (of which the tourist information center is a part): **3** **Provost Skene's House** (*provost* is Scottish for mayor) was once part of a closely packed area of town houses. Steeply gabled and rubble-built, it survives in part from 1545. It was originally a domestic dwelling house and is now a museum portraying civic life, with restored furnished period rooms and a painted chapel. ⊠ *Guestrow, off Broad St.,* ☎ *01224/641086.* ☞ *Free.* ☼ *Mon.–Sat. 10–5.*

In **Upperkirkgate,** at the lowest point, are two modern shopping malls—the **St. Nicholas Centre** on the left, the **Bon-Accord Centre** on the right. Until recent years, George Street, at the foot of the hill here, was a bustling shopping street. But not even Aberdeen, in its far northern perch, exempted itself from the British trend toward chain-store anonymity, and it thus demolished traditional stonework to accommodate the chains. If you do enter the portals of the Bon-Accord Centre, you will eventually emerge at the truncated George Street.

At the top of Schoolhill, as the slope eases off, there is a complex of silver-toned buildings, in front of which stands a statue of General Charles Gordon, the military hero of Khartoum (1885). Interestingly, he is not **4** the Gordon recalled in **Robert Gordon's University** behind the statue.

198

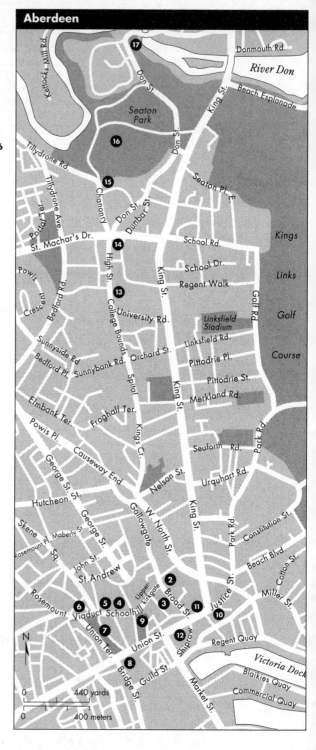

Built in 1731, the structure was originally called Robert Gordon's Hospital and it was used to educate poor boys. It became an independent school later and then an institute of technology, before gaining university status in 1992.

5 **Aberdeen Art Gallery** plays an active role in Aberdeen's cultural life and is a popular rendezvous for locals. It houses a wide-ranging collection—from the 18th century to contemporary work. The sculpture court is worth seeing, with its gallery supported by columns of different shades of polished granite. Next door is Robert Gordon's University. ✉ *Schoolhill*, ☎ *01224/646333.* ▨ *Free.* ☉ *Mon–Wed. and Fri.–Sat., 10–5, Thurs. 10–8, Sun. 2–5.*

6 A library, church, and nearby theater on **Rosemount Viaduct** are collectively known by all Aberdonians as Education, Salvation, and Damnation! Silvery and handsome, the **Central Library** and **St. Mark's Church** date from the last decade of the 19th century, while **His Majesty's Theatre** (1904–08) has been restored inside to its full Edwardian splendor (☞ Nightlife and the Arts, *below*). If you're taking photographs, you can choose an angle that includes the statue of Scotland's first freedom fighter, Sir William Wallace, in the foreground, pointing majestically to Damnation.

🐾 The **Rosemount Celebration Centre** has an activities-based heritage museum and learning center called Jonah's Journey, based on life in a 2,000-year-old Israelite village. The center offers costumes, spinning and weaving, mosaic making, puppet plays, and jigsaw puzzles. ✉ *Rosemount Pl.,* ☎ *01224/647614.* ▨ *£1.50.* ☉ *Mon.–Sat. 10–12, Sun. 2:30–4:30. Closed Dec. 25–Jan. 8.*

7 On **Union Terrace,** a statue of **Robert Burns** stands, addressing a daisy. Behind Burns are the **Union Terrace Gardens,** faintly echoing Edinburgh's Princes Street Gardens in that they separate the older part of the city, to the east, from the 19th-century development of Union Terrace and points west (as well as Union Street itself). Most of the buildings on Union Terrace around the grand-looking Caledonian Hotel are late-Victorian, when exuberance and confidence in style was at its height. The results are impressive. Note for example, at the corner of Union Street, the wonderfully elaborate **Commercial Union Assurance building** (1885). Its Doric portico has been a landmark and meeting place for generations of locals. They call it the "monkey house," though few can tell you why.

8 Smug cats seated primly on its parapet decorate **Union Bridge.** The bridge was built in the early years of the 19th century, as was much of Union Street. The bridge has a gentle rise—or descent, if you are traveling east—and the street is carried on a series of blind arches. The north side of Union Bridge is the most obvious reminder of the grand thoroughfare's artificial levels. (Despite appearances, you'll discover you're not at ground level.) Much of the original work remains.

9 A colonnaded facade from 1829 screens the churchyard of **St. Nicholas Kirk** from the shopping hustle and bustle of Union Street. The Mither Kirk, as this, the original burgh church, was known, is curiously not within the bounds of the early town settlement: that was located to the east, near the end of present-day Union Street. During the 12th century, the port of Aberdeen flourished and room could not be found for the church within the settlement. Its earliest features are the pillars—supporting a tower built much later—and its clerestory windows: Both date from the original 12th-century structure. St. Nicholas was divided into east and west kirks at the Reformation, followed by a substantial amount of renovation from 1741 on. Some early memorials and other works have survived. ⊠ *Union St.* ⊙ *Weekdays 10–1, and for Sun. services.*

At the east end of Union Street, within the original old town, is the **Castlegate.** The actual castle once stood somewhere behind the **Salvation Army Citadel** (1896), an imposing baronial granite tower whose ❿ design was inspired by Balmoral Castle. The impressive **Mercat Cross** (built in 1686 and restored in 1820), always the symbolic center of a Scottish medieval burgh, stands just beyond King Street. Along its ⓫ parapet are 12 portrait panels of the Stewart monarchs. The **Tolbooth,** with its handsome tower, dates from the 17th century.

★ ⓬ **Provost Ross's House** (1593) now houses **Aberdeen's Maritime Museum,** which tells the story of the city's involvement with the sea, from early inshore fisheries by way of tea clippers to the North Sea oil boom. It is a fascinating place for grade-schoolers, with its ship models, paintings, and equipment associated with the fishing, local shipbuilding, and North Sea oil and gas industries. ⊠ *Provost Ross's House, Ship Row,* ☎ *01224/585788.* ☞ *Free.* ⊙ *Mon.–Sat. 10–5.*

Below Ship Row is the **harbor,** which contains some fine architecture from the 18th and 19th centuries. Explore it if time permits and you don't mind the background traffic.

☙ **Satrosphere** is a hands-on exhibition of science and technology that makes science come alive. Children (and adults) of even the most unscientific bent will love it. You will find it off the west end of Union Street. ⊠ *19 Justice Mill La.,* ☎ *01224/213232.* ☞ *£3.50.* ⊙ *Mon.–Sat. 10–5, Sun. 1:30–5; Mid-Oct.–mid-Apr., Mon., Wed.–Fri. 10–4, Sat. 10–5, Sun. 1:30–5, closed Tues.*

Old Aberdeen was once an independent burgh and lies to the north of the city, near the River Don. Although swallowed up by the expanding main city before the end of the 19th century, Old Aberdeen, which lies between King's College and St. Machar's Cathedral, still retains a certain degree of character and integrity. Reach it by taking a bus north from a stop near Marischal College or up King Street, off the Castlegate.

College Bounds has handsome 18th- and 19th-century houses, cobbled ★ ⓭ streets, and paved sidewalks. **King's College,** founded in 1494 and now part of the University of Aberdeen, has an unmistakable flying (or crown) spire to its **Chapel,** which was built around 1500. The fact that it has survived at all was due to the zeal of the principal, who managed to defend his church against the destructive fanaticism that swept through Scotland during the Reformation, when the building was less than a century old. Today the renovated chapel plays an important role in university life. The tall oak screen that separates nave from choir and the ribbed wooden ceiling and stalls constitute the finest medieval wood carving to be found anywhere in Scotland.

On Old Aberdeen's High Street, some restored Georgian houses stand ⓮ out, including the **Town House.** This Georgian work, plain and handsome, uses parts of an earlier building from 1720. Behind the Town House the modern intrusion of St. Machar's Drive destroys some of the old-town ambience. The atmosphere is restored by a stroll down the **Chanonry,** past the elegant houses once lived in by the officials connected with the cathedral nearby. Today, they house mainly university staff. King's College at the University of Aberdeen has a **visitor center** with shop and cafeteria, where you can find out more about one of Britain's oldest universities. *Visitor Center:* ⊠ *High St.,* ☎ *01224/ 273702.* ⊙ *Mon.–Sat. 10–5, Sun. noon–5.*

It is said that St. Machar was sent by St. Columba to build a church on a grassy platform near the sea, where a river flowed in the shape ⓯ of a shepherd's crook. This spot fitted the bill, and **St. Machar's Cathedral** was built in AD 580. However, nothing remains of the original foundation. Much of the existing building dates from the 15th and 16th centuries. The central tower collapsed in 1688, reducing the building to half its original length. The twin octagonal spires on the western towers date from the first half of the 16th century. The nave is thought to have been rebuilt in red sandstone in 1370, but the final renovation was completed in granite by the middle of the 15th century. Along with the nave ceiling, the twin spires were finished in time to take a battering in the Reformation, when the barons of the Mearns stripped the lead off the roof of St. Machar's and stole the bells. The cathedral suffered further mistreatment—including the removal of stone by Oliver Cromwell's English garrison in the 1650s—until a 19th-century scheme restored the church to its former grandeur. ⊠ *Chanonry*, ☎ *01224/ 485988.* ☉ *Daily 9–5.*

⓰ Beyond St. Machar's Cathedral lies **Seaton Park,** with its spring daffodils, tall trees, and herbaceous, boldly colored borders. Until 1827, the only way out of Aberdeen to the north was over the River Don on ⓱ the **Brig o' Balgownie,** a single-arch bridge found at the far end of Seaton Park—a 15-minute walk. It dates from 1314 and is thought to have been built by Richard Cementarius, Aberdeen's first provost.

☾ Aberdeen's other river is the Dee, not far from which is **Duthie Park and Winter Gardens.** A great place to feed the ducks, Duthie Park also has a boating pond and trampolines, carved wooden animals, and playgrounds. In the very attractive (and warm!) Winter Gardens, there are fish in ponds, free-flying birds, turtles, and terrapins to be seen among the luxuriant foliage and flowers. ⊠ *Polmuir Rd., Riverside Dr.* ☒ *Free.* ☉ *Park and gardens year-round; entertainment in summer only. Gardens open daily 10–dusk.*

Dining and Lodging

$$–$$$ ✕ **Silver Darling.** Situated right on the quayside, the Silver Darling is ★ one of Aberdeen's most acclaimed restaurants. It specializes, as its name suggests, in fish. The style is French provincial and an indoor barbecue guarantees flavorful grilled fish and shellfish. Reservations are essential on weekends. ⊠ *Pocra Quay, Footdee, Aberdeen,* ☎ *01224/ 576229. AE, DC, MC, V. Closed Dec. 23 or 24 and 2 wks following. No lunch weekends, no dinner Sun.*

$–$$$ ✕ **Brasserie Gerard's.** On a side street moments from the West End, Gerard's is a long-established part of the Aberdeen dining scene. Classic French cuisine is ably prepared with local produce—fish and red meats in particular. Try the Angus fillet steak, stuffed with pâté, ham, and mushrooms, wrapped in bacon and served in a red-wine sauce. Nouvelle cuisine this is not, but it's satisfying, and the fixed-price set lunch is especially good value. The relaxed, softly lit setting includes a flagstone-floored garden room, with greenery and tile or marble tables. ⊠ *50 Chapel St., Aberdeen,* ☎ *01224/639500. AE, DC, MC, V.*

$$$$ ✕▥ **The Marcliffe at Pitfodels.** The Marcliffe at Pitfodels benefits from ★ the skills and experience of leading Scottish hotelier Stewart Spence. This spacious building in the upmarket West End of the city is made up of an old country house, with later additions; the combination of old and new is impressive. Rooms are individually decorated, some with reproduction antique furnishings, others with a more modern style. There are two restaurants: an informal dining area and the Invery, offering international fare with a Scottish flavor. (A jacket and tie are required). ⊠ *N. Dee-*

side Rd., Pitfodels, Aberdeen, AB1 9PN, ☎ *01224/861000,* FAX *01224/868860. 42 rooms with bath. 2 restaurants. AE, DC, MC, V.*

$$–$$$$ ✕⊞ **Caledonian Thistle Hotel.** Well situated and offering pleasant views over tidy gardens, the Caledonian, one of the larger hotels in the Granite City, is generally considered to be one of the best hotels in the city. Rooms are redecorated regularly, and the attractive restaurant serves such dishes as chicken breasts with brandy, paprika, and cream. Its large size doesn't impede the friendly service. ⊠ *Union Terr., AB9 1HE,* ☎ *01224/640233,* FAX *01224/641627. 80 rooms with bath. Restaurant, coffee shop, wine bar. AE, DC, MC, V.*

$$–$$$ ✕⊞ **Atholl Hotel.** One of Aberdeen's many splendid silver granite properties, the Atholl Hotel is turreted and gabled and set within a leafy residential area to the west of the city. Rooms are done in rich, dark colors; the best views are from the top floor; the larger rooms are on the first floor. The restaurant prepares traditional dishes like lamb cutlets and roast rib of beef. ⊠ *54 Kings Gate, Aberdeen, AB9 2YN,* ☎ *01224/323505,* FAX *01224/321555. 35 rooms with bath or shower. Restaurant. MC, V.*

$$ ✕⊞ **Craighaar Hotel.** Don't be fooled by the plain, modern exterior—this is a hotel with character, a refreshing change from the many indistinguishable business hotels in Aberdeen. That said, the Craighaar is popular with businesspeople (it's very convenient to the airport). But what makes this establishment stand out is the personal service—this is the kind of place where the staff remembers your name. The comfortable restaurant serves cuisine with a Scottish slant: Orkney oysters, smoked trout, crab claws, gourmet scampi, and char-grilled steaks. Bedrooms are cheerful with bright floral prints. The gallery suites—split-level rooms—are outstanding. Ask about the great deals on weekend rooms. ⊠ *Waterton Rd., Bucksburn, Aberdeen, AB2 9HS,* ☎ *01224/712275,* FAX *01224/716362. 55 rooms with bath or shower. Restaurant, bar. AE, DC, MC, V.*

Nightlife and the Arts

As you would expect, Aberdeen is the main nightlife hot spot and cultural center of the region. In part because of the oil-industry boom, Aberdeen has a fairly lively nightlife scene, though much of it revolves around pubs and hotels; theaters, concert halls, arts centers, and cinemas are also well represented. The main Aberdeen newspapers—the *Press and Journal* and the *Evening Express*—and *Aberdeen Leopard* magazine can fill you in on what's going on anywhere in the Northeast. Outside Aberdeen a number of small-town local papers list events under the "What's On" heading. Aberdeen's tourist information center has a monthly "What's On" with a full calendar, as well as contact telephone numbers.

ARTS CENTERS

The Lemon Tree (⊠ 5 W. North St., ☎ 01224/642230) features an innovative and international program of dance, stand-up comedy, folk, jazz, rock and roll, and art exhibitions.

Aberdeen Arts Centre (⊠ King St., ☎ 01224/635208) is a theater and concert venue where experimental theater, poetry readings, exhibitions by local and Scottish artists, and many other arts-based presentations can be enjoyed.

At **Haddo House,** 20 miles north of Aberdeen (⊠ off B9005 near Methlick, ☎ 01651/851770), the Haddo House Hall Arts Trust runs a wide-ranging program of events, from opera and ballet to Shakespeare and Scots language plays to puppetry: truly something for everyone.

CASINO

Visitors interested in trying their luck at the gaming tables can place their bets at the **Stakis Regency Casino** (⊠ 61 Summer St., ☎ 01224/ 645273; membership after 48 hours notice).

CONCERTS

The Music Hall (⊠ Union St., Aberdeen, ☎ 01224/632080) presents seasonal programs of concerts by the Scottish National Orchestra, the Scottish Chamber Orchestra, and other major orchestras and musicians. Its wide-ranging program of events also includes folk concerts, crafts fairs, and exhibitions.

DANCE

His Majesty's Theatre (⊠ Rosemount Viaduct, Aberdeen, ☎ 01224/ 641122)and **Aberdeen Arts Centre** (⊠ King St., ☎ 01224/ 635208) are regular venues for dance companies. Contact the box offices for details of current productions.

DISCOS

Two notes of warning about discos in Aberdeen: Most of these establishments do not allow jeans or athletic shoes, and it's advisable to check beforehand that a particular disco is not closed for a private function. Below is a list of the city's most popular discos.

Cotton Club (⊠ 491 Union St., ☎ 01224/581858). **Eagles** (⊠ 120 Union St., ☎ 01224/640641). **Franklyn's** (⊠ Justice Mill La., ☎ 01224/ 212817). **Hotel Metro** (⊠ 17 Market St., ☎ 01224/583275). **The Ministry** (⊠ 16 Dee St., ☎ 01224/211661). **Mr G's** (⊠ 70–78 Chapel St., ☎ 01224/642112). **The Palace Nightclub** (⊠ Bridge Pl., ☎ 01224/ 581135). **Zig-Zag** (⊠ 2 Diamond St., ☎ 01224/641580).

FESTIVAL

The **Aberdeen International Youth Festival** in August has worldwide recognition and attracts youth orchestras, choirs, dance, and theater companies from many countries. During the festival, many of the companies that appear also take their productions to other venues in the Northeast. For details, contact AIYF Box Office (⊠ Music Hall, Union St., Aberdeen, ☎ 01224/641122).

FILM

Cinemas showing general-release films include:

Cannon (⊠ Union St., ☎ 01224/591477). **Capitol** (⊠ 431 Union St., Aberdeen, ☎ 01224/583141). **Odeon** (⊠ Justice Mill La., ☎ 01224/ 587160).

JAZZ CLUBS

There is jazz on Saturday night at the **Masada Continental Lounge** (⊠ Rosemount Viaduct, Aberdeen, ☎ 01224/641587). The **Lemon Tree** (⊠ 5 W. North St., ☎ 01224/642230) stages frequent jazz events in its wide-ranging music program.

OPERA

Both **His Majesty's Theatre** (⊠ Rosemount Viaduct, Aberdeen, ☎ 01224/ 641122) and **Haddo House** (⊠ off B9005 near Methlick, ☎ 01651/ 851770) present operatic performances at certain times throughout the year; call for details or inquire at the tourist information center (☞ Visitor Information in Aberdeen and the Northeast A to Z, *below*).

ROCK CLUB

The Lemon Tree (⊠ 5 W. North St., ☎ 01224/642230) is the main rock venue.

THEATER

His Majesty's Theatre (⊠ Rosemount Viaduct, Aberdeen, ☎ 01224/ 641122) is one of the most beautiful theaters in Britain. Live shows are presented throughout the year, many of them in advance of their official opening in London's West End.

Outdoor Activities and Sports

BICYCLING

The tourist information center can provide a leaflet of suggested cycle tours. Rates for bicycle rentals vary, depending on the type of bike. An average rate for a mountain bike is £10 a day. You can rent bicycles at: **Aberdeen Cycle Centre** (⊠ 188 King St., Aberdeen, ☎ 01224/ 644542); **Alpine Bikes** (⊠ 70 Holburn St., Aberdeen, ☎ 01224/211455); and **Outdoor Gear** (⊠ 88 Fonthill Rd., Aberdeen, ☎ 01224/573952).

CANOEING

For information on canoeing in the area, contact the **Aberdeen Sports Council** (⊠ Room A18, St. Nicholas House, Aberdeen, ☎ 01224/ 276276, ext. 2838), or the **Scottish Sports Council** (in Edinburgh, ☎ 0131/317–7200).

GOLF

The following courses in and around Aberdeen are open to visitors:

Balnagask (⊠ St. Fitticks Rd., ☎ 01224/876407). 18 holes, 5,986 yards, SSS 69.

Hazlehead (☎ 01224/321830). Course 1: 18 holes, 6,204 yards, SSS 70. Course 2: 18 holes, 5,801 yards, SSS 68.

Murcar (⊠ Bridge of Don, ☎ 01224/704345). 18 holes, 6,240 yards, SSS 70.

Westhill (☎ 01224/740159). 18 holes, 5,921 yards, SSS 68.

HEALTH AND FITNESS CLUBS

Balmedie Leisure Centre (⊠ Eigie Rd., Balmedie, ☎ 01358/743725). **Bon-Accord Swimming and Leisure Centre** (⊠ Justice Mill La., Aberdeen, ☎ 01224/587920). **Kincorth Sports Centre** (⊠ Corthan Dr., Aberdeen, ☎ 01224/879759). **Sheddocksley Sports Centre** (⊠ Springhill Rd., Aberdeen, ☎ 01224/692534). **Westdyke Leisure Centre** (⊠ 4 Westdyke Ave., Skene, ☎ 01224/743098).

Shopping

Aberdeen's shopping scene is in the throes of change. For generations, residents from nearby would come into Aberdeen for the day—the city is a kind of large-scale market town. Their chief delight would be to stroll the length of Union Street and perhaps take in George Street as well. Now this pattern is changing, thanks mainly to the modern and faceless shopping developments (pleasant enough in an anonymous way), the Trinity Centre (Union St.), and the St. Nicholas and Bon-Accord centers (George St.), which have taken the emphasis away from Union Street.

Most of the larger national-name department stores are to be found in the shopping malls or along Union Street. However, note the spacious **John Lewis** store (⊠ George St. [reached via Bon Accord Centre], ☎ 01224/625000, closed Mon.), built in a design that closely resembles a double-decker sandwich, with an illuminated filling and the crusts left on. It has a good-value, wide-ranging stock of clothing, household items, giftware, and much more.

Smaller specialty shops are still to be found, particularly in the Chapel Street/Thistle Street area at the west end of Union Street and on the latter's north side, which has a series of interesting small retailers well worth discovering. **Nova** (⊠ 20 Chapel St., ☎ 01224/641270), where the locals go for gifts, stocks major U.K. brand names, such as Liberty of London, Dartington Glass, and Crabtree and Evelyn, as well as a wide range of Scottish silver jewelry. **Colin Wood** (⊠ 25 Rose St., ☎ 01224/643019) is the place to go for antiques, maps, and prints. **Harlequin** (⊠ 65 Thistle St., ☎ 01224/635716) stocks a large selection of embroidery and tapestry kits, designer yarns, and expensive, colorful knitwear. **Elizabeth Watt's** (⊠ 69 Thistle St., ☎ 01224/647232) is the place to look for smaller antiques, especially china and glassware.

Visitors looking for bargains can try the **Crombie Woollen Mill** (⊠ Grandholm Mills, Woodside, off the A96, ☎ 01224/483201) on the edge of town; a particularly good value are the men's overcoats bearing the Crombie name (known for high quality).

At the **Aberdeen Family History Shop** (⊠ 164 King St., ☎ 01224/646323) you can browse through a huge range of publications related to local history and genealogical research. For a small membership fee, the Aberdeen & North East Family History Society will undertake some research on your behalf.

Aberdeen shops catering to children include **The Toy Bazaar** (⊠ 45 Schoolhill, ☎ 01224/640021), which stocks a range of toys for children preschool age and up. **The Early Learning Centre** (⊠ Bon-Accord Centre, George St., ☎ 01224/624188) specializes in toys with educational value.

ROYAL DEESIDE AND CASTLE COUNTRY

Deeside, the valley running west from Aberdeen down which the River Dee flows, earned its "Royal" appellation when discovered by Queen Victoria. To this day, where royalty goes, lesser aristocracy and freshly minted millionaires from across the globe follow. In fact, it is still the aspiration of many to own a grand shooting estate on Deeside. In a sense, this yearning is understandable, since piney hill slope, purple moor, and blue river intermingle most tastefully here, as you will see from the main road. Royal Deeside's gradual scenic change adds a growing sense of excitement as the road runs deeper and deeper into the Grampians.

There are castles along the Dee and to the north, an area that is indeed known as "castle country," and that well illustrates the gradual geological change in the Northeast: uplands lapped by a tide of farms. Although best toured by car, much of this area is accessible either by public transportation or on tours from Aberdeen.

Banchory

18 *19 mi west of Aberdeen via A93.*

Banchory is an immaculate place with a pinkish tinge to its granite. It is usually bustling with ice cream–eating city strollers, out on a day trip from Aberdeen. If you visit in autumn and have time to spare, drive out to the **Brig o'Feuch** (pronounced fyooch, the "ch" as in loch). Here, salmon leap in season, and the fall colors and foaming waters make for an attractive scene.

East of the town, and passed on the way from Aberdeen, are two castles for castle hoppers to explore. The first is **Drum Castle,** an ancient foursquare tower that dates from the 13th century, with later additions. Note the rounded corners of the tower, said to make battering-ram attacks more difficult. Nearby, fragments of the ancient Forest of Drum still stand, dating from the early days when Scotland was covered by great woodlands of oak and pine. ⊠ *Off the A93, 10 mi west of Aberdeen,*

☎ *01330/811204. ✆ Castle and garden: £3.60; grounds and garden only: £1.60. ☉ Easter, May–Sept., daily 1:30–5:30; Oct., weekends 1:30–5:30 (last admission 4:45). Garden of historic roses: Easter, May–Sept., daily 10–6; Oct., weekends 10–6. Grounds: daily 9:30–sunset.*

⑳ Crathes Castle was once home of the Burnett family. Keepers of the Forest of Drum for generations, the family acquired lands here by marriage and later built a new castle, completed in 1596. Crathes is in the care of the National Trust for Scotland; the trust also looks after the grand gardens, with their calculated symmetry and clipped yew hedges. It is off the A93, 3½ miles east of Banchory. ☎ *01330/844525. ✆ Grounds only: £1.60; castle only: £1.60; castle, garden, and grounds: £4.10. ☉ Castle: Apr.–Oct., daily 11–5:30 (last admission 4:45); garden and grounds: daily 9:30–sunset.*

....

NEED A BREAK?   Sample the National Trust for Scotland's excellent home baking in Crathes Castle's **tearoom** (☎ 01330/844525).

....

Dining and Lodging

$$$–$$$$ ✕🏠 **Raemoir Hotel.** The core of this large mansion dates from the 18th century, though a number of additions have been built over the years. Central heating has been added as well, so there is no need to fear chilly, windy rooms. All the guest rooms are comfortable and well appointed; many are hung with beautiful tapestries. The hotel is set on spacious grounds and overshadowed by the 1,500-foot-high Hill of Fare. Adjoining the hotel's property are 3,500 acres of land on which fishing and shooting can be arranged. Guests who don't want to venture too far from the hotel can make use of the nine-hole golf course and tennis court. ✉ *Raemoir (just north of Banchory, 5 min. from town center), Kincardineshire, AB3 4ED, ☎ 01330/824884, ℻ 01330/822171. 28 rooms with bath. Restaurant, sauna, 9-hole golf course, tennis court, fishing, baby-sitting, helipad. AE, DC, MC, V.*

$$$ ✕🏠 **Banchory Lodge.** With the River Dee running past just a few yards away at the bottom of the garden, the Banchory Lodge, a fine example of a 17th-century country house, is an ideal resting place for anglers. The lodge has retained its period charm and is well maintained inside and out. Tranquility is the keynote here. Rooms, with bold colors and tartan or floral fabrics, are individually decorated. The restaurant has high standards for its Scottish cuisine with French overtones; try the fillet of salmon, roast duckling, or guinea fowl with wild berries. ✉ *Kincardineshire, AB3 3HS, ☎ 01330/822625, ℻ 01330/825019. 22 rooms with bath. Restaurant, fishing. AE, DC, MC, V.*

Kincardine O'Neill

㉑ *9 mi west of Banchory.*

The ruined kirk in the little village of Kincardine O'Neill was built in 1233 and once sheltered travelers: It was the last hospice before the Mounth, the name given to the massif that shuts off the south side of the Dee Valley. Beyond Banchory (and the B974), no motor roads run south until you reach Braemar, though the Mounth is crossed by a network of tracks used in former times by Scottish soldiers, invading armies (including the Romans), and cattle drovers.

If you have the time, there are many other intricate features to examine in the area; for example, the picture-postcard bridge at **Potarch,** just to the east.

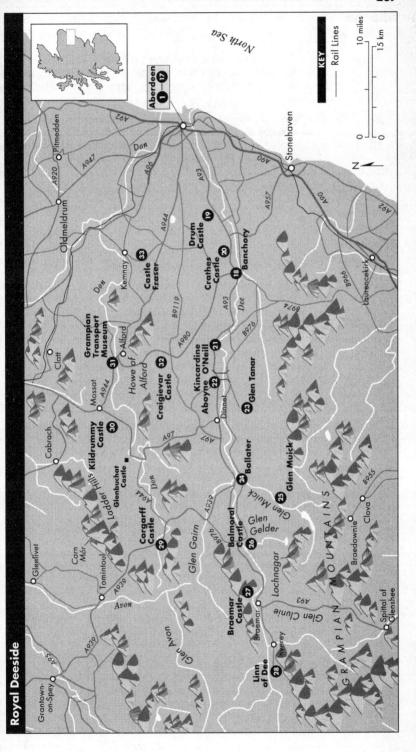

Royal Deeside

Aboyne

㉒ *5 mi west of Kincardine O'Neill.*

The little town of Aboyne is a pleasant and well laid out place, with a village green (unusual for Scotland) that is the setting for an annual Highland Games. There is, however, not a great deal to detain the visitor here.

㉓ The **Braeloine Interpretive Centre** in **Glen Tanar** beyond Aboyne (cross over the River Dee, go right on B976, then left into the glen) has a display on natural history, a café, a picnic area, and walks. ⊠ *Glen Tanar,* ☎ *013398/86072.* ⊙ *Daily 10–5 (extended hours in summer).*

En Route Look for a large granite boulder beside the A93 on which is carved YOU ARE NOW ENTERING THE HIGHLANDS. You may find this piece of information superfluous, given the quality of the scenery.

Ballater

㉔ *12 mi west of Aboyne, 43 mi west of Aberdeen.*

The handsome holiday resort of Ballater, once noted for the curative properties of its local well, has profited from the proximity of the royals, nearby at Balmoral (☞ *below*). Visitors are amused by the array of BY ROYAL APPOINTMENT signs proudly hanging from many of its various shops (even monarchs need bakers and butchers). If you get a chance, take time to stroll around this neat community—well laid out in silver-gray masses. Note that the railway station now houses the tourist information center and a display on the former glories of this Great North of Scotland branch line, closed in the 1960s along with so many others in this country.

Close to the town, visitors have the opportunity to capture the feel of the eastern Highlands—as long as they have their own transportation.

★ ㉕ Start your expedition into **Glen Muick** (Gaelic for pig, pronounced mick) by crossing the River Dee and turning upriver on the south side, shortly after the road forks into this fine Highland glen. The native red deer are quite common throughout the Scottish Highlands, but Glen Muick is one of the very best places to see them in abundance, with herds grazing the flat valley floor. Beyond the lower glen, the prospect opens to reveal not only grazing herds, but also fine views of the battlement of cliffs edging the mountain called Lochnagar.

㉖ The enormous car park is indicative of the popularity of **Balmoral Castle,** the rebuilt castle modified by Prince Albert in 1855 for his queen. Balmoral's visiting hours depend on whether the royals are in residence. In truth, there are more interesting and historic buildings to explore, as the only part of the castle on view is the ballroom, with an exhibition of Royal artifacts. ⊠ *On the A93 7 mi west of Ballater,* ☎ *013397/42334.* 🎟 *£2.50.* ⊙ *May–July, Mon.–Sat. 10–5.*

Dining and Lodging

$$$$ ✕🏨 **Stakis Balmoral Hotel.** This magnificent country house hotel, just outside Ballater on a hillside overlooking the River Dee, really does manage to keep everyone happy. Hotel guests are cosseted in luxurious surroundings and can use the nearby leisure facilities. An even better value are the pine lodges set among the trees around the hotel. These self-catering cottages are geared for families and fitted with every kind of labor-saving appliance. There is also a solid choice of on-site restaurants, including the top-quality **Oaks** for à la carte dinners, and **The Clubhouse** poolside brasserie. ⊠ *Ballater, AB35 5XA,* ☎ *013397/55858,*

FAX *013397/55447. 44 rooms with bath, including 7 suites. 2 restaurants, 2 indoor pools, wading pool, hot tub, beauty salon, sauna, tennis court, exercise room, Ping-Pong, squash. AE, DC, MC, V.*

$$–$$$ ✕⊡ **Darroch Learg Hotel.** Amid tall trees on a hillside, the Darroch Learg is everything a Scottish country-house hotel should be, with the added bonus that the charming town of Ballater is moments away. Built in the 1880s as a country residence, the hotel exudes charm. Most bedrooms—decorated with mahogany furniture and designer fabrics in rich colors—enjoy a stunning panoramic view south across Royal Deeside. Food in the conservatory restaurant is sophisticated—delicately flavored terrines and soups—but also substantial, with the rich flavors of local beef and fish produce. ⊠ *Braemar Rd., Ballater, Aberdeenshire, AB35 5UX,* ☎ *013397/55443,* FAX *013397/55252. 20 rooms with bath. Restaurant. AE, DC, MC, V.*

Shopping

The **McEwan Gallery** (⊠ on A939, 1 mi west of Ballater, ☎ 013397/ 55429) displays a good range of fine paintings, watercolors, prints, and books (many with a Scottish or golf theme) in an unusual house built by the Swiss artist Rudolphe Christen in 1902. For a low-cost gift you could always see what is being boiled up at **Dee Valley Confectioners** (⊠ Station Sq.☎ 013397/55499). You can buy Scottish designer knitwear at **Goodbrand Knitwear** (⊠ 1 Braemar Rd., ☎ 013397/55947). At either of **Countrywear**'s two shops (⊠ 15 and 35 Bridge St., ☎ 013397/ 55453) you'll find everything you need for Scottish country living, including fishing tackle, shooting accessories, cashmere, tweeds, and that flexible garment popular in Scotland between seasons: the bodywarmer.

En Route Continuing west into Highland scenery, further pine-framed glimpses appear of the "steep frowning glories of dark Lochnagar," as it was described by the poet Byron. Lochnagar (3786 ft) was made known to a wider audience than hillwalkers by the Prince of Wales, who published a children's story "The Old Man of Lochnagar."

Braemar

17 mi west of Ballater, 60 mi west of Aberdeen, 51 mi north of Perth via A93.

㉗ The village of Braemar is dominated by **Braemar Castle** on its outskirts, dating from the 17th century, with defensive walls later built in the plan of a pointed star. At Braemar (the braes, or slopes, of the district of Mar), the standard, or rebel flag, was first raised at the start of the spectacularly unsuccessful Jacobite rebellion of 1715. Thirty years later, during the last rebellion, Braemar Castle was strengthened and garrisoned by Hanoverian (government) troops. ⊠ *Braemar,* ☎ *013397/41219, off-season* ☎ *013397/41224.* ⊡ *£2.* ☉ *Easter–Oct., Sat.–Thurs. 10–6.*

Braemar is also associated with the **Braemar Highland Gathering** held every September. Although it's one of many such events celebrated throughout Scotland, Braemar's gathering is distinguished by the presence of the royal family. Find out more about the Braemar Highland Gathering at the **Braemar Highland Heritage Centre,** in a converted stable block in the middle of Braemar. It tells the history of the village with displays and a film, and also has a gift shop. ⊠ *The Mews, Mar Rd.,* ☎ *013397/41944.* ⊡ *Free.* ☉ *Daily 9–5 (extended hours in summer season).*

Although the main A93 slinks off to the south from Braemar, a little unmarked road will take you farther west into the hilly heartlands. In fact, even if you do not have your own car, you can still explore this area by catching the post bus that leaves from Braemar Post Office once a day. The road offers you delectable views over the winding river Dee and the blue hills before passing through the tiny hamlet of Inverey ★ ㉘ and crossing a bridge at the **Linn of Dee.** *Linn* is a Scots word meaning rocky narrows, and the river's rocky gash here is deep and roaring. Park beyond the bridge and walk back to admire the sylvan setting of the river and woodland, replete with bending larch bows and deep, tranquil pools with salmon glinting in them.

Dining and Lodging

$$–$$$ ×⊡ **Invercauld Arms Thistle.** This handsome stone-built Victorian hotel in the center of Braemar makes a good base for exploring Royal Deeside. Interiors are traditional in style and recently refurbished, with plenty of interesting prints decorating the walls. The welcoming entrance lounge, with plush sofas and elegant velvet chairs, leads to beautifully restored public rooms with attractive plasterwork and to comfortable guest rooms with floral drapes and reproduction antique furniture. The restaurant, with magnificent views toward Braemar Castle from its bay windows, serves an international cuisine with Scottish overtones, not least in the use of local fish, game, lamb, and beef. Dishes might include Aberdeen Angus steak with tomato and wild mushroom sauce or chicken with bean sprouts and water chestnuts with oyster sauce. ⊠ *Braemar, AB35 5YR,* ☎ *013397/41605,* 𝖥𝖠𝖷 *013397/41428. 68 rooms with bath and shower. Restaurant, bar. AE, DC, MC, V.*

Outdoor Activities and Sports

GOLF

Braemar has a tricky golf course laden with foaming waters. Erratic duffers take note: The compassionate course managers have installed, near the water, poles with little nets on the end for those occasional shots that may go awry.

En Route From Braemar, retrace the A93 as far as Balmoral. From Balmoral, look for a narrow road going north, signposted B976. Be careful on the first twisting mile through the trees. Soon you will emerge from scattered pines into the open moor in upland Aberdeenshire. Behind is the massif of Lochnagar again, and to the west are snow-tipped domes of the big Cairngorms. Roll down to a bridge and go left on the A939, which comes in from Ballater. Another high moor section follows: As the road leaves the scattered buildings by the bridge, see if you can spot the roadside inscription to the company of soldiers who built the A939 in the 18th century.

Corgarff Castle

㉙ *23 mi northeast of Braemar, 14 mi northwest of Ballater.*

Eighteenth-century soldiers paved a military highway, now the A939, north from Ballater to Corgarff Castle, a lonely tower house with another star-shaped defensive wall—a curious replica of Braemar Castle. Corgarff was built as a hunting seat for the earls of Mar in the 16th century. After an eventful history that included the wife of a later laird being burned alive in a family dispute, the castle ended its career as a garrison for Hanoverian troops. The troops also had the responsibility of trying to prevent illegal whisky distilling, at one time a popular hobby in these parts. ⊠ *Signposted off A939,* ☎ *0131/668–8600.* ⊡ *£2.* ⊙ *Apr.–Sept., Mon.–Sat. 9:30–6, Sun. 2–6; Oct.–Mar., Sat. 9:30–4, Sun. 2–4.*

En Route If you return east from Corgarff Castle to the A939/A944 junction and then make a left onto the A944, the excellent castle signposting will tell you that you are on the **Castle Trail.** The A944 meanders along the River Don to the village of Strathdon, where a great mound by the roadside—on the left—turns out to be a *motte,* or the base of a wooden castle, built in the late 12th century. Surviving mottes are significant

Your passport around the world.

Worldwide access
Operators who speak your language
Monthly itemized billing

MCI. Calling Card

415 555 1234 2244
J.D. SMITH

Use your MCI Card® and these access numbers for an easy way to call when traveling worldwide.

Austria (CC)♦†	022-903-012
Belarus	
From Gomel and Mogilev regions	8-10-800-103
From all other localities	8-800-103
Belgium (CC)♦†	0800-10012
Bulgaria	00800-0001
Croatia (CC)★	99-385-0112
Czech Republic (CC)♦	00-42-000112
Denmark (CC)♦†	8001-0022
Finland (CC)♦†	9800-102-80
France (CC)♦†	0800-99-0019
Germany (CC)†	0130-0012
Greece (CC)♦†	00-800-1211
Hungary (CC)♦	00▼800-01411
Iceland (CC)♦†	800-9002
Ireland (CC)†	1-800-55-1001
Italy (CC)♦†	172-1022
Kazakhstan (CC)	1-800-131-4321
Liechtenstein (CC)♦	155-0222
Luxembourg†	0800-0112
Monaco (CC)♦	800-90-19

Netherlands (CC)♦†	06-022-91-22
Norway (CC)♦†	800-19912
Poland (CC)⋄††	00-800-111-21-22
Portugal (CC)⋄††	05-017-1234
Romania (CC)⋄	01-800-1800
Russia (CC)⋄♦	747-3322
For a Russian-speaking operator	747-3320
San Marino (CC)♦	172-1022
Slovak Republic (CC)	00-42-000112
Slovenia	080-8808
Spain (CC)†	900-99-0014
Sweden (CC)♦†	020-795-922
Switzerland (CC)♦†	155-0222
Turkey (CC)♦†	00-8001-1177
Ukraine (CC)⋄	8▼10-013
United Kingdom (CC)†	
To call to the U.S. using BT ■	0800-89-0222
To call to the U.S. using Mercury ■	0500-89-0222
Vatican City (CC)†	172-1022

To sign up for the MCI Card, dial the access number of the country you are in and ask to speak with a customer service representative.

http://www.mci.com

It helps to be pushy in airports.

Introducing the revolutionary new TransPorter™ from American Tourister® It's the first suitcase you can push around without a fight. TransPorter's™ exclusive four-wheel design lets you push it in front of you with almost no effort–the wheels take the weight. Or pull it on two wheels if you choose. You can even stack on other bags and use it like a luggage cart.

Stable 4-wheel design.

TransPorter™ is designed like a dresser, with built-in shelves to organize your belongings. Or collapse the shelves and pack it like a traditional suitcase. Inside, there's a suiter feature to help keep suits and dresses from wrinkling. When push comes to shove, you can't beat a TransPorter™ For more information on how you can be this pushy, call 1-800-542-1300.

Shelves collapse on command.

American Tourister

Making travel less primitive®

in terms of confirming the history of Scottish castles, but it is difficult for visitors to become enthusiastic about a great grassed-over heap, no matter what its historic content. The A944 then joins the A97 (go left) and just a few minutes later a sign points to Glenbuchat Castle, a plain Z-plan tower house.

Kildrummy

18 mi northeast of Corgarff, 23 mi north of Ballater, 22 mi north of Aboyne.

★ ③ **Kildrummy Castle** is significant because of its age (13th century) and because it has ties to the mainstream medieval traditions of European castle building. It shares features with Harlech and Caernarvon in Wales, as well as with continental sites, such as Château de Coucy near Laon, France. Kildrummy had undergone several expansions at the hands of England's King Edward I when, in 1306, back in Scottish hands, the castle was besieged by King Edward I's son. The defenders were betrayed by a certain Osbarn the Smith, who had been promised a large amount of gold by the English besieging forces. They gave it to him after the castle fell, pouring it molten down his throat, or so the ghoulish story goes. Kildrummy's prominence came to an end after the collapse of the 1715 Jacobite uprising. It had been the rebel headquarters and was consequently dismantled. ☎ *0131/668–8600.* ☎ *£1.50.* ☉ *Apr.–Sept., Mon.–Sat. 9:30–6, Sun. 2–6.*

Kildrummy Castle Gardens behind the castle—with a separate entrance from the main road—are built in what was the original quarry for the castle. This sheltered bowl within the woodlands has a broad range of shrubs and alpine plants and a notable water garden. If the weather is pleasant, it makes for a nice place to pause and plan the next stage of your journey. ⊠ *A97,* ☎ *019755/71264 or 019755/71277.* ☎ *£1.70.* ☉ *Apr.–Oct., daily 10–5 (call to confirm opening times late in the season).*

NEED A BREAK?

The **Mossat Shop,** 4 miles north of Kildrummy, at the junction of the A97 and the A944, is a possible pit stop for tea or some light shopping. If you have more time, however, then stop in the tiny rural community of **Clatt** (7 miles northeast, just off the A97) at its **village hall.** It has a savory reputation for its home baking; local ladies bake the delicious breads and cakes at this cooperatively run establishment (summer weekends only). People come from miles around to sample the results. There is also a produce and crafts shop.

Dining and Lodging

$$$$ ✕☷ **Kildrummy Castle Hotel.** A grand, late-Victorian country house, this hotel offers an attractive blend of a peaceful setting, attentive service, and sporting opportunities. Oak paneling, beautiful plasterwork, and gentle color schemes create a serene environment, enhanced by the views of Kildrummy Castle Gardens next door. The award-winning cuisine features local game and seafood. ⊠ *Kildrummy (by Alford), Aberdeenshire, AB33 8RA,* ☎ *019755/71288,* FAX *019755/71345. 16 rooms with bath or shower. Restaurant, golf privileges, fishing. AE, MC, V.*

Alford

9 mi east of Kildrummy, 28 mi west of Aberdeen.

A plain and sturdy settlement in the Howe (Hollow) of Alford, Alford gives those visitors who have grown somewhat weary of castle hopping a break: It has a museum instead. The **Grampian Transport Mu-**

seum specializes in road-based means of locomotion. One of its more unusual exhibits is the *Craigievar Express,* a steam-driven creation invented by the local postman to deliver mail more efficiently. ⊠ *Alford,* ☎ *019755/62292.* ⊡ *£2.75.* ⊘ *Apr.–Oct., daily 10–5.*

★ ㉜ Two of the finest castles on the Castle Trail are near Alford. **Craigievar**'s historic structure represents one of the finest traditions of local castle building. It also has the advantage of having survived intact, much as the stonemasons left it in 1626, with its pepper-pot turrets and towers, the whole slender shape covered in a pink-cream pastel. It was built in relatively peaceful times by William Forbes, a successful merchant in trade with the Baltic Sea ports (hence he was also known as Danzig Willie). Centuries of care and wise stewardship have ensured that the experience proffered today's visitor is as authentic as possible. The castle is is about 5 miles south of Alford on the A980. ☎ *013398/83635.* ⊡ *£5.20; grounds only, £1 (honesty box).* ⊘ *May–Sept., daily 1:30– 5:30 (last admission 4:45). Grounds open daily 9:30–sunset.*

㉝ The massive **Castle Fraser** is the largest of the castles of Mar. While this building shows a variety of styles reflecting the taste of its owners from the 15th to the 19th centuries, its design is typical of the cavalcade of castles that exist here in the Northeast. It has the further advantages of a walled garden, a picnic area, and a tearoom. It can be found 8 miles east of Alford off the A944. ☎ *01330/833463.* ⊡ *£3.60.* ⊘ *Easter, May, June and Sept., daily 1:30–5:30; July and Aug., daily 11–5:30; Oct., weekends 1:30–5:30 (last admission 4:45). Gardens: daily 9:30–6 (or sunset if earlier); grounds: daily 9:30–sunset.*

THE NORTHEAST

This route starts inland, traveling toward Speyside—the valley or strath of the River Spey—famed for its whisky distilleries, which it promotes in yet another signposted trail. Whisky distilling is not an intrinsically spectacular process. It involves pure water, malted barley, and, sometimes, peat smoke, then a lot of bubbling and fermentation, all of which causes a range of extremely odd smells. The end result is a prestigious product with a fascinating range of flavors that you either enjoy immensely or not at all.

Instead of assiduously following the whisky trail, just dip into it and blend it with some other aspects of the lower end of Speyside—the old county of Moray. Whisky notwithstanding, Moray's scenic qualities, low rainfall, and other reassuring weather statistics are also worth remembering. The suggested route then ranges widely to sample the seaboard of the Northeast, including some of the best, but least-known, coastal scenery in Scotland.

Dufftown

★ ㉞ *54 mi from Aberdeen via A96 and A920 (turn west at Huntly).*

On one of the Spey tributaries, Dufftown was planned in 1817 by the Earl of Fife. One of the most famous malt whiskies of all, the market leader **Glenfiddich,** is distilled here. The independent company of William Grant and Sons Limited was the first distillery to realize the tourist potential of the distilling process. It subsequently built an entertaining visitor center in addition to offering tours. In short, if you do intend to visit a distillery, it may as well be Glenfiddich, especially because it probably offers the most complete range of on-site activities, from floor malting to bottling. In fact, it is the only Speyside distiller that bottles on the premises. The audiovisual show and displays in the visitor center are also worthwhile, and the traditional stone-walled premises with the typical pagoda-roofed malting buildings have a pleasant period ambience. Not all visitors have to like whisky to come away feeling they've learned something about a leading Scottish export. ⊠ *North of Dufftown on the A941,* ☎ *01340/820373.* ☜ *Free.* ☉ *Weekdays 9:30–4:30; Easter–mid-Oct., Sat. 9:30–4:30, Sun. noon–4:30. Closed Dec. 25, Jan. 1.*

On a mound just above Glenfiddich Distillery is a grim, gray, and squat curtain-walled castle, **Balvenie.** This fortress, which dates from the 13th century, once commanded the glens and passes toward Speyside and Elgin. ⊠ *Dufftown,* ☎ *0131/668–8600.* ☜ *£1.20.* ☉ *Apr.–Sept., Mon.–Sat. 9:30–6, Sun. 2–6.*

In the center of Dufftown, the conspicuous battlemented **clock tower**—the centerpiece of the planned town and a former jail—houses a local museum open in summer. **Mortlach Church,** set in a hollow by the Dullan Water, is thought to be one of the oldest Christian sites in Scotland, perhaps founded by St. Moluag, a contemporary of St. Columba, as early as AD 566. Note the weathered Pictish cross in the churchyard and the even older stone under cover in the vestibule, with a strange Pictish elephantlike beast carved on it. Though much of the church was rebuilt after 1876, some early work survives, including three lancet windows from the 13th century and a leper's squint (a hole extended to the outside of the church so that lepers could hear the service but be kept away from the rest of the congregation).

Craigellachie

35 *4 mi northwest of Dufftown via A941.*

Renowned as an angling resort on the Spey, Craigellachie, like so many Speyside settlements, is sometimes enveloped in the malty reek of the local industry. As you arrive in the village, you will notice the huge cooperage, the place where barrels are made and repaired. The Spey itself is crossed by a handsome suspension bridge, designed by Thomas Telford in 1814 and now bypassed by the modern road.

Aberlour

36 *2 mi southwest of Craigellachie via A95.*

Aberlour (often marked as Charlestown of Aberlour on maps) is another handsome little burgh, essentially Victorian in style, though actually founded in 1812 by the local landowner. Glenfarclas, Cragganmore, and Aberlour are the names of the noted local whiskies; if you're interested in something nonalcoholic, take a look at the **Village Store.** After the owners retired in 1978, the shop was locked away intact, complete with stock. In the late 1980s, new owners discovered they had bought a time capsule—a range of products dating from the early decades of the present century—as well as all the paraphernalia, books and ledgers, accounts, and notes of a country business. Part of the premises is now a gift shop, but the remainder is preserved for visitors to enjoy, with stock of a bygone era on the shelves. ⊠ *98 High St.,* ☎ *01340/871243.* ☜ *Free.* ☉ *Mon.–Sat. 10–5, Sun. 1:30–5. Closed Jan.*

NEED A BREAK?
The Old Pantry (⊠ The Square, ☎ 01340/871617) serves everything from a cup of coffee to a four-course spread.

The Northeast

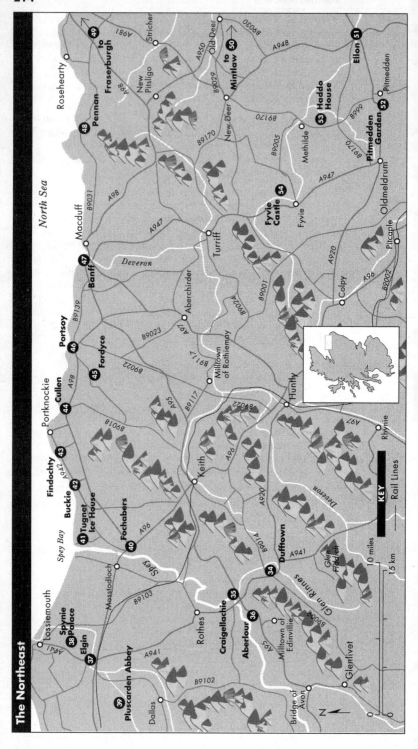

North Sea

Rosehearty

to Fraserburgh **49**

Strichen
A981

New Pitsligo

A950

Old Deer
B9029

to Mintlaw **50**
B9030

A948

Ellon **51**

Pennan **48**

A98

New Deer

B9170

B9005

Haddo House **53**

Pitmedden
B9170

Pitmedden Garden **52**

Methilde

Macduff
B9031

A98

A947

A947

Turriff

B9170

A947

Fyvie Castle **54**

Fyvie

Oldmeldrum

Pitmedden

Deveron

Banff **47**

Aberchirder

B9001

B920

A947

A920

Colpy

Picaple

A96

B9002

Portsoy **46**

B9139

B9023

A97

B9022

Fordyce **45**

B9022

Huntly

Rhynie
A97

Cullen **44**

A98

B9018

B9117

A95

Portknockie

A95

Keith

A96

A920

Deveron

Findochty **43**
A942

Buckie **42**

A96

Dufftown **34**
B9014

A941

Glen Fiddich

Tugnet Ice House **41**

Fochabers

A96

Spey Bay

Lossiemouth
A941

Spynie Palace **38**

Elgin **37**

Mosstodloch
B9103

Spey

Craigellachie **35**

Aberlour **36**

Glen Rinnes

Rothes

Millstown of Edinville
A95

B9009

Glenlivet

Pluscarden Abbey **39**

A941

Dallas

B9102

Bridge of Avon

B9008

KEY
— Rail Lines

10 miles
15 km

N

Dining and Lodging

$$ ✕▥ **Minmore House.** Former home of George Smith, founder of the Glenlivet Distillery, Minmore is now a family-run hotel that retains a strong private-house feel. It's certainly worth the 25-minute drive from Aberlour to reach it. Faded chintz in the drawing room (where afternoon tea is served to guests) and a paneled library (which now houses a bar with nearly 100 malt whiskies) are complemented by very comfortable guest rooms (one, allegedly, with a ghost) with an eclectic mix of antique furnishings. The restaurant serves exceptionally well-cooked food, including such dishes as Highland lamb with a mint and honey glaze; the menu changes daily. The Speyside Way long-distance footpath passes below the house, providing good walks. The area is famous for bird-watching—you might sight buzzards, peregrines, or maybe even a golden eagle. To find the house, take the A95 south from Aberlour, then turn left on the B9008 at Bridge of Avon. ✉ *Glenlivet, Ballindalloch, Banffshire, AB37 9DB,* ☎ *01807/590378,* ℻ *01807/590472. 10 rooms with bath. Restaurant, bar. MC, V. Closed Nov.–Mar.*

Elgin

㊲ *16 mi north of Aberlour via A941, 69 mi northwest of Aberdeen, 41 mi east of Inverness via A96.*

As the center of the fertile Laigh (low-lying lands) of Moray, Elgin has been of local importance for centuries. Like Aberdeen, it is self-supporting and previously remote, sheltered by great hills to the south and lying between two major rivers, the Spey and the Findhorn. Beginning in the 13th century, Elgin became an important religious center, a cathedral city with a walled town growing up around the cathedral and adjacent to the original settlement. Left in peace for at least some of its history, Elgin prospered and became, by the early 18th century, a mini-Edinburgh of the north and a place where country gentlemen came to spend the winter. It even echoed Edinburgh in the wide scale reconstruction of the early 19th century: Much of the old town was swept away in a wave of rebuilding, giving Elgin the fine neoclassical buildings that survive today.

The old street plan of the town survived almost intact until this century, when it succumbed to the modern madness of demolishing great swaths of buildings for the sake of better traffic flow: Elgin suffered from its position on the Aberdeen–Inverness main road. However, the central main street plan and some of the older little streets and wynds (alleyways) remain. Visitors can also recall Elgin's past by observing the arcaded shop fronts—some of which date from the late-17th century—that give the main shopping street its scruffy, aged appeal.

At the center of Elgin, the most conspicuous, positively unavoidable building is **St. Giles Church,** which divides High Street. The grand foursquare building built in 1828 exhibits the style known as Greek Revival: Note the columns, the pilasters, and the top of the spire, surmounted by a representation of the Lysicrates Monument. Past the arcaded shops at the east end of High Street, you can see the **Little Cross** (17th century), which marked the boundary between the town and the cathedral grounds. Near the Little Cross, the **museum** (☉ summer months only) has an especially interesting collection of dinosaur relics.

Cooper Park, a short distance to the southeast across the modern bypass road, is home to a magnificent ruin, the **cathedral,** consecrated in 1224. The cathedral's eventful story included devastation by fire: a 1390 act of retaliation by Alexander Stewart, the Wolf of Badenoch. The illegitimate son-turned-bandit of King David II had sought revenge for his being excommunicated by the bishop of Moray. The cathedral was rebuilt but finally fell into disuse after the Reformation in 1560. By 1567, the highest authority in the land at the time, the regent earl of Moray, had stripped the lead from the roof to pay for his army. Thus ended the career of the religious seat known as the Lamp of the North. Some traces of the cathedral settlement survive, although they have been drastically altered: the gateway Pann's Port and the Bishop's Palace. ☎ 0131/668–8600. 🎫 £1.50. Joint entry ticket with Spynie Palace: £2.50. ⊙ Apr.–Oct., Mon.–Sat. 9:30–6, Sun. 2–6; Nov.–Mar., Mon.–Wed. and Sat. 9:30–4, Thurs. 9:30–12, Sun. 2–4.

❸❽ Just northwest of Elgin is **Spynie Palace,** the large 15th-century former headquarters of the bishops of Moray. It has now fallen into ruin and decay, though the top of the tower has good views over the Laigh of Moray. Find it by turning right off the main A941 Elgin–Lossiemouth road. ☎ 0131/668–8600. 🎫 £1.50. Joint entry ticket with Elgin Cathedral: £2.50. ⊙ Apr.–Oct., Mon.–Sat. 9:30–6, Sun. 2–6; Nov.–Mar., Sat. 9:30–4, Sun. 2–4.

Given the general destruction caused by the 16th-century religious upheaval of the Reformation, abbeys in Scotland tend to be ruinous and **❸❾** deserted, but at **Pluscarden Abbey** the way of life of the monks continues. Originally a 13th-century foundation, the religious community abandoned their abbey after the Reformation. The third Marquis of Bute bought the remains in 1897 and initiated a repair and restoration program that continues to this day. Monks from an abbey near Gloucester, England, returned here in 1948, and today the abbey is an active religious community. The abbey is southwest of Elgin, off B9010. 🎫 Free. ⊙ Daily 5 AM–8:30 PM.

Dining and Lodging

$$$$ ✕🏨 **Mansion House Hotel.** This Scots baronial mansion complete with tower is set on the River Lossie. The rooms are individually decorated; all provide comfort and pleasant surroundings. Head chef John Alexander produces flavorful dishes such as brochette of monkfish and salmon with lime and butter sauce, or breast of pheasant with port sauce; vegetarians are also well catered to. ⊠ The Haugh, IV30 1AW, ☎ 01343/548811, ℻ 01343/547916. 23 rooms with bath. Restaurant, bar, indoor pool, beauty salon, sauna, exercise room. AE, DC, MC, V.

Nightlife

FILM

Moray Playhouse (⊠ High St., Elgin, ☎ 01343/542680) shows mainstream releases.

Shopping

Elgin has, in addition to the usual range of High Street stores, **Gordon and MacPhail** (⊠ South St., ☎ 01343/545111), an outstanding delicatessen and wine merchant that, in addition to wine, stocks a breathtaking range of otherwise scarce malt whiskies. This is a good place to shop for gifts for those foodies among your friends. **Johnstons of Elgin** (⊠ Newmill, ☎ 01343/554099) has a worldwide reputation for its luxury fabrics, including cashmere. The bold color range is particularly appealing.

Fochabers

❹⓪ 9 mi east of Elgin.

Just before reaching Fochabers, you will see the works of a major local employer, Baxters of Fochabers, a family-run firm with an international reputation for fine foods. From Tokyo to New York, upmarket stores stock their soups, jams, chutneys, and other gourmet products—all of which are made here, close to the River Spey. Factory tours yield glimpses of impeccably attired staff stirring great vats of boiling marmalade and other concoctions. The **Baxters Visitors Centre** also offers a video presentation, a re-creation of the Baxters' first grocery shop, as well as a real shop stocking Baxters' goods (among other products), the Best of Scotland shop (specializing in Scottish goods), a store selling quality cooking utensils, cooking demonstrations, and two restaurants that offer an assortment of delectables. It is 1 mile west of Fochabers on the A96. ⊠ *Fochabers,* ☎ *01343/820666.* ⊡ *Free (small charge for cooking demonstrations).* ☉ *Daily 10–5:30 (extended hours in summer). Guided tours on weekdays only, Mon.–Thurs. 10–11:30 and 12:30–4, Fri. 10–11:30 and 12:30–2; no tours during factory holiday weeks in April (1 wk), June/July (2 wks), and Aug. (1 wk).*

Over the Spey bridge, visitors will find that Fochabers itself has the symmetrical village green. Perhaps this pleasing, mellow ambience attracts the antiques dealers to Fochabers, their wares ranging from near-junk to designer pieces. Through one of the antiques shops, you can enter the **Fochabers Folk Museum,** a converted church that has an excellent display of rural items, ranging from carts and carriages to interesting farm implements. ☎ *01343/820362.* ⊡ *Free.* ☉ *Winter, daily 9:30–1 and 2–5; summer, daily 9:30–1 and 2–6.*

Consider diverting up the road that runs south directly opposite the Fochabers Folk Museum. Leaving the houses behind for well-hedged country lanes, you will discover a Forestry Commission sign to the **Earth Pillars.** These curious eroded sandstone pillars are framed by tall-trunked pines and overlook a wide prospect of the lower Spey Valley.

❹❶ Another option is to take the B9108 from Fochabers down to the mouth of the River Spey. Here, by a storm beach with a high stone swell of smooth-washed pebbles, the river enters the sea. Nearby is the **Tugnet Ice House,** once the centerpiece of the local salmon fishing industry. Before the days of mechanical refrigeration, the salmon were stored in icy chambers. The ice was gathered in the winter and lasted in its insulated cellars throughout the fishing season. Now a museum housed in the ice house tells the story. ⊠ *Spey Bay,* ☎ *01309/673701.* ⊡ *Free.* ☉ *May–Sept., daily 11–5.*

Shopping

This is the place for antiques hunters, with several antiques shops all within a few yards of each other on the main street. Try **Sylvan Antiques** (⊠ 23 High St., ☎ 01343/820814) for pottery and bric-a-brac; **Antiques (Fochabers)** (⊠ Hadlow House, The Square, ☎ 01343/820838) for kitchenware and furniture; and **Pringle Antiques** (⊠ High St., ☎ 01343/821204) for small furniture, pottery, glassware, and jewelry. **Just Art** (⊠ 64 High St., ☎ 01343/820500) is a fine art gallery with high-quality ceramics and paintings. **Balance** (⊠ 59 High St., ☎ 01343/821443) stocks homeopathic remedies, potpourris, and the like. At **The Quaich** (⊠ 85 High St., ☎ 01343/820981), you can stock up on gifts, then sit with a cup of tea and a home-baked snack.

Buckie

❹❷ *8 mi east of Fochabers via A98 and A942.*

The fishing port of Buckie and its satellite villages are gray and workaday, with plenty of Victorian architecture added to the original, end-on-to-the-sea fishermen's cottages. The **Buckie Drifter** maritime museum, housed in premises designed to be reminiscent of an old fishing drifter, is a hands-on visitor center that tells the story of the herring industry and of Buckie's development as a herring port. Upstairs, you enter a 1920s quayside scene, with a replica steam drifter that you can board, and barrels you can pack with herring. ⊠ *Freuchny Rd., off Commercial Rd.,* ☎ *01542/834646.* ☞ *£2.50.* ⊙ *Apr.–Oct., Mon.–Sat. 10–6, Sun. noon–6.*

The **Peter Anson Gallery** shows a selection of watercolor works also related to the development of the fishing industry. The gallery is housed in a room accessed through the library. ⊠ *Cluny Pl.,* ☎ *01309/673701.* ☞ *Free.* ⊙ *Weekdays 10–8, Sat. 10–12.*

Dining

$$–$$$$ ✕ **The Old Monastery.** On a broad, wooded slope set back from the
★   coast near Buckie, with westward views as far as the hills of Wester Ross, the Old Monastery was once a Victorian religious establishment. This theme has been preserved and carries through to the restrained decor of the Cloisters Bar and the Chapel Restaurant, with its hand stenciling. The local specialties—the freshest fish from sea and river and Aberdeen Angus beef—make up the major part of the menu, or you can opt for such dishes as chicken breast coated in oatmeal and pan-fried, served with a lemon, mustard, and cream sauce. Homemade soups and delicious puddings are bonuses, as is the no-smoking dining room. This is quite simply the best for miles around. ⊠ *Drybridge, Buckie,* ☎ *01542/832660. AE, MC, V. Closed Sun., Mon., 3 wks in Jan. and 2 wks in Nov.*

En Route   Visitors will find a string of other fishing communities down by the shore, running east. These salty little villages paint a colorful scene with their gable-ended houses and fishing nets set out to dry amid the rocky shoreline.

Findochty

43   *2 mi east of Buckie on A942.*

The residents of Findochty are known for their fastidiousness and creativity in painting their fishing houses, taking the fine art of housepainting to a new level. Some residents even paint the mortar between the stonework a different color. This small town also has a harbor with a faint echo of the Mediterranean about it.

Cullen

★ **44**   *3 mi east of Findochty.*

You will see some wonderfully painted homes again at Cullen, a few miles from Findochty on the A98, in the old fishermen's town below the railway viaduct. But the real attractions of this little resort are its white-sand beach and the fine view west toward the Bowfiddle Rock (the reason for its name is obvious on sight). A stroll along the beach reveals the shape of the fishing settlement below and planned town above. Cullen and its shops are far enough away from major town superstores to survive on local, intermittent trade; most unusual for a town of its size, Cullen has a full range of specialty shops—ironmongers, butchers, a baker, a haberdasher, and a locally famous ice-cream shop among them.

NEED A   **Cullen Restaurant** (⊠ Seafield St.) is a great place for morning coffee,
BREAK?   light lunches, or teas, with a delicious selection of baked goods to choose from, wheeled up to your table, and equally special homemade soups.

Fordyce

45 *5 mi east of Cullen.*

The conservation village of Fordyce lies among the barley fields of Banff-shire like a small slice of rural England gone far adrift. You can stroll by the churchyard; picnic on the old bleaching green (an explanatory notice board tells you all about it); or visit a restored 19th-century carpenter's workshop.

Lodging

$ ☎ **Academy House.** This top-of-the-range bed-and-breakfast offers
★ accommodation in what was once the headmaster's house for the local secondary school. Traditional decor and some well-chosen antique furniture decorate the spacious, well-proportioned rooms. Evening meals are served upon request. ⊠ *School Rd., Fordyce, AB45 2SJ,* ☎ *01261/842743. 3 rooms (no private facilities). No credit cards.*

$ ☎ **Broom Farm.** Set on a hilltop, overlooking Sandend Bay with its beautiful, deserted sandy beach, seals basking on the rocks, and dolphins cruising the Moray Firth, this working farm offers bed-and-breakfast accommodations in a private wing of the main house. Guests have their own bathroom, a master bedroom, dressing room, and another bedroom with bunk beds for children, all with traditional pine furniture and pastel color schemes. ⊠ *Broom Farm, Sandend, Portsoy, Banff-shire, AB45 2UD,* ☎ FAX *01542/840401. 1 suite for couple or family. No credit cards.*

Shopping

Fiona Anderson Gallery (⊠ The Square, Fordyce ☎ 01261/842224) is tucked behind the castle on the main street and has a tempting choice of antique furniture, rugs, paintings, and ornaments.

Portsoy

46 *6 mi east of Cullen.*

The little town of Portsoy has a much more ancient layout than many Northeast communities. It boasts the oldest harbor on the Moray Firth, built in the 17th century. Once a North Sea trading port and later participating in the 19th-century fishing boom, the community thereafter fell into a decline. But thoughtful conservation programs have revitalized much of Portsoy's old fabric.

Shopping

Portsoy Marble (⊠ Old Harbour, ☎ 01261/842404) stocks not only marble items—eggs, platters, etc.—but also local pottery, books, cards, knitwear, and ornaments. (Portsoy marble, which can have a greenish or reddish tone, even found its way to the Palace of Versailles in France.

Banff

47 *36 mi east of Elgin, 47 mi north of Aberdeen.*

Midway along the northeast coast, overlooking Moray Firth and the estuary of the River Deveron, the town of Banff is a fishing town of considerable elegance that feels as though it is a million miles from tartan-clad Scotland. Part Georgian, like Edinburgh's New Town, and part 16th-century small burgh, like Culross, Banff is an exemplary east-coast salty town, with its tiny harbor and fine Georgian domestic architecture. It is also within easy reach of plenty of unspoiled coastline—cliff and rock to the east at Gardenstown (known as Ganrie) and Pennan, or beautiful little sandy beaches westward toward Sandend or Cullen.

The jewel in Banff's crown is the grand mansion of **Duff House,** a splendid William Adam–designed baroque mansion that has been restored as an outstation of the National Galleries of Scotland. Many fine paintings are displayed in rooms furnished to reflect the days when the house was occupied by the Dukes of Fife. ☎ *01261/818181.* 🖃 *£2.50.* ☉ *Apr.–Sept., Wed.–Mon. 10–5; Oct.-Mar., Thurs.–Sun. 10–5.*

Lodging

$$ 🏨 **Eden House.** Surrounded by woodland, this Georgian mansion house set high above the River Deveron has magnificent views and makes an elegant but comfortable base from which to explore the northeast coast east of Inverness. Since it is also the home of the proprietors, you are likely to feel like a houseguest rather than a room number. Tennis, billiards, fishing, and shooting can all be arranged, while numerous golf courses are within easy reach. Relax in the evening surrounded by carefully chosen antiques. Dinner (resident guests only) might include local seafood, Deveron salmon, game, or Scottish beef. ⊠ *AB45 3NT,* ☎ *01261/821282.* 🖷 *01261/821283. 5 rooms, 3 with bath or shower. No credit cards. Closed Dec. 25 and Jan. 1.*

Pennan

48   *12 mi east of Banff.*

A huddle of houses tucked below a crescent of grassy cliffs, Pennan shot to minor fame as the setting for some of the filming of *Local Hero,* which starred Burt Lancaster. The phone box and the inn featured in the film are still there. Pennan is set in a remote cliff coastline about as far from the tourist trail as is possible. Find it off B9031 between Macduff, east of Banff, and Fraserburgh.

Fraserburgh

49   *27 mi east of Banff, 47 mi north of Aberdeen.*

The gray-toned, workaday port of Fraserburgh has two great surprises for visitors. The **beach** should not be missed: Its sands sweep away out of sight, backed by wind-sculpted dunes, and it is often to-
★ tally unoccupied save by seabirds. Past the harbor you will find **Scotland's Lighthouse Museum,** at the northeasternmost point of Scotland, overlooked by a 16th-century castle that was converted into the first lighthouse to be built by the Commissioners for Northern Lights in the 1780s. The museum tells the story of Scotland's lighthouses, vital in the development of the country's maritime history. Highlights include the displays of astonishingly beautiful lenses, which would be the envy of any interior designer, and the tour of the lighthouse itself, right up to the top. ⊠ *Kinnaird Head, Fraserburgh,* ☎ *01346/511022.* 🖃 *£2.50.* ☉ *Apr.–Oct., Mon.–Sat. 10–6, Sun. 12:30–6; Nov.–Mar., Mon.–Sat. 10–4, Sun. 12:30–4.*

Mintlaw

50   *13 mi south of Fraserburgh.*

It can seem to the casual visitor that Mintlaw consists of little except a few houses and a traffic circle. However, here in Aden Country Park, the **Northeast Scotland Agricultural Heritage Centre** tells through videos the moving story of life on the land and the hard toil of the farming folk who battled to tame the ground of the Northeast. Housed in a handsome courtyard of former farm buildings, implements, tableaux, models, and displays create a vivid impression. Aden Country Park is also an important recreational resource for the locals, with trails that meander throughout the park's 230 acres. Find it off A92, just west of Mint-law. ☎ 01771/622857. 🎟 *Heritage Centre: £1.* ☉ *May–Sept., daily 11–5; Apr., Oct., and early Nov., weekends noon–5 (last admission 4:30).*

West of Mintlaw, at **Deer Abbey** are the remains of a Cistercian monastery founded in 1218. ✉ *Old Deer,* ☎ *0131/668–8600.* 🎟 *Free.* ☉ *At all times.*

Dining and Lodging

$$ ✕🎟 **Saplinbrae House.** The restaurant in this country-house hotel is very popular with the locals. As elsewhere in this farming region, with its bounteous salmon rivers, local fish and produce is the basis of the menu. Game pie, roast duck, and hefty steamed puddings require advance planning to ensure that you have the capacity to stay the course (try a light breakfast followed by a day's hill walking before you take a meal here). Rooms have traditional decor with dark color schemes. ✉ *Old Deer, near Mintlaw, Aberdeenshire, AB4 8PL,* ☎ *01771/ 623515,* 🖷 *01771/624472. 14 rooms with bath or shower. Restaurant. AE, DC, MC, V.*

Ellon

🛈 *14 mi south of Mintlaw.*

Formerly a market center on what was then the lowest bridging point of the River Ythan, Ellon is a small town at the center of a rural hinterland as well as a bedroom suburb of Aberdeen.

It is also well-placed for visiting several more of "castle country's" splendid properties. West of Ellon, at Pitmedden, is a unique re-creation by the National Trust for Scotland of a 17th-century garden: **Pitmedden Garden** is best visited in high summer, from July onward, when annual bedding plants form intricate formal patterns of the garden plots. The 100-acre estate also has a variety of woodland and farmland walks, as well as the Museum of Farming Life. ☎ *01651/842352.* 🎟 *£3.10.* ☉ *May–Sept., daily 10–5:30 (last admission 5).*

Created as the home of the earls and marquesses of Aberdeen, **Haddo House**—designed by William Adam (father of Robert)—is now cared for by the National Trust for Scotland. Built in 1732, the elegant mansion has a light and graceful design, with curving wings on either side of a harmonious, symmetrical facade. The Chapel has a stained-glass window by Burne-Jones. To find Haddo, turn off B999, northwest of Ellon. 🎟 *£3.60; garden only, £1 (honesty box).* ☉ *House: Easter and May–Sept., daily 1:30–5:30; Oct., weekends 1:30–5:30 (last admission 4:45). Shop and Stables restaurant: Apr.–Sept., daily 11–5:30; Oct., weekends 11–5:30. Garden and country park: daily 9:30–sunset.*

In an area rife with castles, many are distinguished within their own categories: Craigievar for untouched perfection, Corgarff for sheer loneliness, Haddo House for elegance. Perhaps **Fyvie Castle** stands out in its own category: most complex. Five great towers built by five successive powerful families turned a 13th-century foursquare castle into an opulent Edwardian statement of wealth. There's an array of superb paintings on view, including 12 Raeburns, as well as myriad sumptuous interiors and walks on the castle grounds. Fyvie is praised for its sheer impact, if you like your castles oppressive and gloomy. It's off A947 between Oldmeldrum and Turriff, northwest of Ellon. ☎ *01651/891266.* 🎟 *£3.60; garden only, £1 (honesty box).* ☉ *Castle: Apr.–June and Sept., daily 1:30–5:30; July and Aug., daily 11–5:30; Oct., weekends 1:30–5:30 (last admission 4:45). Grounds: daily 9:30–sunset.*

OFF THE
BEATEN PATH
BULLERS OF BUCHAN – On a stretch of windy cliff and cove coastline—
once used by smugglers—the sea has cut through a cave, collapsing its
roof and forming a great rocky cauldron, fearsome in bad weather. The
Bullers of Buchan is an impressive sight, worth seeing for those explorers
who like their sights austere and elemental, but not for the vertigo-prone.
Approach the cliff edge with great care. (Located off the A952/A975
northeast of Ellon.)

ABERDEEN AND THE NORTHEAST A TO Z

Arriving and Departing

By Bus

Long-distance coach service operates to and from most parts of Scotland, England, and Wales. Main operators include **National Express/Scottish Citylink** (☎ 0990/808080, or ☎ 0990/505050) and **Stagecoach** (☎ 01738/629339).

By Car

It is now possible to travel from Glasgow and Edinburgh to Aberdeen on a continuous stretch of the A90/M90, a fairly scenic route that runs up Strathmore, with a fine hill view to the west. The coastal route, the A92, is a more leisurely alternative, with its interesting coastal resorts and fishing villages. The most scenic route, however, is probably the A93 from Perth, north to Blairgowrie and into Glen Shee. The A93 then goes over the Cairnwell Pass, the highest main road in the United Kingdom. (This route is not recommended in the winter months when snow can make driving over high ground difficult.)

By Ferry

There is a summer (June–August) ferry service between Aberdeen, Lerwick (Shetland), and Bergen (Norway), which means that it is possible to travel from Norway to Aberdeen by boat. It is operated by **P&O Ferries** (contact via Box 5, Jamieson's Quay, Aberdeen, ☎ 01224/572615, FAX 01224/574411) and is subject to annual review; if you plan to use this route, check that the service will be running.

By Plane

Aberdeen's airport—serving both international and domestic flights—is in Dyce, 7 miles west of the city center on the A96 (Inverness). The terminal building is modern (expanded in recent years because of Dyce's prominent role in North Sea oil-rig communications) and generally uncrowded.

Airlines linking Aberdeen with Europe include **Air U.K.,** with flights to Amsterdam (the Netherlands), Paris (France), and Bergen and Stavanger (Norway); **SAS (Scandinavian Airlines),** serving Stavanger; and **Business Air,** with flights to Esbjerg (Denmark). An extensive network of domestic flights linking Aberdeen with most major U.K. airports is operated by **Air U.K., British Airways, Brymon, Business Air, EasyJet, Gill Air,** and **Knight Air.** Consult the individual airlines or your travel agent for arrival and departure times (airport information desk, ☎ 01224/722331).

Note the direct Amsterdam–Aberdeen link enabling transatlantic passengers to visit Scotland's northeast by first flying from the United States to Amsterdam and then flying on to Aberdeen with Air U.K.; this can actually be faster than traveling to Aberdeen from other parts of Scotland or England.

BETWEEN THE AIRPORT AND CITY CENTER

By Bus: Grampian Transport's number 27 bus operates between the airport terminal and Union Street in the center of Aberdeen. Buses (exact fare £1.20) run frequently at peak times, less often in midday and evenings; the journey time is approximately 40 minutes.

By Car: The drive to the center of Aberdeen is very easy via the A96 (which can be busy in the rush hour).

By Train: Dyce is on **ScotRail's** Inverness–Aberdeen route. The rail station is a short taxi ride from the terminal building. The ride by rail into Aberdeen from Dyce takes 12 minutes. Trains run approximately every two hours. If you intend to visit the western part of the area first, it is possible to travel northwest, away from Aberdeen, by rail, direct to Elgin via Inverurie, Insch, Huntly, and Keith.

By Train
Travelers can reach Aberdeen directly from Edinburgh (2½ hours), Glasgow (three hours), and Inverness (2½ hours). See ScotRail time-table for full details, or call Aberdeen Railway Station (☎ 01224/594222). There are also London–Aberdeen routes that go through Edinburgh and the east-coast main line.

Getting Around
Aberdeen is not a large city. Its center is Union Street, the main thoroughfare running east–west. Anderson Drive is an efficient ring road on the western side of the city; inexperienced drivers should be extra careful on its many traffic circles. In general, road signs are clear and legible, and parking near the center of Aberdeen is no worse than in any other U.K. city, though the park-and-ride facility clearly signposted on the northern outskirts of Aberdeen at Bridge of Don is recommended.

By Bus
Grampian Transport operates services throughout the city. There is an inquiry kiosk on St. Nicholas Street, outside Marks and Spencers department store, and timetables are available at the kiosk or from the tourist information center at St. Nicholas House nearby.

By Car
Aberdeen is a compact city, with good signing. Union Street is the main axis, and tends to get crowded with traffic. It is better to leave your car in one of the parking garages (arrive early to get a space), and walk around. Alternatively, make use of the excellent park-and-ride scheme at Bridge of Don, north of the city. Street maps are available from the tourist information center or from newsagents and booksellers. Around the Northeast, roads are generally not busy, but speeding and erratic driving can be a problem on the main A roads. The rural side roads are a pleasure to drive.

By Taxi
Taxi stands can be found throughout the center of Aberdeen: along Union Street, at the railway station at Guild Street, at Back Wynd, and at Regent Quay. Taxis are mostly black, though variations in beige, maroon, or white exist.

Contacts and Resources
Camping
Most of the population centers in the area have campsites. It is possible to camp on private land, but you must obtain the permission of the landowner first. Except for the more remote upland areas, "wild land" camping is better pursued farther west.

Car-Rental Agencies

Alamo (⊠ at Airport Skean Dhu Hotel, ☎ 01224/770955). **Arnold Clark** (⊠ Girdleness Rd., ☎ 01224/248842). **Avis** (⊠ Aberdeen Airport, ☎ 01224/722282; ⊠ 16 Broomhill Rd., ☎ 01224/574252). **Budget Rent a Car** (⊠ Great Northern Rd, Kittybrewster, ☎ 01224/488770). **Eurodollar** (⊠ 46 Summer St., ☎ 01224/626955). **Europcar** (⊠ Aberdeen Airport, ☎ 01224/770770; ⊠ 121 Causewayend, ☎ 01224/631199). **Hertz** (⊠ Aberdeen Airport, ☎ 01224/722373; ⊠ Railway Station, ☎ 01224/210748). **Kenning** (⊠ 240 Market St., ☎ 01224/571445). **Mitchell Self-Drive** (⊠ 35 Chapel St., ☎ 01224/642642). **Watson's Self-Drive** (⊠ 114–126 Hutcheon St., ☎ 01224/625625).

Emergencies

For **fire, police,** or **ambulance,** dial 999 from any telephone. No coins are needed for emergency calls made from public telephone booths.

Grampian Police (⊠ Force Headquarters, Queen St., Aberdeen, ☎ 01224/639111). There is a lost property office here.

Aberdeen Royal Infirmary (⊠ Accident and Emergency Department, Foresterhill, Aberdeen, ☎ 01224/681818).

Dr. Gray's Hospital, Elgin (⊠ Accident and Emergency Department, at end of High St. on A96, ☎ 01343/543131, ext. 77310).

Doctors and Dentists

The **Grampian Health Board** (⊠ Primary Care Department, Woolmanhill, ☎ 01224/681818, ext. 55537) can help you find a doctor or dentist, or consult your hotel receptionist, bed-and-breakfast proprietor, or the Yellow Pages telephone book.

Fishing

Details of beats, boats, and permit prices can be obtained from local tourist information centers. Some local hotels offer fishing packages or, at least, can organize permits. Prices vary widely, depending on the fish and individual river beat.

Golf

The Northeast has more than 50 golf clubs, some of which have championship courses. Tourist information centers can supply leaflets appropriate to their area. All towns and many villages have their nine- and 18-hole municipal links, at which you pay £5–£10 per round. The more prestigious clubs charge up to £40 a day and expect you to book by letter or to bring a letter of recommendation from a member.

Guided Tours

ORIENTATION

City tours are available on most days between June and mid-September. Contact **Grampian Transport** (☎ 01224/637047). **Grampian Coaches** (operated by Grampian Transport), **Bluebird Northern** (☎ 01224/212266), and **McIntyre Coaches** (☎ 01224/493112) all operate tours encompassing the Northeast coastline and countryside. Some of the tours are of general interest, others are based on one of the area's various trails: Malt Whisky, Coastal, Castle, or Royal.

PERSONAL GUIDES

The **Scottish Tourist Guides Association** (⊠ Mrs. Anne Sinclair, 32 Henderson Dr., Skene, Aberdeen, AB31 6RA, ☎ FAX 01224/741314) can supply experienced personal guides, including foreign-language-speaking guides if necessary.

The following firms offer chauffeur-driven limousines to take clients on tailor-made tours: **Alamo Chauffeur Drive** (☎ 01764/663777) and **Scotland Scene Ltd.** (☎ 01343/541468).

WALKING TOURS

The **Scottish Tourist Guides Association** (☞ *above*) organizes an "Old Aberdeen" walk from mid-May through August on Wednesday evenings and Sunday afternoons.

Late-Night Pharmacies

Anderson Pharmacy (✉ 4 Union Grove, ☎ 01224/587148) and **Boots the Chemists Ltd.** (✉ Bon Accord Centre, George St., ☎ 01224/626080), both in Aberdeen, keep longer hours than most. There also is also an in-store pharmacist at **Safeway Food Store** (✉ 215 King St., ☎ 01224/624398, ☉ Mon.–Wed. and Sat. 9–8, Thurs. and Fri. 9–9, Sun. 10–4).

Notices on pharmacy doors will guide you to the nearest open pharmacy at any given time. The police can provide assistance in an emergency.

Skiing

The area's main skiing development is at **Glenshee** (☎ 013397/41320, FAX 013397/41665), just south of Braemar, though the season can be brief here. Visitors accustomed to long alpine runs and extensive choice will find the runs here short, unlike the lift lines. **The Lecht** (☎ 01975/651440, FAX 01975/651426) lies at even lower altitude, also within easy reach of the area, and is mainly suitable for beginners. The development at **Cairngorm** (☎ 01479/861261, FAX 01479/861207) by Aviemore is also nearby (☞ Chapter 10). There is an artificial "dry" slope at **Alford** (☎ 019755/62380).

Visitor Information

Aberdeen (✉ St. Nicholas House, Broad St., Aberdeen, ☎ 01224/632727, FAX 01224/620415); this tourist information center supplies information on all Scotland's Northeast and there is also a currency exchange. **Banff** (✉ Collie Lodge, ☎ 01261/812419, FAX 01261/815807). **Banchory** (✉ Bridge St., ☎ 01330/822000, FAX 01330/825126). **Braemar** (✉ The Mews, Mar Rd., ☎ 013397/41600). **Elgin** (✉ 17 High St., ☎ 01343/542666; FAX 01343/552982).

In summer, also look for tourist information centers in Aboyne, Alford, Ballater, Buckie, Crathie, Cullen, Dufftown, Ellon, Forres, Fraserburgh, Huntly, Inverurie, Keith, Mintlaw, Peterhead, Stonehaven, Tomintoul, and Turriff.

9 Argyll and the Isles

With long sea lochs running into the mountainous interior, Argyll is a picture-postcard interplay of land and water. Rainy Atlantic weather systems make for green, mossy woods and hills. The pastoral Kintyre peninsula at its southern end is a wonderland of sea views and early monuments. On the islands, Mull's main town, Tobermory, with its brightly painted houses, has a Mediterranean feel. The Isle of Islay, synonymous with whisky, produces seven malts. Arran is an outdoor playground, loved by generations of Scots.

By Gilbert
Summers

THIS POPULAR AND ALLURING REGION in western Scotland, divided in two by the long peninsula of Kintyre, is characterized by a splintered, complex seaboard. The west is an aesthetic delight, though it catches the moist—and that's a euphemism—Atlantic weather systems. The same holds true for the Great Glen area. But an occasionally wet foray is the price visitors pay for the glittering freshness of oak woods and bracken-covered hillsides, and for the bright interplay of sea, loch, and rugged green peninsula.

Kintyre also separates the islands of the Firth of Clyde (including Arran), from the islands of the Inner Hebrides, the largest of which are Mull, Islay, and Jura. You could spend all your time touring these larger islands, but keep in mind that there are plenty of small islands that can also be explored—the captivating gem, Colonsay, between Islay and Mull, for example. Those visiting the mainland cannot avoid the touring center of Oban, an important ferry port with a main road leading south into Kintyre.

Pleasures and Pastimes

Dining

This part of Scotland is not usually considered a great gastronomic center, though it does have some restaurants of distinction. Still, the ingredients used in dishes are of good quality and are locally produced: Fish, fresh from the sparkling lochs and sea, could hardly be better. Beef, lamb, and game are also common. In the rural districts, your best bet is to choose a hotel or guest house that can provide a decent evening meal as well as breakfast.

WHAT TO WEAR
Although this is a relaxed area in terms of dress, upscale hotel restaurants expect a smart standard of dress—no T-shirts or shorts.

CATEGORY	COST*
$$$$	over £40
$$$	£30–£40
$$	£15–£30
$	under £15

per person for a 3-course meal, including VAT and excluding drinks and service

Golf

The area has about two dozen golf courses, notably the fine coastal links, of which Machrihanish near Campbeltown is the most famous.

Lodging

Accommodations in Argyll and the Isles range from château-like hotels to modest inns. The traditional provincial hotels and small coastal resorts have been modernized and equipped with all the necessary comforts, yet they retain their sense of personalized service and the charm that comes with older buildings. Apart from these, however, your choices are more limited, and your best overnight option is usually a modest guest house offering bed, breakfast, and an evening meal.

CATEGORY	COST*
$$$$	over £110
$$$	£80–£110
$$	£45–£80
$	under £45

All prices are for standard double room, including service, breakfast, and VAT.

Shopping

Although great shopping is not what lures visitors to this predominantly rural area, there are several interesting crafts outlets; and on Islay, in particular, there are opportunities to sample and purchase fine island whiskies.

Exploring Argyll and the Isles

On mainland-based tours, Loch Fyne tends to get in the way. It is a long haul around the end of this fjordlike sea loch to reach Inveraray, a popular destination. Ferry services provided by Caledonian MacBrayne (☞ Getting Around by Car and Ferry in Argyll and the Isles A to Z, *below*) make all kinds of interisland tours possible and can shorten mainland distances as well. From Ardrossan, southwest of Glasgow, you can reach the island of Arran, then exit westward to Kintyre by a short ferry crossing. You can continue to the islands of Islay and Jura, and from there a ferry can take you northeast to Oban. (All the ferries transport cars and pedestrians.) The routes suggested begin on the mainland but also highlight the main islands.

Great Itineraries

You could easily spend a week here, wandering across the islands. It will take you a day to get around Mull, for instance, especially if you are visiting castles, or it can take even longer if you go to Iona. Arran, too, by the time you have driven around it and gone to Brodick, is more than just a day trip. Overall, allow yourself a good chunk of time, particularly if the weather looks settled. Mainland areas, such as Inveraray, and Oban and its environs, have places of interest that can easily swallow up the day.

IF YOU HAVE 2 DAYS

Numbers in the text correspond to numbers in the margin and on the Argyll and the Isles map.

Make your way to **Inveraray** ⑥ with its choice of attractions, via Loch Lomond and the Rest and Be Thankful. Continue south via **Crarae Gardens** ⑧ to **Crinan Canal** ⑩, then overnight at 🏨 **Oban** ①. Next day follow the A85 east from Oban, taking in the settings of **Dunstaffnage** ② and **Kilchurn** ⑤ castles, before returning to the Loch Lomond/Glasgow area.

IF YOU HAVE 4 DAYS

Starting from Ardrossan in Ayrshire, take the ferry to 🏨 **Brodick** ⑭ on the island of Arran and tour the island, visiting **Brodick Castle and Country Park** ⑳. Take the ferry from **Lochranza** ㉑ for Tarbert, going south to the island of **Gigha** ⑬, then return north to the 🏨 **Crinan Canal** ⑩ area. Go north to **Oban** ①, make an excursion to Mull, for **Iona** ㊱, 🏨 **Tobermory** ㊳, and **Torosay Castle** ㉞, then return to Oban or go farther north, via the Fishnish, to Lochaline ferry.

IF YOU HAVE 7 DAYS

This non-circular route provides a good flavor of the islands. As with the four-day itinerary above, start from Ardrossan in Ayrshire and take the ferry to 🏨 **Brodick** ⑭. Stay overnight on Arran and tour the island, visiting **Brodick Castle and Country Park** ⑯. Take the ferry from **Lochranza** ㉑ for Tarbert, then visit the island of **Islay** ㉔–㉛, staying two nights for its whisky, island life, and nature reserves. Visit **Jura** as well. Return to the mainland to take in the area around Knapdale, staying at 🏨 **Lochgilphead** ⑨ for at least one night. Go north to 🏨 **Oban** ① and take the ferry to Mull, for **Iona** ㊱, 🏨 **Tobermory** ㊳, and **Torosay Castle** ㉞, staying two nights. Then return to 🏨 **Oban** ① to explore the attractions along the A85 to the east: **Dunstaffnage Castle** ②,

Bonawe Iron Furnace ③, Cruachan Dam Power Station Visitor Centre ④, and **Kilchurn Castle** ⑤.

When to Tour Argyll and the Isles

The mainland part of this area is near enough to Glasgow, in particular, to justify its description as a year-round touring ground. This means that you can take advantage of the quiet roads in late autumn or early spring and still find a good selection of accommodations, but if the weather lets you down, you can get back to the main cities with little difficulty. Avoid the islands in winter, when howling gales and frigid temperatures prevail.

AROUND ARGYLL

Take time to get to know the characteristic mix of grandeur and lush greenery that make this bit of Argyll special. Inevitably, Oban, a major ferry gateway and route center, will figure in your explorations hereabouts; and even if you have only a little time, you should try to take to the water at least once. The sea and the sea lochs have played a vital role in the history of the west, since the time of the war galleys of the clans.

Oban

❶ *96 mi north of Glasgow, 50 mi south of Fort William, 118 mi southwest of Inverness, 125 mi northwest of Edinburgh.*

Just as it is impossible to avoid Fort William when touring the north, it is almost impossible to avoid Oban when touring this part of Scotland. Unlike Fort William, however, Oban has a fairly attractive waterfront and several ferry excursions from which to choose. It also has a more pleasant environment, though it does get busy during the peak season. Oban is a traditional Scottish resort where you find *ceilidhs* (song, music and dance) and tartan kitsch, as well as late-night revelry in pubs and hotel bars. There is an inescapable sense, however, that just over the horizon, on the islands or down Kintyre, loom more peaceful and authentic environs.

☝ **A World in Miniature** displays handcrafted miniature rooms and furniture made to a ½ scale. ⊠ *North pier, Oban,* ☎ *01852/316272 or 01631/566300.* ⊡ *£1.50.* ⊗ *Easter–Oct., Mon.–Sat. 10–5, Sun. 2–5.*

❷ North of Oban stands **Dunstaffnage Castle,** once an important stronghold of the MacDougalls. The ramparts offer outstanding views across the **Sound of Mull** and the **Firth of Lorne,** a nautical crossroads of sorts, once watched over by Dunstaffnage Castle and commanded by the galleys (in Gaelic, *birlinn*) of the Lords of the Isles. ☎ *0131/668–8600.* ⊡ *£1.50.* ⊗ *Apr.–Sept., weekdays 9:30–6, Sun. 2–6.*

From Dunstaffnage Castle keep, you should be able to see **Connel Bridge,** 2 miles farther east. This elegant structure once carried a branch railway along the coast, but it has since surrendered to the all-conquering automobile. Below the bridge, in the shadow of the girders, the **Falls of Lora** foam, given the right tidal conditions. Upstream is fjordlike **Loch Etive** (with cruises from Oban); the water leaving this deep, narrow loch foams and fights with the sea tides, creating turbulence and curious cascades.

Dining and Lodging

$$$$ ✕▥ **Glenfeochan House.** This family-run Victorian mansion, set on 350 acres, is 5 miles south of Oban on A816. It offers tastefully decorated rooms with antique furniture and original plasterwork. The owner, once

Argyll and the Isles

Ben Nevis
Fort William
A82
Kinlochleven
A82
Glen Coe
Ardgour
Corron
Inversanda
Ballachulish
A828
Barcaldine Forest
Ben Cruachan
Loch Etive
Dalmally
5 Kilchurn Castle
4 Cruachan Dam Power Station Visitor Centre
3 Bonawe Iron Furnace
Taynuilt
A85
Barcaldine
A819
6 Inveraray
Strachur
7 Auchindrain Museum
Loch Fyne
A83
A815
A861
Strontian
B8043
A884
Loch Sunart
Lochaline
Rudha an Ridire
2 Dunstaffnage Castle
1 Oban
Loch Linnhe
Loch Don
Seil
Easdale Island
A816
Scarba
Gulf of Corryvreckan
Carnasserie Castle
Kilmartin
12
Crinan Canal
Ardnamurchan
B8007
Glenborrodale
Sanna
Fishnish Pier
33 Craignure
34 Torosay Castle
35 Duart Castle
Loch Spelve
Firth of Lorne
B849
Aros
B8073
Salen
A848
Isle of Mull
Sound of Mull
38 Tobermory
Dervaig
37
Calgary Bay
Threshnish Islands
Gometra
Ulva
Ben More
B8035
The Burg
Loch Scridain
Ross of Mull
Carsaig
Carsaig Arches
Fionnphort
36 Iona
Sound of Iona
Colonsay
Arinagour
Coll
I N N E R   H E B R I D E S
Scarinish
Tiree

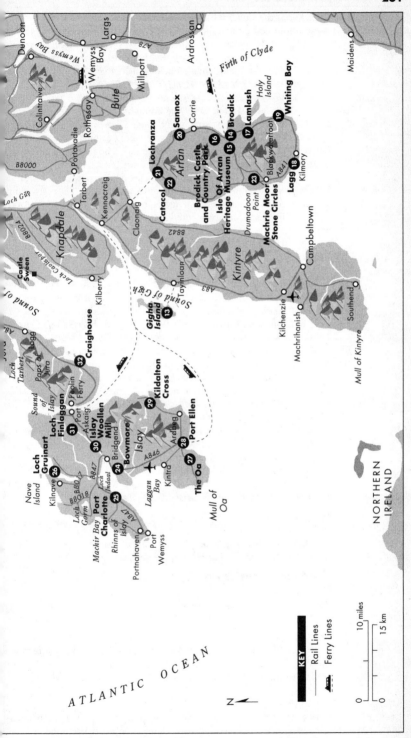

ATLANTIC OCEAN

NORTHERN IRELAND

Firth of Clyde

KEY
Rail Lines
Ferry Lines

10 miles
15 km

Dunoon
Wemyss Bay
Largs
Colintraive
Rothesay
Bute
Millport
Portavadie
Maidens
Ardrossan
Whiting Bay **19**
Holy Island
Lamlash **17**
Brodick **14**
Sannox **20**
Corrie
Lochranza **21**
Arran
Brodick Castle and Country Park **16**
Isle Of Arran Heritage Museum **15**
Catacol **22**
Blackwaterfoot
Lagg **18**
Kilmory
Machrie Moor Stone Circles **23**
Drumadoon Point
Loch Gilp
Knapdale
Tarbert
Kennacraig
Claonaig
Kintyre
Campbeltown
Castle Sween
Kilberry
Loch Caolisport
Sound of Gigha
Tayinloan
Gigha Island **13**
Kilchenzie
Machrihanish
Southend
Mull of Kintyre
Craighouse **32**
Paps of Jura
Loch Tarbert
Feolin Ferry
Kildalton Cross
Port Askaig
Loch Finlaggan **31**
30 Islay Woollen Mill
Bridgend
29
Port Ellen
Ardbeg
28
Bowmore Islay **24**
27 The Oa
Loch Gruinart **26**
Nave Island
Kilnave
Port Charlotte **25**
Loch Gorm
Machir Bay
Rhinns of Islay
Loch Indaal
Laggan Bay
Kintra
Portnahaven
Port Wemyss
Mull of Oa

N

a teacher at the Cordon Bleu School in London, serves lucky resident guests a four-course, completely home-cooked dinner, using only fresh, seasonal, local ingredients—most of the vegetables and fruit come from the walled garden on the estate, the venison comes from the island of Jura, and the shellfish is from local fishermen. ⊠ *Kilmore, PA34 4QR,* ☎ *01631/770273,* FAX *01631/770624. 3 rooms with bath. Dining room, fishing. AE, MC, V. Closed Nov.—Mar.*

$$$$ ✕🏨 **Manor House Hotel.** Once the home of the Duke of Argyll, this 1780 stone house on the shore, just outside Oban, is now a hotel with great views of the sea. It's within easy walking distance of downtown Oban and the bus, train, and ferry terminals. The reception and public areas are furnished with many genuine antiques, and the bedrooms, with reproductions. Bedcoverings and curtains are made of textured fabrics in warm colors, such as gold, pink, and yellow. The restaurant serves both Scottish and French dishes, including lots of local seafood and game in season, complemented by a carefully chosen wine list. Dinner is included in the room rate. ⊠ *Gallanach Rd., Oban, Argyll, PA34 4LS,* ☎ *01631/562087,* FAX *01631/563053. 11 rooms with bath. Restaurant (jacket and tie). AE, MC, V. Closed Jan.*

$$ 🏨 **Kilchrenan House.** A fully refurbished Victorian house only a few minutes' walk from the town center, this is a high-grade bed-and-breakfast, with rooms offering views out to sea and to the islands. ⊠ *Corran Esplanade, Oban, Argyll, PA34 5AQ,* ☎ FAX *01631/562663. 10 rooms, 8 with bath, 2 with shower. MC, V. Closed Nov.–Mar.*

$$ 🏨 **Ronebhal Guest House.** Loch Etive and the mountains beyond can
★   be seen from this stone house east of Oban. Although Connel is on the main road, Ronebhal is set back within its own grounds. It offers bed-and-breakfast in spacious surroundings. ⊠ *Connel, Argyll, PA37 1PJ,* ☎ *01631/710310. 6 rooms with shower. MC, V. Closed Nov.–Mar.*

$ 🏨 **Dungrianach.** This aptly named bed-and-breakfast ("the sunny house on the hill") is set in woodland with superb views of the ocean and islands, yet it is only a few minutes walk from Oban's ferry piers and town center. Both rooms in this late Victorian house have private facilities and are decorated with handsome period furniture. ⊠ *Pulpit Hill, Oban, Argyll, PA34 4LX,* ☎ *01631/562840. 2 rooms with bath or shower. No credit cards. Closed Oct.–Mar.*

The Arts

FILM

The **Highland Discovery Centre** (⊠ George St., Oban, ☎ 01631/562444) shows feature films and also has a theater for plays.

Outdoor Activities and Sports

BICYCLING

Rent bicycles from **Oban Cycles** (⊠ 9 Craigard Rd., Oban, ☎ 01631/566996).

Shopping

Caithness Glass Oban (⊠ Railway Pier, ☎ 01631/563386), a factory shop for Caithness Glass, is a good place to buy a memento of Scotland to treasure. Especially lovely are the paperweights with swirling colored patterns.

OFF THE   **SEA-LIFE CENTRE** – This outstanding place for children (and adults) offers a
BEATEN PATH   fascinating display of marine life, including shoals of herring, sharks, rays, catfish, and seals. To get there, drive south from Glencoe village on A828. ⊠ *Barcaldine, Connel, Argyll,* ☎ *01631/720386,* FAX *01631/720529.* 🎫 *£4.75.* ☉ *Mid-Feb.–Nov., daily 9–6 (until 7, July and Aug.).*

NEED A BREAK? The **restaurant** at the Sea-Life Centre (✉ Barcaldine, ☎ 01631/720386) offers morning coffee with homemade scones; a full lunch menu, which might include homemade soup, fish pie, baked potatoes with various fillings, or oysters; and afternoon teas.

Taynuilt

12 mi east of Oban.

❸ At Taynuilt, the **Bonawe Iron Furnace** is signposted. No industrial activity takes place there now, but once the peaceful wooded slopes overlooked the smoky glow of furnaces burning local timber to make charcoal. The furnaces played a central role in the iron-smelting industry, which flourished here between 1753 and 1876. Today, Historic Scotland cares for the well-preserved buildings. ✉ *Bonawe,* ☎ *0131/ 668–8600.* ⌑ *£2.* ⊙ *Apr.–Sept., Mon.–Sat. 9:30–6, Sun. 2–6.*

★ ❹ Through the narrow Pass of Brander is the **Cruachan Dam Power Station Visitor Centre.** If you want to go underneath **Ben Cruachan,** the mountain seen from Dunstaffnage Castle, but lost to view at close proximity, stop at the visitor center for instructions. A horseshoe-shaped series of peaks, Ben Cruachan has a man-made dam within its confines. Water flows from the dam to Loch Awe, the loch on your right, turning turbines along the way. You can learn about this at the visitor center and on a ½-mile minibus trip down a tunnel into a huge cavern-cum-turbine hall. Be sure to take this trip, which will take you under several cubic miles of mountain. You will find the Visitor Centre off A85, 18 miles east of Oban. ☎ *01866/822673.* ⌑ *£2 adults.* ⊙ *Apr.–mid-Nov., daily 9–4:30.*

Dining and Lodging

$$$$ ★ ✕🏠 **Ardanaiseig House.** Set on the shores of Loch Awe and framed by rhododendron blossoms in May and June (the gardens are famous), this excellent, privately run hotel is worth the extra cost, especially when the rhododendrons are blooming. All the bedrooms, which vary in size, have been decorated individually in traditional style, and the public rooms, with an abundance of chintz and polished wood, are comfortable and inviting. The menu features five imaginative courses prepared with local ingredients. Home-smoked scallops, fresh fruit from the garden, pickled salmon, and wood pigeon are among the choices. ✉ *Kilchrenan, near Taynuilt, Argyll,* ☎ *01866/833333,* 🆇 *01866/833222. 14 rooms with bath. Restaurant. AE, DC, MC, V. Closed mid-Dec.–mid-Mar.*

Shopping

Inverawe Fisheries and Smokery (☎ 01866/822446; ⊙ smokery: mid-Mar.–Dec., weekdays 8:30–4; shop: daily 8–6:30; call ahead in winter) produces smoked salmon and other fish, to eat on the premises or take out. The fish may be impractical to take home, but it's delicious for picnics.

Lochawe

18 mi east of Oban.

Lochawe is a scattered loch-side community squeezed between the broad shoulder of Ben Cruachan and Loch Awe itself. The road gets busy in peak season, filled with people trying to park by Lochawe Station. Cruises on Loch Awe and to Kilchurn Castle start here, aboard the **Lady Rowena Steam Launch,** an Edwardian peat-fired steamboat. ☎ *01838/ 200440 or 01838/200449.* ⌑ *£3.75 per hour. Reservations can be made on the spot or in advance.*

★ ❺ Near Lochawe is **Kilchurn Castle,** a ruined fortress at the eastern end of Loch Awe. The castle was built by Sir Colin Campbell of Glenorchy in the 15th century and rebuilt in the 17th century. The Campbells had their original power base in this area. Park and cross the railway line, then walk across the grassy flats to the airy vantage points, complete with informative signs, amid the towers; from there you'll see more fine panoramas. ☎ *0131/668–8600.*

Near Dalmally, just east of Lochawe, the **Duncan Ban Macintyre Monument** was erected in honor of this Gaelic poet (1724–1812), sometimes referred to as the Robert Burns of the Highlands. The view from here is one of the finest in Argyll, taking in Ben Cruachan and the other peaks nearby, as well as Loch Awe and its scattering of islands. To find it, from Dalmally follow an old road running southwest toward the banks of Loch Awe. At the road's highest point, often called Monument Hill, you'll see the round, granite monument.

En Route The A819 between Lochawe and Inveraray initially runs alongside Loch Awe, the longest loch in Scotland, but soon leaves its pleasant banks, turning south to join the A83. The A83 carries traffic from Glasgow and Loch Lomond by way of the high pass of the Rest and Be Thankful. (Though Loch Lomond is not covered in this chapter, many visitors come up the loch and head west by the A83. The Rest and Be Thankful is perhaps its most scenic point—an aptly named, almost-Alpine pass among high green slopes and gray rocks.)

Inveraray

★ ❻ *21 mi south of Lochawe, 61 mi north of Glasgow, 29 mi west of Loch Lomond.*

On the approaches to Inveraray, note the ornate 18th-century bridgework that carries the road along the loch-side. This is the first sign that Inveraray is not just a higgledy-piggledy assembly of houses. In fact, much of Inveraray was designed as a planned town for the third Duke of Argyll, in the mid-18th century. The present Campbell duke's seat is **Inveraray Castle,** a grayish-green, turreted stone castle that can be seen through the trees on the right. Like Inveraray town, the castle was built around 1743. Much of this powerful family's history can be seen on a tour. ☎ *01499/302203.* ✑ *£4.* ۩ *July–Aug., Mon.–Sat. 10–5, Sun. 1–5; Apr.–June and Sept.–mid-Oct., Mon.–Thurs. and Sat. 10–12:30 and 2–5, Sun. 1–5.*

The **Combined Operations Museum** sits close to Inveraray Castle, a reminder that this sleepy place among the hills was an important wartime training area. ✉ *Cherry Park,* ☎ *01499/500218.* ✑ *£1.* ۩ *Apr.–June and Sept.–mid-Oct., Mon.–Thurs., Sat. 10–5:30, Sun. 1–5:30; July and Aug., Mon.–Sat. 10–5:30, Sun. 1–5:30 (last admission 5).*

The **Inveraray Jail** is one of the latest generation of visitor centers. The old town jail and courtroom now house realistic courtroom scenes, period cells, and much other paraphernalia that enable the visitor to glimpse life behind bars in Victorian times. There is also a Scottish crafts shop within the jail. ✉ *Inveraray,* ☎ *01499/302381.* ✑ *£3.95.* ۩ *Daily, Apr.–Oct. 9:30–6, Nov.–Mar. 10–5 (last admission 1 hr. before closing.)*

Also in Inveraray is the **Arctic Penguin,** a 1911 lightship and a rare example of a riveted iron vessel. She now houses exhibits and displays on the maritime heritage of the River Clyde and Scotland's west coast. ☎ *01499/302213.* ✑ *£2.50.* ۩ *Daily, Apr.–Oct. 10–6, Nov.–Mar. 10–5.*

Ardkinglas Woodland Garden is home to one of Britain's finest collections of conifers, set off by rhododendron blossoms in early summer. Find it around the head of Loch Fyne 12 miles east of Inveraray. ⊠ *Cairndow,* ☎ *01499/600263.* ☒ *£1.50.* ☉ *Daily, year-round.*

NEED A BREAK? The simple decor—wood-top tables and fittings—lets you concentrate on the seafood at the **Loch Fyne Oyster Bar** (⊠ A83, on the approach to Loch Fyne, ☎ 01499/600236). Local oysters and crisp white wine certainly are a far cry from roadside hamburgers and french fries.

★ **7** A reminder of the 18th-century lifestyle can be seen at the **Auchindrain Museum.** Formerly a communal tenancy farm, this 18th-century co-operative venture has been restored. The old bracken-thatched or iron-roofed buildings provide information about early farming life in the Highlands. There is also an interpretation center and shop. The farm is on the A83, 5½ miles south of Inveraray. ☎ 01499/500235. ☒ £2.50. ☉ Apr.–Sept., daily 10–5 (closed Sat. in Apr.).

★ **8** Well worth a visit are **Crarae Gardens,** which are occasionally likened to a wild valley in the Himalayas. Magnolias and azaleas give the area a moist and lush atmosphere, undoubtedly aided by the local rainfall. There are paths through the plantings that will suit hikers of every fitness level. The gardens lie off the A83, 10 miles southwest of Inveraray. ☎ 01546/886614 or 01546/886388. ☒ £2.50. ☉ Daily 9–6 (restricted to daylight hours in winter); visitor center open Easter–Oct.

Dining and Lodging

$$ ✕▣ **Creggans Inn.** This traditional inn overlooking Loch Fyne on its eastern shore, 21 miles from Inveraray, dates to the 17th century. Visitors can enjoy an appetizing lunch in the bar or a more formal dinner in the inn's attractive dining room, with views of the water. Once again, local produce and seafood, including Loch Fyne oysters, are staples on the menu. The bedrooms vary in size from large to rather small, all decorated in pastels. The staff is friendly and hospitable. ⊠ *Strachur, Argyll,* ☎ *01369/860279,* ℻ *01369/860637. 21 rooms, 19 with bath. Restaurant. AE, DC, MC, V.*

Lochgilphead

9 *25 mi south of Inveraray.*

Lochgilphead, the area's main town, is at its aesthetic best when the tide is in: **Loch Gilp,** really a bite out of Loch Fyne, reveals a muddy shoreline at low tide. However, the neat little town with its well-kept, colorful frontages along the main street is well worth a break in your travels.

10 The **Crinan Canal** was opened in 1801 to enable fishing vessels to avoid the long haul around the south-stretching Kintyre peninsula and reach the Hebridean fishing grounds more easily. At the western end of the canal it drops to the sea in a series of locks. This area can be a busy spot, with yachting enthusiasts strolling around and frequenting the coffee shop beside the Crinan Hotel. To reach Crinan, take the A816 Oban road north from Lochgilphead for slightly more than 2 miles and turn left.

11 To capture a glimpse of early Scottish history, visit **Dunadd Fort.** Follow a track to a rocky hump that rises out of the level ground around Crinan; you will find—by clambering up the rock—a basin, a footprint, and an outline of a boar carved on the smooth upper face of the knoll. This breezy refuge was once the capital of the early kingdom of Dalriada, founded by the first wave of Scots who migrated from Ireland. The fort is signed west off A816, 4 miles northwest of Lochgilphead. ☎ 0131/668–8600. ☒ Free. ☉ At all times.

A number of early monuments are located along the road between Dunadd and **Kilmartin** (a small village). At Kilmartin itself, there are finely carved medieval grave slabs and crosses. Keep a sharp lookout: from the road you can see a number of even earlier monuments—notably burial cairns and stone circles from the Bronze Age and earlier.

⑫ A tower house called **Carnasserie Castle** has the distinction of having belonged to the writer of the first book printed in Gaelic. The writer, John Carswell, bishop of the Isles, translated a text by the Scottish reformer, John Knox, into Gaelic and published it in 1567. The castle is off A816, 9 miles north of Lochgilphead. ☎ *0131/668–8600.* 🖼 *Free.* ☾ *At all times.*

Dining and Lodging

$$$$ ✕🖼 **Crinan Hotel.** This turn-of-the-century property, overlooking the
★   picturesque Crinan Canal and the Sound of Jura, has been extensively refurbished. Friendly and helpful, one of the owners is artist Frances Macdonald, who has put her artistic skills to great use in the interior design of the hotel. Two restaurants offer both Scottish cuisine and the freshest local seafood: **The Westward Room** serves dinner in a luxurious, country-mansion setting, where you are surrounded by antiques and floral arrangements; the rooftop **Lock 16** has a nautical theme, and superb sunsets accompany the award-winning fresh seafood. ✉ *Near Lochgilphead, PA31 8SR,* ☎ *01546/830261,* ⒻⒶⓍ *01546/830292. 22 rooms, 21 with bath, 1 with shower only. 2 restaurants (reservations essential; jacket and tie in Lock 16), coffee shop, boating, fishing. AE, DC, MC, V. Lock 16 closed Sun.–Mon.*

Outdoor Activities and Sports

HORSEBACK RIDING

Explorers can take off from **Castle Riding Centre and Argyll Trail Riding,** south of Lochgilphead, with highly qualified trail guides leading them along routes throughout Argyll; instruction in jumping and eventing is also offered here (✉ Brenfield, Ardrishaig, Argyll, ☎ 01546/ 603274, ⒻⒶⓍ 01546/603225).

Shopping

At the **Highbank Porcelain Pottery** (✉ Highbank Industrial Estate, Lochgilphead, ☎ 01546/602044), visitors can watch slip casting, hand painting, and firing, then buy the product at the shop (including reasonably priced seconds); the shop also stocks ceramic giftware from other potteries.

OFF THE
BEATEN PATH

CASTLE SWEEN – The oldest stone castle on the Scottish mainland (12th century) sits on a rocky sea edge, 15 miles southwest of Lochgilphead. The castle is reached by an unclassified road from Crinan, which offers outstanding views of the Paps of Jura across the sound. There are also some attractive white sand beaches here.

SEIL ISLAND – The bridge over the Atlantic leads to the island of Seil. This crossing is less spectacular than it sounds—the island is so close to the mainland that a single-span bridge, built in 1791, carries the road across. From Seil, visitors are ferried to neighboring Easdale Island. Once Easdale and Seil were known as the slate islands: Extensive quarrying for roofing materials was undertaken on both isles. The B844 leads to these islands, west off the A816 at Kilninver, 40 miles north of Lochgilphead, 17 miles south of Oban.

The Kintyre Peninsula

52 mi (to Campbeltown) south of Lochgilphead.

Tarbert, in Gaelic, means a place of portage—there are other Tarbe(r)ts scattered throughout the Highlands—and a glance at the map tells you why: This little town, with a fairly attractive waterfront, has grown up on the narrow neck of land between East and West Loch Tarbert. Long ago, boats were carried across the land to avoid going all the way around the peninsula.

❸ The **Island of Gigha** is a delectable Hebridean island, barely 5 miles long, sheltered in a frost-free, sea-warmed climate between Kintyre and Islay. The isle is noted for the **Achamore House Gardens.** It is possible to take the ferry from Tayinloan (a 20-minute trip), walk to the gardens, and return to the mainland, all on a short day trip. ☎ *01583/ 505254. Gardens: ☞ £2. ☉ Daily 10–dusk. Ferry: ☞ £4 per person; £15.50 cars, plus £4 per passenger. ☉ 8–12, 2–6, hourly on the hour; mid-Oct.–Apr. 8–12, 1– 5.*

Campbeltown is a fairly substantial town with whisky distilling and fishing among its day-to-day activities. It has a reasonable choice of shops—so don't feel you have to stock up on items, such as film, farther up the peninsula.

Famous in song, the **Mull of Kintyre** is, in reality, a narrow road to the lighthouse beyond Campbeltown at the tip of Kintyre. The road crosses moors and sheep pastures. There is a parking place before the road suddenly dips to reach the lighthouse tower, which is well down the steep slope that tilts toward the sea. Do not go down the hill; the best sunset views are from the adjacent moors, from which you can see Ireland clearly.

Outdoor Activities and Sports

GOLF

Machrihanish, near Campbeltown, is the most famous golf course in this area, and deservedly popular; book well ahead, especially for weekends (☎ 01586/810213; 18 holes, 6,228 yards, SSS 70).

Shopping

Campbeltown is the center for local shopping on the Kintyre peninsula; here you will find **Oystercatcher Crafts and Gallery** (✉ 10 Hall St. and 2–4 Main St., ☎ 01586/553070), with original paintings, wood carvings, gifts, and cards.

A few miles north of Campbeltown, at Carradale, is **Wallis Hunter Design** (✉ The Steading, ☎ 01583/431683), which makes gold and silver jewelry. Clachan is the home of **Ronachan Silks** (✉ Ronachan Farmhouse, ☎ 01880/740242), which produces distinctive jewel-colored scarves, cushion covers, kimonos, and caftans.

ARRAN

Many Scots, especially those from Glasgow and the west, are well disposed toward Arran, which reminds them of unhurried childhood holidays. In fact, some of its cafés and boarding houses still exude a 1950s mood—a pleasant reminder of the days when Scots all took their holidays in Scotland. Only a few decades ago, the Clyde estuary was the coastal playground for the majority of the populace living in Glasgow and along the Clydeside. Their annual holiday comprised a trip by steamer to any one of a number of Clyde coast resorts, known as going *doon the watter* (down the water, the estuary of the Clyde). Today the masses go to Spain, but, as with other parts of the Clyde, the island of Arran has for a long time been associated with the healthy outdoor life.

To get to Arran, take the ferry from Ardrossan. During the ride, stroll on deck and note the number of fellow travelers wearing hiking boots. They're ready for the delights of Goat Fell, an impressive peak (2,868 ft) that gives the island one of the most distinctive profiles of any in Scotland. The cone of Goat Fell and its satellites serves as an eye-catching backdrop to the northwest, as the ferry approaches Brodick. As you will have seen while crossing, the southern half of Arran is less mountainous: The Highland Boundary Fault crosses just to the north of Brodick Bay.

Exploring on Arran is easy: the A841 road encircles the island and makes it difficult to get lost.

Brodick

⑭ *1 hour by ferry from Ardrossan.*

The largest township on the island, Brodick is really just a village, with a frontage spaciously set back from a promenade and beach.

⑮ Brodick is the site of the **Isle of Arran Heritage Museum,** which documents the life of the island from ancient times to the present century. A number of buildings, including a cottage and *smiddy* (blacksmith's), have period furnishings and displays on prehistoric life, geology, farming, fishing, and many other aspects of the island's heritage. ⊠ *Rosaburn, Brodick,* ☎ *01770/302636.* 🔄 *£1.50.* ☉ *Apr.–Oct., Mon.–Sat. 10–5.*

In **Glen Rosa,** visitors can walk through a long glen that offers a glimpse of the wild ridges that call so many outdoor enthusiasts to the island. To get there, go just beyond the Isle of Arran Heritage Museum and find the junction where the String Road cuts across the island. Drive up the String Road a short way to a signpost and turn right into the glen. The road soon becomes undrivable, but park the car and walk a little way up the glen.

★ **⑯** Arran's most important draw for those other than the outdoor enthusiasts is **Brodick Castle and Country Park,** on the north side of Brodick Bay, its red sandstone cosseted by trees and parkland. Now under the auspices of the National Trust for Scotland, this former seat of the dukes of Hamilton has a number of rooms open to the public. The furniture, paintings, silver, and sporting trophies are opulent in their own right, but the real attraction is the garden with its brilliantly colored rhododendrons, particularly in late spring and early summer. Though there are many unusual varieties, you will find the ordinary yellow variety unmatched for its scent: Your initial encounter with them is comparable to hitting a wall of perfume. The castle stands 1½ miles north of Brodick pier. ☎ *01770/302202.* 🔄 *£4.10.* ☉ *Easter–Oct., daily 11:30–5 (last admission 4:30). Garden and country park open year-round, daily 9:30–sunset.*

NEED A
BREAK?

In the **Servant's Hall** at Brodick Castle, an award-winning restaurant (open 11–5) serves morning coffee (with six different types of hot scones—try the date and walnut!), a full lunch menu that changes daily (venison casserole or salmon steaks might be available), and afternoon teas with home-baked goods, including the bread. Eat out on the terrace on a fine day, with chaffinches clamoring for crumbs.

A pleasant walk to **Corriegills** offers fine views over Brodick Bay. It is signed from the A841 just to the south of Brodick.

Dining and Lodging

$$–$$$
★
✕▥ Kilmichael Country House Hotel. At the head of Glen Cloy, just outside Brodick, is this 300-year-old mansion, built by the Fullerton family on land granted to them by Robert the Bruce. Now an outstanding small hotel, it is furnished in Georgian oak antiques, Sanderson fabrics, and light, sunny colors. At one end of the blue-and-yellow sitting room, in what was once a private chapel, is a stained-glass window showing the Fullerton family crest. Cuisine in the hotel's restaurant is also exceptional: Salmon en croute with dill sauce, duck with kumquats, and salad of pigeon with walnuts and smoked bacon, are examples of the marriage of fresh Scottish produce and international flair. ✉ *Brodick, Isle of Arran, KA27 8BY,* ☎ *01770/302219,* ℻ *01770/302068. 9 rooms with bath. Restaurant (reservations essential; jacket and tie). MC, V. Closed Nov., Dec.*

Outdoor Activities and Sports

BICYCLING

Rent bicycles from **Brodick Boat and Cycle Hire** (✉ The Beach, ☎ 01770/302009) or **Brodick Cycles** (✉ Opposite Village Hall, ☎ 01770/302460).

HORSEBACK RIDING

Explore Arran on horseback with **Cloyburn Trekking Centre** (✉ Brodick, Arran, ☎ 01770/302108).

Shopping

Arran's shops are particularly well stocked with island-produced goods. **Duchess Court Shops** (✉ The Pier, Brodick, ☎ 01770/302831) include **Something Special** for scented items such as candles, as well as glass ornaments and designer pottery; **The Home Farm Kitchen Shop** for locally made mustards and other preserves, together with kitchenware; and **The Nature Shop** for nature-oriented books and gifts.

Lamlash

⑰ *4 mi south of Brodick.*

Lamlash, with views offshore to steep-flanked Holy Island, has a breezy seaside holiday atmosphere—like the whole island. To reach the highest point accessible by car on the island, go through the village and turn right beside the bridge, onto **Ross Road,** which climbs steeply from a thickly planted valley, Glen Scorrodale, and yields fine views of Lamlash Bay.

Shopping

Patterson Arran Ltd. (✉ The Old Mill, Lamlash, ☎ 01770/600606) is famous for its mustards, preserves, and marmalades.

Lagg

⑱ *10 mi southwest of Lamlash via the Ross Road.*

Lagg, a little community in a hollow beneath the sheltering trees, sits peacefully by the banks of the Kilmory Water.

NEED A
BREAK?
The **Lagg Hotel** (☎ 01770/870255; closed Nov.–Feb.), an inn since 1791, is a warm place offering appetizing buffet lunches on Sunday, and excellent bar lunches and evening meals the rest of the week.

En Route Continuing east on the A841 along the bottom end of the island, past white-painted farmhouses and cottages, there are views across gently tilting fields to the steep hump of Ailsa Craig, offshore in the Firth of Clyde. Cheese connoisseurs will be pleased to know the creamery at

Torrylinn makes Arran Cheddar from local milk. Beyond Kildonan the road twists north; the trees extend to the sea edge, where gannets seem to dive through the branches.

Whiting Bay

⑲ *9 mi east of Lagg.*

Whiting Bay has a string of hotels and well-kept property along the seafront.

Outdoor Activities and Sports

BICYCLING

Rent bicycles from **Whiting Bay Cycle Hire** (☎ 01770/700382).

Shopping

Crafts of Arran (✉ Whiting Bay, ☎ 01770/700251) prides itself on stocking crafts produced in Arran.

En Route   Northward from Brodick the road is built along a raised beach platform, a common phenomenon in Scotland, caused by the lifting of the land after its burden of ice melted at the end of the Ice Age. Large, round boulders rest on softer sandstones in certain places on the shore. These stones, called *erratics,* were once carried by glaciers off the granite mountains that loom in the distance to your left, as you approach Corrie.

Corrie

6 mi north of Brodick.

Corrie is a sparse, spread-out settlement with stores that sell the ubiquitous pottery and crafts items.

Outdoor Activities and Sports

BICYCLING

Rent bicycles from **Spinning Wheels** (✉ The Trossachs, Corrie, ☎ 01770/810640).

Shopping

Corriecraft and Antiques (✉ Corrie, ☎ 01770/810661) sells crafts (though they may come from different parts of Scotland), together with a carefully chosen mix of small antiques and curios.

Sannox

⑳ *2 mi north of Corrie.*

At Sannox, a locale consisting of another cluster of houses, there is a sandy bay of ground granite, washed down from the mountainous interior. There are also outstanding views of the rugged hills of the interior, particularly the steep pyramid of **Cir Mhor.** You can enjoy a good coastal walk from North Sannox.

Lochranza

㉑ *6 mi north of Sannox.*

The attractively situated settlement of Lochranza is one more community that focuses on crafts. It is sheltered by the bay of Loch Ranza, which spills in shallows up the flat-bottomed glacial glen. The village is set off by a picturesque ruin: **Lochranza Castle,** situated on a low sand spit. It's said to have been the landing place of Robert the Bruce, who returned from Rathlin Island in 1307 to start the campaign that won Scotland's independence. ☎ 0131/668–8600. ✉ *Free.* ☉ *Apr.–Sept., Mon.–Sat. 9:30–6, Sun. 2–6; Oct.–Mar., Mon.–Sat. 9:30–4, Sun. 2–4.*

South of Lochranza, the raised beach backed by a cliff continues to make a scenic platform for the road. There are fine views across the Kilbrannan Sound to the long rolling horizon of Kintyre. At **Catacol,** immediately after the Catacol Bay Hotel, sit the **Twelve Apostles,** a row of fishermen's houses, identical except for differences in the window shapes (so they can be recognized from offshore).

Machrie

11 mi south of Lochranza.

Near the scattered homesteads of Machrie—which has a popular beach—a Historic Scotland sign points to the **Machrie Moor Stone Circles,** which are just about 1 mile farther along, although on foot it feels a bit more than that. A well-surfaced track will take you to a grassy moor by a ruined farm, where you will see small, rounded, granite-boulder circles and much taller, eerie, red-sandstone monoliths. The lost and lonely stones out in the bare moor are very atmospheric and well worth a walk to see, if you like solitude. The Machrie area is littered with these sites: chambered cairns, hut circles, and standing stones dating from the Bronze Age.

Outdoor Activities and Sports
HORSEBACK RIDING
Enjoy guided rides on a mount from **Cairnhouse Riding Centre** (⊠ Blackwaterfoot, Arran, ☎ 01770/860466).

Shopping
The **Old Byre Showroom** (⊠ Auchencar Farm, ☎ 01770/840227) sells sheepskin goods, locally hand-knit "jumpers" (sweaters), leather goods, and tweeds.

En Route   Continuing to Blackwaterfoot, you can return to Brodick by the String Road; turn left by the Kinloch Hotel, up the hill. There are more fine views of the granite complexities of Arran's hills: gray notched ridges beyond brown moor and, past the watershed, a vista of Brodick Bay. From this high point the road rolls down to Brodick.

ISLAY AND JURA

Islay has a personality distinct from that of the rest of the Hebrides. The western half, in particular, has large farms rather than crofts. Many of Islay's best beaches—as well as wildlife and historical preserves—are also in its western half, in contrast to the southeast area, which is mainly an extension of Jura's inhospitable quartzite hills. A number of distilleries—the source of the island's delectable malt whiskies—provide jobs for the locals. Islay is also known for its wildlife, especially its birds, including the rare chough—a crow with red legs and beak—and, in winter, its barnacle geese.

Although it is possible to meet an Islay native in a local pub, such an event is statistically less likely on Jura, with its one road, one distillery, one hotel, and six sporting estates. In fact, visitors have a better chance of bumping into one of the island's 5,000 red deer, which outnumber the human population by at least 20 to one. The island has a much more rugged look than Islay, with its profiles of the Paps of Jura, a hill range at its most impressive when basking in the rays of a west-coast sunset.

Bowmore, Islay

24 *11 mi north of Port Ellen.*

The town of Bowmore is compact and about the same size (population 1,000) as the ferry port of Port Ellen, but slightly better suited as a base for touring. Bowmore, which gives its name to the whisky made in the distillery (founded 1779) by the shore, is a tidy town. Its grid pattern was laid out in 1768 by the local landowner Daniel Campbell of Shawfield. Bowmore's Main Street stretches from the pier head to the commanding parish church, built in 1767 in an unusual circular design—so the devil could not find a corner to hide in. The town has a selection of accommodations and restaurants despite its small size.

NEED A BREAK?
Rub elbows with the locals at the **Harbour Inn** (⊠ Main St., ☎ 01496/810330), with its cheerfully noisy and cramped public bar frequented by off-duty distillery workers who are happy to exchange island gossip. The excellent restaurant serves lunch 12–2, high tea 5–7, and dinner 7–9 (closed Sun.).

Shopping

On Islay you'll be spoiled by the sheer number of distilleries from which to choose a holiday purchase. Their delicious products, characterized by a peaty taste, can be purchased at off-license shops on the island, at local pubs, or at those distilleries that have shops. Most of them welcome visitors by appointment:

Bowmore (⊠ School St., Bowmore, ☎ 01496/810441). **Bunnahabhain** (⊠ Port Askaig, ☎ 01496/840646). **Caol Ila** (⊠ Port Askaig, ☎ 01496/840207). **Isle of Jura** (⊠ Craighouse, Jura, ☎ 01496/820240). **Lagavoulin** (⊠ Port Ellen, ☎ 01496/302250). **Laphroaig** (⊠ Port Ellen, ☎ 01496/302418).

En Route   Traveling north out of Bowmore (signposted Bridgend), the road skirts the sand flats at the head of Loch Indaal. To reach Port Charlotte, follow the loch shores all the way past Bruichladdich which, like Bowmore, is the name of a malt whisky, as well as a village with a distillery.

Port Charlotte

25 *11 mi west of Bowmore via A846/A847.*

At Port Charlotte, above the road on the right, in a converted kirk (church), is the **Museum of Islay Life,** a haphazard but authentic and informative display of times past. ☎ *01496/850358.* ⌑ *£1.75.* ☉ *Apr.–Oct., Mon.–Sat. 10–5, Sun. 2–5.*

From Port Charlotte a loop road allows for further exploration into the wilder landscape of the **Rhinns of Islay.** At the southern end are the scattered cottages of **Portnahaven** and its twin, **Port Wemyss.** To reach them, take the A847 south from Port Charlotte. You can return by the bleak, unclassified road that loops westward and passes by the recumbent stone circle at Coultoon and the chapel at Kilchiaran, before reaching Port Charlotte.

En Route   To get a glimpse of Islay's peerless western seascapes, make a left onto the B8018, north of Bruichladdich. After 2 miles, turn left again onto a little road that meanders past Loch Gorm and ends close to Machir Bay and its superb (and probably deserted) sandy beach. Soon after you turn around to go back, make a right, which will lead you to the derelict kirk of Kilchoman. In the kirkyard are some interesting grave slabs and two crosses of late-medieval times, from the Iona school of carving. (There was another Scottish "school" in Kintyre.) They are an excellent introduction to the island's wealth of stone carvings. From Kilchoman turn right and then left to circle Loch Gorm, pausing as the road all but touches the coast at Saligo. It's worth a stroll (beyond the former wartime camp) to enjoy the view of some fine seascapes, especially if the westerlies are piling up high breakers on the rock ridges. On the return journey east, turn right at the B8018, then left on the B8017. Take a left at Aoradh Farm onto a minor road that runs north along the west side of Loch Gruinart.

Loch Gruinart

26 *7 mi northeast of Port Charlotte, 8 mi north of Bowmore.*

Visitors are inevitably drawn to the long reaches of Loch Gruinart. Dunes flank its sea outlet, and pale beaches rise out of the falling tides. Traveling north up its western shore, the road soon brings you to **Cill Naoimh** (Kilnave). Kilnave's ruined chapel is associated with a dark tale in which a group of wounded Maclean clansmen were defeated in a nearby battle with the MacDonalds in 1598. The Macleans sought sanctuary in the chapel; their pursuers set its roof aflame, and the clansmen perished within. In the graveyard is a weathered 8th-century carved cross.

For those who appreciate wide skies, crashing waves, and lonely coast, the best view of Loch Gruinart is northwards up its eastern shore. From the far dunes of the headland, held together with marram grass, there are views of the islands of **Colonsay** and **Oronsay** across Hebridean waters, on which plumes and fans of white spray rise from hidden reefs. The **priory** on the island of Oronsay, with its famous carved cross, is barely distinguishable. To experience this peerless scenery, return to the B8017 from visiting Kilnave, cross the flats at the head of the loch, and then go left up its eastern shore. Park before a gate, where the road deteriorates, and continue on foot.

The Oa

27 *13 mi south of Bowmore; take the long straight of the A846 that passes the island airport just inland from the endless sandy curve of Laggan Bay. Before you reach Port Ellen, go straight ahead to a minor road to Imeraval, then make a right at a junction and then a left.*

The southern peninsula of The Oa is a region of caves rich in tales of smuggling. At its tip, the Mull of Oa, there is a monument recalling the 650 men who lost their lives when the troopships *Tuscania* and *Otranto* went down nearby in 1918.

Port Ellen

28 *11 mi south of Bowmore.*

The sturdy community of Port Ellen was founded in the 1820s, with much of its architecture still dating to the 19th century. It has a harbor, a few shops, and some inns, but not enough commercial development to mortgage its personality.

The road eastward from Port Ellen passes communities bearing several more names known to the malt-whisky connoisseur: the whisky of the **Laphroaig distillery**—which offers tours—is perhaps one of the most distinctive of the local whiskies, with a tangy, peaty, seaweed/iodine flavor. This distillery is 1½ miles along the road to Ardbeg from Port Ellen. ☎ *01496/302418 or 01496/302393.* 🖅 *Free.* ☉ *Tours by appointment.*

From Port Ellen, it is also possible to experience one of the highlights of Scotland's Celtic heritage. Passing through a pleasantly rolling, partly wooded landscape northeastward, take a narrow road signposted from Ardbeg. This leads to a ruined chapel with surrounding kirkyard, in which stands the finest carved cross anywhere in Scotland: the 8th-century **Kildalton Cross.** Carved from a single slab of epidiorite rock, this ringed cross is encrusted on both sides with elaborate designs in the style of the Iona school. Interesting early grave slabs from the 12th and 13th centuries can also be seen in the kirkyard.

★ ㉙

Outdoor Activities and Sports
HORSEBACK RIDING

Ballivicar Pony Trekking (✉ Ballivicar Farm, Port Ellen, ☎ 01496/ 302251) takes riders on trips along nearby beaches and into the surrounding countryside.

Bridgend

3 mi north of Bowmore via A846 (follow signs for Port Askaig).

Bridgend itself is a tiny little community beside the main road, but hardly a mile beyond is a sign for the **Islay Woollen Mill** (☞ Shopping, *below*). Set in a wooded hollow by the river, the mill has a fascinating selection of working machinery to inspect.

★ ㉚

Shopping
The **Islay Woollen Mill** has a shop selling high-quality products that are woven on site. Beside the usual tweed lengths, there is a distinctive range of hats, caps, and clothing made from the mill's own cloth. ✉ *Bridgend,* ☎ *01496/810563,* 🖃 *Free.* ☼ *Year-round, Mon.–Fri. 10– 5; also Easter–Sept., Sat. 10–5.*

Loch Finlaggan

㉛ *7 mi northeast of Bridgend; take a side road (to the left) 1 mi beyond Ballygrant, then drive through a gate.*

At first sight, there is not a great deal to see at Loch Finlaggan. But the little island on the loch, with its scanty traces of early buildings, was the council seat of the Lords of the Isles. This former western power base of the Clan Donald threatened the sovereignty of the Stewart monarchs of Scotland in its heyday; the ruins are a reminder of how independent the Highlands were in those times. A cottage interpretative center is located nearby, with an exhibition relating to the ongoing excavations of the island ruins. ☎ *01496/840644.* 🖃 *Small fee.* ☼ *Apr.–Sept., Sun., Tues., and Thurs. 2:30–5.*

Lodging
$$ ▥ **Kilmeny Farmhouse.** There are fine views over the surrounding countryside from this white-painted traditional farmhouse, also on a working farm. It offers bed-and-breakfast accommodations with an evening meal, if desired. Home baking and homemade preserves make breakfast special. ✉ *Ballygrant, Isle of Islay, PA45 7QW,* ☎ 🖾 *01496/840668. 3 rooms with bath and shower. No credit cards. Closed Dec. 25, Jan. 1.*

Port Askaig

3 mi northeast of Loch Finlaggan via A846.

Tiny Port Askaig is the ferry port for Jura; it is just a cluster of cottages by the pier. Uphill, just outside the village, a side road travels along the coast, giving impressive views of Jura on the way. At the road end, the **Bunnahabhain Distillery** (☎ 01496/840646, visits by appointment) sits on an attractive shore site.

Dining and Lodging

$$ ✕⚑ **Port Askaig Hotel.** This modernized drovers' inn by the roadside, with grounds extending to the shore, overlooks the Sound of Islay and the island of Jura and is conveniently located near the ferry terminal. Accommodations are comfortable without being luxurious, and the food is well prepared, using homegrown produce, but not very imaginative. ✉ *Port Askaig, Isle of Islay, Argyll, PA46 7RD,* ☎ *01496/840245,* FAX *01496/840295. 8 rooms, 6 with bath. Restaurant, 2 bars. No credit cards.*

Jura

5 minutes by ferry from Port Askaig.

Having crossed the Sound of Islay, explorers will find it easy to choose which road to take—Jura only has one. Apart from the initial stretch it is all single-lane. The A846 starts off below one of the many raised beaches, then climbs across poor moorland, providing scenic views across the Sound of Jura. The ruined **Claig Castle,** on an island just offshore, was built by the Lords of the Isles to control the sound. Beyond the farm buildings of Ardfin is **Jura House** in the woodlands, with its sheltered garden walks and fine views. Teas are available in the summer season on weekdays, 10–4. ☎ *01496/820315.* 🎫 *Gardens: £2.* ⊘ *Daily 9–5.*

Beyond Jura House the road turns northward across open moorland with scattered forestry blocks and the faint evidence, in the shape of parallel ridges, of the original inhabitants' lazy beds or strip cultivation. The original settlements were cleared with the other parts of the Highlands when the island became more of a sheep pasture and deer forest. ㉜ The community of **Craighouse** is home to the island's only distillery.

The aptly named **Small Isles Bay** has a superb strip of beach to the north of Craighouse. As the road climbs away from the bay, the little cottage above the creek is a reminder of the history of this island: The cottage is the only survivor of a village with a population of 56 that was destroyed in 1841. Ironically, a sheep *fank* (fold) farther up the creek shows what happened to the stones of the demolished cottages. Although the landscapes of Jura seem devoid of life, they are, in fact, populated with many ghosts, most of which are missed by the casual visitor.

Beyond the River Corran the road climbs, offering austere views of the Paps, with their long quartzite screes, and of the fine, though usually deserted, anchorage in the scoop of **Lowlandman's Bay.** The next section of road is more hemmed in and runs to **Lagg,** formerly a ferry-crossing point on the old cattle-driving road between here and Feolin. Beyond Lagg, the sea views are blocked by conifer plantings. Views of fjordlike **Loch Tarbert,** westward to the left, are at their best beside the forestry plantation a little farther on. At this point the road leads through a stretch of rough, uninhabited landscape. A gate and cattle grid by **Ardlussa** to the north mark the start of a Site of Special Scientific Interest in a shady oak wood. The coast here is rocky and unspoiled. Choose your own picnic site, but be sure to park sensibly: the road is very narrow. Yellow flag (a Scottish iris), bracken, strands of crisp seaweed on the salty grass, and background birdsong from the mossy woods make this an idyllic stretch when the sun shines. Try not to be too loud, so you won't distract the area's resident otter population.

The last house you will see is at **Lealt,** where you cross the river. Shortly beyond this point the tarmac ends rather abruptly, with a turning

space cut into the hill. Ordinary cars should not attempt to go any farther on the remainder of this trail, though Jeeps, Rovers, and other high-
clearance vehicles can make it through. With an ordinary car, you have
no choice but to retrace your route to the ferry pier. The track beyond
the surfaced road continues for another 5 miles to **Kinuachdrach,** a settlement that once served as a crossing point to Scarba and the mainland. The coastal footpath to Corryvreckan lies beyond, over the bare
moors. This area has two enticements: The first, for fans of George
Orwell, is the house of **Barnhill,** where the author wrote *1984;* the second, for wilderness enthusiasts, is the whirlpool of the **Corryvreckan**
and the unspoiled coastal scenery.

Dining and Lodging

$$–$$$ ✕🏠 **Jura Hotel.** In spite of its monopoly, this hotel set in pleasant gar-
dens genuinely welcomes its guests and can be relied on for high-quality accommodations and food. ✉ *Craighouse, PA60 7XU,* ☎ *01496/
820243,* 🗚 *01496/820249. 17 rooms, 11 with bath/shower. Restaurant. AE, DC, MC, V.*

THE ISLE OF MULL

It's possible to spend a long weekend on Mull and not meet a single
resident who was born north of Manchester, England. Though Mull
certainly has an indigenous population, the island is often referred to
as the Officers' Mess because of its popularity with retired military personnel. It has a thriving tourist industry, with several thousand visitors per year making their way across the Ross of Mull to Iona, cradle
of Scottish Christianity and ancient burial site of the kings of Scotland.

Craignure

㉝ *40-minute ferry crossing from Oban (bookable), 15-minute ferry crossing (to Fishnish 5 mi northwest of Craignure, summer-only service, first-
come, first-served) from Lochaline.*

Craignure, little more than a pier with some houses, is close to Mull's
two best-known castles, Torosay and Duart.

★ **㉞** **Torosay Castle** is probably more fun than Duart Castle, and it also has
the novelty of a steam-and-diesel service on a narrow-gauge railway,
which takes 20 minutes to run from the pier at Craignure to Torosay's
grounds. Scottish baronial in style, Torosay has a friendly air. Visitors
have the run of much of the house, which is full of intrigue and humor
by way of idiosyncratic information boards and informal family albums.
The main feature of the castle's gardens—a gentle blend of formal and
informal—is its Italian statue walk. The castle is off the A849, 1½ miles
southeast of Craignure. ☎ *01680/812421.* 🎟 *Castle and gardens £3.50;
gardens £2.* ⊙ *Castle: Easter–mid-Oct., daily 10:30–5:30 (last admission 5); gardens: summer, daily 9–7; winter, daily sunrise–sunset.*

㉟ The energetic can walk along the shore from Torosay to **Duart Castle.**
This ancient Maclean seat was ruined by the Campbells in 1691 but
bought and restored by Sir Fitzroy Maclean in 1911. If you're driving
to Duart, use the A849, then turn off left round the shore of Duart
Bay. ☎ *01680/812309.* 🎟 *£3.30.* ⊙ *May–mid-Oct., daily 10:30–6
(Tearoom closes Sept. 30).*

En Route   Traveling from Craignure to Fionnphort, the double-lane road narrows
as it goes southwest, touched by sea inlets at Lochs Don and Spelve.
Gray and green are the most prevalent colors of the interior, with
vivid grass and high rock faces in Glen More. These stepped-rock
faces, the by-product of ancient lava flows, reach their highest point

in Ben More, the only island *munro* outside Skye. (A munro is a Scottish mountain over 3,000 ft high.) Its high, bald slopes are prominent by the time you reach the road junction at the head of Loch Scridain. Stay on the A849 for a pleasant drive the length of the Ross of Mull, a wide promontory with scattered settlements. There are good views to the right of the dramatic cliff ramparts of Ardmeanach, the stubbier promontory to the north: The National Trust for Scotland cares for the rugged stretch of coast known as The Burg, which is home to a 40 million-year-old fossil tree (at the end of a long walk from the B8035, signposted left off the A849). The A849 continues through the village of Bunessan and eventually ends in a long parking lot opposite the houses of Fionnphort.

Fionnphort

36 mi west of Craignure.

The vast parking space at the small village of Fionnphort is made necessary by the popularity of the nearby island of Iona, which does not allow cars. Ferry service is frequent in summer months.

Iona

★ **36** *5 minutes by ferry from Fionnphort.*

The fiery and argumentative Irish monk, Columba, chose Iona for the site of a monastery in AD 563 because it was the first place he landed from which he could not see Ireland. Christianity had been brought to Scotland (Galloway) by Saint Ninian in 397, but until Saint Columba's church was founded, the word had not spread widely among the ancient northerners, called Picts. Iona was the burial place of the kings of Scotland until the 11th century. It survived repeated Norse sackings and finally fell into disuse around the time of the Reformation. Restoration work began at the turn of this century, and later, in 1938, the **Iona Community** was founded. Today the restored buildings serve as a spiritual center under the jurisdiction of the Church of Scotland. The ambience of the complex is a curious amalgam of the ancient and the earnest. But beyond the restored cloisters the most mystifying aspect of all is the island's ability to absorb visitors and still feel peaceful—a phenomenon often remarked upon by tourists; most people only make the short walk from the ferry pier by way of the nunnery to the abbey. ☎ *01681/700404. ⊙ Abbey gift and bookshop: Mon.–Sat. 10–5, Sun. noon–4; abbey coffeehouse: Apr.–Oct., Mon.–Thurs. and Sat. 11–4:30, Fri. and Sun. noon–4:30.*

Shopping

Iona has one or two pleasant surprises for shoppers, the biggest being **The Old Printing Press Bookshop** (⊠ St. Columba Hotel, ☎ 01681/700304), an excellent antiquarian and secondhand bookshop. The shop at the **Abbey** (☎ 01681/700404) is also worth a visit for its selection of Celtic-inspired gift items.

Carsaig

19 mi east of Fionnphort via A849 and an unclassified road; look for a sign on the right to Carsaig as you approach the head of Loch Scridain.

On your return to Mull, retrace your route eastward, then turn south for a side trip to the remote south coast. From the pier head at the tiny settlement of **Carsaig,** a rough path meanders west below lava cliffs to the impressive **Carsaig Arches.** Taking on the arches is a separate excursion reserved for the agile.

En Route   From the B8035 at Loch Scridain, the road rises away from the loch to the conifer plantations and green slopes of Gleann Seilisdeir. The main road through the glen breaches the stepped cliffs and drops to the shore, offering inspiring views of the island of Ulva guarding Loch na Keil. This stretch of the B8035, with splinters of rock from the heights strewn over it in places, feels remote. The high ledges eventually give way (not literally) to vistas of the screes of Ben More. Continue to skirt the coast by way of the B8073, and you will enjoy a succession of fine coastal views with Ulva in the foreground. Beyond Calgary Bay the landscape is gentler, as the road leads to the village of Dervaig.

Dervaig

37   *42 mi north of Carsaig, 27 mi northwest of Craignure.*

Just before the village of Dervaig, the **Old Byre Heritage Centre** is signposted. An audiovisual presentation on the history of Mull plays here; there is also a crafts shop. ⊠ *Dervaig,* ☎ *01688/400229.* 🎟 *£2.* ☉ *Easter–Oct., daily 10:30–6:30 (last admission 6); AV plays every hr on the half hr.*

NEED A   The wholesome catering at the restaurant at the **Old Byre Heritage Centre**
BREAK?   (⊠ Dervaig, ☎ 01688/400229) certainly will be appreciated by weary travelers, particularly those who enjoy thick and hearty homemade soups.

In Dervaig the Mull Little Theatre (☞ The Arts, *below*) offers a varied program and claims the record as the smallest professional theater in the United Kingdom.

Dining and Lodging

$$–$$$ ✕🏠 **Druimard Country House.** From this attractive Victorian house on the outskirts of the village, there are loch and glen views over the River Bellart. The restaurant is elegantly furnished and offers an original menu with several vegetarian options. Local prawns sautéed with mushrooms in a wine-and-cream sauce, and Argyll lamb with red-wine-and-rosemary sauce and apricot chutney tartlets, are two popular dishes. Rooms are individually decorated with Laura Ashley wallpaper and fabrics, and antique Victorian oak or mahogany furniture. Bed-and-breakfast accommodations are available. ⊠ *Dervaig, Isle of Mull, Argyll, PA75 6QW,* ☎ 𝔽𝔸𝕏 *01688/400345. 6 rooms with bath/shower. Restaurant. MC, V. Closed Nov.–Mar.*

The Arts
THEATER
Mull Little Theatre (⊠ Dervaig, Isle of Mull, ☎ 01688/400267) is Britain's smallest professional playhouse (43 seats) and presents a number of productions throughout the season.

Tobermory

38   *5 mi east of Dervaig.*

Founded as a fishing station, Tobermory gradually declined, hastened by the arrival of the railroad station at Oban, which took away fishing traffic. However, the brightly painted crescent of 18th-century buildings around the harbor, which is now a popular mooring with yachtsmen, gives Tobermory a Mediterranean look.

Dining and Lodging

$$$ ✕⊞ **Strongarbh House.** A stone-built Victorian house with attractive gardens, Strongarbh is decorated throughout in restful pastel shades, with a pleasing blend of modern and antique furniture. Two bedrooms have superb views over Tobermory Bay; the other two overlook the gardens. Seafood reigns supreme in the restaurant: local prawns, lobster, oysters, scallops, halibut, turbot—all imaginatively prepared in palate-stimulating style. (There are also alternative dishes for seafood phobics.) Gourmet seafood weekends are held throughout the year. ⊠ *Tobermory, Isle of Mull, Argyll, PA75 6PR,* ☎ *01688/302328. 4 rooms with bath and shower. Restaurant. MC, V.*

$$ ✕⊞ **Tobermory Hotel.** This 18th-century building by the quay on the northeastern tip of the island of Mull commands superb views. The ambience is crisp and bright, plants dot every windowsill, and rooms are spacious and sunny (weather permitting, of course). ⊠ *Tobermory, Isle of Mull, Argyll, PA75 6NT,* ☎ *01688/302091,* ℻ *01688/302254. 17 rooms, 9 with bath or shower. Restaurant. MC, V.*

Outdoor Activities and Sports

BICYCLING

Rent bicycles from **On Yer Bike** (⊠ Salen, Aros, Isle of Mull, ☎ 01680/300501. ☉ Easter–Nov.).

En Route The route to the ferry lies southward on the A848, which yields pleasant, though unspectacular, views across to Morven on the mainland. On the coast just beyond Aros, across the river flats, stands the ruined 13th-century Aros Castle. The road continues through Salen to either Fishnish, for the ferry to Lochaline, or Craignure, for the ferry to Oban.

ARGYLL AND THE ISLES A TO Z

Arriving and Departing

By Bus

Daily bus service from Glasgow Buchanan Street Station to Mid-Argyll and Kintyre is available through **National Express/Scottish Citylink** (☎ 0990/505050).

By Car

The A85 reaches Oban, the main ferry terminal for Mull, and the A83 rounds Loch Fyne and heads down Kintyre to reach Kennacraig, the main ferry terminal for Islay. Farther down the A83 is Tayinloan, the ferry departure point for Gigha. Brodick (Arran) is reached from Ardrossan on the Clyde coast (A8/A78 from Glasgow). For information on ferry times, contact **Caledonian MacBrayne** (CalMac, main office: ⊠ The Ferry Terminal, Gourock, ☎ 01475/650100, ℻ 01475/637607; for reservations, ☎ 01475/650000, ℻ 01475/637607).

By Plane

Although the nearest full-service airport for the entire area is in Glasgow (☞ Chapter 4), there are two airports within Argyll and the Isles. Both **Campbeltown** (on the mainland Kintyre peninsula) and the island of **Islay** are served weekdays (Islay also on Saturday) by **British Airways Express** (☎ 0345/222111) from Glasgow.

By Train

Oban (☎ 01631/563083) and Ardrossan (☎ 0141/204–2844) are the main rail stations. All trains connect with ferries.

Getting Around

By Bus

The following companies operate in the area: **B. Mundell Ltd.** (Islay, ☎ 01496/840273); **Essbee** (Mull, ☎ 01236/423621); **C. MacLean** (Jura, ☎ 01496/820221); **Oban & District Buses** (Oban and Lorne, ☎ 01631/562856); **Stagecoach Western** (Arran, ☎ 01770/302000); and **West Coast Motor Service** (Mid-Argyll and Kintyre, ☎ 01586/552319).

By Car and Ferry

Negotiating this area is easy except in peak season, when the roads around Oban may be congested. There are some single-lane roads, especially on the east side of the Kintyre peninsula and on the islands. Car-ferry services to and from the main islands are operated by **Caledonian MacBrayne** (CalMac, main office: ✉ The Ferry Terminal, Gourock, ☎ 01475/650100, ℻ 01475/637607; for reservations, ☎ 01475/650000, ℻ 01475/637607). An Island Hopscotch ticket reduces the cost of island-hopping excursions. **Western Ferries** (☎ 0141/332-9766) operates the Islay–Jura ferry service.

By Train

Aside from the main line to Oban, with stations at Dalmally, Loch Awe, Falls of Cruachan, Taynuilt, and Connel Ferry, there is no train service. You can travel from the pier head at **Craignure** on **Mull** to **Torosay Castle,** a distance of about 1 mile, by narrow-gauge railway.

Contacts and Resources

Bicycling

As a popular vacation destination and a ferry gateway, Oban gets a lot of traffic. Main routes to and from town are busy, and there are few side roads. Arran is a popular island for cycling, with a large number of bicycle-rental shops. Island roads may be single-track, so wear high-visibility clothing, especially in the busy summer months, and be *sure* to bring rain gear.

Doctors and Dentists

Information is available from your hotel, the local tourist information center, and the police, or look under "Doctors" or "Dentists" in the Yellow Pages telephone directory. There is an emergency room at **Lorne and Islands District General Hospital** (✉ Glengallen Rd., Oban, ☎ 01631/567500).

Emergencies

For **police, fire,** or **ambulance,** dial 999 from any telephone. No coins are needed for emergency calls from public telephone booths.

Fishing

Tourist information centers (☞ Visitor Information, *below*) provide details. Local fishing literature identifies at least 50 fishing sites on lochs and rivers for game fishing and at least 20 coastal settlements suited to sea angling.

Golf

The area has about two dozen golf courses, including fine coastal links, of which Machrihanish is the most famous. The local tourist information centers can provide detailed information.

Guided Tours

ORIENTATION

The bus companies listed in (☞ Getting Around By Bus, *above*), offer orientation tours.

Bowman's Coaches (⊠ Mull, ☎ 01680/812313) offers trips to Mull and Iona from Oban. **Gordon Grant Marine** (⊠ Staffa Ferries, Isle of Iona, ☎ 01681/700338) offers a "Three Isle" excursion to Mull, Iona, and Staffa, and also trips to the Treshnish Isles and to Staffa, from Mull. Other boat cruises are available on **Loch Etive Cruises** (from Taynuilt near Oban, ☎ FAX 01866/822555, or call the tourist information center at Oban). **Sea Life Surveys** (from Dervaig on Mull, ☎ 01688/400223) offers four-hour day trips, and three-, five-, and seven-day packages where you can assist with an ongoing whale and dolphin survey. **Mac-Dougall's Tours** (⊠ Oban, ☎ 01631/562133) runs half- and full-day touring and sailing expeditions to Mull and Iona. **Turas Mara** (⊠ Penmore Mill, Dervaig, Isle of Mull, ☎ FAX 01688/400242) runs daily excursions from Oban and Mull to Staffa, Iona, and the Treshnish Isles.

Late-Night Pharmacies

Pharmacies are not found in rural areas. In an emergency the police will provide assistance in locating a pharmacist. In rural areas general practitioners may also dispense medicines.

Nightlife and the Arts

This predominantly rural area with a small population relies to a great extent on touring companies and small local exhibitions and events for its cultural fulfillment. Tourist information centers (☞ Visitor Information, *below*) can supply an up-to-date events list.

Visitor Information

Local tourist information centers include:

Bowmore, Islay (⊠ The Square, ☎ 01496/810254). **Brodick, Arran** (⊠ The Pier, Brodick, ☎ 01770/302140, FAX 01770/302395). **Campbeltown** (⊠ Mackinnon House, The Pier, ☎ 01586/552056). **Craignure, Mull** (⊠ The Pierhead, ☎ 01680/812377). **Dunoon** (⊠ 7 Alexandra Parade, Dunoon, ☎ 01369/703785, FAX 01369/706085). **Inveraray** (⊠ Front St., ☎ 01499/302063). **Oban** (⊠ Boswell House, Argyll Square, ☎ 01631/563122, FAX 01631/564273). **Tobermory, Mull** (☎ 01688/302182).

There are also seasonal information centers at Lochgilphead, Lochranza (Arran), and Tarbert.

10 Around the Great Glen

Inverness, Loch Ness, Speyside, Fort William

The Great Glen cuts through the Southern Highlands from Inverness to Fort William—two of the Highlands' best areas for lodging and shopping—and is surrounded by Scotland's tallest mountains and, nearby, some of the country's finest glens. The lochs of the Great Glen include Scotland's most famous, Loch Ness. Ben Nevis, at the south end of the Great Glen, is the highest peak in Scotland and easily reached from Fort William, behind which is Glen Nevis, another scenic treat.

THE ANCIENT RIFT VALLEY of the Great Glen is a dramatic feature on the map of Scotland, giving the impression that the top half of the country has slid southwest. Geologists confirm that this actually occurred, having matched granite from Strontian in Morvern, west of Fort William, with the same rocks found at Foyers, on the east side of Loch Ness, some 65 miles away. The Great Glen, with its sense of openness, lacks the grandeur of Glen Coe or the Torridons, but the highest mountain in the United Kingdom, Ben Nevis (4,406 ft), looms over its southern portals, and spectacular scenery lies within a short distance of the main glen.

By Gilbert Summers

Though it's the capital of the Highlands, Inverness has the flavor of a Lowland town, its winds blowing in a sea-salt air from the Moray Firth. Inverness is also home to one of the world's most famous monster myths: In 1933, during a quiet news week for the local paper, the editor decided to run a story about a strange sighting of something splashing about in Loch Ness. More than 60 years later the story lives on, and the dubious Loch Ness phenomenon continues to keep cameras trained on the deep waters, which have an ominous tendency to create mirages in still conditions. The loch also has the greatest volume of water of any Scottish loch.

Fort William, without a monster on its doorstep, makes do with Ben Nevis and the Road to the Isles, a title sometimes applied to the breathtakingly scenic route to Mallaig, which is best seen by rail. On the way, road and rail routes pass Loch Morar, the country's deepest body of water, which lays claim to its own monster, Morag.

Away from the Great Glen to the north lie the heartlands of Scotland, a bare backbone of remote mountains. The great hills that loom to the south can be seen clearly on either side of Strathspey, the broad valley of the River Spey, an area also commonly known as Speyside.

Pleasures and Pastimes

Beaches
The most extensive beaches are at Nairn, with miles of clean, golden sand. The best-known are at Morar, home of the famous white-and-silver sands.

Bicycling
The Great Glen itself has a very busy main road, not recommended for cyclists, along the west bank of Loch Ness via Drumnadrochit. The B862/B852, which runs by the east side of Loch Ness, has less traffic and is a better bet for cyclists. There are plans to expand off-road routes for cyclists in this area—one option is the tow path of the Caledonian Canal. To the east, there is a good network of back roads around Inverness and toward Nairn. The A9, however, on either side of Aviemore, is not recommended for cyclists.

Dining
No doubt about it, there are some fine places with superb cuisine in this area, with a wealth of country house hotels to choose from, as well as an excellent seafood restaurant in Fort William.

WHAT TO WEAR
As elsewhere in Scotland, the country house hotels expect a high standard of dress in their public rooms. However, the less grand hotels, guest houses, and bed-and-breakfasts are used to dealing with the needs of hikers and other outdoor enthusiasts, and only ask that you

arrive at the table clean and fresh after your day enjoying this beautiful region.

CATEGORY	COST*
$$$$	over £40
$$$	£30–£40
$$	£15–£30
$	under £15

per person for a 3-course meal, including VAT and excluding drinks and service

Fishing

The Great Glen has many rivers and lochs where you can fly-fish for salmon and trout. The fishing seasons are as follows: salmon, depending on the area, early February through September or early October; brown trout, March 15 to September 30; sea trout, May through September or early October; rainbow trout, no statutory-close season. Sea angling from shore or boat is also possible.

Golf

As is the case with most of Scotland, there is a broad selection of courses, especially toward the eastern end of this area. Nairn, with two courses, is highly regarded among Scottish players.

Lodging

The main centers, Inverness, Fort William, and Aviemore, have plenty of accommodations in all price ranges. Since this is such an old, established vacation area, there are few places where you'd have trouble finding a room for a night. However, the area is quite busy in peak season and may soon get busier: local tourism authorities are banking on Ted Danson's 1996 Hollywood film about the Loch Ness monster to bring in even more tourists!

CATEGORY	COST*
$$$$	over £110
$$$	£80–£110
$$	£45–£80
$	under £45

Prices are for a standard double room, including service, breakfast, and VAT.

Nightlife and the Arts

Do not visit this area expecting to have a big-city choice of late-night activities. With the exception of Inverness, evening entertainment revolves around pubs and hotels, with the *ceilidh*, a small, informal, musical get-together; and "Scottish Evening," a staged performance of tartan-clad Highland dancers, being the most popular forms of entertainment offered to visitors.

Walking

The Great Glen area is renowned for its hill-walking opportunities, but walkers should be fit and properly outfitted. Remember that on Ben Nevis, a popular route even for inexperienced hikers, it can snow on the summit plateau at any time of the year. Ben Nevis is a large and dangerous mountain.

Exploring the Great Glen

Of the two routes covered below, the first centers on Inverness, moving east into Speyside, then west down the Great Glen. The second route, originating in Fort William, takes in the special qualities of the birch-knoll and blue island West Highland views. There are many romantic and historic associations with this area. It was here where the rash adventurer Prince Charles Edward Stuart arrived for the final Jacobite rebellion of 1745–46, and it was from here that he departed following the battle.

Great Itineraries

The road between Fort William and Mallaig is one of the classic routes of Scottish touring. Even tour buses sometimes say THE ROAD TO THE ISLES on their destination boards. Similarly, the Great Glen road is a vital coast-to-coast link. The fact that it passes by a loch with a "monster" phenomenon is just a happy coincidence.

IF YOU HAVE 2 DAYS

Numbers in the text correspond to numbers in the margin and on The Great Glen Area map.

Both ⛺ **Inverness** ① and ⛺ **Fort William** ㉚ have a choice of loops running from them. Base yourself anywhere around Fort William, so that you can take in the spectacular scenery of **Glen Coe** ㉘ and Glen Nevis, and also at least glimpse the western seaboard toward **Mallaig** ㉞.

IF YOU HAVE 4 DAYS

Spend two days at one of two bases at each end of the Great Glen, say, ⛺ **Inverness** ① or ⛺ **Nairn** ④ at the north end, and ⛺ **Fort William** ㉚ or ⛺ **Ballachulish** ㉙ at the south end. This will give you adequate time to see what this chunk of Scotland has to offer. The first day, from Inverness travel to Nairn, and from Nairn go southward via **Cawdor Castle** ⑥ and **Lochindorb Castle** to **Grantown on Spey** ⑦. Then follow the Spey as far as you feel like, via **Boat of Garten** ⑧, with its ospreys in spring and early summer; **Aviemore** ⑪ and its mountain scenery; and **Kingussie** ⑭,where the Highland Folk Museum does a good job of explaining what life was really like before modern domestic and agricultural equipment made things easy. The next day, explore Loch Ness, traveling down the eastern bank as far as **Fort Augustus** ㉑, and returning up the western bank via **Drumnadrochit** ㉓; if you have time on a long summer evening, divert northward at Drumnadrochit to discover beautiful glens Affric and Cannich, before returning to Inverness. The third day, travel to ⛺ **Fort William** ㉚, taking in the **Caledonian Canal** ⑳ and **Commando Memorial** ⑲. Spend a day doing the suggested loop to **Mallaig** ㉞ and back through **Glenfinnan** ㊱ to Fort William, or go straight to **Arisaig** ㉝ and take an unforgettable day cruise among the Small Isles.

IF YOU HAVE 7 DAYS

This is plenty of time to visit all the places in the Great Glen area in the order described in this chapter. Base yourself at ⛺ **Inverness** ① or ⛺ **Nairn** ④ for two nights, then spend a night at ⛺ **Kingussie** ⑭ and a night at ⛺ **Drumnadrochit** ㉓ or ⛺ **Whitebridge** ㉕. Moving west to the Fort William area, either stay in ⛺ **Fort William** ㉚ itself, or go farther west to the excellent accommodations of ⛺ **Arisaig** ㉝ for two nights. Either base will allow for exploration of the suggested circular route, a day at sea among the Small Isles, and a half-day or day amid the grandeur of **Glen Coe** ㉘, or Glen Nevis behind Fort William. You may also want to make excursions farther north and west.

When to Tour the Great Glen

This is a spring and autumn kind of area. However, in summer, if the weather is settled, it can be very pleasant in the far west, perhaps on the Road to the Isles, toward Mallaig. Early spring is a good time to sample Scottish skiing at Nevis Range or Glencoe.

The Great Glen Area

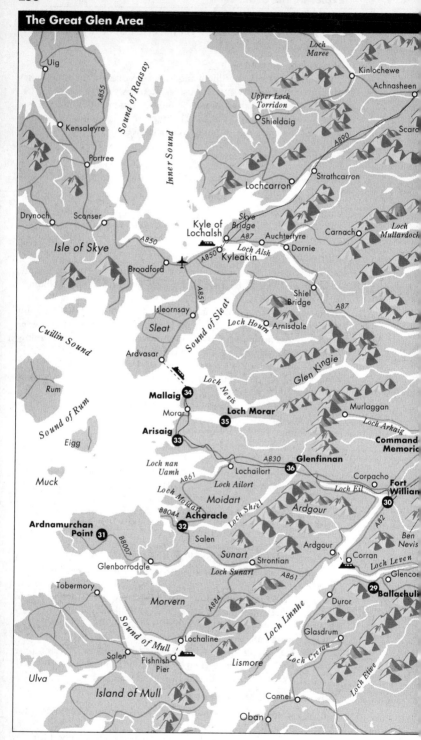

Uig
Kensaleyre
Portree
Drynoch
Sconser
Isle of Skye
Broadford
Isleornsay
Sleat
Ardvasar

Sound of Raasay
Inner Sound
A855
A850

Loch Maree
Kinlochewe
Achnasheen
Upper Loch Torridon
Shieldaig
Scaro
A890
Lochcarron
Strathcarron

Kyle of Lochalsh
Skye Bridge
A87
Auchtertyre
Dornie
Carnach
Loch Mullardoch
Kyleakin
Loch Alsh
A850
A851
Shiel Bridge
A87

Cuillin Sound
Loch Houm
Arnisdale

Rum
Sound of Rum
Eigg
Muck

Mallaig 34
Morar
Arisaig 33
Loch Morar 35
Loch Nevis
Glen Kingie
Murlaggan
Loch Arkaig

Loch nan Uamh
Lochailort
A861
Loch Ailort
A830
Glenfinnan 36
Corpacho
Command Memoric
Loch Eil
Fort William 30

Ardnamurchan Point 31
B8007
B8044
Acharacle 32
Salen
Moidart
Loch Shiel
Ardgour
A82
Ben Nevis

Glenborrodale
Sunart
Strontian
Loch Sunart
Ardgour
A861
Corran
Loch Leven
Glencoe
29 **Ballachuli**

Tobermory
Morvern
A824
Duror
Glasdrum
Loch Creran

Sound of Mull
Lochaline
Loch Linnhe
Loch Etive

Salen
Fishnish Pier
Lismore
Ulva
Island of Mull
Connel
Oban

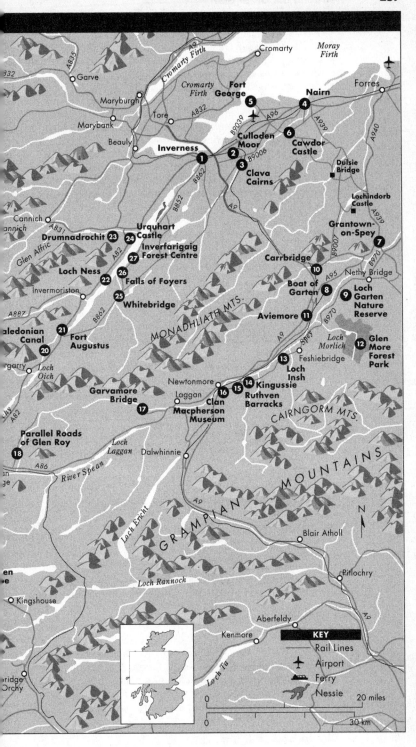

KEY

— Rail Lines

✈ Airport

⛴ Ferry

🐉 Nessie

0 ——— 20 miles

0 ——— 30 km

SPEYSIDE AND LOCH NESS

Inverness itself is not really a town to linger in, unless you need to do some shopping. Because Jacobite tales are interwoven with landmarks throughout this entire area, it is suggested that you first learn something about this thorny but colorful period of Scottish history. One of the best places to do this is at Culloden, just east of Inverness, where a major battle ended in final defeat for the Jacobites. Other points of interest that are highlighted are along the inner Moray Firth and down into Speyside, before moving west into the Great Glen. Loch Ness, star of the recent film of the same name, is just one of the attractions hereabouts, both natural and man-made. In the Great Glen and Speyside, the best sights are often hidden from the main road, an excellent reason to favor peaceful rural byways and avoid, as far as possible, the busy A82 (down Loch Ness's western shore), and the A96 and A9, which carry much of the eastern traffic in the area.

Inverness

❶ *176 mi north of Glasgow, 109 mi northwest of Aberdeen, 161 mi northwest of Edinburgh.*

Inverness seems designed for the tourist, with its banks, souvenirs, high-quality woolens, and well-equipped tourist information center. Compared with other Scottish towns, however, Inverness has less to offer visitors who have a keen interest in Scottish history. Throughout its history, Inverness was burned and ravaged by one or another of the restive Highland clans competing for dominance in the region. Thus, a decorative wall panel, here, and a fragment of tower, there, are all that remain amid the modern shopping facilities and 19th-century downtown developments.

One of Inverness's few historical landmarks is the **castle** (the local Sheriff Court), nestled above the river. The present structure is Victorian, built after a former fort was blown up by the Jacobites in the 1745 campaign.

★ ❷ At **Culloden Moor,** on a sleety April day in 1746, an army of 5,000 Jacobites, under Prince Charles Edward Stuart, faced 9,000 well-armed British troops, under the command of the prince's distant cousin, General Cumberland. The latter became known in Scotland as Butcher Cumberland because of the atrocities committed by his men after the battle ended. The story of the encounter, of how the ill-advised, poorly organized, and exhausted rebel army was swept aside by superior British firepower, is illustrated in the visitor center by a moving audiovisual presentation. The battlefield lies 5 miles east of Inverness via B9006. ☎ *01463/790607.* 🎫 *Visitor center £2.60.* ☺ *Site: daily; visitor center: Apr.–Oct., daily 9–6; Nov., Dec., Feb., and Mar., daily 10–4 (closed Dec. 25).*

❸ Not far from Culloden, on a narrow road southeast of the battlefield, are the **Clava Cairns,** dating from the Bronze Age. In a cluster among the trees, these stones and monuments form a large ring with passage graves, which consist of a central chamber below a cairn of stone, reached via a passage. On-site information placards explain the graves' significance.

Dining and Lodging

$$$$ ✕🏠 **Bunchrew House.** This turreted mansion, on the banks of the Beauly Firth, abounds with handsome wood paneling. The dining room is particularly attractive, with fine antique furniture, and the lounge and comfortable bedrooms are decorated with velvet and chintz. The restaurant serves French-influenced Scottish cuisine, using the best Aberdeen Angus beef, local salmon, and game. The extensive grounds are delightful for a pre-dinner stroll, and the views of the Firth are superb. ✉ *Bunchrew, Inverness-shire, IV3 6TA,* ☎ *01463/234917,* 🆁🅰🆇 *01463/710620. 11 rooms with bath. Restaurant. AE, MC. V.*

$$$$ ✕🏨 **Kingsmills Hotel.** A rambling mansion set in four acres of gardens on the edge of a golf course, the Kingsmills is about 1 mile from the center of Inverness. It's a great place for families: children under 14 stay for free, and the heated indoor pool and extensive leisure facilities offer plenty to do. The bedrooms are particularly spacious, comfortable, and well-equipped. The restaurant serves well-prepared and reliable dishes, such as steak, seafood tagliatelle, and game pâté. ✉ *Culcabock Rd., IV2 3LP,* ☎ *01463/237166,* 🆁🅰🆇 *01463/225208. 84 rooms with bath. Restaurant, indoor pool, golf privileges, 3-hole golf course, health club. AE, DC, MC, V.*

$$–$$$$ ✕🏨 **Dunain Park Hotel.** Guests receive individual attention in this 18th-century mansion set in six acres of wooded gardens. A log fire awaits you in the living room, a good place to sip a drink and browse through books and magazines. Antiques and traditional decor make the bedrooms equally cozy and attractive. The restaurant offers French-influenced Scottish dishes, served on bone china with crystal glasses. Saddle of venison in port sauce and boned quail stuffed with pistachios are two specialties. ✉ *Dunain (2½ mi SW of Inverness on A82), IV38 6JN,* ☎ *01463/230512,* 🆁🅰🆇 *01463/224532. 14 rooms with bath. Restaurant, indoor pool, sauna. AE, DC, MC, V.*

$$ ✕🏨 **Priory Hotel.** A haven in the center of Beauly, west of Inverness, the
★ Priory is a comfortable, traditional-style hotel—cheerful, patterned carpets, peachy color schemes, and modern furnishings—notable for the warmth of its staff and its excellent food. In the restaurant, tradition, in the form of satisfying game, steaks, and seafood, is tempered with imaginative sauces: Try the medallions of beef in port, honey, and ginger sauce. It's all that a good hotel should be, and rarely is, at reasonable prices. ✉ *The Square, Beauly, IV4 7BX,* ☎ *01463/782309,* 🆁🅰🆇 *01463/782531. 22 rooms with bath or shower. Restaurant. AE, DC, MC, V.*

$$ 🏨 **Ballifeary House Hotel.** This well-maintained Victorian property is within easy reach of downtown Inverness. The particularly helpful proprietors offer high standards of comfort and service. Rooms are individually decorated with modern furnishings, while the downstairs has reproduction antiques. ✉ *10 Ballifeary Rd., IV3 5PJ,* ☎ *01463/235572,* 🆁🅰🆇 *01463/717583. 8 rooms with bath. MC, V. No smoking. Closed Nov.–Mar.*

$ 🏨 **Atholdene House.** This family-run, 19th-century stone villa offers a friendly welcome and modernized accommodations. Evening meals can be provided for guests on request. The bus and railway stations are a short walk away. ✉ *20 Southside Rd., IV2 3BG,* ☎ 🆁🅰🆇 *01463/ 233565. 9 rooms, 7 with shower. No credit cards.*

$ 🏨 **Clach Mhuilinn.** This modern family home is set in a pretty garden and has good parking facilities. It offers bed-and-breakfast of a very high standard. ✉ *7 Harris Rd., IV2 3LS,* ☎ *01463/237059.* 🆁🅰🆇 *01463/ 242092. 3 rooms, 2 with bath or shower. MC, V. No smoking. Closed Dec.–Feb.*

$ 🏨 **Daviot Mains Farm.** A 19th-century farmhouse, 5 miles south of In-
★ verness on the A9, provides the perfect setting for home comforts and traditional Scottish cooking for guests only; lucky ones may find wild salmon on the menu. ✉ *Daviot Mains,* ☎ 🆁🅰🆇 *01463/772215. 3 rooms, 2 with bath or shower. MC, V.*

$ 🏠 **Easter Dalziel Farm.** This 210-acre working farm, with livestock, offers plenty of interest for guests staying one night or longer. The Victorian farmhouse, with its log fire, home baking, and pretty gardens, is a welcome change from impersonal hotels. Rooms have antique mahogany, oak, or pine furniture and floral fabrics; tapestries stitched by the owner are displayed throughout the house. ⊠ *Dalcross, Inverness,* ☎ FAX *01667/462213. 3 rooms. MC, V.*

Nightlife and the Arts

BARS AND LOUNGES

Inverness has an array of bars and lounges. **Gunsmith's** (⊠ Union St., ☎ 01463/710519) is a traditional pub offering bar meals. **DJ's Café Bar** (⊠ High St.) serves everything from breakfast to late-night cocktails.

CABARET

Scottish Showtime (⊠ Cummings Hotel, Church St., Inverness, ☎ 01463/232531) offers Scottish cabaret of the tartan-clad dancer and bagpipe/accordion variety.

THEATER

Eden Court Theatre (⊠ Bishops Rd., Inverness, ☎ 01463/221718) offers not only drama, but also a program of music, film, and light entertainment, and an art gallery.

Outdoor Activities and Sports

BICYCLING

Inverness outlets for bicycle rentals include **Thornton Cycles** (⊠ 23 Castle St., ☎ 01463/235078).

GOLF

The following courses welcome visitors: **Inverness Golf Club** (☎ 01463/239882).

Torvean Golf Course (Inverness, ☎ 01463/711434).

Shopping

Although Inverness has the usual High Street stores and department stores—including Arnott's and Marks and Spencer—the most interesting goods are to be found in the specialty outlets in and around town.

The Riverside Gallery (⊠ 11 Bank St., ☎ 01463/224781) sells paintings and prints of Scottish landscapes, natural history, and sporting themes. For contemporary art there's the **Highland Printmakers Workshop and Gallery** (⊠ 20 Bank St., ☎ 01463/712240). **Duncan Chisholm and Sons** (⊠ 49 Castle St., ☎ 01463/234599) specializes in Highland dress, tartans, and Scottish crafts. Mail-order and made-to-measure services are available. **James Pringle Ltd.** (⊠ Holm Woollen Mills, Dores Rd., ☎ 01463/223311) has a shop stocked with a vast selection of cashmere, lamb's wool, and Shetland knitwear, tartans, and tweeds. **Hector Russell Kiltmakers** (⊠ 4/9 Huntly St., ☎ 01463/222781) explains the history of the kilt, shows them being made, and then gives you the opportunity to buy from a huge selection, or have a kilt made-to-measure. The firm offers overseas mail-order.

Highland Aromatics (⊠ Drumchardine, Kirkhill, ☎ 01463/831625, FAX 01463/831405), in a converted church, makes sweet-smelling soaps, perfumes, colognes, and other toiletries with the scents of the Highlands. **Highland Wineries** (⊠ Moniack Castle, Kirkhill, ☎ 01463/831283, FAX 01463/831419) creates wines from Scottish ingredients, such as birch sap, and also makes jams, marmalade, and other preserves.

Nairn

④ *17 mi east of Inverness via B9006/B9091, 92 mi west of Aberdeen.*

Although Nairn has the air of a Lowland town, it is actually part of the Highlands. A once-prosperous fishing village, Nairn has, in fact, something of a split personality. King James VI once boasted that there was a town in his kingdom so large that the residents at either end of town spoke different languages. He was referring to the fact that in past centuries, Nairn's fisherfolk spoke Lowland Scots by the sea, while the uptown farmers and crofters spoke Gaelic.

The fishing boats have since moved to larger ports, but Nairn's historic flavor has been preserved in the **Nairn Fishertown Museum,** a hall crammed with artifacts, photographs, and model boats. This is an informal museum in the best sense, where the volunteer staff is full of information and eager to talk. ⊠ *Laing Hall, King St.,* ☎ *01667/456798.* 🔄 *30p.* ☉ *June–Sept., Mon.–Sat. 2:30–4:30, also Mon., Wed., and Fri. evenings 6:30–8:30.*

★ ⑤ Two contrasting defensive structures lie within easy reach of Nairn. As a direct result of the battle at Culloden, the nervous government in London ordered the construction of a large fort on a promontory reaching into the Moray Firth: **Fort George** was started in 1748 and completed some 20 years later. It survives today as perhaps the best-preserved 18th-century military fortification in Europe. Because it is low-lying, its immense scale can be seen only from within. The huge walls, as broad and high as harbor quays, are large enough to contain a complete military town. A walk along the wall tops affords fine views of the Highland hills in the distance and of the firth immediately below. Even though no one has sighted a Jacobite here for more than 200 years, the army still uses the barracks. And if you happen to meet any of the fort's current military residents, you will find them unfailingly polite. A visitor center and a number of tableaux at the fort portray the 18th-century Scottish soldier's way of life, as does the **Regimental Museum of the Queen's Own Highlanders.** To reach the fort take the B9092 north off A96 west of Nairn. ⊠ *Ardersier,* ☎ *0131/668–8600.* 🔄 *Admission to fort: £2.50. Museum free.* ☉ *Fort and museum open Apr.–Sept., Mon.–Sat. 9:30–6. Sun. 2–6; Oct.–Mar., Mon.–Sat. 9:30–4. Last tickets 45 min before closing.*

★ ⑥ Southwest of Nairn is **Cawdor Castle** (☞ Walking, below). Shakespeare's Macbeth was Thane of Cawdor, but the sense of history that exists within these turreted walls is more than fictional. Cawdor is a lived-in castle, not an abandoned, decaying structure. The earliest part of the castle is the 14th-century central tower; the rooms contain family portraits, tapestries, fine furniture, and paraphernalia reflecting 600 years of history. Outside the castle there are sheltered gardens and walks. The castle is located off the B9090, 5 miles southwest of Nairn. ⊠ *Cawdor,* ☎ *01667/404615.* 🔄 *£4.70; garden and grounds only £2.50.* ☉ *May–mid-Oct., daily 10–5.*

Dining and Lodging

$$$ **★** ✕🏨 **Clifton House.** Here is a unique hotel: original works of art cover the walls, antique furniture graces the rooms, and antique silver gleams in the dining room. The hotel is also licensed as a theater, and each March and November you can enjoy excellent theatrical and musical performances. The restaurant is famous for its classic Scottish cuisine—the Beef Wellington, lamb cutlets, and duck à l'orange are particularly good—and the wine list is probably the longest in the area. ⊠ *Viewfield St., Nairn,* ☎ *01667/453119,* 🕿 *01667/452836. 16 rooms, 15*

*with bath, 1 with shower. 2 restaurants. AE, DC, MC, V. Closed Dec.
and Jan.*

The Arts

Clifton House (☞ Dining and Lodging, *above*) at Nairn runs a program
of concerts, recitals, and plays every March and November.

Outdoor Activities and Sports

GOLF

Nairn's courses, which welcome visitors, are highly regarded by golfers.
They're very popular, so be sure to book far in advance: **Nairn Dunbar Golf Club** (☎ 01667/452741); **Nairn Golf Club** (☎ 01667/453208).

WALKING

Cawdor Castle Nature Trails provides a choice of four hikes through
some of the most beautiful and varied woodlands in Britain. You will
pass ancient oaks and beeches, magnificent waterfalls, and deep river
gorges. ⊠ *Cawdor Castle (Tourism) Ltd., Cawdor Castle, Nairn, near
Inverness, IV12 5RD,* ☎ 01667/404615. ☜ £2.50. ☉ *May–mid-Oct.*

Shopping

Do not miss **Nairn Antiques** (⊠ St. Ninian Pl., near the traffic circle,
☎ 01667/453303) for a wide selection of antique jewelry, glassware,
furniture, pottery, prints, and some unusual giftware. **Culloden Pottery**
(⊠ Gollanfield, midway between Nairn and Inverness, ☎ 01667/
462340) offers you the chance to throw your own pot (which is then
fired, glazed, and mailed to your home) or to choose from an original
and extensive selection of hand-thrown domestic stoneware. There is
also a gift-and-crafts shop and a vegetarian restaurant that prides itself on serving only fresh food; there are fine views from the restaurant as well. **Brodie Country Fare** (⊠ Brodie, east of Nairn, ☎ 01309/
641555) is guaranteed to affect your wallet in a pleasant way. Unusual
knitwear, quality clothing, gifts, toys, and a restaurant beckon from
beyond the food store and delicatessen.

OFF THE
BEATEN PATH

DULSIE BRIDGE AND LOCHINDORB CASTLE – If Cawdor has inspired you
to seek the wild Highlands, use the unclassified roads southeast of Cawdor to find a classic Highland "edge" landscape, where the open moor
contrasts with the improved upland pasture and thickets of birch and fir.
(Clunas may be the first road sign you see, but reaching Dulsie is your
first objective.) As you take to the higher ground, look for the longest
views back over the Firth—you should still just barely be able to see Fort
George in the distance. Follow what was the former military road built
in the 1750s to service the garrison. Look for the point where the road
crosses the River Findhorn by a narrow span, the **Dulsie Bridge.** Just beyond the bridge, on the right, is a parking place and kissing gate. If you
park and go through the gate, a walk of a few yards brings you to a
viewpoint over the birch-scattered rocky confines of the river.

Shortly after Dulsie Bridge, turn right off the unclassified road onto the
B9007. Shakespeare's Thane of Cawdor met the three prophesying
witches on a bare moor very much like this one. Rolling folds of marbled
purple and brown are broken here and there by a roofless cottage. Follow the sign (pointing east) for a view of the lonely ruin of **Lochindorb
Castle.** What appears to be a walled enclosure fills and surrounds an entire island on Lochindorb loch. This 13th-century stronghold was the former power base of the Wolf of Badenoch, the marauding Earl of Buchan
who damaged Elgin Cathedral. The castle was eventually dismantled by
a 15th-century Thane of Cawdor, on orders of the king. (Lochindorb's
iron *yett* [gate] is now on view at Cawdor Castle.)

Grantown-on-Spey

❼ *24 mi south of Nairn via A939, 7 mi southeast of Lochindorb Castle via unclassified road and A939.*

The sturdy settlement of Grantown-on-Spey, set amid tall pines that flank the River Spey, is a classic Scottish planned town. This means it is a community which was planned and laid out by the local landowner, in this case, Sir James Grant in 1776. It has handsome buildings in silver granite and some good shopping for Scottish gifts.

Shopping

Speyside Heather Centre (✉ Skye of Curr, ☎ 01479/851359), has 200–300 varieties of heather for sale (some in sterile planting material). This firm can supply heather plants by mail-order overseas. There is also a crafts shop, floral-art sundries, and a tearoom. **The Kist** (✉ 74 High St., Grantown on Spey, ☎ 01479/873043), is a well-stocked, high-quality gift shop specializing in local crafts.

Boat of Garten

❽ *11 mi southwest of Grantown via B970.*

In the peaceful village of Boat of Garten, the scent of pine trees mingles with an equally evocative smell: This is the terminus of the **Speyside Railway,** and the oily scent of smoke and steam hang faintly in the air near the authentically preserved train station. From here there's a 5-mile train trip to Aviemore, offering a chance to wallow in nostalgia and enjoy superb views of the high and often white domes of the Cairngorms.

NEED A
BREAK?

At the **Boat Hotel** (☎ 01479/831258), in Boat of Garten, you can have a friendly pub lunch while you wait for the train. The malt whisky selection behind the bar may also be of interest.

---

❾ The **Loch Garten Nature Reserve,** administered by the Royal Society for the Protection of Birds (RSPB), is just outside Boat of Garten, to the east. This sanctuary achieved fame when the osprey, a bird that was facing extinction in the early part of this century, returned to breed here. Instead of cordoning off the nest site, conservation officials encouraged visitors by constructing a blind for bird-watching. Now thousands of bird lovers visit annually to get a glimpse of the domestic arrangements of this fish-eating bird, which has since bred in many other parts of the Highlands. ☎ 01479/831694 or 0131/557–3136. ✍ £2. ☉ Osprey observation post: May, daily 10–6, June–Aug., daily 10–8; other areas of reserve: daily year-round.

❿ In **Carrbridge,** just north of Boat of Garten, you'll find the **Landmark Visitor Centre,** an early pioneer in the move toward more sophisticated visitor attractions. It has an audiovisual presentation on the history of the Scottish Highlands; a permanent exhibition; a display on forestry with a working steam-powered sawmill and a Clydesdale horse to haul the logs; a forestry workshop, where you can try out forest skills, such as bark peeling; and a bookshop and restaurant. Outdoors are nature trails, a treetop trail, and a viewing platform, as well as plenty of diversions for children, such as a Wild Forest maze and an adventure playground. Reach Carrbridge on the quiet B9153—keep off the A9. ✉ Carrbridge, ☎ 01479/841613. ✍ £3.35–5.05. ☉ Apr.–mid-July, daily 9:30–6; mid-July–Aug., daily 9:30–8; Sept. and Oct., daily 9:30–5:30; Nov.–Mar., daily 9:30–5.

Aviemore

⓫   *6 mi southwest of Boat of Garten via B970.*

Once a quiet junction on the Highland Railway, Aviemore now has all the brashness and concrete boxiness of a year-round holiday resort. A resort environment translates into a lot of things to do, however, and here you can swim, curl, skate, see a movie, dance, and shop.

⓬   The Aviemore area is a versatile walking base, but walkers must be dressed properly for high-level excursions onto the near-Arctic plateau. Visitors interested in skiing and rugged hiking can follow the B970 from Aviemore, past Loch Morlich in the **Glen More Forest Park,** to the high parking lots on the exposed shoulders of the **Cairngorm Mountains.** The chairlifts take you even higher, during and after the ski season, for extensive views of the broad valley of the Spey. But be forewarned: It can get very cold at over 3,000 feet, and weather conditions can change rapidly even in the middle of summer. ⊠ *Off B9152,* ☎ *01479/861261.* ☞ *Free.* ☉ *Daily, weather permitting.*

While you are on the high slopes, you may see the reindeer herd that was introduced here in the 1950s. By inquiring at the **Cairngorm Reindeer Centre,** by Loch Morlich, you can accompany the keeper on his daily rounds. ⊠ *Loch Morlich, Glen More Forest Park,* ☎ *01479/ 861228.* ☞ *£3.50.; Visitor Centre admission: £1.50.* ☉ *Daily, 10–6; Departures daily at 11 (subject to weather conditions); also at 2:30 from Apr.–Oct.*

★   The place that best sums up Speyside's piney ambience is probably **Loch an Eilean.** A converted cottage on the **Rothiemurchus Estate** houses a visitor center (the area is a National Nature Reserve). Be careful entering the cottage: It has an extremely low door and a very hard lintel! All around the loch you can still see some stands of old Scots pines; look for the characteristic red limbs high up. These are the descendants of the Caledonian Forest that once covered much of Scotland and now survives only in remnants. The loch is signposted off the B970 (parallel with the main A9) slightly more than 1 mile south of Aviemore. ⊠ *Rothiemurchus Estate Visitor Centre, Loch an Eilean* ☎ *01479/810858.* ☞ *Free.* ☉ *Daily 9–5.*

⓭   Many lochs in the vicinity of Aviemore, notably Loch an Eilean and Loch Garten, are what geologists call kettle holes—round depressions that remained after huge blocks of ice melted at the end of the Ice Age. **Loch Insh** is thought to be the remains of a much larger loch that, until recent geological times, filled the valley floor. Loch Insh is known for its recreational diversions and is a popular water-sports center, especially for sailing and canoeing. Beyond the loch, the valley floor broadens into marshland and becomes the haunt of water birds and bird-watchers. Look for ospreys here, close to Feshiebridge on the B970 south of Aviemore.

Nightlife

Crofters (☎ 01479/810624) at the Aviemore Mountain Resort has a bar open all day, with dancing nightly until 1 AM.

Outdoor Activities and Sports

BICYCLING

Aviemore has a wide choice of bicycle rental outlets, among them: **Inverdruie Mountain Bikes** (⊠ at Inverdruie, on the Cairngorms road out of Aviemore, ☎ 01479/810787). **Speyside Sports** (⊠ Main St., ☎ 01479/ 810656). **Sporthaus** (⊠ Main St., ☎ 01479/810655).

SKIING

Aviemore is perhaps the most advanced ski resort in the area, though the word "resort" is only loosely applicable to skiing in Scotland. Sometimes lifts can't operate owing to high winds. The ski area is operated by Cairngorm Chairlift Company (☎ 01479/861261).

Shopping

The **Cairngorm Whisky Centre** has one of the largest selections of malt whiskies in the world—more than 500. There is a tasting room to help you make your choice. ⊠ *Aviemore, on the road to the Cairngorms,* ☎ *01479/810574.* ▣ *Tasting Room £3.50.* ☉ *Daily 9:30–4:30 (longer hrs in summer).*

Kingussie

⑭ *13 mi southwest of Aviemore.*

The village of Kingussie (pronounced Kin-*yoo*-see) is of interest primarily because of the **Highland Folk Museum.** The interior exhibits are housed in what was an 18th-century shooting lodge, its paneled and varnished ambience still apparent. Displays include 18th-century furniture, clothing, and implements. Outside, various types of Highland buildings have been reconstructed. In summer, local weavers and other artisans demonstrate Highland crafts. Visitors can wander around the grounds freely or see the highlights of the museum on a guided tour. ⊠ *Kingussie,* ☎ *01540/661307.* ▣ *£2.50.* ☉ *Apr.–Oct., Mon.–Sat. 10–6, Sun. 2–6; Nov.–Mar., Mon.–Fri. 10–3.*

⑮ **Ruthven Barracks,** which from a distance looks like a ruined castle on a mound, is redolent with tales of the '45 (as the last Jacobite rebellion is often called). The defeated Jacobite forces rallied here after Culloden, but then abandoned and blew up the government outpost they had earlier captured. You'll see it as you approach Kingussie. ⊠ *B970, ½ mi south of Kingussie,* ☎ *0131/668–8600.* ▣ *Free.* ☉ *At all times.*

The rounded **Monadhliath Mountains** (*monadhliath* is Gaelic for gray moors) loom northward over Kingussie and Strathspey (the valley of the River Spey), separating Speyside from the Great Glen. The Monadhliath are less often explored by hikers than the Cairngorms, which form Speyside's southern side.

Dining and Lodging

$$$$ ✕▥ **The Cross.** Meals are superb and the wine list extensive. This is an award-winning "restaurant with rooms" in the French style. Dinner, which could be breast of wood pigeon with onion confit, or mousseline of pike with prawn sauce, is included in the price of your room. Bedrooms—all with king-size beds—are individually decorated, and may have a balcony, canopied bed, or an antique dressing table. ⊠ *Tweed Mill Brae, Kingussie, Inverness-shire, PH21 1TC,* ☎ *01540/661166,* FAX *01540/661080. 9 rooms with bath. Restaurant. MC, V. Closed Dec.–Feb. and Tues. dinner.*

$ ✕▥ **Osprey Hotel.** This friendly hotel in the village of Kingussie is ideally located for skiing and hiking. Rooms have old or antique furniture and floral wallpaper. An impressive wine list complements the much praised cuisine, which might include such dishes as halibut with smoked salmon sauce, or fillet steak with Stilton cheese and port. ⊠ *Kingussie, Inverness-shire, PH21 1HX,* ☎ FAX *01540/661510. 7 rooms with bath. Restaurant. AE, DC, MC, V.*

Newtonmore

3 mi southwest of Kingussie.

⑯ Newtonmore is home of the **Clan Macpherson Museum.** One of many clan museums scattered throughout the old homelands, the Macpherson Museum displays a number of interesting artifacts associated with the '45 rebellion, as well as those of clan chiefs of the even more distant past. ✉ *Newtonmore,* ☎ *01540/673332.* 🎫 *Free (donation box).* ☉ *May–Sept., Mon.–Sat. 10–5:30, Sun. 2:30–5:30 (open at other times by appointment).*

A few miles southwest of Newtonmore on the A86 at **Laggan,** where the main road crosses the young River Spey, an unclassified road runs ⑰ west up the glen to **Garvamore.** If you are not pressed for time, it's worth taking this road to view the **Garvamore Bridge,** about 6 miles from the junction, at the south side of Corrieyairack Pass). This dual-arched bridge was built in 1735 by English General Wade, who had been charged with the task of improving Scotland's roads by a British government concerned that its troops would not be able to travel the Highlands quickly enough to quell an uprising.

En Route The A86 hugs the western shore of **Loch Laggan.** This was the route chosen by later road builders than General Wade, to avoid the high Corrieyairack Pass. Still quite narrow in a few places, this stretch of the A86 is a road to be enjoyed. It offers superb views of the mountainous heartlands to the north, where high shoulders loom; and to the south, over the silvery spine of hills known as the **Grey Corries;** and culminating with views of **Ben Nevis.**

Roybridge

34 mi west of Newtonmore.

In the tiny community of Roybridge you'll find a cul-de-sac diversion ⑱ to the so-called **Parallel Roads of Glen Roy:** three curious terraces, parallel and level, cut across the hillsides on both sides of the glen. Their levelness hints of their origins as former shorelines of lochs dammed by ice that melted in stages at the end of the last Ice Age. ✉ *Unclassified road off A86 at Roybridge.*

Spean Bridge

3 mi west of Roy Bridge.

Uphill and beyond the little village of Spean Bridge, easily visible from ⑲ the road, is the arresting and dignified **Commando Memorial.** The rugged glens and hills of this area were a training ground for elite forces during World War II. Today, three battle-equipped figures on a high stone plinth overlook the panorama, while the veterans and younger generations who visit follow their gaze.

Laggan

30 mi north of Spean Bridge via A82.

Traveling north up the Great Glen takes you parallel to Loch Lochy ⑳ (on the eastern shore) and over the **Caledonian Canal** at Laggan Locks. From this beautiful spot, which offers stunning vistas of lochs, mountains, and glens in all directions, you can look back on the impressive profile of Ben Nevis. The canal, which links the lochs of the Great Glen—Loch Lochy, Loch Oich, and Loch Ness—owes its origins to a combination of military as well as political pressures that emerged at the time of the Napoleonic Wars with France. (Mostly, the British needed a better and faster way to get naval vessels from one side of Scotland to the other.) The great Scottish engineer Thomas Telford surveyed the route in 1803. The canal, which took 19 years to complete, has 29 locks and 42 gates. Because Telford took advantage of the three lochs that lie in the Great Glen, which have a combined length of 45 miles, only 22 miles of canal had to be constructed to connect the lochs and complete the waterway from coast to coast.

Dining and Lodging

$$–$$$ ✕🏨 **Glengarry Castle Hotel.** This rambling, pleasantly old-fashioned mansion makes a good touring base; Invergarry is just south of Loch Ness and within easy reach of the Great Glen's best sights. Rooms have traditional Victorian decor; some have superb views over Loch Oich. The food is in traditional Scottish style; try the poached salmon with hollandaise or the loin of lamb with rosemary. The grounds include the ruins of **Glengarry Castle,** a seat of the MacDonnell Clan. The hotel entrance is south of the A82–A87 road junction. ✉ *Invergarry, Inverness-shire, PH35 4HW,* ☎ *01809/501254,* ℻ *01809/501207. 26 rooms with bath. Restaurant, tennis court, trout and pike fishing. MC, V. Closed Nov.–Mar.*

Fort Augustus

㉑ *53 mi north of Laggan.*

The best place to see the locks of the Caledonian Canal in action is at Fort Augustus, at the southern tip of Loch Ness. Fort Augustus itself was captured by the Jacobite clans during the 1745 rebellion. Later the fort was rebuilt as a Benedictine abbey. In the village center, considerable canal activity takes place at a series of locks that rise from Loch Ness.

㉒ From the B862, just east of Fort Augustus, you'll get your first good long view of the formidable and famous **Loch Ness,** which has a greater volume of water than any other Scottish loch and a maximum depth of more than 800 feet. Early travelers who passed this way included English lexicographer Dr. Samuel Johnson, and his guide and biographer, James Boswell, who were on their way to the Hebrides in 1783. They remarked at the time about the condition of the population and the squalor of their homes. Another early travel writer, Thomas Pennant, noted that the loch kept the locality frost-free in winter. Even General Wade came here, his troops blasting and digging a road up much of the eastern shore. None of these observant early travelers ever made mention of a monster. Clearly, they had not read the local guidebooks—or seen the film.

Drumnadrochit

㉓ *21 mi north of Fort Augustus via A82.*

If you're in search of the infamous beast Nessie, at Drumnadrochit you will find the **Official Loch Ness Monster Exhibition,** which presents the facts and the fakes, the photographs, the unexplained sonar contacts, and the sincere testimony of eyewitnesses. It's then up to you to make up your own mind. ✉ *Drumnadrochit,* ☎ *01456/450573 and 01456/450218,* ℻ *01456/450770.* 🎟 *£4.* ⏰ *Easter–May, daily 9:30–5:30; June and Sept., daily 9:30–6:30; July and Aug., daily 9–8:30; Oct.–Mar., daily 10–4 (last admission 1 hr before closing). Off-season opening times vary; call ahead.*

㉔ **Urquhart Castle,** near Drumnadrochit, is a favorite Loch Ness monster-watching spot. This plundered fortress stands on a promontory overlooking the loch, as it has since the Middle Ages. Because of its central and strategic position in the Great Glen line of communication, the castle has a complex history involving military offense and defense, as well as its own destruction and renovation. The castle was begun in the 13th century and was destroyed before the end of the 17th century to prevent its use by the Jacobites. The ruins of what was one of the largest castles in Scotland were plundered for building material. Today swarms of bus tours pass through after investigating the Loch Ness phenomenon. ⊠ *2 mi southeast of Drumnadrochit,* ☎ *0131/668–8600.* ⊑ *£3.* ☉ *Apr.–Sept., daily 9:30–6; Oct.–Mar., Mon.–Sat. 9:30–4, Sun. 11:30–4.*

Dining and Lodging

$$–$$$ ✕🏠 **Polmaily House.** This country house is located on the northern edge of Loch Ness amid lovely parkland. Books, log fires, and a helpful staff contribute to an atmosphere that is warmer and more personal than that found at grander, more expensive hotels. The restaurant is noted for its traditional British cuisine, which takes advantage of fresh Highland produce. Tay salmon in pastry with dill sauce, roast rack of lamb with rosemary, and cold smoked venison with melon, are examples of some flavorful dishes, cooked modern British style. ⊠ *Drumnadrochit, IV3 6XT,* ☎ *01456/450343,* 🖷 *01456/450813. 11 rooms, 9 with bath, 2 with shower. Restaurant, indoor pool, tennis court, croquet, fishing. MC, V.*

$–$$ 🏠 **Borlum Farmhouse.** Spectacular views over Loch Ness are the outstanding feature of this guest house on a working farm. The rooms are individually decorated, most with light colors and antique furniture, and breakfasts are well cooked. ⊠ *Drumnadrochit, Inverness, IV3 6XN,* ☎ 🖷 *01456/450358. 5 rooms, 2 with bath. No smoking. MC, V.*

OFF THE   **GLENS AFFRIC AND CANNICH** – Two outstanding mountain landscapes,
BEATEN PATH   those of Glens Affric and Cannich, are located toward the northern end and to the west of the Great Glen. These two glens offer a cross section of typical remote Highland landscape, yet are accessible. Glen Cannich is constricted by crags and birch-clad slopes before opening into a broad valley with a hydroelectric dam at its far end. Glen Affric is even more aesthetically appealing, with oak woodlands and hay fields in the lower reaches, and, higher up, wild lochs (also dammed) and pine forests, similar to the Trossachs, but on a grander scale. Reach these glens by taking the A831 west from Drumnadrochit to Cannich village, then turning left onto the respective minor road for each glen.

En Route   A more leisurely alternative to the fast-moving traffic on the busy A82 to Inverness, and one that combines monster-watching with peaceful road touring, is to take the B862 from Fort Augustus and follow the east bank of Loch Ness. The B862 runs around the end of Loch Ness, then climbs into moorland and forestry plantation. Fine views of Fort Augustus can be seen by climbing a few yards up and to the right, onto the moor; here you'll be able to see above the conifer spikes. The half-hidden track beside the road is a remnant of the military road built by General Wade. Loch Ness quickly drops out of sight, but is soon replaced by the peaceful, reedy Loch Tarff.

Whitebridge

㉕   *12 mi north of Fort Augustus via B862.*

The B862 follows the line of the former military route and shows appropriate military precision nearly all the way to Whitebridge, where a handsome single-arch Wade bridge (look for it on your right) has been restored. Just before the bridge is the **Whitebridge Hotel,** a former King-shouse, one of a chain of inns built by the government in the 18th century to service the military roads. The Kingshouse name is still used by a few of Scotland's hotels.

Dining and Lodging

$$$–$$$$
★
✕⊞ **Knockie Lodge.** Set on rising ground not far from Loch Ness, this former shooting lodge has superb views over peaceful surroundings and is especially popular with fishermen and other outdoor-sports enthusiasts. The hotel is decorated with traditional and antique furniture, and there's a restrained elegance throughout. The restaurant offers enticing fixed menus with a choice of desserts. The chef uses top-quality produce and prepares everything with great care: Try the chicken and duck terrine, the beef fillet wrapped in bacon and herbs with red wine sauce, or the salmon fillet phyllo pastry with sole mousse. Bar lunches are also wholesome. The dining room is small and fills up quickly. Inverness is easily accessed from the hotel. ⊠ *Whitebridge, IV1 2UP,* ☎ *01456/486276,* ℻ *01456/486389. 10 rooms with bath. Restaurant (reservations essential). AE, DC, MC, V. Closed Nov.–Apr.*

En Route Beyond Whitebridge the small banks on either side of the road are thought to have survived from the military's original work in 1726; thus you find yourself traveling one of the earliest roads in the Highlands. Take the B852, left at the junction beyond Whitebridge, to regain the shores of Loch Ness by way of some fine woodlands.

Foyers

3 mi north of Whitebridge, 21 mi southwest of Inverness.

㉖ At Foyers, almost back at Loch Ness-side, a sign outside the general store will direct you to the **Falls of Foyers.** Steep paths, strewn with pine cones, lead to a site where a thin waterfall streams into a dark pot and then down a ravine. The original volume of the falls was much reduced shortly before the turn of the century, when the power generated here was harnessed for the first commercial application of hydroelectricity (1896), in an aluminum-smelting plant on a site by Loch Ness.

㉗ The road meanders pleasantly north from Foyers, offering some views of the loch on the way to **Inverfarigaig** and the **Inverfarigaig Forest Centre.** The center has several displays on forestry activities, plus a number of trails leading into the woodlands. ⊠ *Inverfarigaig,* ☎ *01320/366322.* ⊡ *Free.* ☉ *Easter–mid-Oct., daily 9:30–7.*

TOWARD THE SMALL ISLES

Fort William has enough points of interest for visitors—a museum, exhibits, and shopping—to compensate for its less-than-picturesque milieu. The town's primary purpose is to serve the west Highland hinterland; its role as a tourist stop is secondary. Since this is a relatively wet part of Scotland, and since Fort William itself can always be explored if it rains, strike west toward the coast if the weather looks settled: On a sunny day, the Small Isles—Rum, Eigg, Canna, and Muck—look as blue as the sea and sky together. From here you could also visit Skye via the ferry at Mallaig, or take a day cruise from Arisaig to the Small Isles for a glimpse of traffic-free island life. South of Fort William, Ballachulish and Glencoe are within easy striking distance.

Glen Coe

 92 mi north of Glasgow, 44 mi northwest of Edinburgh.

Glen Coe, where great craggy buttresses loom darkly over the road, has a special place in the folk memory of Scotland: it was the site of an infamous massacre in 1692, still remembered in the Highlands for the treachery with which soldiers of the Campbell clan, acting as government militia, treated their hosts, the MacDonalds. According to Highland code, in his own home a clansman should give shelter even to his sworn enemy. In the face of bitter weather, the Campbells were accepted as guests by the MacDonalds. Apparently acting on orders from the British government, the Campbells turned on their hosts, committing murder "under trust." The National Trust for Scotland's **visitor center** at Glencoe (at the western end of the glen) tells the story of the massacre and also offers excellent displays on local geology. ☎ *01855/811307.* ◻ *50p.* ☉ *Apr.–mid-May, Sept.–Oct., daily 10–5; mid-May–Aug., daily 9:30–5:30.*

Outdoor Activities and Sports

SKIING

The **Glen Coe** development (☎ 01855/851226) at the east end of the glen once had a formidable reputation in Scotland: if you could ski there, you could ski anywhere, because of a frequent combination of severe weather and icy runs, as well as fairly primitive facilities. Things have improved in recent years. Although the black runs are still very challenging, there are now extensive, well-maintained beginner and intermediate runs on the lower plateau. There's also a good restaurant.

Ballachulish

 1 mi west of Glencoe, 15 mi south of Fort William, 39 mi north of Oban.

Ballachulish, once a slate-carrying community, acts as gateway to the western approaches to Glencoe. There is a Glencoe village as well. On a little peninsula north of the main road, which is actually reclaimed land using the slate spoils from the old quarry, you will find a hotel and visitor center complex, **Highland Mystery World,** (opened March 1996) which promises a journey into the Highland environment of old, where the spirit world and the mythical world are portrayed as they appeared to our ancestors. You can also enjoy real-life snacks and meals here. ◻ *Ballachulish,* ☎ *01855/821582,* ⅎⅩ *01855/821463.* ◻ *£4.75.* ☉ *Apr.–Sept., daily 10–9:30 (last admission 9); Oct.–Mar., daily 10–5:30 (last admission 5).*

Dining and Lodging

$$$$ ✕▥ **Airds Hotel.** This former ferry inn, dating from the 17th century, has some of the finest views in all of Scotland. Located in a peaceful village midway between Ballachulish and Oban, the long white building, backed by trees, has a friendly feel to it. Quilted bedspreads and family mementos make guests feel right at home. Shooting and fishing trips can be arranged. The restaurant serves Scottish cuisine, including deer and grouse dishes. ◻ *Port Appin, Argyll, PA38 4DF,* ☎ *01631/730206,* ⅎⅩ *01631/730535. 12 rooms with bath. Restaurant (jacket and tie). AE, MC, V.*

$$$ ✕▥ **Holly Tree Hotel.** Railway buffs should enjoy this converted Edwardian railway station, complete with some of its original fixtures and fittings. The spacious restaurant is on the carefully extended former platform. You may see seals in Loch Linnhe from your dinner table, along with memorable sunsets over the Ardgour mountains. The emphasis is on fresh local produce—pigeon, venison, lamb, halibut, and salmon. Bedrooms are modern and well equipped, if on the small side.

✉ *Kentallen, on A828, south of Ballachulish,* ☎ *01631/740292,* FAX *01631/740345. 10 rooms with bath. Restaurant (reservations essential). AE, DC, MC, V.*

Outdoor Activities and Sports

BICYCLING

Mountain Madness (✉ Cameron Court, Onich, by Fort William, Inverness-shire, PH33 6RY, ☎ 01855/821500) rents mountain bikes and can suggest tour routes in the Glen Coe area.

Fort William

③⓪ *15 mi north of Ballachulish, 69 mi southwest of Inverness, 108 mi northwest of Glasgow, 138 mi northwest of Edinburgh.*

As its name suggests, Fort William originated as a military outpost, first established by Cromwell's General Monk in 1655 and refortified by George I in 1715 to help combat an outbreak by the turbulent Jacobite clans. It remains the southern gateway to the Great Glen and to the far west, and is a bustling, tourist-oriented place. The **West Highland Museum,** in the center of town, explores the theme of Prince Charles Edward Stuart and the 1745 rebellion. Included in the museum's folk exhibits is a tartan exhibit. ✉ *Cameron Sq.,* ☎ *01397/702169.* ☞ *£1.50.* ☉ *May–Oct., Mon.–Sat. 10–1 and 2–5 (extended hours in summer).*

Scotland's (and Britain's) highest mountain, the 4,406-foot **Ben Nevis,** looms over Fort William less than 4 miles from the sea. The mountain is a challenge to climb: Only fit and well-equipped hikers should try the hike to its summit.

A huge collection of gemstones, crystals, and fossils, including a 26-pound uncut emerald, is displayed at **Treasures of the Earth,** in a converted church at Corpach on A830 near Fort William. ☎ *01397/772283.* ☞ *£2.50.* ☉ *July–Sept., daily 9:30–7; Oct.–Dec. and Feb.–June, daily 10–5; Jan. by appointment.*

Dining and Lodging

$–$$ ✕ **Crannog Scottish Seafoods.** Set conspicuously on a small pier pro-
★ jecting over the waters of Loch Linnhe, the Crannog has transformed Fort William dining. The sight of a fishing boat drawing up to the pier side to land its catch straight into the restaurant kitchen, says all that needs to be said about the freshness of the seafood. Sitting at a window seat—pine predominates in fixtures and fittings—with the sun going down behind the steep hills on the far side of the loch, is a special treat. The chef's deft touch ensures that the fresh flavors are not overwhelmed. ✉ *Crannog Scottish Seafoods, Town Pier, Fort William,* ☎ *01397/ 705589. MC, V.*

$$$$ ✕▦ **Inverlochy Castle.** A red-granite Victorian castle, Inverlochy stands in 50 acres of woodlands in the shadow of Ben Nevis, with striking Highland landscape on every side. Queen Victoria stayed here and wrote, "I never saw a lovelier or more romantic spot." Dating from 1863, the hotel retains all the splendor of its period, with a fine frescoed ceiling, crystal chandeliers, a handsome staircase in the Great Hall, paintings and hunting trophies everywhere, and plush, comfortable bedrooms. The restaurant is exceptional—a lovely room with wonderful cuisine. Many of the specialties use local produce, such as roast saddle of roe deer or wood pigeon consommé, with orange soufflé as the final touch. ✉ *Torlundy (3 mi northeast of Fort William on A82), PH33 6SN,* ☎ *01397/702177,* FAX *01397/702953. 17 rooms with bath. Restaurant (reservations essential), tennis court, croquet, fishing, billiards. AE, MC, V. Closed Dec.–Feb.*

$$ 🏠 **Crolinnhe.** An elegant Victorian house with colorful gardens, over-
★ looking Loch Linnhe yet only a 10-minute walk from town, Crolinnhe
is an exceptionally comfortable bed-and-breakfast (as its tourist board
deluxe grading confirms). Antique and high-quality reproduction fur-
niture is set off by pastel walls and bold-toned curtains, with each bed-
room individually decorated. The breakfasts are among the best you
will taste in any establishment in any price range in Scotland. ⊠ *Grange
Rd., Fort William, PH33 6JF,* ☎ *01397/702709. 5 rooms, 4 with
shower. No credit cards. Closed Nov.–Mar.*

Nightlife

CABARET

McTavish's Kitchens (⊠ High St., Fort William, ☎ 01397/702406) of-
fers Scottish cabaret in the summer season, of the tartan-clad dancer
and bagpipe/accordion variety.

Outdoor Activities and Sports

BICYCLING

Bicycles can be rented from **Lees Cycle Hire** (⊠ Leesholme, Cameron
Rd., Fort William, ☎ 01397/704204, ☉ May–mid-Aug.) **Off Beat
Bikes** (⊠ 117 High St., Fort William, ☎ 01397/704008).

GOLF

The 18-hole golf course at Fort William welcomes visitors (☎ 01397/
704464).

SKIING

Nevis Range (⊠ Fort William, ☎ 01397/705825), the newest of
Scotland's ski areas, is a fashionable and modern development on the
flanks of Aonach Mor, offering good and varied skiing, as well as su-
perb views of Ben Nevis. There are runs for all ability levels, and a gon-
dola system, unique in Scotland.

WALKING

This area, especially around Glen Coe and Ben Nevis, is very popular
with hikers, but only the fit and properly outfitted should try it. The
tourist information center (☞ Visitor Information, *below*) can offer
guidance on low-level routes. Several excellent guides are available lo-
cally; they can and should be consulted for high-level routes. **Ben Nevis**
is a large and dangerous mountain, where snow can fall on the sum-
mit plateau any time of the year.

Shopping

The majority of the shops here are located along High Street, which
in summer attracts ever-present, bustling crowds intent on stocking up
for excursions to the west. **Ben Nevis Woollen Mill** (⊠ Belford Rd., ☎
01397/704244), at the north end of town, is a major supplier of tar-
tans, woolens and tweeds, and has a restaurant. **The Granite House** (⊠
High St., ☎ 01397/703651) stocks Scottish contemporary jewelry, china
and crystal giftware, wildlife sculptures, and other collectibles. **Scot-
tish Crafts and Whisky Centre** (⊠ 135–139 High St., ☎ 01397/704406)
has the usual range of souvenirs, but it also sells homemade choco-
lates and a vast range of malt whiskies, including miniatures and lim-
ited edition bottlings.

At **Treasures of the Earth** (⊠ Corpach, ☎ 01397/772283) there is a
shop that stocks an Aladdin's Cave assortment of gemstone jewelry,
crystal ornaments, mineral specimens, polished stones, and books on
related subjects. It's a treasure trove of unusual gifts.

En Route Travel down the eastern side of Loch Linnhe to Corran, where a fre-
quent ferry shuttles autos and foot passengers across the loch to Ard-
gour. (From the map you will see you can avoid the ferry by driving

around the head of Loch Eil, but it's not a particularly scenic route.) From Ardgour, the two-lane A861 runs south along Loch Linnhe before turning into Glen Sanda, crossing the watershed, and running down to the long shores of Loch Sunart. This is a typical west Highlands sea loch: Orange kelp marks the tide lines, and herons stand muffled and miserable, wondering if it is worth risking a free meal at the local fish farm. As for the fish farms themselves, visitors will become accustomed to their floats and cages turning up in the foreground of every sea-loch view. The farms were originally hailed as the savior of the Highland economy because of the number of jobs they created, but questions are now being raised about their environmental effects, and the market for their product is being threatened by Scandinavian imports. At the little village of Salen, either turn north immediately, or divert west to Ardnamurchan Point.

Ardnamurchan Point

③① *55 mi west of Fort William via A861 and B8007.*

Along a narrow road blind-bending partly through thickets of rhododendrons, the most western point of mainland Scotland is reached at Ardnamurchan Point. The Ardnamurchan peninsula is a must-see for those who love unspoiled coastal scenery. Here you'll find small farming communities and vacation homes.

Acharacle

★ **③②** *3 mi north of Salen.*

On the way north to Acharacle (pronounced ach-*ar*-ra-kle with a Scots "ch"), you'll pass through deep-green plantations and moorland lily ponds. This spread out settlement, backed by the hills of Moidart, lies at the shallow and reedy western end of **Loch Shiel;** the north end is more dramatic and sits deep within the rugged hills.

A few minutes north of Acharacle—where the main road turns sharply right—a narrow road goes left, overhung in places by mossy trees, to emerge at **Castle Tioram.** This ruined fortress dominates a bracken-green islet, barely anchored to the mainland by a sand spit. The castle was once the home of the chief of the MacDonalds of Clan Ranald, but the last chief burned the castle to prevent its falling into the hands of his enemies, the Campbells, during the 1715 Jacobite rebellion. This fragment of Scottish history guards the south channel of Loch Moidart. ✉ *Reached by an unclassified road north of A861.* ⌨ *Free.* ☺ *At all times.*

En Route   Traveling between Acharacle and Arisaig, you'll reach the upper sandy shores of Loch Moidart by climbing on the A861 over a high moorland pass. On the next ascent, from Loch Moidart, you'll be rewarded with stunning sea views. The sea coast is reached by the mouth of Loch Ailort (pronounced *eye*-ort), and there are plenty of places to pull off among the boulders and birch scrub and sort out the view of the islands. In the distance you'll be able to spot Eigg, a low island marked by the dramatic black peak of An Sgurr. Beyond Eigg is the larger Rum, with its range of hills, the Norse-named Rum Coullin, looming cloud-capped over the island. Loch Ailort itself is another picturesque inlet, now cluttered with the garish floats of fish cages. You meet the main road again at the junction with the A830, the main road from Fort William to Mallaig. Turn left here. The breathtaking seaward views continue to distract you from the road beside Loch nan Uamh (from Gaelic meaning cave, and pronounced *oo*-am). This loch is associated with Prince Charles Edward Stuart's nine-month stay on the mainland, during which he gathered a small army, marched as far south as Derby in England, alarmed the king, retreated to unavoidable defeat at Culloden in the spring, and then spent a few months as a fugitive in the Highlands. A cairn by the shore marks the spot where the prince was picked up by a French ship. Prince Charles never returned to Scotland.

Arisaig

③ *27 mi north of Acharacle.*

Considering its small size, Arisaig offers a surprising choice of high-quality options for dining and lodging (☞ Dining and Lodging, *below*).

To the north of Arisaig, the road cuts across a headland to reach a stretch of coastline where silver sands glitter with the mica in the local rock; clear water, blue sky, and white sand lend a tropical flavor to the beaches—when the sun shines.

Try to visit at least a couple of the **Small Isles: Rum, Eigg, Muck,** and **Canna,** from Arisaig. Contact **Murdo Grant** (⊠ Arisaig Marine, Arisaig, Inverness-shire, ☎ 01687/450224, FAX 01687/450678), who runs a service from the harbor at Arisaig. The MV *Shearwater,* a former naval inshore minesweeper, delivers supplies and mail as well as visitors to the diminutive island communities. What sets Grant's operation apart from the tourism-oriented excursions is that it offers visitors a glimpse of island life from a working vessel going about its summer routine.

Dining and Lodging

$$$$ ✕🗗 **Arisaig House Hotel.** This secluded and grand Victorian mansion offers tranquillity and some marvelous scenery, including views of the Inner Hebrides. The bedrooms are plush and restful, with soft pastels, original moldings, and antique furniture. The cuisine showcases fresh local produce, such as salmon or venison cooked in the modern British style: Try the local scallops and prawns with fresh basil and coriander or the spring lamb with fresh herbs. ⊠ *Beasdale, 6 mi south of Mallaig on A830, west of Glenfinnan, PH39 4NR,* ☎ *01687/450622,* FAX *01687/450626. 2 suites, 12 rooms with bath. Restaurant, 9-hole golf course at Crigh, croquet, boating, fishing, billiards, island trips, library. No children under 10. AE, MC, V. Closed Nov.–Mar.*

$$$ ✕🗗 **Old Library Lodge and Restaurant.** This guest house, a converted barn situated on the waterfront, has a fine restaurant, giving visitors another reason to believe that the village of Arisaig is unusually well endowed with good places to eat at all price levels. It offers local produce prepared in a French bistro style, served in a whitewashed, airy dining room. The bedrooms are very comfortable, from the flowery duvets to the cozy armchairs. ⊠ *Arisaig, PH39 4NH,* ☎ *01687/450651,* FAX *01687/450219. 6 rooms, 4 with bath, 2 with shower. Restaurant. MC, V. Closed Nov.–Mar.*

$$ ✕🗗 **Arisaig Hotel.** An old coaching inn close to the water, with magnificent views of the Small Isles, this hotel offers a slightly more modest environment than Arisaig House. The inn has retained its provinciality with simple decor and home cooking. High-quality local ingredients are used here to good advantage; locally caught lobster, langoustines, and crayfish are specialties, as are proper puddings, such as fruit crumbles. ⊠ *Arisaig, PH39 4NH,* ☎ *01687/450210,* FAX *01687/450310. 15 rooms with bath or shower. Restaurant. MC, V.*

Outdoor Activities and Sports

BICYCLING

Bespoke Highland Tours (⊠ The Bothy, Camusdarach, Inverness-shire, (☎ 01687/450272) rents bicycles and arranges tours of the Great Glen and the Highlands.

Mallaig

34 *8 mi north of Arisaig, 44 mi northwest of Fort William.*

After the approach along the coast, the workaday fishing port of Mallaig itself is anticlimactic. It has a few shops, and there is some bustle by the quayside when fishing boats unload or the Skye ferry departs: this is the departure point for the southern ferry connection to the Isle of Skye, the largest of the Inner Hebrides. Mallaig is also the starting point for day cruises up the Sound of Sleat, which separates Skye from the mainland. For cruises, which operate all year, contact **Bruce Watt Sea Cruises** (✉ Western Isles Guest House, Mallaig, ☎ 01687/462320). It offers views into rugged Knoydart and its long, fjordlike sea lochs, **Lochs Nevis and Hourn.** The area to the immediate north and west, beyond Loch Nevis, one of the most remote in Scotland, is often referred to as the Rough Bounds of Knoydart. In Mallaig itself, the **Heritage Centre** has exhibits, films, photographs, and models on all aspects of the local history. ✉ *Station Rd.,* ☎ *01687/462085.* ☑ *£1.80.* ☉ *Apr., May and Oct., Mon.–Sat. 11–4; June–Sept., Mon.–Sat. 9.30–5, Sun. 1–5.*

Beside the harbor, **Mallaig Marine World** shows you what goes on beneath the surface of the Sound of Sleat: live fish and shellfish, and a display on the local fishing traditions are among the attractions here. ✉ *The Harbour,* ☎ *01687/462292.* ☑ *£2.50.* ☉ *Daily 10–5; closed Dec. 25, Jan. 1 and Jan.–early Feb.*

35 A small, unclassified side road leads east just south of Mallaig, to an even smaller road that will bring you to **Loch Morar,** the deepest of all the Scottish lochs (over 1,000 ft); the next deepest point is miles out into the Atlantic, beyond the Continental Shelf. Apart from this short public road, the area around the loch is all but roadless.

Glenfinnan

36 *26 mi southeast of Mallaig.*

Glenfinnan, perhaps the most visitor-oriented stop on the route between Mallaig and Fort William, has the most to offer visitors interested in Scottish history. Here the National Trust for Scotland has capitalized on the romance surrounding the story of the Jacobites and their intention of returning a Stuart monarch and the Roman Catholic religion to a country that had become staunchly Protestant. In Glenfinnan, in 1745, the sometimes-reluctant clans joined forces and rallied to Prince Charles Edward Stuart's cause. The raising of the prince's standard is commemorated by the **Glenfinnan Monument** (an unusual tower on the banks of Loch Shiel), and the story of his campaign is told in the nearby visitor center. Note that the figure at the top of the monument is of a Highlander, not the prince. The view down Loch Shiel from the Glenfinnan Monument is one of the most photographed views in Scotland. ✉ *A830,* ☎ *01397/722250.* ☑ *£1.* ☉ *Apr.–mid-May and Sept.–Oct., daily 10–1 and 2–5; mid-May–Aug., daily 10–6.*

As impressive as the Glenfinnan Monument (for visitors who have tired of the Jacobite "Will He No Come Back Again" sentiment) is the curving railway viaduct that stretches across the green slopes behind the monument. The **Glenfinnan Viaduct,** 21 spans and 1,248 feet long, was in its time the wonder of the Highlands. The railway's contractor, Robert MacAlpine, known as Concrete Bob by the locals, pioneered the use of mass concrete for viaducts and bridges when his company built the Mallaig extension, which opened in 1901.

The train is the most relaxing way to take in the landscape of birch- and bracken-covered wild slopes; rail services (☎ 01397/703791) run all year on the stretch of line between Fort William and Mallaig, with steam engines operating in the summer season only.

AROUND THE GREAT GLEN A TO Z

Arriving and Departing

By Bus
There is a long-distance **Scottish Citylink** service from Glasgow to Fort William (☎ 0990/505050). Inverness is also well served from the central belt of Scotland (Inverness coach station, ☎ 01463/233371).

By Car
As in all areas of rural Scotland, a car is a great asset for exploring the Great Glen and Speyside, especially since the best of the area is away from the main roads. The fast A9 brings you to Inverness in roughly three hours from Glasgow or Edinburgh, even if you take your time.

By Plane
Inverness Airport (Dalcross, ☎ 01463/232471) has flights from London, Manchester, and Glasgow, and a wide range of internal flights covering the Highlands and islands. All flights are operated by **British Airways** (☎ 0345/222111). Fort William has bus and train connections with Glasgow, so **Glasgow Airport** can be an appropriate access point. (☞ Chapter 4, Glasgow, for further information.)

By Train
The area is well served by train. There are connections from London to Inverness and Fort William, as well as reliable links from Glasgow and Edinburgh. For information call **ScotRail** (Fort William, ☎ 01397/703791; Inverness, ☎ 01463/238924) or contact any main-line station in Scotland.

Getting Around

By Bus
There is limited service available in the Great Glen area and some local service running from Fort William. **Highland Bus and Coach Company/GaelicBus** (☎ 01397/702373) operates buses down the Great Glen, around Fort William, and in the Lochaber area, and also a service from Fort William south to Oban. A number of post-bus services will help get you to the more remote corners of the area. The timetable is available from the **Royal Mail** (✉ 7 Strothers Lane, Inverness, IV1 1AA ☎ 01463/256200).

By Car
You can use the main A9 Perth–Inverness road (via Aviemore) to explore this area or use one of the many other smaller roads (some of them old military roads) to explore the much quieter east side of Loch Ness. The same applies to Speyside, where a variety of options open up away from the A9, especially through the pinewoods by Coylumbridge and Feshiebridge, east of the main road. Mallaig, west of Fort William, also has improving road connections, but rail remains the most enjoyable way to experience the rugged hills and loch scenery between these two places. In Morvern, the area across Loch Linnhe southwest of Fort William, you may encounter single-lane roads, which require slower speeds and concentration.

By Train
Though the Great Glen has no rail connection (in Victorian times Fort William and Inverness had different lines built by companies that could not agree), this area has the **West Highland line,** which links Fort

William to Mallaig, a small fishing and ferry port on the west coast; a trip on this scenic line is highly recommended. There is also train service between Glasgow (Queen Street) and Inverness, via Aviemore, which gives access to the heart of Speyside. For information call **ScotRail** (Fort William, ☎ 01397/703791; Inverness, ☎ 01463/238924).

Contacts and Resources

Car Rentals
Europcar Ltd. (✉ The Highlander Service Station, Millburn Rd., Inverness, ☎ 01463/235337. **Hertz** (✉ Dalcross Airport, Inverness, ☎ 01667/462652.

Emergencies
For **police, fire,** or **ambulance,** dial 999 from any telephone. No coins are needed for emergency calls from phone booths.

Fishing
The Great Glen offers many rivers and lochs where you can fly-fish for salmon and trout. Tourist information centers (☞ Visitor Information, *below*) can provide information on locations, permits, and fishing rights (which differ from those in England and Wales). The fishing seasons are as follows: salmon, depending on the area, early February through September or early October; brown trout, March 15 to September 30; sea trout, May through September or early October; rainbow trout, no statutory-close season. Sea angling from shore or boat is also possible.

Guided Tours
ORIENTATION
From Fort William, **Highland Bus and Coach Company** (✉ Travel Centre, Fort William, ☎ 01397/702373) operates coach tours in the summer season. **ScotRail** (☎ 01397/703791) runs services on the outstandingly beautiful West Highland Line to Mallaig. **Caledonian MacBrayne** runs scheduled service and cruises to Skye, the Small Isles, and Mull from Mallaig (☎ 01475/650100, FAX 01475/637607). **Arisaig Marine** (☎ 01687/450224) operates highly recommended Hebridean day cruises on the MV (motor vessel) *Shearwater* to the Small Isles and Skye at Easter, and daily from May to September. Also available for charter from Arisaig Marine is a fast twin-engine motor yacht, which can take up to 12 passengers for go-where-you-please cruises around the Small Isles and farther afield.

From Inverness, the following companies offer coach tours during the summer season: **Highland Bus and Coach Company** (✉ Inverness bus station, ☎ 01463/233371). **Macdonald's Tours** (☎ 01463/240673).

SPECIAL-INTEREST
From Inverness, **Highland Insight Tours and Travel** (☎ 01463/831403), offers personalized touring holidays and full-day or half-day tours that cater to any interest. **James Johnson** (☎ 01463/790179) will drive you anywhere, but he has a particularly good knowledge of the Highlands and islands, including the Outer Isles. **Jacobite Cruises Ltd.** (✉ Tomnahurich Bridge, Glenurquhart Rd., Inverness, ☎ 01463/233999, FAX 01463/710188) runs morning and afternoon cruises to Loch Ness, morning and afternoon excursions to Urquhart Castle, and boat and coach excursions to the Monster Exhibition. **Macaulay Charters** (✉ 12 Pict Ave., Inverness, ☎ 01463/225398) provides trips by boat from Inverness to Nairn and the surrounding coastline, offering visitors the chance to see dolphins in their breeding area.

An unusual option from Inverness is a day trip to Orkney: **John o'Groats Ferries** (☎ 01955/611353) offers day tours from Inverness to Orkney daily from June to August.

Hospitals

Emergency rooms are located at the following hospitals: **Belford Hospital** (✉ Belford Rd., Fort William, ☎ 01397/702481), **Raigmore Hospital** (✉ Perth Rd., Inverness, ☎ 01463/704000), and **Town and County Hospital** (✉ Cawdor Rd., Nairn, ☎ 01667/452101).

Late-Night Pharmacies

Pharmacies are not common away from the larger towns. In an emergency, the police will assist you in locating a pharmacist. In Inverness, **Kinmylies Pharmacy** (✉ 1 Charleston Court, Kinmylies, ☎ 01463/221094) is open weekdays until 6 and Saturdays until 5:30. The pharmacy at the **Scottish Co-op** superstore (✉ Milton of Inshes, Perth Rd., outside Inverness, ☎ 01463/242525), is open Monday to Wednesday 9–8, Thursday and Friday 9–9, Saturday 8–6, and Sunday 10–5. In Fort William, **Boots the Chemist** (✉ High St., ☎ 01397/705143) is open Monday to Saturday 8:45–6. A rotation system provides limited Sunday service—consult the list on any pharmacy door.

Visitor Information

The principal tourist information centers in the area are: **Aviemore** (✉ Grampian Rd., ☎ 01479/810363, ℻ 01479/811063). **Fort William** (✉ Cameron Centre, Cameron Sq., ☎ 01397/703781, ℻ 01397/705184). **Inverness** (✉ Castle Wynd, ☎ 01463/234353, ℻ 01463/710609).

Other tourist information centers, open seasonally, include those at Ballachulish, Carrbridge, Daviot Wood (A9), Fort Augustus, Grantown on Spey, Kilchoan, Kingussie, Mallaig, Nairn, Ralia (A9), Spean Bridge, and Strontian.

11 The Northern Highlands

Red sandstone, black gabbro, and silver-gray gneiss, scoured by now-vanished glaciers, are the region's building blocks and make for some of Scotland's most breathtaking scenery. Drive through Glen Torridon or walk through the bare-bones landscape around Lochinver, and the last Ice Age doesn't seem so long ago. The area ranges from the long rolling moors of Caithness to the jagged profile of the Cuillin Mountains of Skye. By road, air, and ferry, you can explore the ruined croft (farm) houses in a deserted glen from which the old population has long vanished.

THE OLD COUNTIES OF ROSS AND CROMARTY (sometimes called Easter and Wester Ross), Sutherland, and Caithness constitute the most northern portion of mainland Scotland. The population is sparse, mountains and moorland limit the choice of touring routes, and distances are less important than whether the winding, hilly roads you sometimes encounter are two lanes or one. On a map, this area seems far from major urban centers, but it is easy to get to. Inverness has an airport with direct links to Glasgow, and you can reach destinations such as the fishing town of Ullapool in an hour by car from Inverness. In fact, much of the western seaboard is easily accessible from the Northern Highlands.

By Gilbert Summers

The area contains some of Scotland's most intriguing scenery. Much of Sutherland and Wester Ross, for example, is comprised of a rocky platform of Lewisian gneiss, certainly the oldest rocks in Britain, scoured and hollowed by glacial action into numerous lochs. On top of this rolling wet moorland landscape sit strangely shaped quartzite-capped sandstone mountains, eroded and pinnacled.

Many of the place-names in this region reflect its early links with Scandinavia. Sutherland, the most northern portion of mainland Scotland, was once the "southern land" of the Vikings. Scotland's most northern point, Cape Wrath, got its name from the Viking's word *hvarth*, (turning point) and Laxford, Suilven, and dozens of other names in the area have Norse rather than Gaelic derivations.

The islands of Skye and especially the Outer Hebrides, which are now often referred to as the Western Isles, are the stronghold of the Gaelic language. Skye is famous for its misty mountains called the Cuillins, while the Outer Hebrides have some of Scotland's finest beaches.

Pleasures and Pastimes

Bicycling

Be prepared to meet holiday traffic at peak season, especially on the mainland. Some side roads (and even, in the far northwest, some main roads) are single-track and narrow, meaning there will be traffic coming the other way between passing places. High-visibility clothing is advised. The landscapes are great, but the open and rugged terrain has not favored the development of a pleasing network of rural back roads as exists in other parts of Scotland.

Dining

In an area with such a low population, the choice of restaurants is a bit more restricted in comparison with other parts of Scotland. The places selected in this chapter can be relied upon for acceptable standards in the dining room.

WHAT TO WEAR

In mainland hotels and guest houses in the northern Highlands, your fellow guests will be walkers and fishermen, and the dress code will be relaxed. At upscale country houses you'll be more comfortable if you dress up a bit.

CATEGORY	COST*
$$$$	over £40
$$$	£30–£40
$$	£15–£30
$	under £15

*per person for a three-course meal, including VAT and excluding drinks and service

Fishing

The possibilities for fishing are endless here, as a glance at the loch-littered map of Sutherland suggests. Trout-fishing permits on several hill lochans should be available locally. Inquire at your accommodation or at the nearest tourist information center. Your host(ess) will probably be perfectly willing to cook the tasty, apricot-flesh loch trout that you just might catch.

Golf

There are only about 15 courses in the area—not many compared with other regions of Scotland—with almost no courses on the west coast, although Gairloch Golf Club has its enthusiasts. The best-known club in the area is Royal Dornoch on the east coast north of Inverness. Were it not for its northern location, the club, sometimes described as the "St. Andrews of the north," could be a candidate for the Open Championship.

Lodging

This region of Scotland has some good modern hotels and some charming inns but not many establishments in the more expensive categories. Travelers often find that the most enjoyable accommodations are low-cost guest houses (often family-run), offering bed-and-breakfast. Dining rooms of country-house lodgings frequently reach the standard of top-quality restaurants.

CATEGORY	COST*
$$$$	over £110
$$$	£80–£110
$$	£45–£80
$	under £45

All prices are for a standard double room, including service, breakfast, and VAT.

Nightlife

The nightlife here is confined mainly to hotels and pubs. *Ceilidhs* (song, music and dance), dances, and concerts are performed on a sporadic basis and advertised locally.

Pony Trekking

Pony trekking was invented to give the sturdy Highland ponies a job to do when they weren't carrying dead deer off the hills during the "stalking" (deer-hunting) season. Treks last from two hours to a whole day, and ponies can be found to suit all ages and levels of experience.

Shopping

As in Argyll and the Western Isles, shopping in the Northern Highlands tends to be more interesting for the variety of crafts available rather than for the number and types of shops. After all, the population of the area is scattered, and if the locals have any special needs, they can travel to the larger population centers, as well as to Inverness. In the Outer Hebrides, the specialty to look for is Harris tweed, woven by individuals working at home, and available either directly from the weaving shed or at local crafts shops.

Exploring the Northern Highlands

From Inverness, gateway to the Northern Highlands, roads fan out like the spokes of a wheel to join the coastal route around the rim of mainland Scotland. The routes described below first explore the mainland as far northwest as Cape Wrath, and to Duncansby Head in the far north, then travel to Skye, and the Outer Hebrides.

Great Itineraries

The quality of the northern light and the sheer ambience of the landscapes add to the touring adventure. Above all, don't rush things. And take a good look at how multiple-journey ferry tickets—the Island Hopscotch, for example—can help you stay flexible (☞ Getting Around by Car and Ferry, in The Northern Highlands A to Z, *below*).

IF YOU HAVE 2 DAYS

Numbers in the text correspond to numbers in the margin and on The Northern Highlands and Skye and The Outer Hebrides maps.

In only two days, you should stay on the mainland and take in the western seaboard, particularly around 🏨 **Shieldaig** ㉑ and **Glen Torridon** ㉒ or between 🏨 **Ullapool** ③ and 🏨 **Lochinver** ⑥.

IF YOU HAVE 5 DAYS

If the weather looks settled, then head for Skye, which needs two days at least if you are going to take in some of its attractions as well as enjoy the scenery. Base yourself at 🏨 **Portree** ㉗. You could then hop over from Uig in the north of Skye to 🏨 **Tarbert** ㊸ in the Western Isles for **Callanish Standing Stones** ㊶, the **Arnol Black House** ㊳, and some deserted beaches, returning to 🏨 **Ullapool** ③ in the north, and travelling to Inverness via **Strathpeffer** ①. Otherwise, stay on the mainland and do the entire north of Scotland loop, staying overnight at 🏨 **Ullapool** ③, 🏨 **Scourie** ⑧, 🏨 **Thurso** ⑪, 🏨 **Wick** ⑬, or 🏨 **Dornoch** ⑰.

IF YOU HAVE 8 DAYS

Tackle the north of Scotland coastal loop counterclockwise, taking the ferry at 🏨 **Ullapool** ③ for 🏨 **Stornoway** ㊱ and the Western Isles, returning to the mainland via the ferry from 🏨 **Tarbert** ㊸ to Uig on Skye, then over the Skye Bridge.

When to Tour the Northern Highlands

There is no best season to tour this area, though you should avoid the depth of winter, with its short days. The earlier in the spring or later in the autumn you go, the greater the chances of your encountering the elements in their extreme form. But although you may not want a western sea passage in a gale, the area is spectacular in all seasons.

THE NORTHERN LANDSCAPES
Wester Ross and Sutherland

The northern landscapes offer some of the most distinctive mountain profiles in all of Scotland, although the coastal rim roads are more interesting than the cross-country routes. In recent years, an influx of newcomers from other parts of the United Kingdom has improved the choices in lodging and dining. Your host in the northwest may not turn out to be a native, but that should make no difference to your enjoyment of this part of Scotland.

The essence of Caithness, the area at the top of Scotland, is space, big skies, and distant blue hills beyond endless rolling moors. There is a surprising amount to see and do on the east coast, beyond Inverness—so make sure you allow enough time to see the visitor centers, croft houses open to view, and so on.

Strathpeffer

❶ *19 mi northwest of Inverness via A9, A835 and A834.*

At the former Victorian spa town of Strathpeffer you can still taste the waters. Not far from Strathpeffer are the tumbling **Falls of Rogie** (signposted off the A835), where an interestingly bouncy suspension bridge leaves visitors with a fine view of the splashing waters below.

En Route   Follow the A835 through Garve and on across the bare backbone of Scotland. As the road begins to drop down from the bleak lands of the interior, look for Braemore junction and continue on the A835. Shortly after, as you draw closer to the woods, you'll see the Corrieshalloch Gorge parking lot on the left.

Corrieshalloch Gorge

★ ➋   *39 mi west of Strathpeffer.*

For a touch of vertigo, the Corrieshalloch Gorge is not to be missed. A burn draining the high moors plunges 150 feet into a 200-foot-deep, thickly wooded gorge. There is a suspension-bridge viewpoint and an atmosphere of romantic grandeur, like an old Scottish print come to life.

Ullapool

➌   *5 mi west of Corrieshalloch Gorge, 238 mi north of Glasgow.*

Set by the shores of salty **Loch Broom,** Ullapool was founded in 1788 as a fishing station, to exploit the local herring stocks. In recent years the fishing activity here has included "klondyking," the direct purchase of fish from local boats by large Eastern European factory ships. Ullapool has a cosmopolitan air and comes alive when the Lewis ferry docks and departs.

NEED A BREAK?   **Ceilidh Place** (⊠ W. Argyle St., ☎ 01854/612103) is a warm, friendly coffeehouse and restaurant where the prices are sensible and there is a regular program of music and drama. It also offers excellent, reasonably priced accommodation (☞ Dining and Lodging, *below*).

North and west from Ullapool lies the strange landscape of Wester Ross, with the little mountain Stac Polly, resembling a ruined fortress, and the humps of Suilven. At **Knockan,** about 15 miles north of Ullapool, a nature trail along a cliff illuminates some of the interesting local geology, as well as the area's flora and fauna. If this jaunt sounds too energetic, a more restful alternative may be to stay on the road and enjoy the good ➍ views of the mountains in the **Inverpolly National Nature Reserve.**

Dining and Lodging

$–$$$ ✕☷ **Ceilidh Place.** This hostelry is extremely comfortable; guests can while away the hours on deep luxurious sofas in the first-floor sitting room—which overlooks the bay—or borrow one of the many books scattered throughout the inn to read back in the room or over breakfast. About as far away in style as you can get from a major chain hotel, the Ceilidh Place must be taken strictly on its own terms—relax and fit in and you will thoroughly enjoy a stay here. Rooms have cream bedspreads and rich, warm color schemes. The inn's restaurant specializes in seafood and vegetarian food (try the mushroom-and-walnut pâté, poached wild salmon, monkfish and prawn brochettes, or venison casserole) and ceilidhs and other musical events are held here frequently. There is a bunkhouse across the road for guests desiring less expensive accommodations. ⊠ W. Argyle St., Ullapool, IV26 2TY, ☎ 01854/612103, ℻ 01854/612886. 26 rooms, 13 with bath and showers. Restaurant (reservations essential). AE, DC, MC, V.

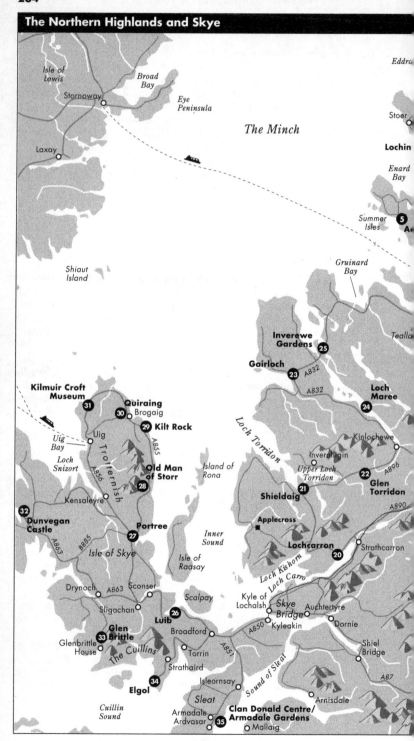

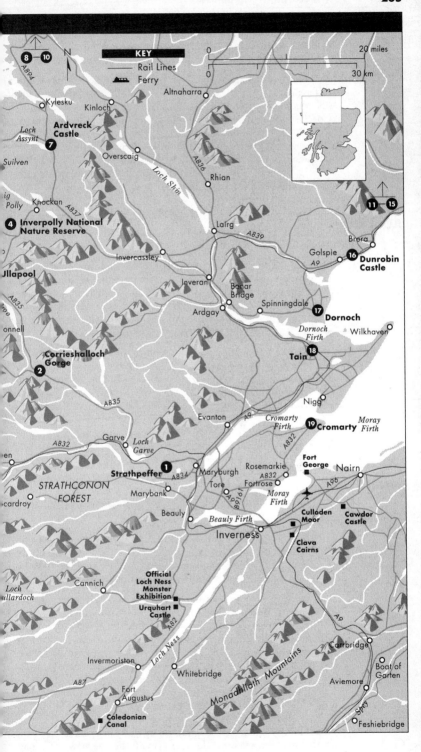

0 ___ 20 miles
0 ___ 30 km

N

8 → **10**

A894

Kylesku
Kinloch

Ardvreck Castle
7

Loch Assynt

Suilven

Altnaharra

Overscaig

Loch Shin

A836

Rhian

ig Polly

Knockan

A837

4 **Inverpolly National Nature Reserve**

Lairg

A839

11 → **15**

Brora

Golspie

A9

16 **Dunrobin Castle**

Invercassley

Jllapool

A835

Inveran

Bonar Bridge

Spinningdale

17 **Dornoch**

Dornoch Firth

Wilkhaven

Ardgay

onnell

Corrieshalloch Gorge
2

Tain **18**

A835

Nigg

Cromarty Firth

Moray Firth

Evanton

A9

19 **Cromarty**

A832

Garve

Loch Garve

en

A832

Strathpeffer **1**

A834

Maryburgh

Rosemarkie

A832

Fort George

Nairn

cardroy

STRATHCONON FOREST

Marybank

Tore

Fortrose

Moray Firth

A96

A9161

A9

Beauly

Culloden Moor

Cawdor Castle

Inverness

Beauly Firth

Loch ullardoch

Cannich

Clava Cairns

Official Loch Ness Monster Exhibition

Urquhart Castle

Loch Ness

A82

Carrbridge

Boat of Garten

Invermoriston

Whitebridge

Monadhliath Mountains

Aviemore

A87

Fort Augustus

Spey

Feshiebridge

Caledonian Canal

Nightlife and the Arts

The Ceilidh Place (☞ Dining and Lodging, *above*) frequently presents ceilidhs and has a regular program of musical and dramatic productions—chamber music, folk music, and opera all find a place here.

En Route Drive north of Ullapool and there is a strong sense of passing into a different kind of landscape. You won't find the broad flanks of great hills that hem you in here, as you do, say, in the Great Glen or Glen Coe. Instead, the mountains rear out of the hummocky terrain and seem to shift their position, hiding behind one another in a slightly bewitching way. Even their names seem different from those of the *bens* (mountain peaks or high hills) elsewhere: Cul Mor, Cul Beag, Stac Polly, Canisp, Suilven . . . some owing their origins to Norse words rather than to undiluted Gaelic—a reminder of the Vikings who used to sail this northern seaboard.

Achiltibuie

❺ *25 mi northwest of Ullapool.*

A spread-out line of crofts, many now owned by newcomers, marks the approach to Achiltibuie. Offshore are the **Summer Isles,** romantic enough in theory, but in reality bleak and austere. In Achiltibuie there's a smokehouse that serves succulent smoked cuts of venison and other delicacies, and the Hydroponicum, a huge glass house that looks out of place but is effective in producing giant strawberries.

En Route A single-lane unclassified road winds north from Achiltibuie, through a wild though harmonious landscape of bracken and birch trees, heather and humped-hill horizons, with outstanding sea views on the second half of the route. Do not fall victim to the breathtaking landscape, however: The road has several blind bends that demand special care. Along this road, you will be near what is perhaps Scotland's most remote bookshop. Just before Inverkirkaig is a parking lot beside the River Kirkaig, and a short stroll away is Achins Book and Craft Shop (☞ Lochinver Shopping, *below;* look for signs by the river bridge).

Lochinver

❻ *18 mi north of Achiltibuie via unclassified road, 38 mi north of Ullapool via A835/A837.*

Lochinver is a charming community with a few dining and lodging options. Behind the town the mountain Suilven rises abruptly. This unusual monolith is best seen from across the water, however: Take the cul-de-sac, **Baddidarach Road,** for the finest photo opportunity.

Bold souls spending time at Lochinver may enjoy the interesting single-lane B869 **Drumbeg loop** to the north of Lochinver—it has several challenging hairpin turns along with breathtaking views. (The junction is just north of the River Inver bridge on the outskirts of the village, signed Stoer and Clashnessie.) Just beyond the scattered community of Stoer, a road leads west to **Stoer Point Lighthouse.** Energetic walkers can hike across the short turf and heather along the cliff top for fine views east toward the profiles of the northwest mountains. There is also a red-sandstone sea stack to view: the **Old Man of Stoer.** This makes a pleasant excursion on a long summer evening. If you stay on the Drumbeg section, there is a particularly tricky hairpin turn in a steep dip that may force you to take your eyes off the fine view of Quinag, yet another of Sutherland's shapely mountains.

7 Beside Loch Assynt, on the road east from Lochinver, stand the abandoned ruins of **Ardvreck Castle.** This was a clan MacLeod stronghold, built in the 15th century.

Lodging

$ **Linne Mhuirich.** This modern croft house bed-and-breakfast offers cooking with a Taste of Scotland theme. The evening meal (for guests only) may consist of salmon with lime and almonds, local mussels and prawns in garlic butter, or cashew-and-mushroom flan. The property is set in the middle of open country surrounded by superb mountain and loch scenery. Rooms have pine furniture and tartan or floral fabrics. No smoking is permitted throughout the property. ⊠ *Unapool Croft Rd., Kylesku, via Lairg, Sutherland, IV27 4HW,* ☎ *01971/502227. 3 rooms, 1 with bath. No credit cards.* ☉ *May–Oct.*

Shopping

Highland Stoneware (⊠ Baddidarroch, Lochinver, ☎ 01571/844376) manufactures tableware and decorative items with hand-painted designs of Highland wildflowers, animals, and landscapes. There is a showroom where you can browse and purchase wares.

At Inverkirkaig, just south of Lochinver, do not miss **Achins Book and Craft Shop** (⊠ Inverkirkaig, ☎ 01571/844262) for Scottish books on natural history, hill walking, fishing, and crafts as well as a well-chosen variety of crafts: knitwear, tweeds, and pottery. Its pleasant coffee shop is open Easter through October, daily (except Sunday) 10–5.

OFF THE
BEATEN PATH

EAS COUL AULIN WATERFALL – This is the longest waterfall in the United Kingdom. At the head of Loch Glencoul, the falls have a 685-foot drop. A rugged walk that leads to the falls is popular with hikers; in summer, cruises offer a less taxing alternative. The falls are located 3 miles southeast of the Kylesku Bridge off the A894; contact the tourist information center in Ullapool or Lochinver for more information.

Scourie

8 *28 mi north of Lochinver.*

Scourie is a small settlement catering to visitors—fishermen especially—with a choice of local accommodations and a shop. It also makes a good base for a trip to the bird sanctuary on the island of Handa.

Dining and Lodging

$$ **✕ Eddrachilles Hotel.** This old, established, traditional inn has one of the best views of any hotel in Scotland—across the islands of Eddrachillis Bay (which can be explored by boat from the hotel). The hotel sits on 320 acres of private moorland and is just south of the Handa Island bird sanctuary. Inside and outside, the hotel is well-preserved. The bedrooms are modern and comfortable, and each is outfitted with tea- and coffee-making facilities. The chef uses local produce to prepare meals cooked in straightforward Scottish style, with the emphasis on fish and game; try the saddle of venison or the poached salmon. ⊠ *Badcall Bay, Scourie IV27 4TH,* ☎ *01971/502080,* ⅁ *01971/ 502477. 11 rooms with bath or shower. Restaurant (reservations essential), bar. MC, V. Closed Nov.–Feb.*

En Route From Scourie northward, the A894 traverses the most northerly landscapes, with the empty quarter below Cape Wrath on the western side. You can sample this by way of a hike to Sandwood Bay, at the end of the B801, beyond the fishing port of Kinlochbervie. Sandwood has rock stacks and a white beach and also its own ghost, said to frequent a cottage (or bothy) near the shore: truly a haunting area.

Durness

❾ *55 mi north of Lochinver.*

Durness is strung along the north-facing coast, the sudden patches of greenness hereabouts caused by the richer limestone outcrops amongst the acid moorlands. The limestone's most spectacular feature is **Smoo Cave,** a cave system hollowed out of the limestone by water action. There are boat tours available daily from April to October (maximum six per tour, lasting 20 minutes). The seasonal tourist information center in Durness has full information (☎ 01971/511259).

❿ If you have toured this far north, you will probably want to go all the way to **Cape Wrath** at the northwest tip of Scotland. You can't drive your own vehicle, though, as a small boat ferries only people across the Kyle of Durness, a sea inlet, then a minibus takes you to the lighthouse. The highest mainland cliffs in Scotland lie between the Kyle and Cape Wrath. These are the 800-foot **Cleit Dubh** (the name means "black cleft" in Gaelic and comes from the Old Norse *klettr,* (crag).

En Route   The north coast road along the top of Scotland is both attractive and austere. It runs, for example, round the head of Loch Eriboll, which was a World War II convoy assembly point and was usually referred to as "Loch 'orrible" by the crews. Yet it has its own bleak charm. There are little beaches and bays to explore along this road, and the landscape gradually softens as you journey east.

Thurso

⓫ *74 mi east of Durness.*

Thurso is a town that is hard to categorize. Quite substantial for a community so far north, since the 1950s its development has been related to the atomic reactor (Britain's first) along the coast at Dounreay—situated there, presumably, to be as far away from the seat of government in London as possible. There is not much to see in the town itself, though there are fine beaches, particularly to the east at Dunnet Bay. Many people make the trip to the truly most northern point of mainland Britain at **Dunnet Head,** with its fine views to Orkney.

Lodging

$ 🏠 **Murray House.** This Victorian town house in the center of Thurso offers bed-and-breakfast of a very high standard, including en suite facilities for two of its bedrooms. ⊠ *1 Campbell St., Thurso, KW14 7HD,* ☎ *01847/895759. 4 rooms, 2 with bath/shower. No credit cards.*

Outdoor Activities and Sports

BICYCLING

Bikes can be hired from **The Bike Shop** (⊠ 35 High St., Thurso, ☎ 01847/896124 or 01847/894223).

John o'Groats

⓬ *21 mi east of Thurso via A836.*

The windswept little outpost of John o'Groats is usually taken to be the most northern community in the Scottish mainland, though that is not strictly accurate, as an exploration of the little network of roads between Dunnet Head and John o'Groats will confirm. However, John o'Groats has some high-quality crafts shops and should be visited. Go east to **Duncansby Head** for spectacular views of cliffs and sea stacks by the lighthouse—and puffins, too, if you know where to look.

The Arts

The **Lyth Arts Centre,** between Wick and John o'Groats, is set in an old country school. From April to September each year, it hosts frequent performances by quality touring music and theater companies (it forms part of the circuit of British Arts Centres). In July and August there are also local and touring exhibitions of contemporary fine art (small admission fee). ⊠ *Lyth, 4 mi off A9,* ☎ *01955/641270.* ✑ *£7, £4 concessions.* ☉ *Apr.–Sept. daily 10–6.*

Outdoor Activities and Sports

CRUISES

Wildlife cruises are operated from John o'Groats harbor by **John o'Groats Ferries.** The trip takes passengers into the Pentland Firth, to Duncansby Stacks and the island of Stroma, and offers spectacular cliff scenery and bird life. ☎ *01955/611353.* ✑ *£12.* ☉ *Cruise daily from mid-June to August, 2:30 PM (cruise lasts 1¼ hours).*

Wick

🔞 *17 mi south of John o'Groats, 22 mi southeast of Thurso via A882.*

Wick is a substantial town that was built on its fishing industry. For details on how this town grew, visit the **Wick Heritage Centre**—it's run by local people in part for the local community, and they are real enthusiasts. ⊠ *18 Bank Row,* ☎ *01955/605393 or 01955/603385.* ✑ *£1.50.* ☉ *June–Sept., Mon.–Sat. 10–5.*

The gaunt, bleak ruins of **Castle Sinclair** and **Castle Girnigoe** teeter on a cliff top to the north of Wick. The **Northlands Viking Centre,** which highlights the role of Scandinavian settlers in this area, includes models of the Viking settlement at Freswick and of a Viking long ship, and artifacts such as coins. ⊠ *The Old School, Auckengill,* ☎ *01955/603761, ext. 242.* ✑ *£1.05.* ☉ *June–Sept., daily 10–4.*

Lodging

$ 🏠 **Greenvoe.** This bed-and-breakfast offers perhaps one of the best values anywhere in Scotland. A well-appointed modern house, fresh and beautifully maintained, Greenvoe has unfussy, functional, and comfortable bedrooms. It's the ideal base for touring the far north of Scotland around John o'Groats, or for catching the Orkney ferry. A delicious substantial breakfast is included in the room rate, and late-night snacks are a hospitable touch. Smoking is prohibited. ⊠ *George St., Wick, Caithness, KW1 4DE,* ☎ *01955/603942. 3 rooms with shared bathroom and shower room. No credit cards. Closed 2 weeks Christmas/New Year's.*

Shopping

Perhaps the best-known purveyor of crafts in the area is **Caithness Glass** (⊠ Wick Industrial Site, Wick Airport, ☎ 01955/602286). Producing a distinctive style of glassware and paperweights familiar to those traveling around Scotland (most of the better gift shops stock Caithness Glass), the factory has tours of the glassblowing workshops and a shop stocking the full product range.

Dunbeath

🔞 *21 mi south of Wick.*

As the moors of Caithness roll down to the sea, at Dunbeath, the **Dunbeath Heritage Centre** is an old school that the local community—concerned that their past should be recorded—turned into a museum. It displays photographs, and domestic and crofting artifacts that relay the history of the area from the Bronze Age to the oil age, and it's particularly helpful to those researching their family histories. ☒ *Dunbeath,* ☎ *01593/731233.* 🎫 *£1.50.* ☼ *Apr.–Sept., Mon.–Sat. 10–5, Sun. 11–6.*

Just north of Dunbeath, the **Lhaidhay Croft Museum** feels, appropriately, more like a private home than a museum. It was built around 1842, comprising a longhouse and barn—animals and people lived under the same long roof—furnished as it would have been during its working life. ☒ *Dunbeath,* ☎ *01593/731244.* 🎫 *£1.* ☼ *Easter–mid-Oct., daily 10–6.*

Helmsdale

⑮ *15 mi south of Dunbeath.*

At Helmsdale, the **Timespan Heritage Centre,** a thought-provoking mix of tableaux, artifacts, and audiovisual materials, portrays the history of the area, from the Stone Age to the 1869 gold rush in the Strath of Kildonan. ☒ *Helmsdale,* ☎ *01431/821327.* 🎫 *£2.75.* ☼ *Apr.–Oct., Mon.–Sat. 10–5, Sun. 2–5 (closes at 6 PM in summer).*

Nearby, at **Baile an Or (Gold Town),** on the site of the 1869 gold rush, panning is still possible, using pans supplied by **Strathullie Local and Scottish Crafts.** ☒ *Dunrobin St., Helmsdale,* ☎ *01431/821343.* 🎫 *£2 a day to hire pan, riddle, and trowel.* ☼ *Daily, 9–5:30.*

Golspie

18 mi south of Helmsdale.

Golspie is a little coastal town with a number of shops and accommodations, though it has the air of a place that visitors pass through on their way to sites such as the nearby Dunrobin Castle (☞ *below*).

⑯ The Scottish home of the Dukes of Sutherland is **Dunrobin Castle,** which is one of the largest houses in the Highlands and is open to visitors. ☒ *Golspie (on the A9),* ☎ *01408/633177.* 🎫 *£4.50.* ☼ *Easter–May and Oct., Mon.–Sat. 10:30–4, Sun. 1–4; June–Sept., Mon.–Sat. 10:30–5, Sun. 1–5.*

Shopping

The **Orcadian Stone Company** (☒ Main St., Golspie, ☎ 01408/633483) makes stone products (including items made from local Caithness slate and modern versions of the carpet bowls, beloved of the Victorians and of today's interior designers), jewelry, incised plaques, and prepared mineral specimens. There is also a geological exhibition on site.

En Route Traveling south on the A9, you'll see the controversial statue of the 1st Duke of Sutherland, like some Eastern Bloc despot, on Beinn a Bragaidh (Ben Braggie), the hilltop to the west. 1994 saw the initiation of a campaign to have it removed, as the "improving" policies of the Duke were ultimately responsible for the brutality associated with the Sutherland Clearances of 1810–1820. This was a kind of ethnic cleansing when thousands of native Gaels were evicted from settlements in the interior and forced to settle at sites on the coast or to emigrate.

Dornoch

⑰ *10 mi south of Golspie.*

A town of mellow sandstone and tiny, rose-filled gardens, with a 13th-century cathedral, Dornoch is noted for its golf—you may hear it referred to as "the St. Andrews of the north." Visit the **Town Jail Craft Centre,** which occupies the former town jail; here you can watch weavers at work weaving tartan cloth. There's also an exhibition of prison life in past times, just to remind you of the building's origins. ⊠ *Castle St.,* ☎ *01862/810555.* ⊠ *Free.* ☉ *Easter–Sept., daily 9–5; Oct.–Easter, weekdays 10–1 and 2–4.*

Lodging

$–$$ 🏠 **Highfield.** In its own grounds on the edge of town, Highfield (a no-smoking establishment) offers deluxe bed-and-breakfast accommodations in a modern family home. ⊠ *Evelix Rd., Dornoch, IV25 3HR,* ☎ 📠 *01862/810909. 3 rooms with bath/shower. No credit cards.*

$ 🏠 **Burnside Guest House.** Conveniently yet quietly situated in the center of town, moments from the cathedral, Burnside is a traditional-style, good-value establishment without frills, offering comfortable, clean bed-and-breakfast accommodation. ⊠ *Shore Rd., Dornoch, IV25 3LS,* ☎ *01862/810919. 5 rooms, 1 with shower. MC, V.*

Outdoor Activities and Sports

GOLF

Were it not for its northern location, **Royal Dornoch** would undoubtedly be a candidate for the Open Championship. It is a superb, breezy, and challenging links course. ☎ *01862/810219. 18 holes, 6,581 yards, SSS 72.*

Shopping

The **Town Jail Craft Centre** (⊠ Castle St., Dornoch, ☎ 01862/810555) is a textile-and-crafts center where you can buy tartans woven on the premises.

Tain

18 *11 mi south of Dornoch.*

Over the Dornoch Firth—there is a bridge—lies Tain, another attractive community and once a place of pilgrimage of the Scottish kings. The ruins of St. Duthac's Chapel, built from 1065 to 1256, mark the site of the birthplace of St. Duthac, an early missionary to the Picts. The chapel was a pilgrimage site for centuries. The **Pilgrimage Visitor Centre** (under the theme of 'Tain through Time') (⊠ Tower St., ☎ 01862/894089) has an audiovisual (just a little tedious) in its visitor center as well as a tape tour (much more interesting) and an on-site museum.

Cromarty

19 *42 mi south of Tain via A9 and B9163, 23 mi north of Inverness via A832, B9161, A9.*

Set at the tip of the Black Isle, a pleasant mixture of woods and farmland, Cromarty is a good example of a Scottish eastern seaboard town, with narrow, winding streets and old cottages interspersed with a few Georgian mansions, the town houses of landowners living 200 years ago. Thanks to the conversion of the **Cromarty Courthouse** into a visitor center, you can learn all about life in an 18th-century Scottish *burgh* (a town with trading rights); take a self-guided walking tour of the town—the center's cassette and headphones will keep you on track. ⊠ *Church St.,* ☎ *01381/600418.* ⊠ *£3.* ☉ *Mar. daily 11–4; Apr.–Oct., daily 10–6; Nov.–Dec. 23. and Feb., daily noon–4; closed Dec. 24–Jan. except by appointment.*

Hugh Miller's Cottage is close to Cromarty Courthouse. Hugh Miller was a 19th-century stonemason, theologian, and self-taught geologist who advanced the science of geology by his fossil discoveries in Scotland. The cottage itself is whitewashed, thatched, and dates from 1711, when it was built by Miller's great-grandfather. It contains an exhibition on Miller's life and work, and it is decorated in period style. ⊠ *Church St.,* ☎ *01381/600245.* 🖃 *£1.60.* ⊘ *May–Sept., Mon.–Sat. 10–1 and 2–5:30, Sun. 2–5:30.*

THE TORRIDONS

The Torridons have a grand and wild air that feels especially remote, yet it is not much more than an hour from Inverness before you reach Kinlochewe at the east end of Glen Torridon. The western end is equally spectacular. There are plenty of opportunities to enjoy mountain panoramas as well as walks and trails.

En Route   The A890 is a single-lane road in some stretches, with plenty of open vistas across the deserted heart of northern Scotland.

Lochcarron

⑳   *66 mi west of Inverness via A832/A890.*

Lochcarron is a village strung along the shore without a recognizable center. It does, however, function as a local hub for shopping, garage facilities and so on.

Shopping

The premises of **Lochcarron Weavers** (⊠ North Strone, Lochcarron, ☎ 01520/722212) are open to the public: Weavers can be seen at work, producing pure-wool worsted tartans that can be bought on site or at the firm's other outlets in the area.

East of Lochcarron, at Achnasheen, is the **Highland Line Craft Centre** (⊠ center of Achnasheen, ☎ 01445/720227), where silver and gold jewelry is made. You can watch the silversmiths; their products are available in the shop on the premises.

En Route   Driving north by the A896, the road passes **Rassal Ash Wood** (on your right). The lushness of the fenced-in area within this small nature reserve is a reminder of what Scotland might have been had sheep and deer not been kept here in such high numbers. The combined nibbling of these animals ensures that Scotland's natural tree cover does not regenerate without human intervention.

Shieldaig

㉑   *16 mi northwest of Lochcarron.*

Not too far from the southern coast of Upper Loch Torridon is Shieldaig, a village that sits in an attractive crescent over a loch of its own, **Loch Shieldaig.** For an atmospheric evening foray, walk north toward Loch Torridon at the northern end of the village, by the church. The path is fairly well made, though hiking shoes are recommended. You will find exquisite views and tiny rocky beaches.

★ **㉒**   The scenic spectacle of **Glen Torridon** lies east of Shieldaig. Some say that Glen Torridon has the finest mountain scenery in Scotland. It consists mainly of the long gray quartzite flanks of **Beinn Eighe** (rhymes with *say*), which make up Scotland's oldest national nature reserve, and **Liathach** (*leea*-gach), with its distinct ridge profile that looks like the keel of an upturned boat. At the end of the glen the National Trust for Scotland operates a **visitor center** that explains the ecology and geology of the area. ☎ *01445/791221.* 🖃 *Audiovisual display and deer* *museum, £1.* ☉ *Countryside Centre, May–Sept., Mon.–Sat. 10–5, Sun. 2–5; estate, deer park, and deer museum, year-round, daily.*

Dining and Lodging

$$ ✕🏨 **Loch Torridon Hotel.** Once a shooting lodge, and right on the shore of Loch Torridon with forest and mountains rising behind, the hotel provides a real Highland welcome. Log fires, handsome plaster-work ceilings, mounted stag heads, and traditional furnishings set the mood downstairs, while bedrooms are decorated in restrained pastel shades with antique mahogany furniture. The restaurant makes elaborate use of local seafood, salmon, beef, lamb, and game, and the cellar includes many fine wines. ⊠ *Torridon, by Achnasheen, Wester Ross, IV27 2EY,* ☎ *01445/791242,* 🖷 *01445/791296. 21 rooms, 20 with bath, 1 with shower. Restaurant (reservations essential). AE, MC, V.*

OFF THE BEATEN PATH	**APPLECROSS** – The tame way to reach Applecross, a small community facing Skye, is by a coastal road from near Shieldaig; the exciting way is via the A896 a few miles farther south. A series of hairpin turns corkscrews up the steep wall at the head of a corrie (a glacier-cut mountain valley), over the **Bealach na Ba** (Pass of the Cattle). There are spectacular views of Skye from the bare plateau on top, and you can boast afterward that you have been on what is probably Scotland's highest drivable road. The town of Applecross itself is pleasant but not riveting.

Gairloch

㉓ *38 mi north of Shieldaig.*

This region's main center, with some shops and accommodations, Gairloch has one further advantage: Lying just a short way from the mountains of the interior, this small oasis often escapes the rain clouds that sometimes cling to the high summits. Guests can enjoy a game of golf here and perhaps stay dry, even when the nearby Torridon hills are deluged. In the village is the **Gairloch Heritage Museum,** with exhibitions covering prehistoric times to the present.

NEED A BREAK?	The **Myrtle Bank Hotel** (☎ 01445/712004) serves cream-scone teas as well as bar meals.

★ ㉔ Southeast of Gairloch stretches one of Scotland's most scenic lochs, **Loch Maree.** The harmonious environs of the loch, with its tall Scots pines and the mountain Slioch looming as a backdrop, witnessed the destruction of much of its tree cover in the 18th century. Iron ore was shipped in and smelted using local oak to feed the furnaces. Oak now grows here only on the northern limits of the range. **Scottish Natural Heritage** has an information center and nature trails by the loch side. Red deer sightings are virtually guaranteed; locals say the best place to spot another local denizen, the pine marten, is around the trash containers in the parking turnoffs. Further on, look for the sign for **Victoria Falls,** a waterfall named after the queen who visited them.

★ ㉕ The highlight of this area for most travelers is **Inverewe Gardens,** 6 miles northeast of Gairloch. The reputation of the gardens at Inverewe, in spite of their comparatively remote location, has grown steadily through the years. The main attraction lies in the contrast between the bleak coastal headlands and thin-soiled moors and the lush plantings of the garden behind the dense shelterbelts. These are proof of the efficiency of the warm North Atlantic Drift, part of the Gulf Stream, which takes the edge off winter frosts. (Inverewe is sometimes described as subtropical, but this is an inaccuracy that irritates the head gardener;

do not expect coconuts and palm trees here.) ✉ *Poolewe,* ☎ *01445/ 781200.* 🖾 *£3.60.* ⏳ *Gardens: Apr.–Oct., daily 9:30–9; Nov.–Mar., daily 9:30–5. Visitor center: Apr.–Oct., daily 9:30–5:30. Guided walks with the head gardener Apr.–Oct., weekdays at 1:30.*

NEED A
BREAK?
The National Trust for Scotland, which looks after the gardens, also runs a **licensed restaurant** (☎ 01445/781200, ⏳ 10–5) offering light lunches (soup, salads, baked potatoes, sandwiches, and one hot dish daily) and a selection of cakes and biscuits.

Dining and Lodging

$$$ ✕🗺 **Dundonnell Hotel.** Set on the roadside by Little Loch Broom, east of Gairloch, this hotel has been a family-run enterprise since 1962 and has cultivated a solid reputation for hospitality and cuisine. The bedrooms are decorated in a fresh, modern style, with light, floral curtains and bedspreads, contemporary furnishings, and modern comforts including tea- and coffee-making equipment. Many bedrooms have stunning views over pristine hills and lochs, as do the public rooms. The Taste of Scotland menu features homemade soups, fresh seafood, and desserts well worth leaving room for. ✉ *Dundonnell, near Garve, Ross-shire,* ☎ *01854/633204,* 🅵🅰🆇 *01854/633366. 30 rooms with bath. Restaurant, bar. AE, MC, V. Closed Jan., Feb.*

Outdoor Activities and Sports

GOLF

Gairloch Golf Club, one of few on this stretch of coast, has its enthusiasts. ☎ *01445/712407. 9 holes, 1,942 yards, SSS 71.*

En Route   The road between Gairloch and the Corrieshalloch Gorge (☞ The Northern Landscapes, *above*) initially offers coastal scenery with views of **Gruinard Bay** and its white beaches, then woodlands around **Dundonnell** and Loch Broom. Soon the route traverses wild country: The toothed ramparts of the mountain **An Teallach** (pronounced *tyel* lach, with Scots *ch,* of course) can be seen on the horizon. The moorland route you travel is known chillingly as **Destitution Road.** It was commissioned in 1851 to give the local folk (long vanished from the area) some way of earning a living following the failure of the potato crop; it is said the workers were paid only in food. At Corrieshalloch, the A832 joins the A835 for Inverness.

SKYE, THE MISTY ISLAND

Skye ranks near the top of most visitors' priority lists: The romance of Bonnie Prince Charlie, the misty **Cuillin Mountains,** and its nearness to the mainland all contribute to its popularity. You can tour comfortably around the island in two or three days. Orientation is easy: Follow the only roads around the loops on the northern part of the island. There are some stretches of single-lane road, but none poses a problem.

Luib

㉖   *15 mi from Kyle of Lochalsh via Skye Bridge and A850.*

At Luib, note the **Old Skye Crofter's House,** with its traditional thatch and 19th-century furnishings.

En Route   The hills north have a reddish hue—they comprise the Red Cuillin, the gentler companions of the Black Cuillins, which swing spectacularly into view on the approaches to Sligachan. Turning away from the hills, the road goes north through tranquil scenery.

Portree

㉗ *19 mi north of Luib.*

The population center of the island, Portree is not overburdened by historical features, but it's a pleasant center clustered around a small and sheltered bay, and it makes a good touring base.

Dining and Lodging

$$$ ✕🏠 **Cuillin Hills Hotel.** Situated on lovely grounds just outside Portree, this gabled hotel is within easy walking distance of the town center. Many of the rooms have outstanding views over Portree Bay toward the Cuillin Hills. Bedrooms are reasonably spacious and well equipped, and individually decorated in bold floral patterns. The public rooms give you a choice of sitting areas and a friendly bar. The meals, especially seafood dishes, are prepared in straightforward fashion, with few gimmicks and a lot of flavor—try the local prawns, lobster, or scallops, or glazed ham carved from the bone. ⊠ *Portree, Isle of Skye,* ☎ *01478/ 612003,* 🅵🅰🆇 *01478/613092. 25 rooms with bath and/or shower. Restaurant, bar. AE, MC, V.*

Shopping

Skye Original Prints (⊠ Portree, ☎ 01478/612388) stocks original works by local artists, together with a good range of original greeting cards.

Trotternish Peninsula

16 mi north of Portree via A855.

As the road goes north from Portree, **cliffs** rise to the left. They are actually the edge of an ancient lava flow, set back from the road, that runs for miles as your rugged companion. In some places the hardened lava has created spectacular features, including a curious pinnacle called the **㉘ Old Man of Storr.** The road continues past neat white crofts and forestry **㉙** plantings to **Kilt Rock.** Everyone on the Skye tour circuit stops here to peep over the cliffs (there is a safe viewing platform) for a look at the curious geology of the cliff edge: bands of two different types of rock have a folded, pleated effect just like the material of a kilt.

★ ㉚ The spectacular **Quiraing** dominates the horizon 5 miles farther. For a closer view of the strange pinnacles and rock forms, make a left onto a small road at **Brogaig** by **Staffin Bay.** There is a car park near the point where this road breaches the ever-present cliff line, though you will have to be physically fit to walk back toward the Quiraing itself, where the rock formations and cliffs are most dramatic. The trail is on uneven, stony ground, and it's a steep scramble up to the rock formations. In ages past, stolen cattle were hidden deep within the Quiraing's rocky jaws.

The main A855 continues around the top end of Trotternish, to the **㉛ Kilmuir Croft Museum,** where you can see the old farming ways brought to life. Included in the displays and exhibits are documents and photographs, reconstructed interiors, and implements. Flora Macdonald, helpmate of Prince Charles Edward Stuart, is buried nearby.

The west coast of Trotternish is pleasant, as the route carries you back to Portree.

Dunvegan Castle

㉜ *22 mi west of Portree.*

In a commanding position above a sea loch, Dunvegan Castle has been the seat of the chiefs of Clan Macleod for more than 700 years. Though greatly changed over the centuries, a gloomy ambience prevails, and there is plenty of family history on display, notably the fascinating "Fairy Flag"—a silk banner, thought to be originally from Rhodes or Syria and believed to have magically saved the clan from danger. The banner's powers are said to suffice for only one more use. ⊠ *Dunvegan*, ☏ *01470/521206.* 🖼 *£4.50; garden only, £3.* ⊘ *Mid-Mar.–Oct., daily 10–5:30 (last entry 5).*

Shopping

For wood-fired stoneware, try **Edinbane Pottery** (⊠ Edinbane, ☏ 01470/582234), 8 miles east of Dunvegan. **Skye Silver** (⊠ The Old School, Colbost, ☏ 01470/511263), west of Dunvegan, designs gold and silver jewelry with a Celtic theme.

Glen Brittle

★ ㉝ *26 mi southwest of Portree.*

Spectacular mountain scenery can be enjoyed in Glen Brittle, with some fine views of the Cuillin ridges—not a place for the ordinary walker (there are many dangerous ridges and steep faces). Glen Brittle extends off the A863 on the west side of the island.

Elgol

40 mi southwest of Portree via A881.

A small cul-de-sac resembling Glen Brittle leads from **Broadford** to one of the finest views in Scotland. This road passes through **Strath Suardal** and little **Loch Cill Chriosd** (Kilchrist) by a ruined church. If there are cattle wading in the loch and the light is soft—typical of Skye—then this place takes on the air of a romantic Victorian oil painting. Skye marble, with its attractive green veining, is produced from the marble quarry at **Torrin**. Breathtaking views of the mountain **Blaven** can be ㉞ appreciated as the road continues to **Elgol**, a gathering of crofts along the suddenly descending road, which ends at a pier. You can admire the heart-stopping profile of the Cuillin peaks from the shore or, at a point about halfway down the hill, find the path that goes toward them across the rough grasslands.

Outdoor Activities and Sports
BICYCLING

Broadford Bicycle Hire (⊠ Fairwinds, Elgol Rd., Broadford, ☏ 01471/822270), rents bicycles in the summer season.

Shopping
Craft Encounters (⊠ Broadford, ☏ 01471/822754) stocks an array of Scottish crafts, including marquetry and jewelry.

Armadale

43 mi south of Portree, 5 mi (ferry crossing) west of Mallaig.

㉟ At Armadale the popular **Clan Donald Centre** and **Armadale Gardens** tell the story of the Macdonalds and their proud title: the Lords of the Isles. In the 15th century they were powerful enough to threaten the authority of the Stuart monarchs of Scotland. There is also a major exhibition in a restored part of the castle, as well as extensive gardens and nature trails. ⊠ *Armadale, ½ mi north of Armadale Pier,* ☏ *01471/ 844305 or 01471/844227.* 🖼 *£3.40.* ⊘ *Clan Donald Centre: Apr.–Oct., daily 9:30–6 (last entry 5). Gardens open at all times.*

Bicycling

The Ferry Filling Station (⊠ Ardvasar, ☎ 01471/844249) rents bicycles in the summer season.

Dining and Lodging

$$$–$$$$ ✕⊞ **Kinloch Lodge.** Just a few miles up the road from Armadale, this hotel offers elegant comfort on the edge of the world. Run by Lord and Lady MacDonald with flair and considerable professionalism, Kinloch Lodge is a supremely comfortable country house, with warm, restful lounges with antique furnishings, chintz fabrics, and family photographs; snug bedrooms individually decorated with quilted bedspreads and pastel wallpaper; and a handsome dining room that serves imaginative cuisine such as warm chicken-liver salad with croutons, herb crepe filled with smoked trout and cucumber, and monkfish stir-fried with tomatoes and garlic. ⊠ *Isleornsay, Sleat, IV43 8QY,* ☎ *01471/833333,* FAX *01471/833277. 10 rooms with bath. Restaurant, fishing. AE, MC, V. Closed Dec.–mid-Mar.*

Shopping

Ragamuffin (⊠ Armadale Pier, ☎ 01471/844217) specializes in designer knitwear and clothing. **Skye Batiks** (⊠ Armadale, ☎ 01471/844396) has designs influenced by Celtic motifs, and sells wall hangings and cotton, silk, and linen clothing at reasonable prices. **Harlequin Knitwear** (⊠ Duisdale, Sleat, ☎ 01471/833321) sells colorful wool sweaters created by local designers.

THE OUTER HEBRIDES (WESTERN ISLES)

The Outer Hebrides—in common parlance also known as the Western Isles—stretch about 130 miles from end to end and lie about 50 miles from the Scottish mainland. This splintered archipelago extends from the pugnacious Butt of Lewis in the north to the 600-foot Barra Head on Berneray in the south, whose lighthouse has the greatest arc of visibility in the world. The **Isle of Lewis and Harris** is the northernmost and largest of the group. The island's only major town, **Stornoway,** is situated on a big, nearly landlocked harbor on the east coast of Lewis and is probably the most convenient starting point for a driving tour of the islands if you're approaching the Western Isles from the Northern Highlands.

Just south of the Sound of Harris is **North Uist,** rich in monoliths and chambered cairns and other reminders of a prehistoric past. Though it is one of the smaller islands in the chain, **Benbecula,** sandwiched between North and South Uist and sometimes referred to as the Hill of the Fords, is in fact less bare and neglected looking than its bigger neighbors to the north. **South Uist,** once a refuge of the old Catholic faith, is dotted with ruined forts and chapels; in summer its wild gardens burst with riots of Alpine and rock plants. **Eriskay** and a scattering of islets almost block the 6-mile strait between South Uist and **Barra,** the southernmost major formation in the Outer Hebrides, an isle you can walk across in an hour.

Harris tweed is available at many outlets on the islands, including some of the weavers' homes; keep an eye out for signs directing you to weavers' workshops. Note that on the islands Sunday is strictly observed as a day of rest, and nearly all shops and visitor attractions are closed.

Stornoway

36 *2½-hour ferry trip from Ullapool.*

The port capital for the Outer Hebrides is Stornoway on Lewis. The **An Lanntair Gallery** offers a varied program of contemporary and traditional exhibitions that change monthly, as well as frequent musical and theatrical events emphasizing traditional Gaelic culture. ⊠ *Town Hall, S. Beach St., Stornoway,* ☎ *01851/703307.* 🎟 *Free.* ☽ *Mon.–Sat. 9–5:30.*

Lodging

$ 🏠 **Ravenswood.** A quiet residential street just a few minutes' walk from the harbor and town center is the location of Ravenswood. The house dates from the turn of the century and offers high-quality bed-and-breakfast accommodation, with a residents' lounge and attractive gardens. ⊠ *12 Matheson Rd., Stornoway, Lewis, HS87 2LR,* ☎ *01851/702673. 3 rooms, 2 with bath/shower. No credit cards.*

Nightlife and the Arts

An Lanntair (☎ 01851/703307), in the Town Hall, conducts an eclectic program of monthly exhibitions and evening events.

Outdoor Activities and Sports

BICYCLING

Hire bicycles from **Alex Dan Cycle Centre** (⊠ 67 Kenneth St., Stornoway, ☎ 01851/704025).

Shopping

Beatrice Schulz sells craft items, knitwear, and tweed lengths in a kaleidoscopic range of colors at **Gifts Unlimited** (⊠ 9 Bayhead St., ☎ 01851/703337).

En Route The best road to use to explore the territory north of Stornoway is the A857, which runs first across the island to the northwest and then to the northeast all the way to Port of Ness (about 30 miles).

Port of Ness

30 mi north of Stornoway.

The stark, windswept community of Port of Ness cradles a small harbor squeezed in among the rocks.

37 At the northernmost point of Lewis stands the **Butt of Lewis lighthouse,** designed by David and Thomas Stevenson (of the prominent engineering family, whose best-known member was, ironically, the novelist Robert Louis Stevenson). The lighthouse was first lit in 1862. The adjacent cliffs provide a good vantage point for viewing seabirds, whales, and porpoises. The lighthouse is just a few minutes northwest of Port of Ness along the B8014.

Shopping

At **Borve Pottery** (⊠ Borve, on the road to Ness, ☎ 01851/850345) you can buy attractive hand-thrown studio pottery made on the premises, including lamps, vases, platters, mugs, dishes, and candleholders.

Arnol

21 mi southwest of Port of Ness, 16 mi northwest of Stornoway.

In the small community of Arnol, look for signs off the A858 for the **38** **Arnol Black House,** a well-preserved example of an increasingly rare type of traditional Hebridean home. Once in common use throughout the islands (as recently as 50 years ago), these dwellings were built without

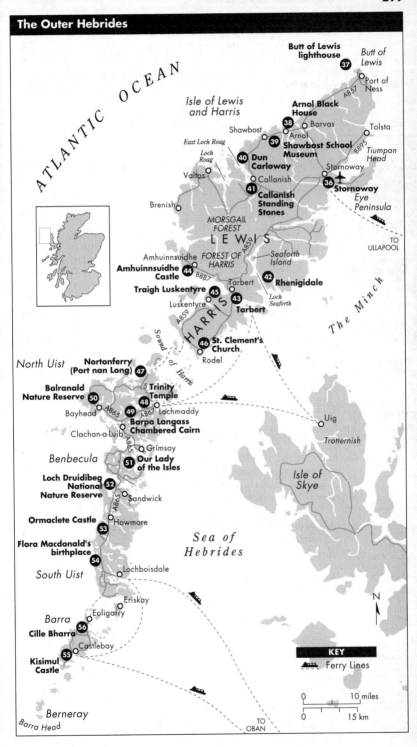

mortar and thatched on a timber framework without eaves. Other characteristic features include an open central peat hearth and the absence of a chimney—hence the sooty atmosphere and the designation "black." On display inside are many of the house's original furnishings. To reach Arnol from Port of Ness, go back south on the A857 and pick up the A858 at Barvas. ⊠ *Arnol,* ☎ *0131/668–8600.* 🎫 *£1.50.* ☉ *Apr.–Sept., Mon.–Sat. 9:30–6; Oct.–Mar., Mon.–Thur. and Sat. 9:30–4.*

Shawbost

5 mi south of Arnol.

㊴ Shawbost is home of the **Shawbost School Museum.** This museum came to life as a result of the so-called Highland Village Competition in 1970, during which school pupils gathered artifacts and contributed to displays aimed at illustrating a past way of life in Lewis. Though it has, sadly, become a bit dog-eared and dusty, the museum does provide a glimpse at the old life and customs of the island. ⊠ *Shawbost,* ☎ *01851/ 710213.* 🎫 *Voluntary donation.* ☉ *Apr.–Nov., Mon.–Sat. 10–6.*

Carloway

8 mi south of Shawbost.

㊵ The scattered community of Carloway is dominated by **Dun Carloway,** one of the best-preserved Iron Age *brochs* (circular stone towers) in Scotland. The mysterious circular defensive tower of the Dun Carloway broch, built about 2,000 years ago possibly as protection against seaborne raiders, provides fine views of a typical Lewis landscape. Parts of the storied walls still stand as high as 30 feet. ⊠ *Carloway,* ☎ *0131/ 668–8600.* 🎫 *Free.* ☉ *At all times.*

Callanish

10 mi southeast of Carloway.

㊶ At Callanish are the **Callanish Standing Stones,** lines of megaliths rated second only to Stonehenge in England. Probably positioned in several stages between 3,000 and 1,500 BC, this grouping is made up of an avenue of 19 monoliths extending northward from a circle of 13 stones, with other rows leading south, east, and west. It's believed they may have been used for astronomical observations. The site is accessible at any time. The recently opened **visitor center** (☎ 0131/668–8600) has an exhibition on the stones, a shop, and a tearoom.

NEED A BREAK?   **Callanish Stones Tearoom** (☎ 01851/621373) has an interesting crafts shop with locally woven tweeds in the restored black house beside the gate leading to the Standing Stones. The tearoom serves home-baked scones, cakes, shortbread, and hearty soups.

Rhenigidale

㊷ *36 mi south of Callanish, 33 mi south of Stornoway.*

Considered to be the most isolated inhabited village in Harris, Rhenigidale was for a long time accessible only by sea or via a rough hill path. A road completed in the early 1990s, which offers fine views high above Loch Seaforth, has now linked the village with the rest of Scotland.

Tarbert

43 *11 mi south of Rhenigidale.*

Tarbert is the main port of Harris, with one or two shops and accommodations. About 10 miles northwest of Tarbert on the B887
44 stands **Amhuinnsuidhe Castle** (the name is almost impossible to pronounce—try *avun-shooee*), a turreted structure built in the 1860s by the earls of Dunmore as a base for fishing and hunting in the North Harris deer forest.

45 **Traigh Luskentyre,** roughly 5 miles southwest of Tarbert, is a spectacular example of Harris's tidy selection of beaches—2 miles of yellow sands adjacent to **Traigh Seilebost** beach, where there are superb views northward to the hills of the Forest of Harris.

Dining and Lodging

$$–$$$ ✕🏠 **Ardvourlie Castle.** A former Victorian hunting lodge that still re-
★ tains its character, Ardvourlie is set in splendid isolation amid the dramatic mountain scenery of Harris, an ideal habitat for hill walking. The bathrooms are magnificent, with mahogany paneling and Victorian-style fixtures, and the decor of the bedrooms and public rooms is bold, idiosyncratic, and entirely in keeping with the High Victorian atmosphere of the castle. The country-house hospitality is perpetuated by the well-stocked library and roaring fires. The cooking is along traditional lines and is of a high standard, favoring fresh local produce and, often, wild game. The portions are generous. You will find the castle north of Tarbert, signed off the A859. ✉ *Isle of Harris, HS3 3AB,* ☎ *01859/ 502307,* 📠 *01859/502348. 4 rooms with bath. Restaurant (reservations essential). No credit cards.*

Rodel

20 mi south of Tarbert.

At the southernmost point of Harris is the community of Rodel. Here
46 you'll find **St. Clement's Church,** a cruciform church standing on a prominent site right on route A859. It was built around 1500 and contains the magnificently sculptured tomb (1528) of the church's builder, Alasdair Crotach, MacLeod chief of Dunvegan Castle. An arched recess contains sculpted panels showing, among other scenes, a galley in full sail, a hunting scene with deer, and St. Michael and Satan weighing souls. There are also other effigies and carvings within the building, which is regarded as the most impressive pre-Reformation church in the Outer Hebrides.

North Uist

8 mi south of Rodel via ferry from Leverburgh, Harris.

47 At **Newtonferry (Port nan Long),** by Otternish and the ferry pier for the Leverburgh (Harris) ferry service, stand the remains of what was reputed to be the last inhabited broch in North Uist, **Dun an Sticar.** This defensive tower, approached by a causeway over the loch, was occupied by Hugh MacDonald, a descendant of MacDonald of Sleat, until 1602.

48 The ruins of **Trinity Temple (Teampull na Trionaid),** a medieval college and monastery said to have been founded in the 13th century by Beathag, daughter of Somerled, the progenitor of the Clan Donald, can be seen 8 miles southwest of Lochmaddy, off the A865. 🎫 *Free.*

49 The **Barpa Langass Chambered Cairn,** dating from the third millennium BC, is the only chambered cairn in the Western Isles known to have retained its inner chamber fully intact. It sits very close to the A867 on the stretch between Lochmaddy and Clachan.

50 The **Balranald Nature Reserve,** administered by the Royal Society for the Protection of Birds, is home to large numbers of waders and seabirds, including red-necked phalarope, living in a varied habitat of loch, marsh, *machair* (grasslands just behind the beach), and sandy and rocky shore. The reserve can be viewed anytime, but visitors are asked to keep to the paths during breeding season (March to July) so as not to disturb the birds. It is sited on the western side of North Uist, about 3 miles northwest of Bayhead, which you can reach via A865. ⊠ *Visitor Centre at Goular,* ☎ *01463/715000 or 0131/557–3136.* 🖾 *Free.* ⊙ *Daily.*

South Uist

34 mi south of Newtonferry via Grimsay, Benbecula, and three causeways.

You can travel the length of South Uist along route A865, making short treks off this main road on your way to Lochboisdale on the southeastern coast of the island; at Lochboisdale you can get ferries to Barra, the southernmost principal island of the Outer Hebrides, or to Oban on the mainland.

About 5 miles south of the causeway from Benbecula, atop Reuval Hill, stands the 125-foot-high statue of the Madonna and Child known as
51 **Our Lady of the Isles.** The work of sculptor Hew Lorimer, the statue was erected in 1957 by the local Catholic community. A few miles far-
52 ther south, to the west of A865, you will come to the **Loch Druidibeg National Nature Reserve.** One of only two remaining British native—nonmigrating—populations of greylag geese make their home here in a fresh and brackish loch environment. (Stop at the warden's office for full information about access.)

A few miles south of Howmore, just west of A865, stand the ruins of
53 **Ormaclete Castle,** which was built in 1708 for the chief of the Clan Ranald, but was accidentally destroyed by fire in 1715 on the eve of the Battle of Sheriffmuir, during which the chief was killed. At Gearraidh Bhailteas (just west of A865 near Milton), you can see the ruins
54 of **Flora Macdonald's birthplace.** South Uist's most famous daughter, Flora helped the Young Pretender Prince Charles Edward Stuart avoid capture and was feted as a heroine afterward.

Shopping
Hebridean Jewelry (⊠ Garrieganichy, Lochdar, ☎ 01870/610288) makes decorative jewelry and framed pictures; the owners also run a crafts shop.

Barra

1 hour 50 minutes by ferry from Lochboisdale.

Barra is an island with a rocky east coast and a west coast of sandy
55 beaches. **Kisimul Castle,** the largest ancient monument in the Western Isles, is situated on an islet in Castlebay, Barra's principal harbor. Kisimul was the stronghold of the Macneils of Barra, noted for their lawlessness and piracy. The main tower dates from about AD 1120. A restoration that was completed in 1970 was started by the 45th clan chief, an American architect. *Contact tourist information center for opening times and admission prices.*

Craigston Museum, in a thatched cottage at Baile ne Creige (Craigston), displays artifacts of local crofting life. (It's open only during the main

summer season.) At Eolaigearraidh (Eoligarry), the departure point for
the passenger ferry to South Uist, you can view **Cille Bharra,** the ruins
of the church dedicated to the saint who gave his name to the island.
The restored **chapel of St. Mary** stands near part of a medieval monastery
and cemetery.

Barra's airport is at the north end of the island on a simple stretch of
sand known as **Traigh Moor** (the Cockle Strand)—which is washed twice
daily by the tides. The departure and arrival times for the daily flights
to and from Glasgow, Benbecula, and Stornoway are scheduled to co-
incide with low tide.

Outdoor Activities and Sports
BICYCLING
Hire a cycle from **MacDougall Cycles** (⊠ 29 St. Brendan Rd., Castle-
bay, ☎ 01871/810284).

THE NORTHERN HIGHLANDS A TO Z

Arriving and Departing

By Bus
National Express/Scottish Citylink (☎ 0990/505050) runs buses from
England to Inverness, Ullapool, and Dingwall. There are also coach
connections between the ferry ports of Tarbert and Stornoway; consult the local tourist information center for details.

By Car and Ferry
The fastest route to this area is the A9 to the gateway town of Inverness. The ferry services run by **Caledonian MacBrayne,** called CalMac,
link the Outer Hebrides (☞ Getting Around by Car and Ferry, *below*):
Ferries run from Ullapool to Stornoway (☎ 01854/612358, FAX
01854/612433), from Oban to Castlebay and Lochboisdale (☎
01631/562285, FAX 01631/566588), and from Uig on the island of
Skye to Tarbert and Lochmaddy (☎ 01470/542219, 01470/542387).
Causeways link North Uist, Benbecula, and South Uist.

By Plane
The main airports for the Northern Highlands are **Inverness** and **Wick**
(both on the mainland). There is direct air service from Edinburgh and
Glasgow to Inverness and Wick. Contact **British Airways** (☎
0345/222111). **Gill Air** (☎ 0191/214–6666) operates the Aberdeen–Wick
service (Mon.–Fri.). There are island flight connections to Stornoway
(Lewis), and Barra and Benbecula in the Outer Hebrides; contact
British Airways for details.

By Train
Main railway stations in the area include Oban (for Barra and the Uists)
and Kyle of Lochalsh (for Skye) on the west coast or Inverness (for points
north to Thurso and Wick). There is direct service from London to Inverness and connecting service from Edinburgh and Glasgow.

Getting Around

It is in the Highlands and Islands that the **Freedom of Scotland Trav-
elpass** really becomes useful, saving you money on ferries, trains, and
some buses. *See* the Gold Guide for details.

By Bus
Highland Bus and Coach Company (mainland and Skye, ☎ 01463/
233371) provides bus service in the Highlands area. On the Outer Hebrides a number of small operators run regular routes to most towns

and villages. The **post-bus** service—which also delivers mail—becomes increasingly important in remote areas; it supplements the regular bus service, which runs only a few times per week because of the small population in the region. A full timetable of services for the Northern Highlands (and the rest of Scotland) is available from the **Royal Mail** (✉ 7 Strothers Lane, Inverness, IV1 1AA ☎ 01463/256200).

By Car and Ferry
Note that in this sparsely populated area, distances between gas stations can be considerable. Although getting around is easy, even on single-lane roads, the choice of routes is restricted by the rugged terrain. Because of the infrequent bus services and sparse railway stations, a car is definitely the best way to explore this region.

The **Island Hopscotch** planned route ticket and the **Island Rover** pass, both offered by CalMac, give considerable reductions on interisland ferry fares; for details, contact Caledonian MacBrayne Ltd. (✉ The Ferry Terminal, Gourock, PA19 1QP, ☎ 01475/650100, 𝐅𝐀𝐗 01475/637607).

An important caveat for visitors driving in this area: There are still some single-lane roads in this part of Scotland. These twisting, winding thoroughfares demand a degree of driving dexterity. Local rules of the road require that when two cars meet, whichever driver reaches a passing place first must stop in it or opposite it and allow the oncoming car to continue. Small cars tend to yield to large commercial vehicles. Never park in passing places, and remember that these sections of the road can also allow traffic behind you to pass; don't hold up a vehicle trying to pass you—tempers can flare over such discourtesies.

By Plane
British Airways (☎ 0345/222111) operates flights between the islands of Barra, Benbecula, and Stornoway in the Outer Hebrides.

By Train
Stations on the northern lines (Inverness to Thurso/Wick and Inverness to Kyle of Lochalsh) include Muir of Ord, Dingwall; on the Thurso/Wick line, Alness, Invergordon, Fearn, Tain, Ardgay, Culrain, Invershin, Lairg, Rogart, Golspie, Brora, Helmsdale, Kildonan, Kinbrace, Forsinard, Altnabreac, Scotscalder, and Georgemas Junction; and on the Kyle line, Garve, Lochluichart, Achanalt, Achnasheen, Achnashellach, Strathcarron, Attadale, Strome Ferry, Duncraig, Plockton, and Duirinish.

Contacts and Resources

Car Rentals
Europcar Ltd. (✉ The Highlander Service Station, Millburn Rd., Inverness, ☎ 01463/235337). **Hertz** (✉ Dalcross Airport, Inverness, ☎ 01667/462652).

Emergencies
For **police, fire,** or **ambulance,** dial 999 from any telephone. No coins are needed for emergency calls from public telephone booths.

Fishing
As in other parts of Scotland, post offices, local shops, and hotels usually sell permits to fish in local waters, and tourist information centers carry lists of the best locales for fishing.

Guided Tours

ORIENTATION

From Inverness, the following companies offer offers coach tours during the summer season: **Highland Bus and Coach Company** (✉ Inverness bus station, ☎ 01463/233371). **Macdonald's Tours** (✉ 65 Fairfield Rd., ☎ 01463/240673). **Spa Coach Tours** (✉ Strathpeffer, ☎ 01997/421311).

SPECIAL-INTEREST

From Inverness, **Highland Insight Tours and Travel** (☎ 01463/831403) offers personalized touring holidays and full-day or half-day tours that cater to any interest. **James Johnson** (☎ 01463/790179) will drive you anywhere, but he has a particularly good knowledge of the Highlands and islands, including the Outer Isles.

Dunvegan Sea Cruises, at Dunvegan Castle (☎ 01470/521206) offers a boat trip to the nearby seal colony (£3.50) and also a spectacular trip up Loch Dunvegan to see seals and many different kinds of birds (£7).

Wildlife cruises are operated from John o'Groats harbor by **John o'Groats Ferries** (☎ 01955/611353. ☉ Daily from mid-June to August). The trip takes passengers into the Pentland Firth, to Duncansby Stacks and the island of Stroma, and it offers spectacular cliff scenery and bird life.

A number of small firms run boat cruises along the spectacular west-coast seaboard. Contact the local tourist information center for details of local operators. On Skye there is also a broad selection of mountain guides. A list can be obtained from Skye's tourist information center (☞ Visitor Information, *below*). **Cycle Caithness** (✉ Thorval, 7 Campbell St., Thurso, ☎ 01847/896124 or 01847/894223) organizes cycling and accommodation packages in ideal flat cycling territory.

Raasay Outdoor Centre (✉ Raasay House, Isle of Raasay (reached by ferry from Sconser, Isle of Skye), ☎ 01478/660266) offers a variety of courses in canoeing, sailing, windsurfing, and navigation skills.

Late-Night Pharmacies

These are not found in rural areas. Pharmacies in the main towns—Thurso, Wick, Stornoway—keep normal shop hours. In an emergency the police will provide assistance in locating a pharmacist. General practitioners may also dispense medicines.

Visitor Information

Tourist Information Centres are located in: **Dornoch** (✉ The Square, Dornoch, ☎ 01862/810400, FAX 01862/810644). **Gairloch** (✉ Auchtercairn, ☎ 01445/712130). **North Kessock** (✉ North Kessock, ☎ 01463/731505, FAX 01463/731701). **Portree,** Isle of Skye (✉ Meall House, ☎ 01478/612137, FAX 01478/612141). **Stornoway,** Lewis and Harris (✉ 4 S. Beach St., ☎ 01851/703088, FAX 01851/705244). **Wick** (✉ Whitechapel Rd., off High St., ☎ 01955/602596, FAX 01955/604940).

Seasonal tourist information centers can be found at Bettyhill, Broadford (Skye), Castlebay (Barra, Outer Hebrides), Durness, Helmsdale, John o' Groats, Kyle of Lochalsh, Lairg, Lochboisdale (South Uist, Outer Hebrides), Lochcarron, Lochinver, Lochmaddy (North Uist, Outer Hebrides), Shiel Bridge, Strathpeffer, Thurso, Uig, and Ullapool.

12 The Northern Isles

Orkney, Shetland

The wind and frequent rains, the exposure and the proximity to the sea: These qualities make a visit to the northern islands as much a challenge as an adventure. Orkney—a cluster of almost 70 islands, 20 of them inhabited—has the greatest concentration of prehistoric sites in Scotland. Shetland's islands, with their awesome cliffs on the coastline and their dramatic "geos," or fissure-like sea inlets, and barren moors in the interior, do not feel "British" at all.

BOTH ORKNEY AND SHETLAND possess a Scandinavian heritage that gives them an ambience different from any other region of Scotland. For mainland Scots, visiting this archipelago is a little like traveling abroad without having to worry about a different language or currency. Both of these isles are bound by the sea, and both are essentially bleak and austere, with awesome seascapes and genuinely warm, friendly people. Neither Orkney nor Shetland has yet been overrun by tourists. Orkney is the greener of the two island groupings, which number 200 islets between them.

By Gilbert Summers

There are more prehistoric sites in Orkney than anywhere else in the United Kingdom, although Shetland also has a number of historic sites of great interest. Orkney's wealth of places includes stone circles, burial chambers, ancient settlements, and fortifications that emphasize many centuries of continuous settlement.

The differences between Orkney and Shetland can be summed up with the description that an Orcadian is a farmer with a boat, while a Shetlander is a fisherman with a croft (small farm). Shetland, rich in ocean views and sparse landscapes, is endowed with a more remote atmosphere than its neighbor Orkney. However, don't let Shetland's bleak countryside fool you—it's far from being a backwater island. Oil money from the mineral resources around its shores and the fact that it has been a crossroads in the northern seas for centuries have helped make it a cosmopolitan place.

Pleasures and Pastimes

Dining

Seafood is first class and so is Orkney's malt whisky. At its best, dining in the islands is as good as anywhere else, but vegetable gardeners do face some extra challenges from the northerly latitude. Look out for Orkney *bere bannocks* (bere is a kind of primitive barley, while a bannock is a kind of oatcake) and local cheese.

WHAT TO WEAR

Casual attire is acceptable at all but the most expensive establishments. At country-house hotels you may wish to dress up for dinner.

CATEGORY	COST*
$$$$	over £25
$$$	£15–£25
$$	£10–£15
$	under £10

per person for a three-course meal, including VAT and excluding drinks and service

Diving

Orkney, especially the former wartime anchorage of Scapa Flow, claims to have the best dive sites in Britain. Part of the attraction is the remains of the German navy, scuttled here in 1919. Many boat-rental firms offer diving charters. Shetland also has exceptional underwater visibility, perfect for viewing the treasure wrecks and abundant marine life.

Festivals

Shetland has quite a strong cultural identity, thanks to its Scandinavian heritage. There are, for instance, books of local dialect verse, a whole folklore contained in knitting patterns, and a strong tradition of fiddle-playing. In the middle of the long winter, at the end of January, the Shetlanders celebrate their Viking culture with the **Up-Helly-Aa festival,** which involves much merrymaking, dressing up, and the burning of a replica of a Viking long ship. The end of January, however, is hardly a peak time for tourists. The **Shetland Folk Festival,** held in April, and the **Shetland Accordion and Fiddle Festival,** in October, both attract large numbers of visitors.

Orkney's cultural highlight is the **St. Magnus Festival,** a festival of music based in Kirkwall and usually held the third week in June. Orkney also has an annual folk festival at the end of May.

Lodging

The northern isles' exoticism does not translate as "primitive": At its best, accommodations are about as good as anywhere else in Scotland.

CATEGORY	COST*
$$$$	over £110
$$$	£80–£110
$$	£45–£80
$	under £45

All prices are for a standard double room, including service, breakfast, and VAT.

Shopping

Neither Orkney nor Shetland is visited expressly for shopping. However, both have attracted high-quality crafts workers, and in the United Kingdom, Shetland is almost synonymous with distinctive knitwear.

Exploring the Northern Isles

Both island groupings need at least a couple of days if you are to do more than just scratch the surface of their characters. The extra effort required to get there means that Shetland certainly deserves four or five days: the Northern Isles in any case generate their own "laid-back" approach to life, and once there you will not want to hurry around. Orkney, being more accessible, is a possibility for a short visit, but again, to get to know the area well, stay a few days.

Great Itineraries

Getting around is quite straightforward—the roads are good on both Shetland and Orkney. A fast and frequent interisland ferry service makes island-hopping perfectly practical. Only at peak season are reservations advisable.

IF YOU HAVE 1 DAY

Numbers in the text correspond to numbers in the margin and on The Shetland Islands and Orkney Islands maps.

Launch yourself from Inverness (☞ Chapter 10) on a day trip—though it will be a long one—by bus and ferry (☞ Arriving and Departing in The Northern Isles A to Z, *below*), which will take you to some of Orkney's top historic sites. Shetland is not practicable for such a short length of time.

IF YOU HAVE 4 DAYS

You could get a good flavor of Orkney and take in the main sites—St. Magnus Cathedral and Earl Patrick and the Bishop's Palace in ⌂ **Kirkwall** ⑳—then go out to **Skara Brae** ⑯, **Maes Howe** ⑮ and the **Ring of Brogar** ⑭. (You could probably get on to one of the other islands as well.) You could see a bit of Shetland in this length of time, too, if you get a good night's sleep on the direct Orkney/Shetland ferry, leaving you a full day as soon as you arrive to take in the south of the island: **Shetland Croft House Museum** ④, **Jarlshof** ⑤, Sumburgh

Head, **St. Ninian's Isle** ⑥, and so on. Staying overnight in 🏨 **Lerwick** ①, you could make a trip up to **Esha Ness** to get flavor of the north of Mainland, leaving Lerwick itself and **Scalloway** ⑦ for the fourth day. In theory, in this length of time it is possible to get out to the very end of Scotland at Muckle Flugga, but Shetland is such an extraordinary place that it merits more time.

IF YOU HAVE 8 DAYS

This is enough time in the Northern Isles for you to see all the main sites on Orkney and then catch a midweek ferry to Shetland, with enough time to get to the far north of Shetland as well.

When to Tour the Northern Isles

Go in the early summer when the bird colonies are at their most spectacular and the long northern daylight hours give you plenty of sightseeing time.

AROUND SHETLAND

The Shetland coastline is an incredible 900 miles owing to all the indentations, and there isn't a point on the island farther than 3 miles from the sea. Settlements away from Lerwick, the primary town, are small and scattered—ask the friendly locals for directions.

Lerwick

❶ *14 hours by ferry from Aberdeen.*

Visitors would be remiss if they failed to explore some of Lerwick's nearby diversions before venturing beyond it. **Fort Charlotte** is a 17th-century Cromwellian stronghold, built to protect the Sound of Bressay. ☎ *0131/668–8600.* 🎫 *Free.* ⊙ *Apr.–Sept., Mon.–Sat. 9:30–6, Sun. 2–6; Oct.–Mar., Mon.–Sat. 9:30–4, Sun. 2–4.*

The **Shetland Museum** in Lerwick gives an interesting account of the development of the town and includes displays on archaeology, art and textiles, shipping, and folk life. ⊠ *Lower Hillhead,* ☎ *01595/695057.* 🎫 *Free.* ⊙ *Mon., Wed., Fri. 10–7, Tues., Thurs., Sat. 10–5.*

NEED A BREAK?
Near the harbor in Lerwick, the **Kvelsdro House Hotel** (☎ 01595/692195) serves hearty pub grub meals; try the breaded haddock or steak pie.

❷ **Clickhimin Broch** (broch are circular stone monuments), on the site of what was originally an Iron-Age fortification, can be your introduction to the mysterious Pictish monuments, whose meaning is still largely obscure. South of the broch there are vivid views of the cliffs at the south end of the island of Bressay, which shelters Lerwick harbor. ⊠ *1 mi south of Lerwick,* ☎ *0131/668–8600.* 🎫 *Free.* ⊙ *Apr.–Sept., Mon.–Sat. 9:30–6, Sun. 2–6; Oct.–Mar., Mon.–Sat. 9:30–4, Sun. 2–4.*

Dining and Lodging

$$–$$$ ✕🏨 **Shetland Hotel.** Modern and well appointed (a result of the oil boom in the area and the needs of high-flying oil executives), the Shetland is located directly opposite the ferry terminal in Lerwick. The hotel is decorated in an attractive blend of peach, burgundy, and blue color schemes. The food is rich and filling, with sometimes wildly clashing flavors. One entrée consists of a folded filet of beef with Stilton cheese inside, coated in oatmeal and served with a rich red-currant sauce: enough of a meal to sink the Shetland ferry! ⊠ *Holmsgarth Rd., Lerwick, ZE1*

Shetland Islands

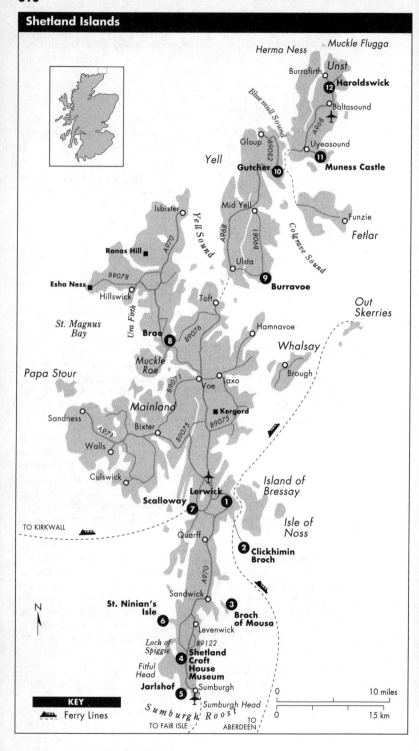

Muckle Flugga

Herma Ness

Burrafirth • *Unst*

⑫ Haroldswick

Baltasound ✈

Blue mull Sound

Gloup • B9082

Gutcher ⑩

Uyeasound •

⑪ Muness Castle

A968

Yell

Isbister •

Mid Yell •

Funzie •

Ronas Hill ■

A970

Fetlar

Yell Sound

A968

B9081

Esha Ness ■

B9078

Ulsta •

Colgrave Sound

Hillswick •

Toft •

⑨ Burravoe

Ura Firth

St. Magnus Bay

Brae ⑧

B9076

Hamnavoe •

Out Skerries

Muckle Roe

B9071

Voe • Laxo •

Whalsay

Papa Stour

Brough •

Mainland

■ **Kergord**

Sandness •

A971

B9075

B9075

Bixter •

Walls •

Culswick •

Island of Bressay

Lerwick ①

✈

Scalloway ⑦

Isle of Noss

TO KIRKWALL ⛴

Quarff •

② Clickhimin Broch

A970

Sandwick •

③

St. Ninian's Isle ⑥

Broch of Mousa

Levenwick •

Loch of Spiggie

B9122

Shetland Croft House Museum ④

Fitful Head

Jarlshof

Sumburgh •

⑤ ✈

Sumburgh Head

Sumburgh Roost

| 0 | 10 miles |

| 0 | 15 km |

TO FAIR ISLE

TO ABERDEEN

KEY

⛴ Ferry Lines

N ↑

0RB, ☎ *01595/695515,* 𝔽𝔸𝕏 *01595/695828. 66 rooms with bath. 2 restaurants, 2 bars. AE, DC, MC, V.*

$ ✕⌂ **The Old Manse.** The oldest inhabited building in Lerwick is now a friendly guest house, located on a quiet side street in the town center. The house dates from 1685 and was built for Lerwick's first minister. Furnishings are traditional, in keeping with the pleasantly aged feel of the house. Dinners are also traditional Scottish, mostly fish, beef, and stews. ✉ *9 Commercial St., Lerwick, ZE1 0AN,* ☎ *01595/696301. 1 room with shower, 2 with shared bath. No credit cards.*

Outdoor Activities and Sports
BICYCLING

Bicycles can be rented from **Eric Brown Cycles** (✉ Grantfield Garage, Grantfield, Lerwick, ☎ 01595/692709).

Shopping
There are many places for knitwear and woolen goods in Lerwick. **The Spider's Web** (✉ 41 Commercial St., ☎ 01595/693299) sells hand-spun and hand-knit goods in neutral earth tones, as well as pottery made in Shetland. **Anderson & Co.** (✉ The Shetland Warehouse, Commercial St., ☎ 01595/693714) sells handmade knitwear and has a small stock of machine-made items and tourist souvenirs. **Millers** (✉ 108–110 Commercial St., Lerwick, ☎ 01595/692517) stocks machine-made knitwear in Shetland and Argyle patterns, Aran sweaters, and capes, rugs, and scarves made elsewhere in Scotland.

J. G. Rae Limited (✉ 92 Commercial St., ☎ 01595/693686) stocks Shetland Silvercraft and gold and silver jewelry with Norse and Celtic motifs. **Hjaltasteyn** (✉ 161 Commercial St., Lerwick ☎ 01595/696224) handcrafts gems and jewelry. **Shetland Jewelry** (✉ Sound Side, Weisdale, ☎ 01595/830275) makes jewelry and other small goods, which are stocked at J. G. Rae (☞ *above*). **Shetland Workshop Gallery** (✉ Burns La., ☎ 01595/693343) has a good selection of pottery, knitwear, and crafts.

Sandwick

14 mi south of Lerwick via A970.

★ ❸ The community of Sandwick is the departure point for boat trips to see the **Broch of Mousa,** the most fully extant of all the broch towers remaining in Scotland. ✉ *Mousa,* ☎ *0131/668–8600.* 🎫 *Broch free, boat trip £4.50.* ☉ *Apr.–Sept., Mon.–Sat. 9:30–6, Sun. 2–6; Oct.–Mar., Mon.–Sat. 9:30–4, Sun. 2–4. Boat for hire operated by Mr. Jamieson (☎ 01950/431367); times subject to his schedule.*

Shopping
Lawrence J. Smith Ltd. (✉ Hoswick, ☎ 01950/431215) sells Shetland knitwear—both hand- and machine-made—at all prices and for all ages, in a wide range of colors.

Voe

7 mi south of Sandwick.

★ ❹ The scattered village of Voe is the location of the **Shetland Croft House Museum.** This traditionally constructed 19th-century thatched house contains a broad range of artifacts that depict the former way of life of the rural Shetlander, which the museum attendant will be delighted to discuss with you. ✉ *Voe, Dunrossness, unclassified road east of A970,* ☎ *01595/695057.* 🎫 *£1.50.* ☉ *May–Sept., daily 10–1 and 2–5.*

Sumburgh

4 mi south of Voe.

★ **⑤** The big attraction at Sumburgh is **Jarlshof,** a centuries-old site that includes the extensive remains of Norse buildings, as well as prehistoric wheelhouses and earth houses representing thousands of years of continuous settlement. The site also includes a 17th-century laird's (landowner's) house built on the ruins of a medieval farmstead. ⊠ *Sumburgh Head,* ☎ *0131/668–8600.* ☑ *£2.* ⊙ *Apr.–Sept., Mon.–Sat. 9:30–6, Sun. 2–6. Closed Oct.–Mar.*

St. Ninian's Isle

⑥ *8 mi north of Sumburgh via A970 and B9122 (turn left at Skelberry).*

It was on St. Ninian's Isle—actually a "tombolo," a spit of sand that moors an island to the mainland—that archaeologists in the 1950s uncovered the St. Ninian treasure, a collection of 28 silver objects from the 8th century. This Celtic silver is now in the Royal Museum of Scotland in Edinburgh (☞ Chapter 3), though good replicas are on view in the Shetland Museum in Lerwick (☞ *above*).

Scalloway

⑦ *21 mi north of St Ninian's Isle, 6 mi west of Lerwick.*

On the western coast of Mainland Island is Scalloway. Look for the information board just off the main road (A970), which overlooks the settlement and its castle. **Scalloway Castle** was built in 1600 by Earl Patrick, who coerced the locals to build it for him. He was executed in 1615 for his cruelty and misdeeds, and the castle was never used again. ⊠ *Scalloway,* ☎ *0131/668–8600.* ☑ *Free.* ⊙ *Apr.–Sept., Mon.–Sat. 9:30–6, Sun. 2–6; Oct.–Mar., Mon.–Sat. 9:30–4, Sun. 2–4.*

Shopping

The **Shetland Woollen Company** (⊠ Castle St., ☎ 01595/880243) is one of many operators with a selection of Shetland knitwear.

OFF THE   **KERGORD** – Take the B9075 east off the A970, at the head of a narrow
BEATEN PATH   sea inlet. This leads into the unexpectedly green valley of Kergord,
                noted for its woodland. This would be unremarkable farther south, but
                here it is a novelty.

Brae

⑧ *24 mi north of Scalloway.*

Brae is the home of the Busta House Hotel (☞ Lodging, *below*), probably the best hotel on the island. Beyond Brae the main road meanders past **Mavis Grind,** a strip of land so narrow you can throw a stone—if you are strong—from the Atlantic, in one inlet, to the North Sea, in another.

NEED A   Follow the A970 left for Hillswick to reach the **St. Magnus Hotel**
BREAK?   (☎ 01806/503371), which serves fresh fish in a wood-panel bar
                and dining room.

Dining and Lodging

$$–$$$ ✕🏠 **Busta House.** Busta House dates in part from the 16th century and
★   is surrounded by terraced grounds. Bedrooms are well furnished in traditional style—floral chintzes and antique furniture—and the 16th-cen-

tury Long Room is a delightful place to sample the hotel's selection of malt whiskies while sitting beside a peat fire. The dining room features a Taste of Scotland menu, with Shetland salmon and lamb usually available. ✉ *Brae, Shetland, ZE2 9QN,* ☎ *01806/522506,* FAX *01806/ 522588. 20 rooms with bath or shower. Restaurant, bar. AE, DC, MC, V. Closed 2 weeks Christmas/New Year's.*

OFF THE
BEATEN PATH

ESHA NESS AND RONAS HILL – For outstanding views of the rugged, forbidding cliffs around Esha Ness, drive north, then turn left onto the B9078. On the way, look for the sandstone stacks in the bay that resemble a Viking galley under sail. After viewing the cliffs at Esha Ness, return to join the A970 at Hillswick and follow an ancillary road from the head of Ura Firth. This road provides vistas of rounded, bare Ronas Hill, the highest hill in Shetland. Though only 1,468 feet high, it is noted for its arctic-alpine flora growing at low levels.

Yell

11 mi northeast of Brae, 31 mi north of Lerwick via A970, A968, or B9076, and ferry from Toft.

⑨ After crossing to Ulsta, on the island of Yell, take the B9081 east to **Burravoe.** There's not a lot to say about the blanket bog that covers two-thirds of Yell, but the **Old Haa** (hall) of Burravoe, the oldest building on the island, is architecturally interesting and has a museum upstairs. One of the displays tells the story of the wrecking of the German sail ship, the *Bohus,* in 1924. A copy of the ship's figurehead is displayed outside the Old Haa itself; the original is at the shipwreck site overlooking Otters Wick, along the coast on the B9081. ☎ *01957/ 722339 or 01957/702127.* ✉ *Free.* ☉ *Apr.–Sept., Tues., Wed., Thurs., and Sat. 10–4, Sun. 2–5.*

NEED A
BREAK?

The **Old Haa,** formerly a merchant's house, serves light meals with home-baked buns, cakes, scones, and other goodies; has a crafts shop; and acts as a kind of unofficial information point. The staff are friendly and give advice to sightseers.

⑩ Rejoin the main A968 at Mid Yell to reach **Gutcher,** the ferry pier. If time permits, turn left on the B9082 for a pleasant drive to **Gloup,** a cluster of houses at the end of the road. Behind a croft, in a field overlooking a long *voe* (sea inlet) is the **Gloup Fisherman's Memorial,** which recalls an 1881 tragedy involving all hands of 10 six-oared local fishing boats.

Unst

49 mi north of Lerwick via ferry from Gutcher.

The ferry crosses the Bluemull Sound to Unst, the northernmost inhabited island in Scotland. Because of its strategic location—it protrudes well into the northern seas—Unst is inhabited by the military.

⑪ **Muness Castle,** Scotland's northernmost castle, was built just before the end of the 16th century. Those visiting the castle will be pleasantly surprised to find some photogenic Shetland ponies in the field nearby. Just to the north of Muness Castle is the **Keen of Hamar** national nature reserve. To reach the castle, in the southeast corner of Unst, follow the A968 then turn right on the B9084. ☎ *0131/668–8600.* ✉ *Free. Ask for the key-keeper.* ☉ *Apr.–Sept., Mon.–Sat. 9:30–6, Sun. 2–6; Oct.–Mar., Mon.–Sat. 9:30–4, Sun. 2–4.*

⑫ In the far north of Unst is **Haroldswick**, with its post office and heritage center. If you take the B9086 at Haroldswick you will go around the head of **Burrafirth** (a sea inlet) and eventually reach a parking lot. From there a path goes north across moorland and up a gentle hill. Bleak and open, this is bird-watchers' territory and is replete with diving skuas—single-minded sky pirates that attack anything that strays near their nest sites. Gannets, puffins, and other seabirds nest in spectacular profusion by the cliffs on the left as you look out to sea. Visitors should keep to the path; this is a national nature reserve.

At the top of the hills, amid the windy grasslands, you can see **Muckle Flugga** to the north, a series of tilting offshore rocks; the largest of these sea-battered protrusions has a lighthouse. This is the northernmost point in Scotland; the sea rolls out on three sides; no land lies beyond.

Lodging

$ ⊡ **Bremner's Guest House.** Comfortable and relaxed, this modern house boasts stunning sunset views which rival those anywhere in the United Kingdom. The rooms are clean and functional, much like the rest of this family-run bed-and-breakfast inn. ⊠ *Barns, Newgord, Westing, Uyeasound, Unst, ZE2 9DW,* ☎ *01957/755249. 2 twin rooms share 1 bath. AE, MC, V.*

AROUND ORKNEY

Orkney has the greatest concentration of prehistoric sites in Scotland. Most of the sites are open to view, offering an insight into the life of bygone eras. At Maes Howe, for example, visitors will discover that graffiti is not solely an expression of today's youths: The Vikings left their marks here in the 8th century.

Stromness

⑬ *1 hour, 45 minutes north of Thurso via ferry from Scrabster.*

You will find two points of interest in Stromness as soon as you arrive. The **Pier Arts Centre** is a former Stromness merchant's house (circa 1800) and has adjoining buildings that now serve as a gallery with a permanent collection of 20th-century paintings and sculptures. ⊠ *Victoria St.,* ☎ *01856/850209.* ▣ *Free.* ⊙ *Tues.–Sat. 10:30–12:30 and 1:30–5.*

The **Stromness Museum** has a varied collection of natural-history material on view, including preserved birds and Orkney shells. The museum also displays exhibits on fishing, shipping, whaling, and the Hudson Bay Company, as well as ship models and a feature on the German fleet that was scuttled on Scapa Flow. ⊠ *Alfred St.,* ☎ *01856/850025.* ▣ *£1.50.* ⊙ *Mon.–Sat. 10:30–12:30 and 1:30–5.*

★ ⑭ The **Ring of Brogar** is a magnificent circle of 36 stones (originally 60) surrounded by a deep ditch. When the fog descends over the stones— a frequent occurrence—their looming shapes seem to come alive. Though their original use is uncertain, it is not hard to imagine strange rituals taking place here in the misty past. The stones stand between Loch of Harray and Loch of Stenness, 5 miles northeast of Stromness. ☎ *0131/668–8600.* ▣ *Free.* ⊙ *At all times.*

★ ⑮ The huge burial mound of **Maes Howe** (circa 2,500 BC) measures 115 feet in diameter and contains an enormous burial chamber. It was raided by Vikings in the 12th century, and Norse crusaders sheltered here, leaving a rich collection of runic inscriptions. Maes Howe is 1 mile farther on the A965 from the Ring of Brogar, 10 miles northeast of Stromness. ☎ *0131/668–8600.* ▣ *£2; joint entry ticket to all Historic Scot-*

Orkney Islands

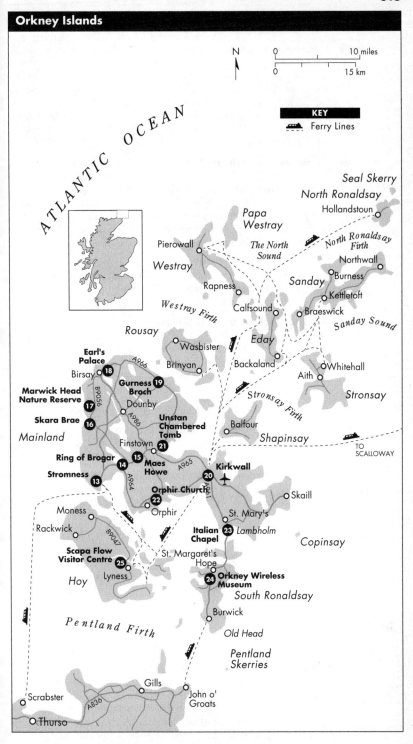

N

0 — 10 miles
0 — 15 km

KEY
Ferry Lines

ATLANTIC OCEAN

Seal Skerry
North Ronaldsay
Hollandstoun

Papa Westray

North Ronaldsay Firth

Pierowall
The North Sound
Westray

Northwall
Burness
Sanday
Kettletoft

Rapness
Calfsound
Braeswick

Westray Firth
Sanday Sound

Rousay
Wasbister
Eday
Whitehall
Aith
Stronsay

Brinyan
Backaland

Earl's Palace
Birsay **18**
A966
Gurness Broch **19**

Marwick Head Nature Reserve **17**
B9056
Dounby

Skara Brae **16**
A986
Unstan Chambered Tomb

Mainland
Finstown **21**

Ring of Brogar **15**
Maes Howe
A965
Kirkwall **20**

Stromness **13** **14**
A964
Orphir Church **22**
Orphir

Skaill

Moness
St. Mary's

Rackwick
B9047
Italian Chapel **23** Lambholm
Copinsay

Scapa Flow Visitor Centre **25**
Lyness
St. Margaret's Hope
Orkney Wireless Museum **24**

Hoy
South Ronaldsay
Burwick

Pentland Firth
Old Head

Pentland Skerries

Gills

Scrabster
John o' Groats

Thurso
A836

Stronsay Firth

Balfour
Shapinsay
TO SCALLOWAY

land's Orkney sights: £6. ☉ Apr.–Sept., Mon.–Sat. 9:30–6, Sun. 2–6; Oct.–Mar., Mon., Tues., Fri.–Sat. 9:30–4, Thur. 12–4, Sun. 2–4.

★ ⓰ At the Neolithic village of **Skara Brae** you will find houses, joined by covered passages, with stone beds, fireplaces, and cupboards that have survived since the village was first occupied around 3,000 BC. The site was preserved in sand until it was uncovered in 1850, and it can be found 8 miles north of Stromness off the A967/ B9056. ☎ 0131/668–8600. ▭ *£2.50; joint entry ticket to all Historic Scotland's Orkney sights: £6. ☉ Apr.–Sept., Mon.–Sat. 9:30–6, Sun. 2–6; Oct.–Mar., Mon.–Sat. 9:30–4, Sun. 2–4.*

⓱ The **Marwick Head Nature Reserve,** with its spectacular seabird cliffs, is tended by Scotland's Royal Society for the Protection of Birds. The **Kitchener Memorial,** which recalls the 1916 sinking of the cruiser HMS *Hampshire* with Lord Kitchener aboard, can also be seen in the reserve, on a cliff-top site. The reserve lies to the north of Skara Brae, up the B9056; access to the reserve is along a path north from Marwick Bay. ☎ *01856/850176.* ▭ *Free. ☉ At all times.*

The Arts

The Pier Arts Centre (✉ Victoria St., ☎ 01856/850209) focuses on artistic life in Stromness, with an eclectic display of paintings and sculptures and changing exhibitions, often by local artists.

Outdoor Activities and Sports

BICYCLING

Bicycles can be rented from the **Baby Linen Shop** (✉ 54 Dundas St., Stromness, ☎ 01856/850255).

Birsay

12 mi north of Stromness, 25 mi northwest of Kirkwall.

⓲ At Birsay is **Earl's Palace,** the impressive remains of a 16th-century palace built by the earls of Orkney. ✉ *Birsay,* ☎ *0131/668–8600.* ▭ *Free. ☉ At all times.*

The **Brough of Birsay,** the remains of a Romanesque church (and a Norse settlement), stands close to Birsay on an island accessible only at low tide. To ensure that you won't be swept away, check the tide tables before setting out. ✉ *Birsay,* ☎ *0131/668–8600.* ▭ *Free. ☉ Daily, subject to tides.*

⓳ The **Gurness Broch** is an Iron-Age tower standing more than 10 feet high, surrounded by stone huts. It is located off the A966, about 8 miles from Birsay along Orkney's northern coast. ✉ *Aikerness,* ☎ *0131/668–8600.* ▭ *£2; joint entry ticket to all Historic Scotland's Orkney sights: £6. ☉ Apr.–Sept., Mon.–Sat. 9:30–6, Sun. 2–6.*

Kirkwall

⓴ *16 mi east of Stromness.*

In bustling Kirkwall, the main town on Orkney, there are plenty of interesting things to see in the narrow, winding streets, extending from the harbor, which retain a strong medieval feel. **Earl Patrick's Palace,** built in 1607, is perhaps the best surviving example of Renaissance architecture in Scotland. The **Bishop's Palace** nearby dates from the 13th century, though its round tower was added in the 16th century. ✉ *Kirkwall,* ☎ *0131/668–8600.* ▭ *Admission to both: £1.20; joint entry ticket to all Historic Scotland's Orkney sights: £6. ☉ Both open Apr.–Sept., Mon.–Sat. 9:30–6, Sun. 2–6.*

Founded by Jarl Rognvald in 1137 and dedicated to his uncle St. Mag-
★ nus, **St. Magnus Cathedral** in Kirkwall was built between 1137 and 1200;
however, additional work was carried out during the following 300
years. The cathedral is still in use and contains some of the best examples of Norman architecture in Scotland. The ornamentation on some
of the tombstones is particularly striking. ☉ *All year, Mon.–Sat. 9–1
and 2–5, open Sun. for services and 2–6.*

㉑ The **Unstan Chambered Tomb** is a 5,000-year-old cairn containing a
chambered tomb. Pottery that has been found within the tomb is now
known as Unstan ware. The tomb is midway between Kirkwall and
Stromness, roughly 3.5 miles from each. ☎ *0131/668–8600.* ☜ *Free.*
☉ *Apr.–Sept., Mon.–Sat. 9:30–6, Sun. 2–6; Oct.–Mar., Mon.–Sat.
9:30–4, Sun. 2–4.*

㉒ The remains of the 12th-century **Orphir Church,** Scotland's only circular medieval church (12th century), lie near the A964, 8 miles southwest of Kirkwall. ☎ *0131/668–8600.* ☜ *Free.* ☉ *At all times.*

Dining and Lodging

$$–$$$ ✕🏠 **Foveran Hotel.** Surrounded by 34 acres of grounds just outside
Kirkwall, and overlooking Scapa Flow, this warm hotel has an attractive
light-wood, Scandinavian-style dining room and an open fire in its sitting room. The menu features Taste of Scotland, and the homemade
soups, pâtés, and seafood have helped secure the restaurant's reputation as a very dependable place to eat. ⊠ *St. Ola, Orkney, KW15 1SF,*
☎ *01856/872389,* ℻ *01856/876430. 8 rooms with bath. Restaurant,
2 lounges. MC, V. Closed Jan.*

$ 🏠 **Polrudden Guest House.** Quietly situated yet close to the town cen-
ter and public parks, this modern guest house offers a high standard
of accommodation for the price. Multicolored matching curtains and
quilt covers complement the cream-colored rooms and pine furnishings. ⊠ *Pickaquoy Rd., KW15 1UH,* ☎ ℻ *01856/874761. 7 rooms
with shower. No credit cards.*

The Arts

FESTIVALS
Orkney's cultural highlight is the **St. Magnus Festival,** a festival of music
based in Kirkwall and usually held the third week in June (☎ 01856/
872669 for details). Orkney also has an annual folk festival at the end
of May.

Outdoor Activities and Sports

BICYCLING
Bicycles can be rented from **Orkney Two Wheels** (⊠ Tankerness Lane,
Kirkwall, ☎ 01856/873097).

Shopping

Kirkwall is the main shopping hub. Do not miss **Ola Gorrie at the Long-
ship** (⊠ 7–9 Broad St., ☎ 01856/873251). The shop designs gold and
silver jewelry with Celtic and Norse themes, including a delightful rep-
resentation of a dragon, originally drawn on the wall of the burial chamber at Maes Howe. **Ortak Jewelry** (⊠ 10 Albert St., ☎ 01856/873536)
stocks a potpourri of gifts: Celtic-theme jewelry, crystal, barometers,
and many other craft items, many made locally. At **Judith Glue** (⊠ 25
Broad St., ☎ 01856/874225) visitors can purchase designer knitwear
with traditional patterns, as well as Orkney-made crafts. Many outlets in Kirkwall stock items made by **Joker Jewelry** (⊠ East School,
Holm, ☎ 01856/781336): eye-catching and whimsical clocks, brooches,
and other jewelry using animal motifs (especially puffins).

South Ronaldsay

18 mi south of Kirkwall.

★ ㉓ Travelers can reach South Ronaldsay via the A961 causeway heading south from Kirkwall. The island's first distinctive point is the **Italian Chapel,** located below the small village of St. Mary's. It was here, by the shore at Lambholm, in 1943, that Italian prisoners of war, using a Nissen hut, created a beautiful chapel from scrap metal and concrete. ⊠ *Lambholm.* ☎ *Free.* ⊘ *At all times.*

㉔ The **Orkney Wireless Museum,** at St. Margaret's Hope, is a museum of wartime communications at Scapa Flow. Thousands of service men and women were stationed here and used the equipment displayed to protect the Home Fleet. The museum also contains many handsome 1930s wireless radios. It is 11 miles south of Kirkwall. ⊠ *St. Margaret's Hope,* ☎ *01856/874272.* ☎ *Small fee.* ⊘ *June–Aug.; check with tourist information center for opening hours.*

Dining and Lodging

\$\$–\$\$\$ ✕ 🏠 **The Creel Restaurant.** This seafront restaurant with a cottage-style interior serves local seafood (including lobster) as its specialty, prepared personally by the owner/chef. The Creel also has some modest accommodations: Three spacious rooms with sea views are offered in an inexpensive bed-and-breakfast style. ⊠ *Front Rd., St. Margaret's Hope,* ☎ FAX *01856/831311. 1 room with bath, 2 with shower. Restaurant (reservations essential). MC, V. Closed Jan.*

Hoy

14 mi from Kirkwall, 6 mi from Stromness via ferry.

㉕ The **Scapa Flow Visitor Centre,** on Hoy, has a growing collection of material portraying the strategic role of the sheltered anchorage of Scapa Flow (said to be Britain's best diving site) in two world wars. It can be found off the B9047. ⊠ *Lyness,* ☎ *01856/791300.* ☎ *£1.50.* ⊘ *May–Sept., Mon.–Fri. 9–4, Sat. 9–3:30, Sun. 9–6; Oct.–Apr., Mon.–Fri. 9–4.*

Tended by the Royal Society for the Protection of Birds, the **North Hoy Nature Reserve,** home to vast numbers of land birds and seabirds, comprises high ground and moor. Huge cliffs nearby include the Old Man of Hoy, a 450-foot sea stack. ☎ *01856/791298.* ☎ *Free.* ⊘ *At all times.*

OFF THE   **KNAP OF HOWAR** – This is one of the oldest inhabited sites in Europe. Its
BEATEN PATH   two 5,000-year-old dwellings—which have yielded some unusual artifacts, such as whalebone mallets, a spatula, and stone grinders—can be found on the west side of Papa Westray, off the island of Westray. ⊠ *West of Holland House,* ☎ *0131/668–8600.* ☎ *Free.* ⊘ *At all times.*

THE NORTHERN ISLES A TO Z

Arriving and Departing

By Bus

Aberdeen and Thurso have reliable bus links to and from all over Scotland: **National Express/Scottish Citylink** (☎ 0990/505050). **John o'Groats Ferries** (☎ 01955/611353) operates the **Orkney Bus,** a direct express coach from Inverness to Kirkwall that runs daily from mid-April to mid-September. The same company offers a **day tour** from Inverness to Orkney daily from June to August.

By Car and Ferry

To get to Lerwick, Shetland, take the ferry from the port in Aberdeen. To reach Stromness, Orkney, take the ferry from the port in Scrabster. Contact **P & O Ferries** (Orkney and Shetland Services, PO Box 5, Jamieson's Quay, Aberdeen, ☎ 01224/572615, FAX 01224/574411) for reservations. Alternatively, take the ferry from John o'Groats to Burwick operated by **John o'Groats Ferries,** with up to 8 sailings daily from mid-April to mid-September (☎ 01955/611353 for details).

By Plane

British Airways (☎ 0345/222111) provides regular service to **Lerwick** (in Shetland) and **Kirkwall** (in Orkney) from Edinburgh, Glasgow, Aberdeen, and Inverness. **Business Air** (☎ 01382/566345) operates flights to **Lerwick** from Edinburgh and Aberdeen.

By Train

There are no trains on Orkney or Shetland, although Aberdeen (which has a ferry to Shetland) is well served by train, and Thurso is the terminus of the far-north line. For information, contact the British Rail information line (☎ 0345/212282). From Thurso a bus connects to Scrabster for Orkney.

Getting Around

By Bus

The main bus services on Orkney are operated by **James D. Peace & Co.** (☎ 01856/872866), **Causeway Coaches** (☎ 01856/831444), and **Shalder Coaches** (☎ 01856/850809); on Shetland by **Shalder Coaches** (☎ 01595/880217) and **J. Leask** (☎ 01595/693162).

By Car

Because of the oil wealth, the roads on Shetland are in very good shape. Both Orkney and Shetland are part of a network of islands with interconnecting ferries that are heavily subsidized. It's a good idea to book ferry tickets in advance. In Shetland, for ferry information, contact the tourist information center (☞ Visitor Information, *below*) or ☎ 01957/722259 or 01957/722268 if you are visiting during peak season. Shetland visitors who want to get to Orkney can do so by way of ferry from Lerwick on Shetland to Stromness, in Orkney (☞ P & O Ferries, *above*).

In Orkney, for details of ferry services operated interisland, call Orkney Ferries (☎ 01856/872044). Orkney also has causeways connecting some of the islands, but using these roads will, in some cases, take you on fairly roundabout routes, thus making for a longer journey than you might have if you took a ferry.

By Plane

Note that because of the isolation of Orkney and Shetland there is a network of interisland flights. Tourist information centers (☞ Visitor Information, *below*) will provide details, or call British Airways (☞ Arriving and Departing by Plane, *above,* or in Orkney, ☎ 01856/872494 for interisland flights).

By Train

There are no trains on Shetland or Orkney.

Contacts and Resources

Car Rental

Although Shetland has a number of car-rental firms, you have the option of taking your car from Aberdeen by sea. The rule of thumb is that for any visit under five days it is cheaper to rent a car in Shetland.

Most of the rental companies are based in Lerwick; they include **Star Rent-a-Car** (✉ 22 Commercial Rd., Lerwick, ☎ 01595/692075, FAX 01595/693964) and **Bolts Car and Minibus Hire** (✉ 26 North Rd., Lerwick, ☎ 01595/693636, FAX 01595/694646). On Orkney try **J & W Tait** (✉ Sparrowhawk Rd., Hatston Industrial Estate, Kirkwall, ☎ 01856/872490) or **James D. Peace & Co.** (✉ Junction Rd., Kirkwall, ☎ 01856/872866).

Discount Pass

A joint entry ticket to all of Historic Scotland's Orkney sites is available from the sites themselves. The ticket lasts until you've seen all the sites and costs £6.

Diving

Orkney, especially the former wartime anchorage of Scapa Flow, claims to have the best dive sites in Britain. Part of the attraction is the remains of the German navy, scuttled here in 1919. Consult the Orkney Tourist Board (☞ Visitor Information, *below*) for information on boat rental firms offering diving charters. Shetland also has exceptional underwater visibility, perfect for viewing the treasure wrecks and abundant marine life. The Shetland Isles tourist information center (☞ Visitor Information, *below*), as well as the **Skolla Diving Centre** (✉ Gulberwick, ☎ 01595/694175), can provide the necessary information.

Doctors and Dentists

Most general practitioners will see visitor patients by appointment or immediately in case of emergency. Your hotel or local tourist information center can advise you accordingly. You can also consult the Yellow Pages of the telephone directory, under "Doctor" or "Dentist." Hospitals with emergency rooms are **Gilbert Bain Hospital** (✉ South Rd., Lerwick, Shetland, ☎ 01595/695678) and **Balfour Hospital** (✉ New Staffa Rd., Kirkwall, Orkney, ☎ 01856/885400).

Emergencies

For **police, fire,** or **ambulance,** dial 999 from any telephone. No coins are needed for emergency calls from public telephone booths.

Fishing

Sea angling is such a popular sport in Orkney that the local tourist board advises fishermen to book early. There are at least seven companies offering sea-angling boat rentals, with fishing rods available in most cases. Loch angling in Orkney is also popular; Loch of Harray and Loch of Stenness are the best-known spots. Contact the Orkney Tourist Board (☞ Visitor Information, *below*) for information. Shetland, also renowned for sea angling, holds several competitions throughout the year. Contact the **Shetland Association of Sea Anglers** via the tourist information center (☞ Visitor Information, *below*) for further information.

Guided Tours

ORIENTATION

In addition to the bus companies mentioned above, well-run personally guided day tours are offered in Orkney by **Go-Orkney** (☎ 01856/874260). Other companies that schedule general orientation tours include **Causeway Coaches** (☎ 01856/831444) and **Shalder Coaches** (☎ 01856/850809). The tour companies that service Shetland are **J. Leask** (☎ 01595/693162) and **Shalder Coaches** (☎ 01595/880217).

SPECIAL-INTEREST

All the above companies run special-interest tours to specific places of interest on the islands, and most can also tailor tours to your interests. Guided walks are available on Orkney: Contact **Wildabout** (through

Orkney Tourist Board) for details of early morning, late evening, and all-day walks with an environmental theme. In Shetland, several companies tour the spectacular Noss Bird Sanctuary—a National Nature Reserve—in the summer, weather permitting. The tourist information center can provide details and take reservations.

Late-Night Pharmacies

There are no late-night pharmacies on the islands. In case of emergency, police can provide assistance in locating pharmacists. Doctors in rural areas also dispense medication.

Nightlife

No one goes to Orkney or Shetland for the nightlife, although there are bars and lounges with live entertainment in Lerwick on Shetland, thanks to the fluctuating population of oil workers and boat crews. The same is true in Kirkwall. Tourist information centers (☞ Visitor Information, *below*) will provide details on local concerts and summer programs for visitors.

Pony Trekking

There is only one riding center on Shetland: **Broothom Ponies** (✉ Braeside, Dunrossness, ☎ 01950/460464). There are no riding centers on Orkney.

Visitor Information

The main tourist information centers in the area are: **Kirkwall, Orkney** (✉ 6 Broad St., ☎ 01856/872856, FAX 01856/875056. **Stromness, Orkney** (✉ Ferry Terminal Building, ☎ 01856/850716). **Lerwick, Shetland** (✉ Market Cross, ☎ 01595/693434, FAX 01595/695807).

Water Sports

There are good anchorages among Orkney's many islands. Contact the tourist information centers for details. There are also sailboats available on Shetland. Details may be obtained from the **Lerwick Boating Club,** which can be contacted through the tourist information center (☞ Visitor Information, *above*).

13 Portraits of Scotland

Scotland at a Glance: A Chronology

Hollywood Comes in for the Kilt

SCOTLAND AT A GLANCE: A CHRONOLOGY

ca. 3000 BC Neolithic migration from Mediterranean: "chambered cairn" people in north, "beaker people" in southeast.

ca. 300 BC Iron Age: infusion of Celtic peoples from the south and from Ireland; "Gallic forts," "brochs" built.

AD 79–89 Julius Agricola, Roman governor of Britain, invades Scotland; Scots tribes defeated at Mons Graupius (Grampians): "they make a desert and call it peace." Roman forts built at Inchtuthil and Ardoch.

142 Emperor Antoninus Pius orders Antonine Wall built between the Firths of Forth and Clyde.

185 Antonine Wall abandoned.

367 Massive invasion of Britain by Picts, Scots, Saxons, and Franks.

392 Ninian's mission to Picts: first Christian chapel at Whitehorn.

400–1000 Era of the Four Peoples: redheaded Picts in the north, Gaelic-speaking Scots and Britons in the west and south, Germanic Angles in the east. Origins of Arthur legend (Arthur's Seat, Ben Arthur). Picts, with bloodline through mothers, eventually dominate.

563 Columba establishes monastery at Iona.

780–1065 Scandinavian invasions; Hebrides remain Norse until 1263, Orkney and Shetland until 1472.

1005–1034 Malcolm II unifies Scotland and (temporarily) repels the English.

1040 Malcolm's heir, Duncan, is slain by his rival, Macbeth, whose wife has a claim to the throne.

The House of Canmore

1057 Malcolm III, known as "Canmore" ("Big Head"), murders Macbeth and assumes the throne.

1093 Death of Malcolm's queen, St. Margaret, founder of modern Edinburgh.

1124–1153 David I, "soir sanct" (sore saint), builds the abbeys of Jedburgh (1118), Kelso (1128), Melrose (1136), and Dryburgh (1150) and brings Norman culture to Scotland.

1290 The first of many attempts to unite Scotland peacefully with England fails when the Scots queen Margaret, "the Maid of Norway," dies on the way to her wedding to Edward, son of Edward I of England. The Scots naively ask Edward I (subsequently known as "the hammer of the Scots") to arbitrate between the remaining 13 claimants to the throne. Edward's choice, John Balliol, is known as "toom tabard" (empty coat).

1295 Under continued threat from England, Scotland signs its first treaty of the "auld alliance" with France. Wine trade flourishes.

1297 Revolutionary William Wallace, immortalized by Burns, leads the Scots against the English.

1305 Wallace captured by the English and executed.

1306–29 Reign of Robert Bruce (Robert I). Defeats Edward II at Bannockburn, 1314; Treaty of Northampton, 1328, recognizes Scottish sovereignty.

1368 Edinburgh Castle rebuilt.

The House of Stewart

1371 Robert II, son of Robert Bruce's daughter Marjorie and Walter the Steward, is crowned. Struggle (dramatized in Scott's novels) between the crown and the barony ensues for the next century, punctuated by sporadic warfare with England.

1411 Founding of University of St. Andrews.

1451 University of Glasgow founded.

1488–1515 Reign of James IV. The Renaissance reaches Scotland. The "Golden Age" of Scots poetry includes Robert Henryson, William Dunbar, Gavin Douglas, and the king himself.

1495 University of Aberdeen founded.

1507 Andrew Myllar and Walter Chapman set up first Scots printing press in Edinburgh.

1513 At war against the English, James is slain at Flodden.

1542 Henry VIII defeats James V at Solway Moss; the dying James, hearing of the birth of his daughter, Mary, declares: "It came with a lass [Marjorie Bruce] and it will pass with a lass."

1542–67 Reign of Mary Queen of Scots. Romantic, Catholic, and with an excellent claim to the English throne, Mary proved to be no match for her barons, John Knox, or her cousin, Elizabeth of England.

1560 Mary returns to Scotland from her childhood in France, at the same time that Catholicism is abolished in favor of Knox's Calvinism.

1565 Mary marries Lord Darnley, a Catholic.

1567 Darnley is murdered at Kirk o' Field; Mary marries one of the conspirators, the earl of Bothwell. Driven from Scotland, she appeals to Elizabeth, who imprisons her. Mary's son, James (1566–1625), is crowned James VI of Scotland.

1582 University of Edinburgh is founded.

1587 Elizabeth orders the execution of Mary.

1603 Elizabeth dies without issue; James VI is crowned James I of England. Parliaments remain separate for another century.

1638 National Covenant challenges Charles I's personal rule.

1639–41 Crisis. The Scots and then the English Parliaments revolt against Charles I.

1643 Solemn League and Covenant establishes Presbyterianism as the Church of Scotland ("the Kirk"). Civil War in England.

1649 Charles I beheaded. Cromwell made Protector.

1650–52 Cromwell roots out Scots royalists.

1658 First Edinburgh—London coach: the journey took two weeks.

1660 Restoration of Charles II. Episcopalianism reestablished in Scotland; Covenanters persecuted.

1688–89   Glorious Revolution; James VII and II, a Catholic, deposed in favor of his daughter Mary and her husband, William of Orange. Supporters of James ("Jacobites") defeated at Killiecrankie. Presbyterianism reestablished.

1692   Highlanders who refuse oath to William and Mary massacred at Glencoe.

1698–1700   Attempted Scottish colony at Darien fails.

1707   Union of English and Scots Parliaments under Queen Anne; deprived of French wine trade, Scots turn to whisky.

The House of Hanover

1714   Queen Anne dies; George I of Hanover, descended from a daughter of James VI and I, crowned.

1715   First Jacobite Rebellion. Earl of Mar defeated.

1730–90   Scottish Enlightenment. The Edinburgh Medical School is the best in Europe; David Hume (1711–1776) and Adam Smith (1723–1790) redefine philosophy and economics. In the arts, Allan Ramsay the elder (1686–1758) and Robert Burns (1759–1796) refine Scottish poetry; Allan Ramsay the younger (1713–1784) and Henry Raeburn (1756–1823) rank among the finest painters of the era. Edinburgh's New Town, begun in the 1770s by the brothers Adam, provides a fitting setting.

1745–46   Last Jacobite Rebellion. Bonnie Prince Charlie, grandson of James VII and II, is defeated at Culloden; wearing of the kilt is forbidden until 1782. James Watt (1736–1819) of Glasgow is granted a patent for his steam engine.

1771   Birth of Walter Scott, Romantic novelist.

1778   First cotton mill, at Rothesay.

1788   Death of Bonnie Prince Charlie.

1790   Forth and Clyde Canal opened.

1800–1850   Highland Clearances: overpopulation, increased rents, and conversion of farms to sheep pasture leads to mass migration, sometimes forced, to North America and elsewhere. Meanwhile, the lowlands industrialize; Catholic Irish immigrate to factories of southwest.

1828   Execution of Burke and Hare, who sold their murder victims to an Edinburgh anatomist, a lucrative trade.

1832   Parliamentary Reform Act expands the franchise, redistributes seats.

1837   Victoria accedes to the British throne.

1842   Edinburgh–Glasgow railroad opened.

1846   Edinburgh–London railroad opened.

1848   Queen Victoria buys estate at Balmoral as her Scottish residence. Andrew Carnegie emigrates from Dunfermline to Pittsburgh.

1884–85   Gladstone's Reform Act establishes manhood suffrage. Office of Secretary for Scotland authorized.

1886   Scottish Home Rule Association founded.

1901   Death of Queen Victoria.

The House of Windsor

1928 Equal Franchise Act gives the vote to women. Scottish Office established as governmental department in Edinburgh. Scottish National Party founded.

1931 Depression hits industrialized Scotland severely.

1945 Two Scottish Nationalists elected to Parliament.

1959 Finnart Oil Terminal, Chapelcross Nuclear Power Station, and Dounreay Fast Breeder Reactor opened.

1964 Forth Road Bridge opened.

1970 British Petroleum strikes oil in the North Sea; revives economy of northeast.

1973 Britain becomes a member of the European Economic Community ("Common Market").

1974 Eleven Scottish Nationalist MPs elected. Old counties reorganized and renamed new regions.

1979 Referendum on "devolution" of a separate Scotland: 33% for, 31% against; 36% don't vote.

1981 Europe's largest oil terminal opens at Sullom Voe, Shetland.

1988 Revival of Scots nationalism under banner of "Scotland in Europe," anticipating 1992 economic union.

1992 Increasing attention focused on Scotland's dissatisfaction with rule from London, England. Poll shows 50% of Scots want independence.

1995 In the face of a Tory Government increasingly looking like a "lame duck" and divided on the issue of Europe, Scotland continues to argue its own way forward. The Labour Party promises a Scottish Parliament but wants to keep Scotland within the United Kingdom; the Scottish National Party still wants independence and sees Labour's Scottish Parliament as a stepping-stone to full autonomy.

HOLLYWOOD COMES IN FOR THE KILT

THE RECENT SUCCESS OF movies such as *Rob Roy* and, to an even greater extent, *Braveheart,* has virtually created a new genre—the so-called kilt movie. In 1996, Scotland became hot, Scotland's scenery a greater than ever attraction to Hollywood. So what if big chunks of *Braveheart* were actually filmed in Ireland?

Not that there is anything new about Scotland as a dramatic backdrop. In 1922, a silent film described at the time as "the first Scottish epic" featured Rob Roy and a cast of two thousand. It was shot partly around Loch Lomond, onetime homeland of the real-life Rob Roy Macgregor. As defender of the downtrodden and scourge of the authorities, Macgregor is known as a tartan Robin Hood. In 1953 Rob Roy's adventures again made it to the screen, in Walt Disney's *The Sword and the Rose,* starring Richard Todd. Locations for this version of the much revered Highland outlaw's story included Aberfoyle, the southern gateway to the Trossachs.

The 1995 *Rob Roy,* starring Liam Neeson, was shot at and around Glen Nevis and Glencoe, both near Fort William; the gardens of Drummond Castle near Crieff; and Crichton Castle near Edinburgh. Another 1995 release, and winner of the Academy Award for that year's Best Picture, Mel Gibson's *Braveheart* is the story of Scotland's first freedom-fighter, Sir William Wallace. It also uses the spectacular craggy scenery of Glen Nevis, a spot well worth a visit if you find yourself in Fort William; it offers a big change from the many woolen shops.

The Prime of Miss Jean Brodie (1969), based on the Muriel Spark novel, starred Dame Maggie Smith in the title role. She won an Academy Award for Best Actress for her performance as an eccentric teacher who reigns over an Edinburgh girls' school. (Pauline Kael praised her for being "very funny—snobbish, full of affectations, and with a jumble shop of a mind.") Filmed in a variety of locations around Edinburgh (as well as in London), it is a Scottish classic. Even Greyfriars Bobby—the Skye terrier who watched over his master's grave at Greyfriars for fourteen years, beginning in 1858, and who was made a citizen of Edinburgh to save him from being destroyed as a stray—had his moment on the silver screen, in the eponymous 1961 Walt Disney film.

Mel Gibson's *Hamlet* (1990) was filmed at Dunnottar Castle at Stonehaven in the east. Looking further back, *Highlander* (1986) with Christopher Lambert and Sean Connery, also used the spectacular crags of Glencoe, along with the prototypical Scottish castle, Eilean Donan—almost a visual cliche in Scottish terms. Starring Peter Riegert and Burt Lancaster, *Local Hero* (1983) put together the best of east and west coast Scotland. The village of Pennan, an hour's drive north of Aberdeen, huddles below spectacular cliffs and became Ferness, the village threatened by oil developments. The village phone box, which plays an important part in the film script, has been carefully preserved. (And, yes, you can see the Aurora Borealis—the Northern Lights—from it, sometimes.) In fact, the phone box has become something of a local landmark and lots of visitors still travel especially to see it.

Hollywood's devotion to Scotland continued apace in 1996, with the release of *Loch Ness* starring Ted Danson. *Trainspotting,* based on the novel of the same name by Irvine Welsh, is about heroin addicts in an economically depressed Scotland. Although it was produced in Britain, it found a large North American audience. And with the story of Robert the Bruce about to be released and a *Macbeth* in the making, it looks like Scotland will remain fertile ground for moviemakers for some time to come.

— *Gilbert Summers*

INDEX

CNN ✈
Airport Network

Your
Window
To The
World
While You're
On The
Road

Keep in touch when you're traveling. Before you take off, tune in to CNN Airport Network. Now available in major airports across America, CNN Airport Network provides nonstop news, sports, business, weather and lifestyle programming. Both domestic and international. All piloted by the top-flight global resources of CNN. All up-to-the minute reporting. And just for travelers, CNN Airport Network features two daily Fodor's specials. "Travel Fact" provides enlightening, useful travel trivia, while "What's Happening" covers upcoming events in major cities worldwide. So why be bored waiting to board? TIME FLIES WHEN YOU'RE WATCHING THE WORLD THROUGH THE WINDOW OF CNN AIRPORT NETWORK!

WHEREVER YOU TRAVEL, *H*ELP IS NEVER FAR AWAY.

From planning your trip to providing travel assistance along the way, American Express® Travel Service Offices are always there to help.

Scotland

Premier Travel Ltd. (R)
2C Boswell Park
Ayr
01292/282 822

American Express Travel Service
139 Princess Street
Edinburgh
0131/225 7881

American Express Travel Service
3 Queen Street
Cardiff
01222/668 858

American Express Travel Service
115 Hope Street
Glasgow
0141/221 4366

D. P. & L. Travel Ltd. (R)
11 Albert Square
Dundee
01382/227 232

Alba Travel (R)
43 Church Street
Inverness
01463/239 188

D. P. & L. Travel Ltd. (R)
8 Mercat Wynd
St. Andrews
01334/474 404

Travel

http://www.americanexpress.com/travel

American Express Travel Service Offices are found in central locations throughout the United Kingdom.